BERYL BAINBRIDGE

BERYL BAINBRIDGE

Love by All Sorts of Means
A Biography

BRENDAN KING

BLOOMSBURY
LONDON · OXFORD · NEW YORK · NEW DELHI · SYDNEY

Bloomsbury Continuum
An imprint of Bloomsbury Publishing Plc

50 BEDFORD SQUARE   1385 BROADWAY
LONDON   NEW YORK
WC1B 3DP   NY 10018
UK   USA

www.bloomsbury.com

Bloomsbury, Continuum and the Diana logo are trademarks of Bloomsbury Publishing Plc

First published 2016

Paperback, 2017

British Library Cataloguing-in-Publication Data
A catalogue record for this book is available from the British Library.

Library of Congress Cataloguing-in-Publication data has been applied for.

ISBN: HB: 978-1-4729-0853-7
         PB: 978-1-47294-733-8
         EPDF: 978-1-4729-0855-1
         EPUB: 978-1-4729-0854-4

2 4 6 8 10 9 7 5 3 1

Typeset by Integra Software Services Pvt. Ltd.
Printed and bound in Great Britain by CPI Group (UK) Ltd, Croydon CR0 4YY

To find out more about our authors and books visit www.bloomsbury.com.
Here you will find extracts, author interviews, details of forthcoming
events and the option to sign up for our newsletters.

'I go on making messy relationships, fail, and fling myself into a fresh one. I seem to have an intense craving for narcissistic gratification. I have to get love by all sorts of means . . .'

Beryl Bainbridge, letter to Judith Shackleton,
October 1963

CONTENTS

CONTENTS

NOTE ON THE TEXT

Beryl was a notoriously erratic speller and her unique and idiosyncratic orthography contributed to the way her correspondents perceived and interacted with her. In quoting from her diaries, journals and letters I have therefore left her original spelling for the most part unchanged, correcting only instances where the sense was difficult to follow. Minor slips in punctuation, such as forgetting to close quotation marks, have also been corrected.

INTRODUCTION

I FIRST STARTED WORKING FOR Beryl Bainbridge in 1987. Initially, I went round to her house in Camden Town once a week to help her deal with the increasing volume of letters and phone calls she had been receiving in the wake of two television series for the BBC, *English Journey* (1984) and *Forever England* (1986), and her weekly column for the *Evening Standard*. My job, insofar as it had a description, was to sort out anything that got in the way of her real work – that of being a novelist. Over the course of the next twenty-three years, until her death in 2010, we established a working relationship that functioned surprisingly well given the difference in age and background. This was especially the case after 1992, as with the departure of her regular typist at Duckworth I took over the task of preparing the manuscripts of her novels, a process that included frequent telephone calls to query her over issues of style, grammar, form and structure – and writers, like most creative artists, often find criticism of their work difficult to take.

Sometimes, when she was bogged down with writer's block or struggling to come up with an idea for a novel, I would suggest that she write her autobiography, as it seemed to me that over the years she had told me many things about herself she'd never made use of in her writing. But she always declined, saying that it was too difficult, that she couldn't remember things well enough, that she didn't have the energy. Instead, it became a kind of in-joke that I was her 'biographer in waiting'. Then, over time, it turned into a settled notion.

After Beryl's death the question of a biography inevitably arose. With her family's permission I began searching through the massive archive of material she had kept and stored in various filing cabinets and trunks in her work room at the top of the house – 'the laboratory' as she called it – and the sizeable collection of manuscripts and other literary material she had sold to the British Library in 2005.

Many of the circumstances and events of Beryl's life were already familiar to me: not only had she told me about them herself, she had written about them in pieces of journalism, spoken about them in interviews, and famously used them as the basis of her novels. But I soon began to notice a considerable difference between the story revealed by her private diaries, journals and correspondence, and the version of her life she had published, whether in fictional or non-fictional form. And the more I researched the more discrepancies I found, until it began to seem as if everything that had been published about her was either misleading or riddled with factual errors. Yet the source of much of this information had been Beryl herself. Surely, if anyone knew the facts of their own life, it would be the person who actually lived it?

There is, of course, a simple reason why the published accounts of Beryl's life don't always match the private record. Whether in interviews or in the articles and books she was writing, she tended to rely on her memory for the details of the stories she was telling. Beryl was very proud of her memory. In an interview in 1973 she claimed to have 'what's called total recall',[1] and a few years later she told another journalist, 'I can actually think myself back into a day 30 years ago, and recall it in exact detail.'[2]

But she did not have total recall and her memory was as prone to inaccuracy as anyone else's. Memory is a notoriously unreliable instrument – the notion that it is a kind of permanent storage device, faithfully recording human experience, fixing it once and for all in the mind so that it can be recalled again and again in exactly the same form, is no longer one accepted by psychologists. Memories are more dynamic, more unstable, than we would like to believe; our recollections alter and adapt over time, they are shaped, consciously or unconsciously, by emotions, by new experiences, by changes in circumstance. It's not just that we forget certain things or emphasize others; we condense events in our mind, confuse one thing with another.

To give just a few examples. In *Forever England*, Beryl recalled that as a thirteen-year-old she went to see the great Polish pianist, Ignacy Paderewski, at the Floral Hall in Southport. After the performance she was taken backstage, dressed in her mother's best fox fur, to meet the musical legend. As Beryl described it: 'He was a small man with a lot of mad white hair and he said he thought I had some kind of specialness – I remember the exact word – but it was only because I was looking at him in a very intense way, out of politeness. My mother never got over it, me shaking hands with a famous pianist, though she too didn't know him from Adam.'[3]

Despite the seemingly unforgettable nature of this experience, and the precise detail with which it is recalled, there is a problem: Paderewski died in 1941, when Beryl was nine years old, and there is no record of him performing in Southport. It is still possible she saw him play, though his last recital in Lancashire was at the Manchester Free Trade Hall in October 1938, when Beryl was almost six. Or it may be that she has simply mistaken some other distinguished white-haired pianist for Paderewski. Either way, the anecdote loses much of its value as an autobiographical memoir given its essential unreliability.

A second example shows that this kind of inconsistency is not an exception. Beryl mentioned as a key early experience in her theatrical career a week-long stint at a theatre in Bulwell, in which she and a schoolfriend performed a series of variety acts after having won a talent contest.[4] Again a memorable event, one which Beryl herself said she had never forgotten. She duly records that prior to ending her turn with a recited monologue, the two girls performed the umbrella dance from *Singin' in the Rain*. The problem here is that the film wasn't released until 1952, three years after she remembered dancing the routine for which it became so famous.

Our confidence in the reliability of such memories is shaken still further when we find that the talent contest in Bulwell was covered quite extensively in the local newspaper at the time, from which it becomes apparent that every verifiable detail Beryl recounts is wrong, including the name of the theatre and that of the other acts that performed alongside her. In fact the two girls did not win the talent contest, they were simply taking part in it, and they did not get to perform for a week, but only for two shows on the same evening, one at 6.15 and another at 8.00, as the rules of the contest required.

Perhaps the most striking, and in some ways the most troubling, example of this tendency of the memory to play tricks, is Beryl's recollection of being taken, along with the whole of her school, to the Philharmonic Hall in Liverpool to see 'the unexpurgated version of the film taken by British troops entering Bergen-Belsen'.[5] Beryl described the experience many times in later life, adducing a huge significance to it in terms of the effect it had on her psychologically and on the kind of novelist she would become. Yet no visit under the auspices of Merchant Taylors' School was ever made to see the newsreel footage, which in any case would have been the standard edited footage presented by Pathé – there were no unexpurgated versions floating around. Despite Beryl's vivid memory that 'the entire school, from the ages of 7 to the 6th form' were marched in file to see the film, there is no record of any such visit, and not a single pupil or alumni of the school remembers the event.

One explanation is that the memory is a conflation of two very different experiences. Merchant Taylors' did have a close connection with the Philharmonic Hall: it was where concerts and the annual prize-giving ceremony were held, and on such occasions the whole school would attend. On 30 April 1945 – as it happens the same day the Bergen-Belsen newsreels were first shown in cinemas[6] – the whole school did go to the Philharmonic Hall, but it was to see a concert conducted by Herbert Bardgett. This visit seems to have become fused in Beryl's mind with a memory of having seen the newsreel in the course of her regular film-going. Although some theatres and cinemas posted warnings about the material contained in the newsreels, for the most part they were shown – as all the other Pathé and Gaumont newsreels were – before the main feature and would have been seen by everyone, young and old alike.

Significantly, Beryl's first public reference to having seen the footage was only in 1978, during a round of publicity interviews for the launch of her novel *Young Adolf*. Perhaps of equal significance was the fact that she had visited Israel on a literary tour the year before and been taken to see the Holocaust Museum at Yad Vashem. No doubt the experience of Yad Vashem forcefully brought back to mind all the Holocaust and concentration camp material she had seen over the years and in retrospect emphasized its importance. She may indeed have found the sight of the newsreels disturbing as a child, but there is nothing in her diaries to suggest that such images shaped her adolescent imagination or her creative impulses.[7]

But aside from the inconsistencies caused by slips of memory, there is another, more complex, reason why the published version of Beryl's life differs so radically from the unpublished one: she wanted it that way. Beryl was someone Janet Malcolm described as an 'auto-fictionalizer', someone with an instinct, or perhaps even a psychological need, to turn herself into a character in the drama of her own life. Beryl wasn't interested in giving the facts of a situation per se, only with the narrative or dramatic form in which the elements of her life could be presented. Ordinarily, when people talk to us in a confessional voice using the 'I' pronoun, we tend to take it for granted that what is being said is true, and that the person saying it knows it to be true. But for Beryl the truth, mere fact, was not the point. Her interviews and her written memoirs are always brilliant, full of memorable quotes and anecdotes, but that was partly because she was never hampered by the feeling that she had to be literally accurate about the facts when recounting them. If it sounded better, more dramatically satisfying, to say she had become a successful writer after leaving school at fourteen, then that was the story she told. Even though she knew that she actually left school at sixteen and a half, no earlier than many other girls her age. This subtle manipulation of the facts was not accidental, it was a way of representing in dramatic form what she felt to be true: she believed she'd had an incomplete education, so she literally gave herself one.

The most obvious example of this massaging of fact was in relation to her age. Beryl repeatedly gave 1934 as the year she was born, rather than 1932, the date that figures on her birth certificate. Of course Beryl knew exactly which year she was born in, but she had long been in the habit of knocking a couple of years off, even when she was only in her early twenties. This is perfectly understandable: a little vanity is excusable in anyone, and telling lies about one's age is the most socially acceptable of untruths. But after she became a public figure, amending the date of her birth had the effect of heightening the dramatic events of her youth whenever she recounted them. Predicated as they now were on her having been born in 1934, Beryl presented her experiences as a young adult as happening to her as an adolescent, and portrayed herself as having to deal with traumatic or emotional events at a younger, more formative age than she had in reality been. Beryl was fourteen and a half when she began her secret assignations with a German prisoner of war in the Formby pine woods, not eleven or twelve as she frequently claimed; she began working in her junior position at the Liverpool Playhouse when she was two months short of her seventeenth birthday, not when she was fifteen; she was nineteen when she left home for London, not sixteen.

On occasion, Beryl did consult her diaries and her youthful auto-biographical reflections. But even here, when she published extracts from them, she was careful to change the details to suit the story she wanted to tell, embroidering what she had originally written or altering dates and inventing new 'facts' to give her narrative a more satisfying shape. In an article on her childhood written in 1999, she transformed an innocuous and pithy comment about international events recorded in her diary – '17 February 1944: A great fight in Stalin-grand. Marshall Stalin worried not a bit'[8] – in order to present an image of herself as a young child with a problematic relationship with her father:

> Nov. 26. 1942. Siege of Stalingrad begun. It's cruchal.
> 27th Nov. 1942. Stalin worried not a bit. I hate my Dad.[9]

The words 'I hate my Dad' appear nowhere in any of Beryl's diaries or letters,[10] and indeed an entry for 23 January 1946 – 'I do love Mummy and Daddy'[11] – suggests the opposite, though such conventional sentiments make for poor copy. Beryl's indifference to factual accuracy can be gauged by the fact that in another article written five years later, she used the same entry from her 1944 diary but changed the words yet again, this time to read:

> September 2 1942. The Germans kill 50,000 Jews in Warsaw ghetto. Daddy upset.
> September 18. Battle of Stalingrad. Uncle Joe worried not a bit.[12]

The way Beryl manipulated these entries reveals something about her habitual method when it came to presenting an image of herself. The earlier piece was nominally about childhood, so she tweaked it to provide a 'proof' of her confrontational relationship with her father. By contrast, the later article was about attitudes to the Iraq war, and here the entry is altered to reflect the view of herself as a writer moulded by Nazi atrocities against the Jews in the Second World War. It goes without saying that there are no references to the Warsaw ghetto, to Jews, or to Jewish persecution in her 1944 or 1946 diaries.[13]

In order to present herself as a child with a precocious fascination with death, she wrote that her diary for 1945 had only one, wordless entry for the date of 28 April: a pasted-in 'photograph of Mussolini, Il Duce, chest exposed, bullet-holed and hanging upside-down beside his mistress on the facade of a petrol station in Milan'.[14] But in reality she hadn't kept a diary for 1945, nor is there a photograph of Mussolini, dead or alive, in either of her other two diaries from the period. In any case, the information about Mussolini was garnered from a copy of *Chronicle of the 20th Century*, an invaluable source-book for the details and dates she frequently used in her journalism, as is evidenced by the fact that the last part of her description of the photograph is copied word for word from the book.[15]

Such embellishments were systematic and designed to produce a particular public image, to contribute to the myth of herself as a writer steeped in, and shaped by, the effects of violent death and family dysfunction. The 'extracts' she reproduced from her 1953 diary would recount how as an out-of-work actress in London she had been so hungry she had stolen a jar of pickles, and that she had taken her mother to Hanbury Street in Whitechapel to show her 'where Jack the Ripper once wielded his knife'.[16] But the diary makes no mention of stolen pickles or Jack the Ripper, and in fact reveals that Beryl spent her time with her mother looking at religious pictures in the National Gallery and having tea and sandwiches in the Regent Palace Hotel.[17] Although the diary contains many more genuinely revealing insights into Beryl's emotional life than the ones she chose to fabricate – she was not only engaged, unengaged and re-engaged to the man who would become her husband during this period, she was also proposed to by three different men, all of whom she was emotionally involved with to a varying degree – she passes over them in silence.

The extent to which this resistance to literal truth-telling became an ingrained habit can be seen in an article she wrote for *The Times* in 1981, about the revised Duckworth edition of her first published novel, *A Weekend with Claud*. To justify the decision to publish a new version, she reproduced a passage from the original 1967 edition to show how 'bad' it was. But she didn't quote the text of the novel as it was actually printed, instead she amended it in order to make it seem more ludicrous and more opaque than it really was, presumably thinking that no one would bother to check the original.[18]

The point here is not to pick Beryl up on every inaccuracy or inconsistency, but to show the extent to which she self-consciously manipulated her image, even if it meant fabricating incidents or recollections, or altering the accounts she had kept at the time. This cavalier attitude to the notion of truth and what constituted lying was formed at an early age: 'I remember going to my first school. I was about five and I can remember sitting there and pretending that I'd hurt myself, so as to draw attention. I was a terrible liar, lying about things that had happened. Making things up. For no reason at all I'd create some story about something happening on the train home, or something I'd seen from the window and it wouldn't be true at all, but I'd go into great detail about it. Because people listened. You got some attention that way.'[19]

Lying also served as a self-protective mechanism. When she began meeting a German prisoner of war down by the Formby dunes, she didn't tell her parents, justifying her mendacity on the grounds that the truth would hurt them: 'Much better to say I was chased by a Nazi than to say I was friendly with a German prisoner.'

The fact that Beryl had no compunction about publishing anecdotes she knew to be false in order to provide more exciting or dramatic copy may make the job of untangling truth from fiction in the numerous accounts she gave of her life that much harder, but there was a reason for it. Such myth-making, whether conscious or unconscious, was a psychological necessity, a way of dealing with emotional trauma, a means by which she kept her private self and her public image separate. Like everyone, Beryl needed an element of privacy in her life, a space in which to forget or hide things that were too personal, too painful, or too embarrassing to be part of the story she wanted to tell about herself. As she herself put it: 'All memory is fiction, which is why autobiographical accounts and historical ones, for that matter, are notoriously inaccurate. We censor memories by recalling only those fragments we wish to remember.'[20]

It was an awareness of just how much she had fictionalized her past that made Beryl sceptical of the very notion of a biography: 'I'm the only one who knows what it was like, so how can anyone else write it?'[21] This must have seemed especially true as regards some of the most intimate relationships in her life, which, for the most part, she had never publicly written or spoken about.

One of the many paradoxes of Beryl's personality was that despite her casual disregard for facts and the frequency with which she gave misleading or distorted accounts of her life, she went out of her way to preserve the documentary evidence that would undercut much of what she had said in print. Aside from diaries, journals and photographs, she kept a vast archive of contemporary material relating to her life, including hundreds of letters – from her parents, her brother, her husband, her lovers, her schoolfriends, her close friends, her publishers and other writers. Not only did she keep them, she made periodic attempts to annotate them,[22] clarifying the names of those involved or giving details about what they had done, as if she wanted the real facts of her life to be understood in the future, even though she didn't want to talk about them in the present. Using this vast array of material, supplemented by Beryl's own letters, many of which, dating back to the 1950s, have come to light since her death, it is now possible to present the details of her life accurately and honestly for the first time.

But the function of a biography goes beyond the simple task of setting out facts or correcting chronology. Its aim is to give an account of a life as it unfolds, to show the impact of traumatic events as they are experienced at the time, not as they might be recounted some thirty or forty years afterwards, reframed in the context of a career as a writer or passed off as an amusing anecdote. If anything, Beryl did herself an injustice by limiting the account of her life to the myths and stories she fabricated, or to the events she retained in her not always reliable memory. The letters, journals and diaries she preserved tell a story that is by turns poignant and heartbreaking, every bit as dramatic and laden with irony as the brilliant fictions she crafted.

ONE

Winnie and Dick

Poor little darling Mummy. Poor little dearest Daddy. The fearful incompatability of human beings, the torture of living together, the crystal glass of true love that shatters and is pasted painfully together with tape, so that in twenty years some of the pieces fuse together again and the clarity is completely forgotten.[1]

AFTER SHE BECAME A published novelist, Beryl attributed a huge importance to the influence of her parents on the shaping of her personality – and more specifically to what she felt was the emotionally destructive result of their mutual incompatibility. Anecdotes about her mother and father can be found in numerous articles she wrote for newspapers and in interviews, and thinly disguised portraits of them appear in a handful of her novels. Inevitably, these representations have tended to focus on moments of conflict or high drama, and consequently our picture of what Beryl's family life was like is somewhat distorted.

Beryl herself was aware of this, and would occasionally admit that what she had presented was only a partial truth: 'I've really only shown the bad side,'[2] she told one journalist. 'I've maligned my parents in every book I've written,'[3] she confessed to another. Nor was everything she wrote about them based on fact: 'Some of it I think I may possibly have made up.'[4] She was aware, too, that her parents themselves would not have recognized their portraits: 'I have spent five or six books giving my version of my own mother and father, which, if they were alive, they would say was lies from start to finish.'[5] Even her older brother, Ian, didn't share her assessment of their formative years: 'His memories of events don't coincide with mine. Whenever we've met,

I've said, "Do you remember so-and-so?" And he says, "Don't be so bloody stupid. You're mad." [6]

But even taking into account the necessarily subjective way in which Beryl interpreted her memories, trying to reconstruct an accurate account of her family history from her interviews and published writings is like entering a minefield. The problem is perhaps best illustrated by quoting an article she wrote about her father, in which she sketched a portrait of him as a boy, supposedly in the year 1900:

> An eleven year old boy sits at a table with a pot of ink and a sheet of exercise paper in front of him. His name is Richard Bainbridge and he's the youngest of nine children. His sister Sally, four years his senior, lies on the sofa under the window, coughing into a piece of rag. Jim, five years older, left Liverpool six years ago and doesn't write. Mother has the notion he's enlisted to fight the Boers in South Africa, but Margo holds that's rubbish. She remembers Jim taking to his heels with fright when a cow escaped from the abattoir and slid in its own blood down the cobbles of Mount Pleasant. John works as a butcher's lad on the Breck Road and sleeps above the shop. Two other brothers neither of whom the boy knew, sailed away to the New World before he could walk . . . Only Nellie, Margo and Sally live at home with him and Mother. [7]

This evocation is clearly an imaginative reconstruction, but it is one rooted in specific and concrete details. Yet every piece of information it contains is false: Richard was not born in 1889, but 1891. Beryl liked the idea of her father being born in 1889, as that was the year of Hitler's birth and it gave an added frisson to link them in this way. Nor was he the youngest, and there were ten children in the family, not nine. Richard's younger sister, christened Sarah Ann, was four years his junior not four years his senior; Jim (James) wasn't five years older but ten years older, and in any case he was a glazier by trade who was still living in the family home in 1900, so their mother Ellen would have been under no illusion he had fought in the Boer War. His brother John was not a butcher's lad, but worked as a draper's clerk; it was *his* son John B. Bainbridge, born in 1911, who became a butcher with a shop on West Derby Road, not Breck Road. Neither of the two remaining brothers emigrated to America: William, a waterman at the Liverpool Corporation, lived in the city until his death in 1931. Finally, following the death of Richard's father William Bainbridge in 1899 (not three months after Richard's birth, as Beryl states later in her article and elsewhere),[8] Ellen became the head of the family, and in the year 1900, as in the past, the household was bursting at the seams. Not only were John, James, Nellie, Margo, George, Richard and Sarah living with her in the small terraced house in Spencer Street, Ellen was also giving house room to Archibald and Elizabeth Kidd, two of her brother Thomas's grown-up children.

Unfortunately Beryl inherited little in the way of documentary material relating to the history of her family. This is frustrating, but not wholly irremediable. Genealogical databases and other sources of information make it possible to cut through some of the morass of misinformation.[9]

The Bainbridges, or the line that Beryl descended from at least, originated in Ulverston, Lancashire. Among the eight children of an agricultural labourer, John Bainbridge, and his wife Deborah, was their fourth son William – Beryl's paternal grandfather – who was born on 26 July 1846 in Flookburgh, a fishing village on the Cartmel peninsula. Although William started out like his father as a farm labourer, working on a nearby farm from the age of fourteen, by the 1870s he had moved to West Derby, one of the many areas around Liverpool that underwent rapid population growth as a result of industrialization and the influx of immigrant labour. Here he found work as a cooper in Threlfall's brewery, or a 'brewer's labourer' as the census of 1881 more bluntly puts it.

In the early 1870s William met Ellen Kidd – Beryl's paternal grandmother – another Liverpool immigrant. Ellen was the daughter of Archibald Kidd, a tin-plate worker from Edinburgh whose life seems to have been plagued by work and money problems. After a short spell in Glasgow where he met and married Margaret Horn in 1840, Archibald and his new wife returned to Edinburgh. As the Kidd household grew – Ellen, born in 1849, was the fifth child in what would become a sprawling family of thirteen – money became so tight that Margaret was reduced to stealing to get by. In 1851 she was convicted of theft and, together with her nine-month-old baby, spent thirty days in Edinburgh prison.

Following Margaret's early death in 1865 at the age of forty-one,[10] Archibald moved his family to West Derby, where, a few years later in

1871, Ellen began working as a live-in domestic servant, her unemployed father and the rest of the extended family acting as childminders for her two-year-old daughter, Marion.[11] It was around this time that Ellen met William Bainbridge, and the two lived together as common-law man and wife for the rest of the 1870s before legally marrying in August 1879. (At the age of thirty Ellen was still unable to write and her wedding certificate had to be signed with a cross.)

Ellen was nothing if not physically robust: she had her first child at the age of nineteen and her tenth twenty-seven years later. After Marion came Deborah (1875), William (1878), John (1880), James (1883), Ellen ('Auntie Nellie', 1884), George (1887), Margaret ('Auntie Margo', 1888), Richard (Beryl's father, 1891) and Sarah Ann (1895). During the 1890s the Bainbridges lived in a small terraced house (now demolished) in Hughes Street, Everton, in conditions it would be an understatement to describe as cramped. The household comprised eleven people: William and Ellen, their eight children ranging in age from two to twenty-three, and their widowed son-in-law, Robert Thompson, who had married Marion two years before she died in 1891.

The Bainbridges were a respectable working-class family. Most of William's children 'got on' in their working life, though it tended to be in trade. (None went to university or 'entered the professions', as it would have been put at the time, and in fact Beryl's brother, Ian, would be the first of the Bainbridges to go to university.) Richard was baptized in Emmanuel church, just off West Derby Road, a short walk from the family home in Hughes Street. He attended Emmanuel Church of England School in Mill Road, and though, according to Beryl, he wasn't happy there, he seems to have been a diligent student. It was probably at school that he acquired his love of Dickens, whose works he would later read aloud to his daughter. Beryl would always say that it was her mother who pushed her into the theatre, but her childhood recollection of coming across a photograph of her father, aged about seven, on the stage of Emmanuel church hall 'dressed in velvet knickerbockers and about to sing Lily of Laguna'[12] shows that Richard was not without his dramatic side.

By 1911 the Bainbridges – Ellen, Richard (or 'Dick' as he was known in the family), Nellie, Margo and Sarah – were living in a small terraced house in Sunbury Road, in a working-class district of Anfield. Richard was now nineteen, and on the census for that year he is listed as a shipping clerk. The origin of his connection to the shipping industry isn't clear. Beryl recalled her father telling her he'd gone away to sea in his teens to serve as a cabin boy on the White Star line, but there is no evidence to confirm this, though his perennial toast at formal occasions – 'Absent and Sea-faring friends'[13] – hints at a nostalgic recollection of sea life. In any event, in the first decades of the twentieth century the Liverpool docks provided numerous opportunities for work: Richard's older brother, George, worked on the docks as a sheet-metal worker, and his brother-in-law was also a shipping clerk.

Richard's war years are as opaque as those of his adolescence: whether he fought, or how he managed to avoid conscription if he didn't, isn't known. There seems to be no proof he was in Ireland during the 1916 Easter uprising, something Beryl claims he told her.[14] He next turns up on the electoral register in 1921, living with Ellen and Nellie in an even smaller terraced house at 21 Bingley Road, a short distance from their former home. One reason for the move was a reduction in the size of the household following the departure of Sarah and Margo, both of whom had brief, but ultimately tragic, experiences in love. Their twin stories became part of Beryl's public mythology, a proof that doomed relationships were part of her family heritage, though the form in which she recounted them doesn't correspond to the facts and she added more dramatically satisfying deaths – poison gas, the heat of battle and a broken heart – to replace the more prosaic one of disease.

Margo left home first, having fallen in love with James Murray Bickerton, a plumber by trade. After the outbreak of the First World War he enrolled as a sapper in the Royal Engineers and it was while on leave in 1917 that he and Margo married. He was sent to France and returned in February 1919, leaving the army with a Medical Category A rating, meaning he was fully fit. When James was demobbed shortly afterwards it was with a Class Z rating, signifying he was liable to be recalled if it was deemed necessary. However, on 3 November 1919 he died at Bingley Road, with Richard in attendance. Beryl's version was that it was the result of mustard gas, but the only medical problem listed on James's army papers was a spell in hospital, complaining of pains in his stomach. Apart from a period of observation no further action was taken, and given that he died from cancer of the stomach and liver a year or so later the army may have accepted that medical negligence was a contributory factor in his death – at any rate the following year Margo received a war pension. After her husband's death, Margo briefly attempted to escape the family orbit, but by 1925, probably in order to economize on her pension, she moved back in with Ellen, Nellie and Richard at Bingley Road, where she lived until her death some forty years later.

Sarah's story was, if anything, even more tragic. In 1922 she married George Ripon Towers, who had enlisted in the Navy as a seventeen-year-old in 1911. During the war he served as a Leading Signalman, receiving a decoration for his service, before being invalided out in April 1919 due to problems with his eyes. Four years later, on 17 December 1923, he died, and within a fortnight Sarah was also dead. Beryl's account of the tragedy – 'Auntie Sally lost her man in the battle of the Somme; she died a month later from something diagnosed as a broken heart'[15] – was clearly a garbled version of these events. In fact both George and Sarah succumbed to pneumonia, and once again it was Richard who had the grim duty of being in attendance during their final moments.

By the 1920s, having not only outlived her husband and two of her daughters, Ellen was established in Bingley Road as something of a matriarchal figure. Richard – the only male in the household after his brothers had married and moved out – seems to have felt obliged to remain with his mother and play the role of dutiful son and responsible breadwinner. Even at the peak of his success as a businessman he continued to live at home with his mother and sisters, which no doubt gave rise to a certain tension when he began courting Winifred Baines, sometime around 1925 or 1926.

Where or how Beryl's parents met is uncertain. Beryl claimed it was on top of a tram, though in one account it was in Lord Street and in another between Everton Brow and Anfield. In yet another article she says it was underneath a gaslamp, so it is fair to say she didn't know.[16] It may be no coincidence that when Winnie and her parents moved from Ettington Road to a new house in the lush suburban environs of Leyfield Road in 1925 one of their close neighbours was George Reginald Bainbridge – though what his connection to Richard's side of the family was, or even if there was one, isn't clear.

The first photograph showing Richard and Winnie together was taken at Leyfield Road shortly after, at Easter 1926. Details of their courtship are sparse, but what is certainly not true is another of Beryl's stories – that Richard broke off a seven-year engagement to a woman called Annie Mudd (or Ann Moss in another version) in order to marry

Winnie. Despite the unlikely sounding name, Annie Mudd was a real person, but her protracted engagement was to Richard's older brother John some twenty years before.

Richard remains an enigmatic figure. While photographs of him in later life often show him as stern-faced, not the sort of person you would want to get on the wrong side of, those from the 1930s show him with a sardonic twinkle in his eye, as if on the point of making some ironic jest or quip, his paternalistic rectitude softened by a jaunty pipe or a party hat. Although there are many pictures in which Richard and Winnie feature together, there are few where they are actually side by side, let alone touching. One curious photograph, probably taken at Chirbury in the 1930s, shows Richard standing at the back of a group while Winnie lies on the ground at the front, her elbow propped on another man and an animated grin on her face. That Winnie and Richard had good times is undoubted – many of the photographs capture their laughter and smiles – though whether they were both having the same good time is not so clear.

During the early 1920s Dick Bainbridge must have felt that he was getting on in the world, a self-made man who, in relative terms, was doing spectacularly well. While most of William and Ellen's other children worked in some form of trade – Deborah was a tailoress, Margo a dressmaker and James an ecclesiastical lead-light maker, and both John and William Jr had worked their way up to become foremen at the Liverpool Corporation waterworks – by 1921 Richard was listed as a shipping agent with his own company. Richard Bainbridge & Co. had an office in South John Street, part of the city's mercantile business quarter, and by the middle of the decade it had a second shipping office in nearby Lord Street.

Richard's rise was rapid, but it didn't last. By 1925 there were already signs the business was in difficulty. Beryl's explanation for the firm's failure was, as she put it, 'a decline in the gold standards'.[17] Although she muddled the meaning of the phrase – there could be no 'decline' of the Gold Standard, only the currencies linked to it – it seems to be based on a genuine recollection, and in it one can hear a faint echo of Richard's impotent rage against Winston Churchill and the international financiers he felt were ruining him. It was Churchill's decision as

Chancellor of the Exchequer in 1925 to return to the Gold Standard at pre-war exchange rates (Britain had abandoned it in 1914 to print money for the war effort) that effectively increased the price of exports and caused a massive slump in trade.

Bainbridge & Co. struggled to compete, along with hundreds of similar businesses at the mercy of global forces. In February 1926 a move was made to wind up the firm and in June liquidators were appointed. Richard was effectively declared bankrupt on 2 February 1931. The years of litigation prior to the bankruptcy no doubt took their toll psychologically and put an added strain on the early years of his marriage. It is easy to imagine that the loss of social prestige and independence that the bankruptcy process entailed was at the root of what Beryl would later describe as her father's unpredictable outbursts of anger, his bouts of melancholy, and his resort to drink.

Winnie would later tell Beryl that when she met Richard he was a successful businessman, and it was only after their marriage that everything collapsed, painting herself as a victim of her husband's financial incompetence. But looking at the timing of Richard's fall there seems to be a self-serving element to her narrative, an attempt to justify her resentments retrospectively. The first petition to wind up Bainbridge & Co. was presented at the County Court in November 1925, almost two years before their marriage. Nor does there seem to be anything to indicate that the collapse of the business was due to Richard's poor management rather than the unhealthy economic climate.[18]

During his successful period in the early 1920s, Richard had possibly benefited from his business connections as a Freemason. A certificate from the St George's Lodge in Wallasey affirms he had 'advanced to the second and third degrees' by 1922. These connections may also have been of use after his bankruptcy, helping him to start a viable business in 1931, even if it was one of freelance dealing negotiated through personal contacts, rather than the official channels of a limited company. There is little concrete information about Richard's work as a commercial agent. Beryl's first public reference to his occupation was in 1953, where she described him as 'an agent for cork and tin plate'.[19] Despite his bankruptcy, Dick Bainbridge remained a recognizable and respected figure in and around Liverpool over the next two decades, and many people recalled seeing him meeting his cronies and doing business in pubs, even if they weren't entirely sure what exactly his business was.

If Richard's life seemed to be a classic story of rise and fall, Winnie could look at her father's career as one of unqualified success. In the 1911 census, John James Baines was listed as a paint manufacturer's clerk, but he would work his way up to become a manager at the Liverpool paint giant Walpamur. During the early 1920s, while Richard was at the height of his success transporting goods across the sea, John James had begun prospecting for raw materials underground, having become secretary of the Ridge Hill Barytes Mine. Located near Chirbury in Montgomeryshire and with offices in Liverpool, the mine was a small but significant source of baryte, a mineral used as a white pigment in paint.[20]

John James's commercial connection to the mine also had an unexpected social bonus: it brought him into contact with Charles V. White, the proprietor of the Herbert Arms Hotel in Chirbury. The Baineses, and subsequently the Bainbridges, would maintain a close connection to the Whites for many years, with Richard and Winnie making regular visits during Beryl and Ian's school holidays.

By 1926, John James had moved his family to a more substantial house, 'Lyndhurst', in Leyfield Road, West Derby. This was a considerable step up from the small terraced house in Ettington Road in which he and his wife Janet ('Nana Baines') had spent the last twenty years and in which Winnie had been born in 1903. By contrast, 'Lyndhurst' was a large suburban semi, not showy or extravagant but indicative of his new social status. Nevertheless, for all of Winnie's later posturing about her family's social superiority, to an outsider there wouldn't have been much to choose between the Baineses and the Bainbridges in the early years of the century, living as they did in practically identical houses, almost literally side by side. If anything, the house in which Winnie grew up was even smaller than that in which Richard lived with his mother and sisters.

To be fair to Winnie, the Baineses were a few rungs higher up the social ladder. John James's father, Albert Baines, rose to become a clerk at a firm of stockbrokers and by the 1880s was sufficiently well off to afford a live-in domestic servant. Clerical work ran in the family, with both John James and his younger brother Thomas starting their working lives as clerks.

Despite her father's professional success, Winnie's childhood was not without its tragedies. Her younger brother, Reginald, died shortly after he was born in 1906, and an older sister, Dorothy ('Fondly remembered by her Mamma, Dadda and Winnie'),[21] died a year later at the age of six. Although her own childhood seems to have passed off without incident, Winnie's later medical complaints, such as the anaemia she suffered from in the 1930s, may have had an inherited component. With her round face she was not an unattractive child, but she seems to have been afflicted with ptosis in her right eye, a condition in which the eyelid droops or doesn't open properly. In her youth it resulted in a slight squint that had a certain gauche attractiveness, but as she got older it became more pronounced, giving her an odd facial expression that added to her self-consciousness.

Winnie's younger brother, Leonard ('Uncle Len'), born in 1908, would frequently figure in later Bainbridge family get-togethers. He was also a regular visitor to Chirbury, and along with his wife Lilian ('Auntie Lil') and their two children, Hilary and Trevor, would spend summer holidays there with the Bainbridges. Like his father, Len went into the paint business, and in 1934 set up his own company, Colours & Chemicals, which specialized in developing pigments and paints. His success gave Winnie another needle with which to prod Richard over his supposed lack of business acumen.

In contrast to the frosty relations between Winnie's father and her husband, Richard and Len got on well. Richard's letters to Beryl include a number of amiable anecdotes about their sorties and social gatherings, and one of Winnie's letters captures a flavour of their male bonhomie, describing how Richard returned home 'in a very peculiar condition' after he and Uncle Len had been out for a lunchtime drink: 'They were both very much the worse for it.'[22]

It is possible that some of the inter-family arguments that Beryl later adduced to her father's touchiness were in fact due to Winnie's difficult relationship with Len. As Len's daughter Hilary recalled: 'My father and Auntie Winnie used to fall out quite a lot . . . there was always this sort of conflict. My father was a difficult man, he didn't tolerate people well. Maybe there was a little bit of looking down. I think Winnie was jealous of my father doing quite so well.'[23] One argument between them at Chirbury was so vociferous that Hilary and Beryl got out of bed and sat on the stairs listening to the row going on below.

According to Beryl, Winnie adored her father but didn't get on with her mother, being embarrassed by her 'lowly' origins (Janet's father having worked as a gatekeeper at the docks). Insecurity about one's social standing is often at the root of feelings of snobbery, and Winnie was a classic example. Fearful lest others might think that she too came from a working-class background, she exaggerated the social gap between herself and the Bainbridges, and tried to distance herself from any hint of social inferiority in her own family. But the invariably unsubtle manner in which she did it – her nephew recalled that she would wear 'a hat with a veil and full make-up if she stepped outside the front door to collect the paper'[24] – wasn't calculated to win friends. Those who didn't warm to Winnie described her as 'putting on airs' and felt that she came across as a snob, her veneer of sophistication being exactly that: a veneer.

Winnie's showiness in public gained her the nickname 'The Duchess', but her seemingly obsessive concern over her self-image wasn't just an affectation stemming from social snobbery. While she was pregnant with Beryl, she suffered an attack of pernicious anaemia, a serious blood disorder that prevents the body processing Vitamin B_{12} and can cause hair, and even teeth, to fall out. Winnie was not, as Beryl claimed, 'injected with a hypodermic used on horses, full of raw liver',[25] but she was given injections of liver extract, a relatively new treatment developed in 1928.[26] The physical effects of the disease – Winnie lost her teeth and had to have dentures, and her thinning hair was cut and replaced by a wig – left her feeling self-conscious about her appearance and she would frequently use heavy make-up. All of which helps explain the distinctly artificial look about her in so many photographs from the 1940s and 1950s. Other symptoms of the disease included fatigue and depression, which may account for the family jokes about her spending so much time in bed, and the fact that Winnie told Beryl shortly before she died that she had 'tried to do away with herself'[27] when pregnant with her.

Winnie had initially been educated at Queen Mary High School, Anfield ('Fees £6 9s to £9 12s per annum'),[28] a respectable institution with a good reputation, but she was fortunate enough that her adolescence coincided with John James's commercial success. By the time she was sixteen he was sufficiently established to send his daughter to a finishing school in Eeklo, northern Belgium. Located between Bruges and Ghent, the Institut Notre-Dame aux Épines described itself as a 'High Class Boarding School for Young Ladies',[29] and during her time in Eeklo, in 1920–21, Winnie was instructed in all the attainments expected of a young lady: deportment, elocution, the rules of etiquette, tennis, speaking French and playing the piano. After her marriage she would have little opportunity to use such skills, which must have acted as a perpetual and irritating reminder of her failure to achieve any kind of social distinction. Nor was Richard particularly impressed: whenever Winnie tried to assert her social superiority he would remark sarcastically that playing the piano and speaking French were 'two blasted accomplishments essential to a housewife in the North of England'.[30]

On her return from Belgium, Winnie seems to have lived a comfortable and sociable life: a photograph album for 1924 shows her and her friends, Doris, Mabel and Joy, in their cloche hats and three-quarter-length dresses doing a passable suburban impression of 1920s Bright Young Things.[31]

It is unlikely that Winnie and Ellen Bainbridge got on well, though the anecdote Beryl later offered as proof can be discounted. According to this version, after her parents were married Richard suggested to his new bride that they look after his bedridden mother, to which Winnie responded with a brusque 'Over my dead body.'[32] However, the story seems to be an exaggeration, as it was only after 'the saintly Ellen' had died, in early 1927,[33] that Richard and Winnie were married, on 6 July, at Holy Trinity, Walton Breck.

Two years after their marriage, despite Richard's ongoing bankruptcy litigation, they moved into a large house in Abbey Road, West Kirby, an affluent suburb of Liverpool. The house featured a Doric-columned portico, spacious rooms, and a large garden front and back; there was also a twenty-three-year-old live-in maid, Margaret Powell. This was where Ian – or Reginald Ian as his name is recorded on the birth certificate in memory of Winnie's dead brother[34] – was born in 1929.

But in the wake of the official bankruptcy, reality began to catch up, not just for Richard in purely financial terms, but for Winnie, in the realization of what her life would now become. She seems to have gone through a period of disillusion, almost of depression, that had a lasting effect on her married life.[35] At the end of 1931 the family moved to a smaller, less impressive semi-detached property in Menlove Avenue, and it was here, on 21 November 1932, that Beryl was born.

TWO

Mummy and Daddy

Often and often my parents tell me angrily, sadly, I am mad
or very young, because my ideas do not corrispond with theirs
and they are at a loss to understand it.

To my parents I show a thoughtless comic exterior, and make
them laugh, when I am not upsetting them by my manners
and ideas.

My parents I hurt continually, although I love them deeply.
They cause me to despise myself greatly, for my lack of
tolerance towards their way of life.[1]

B ERYL'S BIRTH COINCIDED WITH what was probably the
lowest point in her father's career. Not only was Richard having
to start his working life from scratch, he had to cope with the financial and emotional pressures of maintaining a family. To economize,
the family moved again in 1933, to a smaller, cheaper property in
Ravenmeols Lane, Formby, a small village some twelve miles up the
coast from Liverpool. The money for the mortgage came, it was said,
from Winnie's father.[2]

To most people 'Goodacre', as the house was called, would have
seemed what it was, a new, reasonable-sized semi, albeit a distinctly
suburban one. If it wasn't as spacious as the house on Menlove Avenue,
it was by no means unattractive. Beryl's cousin Hilary found it welcom-
ing: 'I used to love going round to that house . . . sitting there in that
little back room, Auntie Winnie sitting with her feet up on the fender.'[3]
But in Beryl's memory the house was always cold, damp and cramped:
'We spent our lives cooped up in the side-room . . . jostling each other as

we took it in turns to get warm at the fire. If anybody called, perish the thought, my brother had to stand out in the hall. It was no use ushering visitors into the front-room; without a fire laid hours in advance, they ran the risk of frostbite.'[4]

The notion of keeping the front room standing idle, to be used only for visitors, was a common practice among lower middle-class households at the time. It was certainly not unique to the Bainbridges, and was more a sign of their conventionality than their perversity. Like the idea of a 'Sunday best' suit, it belonged to a period when maintaining appearances was considered important.

Beryl's childhood memories of cold and damp were in part due to growing up during the war years, when coal was rationed along with food and clothing. To save heating the small boxrooms that nominally served as children's bedrooms may have been one reason for the family's unusual sleeping arrangements; Ian slept with his father in one room, while Beryl and Winnie shared a bed in another. A second factor may have been the bout of pneumonia Beryl contracted in 1940, at the age of eight, which left her with 'a chronic unproductive cough for some years'.[5] Over the next decade or so she would suffer recurrent attacks of bronchitis, and Winnie may have felt that sleeping in a damp, unheated room was not ideal on health grounds.

Beryl would later adduce the sleeping arrangements, which seem to have lasted through the war years, as proof of her parents' temperamental incompatibility. There was probably some truth in this, though the concern about damp wasn't entirely imaginary, as a poem she wrote entitled 'My Little Room' shows: 'My little room . . . smells of damp grain and sweet ripe cheese.'[6] By the time she left for boarding school at the beginning of 1948 she seems to have had her own room, which she described as a place of peace with pictures of Lenin and George Bernard Shaw on the wall.

Although Richard's bankruptcy had an impact on the family finances, this has to be seen in context. The Bainbridges continued to give the outward appearance of doing well: they had a car and a telephone when the possession of such items was by no means common, and they took regular holidays. No expense was spared when it came to Ian and Beryl's education: both attended fee-paying schools and both benefited from private, extracurricular lessons and activities – Latin and music in Ian's case, and piano, dancing and elocution in Beryl's. Her childhood diaries, with their references to her father buying a diamond ring for her mother's birthday and numerous entries noting her parents' trips to the cinema, to the theatre, and to evenings spent playing cards with friends, contain little that would indicate undue concern about money.

Perceptions, though, are relative, and what would have been seen as necessary economies to a parent earning money and trying to cope with the shortages caused by war, might seem like parsimony or hardship to a child. Among the girls Beryl mixed with at school were many who came from families who were considerably better-off, so it is easy to see why she felt her childhood to be more financially impoverished than it was. Although it filled her with guilt, she couldn't stop herself being irritated by what she regarded as her father's thrift, 'switching off the lights as if liquid gold leaked from the bulbs',[7] or feeling embarrassed when she compared the state of the household, with its scuffed table, cracked mugs and tarnished cutlery, to that of her richer schoolfriends.

If the move to Ravenmeols Lane represented a backward step economically speaking, the house did have one positive advantage in Beryl's eyes: its proximity to the sea – and more specifically to an expanse of pine woods that bordered the dunes on the shoreline. As she grew older, it was to the pine woods she would go in order to escape the tensions of home life (though the late evenings she spent walking down by the dunes as a teenager were themselves one of the causes of that tension). The seashore was a space in which family rules and regulations didn't apply, it was where Beryl would develop a sense of her own independence and could let her imagination run free. It would also be where she first started to write seriously, and where she would fall in love for the first time.

––––––––

The precise extent to which Richard and Winnie's marital problems constituted an actual breakdown in their relationship isn't easy to determine. Beryl's diaries for 1944 and 1946 contain no hints of a troubled home life, nor do the letters her parents wrote to her when she was at boarding school. Nevertheless, there were periods when the tension between her parents was almost palpable. One of Beryl's early memories of childhood, written in a notebook in the 1950s, recalls how a peaceful evening could quickly descend into an almost literal struggle for mastery:

My mother and father . . . used to play a game, or so I believed. They would sit reading by the fire, their feet on a chair between them. And quite suddenly in the safe seeming kitchen with the warm fire they would begin to push hard at one anothers feet. Sole to sole they put their feet and pressed with all their might to bend their knees. And quite suddenly my fathers face so white always would break across into a scowl and then he would fling his feet away and the words would begin, and my mother weeps in her chair.[8]

Perhaps the most expressive of Beryl's agonized reflections about her parents' marriage is a diary entry in January 1949: 'Why don't Mummy and Daddy love each other?' It is followed by another entry a few days later, after she had returned to school: 'Oh God poor little Mummy left among the dishes and his everlasting bad temper.'[9] But as in most relationships there were ebbs and flows, and shortly after one flare-up Beryl noted in her diary: 'Daddy and Mummy are happy again.'[10] A memory of her parents during a period of calm – 'I'd come back from school one day to find my mother in the bath with my father scrubbing her back'[11] – implies the bond between them hadn't broken entirely. By her own admission Beryl had a tendency to misjudge the state of her parents' relationship. At one point she was so convinced her mother was about to leave her father that she booked a room for her at the Aber House Hotel, in Falkner Street, but when she told her what she'd done Winnie was 'absolutely horrified'.[12]

Ian's assessment was certainly less fraught than Beryl's. Being a few years older he seems not to have been unduly perturbed by Richard and Winnie's arguments, seeing them as a normal fact of life. When he and Beryl stood 'huddled together on the landing and listened to our parents seemingly bent on murder in the kitchen below', Ian would tell her soothingly: 'It's just an argument, Face-ache . . . We won't be orphans. They don't really hate each other.'[13]

But such reassurances had little effect. Beryl's view of her parents' marriage seems to have been conditioned by a deep feeling of insecurity. A clue to its origin is a recurring image of abandonment – not of herself being abandoned as such, but of being forcibly separated from her mother. This was based on an incident in which her father, irritated at Winnie's tardiness while shopping in a fruit store, drove off with Beryl, leaving her mother behind: 'I felt I should never see her again . . .

I mention this because from that time onward I retained, at least from time to time, a dreadful feeling of ugliness and worry inside me.'[14] Beryl saw her father's impatience as an expression of 'hate', and this fed into her anxiety about the state of her parents' relationship, as well as her perception of him.

The reverse of this anxiety was the sense of security she felt in her mother's presence. The contrast between these two states is highlighted by a childhood recollection of an argument between her parents at her aunties' house, during which she had 'cried and cried': 'Next I am in bed at home in the light and Mummy comes upstairs and says "And haven't you had your bath", [in] the most beautiful kindly voice . . . And then Mummy puts her two cool arms round me and strokes my face and already I have forgotten why the door slammed and why I have been waiting and crying, crying and waiting for Mummy to come in and for me to have my bath.'[15]

As Beryl grew older, recalling this maternal security affected her with an almost inexpressible emotion. She was 'unable to put into words exactly the feeling of safety and love' her mother gave her, and the loss of this feeling coloured her view of the present: 'Even now at moments of near suxcess,' she wrote shortly after leaving home for London in 1952, 'like a new job or being happy on a train with money to buy food and a new white coat, my mind suddenly recalls the security I knew, and nothing comes up to the complete happiness of that moment.'[16]

The childhood fear of abandonment and the corresponding desire for security would shape Beryl's experience of love in her subsequent relationships. In reaction to what she saw as the antagonism between her parents she formed an overly idealized conception of romantic love, and determined that when she grew up she would not be like them: 'I shall never marry, not like that anyway.'[17]

Beryl would write more about her father than about any other member of her family, though it is not always easy to square the tenderness of one anecdote with the hostility of another. One of her most affectionate and nostalgic portraits is an early recollection of being with him on one of his trips to Liverpool, during the course of which he would regale her with stories and bits of local history or invent elaborately imaginative games with her: 'He was very fond of playing a game called Departures . . . He would take me down to the pierhead and put me on the ferry boat to New Brighton. I would stand on the deck of the Royal Daffodil and watch him dwindling on the landing stage. Sometimes he waved his pocked handkerchief and sometimes he raised his homburg hat in a last emigration gesture of farewell.'[18]

But there are other recollections of a more confrontational nature, often provoked by what Beryl felt was her father's unfair treatment of her mother, with whom she identified and whose side she took in disputes. The petulant and violent outbursts that Beryl directed at him – she recalled jumping on his back and wrestling him to the ground during one of his arguments with Winnie – were prompted by a desire to protect her mother and hurt him for making her unhappy. Another childhood memory of an argument that erupted during a car journey shows that money was sometimes a factor in these domestic disputes: 'I can remember my father in the front with my grandfather, and my mother beside me on the seat. I was jubilant I remember because it seemed as if all the shouting was to be over. And they talked quietly together, till my mother raised her voice and my grandfather said "Winnie you can't get blood from a stone you know." And then I raised my two fists and beat my father on his back, quite hard many times.'[19]

Beryl's sense of despair at her parents' marriage – and her hostility towards her father in particular – seems to have reached its peak in the two or three years immediately prior to her leaving home for London in 1952. She would later recall this period in her diary: 'The foul language, the raised voices, the curses, the unnutterable misery year upon year till I left home. The wireless turned up to shut out the noise from the neighbours, the tenseness, the coarseness, trying to think of ways to kill him.'[20]

In her later journalism, when seeking to present a portrait of her home life, Beryl frequently drew on this difficult period. But genuine though her feelings might have been, they were not representative of Beryl's childhood as a whole, or of the full extent of her relationship with her father, especially given the fact that this was a period in which she went through a number of emotional crises of her own that undoubtedly contributed to the escalation of misunderstandings and tensions between them.

Admittedly, treading a path between the extremes of tenderness and hostility that characterize Beryl's recollections of her father isn't easy, and it is certainly difficult to convey in a newspaper profile. Journalists tended to focus on the darker, more dramatic side of their relationship, and the myth of Beryl as a writer forged in the emotional disturbance of a dysfunctional family served as the prominent narrative to explain why she became a novelist and account for the dark subject matter of her novels. Beryl herself was aware that such dramatic portrayals made good copy, with the result that she deliberately represented her father as an unrelenting monomaniac and her childhood as one in which his verbal violence and threats, his 'shouting and swearing',[21] set the prevailing tone. As she succinctly put it: 'From a writer's point of view, it was an ideal childhood.'[22]

There was at least an element of exaggeration in all this and, as has been seen, Beryl was not above fabricating 'proofs' of an antipathy between herself and her father. Although none of Beryl's letters to him have survived, there is one early postcard, written in the late 1940s, which gives an idea of the playfulness that existed between them when things were going well. Written as if to give her father news while he was away on a business trip, the card relies on family in-jokes, and the comical nickname for Beryl and her mother alludes to Richard's habitual complaints about Winnie's indolence:

Darling Daddy,
Another up to date epistle from the Dundonothins. It is now 11.30 in the morning. Mummy is still in bed watching the wardrobe.
    All love, Beryl xxxxxxx[23]

Richard's letters to his daughter are similarly playful, and though they aren't without a certain patriarchal formality, they are tender and considerate. He reassures Beryl she is loved, takes her requests seriously, and tries to deal with her problems at school. He addresses her with extravagant pet-names, 'My darling little humbug' or 'Darling cherry blossom Berry', and spends hours writing to her. He would send her long, fantastical stories in an attempt to amuse her – often adopting a comic, mock-Irish accent as part of his narrative persona, which was a shared joke between them – and sign himself 'Your fatty daddy'. The image projected by these letters bears little resemblance to the portrait she later painted.

This is not to say that Richard couldn't also be moody, irritable or depressed, or that Beryl wasn't deeply affected by his behaviour, just that it is misleading to leave out the counterbalancing feeling of affection she felt towards him and only see his influence on her in negative, one-dimensional terms. Her recollection that 'he might be full of fun for weeks at a stretch – listening to the wireless in the dark; taking us for runs in the car; treating us to afternoon tea in Southport',[24] betrays an affection that belies her caricature of him as a domestic tyrant.

Richard was undoubtedly a key figure in Beryl's psychological development. His significance can be seen by the fact that he stalks so many of her novels as a recurring figure, that of the homburg-wearing older man, a symbol of vague threat but also, importantly, one of attraction and fascination. After his death in 1961, Beryl would attempt to explore her contradictory feelings for 'my little Dad' in a radio play, 'Another Friday'. She would continually rework this piece over the years, turning it first in 1967 into a television play, 'I'm Not Criticising . . . I'm Remembering' (revised and retitled as 'O My Darling' in 1973), and then incorporating elements of it into *Words Fail Me*, a television adaptation of *A Quiet Life*, broadcast in 1979. The thread running through them all is a primal memory about her father ('Once he was all love for his little girl . . . sacrificing his all for her'),[25] and the loss of the love she knew as a child, symbolized in his rejection of her attempt to hold his hand, as if he was repelled by her touch: 'And once we went for a walk . . . and I tried to hold his hand and he pushed me away, like I was making advances to him.'[26]

This sense of having been physically rejected by her father had a long-lasting effect, and the fear of rejection would haunt her, undermining her feelings of self-worth and leaving her fundamentally insecure about her relationships with men. Ironically, it was her almost pathological anxiety that she was no longer loved, often expressed through an obsessive jealousy, that would be a contributory factor in the very rejection she most feared.

Beryl herself recognized this, seeing a connection between her fear of rejection, her low self-esteem and her desire for love: 'A very early rejection of love or withdrawal by ones parents, a repeat of this later on in puberty, and everything is a pattern afterwards . . . For some perverted form of self hatred I go on making messy relationships, fail and fling myself into a fresh one. I seem to have an intense craving for narcissistic gratification. I have to get love by all sorts of means.'[27]

During much of her childhood Beryl's attitude towards her mother was almost one of idolatry: 'I adored her, I thought she was the most wonderful person in the world. I was always hugging and cuddling her.'[28] This is borne out by the handful of surviving letters and notes that Beryl wrote to her, the earliest of which is a postcard from the early 1940s addressed to 'Miss'es Mummykin Bainbridge'.[29] A verse written in a birthday card a few years later gives some idea of the typically effusive outbursts of which her mother was the focus:

> To my little mummy
> The pride of my heart
> I know t'would kill me
> If we were to part[30]

Extravagant expressions of love between a child and a parent are not uncommon, but the notion expressed here – that the loss of the love object would result in one's own death – is a convention more commonly used between lovers, as is the symbol of the red rose, which Beryl had drawn on the card's cover.

That these outbursts were more than just simple effusions of childhood affection is evidenced by an extraordinary letter she wrote to her mother shortly after going to boarding school, at the age of fifteen:

> For my own Mummy,
> Mummy darling you don't know how much I love you. I've been writing this for weeks, ever since I came here, and I've written it with the day grey outside, or blue and blind with sun. Mummy, when I grow up I'm going to be great, and I promise, oh so much that you will be proud of me. I don't want you to laugh at this, because I love you, and I miss you with a pain so great. I've dreamt of home and you and Dad and Ian, and I know you understand. Its very hard being young, and aching to be old and wonderful. I lie awake and scheme and dream and fashion all the wonderful things I'm going to do one day with you down there so happy with Dad, and a great love within my heart swelling and hurting, because I love you. And I know, because if there is a God, he knows too, that I am going to be all that you are praying I will be. Mummy, please believe me and be happy, because as I write

this I am crying with all I hold and want to tell you. It is so lonely here, not because there are no friends, but because I feel as if there is a hundred years of space and time all laughing at me, because I want to do so much. To act and grow and feel the wind in my throat, and know that I am getting somewhere, and that I have you both so happy made. Oh Mummy, Mummy, please read this and believe what I am writing. I want to cry so much, and that is foolish, but I love you so, and my heart is spilling out words and thoughts as fast as it is able, and I am lonely.

Mummy, darling Mummy, I do love you so. When I am older and my dreams are all coming true I want to see your eyes come happy in your face, and all my love is pouring at your feet. I love you so. Oh Mummy, listen to what I'm writing, and believe, because I'm crying now, and oh I want you to understand so much.

Please love me always Mummy, because you don't know how much I love you, and how I am crying. I want to be more famous and more wonderful than you have ever dreamed, and one day Mummy, it will come true . . . Oh darling Mummy please please believe in me and think me wonderful, because the world is going to be lovely for me, and you and Daddy are going to be so proud.[31]

It would be hard to imagine any response that would reassure the writer of such a letter that they were loved. But aside from an almost obsessive need for affection, the letter also reveals Beryl's anxiety about being unworthy of love in her mother's eyes, and – significantly – her assumption that worldly success was a way of earning that love.

Beryl would refer to Winnie as 'Mummy' until she was in her mid-thirties, hinting that their relationship had an infantilizing effect and that at an unconscious level she continued to see herself as a child. As an adult, this would find expression in her habit of pouting and adopting 'a funny little girl's voice',[32] as A. N. Wilson put it, whenever she was accused of wrongdoing or confronted with difficult emotional situations in which she thought she was being criticized.

After her father's death Beryl went through a period of reassessment. She came to a realization that her own psychological make-up was similar to his and that she shared his depressive moods, which as a child she had naively attributed to meanness or emotional coldness. In that peculiar geometry of family relationships, affection for one parent is often in inverse proportion to disaffection with the other, and Beryl's view of her mother went through a corresponding reversal. She began to see Winnie's manipulation of those around her with a more censorious eye, and the idealized love she once felt turned to irritation and even dislike. By the 1960s her antagonism to her mother's visits was such that she warned a friend, 'my reverend Mama is arriving, so don't be cross if I am somewhat strained. The thought of it strikes chill to my heart.'[33]

Confronted by the dramatic emotional triangle formed by Beryl and her parents, it is easy to forget there was a fourth member of the household: her older brother, Ian. He was a significant figure in her childhood and fulfilled many of the roles of the older brother: ground-breaker, mentor, protector and occasional bully.[34] If at times he treated her with the condescension that is a cliché of brother and sister relationships, there was nevertheless a deep, unstated affection between them.

In many ways Ian and Beryl were a perfect example of the diverging character traits seen in older and younger siblings. Parents tend to be stricter and more nervous with a first child than with subsequent children, and if they have social aspirations they tend to push them harder in terms of education. As a result the first child is often more conventional and less likely to challenge parental authority. Ian certainly fulfilled his parents' expectations: neat, conscientious and an academic high achiever, he went on to university to study Law and became what was once the defining occupation of the aspiring middle classes, a solicitor.

By contrast, parents are often more relaxed – indulgent even – with a second child, who consequently becomes less disciplined and less willing to accept discipline. As a second child, Beryl was given more freedom, and took more liberties, than Ian, and she was always having to play catch-up, her academic achievements being compared – to their detriment – to his. Beryl quickly realized she couldn't compete with Ian on his terms so she didn't even try. Instead, she used alternative strategies to get her way. Where Ian was careful, respectful of authority and academically successful, Beryl was reckless, rebellious, and drawn to non-academic subjects like drama and art. Where Ian relied on knowledge and learning, Beryl trusted in instinct and imagination. In retrospect it was almost inevitable that Ian would be seen as the clever one, and Beryl the artistic one.[35]

The difference in their personalities was reflected in the way each was viewed by their Uncle Len and Auntie Lil. While Ian was a frequent and welcome visitor to their house, joining them for games of bridge, Beryl was distinctly *persona non grata*: Auntie Lil considered her a bad influence on Hilary, and Uncle Len never got over the time he had seen Beryl eating in the street, a terrible social *faux pas* in his eyes, which he described as 'appalling behaviour'.[36]

In later life Beryl's relationship with Ian was more distant, especially after she became a published writer. She was not always tactful or discreet in her references to Ian in print. Her comments about him having a 'breakdown' when he was eighteen or having suffered from abuse,[37] or her depiction of him in *A Quiet Life* as timid and repressed, may have led to a certain reserve on his part and a desire to keep some distance between them.

During the 1960s and early 1970s, Beryl would take her family to visit Ian's at their house in Montgomery, but this gradually ceased as the children grew older. If she was asked about Ian in interviews she would confess to knowing 'very little about him',[38] and in an article written during the 1980s she admitted to exchanging Christmas greetings with him over the phone, but little else: 'We never speak to each other during the rest of the year.'[39]

After Ian died in November 1987, Beryl retrospectively tried to find some shared ground, seeing a connection between them in the fact that he had become a country coroner: 'So we were alike after all, in that we both had an interest in death.'[40]

———

Despite the number of Bainbridges and Baineses further up the family tree, Beryl's childhood revolved round a comparatively small circle of relatives, the most significant of which were her two paternal aunts, Nellie and Margo. Visits to 'the aunties' – they were most commonly referred to in the plural – abound in Beryl's early diaries. Many of Winnie's references to Margo in her letters are to do with dressmaking, and the two aunts would famously feature in Beryl's novel *The Dressmaker*, though for dramatic purposes she made Nellie the dressmaker rather than Margo.

The two women were very different in temperament: 'Aunt Nellie was very sweet when I was little. I can remember how cuddly she was; she was the one who did the cooking and the looking after. In the end she annoyed me, though, she was so convinced she was right about everything. Whereas Aunt Margo, who could be an absolute melodramatic bitch, questioned everything, she was curious about things.'[41] Of the two, Beryl preferred Auntie Margo, not just for her unconventional attitude but for the tragically romantic story of her brief marriage. In an anecdote that says much about Winnie's attitude to her daughter, to her sister-in-law, and to the past, Beryl recalled that when Auntie Margo died in 1964, leaving her the contents of the house in Bingley Road, her mother asked her what she wanted to keep: 'I said I didn't mind about the furniture, that I was only interested in the letters and the photographs. Before I got there she wangled the key out of the next-door neighbours and took the bottom drawer of the wardrobe into the backyard. Tipping the letters and the snapshots into a metal bin she made a bonfire of the lot.'[42]

On the Baines side of the family there were regular visits to and from her maternal grandparents, as well as from Uncle Len and his family. To these actual relatives were added a number of other *faux* aunts and uncles: most notably Uncle Charlie, otherwise known as Charles White, the proprietor of the Herbert Arms Hotel in Chirbury, and his wife Elizabeth ('Auntie White'). Beryl, like Winnie, enjoyed her frequent stays in Chirbury. Photographs show games of bowls on the lawn, horse-riding expeditions, and convivial, sociable evenings set against the hotel's elegantly rustic decor. Other entertainments included plays Beryl had written during the day and which would be performed in the evening. One piece was inspired by the popular song 'Open the door Richard',[43] no doubt because of its comic refrain, 'Hey Dick! Open that door!' Although Richard was an enthusiastic participant in these theatrical performances,[44] Winnie was not: 'She was quite remote', as Hilary recalled.[45]

Chirbury also offered the opportunity for numerous outings, whether to the Sun Inn at Marton, managed by Charlie's brother Stanley and his wife Elizabella ('Auntie Belle'), or walks across country. On one of her walks at Chirbury, Beryl met a seventeen-year-old boy, Terry Alderman (no. 3 on her boyfriend list), with whom she had a brief and entirely platonic holiday romance. Terry was staying at Marrington Hall nearby, a magnificent, half-timbered property being used by the British educationalist and psychotherapist, George Lyward, to house a community of 'delinquent, disturbed or disturbing boys'.[46] Terry's ardent letters ('I love you <u>very very very</u> much!')[47] give the impression that Winnie didn't approve of Beryl going out with boys ('Could you come out with me some time or would your mother object?'),[48] though whether this was because she felt Beryl was too young – she was thirteen at the time – or because the boys at Marrington Hall weren't suitable, isn't clear.

The only dark spot regarding Chirbury was an incident Beryl first mentioned in *Forever England*, some forty years after it supposedly happened. According to Beryl the Herbert Arms Hotel had a staff of three, a land girl called Sybil,[49] Mrs Parry the cleaning lady, and 'Fred the cowman', who slept in the attic room of the hotel, close to the bedroom in which Beryl and her parents stayed. Fred, as she put it, 'bothered' her: 'When I was little Fred used to come into my room to kiss me goodnight.'[50] One evening to deter him she locked the door to the bedroom before she fell asleep, and the resulting drama – a ladder had to be fetched so that Uncle Charlie could climb in through the window – put an end to the visits.[51]

In an interview given a year before she died, Beryl was more explicit: 'When I was about eight I suppose, for at least three years he would come up to bed, wake me up [and] fiddle with me.' She added that sexual abuse was common at the time – 'I wasn't the only one' – and that the local milkman used to 'grope' her brother and other boys in exchange for letting them ride around on his milk cart.[52]

There are strong reasons to doubt this recollection – or rather Beryl's later presentation of it. In the first instance, she refers to Fred at Chirbury a couple of times in her 1946 diary and it is clear she had no feelings of repugnance or anxiety about him: 'We are going to Chirbury at Easter. Longing to see Fred and the puppies.'[53] Secondly, Beryl actually talked about Fred's attentions at the time, only the way she framed the matter then was very different to her later protrayal of it.

When Beryl was about thirteen or fourteen she talked quite openly, almost boastingly, about Fred to her cousin Hilary, telling her she was having 'an affair with him'.[54] Even at the time Hilary didn't believe her – Fred certainly liked Beryl, but then everyone did – and as there were other people sleeping on the top floor aside from Fred, she doubted he had the opportunity. Hilary was also adamant that Ian wouldn't have let himself be subjected to the things Beryl later claimed – claims that Hilary had never heard before despite having spent as much time in Chirbury as Beryl.

Did Beryl exaggerate or invent the story for Hilary's sake, to project an image of herself as an object of male desire and show off to her younger, more impressionable cousin? Or was her later portrayal of it as abuse a belated admission of something she'd hitherto been unable to confront? Both interpretations are possible, but there isn't enough evidence to be certain either way.

That Beryl was the subject of unwanted male attention is clear – her diary records several incidents in which men tried to kiss or touch her. Yet one is left with the suspicion that the 'affair' with Fred was not unlike those with thirty-two-year-old Jim Palmer or twenty-eight-year-old Jimmy Clunie, older men with whom the fourteen-year-old Beryl flirted, testing social and sexual boundaries in the way pubescent girls often do. That Beryl enjoyed these kind of flirtatious encounters – and felt confident enough to deal with them in her own way – is shown by a diary entry from 1949, in which a man in the cinema sat next to her and started stroking her thigh: 'I smiled and took his hand away, and we became friendly. He told me all about New York and Chicago etc. He was a sailor. Its funny, people aren't bad if you behave sensibly. Mummy would be horrified.'[55]

It is probably no coincidence that Beryl first published her account at a time when feminism was crossing into the mainstream. Her contrarian response was that there was a certain 'cant' in feminist protestations about the predatory nature of male sexuality. She felt that younger women were making a fuss over nothing as regards sexism or sexual harassment, and as a way of making her point she tended to exaggerate her own experiences to show she had suffered things that were as bad, if not worse, but that they hadn't affected her.

As with her father's violent temper and the notion of parental abuse, Beryl knew child sex abuse was a taboo issue and she enjoyed the frisson of shock provoked in an interviewer when she passed it off as commonplace. 'It was completely natural for men on trains to fiddle with you,' she told the British Library interviewer in 2008, and when she recounted her story about Ian and his friends being the subject of abuse, she even laughed, adding 'Well, they didn't mind . . .'[56]

The problem is that most people do mind, and the more Beryl kept trying to insist this form of abuse was normal, the more untenable her position seemed and the more bizarre it was to maintain it: 'My theory is that as long as there is no violence – no holding a knife to you – it can't be classified as rape. A husband can't rape a wife; I don't think it is possible. As long as you're not a virgin I don't understand what all the fuss is about. When I was younger you just didn't mention abuse, whether it was by strangers or your husband. You just got on with it.'[57]

Beryl's attitude is shocking in its attempt to dismiss what most people would consider a normal response to unwanted sexual attention. Is she really saying that she would be completely indifferent to an act of non-consensual sex? And if that were true, what does it say about her attitude to sex? Mary Kenny was one of many women who were angered by Beryl's comments. She criticized her for attempting to turn sexual abuse into something that should be submitted to in silence:

> Beryl Bainbridge has also written quite jokily about the number of times adults 'groped' or otherwise sexually molested children when she was a child in Liverpool. Her view is that the fuss about this kind of thing is entirely overdone. My reaction to Beryl's memoir was rather horrified. I am thankful that I never experienced any form of such adult molestation as a child, or any improper conduct from an adult. And I don't think it a sardonic point of merriment. But that is Beryl's take on it.[58]

Beryl's attitude was all the more problematic in that she kept the fact she had been raped during the early 1950s a secret. That she had been emotionally scarred by the assault at the time but would later try to downplay its psychological effect seems to be a perplexing paradox. Perhaps the simplest explanation is that Beryl was, to use a popular pseudo-psychological term, 'in denial', and that in denying that rape or abuse had a damaging psychological effect on others, she persuaded herself that she was unaffected by it too.

THREE

Education

> At school I began by being unpopular and then extremely
> popular. When I was unpopular I seemed small and plain and
> weak, when I became popular I assumed height and weight
> and a loudness that I kept till I left school . . .[1]

BERYL'S EARLY SCHOOL YEARS up to the age of nine were spent
at the Girls College in Formby. Located on Freshfield Road, a short
walk from Ravenmeols Lane, the college was actually a private school
run from a large house, with extensive gardens that doubled as a tennis
court and croquet lawn. The school's principals, the Misses Gill, who
had been running the school since the 1890s, lived next door in an
almost equally large house that accommodated boarders and the 'fully
qualified resident and visiting staff'.[2] The Misses Gill promoted the
college as a genteel Prep school helping pupils pass exams for a variety
of boards – but with the added benefits of 'foreign mistresses', 'individual care', and 'country and sea air'.[3]

The refined atmosphere of the Girls College – at one end of the
garden there was a cart that girls could practise stepping up onto and
descending from as if getting into or out of a carriage,[4] and French
was spoken one afternoon a week – no doubt reminded Winnie of her
time at finishing school in Belgium. Mindful of the need to instil in
her daughter the accomplishments necessary for a young lady, Winnie
also sent Beryl for extracurricular music lessons in Southport, eight
miles north of Formby, where she gained her certificate for elementary
piano playing.

The Misses Gill lived up to their advertising: Beryl succeeded in
passing the entrance exam to Merchant Taylors', a fee-paying school
for girls in Crosby. In September 1942, two months short of her tenth

birthday, Beryl entered Form LII, the penultimate junior year. The academic level at Merchant Taylors' was considerably higher than she had been used to, and though bright she was temperamentally unsuited to the discipline of scholarly study. As a result, she constantly struggled to keep up during her time there; she would remain at Merchant Taylors' for the next six years, but it was not a particularly happy period.

Most of the other pupils came from backgrounds that were more financially comfortable than her own. Faced with peers who were also educationally superior and socially more confident, Beryl's reaction was to become the rebel, an aggressive defence mechanism that was the cause of her initial unpopularity. She adopted a generally contrarian attitude to school authority and early on acquired the nickname 'Basher'. In later life she described herself as being 'loutish'[5] at school, and claimed she once challenged the whole of her form to a fight. Her subsequent popularity was simply the flip side of this: as pupils get older and less tolerant of school regulations and authority, the rebel becomes a figure to be admired. It is easy to imagine Beryl's subversive sense of humour enlivening a boring lesson, and her impudence towards unpopular teachers gaining her the respect of her peers.

This combative attitude wasn't quite what it seemed, being not so much an attempt to assert herself as a means of ingratiating herself, and she tended to attack older girls – or bothersome boys – rather than those her own age. Fighting to prevent her friends being bullied was analogous to the way she had attacked her father to protect her mother. This attitude even extended to taking punishment on her friends' behalf; when a teacher demanded that someone in the class own up to a misdemeanour, Beryl would take the blame even if she wasn't the culprit.[6]

Beryl's first year at Merchant Taylors' can be sketched in outline. School records show that she engaged in the usual activities: she acted in the Christmas *tableau*; performed in a play called *The Tables Turned* in the spring term of 1943; and took part in a gym display by the girls in her form.

A more detailed picture of school life emerges after 1944, as Beryl began to keep a diary at the start of the year. From this it becomes clear that her performance at school was very inconsistent. Her attention was divided sharply between a small number of subjects that interested her and which she would consequently do well in, and the majority of subjects that did not interest her. Beryl's inability to concentrate on these left her constantly at odds with her teachers.

Drama was one of her highlights, and though it wasn't taught as a separate subject, plays were regularly staged throughout the year. Beryl's diary entry for 10 March, 'Dramatic's. Tailor of Gloster',[7] is confirmed by school records showing that Form II put on *The Tailor of Gloucester*, an adaptation of Beatrix Potter's story about a tailor whose work on a waistcoat is finished by the mice he rescued from his cat. Beryl played the role of the tailor and the production won a prize in the school's acting competition. As Beryl put it in her diary: 'Have competion and win it. Celarbrate.'[8]

English, taught by Miss Bertha Peck, was another subject in which Beryl, if not excelled, at least showed a definite talent, even though this is belied by the standard of her handwriting. On the face of it Miss Peck might not have seemed like a typically inspirational teacher – a spinster in her late forties, she 'wore her hair in plaited coils that looked like earphones' and was described as being 'very thin and wizened'[9] – but her impact on Beryl's development is shown by the dramatic improvement in her writing over the next few years. She encouraged Beryl to read books by Dickens, Kipling and Henry Williamson. It was during an English class with Miss Peck, who also ran a Junior Dramatic Society at a Catholic church in Crosby,[10] that Beryl first studied *Richard II*, which she would always cite as one of her favourite Shakespeare plays.[11]

Beryl's success in English and drama, however, seemed to be the only bright spots in her school career, and elsewhere the 1944 diary records a succession of poor performances and confrontations with teachers:

28 February: In Miss Martens lesson I have a row about going to pictures in a lesson.
29 February: Mr Simmons wants arithmetic paper. Can [not] find it. Sent out of room.
6 March: With Miss Martin an awful row.
15 June: Trouble at school.
22 June: History absolutely daft.
27 June: Rotten day.
13 July: Awful Geography lesson. No fun at all to-day worse luck.[12]

On 27 April she confided to her diary that she was to 'Go in for scoler-ship soon', and two days later she noted 'Exam or scolorship today'. It is not difficult to see why she wasn't successful.

Despite her less than stellar school performance, when she moved up to Form III Beryl was put into the academic stream (the other stream being euphemistically termed 'housecraft'). If the intention was to push her to work harder, it failed. It soon became clear she was never going to be an academic success and her diary for 1946 continued the litany of clashes with school authority:

15 January: Got in to trouble at school.
28 January: School once more. How I hate it.
5 February: School. More trouble. I've got to work.
6 February: Damn it, These Teachers.
11 February: Oh School how I hate you.
7 March: Got told of at school today I don't think Miss Galbraith likes me at all.[13]

In February 1944 Beryl's diary mentions another significant event, one that would set her on course for her subsequent acting career: 'Go to Crane Hall with mummy and fix up lessons.'[14] The lessons were in what Mrs Harold Ackerley termed 'Dramatic art', and took place in her studios on the fourth floor of Crane's Music Hall, a huge five-storey brick building in Hanover Street that housed both a music store and a theatre.

For the next year or so Beryl would go to Mrs Ackerley's studios on Wednesday afternoons after school[15] for her half-hour lesson, which involved improving her elocution, practising accents, and reciting a dramatic piece or monologue that she had taken home to memorize the previous week. Mrs Ackerley began by correcting pronunciation, stressing the value of certain vowels and consonants: she was not fond of the short 'a' sound – one of the characteristics of the Liverpool accent – and would teach her pupils to say 'parse the glarse', rather than 'pas the glas'.[16] Although Mrs Ackerley was, as the nameplate on the door of her studio announced, a 'teacher of elocution and drama', her lessons encompassed much more. Her emphasis was not so much on 'speaking posh' as on appreciating the beauty and harmony of the language, and to

Mrs Ackerley elocution and good manners went hand in hand – it was almost like attending a finishing school.

Mrs Ackerley, who had established her 'school' in 1919 and continued as its head until she died, almost blind, in 1964, was a distinguished and distinctive figure. Known as the 'star maker' for her ability to spot acting talent, she was easily recognizable in the street, always elegantly dressed with lustrous auburn hair and emerald-tinted spectacles. Her voice was a little on the smoky side – she was a heavy smoker of Craven A cigarettes – but it had a soft richness that combined gravitas and warm friendliness. She kept a bottle of sherry in her studio and would sip at a glass during lessons, occasionally offering one to a student if they got overexcited at having passed an exam: 'Now dear, have a Dry Fly Sherry and calm down.' In marked contrast to her feelings about school, Beryl looked forward to her time at Mrs Ackerley's: 'A lesson soon. Glad am I',[17] as she noted in her diary.

Mrs Ackerley wasn't Beryl's first contact with the world of theatre and performance. Before the war, at the age of four, she had been enrolled in the Ainsdale School of Dancing,[18] just outside Southport. It had been the first step in Winnie's plan for her daughter's future, and initially it seemed to pay off. In June 1937 the *Southport Visitor* reported on the Ainsdale School's matinee performance of the ballet 'The Little Dressmakers' Dance' at the Garrick Theatre, Southport, and the accompanying photograph of the dancing troupe, whose ages ranged from three to six, marked Beryl's first public appearance as a performer.

But there were aspects of dancing that were problematic for a girl who was overly self-conscious about her body. Beryl's description of an impromptu dance performance at her cousin's butcher shop, when she and her father called in to buy meat, shows how humiliating and embarrassing she found it:

> I didn't care for my cousin Jack or my Uncle John. When my Uncle John saw me he made me tap-dance on the sawdust spot because he knew I went to dancing classes. He said I had bonny legs. On a bad day I had to sing 'Kiss me Goodnight, Sergeant-major', my

cousin Jack in his bloody apron thumping the chopping board with his cleaver to give me a beat. There was the head and shoulders of a pig on the shelf beneath the clock. It looked more like a simpering girl than a porker, with its stiff yellow eyelashes, its coquettish shoulders rounded above its cut-off trotters.[19]

The images of dead meat clearly have a symbolic quality, reflecting Beryl's distaste for what she saw as the physicality of her own body. As a young child this was less of a problem, but when she reached puberty she became increasingly sensitive about her body and its size, especially her legs, and grew to dislike dancing entirely.

Drama was different: Beryl was perfectly happy to follow the path laid out for her by her mother. She found the business of rehearsing and putting on plays exciting, and success in drama was as important to her as it was to Winnie. Much of Beryl's 1944 diary is taken up with entries recording the names of plays she had listened to on the radio or seen at the theatre, and almost every Wednesday she noted down a brief précis of the pieces she had to learn for her lesson at Crane Studios, such as Clemence Dane's *Bill of Divorcement* or J. B. Priestley's *Time and the Conways*.

Within a month of enrolling at Mrs Ackerley's, Beryl began preparing for the London Academy of Music, Drama and Art exams in acting, or as she put it in her diary: 'Go in for Bronze medle on April 17th. Very excited.' The staging of the exams was almost a performance in itself. When the LAMDA examiner came to Liverpool to see those taking the exam, candidates would be sent down in the lift to the Crane theatre wearing full stage make-up, which Mrs Ackerley helped to apply. After being called to the stage they would perform their three acting pieces, and when it was over they talked to the examiner, who would tell them, there and then, whether they had passed.[20]

Beryl made rapid progress through the grades, gaining the bronze medal in April – along with a ten-shilling bonus promised to her by her father – and the silver in August. In the Christmas examinations of 1944 she received the gold medal, prompting an item of news in the *Liverpool Echo* with the heading 'A Liverpool success': 'Liverpool once again furnishes a notable recruit to the ranks of dramatic art. The newcomer is Beryl Margaret Bainbridge, who, at 12, is believed to be the youngest Associate of Dramatic Art.'[21]

Another piece in the *Formby Times* featured a photograph of a smiling Beryl with a perm, looking sophisticated and much older than her twelve and a half years.[22] Her family were understandably pleased, and the congratulatory letter Beryl received from her maternal grandparents ('Who knows? You might soon find your way to the Playhouse!')[23] shows that a career in the theatre was already being considered as a possibility.

A few years later, Winnie took another step in her vicarious plan to advance Beryl's dramatic career by encouraging her to answer a BBC advertisement calling for child actors. Beryl's first job came in April 1947,[24] after she received a telegram from *Northern Children's Hour* organizer Nan MacDonald asking her to play a part in *A Cabin for Crusoe*, an adaptation of David Severn's 'camping and tramping' novel about self-sufficiency and living in the wild. Other cast members included BBC regulars such as Brian Trueman, Herbert Smith and Fred Fairclough, and another young child actor, Billie Whitelaw. The novel's sequel, *Wagon for Five*, was also adapted six months later, and Beryl reprised her role as Pamela Sanville, a farm girl who befriends the novel's adventurous hero.

Beryl's involvement with *Northern Children's Hour* was relatively brief, effectively curtailed by her move to boarding school in Tring in January 1948. Nevertheless, the experience was significant in that it was her first taste of professional acting and it established contacts that would be useful in later life. It was on *Children's Hour* in 1956 that Beryl's first stories would be performed and broadcast.

Perhaps inevitably given that she grew up during a time of war, Beryl became interested in political and social issues. After her lesson with Mrs Ackerley on Wednesdays, she would go to the Tatler News Theatre, a five-minute walk away, where a typical programme would include a newsreel, a travelogue, an item of Hollywood news, a musical short and a cartoon. She would also listen regularly to *The Brains Trust* (or 'the brian's Trust' as she repeatedly referred to it in her diary), a radio programme in which a panel of experts explored philosophical and scientific ideas through questions put by listeners.

Beryl kept up with the progress of the war, noting down important events and battles in her diary,[25] so the end of hostilities was a significant event. It formed the subject of one of her earliest surviving poems, entitled 'I Remember Peace Day', which she composed after taking her dog Pedro out for a walk on 7 May 1945, the day Germany signed the act of military surrender at Reims:

I remember Peace Day. There were workers in the fields of corn
Singing, bekoning. I held Pedro close because
My chest was growing, and I was [self] concious.
Italians on the hay, laughing, kind.
Birds high in the starless wide.
I remember Peace Day. Warm brown chin
Rubbing my forehead, impudent teeth,
More laughter. Confusion, blessed youth.
Germany has signed, the war is over . . .
I remember Peace Day. Blackberries warm
Upon my mouth, Pedro fast asleep across
My chest. Lazy day, sleep, and hot oblivion.[26]

Although the poem as a whole is halting in expression and suffers in terms of clarity as a result, the image of Beryl holding Pedro in order to hide her embarrassment at the burgeoning physicality of her body, and her self-consciousness at the gaze of the Italian prisoners of war working in the fields, is nevertheless revealing.[27]

The final lines invoke a complex of sensations, linking the warm brown chin of one of the workers rubbing against her forehead as he tries to kiss her, to the sensuous evocation of the warm blackberries on her mouth and the dog lying against her breasts.

Beryl's incipient interest in social issues was stimulated by the school through a series of extracurricular debates and talks, with titles such as 'Nurseries and Nursery Schools', 'Patriotism and Nationalism' and 'Careers for Women'.[28] In 1946 Beryl took part in the school's inter-house public-speaking competition, helping her house (Fordham) to come second in the debate, the topic of which was 'How youth can promote international friendship'. Inspired by this, she began corresponding with a number of penpals from around Europe: Harry Wesseling in Holland, who shared Beryl's interest in stamp-collecting; Paul Vigo, a twenty-one-year-old Italian studying to become a Catholic priest; and Jacques Delebassée, a student in France.

Over the next few years she would also be encouraged in her new-found political interests by left-leaning local benefactors. One of these was a Formby woman, the wife of a newspaper reporter on the *Liverpool Echo*, who sought to broaden Beryl's cultural education by taking her to classical concerts. It was at her house after one such performance that Beryl met Helah Criddle, the wife of John Frankland Criddle, and she was subsequently taken up by them. The Criddles were committed and active socialists, and meetings at their house, a fifteen-minute walk from Ravenmeols Lane, opened Beryl up to a whole new world of politics and culture:

> Mrs Criddle lent me books to take home. My father was in sympathy with the titles. They were all left-wing book choices dealing with the Russian Revolution and the Socialist Movement and he said he approved. I did a pen-and-ink drawing of Marshal Stalin and he pinned it up on the wall under the Swansea Tin-Plate Company calendar. My brother called him Joe after that. The Criddles lived over the railway line in Wicks Lane in a wonderful house covered in dust, gloomy and full of books and sepia photographs of men with staring eyes under peaked caps . . . The house was always full of people, some of whom must have come on trains from somewhere strange because they all looked like tramps and spoke like teachers and called each other comrade.[29]

Winnie was undoubtedly discomfited by Beryl's political activism, albeit for very different reasons. She couldn't bring herself to even mention the word 'communism' and warned her daughter to be discreet in social situations:

> Darling I do hope you are not letting your little world know of your political views. There is a great deal of trouble going on at the moment in the outside world through certain beliefs (you know what I mean) and your whole career could be ruined through your beliefs. The British C.I.D. have been told to arrest anyone having views in this direction. Be told, darling, through your ignorance of the subject . . . you could ruin all our plans for you. The situation is really serious and the least you have to say in public on the subject the better. So please be sensible.[30]

That there was a class element to all this is clear. Richard Malthouse, who went to Uppingham public school and acted as Beryl's informal boyfriend – one vetted as it were by Winnie – ridiculed her political enthusiasms: 'After getting your last letter, I rather feel now as if I ought to call you "comrade", you and all your communism tripe!'[31]

Beryl's diaries for 1944 and 1946 also provide a glimpse of her other interests and activities at the time. She was a fan of the comedian Tommy Handley's BBC radio programme *ITMA*, for example, and when Handley died in 1949 she cut out newspaper reports of his funeral and stuck them into her diary. A few weeks later she and her friends held a seance using an ouija board and tried to contact him: 'We had a wow of a night yesterday night. We tried to get Tommy Handley back, but of course nothing whatever came of it, much to my dissappointment.'[32]

Beryl's diaries are almost as revealing for what they don't mention as for what they do: while she records her troubles at school, she makes no reference to any disagreements at home, and though her desire to be an actress or an artist is often mentioned, being a writer isn't. While there are frequent references to the films she saw and the plays she heard on the radio – Beryl went to the cinema either on her own or with Winnie at least two or three times a week, and to the theatre about once a week – there is no mention of books or reading (apart from scenes in plays she had to learn for Mrs Ackerley). This early emphasis on the spoken rather than the written word perhaps accounts for Beryl's later obsession with the rhythmical qualities of her prose and the way it had to sound when read aloud. It also helps to explain why her vocabulary was so extensive yet her spelling so poor, as she initially learned words through hearing them spoken, rather than reading them.

Another important feature of her childhood that figures prominently in Beryl's diaries is her relationship with her pet dog, Pedro, originally one of a litter of puppies belonging to the Whites' dog in Chirbury. Beryl quickly became attached to Pedro, and her parents agreed she could have him once he was old enough. In February 1944 Auntie White sent news that 'little Pedro' was ready to be taken home and during her half-term in April, Beryl collected him: 'Lovely puppy. Super.'[33]

Pedro was more than just a pet, however, and he would play a significant role in two key areas of Beryl's childhood development. In the first place, he became a character in his own right, and his activities became a frequent topic of conversation in the family's letters. A spaniel 'with Labrador overtones', Pedro was independent and intelligent enough to ride the local train unaccompanied, going backwards and forwards between Formby and Liverpool, sitting on a seat and looking out of the window.

Richard was also very attached to Pedro. According to Beryl, her father treated the dog 'like a kind of hairy child and fed him with a spoon'.[34] One Christmas Eve, after a train passenger took Pedro to the police station in Southport thinking he was lost, Richard drove around for hours frantically looking for him. When Beryl was at school in Tring, he would write letters to her that included a series of fantastical stories in which 'the exploits of Pedro'[35] formed a recurring theme, and he would frequently add a postscript as if written by 'Mr Pedro'.

The second area in which Pedro came to have an important impact on Beryl's childhood was the opportunity he offered for liberty. A dog needs to be taken for walks – and for Beryl taking Pedro out meant freedom. By 1946 she was regularly taking Pedro for long walks down by the pine woods and the seashore:

20 January: Took Pedro out for long walk. Over the hills. Had a wonderful time.
27 January: Took Peddy long walk. The sea is very blue. Sky blue too but cold.
3 February: Went another walk. Sea very perculiar.
10 March: Took Pedro out. Not a bad day. I must swot hard. Must not bite my nails. Wish I was on stage, married or an artist.[36]

Walking Pedro provided time and solitary peace for thinking, and the 1946 diary records a succession of musings about God and the landscape: 'Saw God in the sky today.'[37] The sense of liberty that walking alone gave Beryl was reflected in a more mature conception of herself as an individual, and she began to write outside too: 'Glorious morning. Am writing this in the pinewoods in a small glade. The sun is lighting up the brown and gold on the pine-needles. Its good to be alive.'[38]

It was also while out walking Pedro that Beryl first became friends with Lynda South, and where she would later meet Harry, the German prisoner of war with whom she had her first serious teenage romance. During her formative years, from the age of twelve till she left home for boarding school at fifteen, Pedro not only provided her with an excuse to leave the house and spend hours down by the seashore or in the woods, but also acted as her chaperone, it being deemed safer for Beryl to be out with the dog than out on her own. For Beryl, Pedro was a symbol of her childhood, and when he died in 1953 it struck her as the end of an era.

FOUR

Us Versus Them

> Us Versus Them
> Being an account of Us (Bash, me and our dogs) versus
> everyone else. By Basher Bainbridge & Lyn. South. All the
> characters are <u>not</u> fictitious by any means an' if they recanise
> themselves an' try an' prosecute us they can just see what they
> will bloomin well get.
> Yours truly Us.[1]

BERYL'S 1944 DIARY REPRESENTS her first appearance as a
writer, but one would be hard pushed to see in it any incipient
signs of the novelist she would become. Indeed, its entries are so
poorly written – almost all of them contain basic errors in spelling and
grammar – it seems impossible that the writer of them would, in the
space of two years, be capable of attempting a full-length novel.

Although the ability to spell is hardly an indicator of intelligence –
or even a prerequisite for a successful writing career – it has been
regarded as such in the past, and if Beryl's spelling at school was
anything like that in her early diaries her English teachers must have
despaired. She writes repeatedly of going to the 'picartures', she goes
to see the 'Phampton of the opero', and she could never quite get
the hang of Mrs Ackerley's name, referring to her variously as 'Miss
Ackerly', 'Mrs Ackely' and 'Ackaly'. However, the kind of errors she
made, as well as their consistency, hint at a more systemic problem
than mere inattention or carelessness – though this undoubtedly also
played a part – and today she would almost certainly have been diagnosed as dyslexic. Her most common spelling mistake was transposing
letters, a typical feature of dyslexia, especially the letters 'i' – in 'panio'
(piano) and 'buisness' (business) – and 'e' – in 'minuet' (minute) and

'quite' (quiet). She also persisted in various other quirks of orthography, invariably writing 'noone' rather than 'no one', 'loose' when she meant 'lose', and misplacing apostrophes in contractions such as 'could'nt' and 'did'nt'.

Despite these problems with articulacy, Beryl's literary development between 1944 and 1946 was remarkable, and her diary for the latter year shows a considerable improvement both in spelling and in expression – though her level of attainment would still be considered under par for someone of her age and schooling.

Although Beryl had probably written stories from an early age, as many children tend to do, it was for poetry rather than prose that she was initially considered to have a precocious talent. The first public reference to Beryl's writing is in relation to her poetry – the *Formby Times* noted in 1945 that she 'was blossoming out as an extremely youthful poet'[2] – and her enthusiasm can be seen in the number of poems she would write and keep over the next few years, as well as in her 1947 and 1949 diaries, into which she copied out verses by her favourite poets, such as Rupert Brooke and Gerard Manley Hopkins. Indeed, poetry would continue to be the form in which she expressed her most personal feelings until she left home, and even in later life she would resort to it at moments of extreme emotion.

In February 1946, during half-term, Beryl began a short novel called 'The Medvale Bombshell',[3] which she wrote out in pencil in a school exercise book and which ran to a little over 6,000 words. Set in London – which she had visited a few months before to collect her LAMDA award[4] – the novel has a vaguely Dickensian air, concerned as it is with issues of work, poverty, convoluted family relationships and unexpected inheritances. It opens with Sam Medvale, the reclusive patriarch of a dysfunctional family, turning up one evening at their 'outrageiously victorian'[5] house to make the unlikely proposal that he will leave the entire Medvale fortune 'to the person who makes the most improvement in the next 6 years'. The rest of the novel follows Anthony Medvale's misguided and ultimately unsuccessful attempt to make his way in life and win his uncle's fortune, before it ends abruptly and inconclusively part way through Chapter Seven.

In terms of characterization and narrative the story is all over the place, and it is practically impenetrable as regards plot. But what is noticeable is a certain facility in adapting the clichés of popular literature – one or two expressions are copied from Kipling's *Stalky & Co.* – and in pastiching the convoluted phraseology of the nine-teenth-century novel:

> Nina, was the half sister of Anthony, a higly colourful ~~young~~ woman of 8 and ~~twenty~~ 30. Her bright yellow hair was swept startlingly and not altogether unbecomingly to the top of her well shaped head. A man of about 40 sat reading in the armchair by the fire. He was a handsome dry looking person, with hair, somewhat grey at the temples, and a rather natty way of dressing. This was Godfery, Nina's husband. At the last remark of Nina's, he raised his head and said, 'Considering also, my dear wife, that you yourself are always making uncalled for statements, it must be rather a change for you to hear Anthony make one.'

Although there is not much in the way of obvious autobiographical representation, there are echoes of the tensions of home life and of Richard's feelings about his in-laws. Sam Medvale's criticism of his niece Nina and her husband Godfery – 'Look what a mess your marriage is. You do nothing but bicker, bicker, bicker' – seems to be directed at Winnie and Richard, while an early scene that takes place in the kitchen, in which Sam admonishes Godfery to 'be a man and stop living on Stuat', has parallels with Beryl's recollections of fractious family conferences in the front room and her father's reliance on money from John James Baines.

Beryl's next attempt at a novel showed more promise. Despite having been begun during her summer holiday in June 1946 just a couple of months after 'The Medvale Bombshell', 'The Tragedy of Andrew Ledwhistle and Martin Andromiky'[6] already shows a much firmer grasp of character and narrative line, and is more mature as regards style and expression. Its themes are similar to those of 'The Medvale Bombshell', involving family connections, issues of inheritance and the threat of poverty, but this time they are handled more lucidly and the character-ization is stronger and more consistent.

Although Beryl didn't find out about her father's bankruptcy until after his death in 1961, she seems to have picked up something of the murky current of financial failure surrounding his past. 'The Tragedy of Andrew Ledwhistle' not only revolves around the ruin of a business, it makes a number of references to failed stock-market speculations and bankruptcy. The central character also happens to be called Richard.

Ironically, given the novel's subject, the manuscript was written in a large notebook that Beryl had originally given to her father for Christmas in 1944, and the inside front cover bears her gift inscription:

> To Daddy
> From Beryl
> Year 1944
> I hope this book will useful be
> And when you write in it remember me.

This inscription had nothing to do with the novel itself, yet when Beryl came to publish the book in 1986, under the title *Filthy Lucre*, she nevertheless copied out the final rhyming couplet, but left off the reference to 'Daddy', and by changing the last line to 'When you read it remember me' made it seem as if it was the infant writer's message to posterity rather than a daughter's affectionate note to her father.

'The Tragedy of Andrew Ledwhistle' is essentially a pastiche of the Victorian popular novel, and while Beryl's familiarity with the clichés and conventional expressions of popular literature is again evident, there are flashes of individuality. Her descriptions are rarely copied directly and it is impressive how many of the distinctive turns of phrase that feature in the book are unique to her. Take the opening paragraph of Chapter Two:

> We will leave now dear readers, the bright Ledwhistle parlour and like a bird pass out into the dark november night. We will journey down to a wharf where the slimy Thames moves like some loathsome reptile, and the houses huddle together in squalid ruins. Here the lamp light falls on wasted limbs and quivering hands. It shines on sin and filth, while all aware the cruel river pursues its fitful course.[7]

While individual phrases sound like borrowings from other writers, and indeed 'like some loathsome reptile' is an adaptation of Dickens's description of Fagin in *Oliver Twist*, the evocation of the murk and gloom of the Thames is brilliantly achieved through the construction of her own newly minted clichés. The novel marked a significant improvement over its predecessor, though it is still flawed in terms of its narrative structure. Reading Robert Louis Stevenson's *Treasure Island* while writing the book seems to have distracted Beryl from her original intention, for its middle section turns into a wholly redundant subplot, involving murderous pirates and a treasure island.

Although much of the text of *Filthy Lucre* is identical with the manuscript of 1946, there are nevertheless some distinct and deliberate changes that go some way to altering our perception of it as a piece of juvenilia. In the first instance the text has been thoroughly copy-edited, certain infelicities of style have been smoothed out, and spelling and grammatical errors have been corrected, making it appear much less childish than the original. The manuscript of 'The Tragedy of Andrew Ledwhistle' also contained a number of painted and drawn illustrations, for the most part either simple portraits or general landscape scenes, none of which were reproduced in the published book. Despite Beryl's statement that the drawings in *Filthy Lucre* were 'copies of those done at the time', they were in fact a new set that had no relation to the originals, being not only more technically competent, but also more ironic. The drawing to illustrate the line 'a queer friendship sprang up between the two men' hinted knowingly at the modern meaning of the word 'queer', for example, something entirely absent from the original.

At the end of the manuscript of 'The Tragedy of Andrew Ledwhistle' there is a hastily scribbled outline for what Beryl planned to be her next novel. It shows that at this stage she was still more interested in fiction as a way of exploring genuinely imaginative stories and plots, even extending to the realm of the supernatural and the fantastical, rather than as a means of expressing her own feelings or life experiences: 'Story of a man who was in a London Blitz. Looses his memory and finds himself in another world. He comes back an old man but time has stood still for the rest of the earth. John Answelwain.'

Beryl got as far as listing a cast of potential characters – 'Leslie Bishop, Carrie Wesly, Jasper Corely, Tod, Busty, Dr Anselwain' – showing that her talent for names was already well developed, but the novel was never begun.

The most significant influence on Beryl's desire to write was her friendship with another pupil at Merchant Taylors', Lynda South. Although they lived only a few houses down from each other on opposite sides of Ravenmeols Lane, the two girls don't seem to have become friends immediately, possibly because Lyn's birthday was in May so she was a year above Beryl at school. According to a story written in 1949, in which Lyn appears thinly disguised as a 'confident looking girl' called Christie, and in which Beryl portrays herself as Loo, they first got to know each other while out taking their respective dogs for a walk, probably in the spring or early summer of 1946. 'The lane to the sea was to Loo the lane to everywhere. It was there she met Christie and the yellow dog, and that was the begining of her youth.'[8]

Beryl and Lyn quickly developed a close, secretive friendship, one that allowed them to recreate themselves outside of what each considered to be the restrictive and oppressive confines of their home life. The significance of the friendship for Beryl can hardly be overstated: for the first time she had met someone of her own age whose passion for art and literature matched – or even surpassed – her own, someone she looked up to and whom she wanted to emulate. She even modelled her handwriting on Lyn's, so much so that it is difficult to tell the two scripts apart. Nevertheless, in spite of their similar interests and enthusiasms, and despite their shared sense of dissatisfaction with and growing alienation from their parents, the two girls were very different in temperament and personality.

Lyn seemed older than her years, more disciplined and more focused on what she wanted to do in life, which was to be an artist like her older sister Maureen, who had also attended Merchant Taylors' and was now studying at the Liverpool School of Art. Lyn was academically gifted in a way that Beryl wasn't. Not only had she won a Junior School Scholarship to attend Merchant Taylors', she featured among the school's annual prizewinners for good work, which Beryl conspicuously failed to do. Not that Lyn was a swot or deferred to school authority. But unlike Beryl, whose rebelliousness was instinctive, Lyn's rebellion had its origins in her sense of her own intellectual superiority. She was also fearless, with a kind of devil-may-care attitude that impressed her peers – she once climbed out of the library window on the upper floor and scaled down the drainpipe, a feat that remained in the memories of her fellow pupils and may have inspired Beryl's description of the vertiginous escape through a church window in *Harriet Said*.

Lyn shared Beryl's sense of humour, but was daring enough to take it to extremes that Beryl never would on her own. The two travelled to and from school together by train, and in the winter, coming home in the dusk 'with the rain heavy on their cheeks, and their legs damp', Lyn would pretend to heave inside and begin to cough very loudly. Beryl would put her arm round her, as if she were helping a 'staggering consumptive', and though the two girls found it difficult to suppress their giggling, 'old ladies would stop and watch them worriedly'.

Lyn also took the lead in other areas: the year Beryl met Lyn was also that in which she 'learnt about boys'. Together they would discuss the merits of the local boys vying for their attention, in Beryl's case Don Dean and Lionel Barras. They would flirt with the porters who worked at Formby railway station, Eric, Ivan and Frank, inventing fantastic stories about them and giving them equally fanciful nicknames. While out together in the pine woods, they would encounter an assortment of male figures – respectably married men, German prisoners of war, local lads up to no good – with whom they would talk, tease, insult or lead on, according to humour or circumstance. In 1947 Beryl started to keep a list of all the boyfriends she'd had, dating back to when she was twelve. Along with their names, she included their nationality, their age, her age when she met them, and the length of time their relationship had lasted. The last name to figure on it dates from 1949, by which time her tally had reached seventeen.

For the next few years the two girls would write effusively and copiously to each other, Lyn addressing Beryl as 'Darling Lickle Girl' or 'Dearest Bashie', to exchange advice or relay news about various boys: 'Your letter came a bit too late because I'd practically (with a few exceptions) finished with Sandy. Geoff is wolfing after me in full cry.'[9] Inevitably there were occasional conflicts: an early letter from Lyn hints at a falling out between them after Beryl started going out with a boy that Lyn fancied: 'Dear Kid, I told you once I would always love you. I wasn't kidding either and I always will but please don't ask me why I have broken. It's harder for me than it is for you.'[10] The break didn't last long but it left its mark: though there was no more poaching, Lyn's letters are sporadically dotted with injunctions to Beryl about certain boys, reminding her that 'he's mine'.[11]

Winnie viewed Beryl's friendship with Lynda with suspicion, feeling that her daughter was being led astray and made yet more unmanageable by Lynda's bad example. The Souths similarly felt that it was Beryl who was an unhealthy influence on their daughter. This mutual parental disapproval only sealed the bond between the two girls.

Lyn's letters and Beryl's diaries are scattered with passionate outbursts of mutual love and adoration, and neither seems to have been immune from the tendency to form what were then called 'pashes'. A poem Beryl wrote during her last year at Merchant Taylors' and entitled 'To Lyn' expresses an envious yearning to be the object of her affection:

> When we found the horse, it rolled
> Its yellow teeth and danced for you.
> I was jealous. My teeth were yellow too.
> I could'nt dance. You were coarse
> And hit its shining bottom with a stone.
> I was jealous then. I felt that I should bear
> The pain you gave, and I alone.
> You knew a lot about flowers. You called them
> Dear Latanic names, you never called me such, and I was envious.
> The tree with the house upon its bough
> Received you as a child, glorious,
> And pleased it danced again beneath
> Your body. It should have been passive.
> I will always be.[12]

Here, as in her willingness to win the affection of her peers by taking on their punishments, Beryl seems to identify passively with each of the objects on which Lyn lavished her attention, even to the extent of masochistically envying the horse's pain. Nor was this sensual element, subliminal though it may have been, absent on Lyn's side, as is clear in one of her letters to Beryl, urging her to return home from school: 'When you come back dear we'll go down to the shore and the night will be sort of grey and dark and warm. And the frogs in the tadpole pools will croak all the time and we'll smell the pines and the wet grass and sand and then we'll lie on our backs in the sand and watch the channel lights go up and down and we'll love each other and be terribly happy, and we'll talk and talk and laugh like we used to, dearest. I can't wait to see you once more.'[13]

There was no doubt a conventional element to such outpourings of affection – many girls of their age and class addressed each other in similar fashion – but it is clear, too, that at certain points they felt their relationship to be so close that they suspected, or feared, a lesbian component to it. In some of the later letters they both seem to be aware of this danger. After one particularly emotional outburst in which Lyn remarked that she wanted to see Beryl more than anyone else in the world, she added as an ironic afterthought: 'Hands up those who are perverted, I don't know. Horrid thought.'[14] The only extract that survives of one of Beryl's letters to Lyn also seems to evoke the line across which they could not go. Drawing a comparison between her physical intimacy with her boyfriend at the time and her love for Lyn, Beryl told her: 'And I would wish to write this to him not you because it is not ever for us to lie together in such love, and wake cool beneath the open window.'[15]

The correspondence between the two was something that even at the time was a self-conscious sign of their relationship. Both Beryl and Lyn had special places where they kept each other's letters; this was partly for the practical reason of hiding them from the prying eyes of their mothers, but it was also symbolic, indicating how important they were to each other. While Lyn used her grandmother's old sewing box, which after a few years was stuffed to overflowing, Beryl kept her letters in a large metal ammunition box, an old olive-green cartridge case from the war inside the lid of which she pasted this warning:

Berry Bainbridge
    Think before you look inside. The contents belong to me and are private. In case of death please give untouched this box and its contents to Miss Lyn South, Fyfield, Ravenmeols Lane, Formby Lancs.
    Important.[16]

Equally significant is the fact that after the friendship ended, Beryl kept all of Lyn's letters whereas Lyn destroyed all of Beryl's. There can be no greater indication of Lyn's desire to completely reject her own past than this attempt to obliterate the relationship that was so emblematic of it. Beryl's long and intimate letters to her, written over the course of the eight years during which they were such close friends, would have thrown light on many aspects of her adolescence and the troubled periods she went through, so her story is considerably the poorer for their loss.

Given Beryl and Lyn's shared interest in literature and art, it was perhaps only a matter of time before they collaborated, though the impulse behind 'Us Versus Them' seems to be less a desire to create a work of literature than an expression of their joint defiance of the adult world, the novel being 'an account of Us (Bash, me and our dogs) versus everyone else'.[17]

It is clear that Lyn was, and saw herself as, the more dynamic and dominant of the two. She was more literate than Beryl and her drawing was more technically proficient: at the time most people would have judged that Lynda had more chance of becoming a writer or an artist. It was Lyn who wrote the opening chapter to the new joint novel and Lyn who did all the illustrations. The story, such as it is, proceeds by way of Lyn and Beryl each taking turns to write a chapter. It opens with Lyn finishing her school homework and in the process of leaving home in search of adventure, armed with a Swedish sheath knife and accompanied by her two dogs, Pan and Captain Scott: 'A soft rain was falling and the road was glistening golden in the rain. I raced down the road, Captain Scott and Pan gaily prancing after me, grinning all over their doggy faces. They knew what was afoot all right, dogs always do. Well, anyway, we came to rest outside Basher's house and whistled three times (I did, not the dogs). I heard Basher's cheerful shout "Goodbye Mum, Cheerio Dad," little did they know that she was gone for ever.'

After they commandeer a boat down at the docks – Lyn dispatches its sole occupant, the drunken Captain Toofpooste, by slitting his throat with her knife and throwing him overboard – the narrative baton is handed over to Beryl, who sets the tone of what is to come as they embark on a series of fantastical, tenuously linked escapades: 'Our world, Lyn's and I's, [is] a world made up of Magic, beautiful green magic.'

Beryl's subsequent chapters shift the setting to 'Juppiter' and Saturn, with its 'rattling houses, cold, all-powerful hurricanes, and men and women with large, bubble like eyes that held strange evil powers and unfilled lusts', and then to an imaginary 'Planet of Fiction'. The range of authors alluded to is interesting: Arthur Conan Doyle, R. D. Blackmore, Lewis Carroll, Dickens, Robert Louis Stevenson and Peter Cheyney, as is a dig at James Barrie's most famous literary creation: 'A regular Sissy of a little twerp spoke next on behalf of the Temperance Society, that curly haired saccahine pill of the Nursery world Peter Pan.'

Beryl's chapters are distinguished not only by her erratic spelling, but by flowing passages that are undercut by comical turns of phrase and incongruous images:

> Daffodil was a darling boy of some 10 and 20 years, very dapper and cynical. He told us his history one night, very sad it was. Full of errors and dissipointments, how his love of minced dough-nuts had been frustrated early in life, how his 9th wife Holly had left him for a New York jail bird. Oh very sad it was. Lyn wept bucketfuls over the deck, which was a very good thing for it was my turn to scrub it.
>
> On we sailed, and then we reached the edge of the night, and our ship grew little pink wings and we floated about as gently as an elephant into the dawn. Dawn was a lovely place, full of cherubs and weepin' willows and Imperial Palaces. Up and up we sailed, up into a world of blue, blue as an artic sea, triumphant as a set of teeth.

The book was probably more fun to write than it is to read, but it nevertheless reveals something of the interests and personalities of its two authors. In Beryl's case, her descriptions of voyages into space and sea landscapes mirror the fascination she expressed in her diaries about the physical world, her wonder at the expanses of infinite sea and sky encountered on Formby beach. On a more prosaic level, her secret, almost guilty fascination with boxers and boxing, a result of having listened to the sport on the radio with her father, is captured in her enthusiastic description of a fist fight and her expert use of the sports commentator's jargon:

> We landed among them. South dancing neatly round Stanley. A lovely uppercut to the nose. South is covering up, her chin well in, dancing airly round Hyacinth. A beautiful smash to the solar plexus. Cedric is landing wonderful blows. Oh well done. A nice smash to the head. Stanley is appealing to the crowd. Bainbridge once more appears. She tears in, tears out, tears in, stays out. South slams two shaking lefts, Stanley takes it on his gloves. Oh he's regretting it. He calls a halt while he takes off his gloves, and lays them carefully in a hedge. Then Bash wades in, swims out, Lyn nips in, gives one wild yell and the fight is over.

In one sense 'Us Versus Them' represented a backward step for Beryl, its subject matter and style are just a bit too childish, even for two fourteen-year-olds. But its significance lies not so much in its literary qualities as in the simplicity of its form. Its casual, write-the-first-thing-that-comes-into-your-head mode of production put an end to the formulaic and derivative pastiches of Victorian literature Beryl had produced up to that point. Writing 'Us Versus Them' allowed Beryl for the first time to inhabit her own prose, to imagine herself as a fictional character and use fiction as a form of self-expression, albeit in a fantasized and self-conscious way. This was undoubtedly a vital lesson; there would be no more literary pastiches from now on. The next thing she would write would be about herself, her life, her experiences and her feelings.

FIVE

Harry

At fourteen I met a german prisoner of war, whose face I can
no longer fully remember, who filled all my life for one brief
summer after the war. I was filled with guilt and happiness
and a dread of being discovered . . .[1]

SINCE THE ARRIVAL OF Pedro, Beryl had been in the habit of
spending her evenings taking the dog for walks in the woods, or
along the dunes at Formby. Turning right out of the drive, she would
head towards the sea, a good fifteen-minute walk down Ravenmeols
Lane, past Lynda's house, past Mr Greggs' house with its strange gothic
tower, its roof pointed like a witch's hat, and past the railway crossing.
Eventually the road petered out; straight ahead were the woods, and to
the left a lane that led to St Luke's church and the graveyard. Here, she
would take off her shoes and socks, and walk the rest of the way bare-
foot, not just because she liked the sensation of the cold sand beneath
her feet, but to avoid ruining her shoes and getting into trouble with
her mother.

The sense of liberty she felt is captured in a poem from this
period:

I liked to wander with my feet devoid of shoes
And my elder brothers trousers rolled way up past my knees;
And an old old shirt so ancient that my skin was showing through
And though my mother wept for me, nothing else would do.
She used to think me slightly mad, and I would catch her
Looking in a patient way to see
The frequent signs and habits
Of a mental faculty.

But when the lane was empty, though I knew folks
Were watching sly, I'de dance and twirl and laugh aloud
And toss the scarlet lines of blossem trees
And hope the crowd of women behind their curtains
Would think me slightly gone,
And wonder in their beds at night
While I danced wildly on.[2]

The poem is revealing not so much for its flouting of conventional values, but for the fact that Beryl needed other people to *see* her acts of rebellion. Despite its metrical flaws, the poem also demonstrates an impressive concision: within the space of three lines Beryl manages to convey the sensual liberty of casting off her shoes, the blurring of gender roles in the wearing of her brother's trousers, and a hint of sexual exhibitionism in the worn shirt that reveals her flesh. Given how conscious Beryl herself was about the transgressive liberties her beach-walking offered her, it was no wonder her parents frowned at it.

Beryl wasn't the only person who enjoyed the liberty the woods and sand dunes offered, and the area became not just the haunt of courting couples, but also of prisoners of war, who were held at a nearby internment camp at Altcar but who were free to leave its confines during daylight hours. As early as January 1946, Beryl had been aware of their presence on the beach: 'Saw some German soldiers', she noted in her diary.

Another memorable figure she occasionally encountered was a 'recluse who lived in a lean-to arrangement of odd planks and boxes in the sandhills, with his dog'.[3] His name was Billy Tasker, an ex-soldier who had been decorated in the First World War but who had abandoned civilized society on his return to Liverpool. By 1947 he had lived his hermit-like existence on the Formby shoreline for nearly thirty years: 'My life has been solitary,' he told a reporter for the *Formby Times*, 'but I have found here what I was seeking – peace and people who understand.'[4] Beryl would later give him a walk-on part in her first and her last novel, as Perjer in 'The Summer of the Tsar' and as Billy Rotten in *The Girl in the Polka Dot Dress*. In both, he features as a child-molester, though there are no suggestions elsewhere in her writing that he tried to take advantage of her, and he was always well regarded by Formby locals, who nicknamed him the 'Holy Hermit'.

Due to post-war fuel shortages, British Double Summer Time was in effect during 1947, which meant that evenings were much lighter than normal. It was while out walking through the pine woods one evening in late spring that Beryl met Harry Franz,[5] a twenty-four-year-old prisoner of war, who was awaiting transferral to his native Bavaria. Harry wasn't the first prisoner Beryl had spoken to among the dunes of the Formby shoreline. The previous year she had become friends with another German in his mid-twenties called Heinz, from the Ruhr valley. On Beryl's list of boyfriends his name appears before Harry's (numbers 5 and 6 respectively), along with a note that the 'length of time' of their relationship was three months. Beryl wrote little about Heinz, but in a letter to Harry she later described how he had seemed 'God-like'[6] to her because of the difference in age. For the same reason – she was just thirteen at the time – Heinz probably didn't take Beryl seriously as a girlfriend, though he may have tried to take advantage of her. Harry, who was more sensitive and less assertive, made a point of comparing himself to Heinz, saying that unlike him he would remain faithful to her, that he was not a 'bad man . . . like Heinz'.[7]

Harry was by far the most important of Beryl's early boyfriends. In physical terms the relationship didn't venture much beyond kisses and cuddles. Beryl may have looked more mature than her years, but she was still only fourteen and a half when they met, nearly ten years younger than Harry, and this probably prevented him from trying to take things any further. On an emotional and imaginative level, however, the relationship was hugely significant: thoughts of Harry would preoccupy Beryl for the next two or three years, and his memory left a lasting, idealized image of what the experience of being in love was like. Harry would also inspire the next stage in her writing. After his return to Germany, she began to write about her experiences and feelings in prose, instead of poetry, and their relationship formed the basis of an autobiographical novella entitled 'My Song is Done', which she began at Tring in 1948 and finished in January 1949.[8]

———

As with many young men caught up in the war, Harry's experiences had left their mark, physically and emotionally. He recalled witnessing brutality on both sides: drunken SS officers executing their own soldiers; English soldiers shooting wounded Austrians. He himself had been shot at, and a ricochet had caught him a glancing blow, leaving him with a white scar beneath his eye. In the portrait Beryl drew of him on the cover of 'My Song is Done' she captured his distinctive Germanic features, his gaunt, scarred face and his closely cropped blond hair.[9]

Before being transferred to Formby, Harry had already spent over a year in an internment camp in America. It was here, as he later told Beryl, that he discovered that the sixteen-year-old brother of his German girlfriend, Ilse, had been killed in the Russian offensive. He had also learned for the first time about the concentration camps, from a Jewish officer from New York.

These experiences had left him nervous and withdrawn, something reflected in Beryl's portrayal of him as Franzi in 'My Song is Done': 'He was utterly twisted with shot nerves inside. When he laughed he shook and could not control himself.'[10] This nervousness allowed the relationship to develop at a slower pace: Harry's lack of confidence, and the fact that he was less sexually predatory than most of the other men Beryl encountered down by the seashore, meant that for the first time she could experience physical contact with an older man in a relatively unthreatening context. For his part, Harry benefited emotionally from her affectionate sympathy and her simple romantic passion for him. Walking hand in hand with her, he felt calmer: 'He did not jerk so much now, his nerves were well under control, he was quieter and he loved her very much.'[11]

A warm intimacy quickly developed and the element of secrecy that necessarily surrounded the relationship gave it an added frisson. In another autobiographical sketch written in London a few years afterwards, she captured both the tenderness of their relationship and the constant nervous tension that she might be found out:

Walking to meet Harry in the dreamy summer evenings, and the passionless mouth-lovely kisses under the white beach leaves in the pine woods. I cannot remember clearly except . . .

He laughed uncontrollably and frantically the first evening rolling a ball for Pedro to chase.

The white woollen socks and the black diamond on his back.

Oh just suddenly it is painful. The wide eyes and the ernest talking, the promises, and the smell of the grass. And the way he thought my legs were made of pearl, dappled under the leaves, and the dark growing and the ships winking in and out far away in the Mersey. And when a rustle was heard and it was a noise of an animal or bird, not a prying woman, I would cry out as he had taught 'Keine men[s] ch, keine men[s]ch.' [It's no one.]

It was such an exciting restless summer, surely the wheather has never been as good. Holding hands tightly on the cindar path going home in the dark, the heart beating terribly with fear as a car came, and the headlights would surely show my half averted face to the occupants, and all would be discovered. The meetings in the bushes so pityful almost. If I was there first I would lie down and sit up and rearrange myself a dozen times for the best affect, rubbing my lips to make them red, sweating in the warmth. And then the movement beyond the gorse, then the crackling and trampling of twigs and the stooping figure. Very shyly we would look again through the dictionary for words, and only after an endless breathless time would he place his hand on my cheek and turn my pale mouth to his. And I cannot recall the sweetness of it, though it exsisted.

If he was there before me, I would creep and surprise him, putting my arms round his neck from behind and then laugh on his neck. And never never did I shiver with an unusual feeling, nothing disturbed me except the desperately real joy of school over for the day and tea in the sullen house, and then Harry and I alone under the leaves, and him kissing me.[12]

Beryl seems to have known that what she was doing had potentially dangerous repercussions and took care to keep the relationship quiet, telling only a few close friends at school like Lyn. 'My Song is Done' includes a scene in which a young English soldier discovers that Loo – Beryl's alter ego in the novella – is going out with a German and tries to strangle her, shouting 'a lot about bitches that played innocent and gave bloodey all to bleeding jerries'.[13] This may have been a fictional embellishment, but it shows that Beryl was aware of the risk she was running.

'What would happen if someone found out?' her friend Alan replied when she asked his advice about Harry. 'I've got nothing against him, but a great amount of people have against all Germans and if they found out in a place like Formby, then as far as I can see it would be awful, life would hardly be worth living.'[14] Coincidentally or not, Beryl would use the name Alan for the fictionalized portrayal of her brother, who expressed a similar disapproval in her novel about that period, *A Quiet Life*. After coming across his sister lying in the dunes with a German, Alan tells her: 'Do you realise . . . only a few years back you would have had your head shaved?'[15] This was a real possibility and other women at the time have testified to the violent reaction their relationships with German prisoners provoked. 'People were very hostile. They would come up to me in the street and punch me or spit on me and ask "Aren't our boys good enough for you?"'[16]

Although she could not have been insensible to the effect her physical appearance had on men, Beryl, like many girls her age, had a negative self-image and was prone to feelings of insecurity about her looks. 'I wish I had not appeared so ugly to myself,' she reflected about her time with Harry, 'white and plump with a poor skin and large pale lips, and the loudness of me.'[17] It was psychologically important to her that Harry should find her physically attractive, though his persistent and often tender declarations of affection seem to have done little to boost her self-confidence. This sense of being found wanting in comparison to other girls – and specifically to Harry's German girlfriend Ilsa – is captured in a poem from this period:

Oh when you walk you only walk with Ilse
And when you talk you only talk of Ilse
And when you dream
Or so it must seem
You wander far from me
For your off high above
Deep in love
With Ilse.
And when you sing
You only sing of Ilse
My kisses bring, only tears for Ilse
I'm dreading it so
Cause you'll want me to know
Your going back to Ilse.[18]

Even at this early stage her anxiety about rejection by the love object seems to be particularly acute, and throughout her life she would continue to look to men for reassurance that she was loved, that she was beautiful, even if nothing they said was ever quite enough.

———

At the end of July 1947 the idyllic period of their secret meetings came to a temporary end when Beryl went on holiday with her mother and brother to Cleish Castle in Kinross-shire, Scotland. Overcome by feelings of insecurity, she immediately wrote to Harry and he tried to reassure her, though his command of English was poor and his vocabulary limited and repetitive:

> My Darling Berry!
> I received your two very nice letters, and I thank you very much for these . . . I am sorry that I can not write English perfect, but I hope you can read it. In your first letter you did write you are afraid that I find another Girl-friend, I promise I don't it. My thoughts are only with you, and I wait full longing till you come back to me . . . I know it first now, how much I love you, and I have broken heart, because I can not be with you . . . Three weeks are a long time, but I hope that these are soon over, and you come back to me, that I can again be happy.
> With all my love, Harry[19]

Beryl's emotional involvement with Harry, genuine though it was, didn't prevent her engaging in a brief holiday romance with a local from nearby Kinross, Jimmy Clunie, whose age is given as twenty-eight on her list of boyfriends.[20] Although the exact nature of their encounter is unclear, Beryl made a couple of cryptic references to him later in her journal, from which it seems she came to a realization that she could arouse sexual desire in men and that it represented a kind of power: 'I remembered the holiday in the castle and Jimmy Clunie in the bushes and the first hard wakenings of power over men.'[21]

Despite listing the duration of their 'relationship' as three weeks – the length of her stay in Scotland – she seems to have looked on him more as a holiday distraction than anything else. Her romantic thoughts remained firmly attached to Harry and one day she rode on a bike to Rumbling Bridge, a small village ten miles from Cleish, where she wrote

'I love Harry Franz' on a piece of paper, put it in a bottle, and 'threw it over the falls and watched it swirl away between the high gloom green banks, down the years'.[22]

Beryl returned to Formby on 15 August and her meetings with Harry resumed, though they were not to last long. On 5 September, unable to meet Beryl himself, he arranged for a letter to be given to her, explaining that he was being transferred to Garswood Park Camp, near Wigan:

> I'm so very miserable and sad that I can't meet you not more to-day, because I go this morning already back to Camp 50. I'm so unhappy that I could not see you last night. I have been yesterday in the afternoon and in the night in Formby looking for you in the Street where is your home, but I must go back again with broken heart then I saw only Pedro sitting in front of your home. I hope that you keep what you have promised to me and once more don't vorget what you did to promise me. With kindly regards, your everlasting Darling, Harry.[23]

The news of his sudden departure was a terrible blow: 'Nothing will ever be as real and terrible or choking as the rude parting on the Friday night,' she wrote, 'the letter by hand, and the lorry having thundered off in the night to Southampton.' To make matters worse, as she was walking back down the lane to go home she was the victim of a casual predatory sexual assault, by a 'blue jowelled man' who was sitting waiting on a bank of grass: 'He came down the bank and kissed me, not like Harry, but drowning me with his mouth, and his tongue wet and strong between my teeth. And all like a dream.'[24]

The next day she wrote to Harry lamenting what had happened: 'Why did it have to end like that?'[25] – a sentiment echoed in a poem she wrote shortly after:

> All along the seashore
> We used to walk
> Overhead the seagulls massed
> I hear you say, I love you
> My heart still cries, I love you too
> What a pity it had to end
> What a pity it could'nt last

Day by day we wandered
Together hand in hand
Oh the time would go so fast
Oh I cried, when
You whispered soft, Aufwiedersehn
What a pity it had to end
What a pity it could'nt last.[26]

A few days later Harry replied from the camp at Sudbury, protesting his love and urging her to keep 'her promise and not go out with anyone', and to try and visit him the following Sunday. Across the back of his note, in his neat italic script, were the words: 'Love once given, can not be recalled.' Somewhat rashly she said she would come to Sudbury, some eighty miles south-east of Formby, though this was no easy thing to arrange given that she had to keep the journey secret from her parents. But despite Harry's carefully organized plan – 'We meet us on the Station of Sudbury and I come to the place there after dinner and I will wait so longing'[27] – things went awry. Harry waited for five hours in vain: Beryl arrived too late.

This was to be their last chance. At the beginning of October, Harry was repatriated to Bavaria.

Although they would never meet again, the relationship was far from over. Between October 1947 and December 1949 Harry would write nearly thirty letters and cards to Beryl, expressing his love for her, urging her to be faithful to him, and asking for help in trying to find a job and arrange references that would enable him to return to England and marry her. Beryl's letters to Harry were equally prolific: she would write over fifteen times in the first six months of 1948 alone, and for years afterwards he would continue to exert a powerful hold on her imagination, especially during periods of loneliness or emotional distress.

From the surviving correspondence – Harry's habit of quoting extracts from Beryl's letters verbatim allows us to glimpse her state of mind as well as his – it is clear that both seemed to take the relationship seriously and both believed in, or hoped for, its continuance. But it is also true that Beryl came to a realization much sooner than Harry that the relationship wasn't one that could realistically work. Nevertheless, in the months following his departure her protestations of fidelity and her reassurances of her love seemed genuinely heartfelt.

In November, shortly after his return to Bavaria, she wrote to tell him that she was unhappy, that she missed him and wanted to be faithful to him. In December she was even more insistent: 'Please promise me Harry that one day you will come back to me and I can see you again.'[28] A week later she assured him that she didn't want another sweetheart, that she had sent her heart to him for Christmas, and that 'to be in your arms again in a "honeymoon" would be so very wonderful'.[29]

In the New Year she went so far as to make the impractical promise that 'if it is at all possible I will try and come to you this summer, only I don't know if my parents would allow me to go to Europe so young, on my own'.[30] A few months afterwards, as a proof of her continuing feelings for him, she wrote him a letter from the special place where they used to meet, 'in our place in love, in the bushes near the forest'.[31]

But as time passed her unequivocal declarations were tempered by more ambivalent statements that seemed to offer him a way out should he want to take it, such as suggesting that he should try to 'fall in love just a little with a german girl this summer and be happy because in summer one should be'.[32] More pertinent, perhaps, is the fact that other names were soon added to her boyfriend list after Harry's: these included Bernard Blundell ('I want to see you again and take you for a walk to the shore and have a bit of fun together . . .'),[33] and Jim Palmer, a thirty-two-year-old married man who developed a crush on her over Christmas and New Year, 1947–8 ('Little did we think a fortnight ago that we would be so attached to one another . . . I do love you').[34]

Another poem about Harry, composed later at Tring, captures both the tenderness of their time together and a sense of her nostalgic melancholy at its passing. Here she uses an image of the sea erasing his message of love written in the sand as a metaphor for the inevitable erosion of her feelings over time. Significantly she also alludes to having found someone else:

> They took a stick and he lifting it and pointing it towards the dying sky
> Looked at her and smiled, and they stood for but a moment
> While the sea tingled against the stars
> And the sea-birds sang a melodey in orange bar
> And twists of dull green foam.

And then he bent and she watched him
Draw their names together and twine
Them with a kiss, and then he took her home . . .

And then he went away to his own land
And she soon found another and laughed
Again and cried; and never stopped to think
Of his name twined so with hers . . .[35]

Perhaps the fullest expression of her feelings about Harry at this period
is given in a letter she wrote to him in August 1948, but which for some
reason she seems not to have sent. Like her poem, a sense of her affection for him is unmistakeable, as is its nostalgic, almost elegaic tone, as
if deep down she knew the relationship belonged in the past:

Harry: You have been away a long while now, at least it seems a long
while to me. It is summer again, and it was in the Summer I met you,
so that our love belonged to the flowers and the sun and to Summer
Madness. You were my first real love. I had known agonies over Heinz
because he was so God-like, and I was so young. I had even lain awake
nights over Terry, because he came after Heinz and I wanted so much
an anchor.

But you were different. We had a lot of happiness I think, at least
I dream we had. Perhaps you could not understand why I would not
be wholly yours, perhaps you were puzzled and unhappy and full of
longing for something more, to drown your loneliness for your own
country.

Only it did not matter because we both felt that our love was for
just a gap in Time, and what had gone before, or what was to come,
had no place in our lives.

You arn't ever by the little forest now, and you don't ever caress my
body with your thin hands till I grow excited and want to live fully.
You don't ever call me 'Chaste little English Girl', and laugh with
your head on one side to see if I am laughing with you.

And we kissed a lot and made love a lot and together watched the
first star come up behind the hills from the sea. And now you are
gone. I still dream of you, and wait so lonely for your letters.

All the lovely memories. And lying in the dull green glow with
your hands making me think and feel things I once never knew of,

and most of all just being with you, and you being so gentle with me, and never impatient.

I don't love you in the way other people love, you see its all such a long while ago, and I am confused, till you are somewhere in a forest of pine, and wild shores and green seas.

I am very lonely without you.

It is all so long ago . . .

Ich liebe dich auf immer [I love you forever]

Berry xx[36]

Even so, almost a year later she was still writing to Harry and telling him she was chaste and solid in her virtuous life, and that she wanted to see him again: 'I would give anything in this world to say to you . . . Harry look out of the window of your train, I am there waiting for you at the station by your home.'[37]

This prevarication wasn't coquettishness: her feelings for him were genuine enough, as is witnessed by the number of spontaneous thoughts of him recorded in her diary when she felt lonely or experienced some emotional setback: 'Oh Harry liebchen. Write,'[38] she implored in February 1949, during a period in which she was feeling depressed about her life at Tring and alienated from her schoolfriends. Two weeks later, during a return visit to Formby, she was again going down to the dunes and thinking melancholy thoughts: 'I went to see Harry and the little place in the forest, but I didn't find him. The little wood was full of whisperings, and birds were quiet. I felt cold and lonely.'[39]

Yet whenever Harry implied he might be able to get to England sooner rather than later, she would get cold feet again and try and put him off, using the hostility of her parents as an excuse. Such mixed messages only served to prolong the confusion and add to his distress. To be fair, the situation was a demanding one for any sixteen-year-old to deal with. Caught between fear of her parents finding out and guilt about Harry's reaction if she were to break with him, Beryl found it difficult to be open, and dealt with matters in an evasive, disingenuous way.

In fact, it would really only be after she started working at the Playhouse in August 1949 that the memory of Harry started to fade from her emotional landscape, and almost a year and a half after that before she would write to tell him the truth – that she had fallen in love with someone else.

———

The psychological repercussions of her relationship with Harry were considerable. The circumstances surrounding it – its secrecy, its existence outside the bounds of her normal life, the difference in age between them, the barrier of language – all served to keep the illusion of an idyllic love alive in Beryl's mind: 'Nothing is ever as sweet again as the first love. Nothing is ever as sweet again as the first love unfulfilled. So gentle was my Harry . . . How shall anything ever be like that again? All the blue-bells picked and garlanded and all the grasses sucked in the mouth, and all the repeated phrases, over and over because of innocence.'[40]

Had the relationship lasted longer, her romantic ideals might have been tempered a little by reality. As it was, its sudden and unexpected end meant her fantasy was never shattered, never tested against the hard edge of reality the way so many youthful illusions about love are. As a result she would yearn to recreate the same idyllic situation in her later relationships, and when her unrealistically high expectations of romantic fulfilment inevitably unravelled, it would leave her feeling lost and disillusioned.

SIX

Tring

Shortly after fifteen I left school somewhat under a cloud and went to an artistic boarding school in Hartfordshire. There I became quieter and filled with a sense of how unworthy I was and how I was ugly, but how I should become beautiful.[1]

Please God make me beautiful . . . and let me be loved.[2]

A S OFTEN HAPPENS AT school, children of a certain age pass round material considered morally unsuitable by their parents. In Beryl's case, her friend Rita Moody had given her a dirty poem and she inadvertently stuffed it into her gymslip pocket. To make matters worse, Beryl had illustrated it, which only confirmed Winnie in her mistaken notion that her daughter was its author:

It's only human nature after all
For a boy to take a girl against a wall
To pull down her protection
And plug in his connection
It's only human nature after all.

Today, it would barely raise a murmur, but when Winnie found the poem during the summer term of 1947, she took it straight to Miss Brash, the headmistress of Merchant Taylors'. In later life, Beryl would always say that she'd been expelled over the incident, though the word was never used by the school, or even by Beryl at the time, because to saddle a young girl with a public expulsion would have caused something of a scandal.

The poem was certainly a factor, but Beryl's weak academic performance was another. If she'd had a realistic chance of passing her School

Cert it is hard to imagine the school would have forced her to leave over such a minor issue.[3] As it was, Beryl's removal suited both parties: the school was unburdened of a disruptive pupil who wasn't expected to do well academically, and Winnie, under the guise of protecting her daughter's morals, could place Beryl in a school more suited to her own ambitions for her as an actress.

Although Beryl didn't finish at Merchant Taylors' until December 1947, by the end of July she had already written to Harry to tell him she would be going to a boarding school in Tring in January 1948.[4] Some girls of Beryl's age and class, influenced by popular fantasies of boarding school life, would have looked forward to the prospect. But for Beryl the idea of living away from home, however much she may have complained about it, was not a pleasant one. In August she wrote to her French penfriend Jacques Delebassée expressing her fears, but his reply didn't do much to alleviate her anxiety: 'Vous n'aimez pas aller au pensionnat! It is not very good. I do not like no more pensionnat!'[5]

The Arts Educational School in Tring, Hertfordshire, was directed by two enterprising Jewish women, Grace Cone and Olive Ripman, both of whom had been ballet dancers before turning to teaching and education. Joining forces in 1939, they founded the Cone-Ripman College, with the aim of preparing students for a professional life in the arts, combining a general academic education with specialized training in dance, drama, music or art. It wasn't the most exclusive of private schools, but at £65 a term it wasn't exactly cheap either.

The school was housed in a rambling old mansion previously owned by the Rothschilds.[6] Although its large reception rooms made for excellent dance studios, the sheer size of the building had its drawbacks, especially in winter when the dormitories were bitterly cold.

Beryl's first day wasn't encouraging. After travelling to London by train, she made her way to Tring by coach and it was dark by the time she reached the school. An administrative mix-up meant she had to share a room with two older girls, not in the main school itself but in a draughty building that had formerly served as a stable. When one of her fellow boarders told her to make up her bed, Beryl was mortified that she didn't know how, her mother having always done it: 'I turned my back and fiddled with my bedding and looked at the name tapes my mother had sewn on to the blankets, and tears came into my eyes.'[7]

After a few days the mix-up was discovered and Beryl was moved back into the main school. Even so, she found her first weeks at Tring something of a strain. Her antipathy to dance, and ballet in particular, was not calculated to endear her to her teachers. Grace Cone was a dangerous person to get on the wrong side of. Julie Andrews, who attended the school in 1942, prior to its move to Tring, described her as 'a real martinet',[8] while another former pupil recalled that she ruled the school 'with a rod of iron . . . she was feared and respected by all'.[9] Beryl's tap-dancing teacher was equally imposing: 'Miss Mackie was a tough woman and quite cruel' and had 'no tolerance for anyone timid or unsure'.[10] When she picked on someone she could be relentless.

This was Beryl's first experience of living away from home and the combination of alienation and physical discomfort prompted an immediate flurry of anxious letters to her parents and her brother Ian, who dismissively tried to make light of things: 'I don't know why you want to come home. If I was away on a holiday like you, I'd jolly well be dreading the day when I had to return home.'[11]

Beryl may have missed her old life, but her absence was also being felt by those who remained. Shortly after her arrival at Tring, Ian sent her a letter, written in the arch, slightly condescending tone he often used with her, that wittily captured the new state of affairs:

Dear Twirp,
It is now eleven days since you departed from the austere precincts of this house to the more austere environ of your present abode. That eleven day old event has altered the whole place, I might even add body, soul and mind, of family life here at home.

First let us deal with our parental antecedent. No longer having a Communist-Conservative in the house . . . the political fermentation has considerably decreased. In its place has developed a completely new procedure. The 'Manchester Guardian', that stalwart publication of a decayed body politic (and maybe heralder of a new and triumphant liberalism), is violently torn from its habitation in my newly-acquired brief case, even more violently turned from Crossword page 2 to Political page 3, & opened out so as to form a barrier between the reader and the outside world; then follows a series of 'umphs', 'Peshaws' and (exasperatedly) 'I don't know', emitted by the aforementioned reader during the course of his perusal of the proceedings in Parliament; then, as if the burden of the whole world's problems lay upon his shoulders, this modern Atlas verbally attacks, in the most heated manner, the cause of the earth's troubles, namely his loving wife and dutiful son. The only one to escape his scathing remarks is his faithful companion, that illustrious member of the canine race, Pedro.

Secondly, our maternal predecessor. This starving outpost of the Housewives' League eats only three eggs a day, half a pound of swine's flesh, a pint of milk, innumerable cups of tea, each one with a piece of cake or a biscuit, and sleeps 23 hours a day, rousing herself for the odd hour to listen to Twenty Questions, Country Ramble, Itma, or Merry-Go-Round.[12]

The volume of letters that criss-crossed between Formby and Tring during this period is truly impressive. Winnie, Richard and Ian all wrote to Beryl every Sunday, with Winnie often adding another letter or two in mid-week. Beryl also regularly received letters from Lyn, Harry, her foreign penpals, public school friends such as Richard Malthouse and Neil Briggs, former schoolfriends from Merchant Taylors' such as Annette Moore and Rita Moody ('How's Harry getting on? Are you still in love with him or have you got your eye on someone else! Knowing you, you will most probably have another one as you are a big flirt . . .'),[13] and from a range of Formby admirers. These included Albert 'Lochie' Riley, one of the porters at Formby railway station ('I miss you of a morning . . . I am going to <u>Bed</u> in a minute I wish you could come with me . . .'),[14] and Jim 'Bang' Seaford, an eighteen-year-old squaddie (no. 10 on her boyfriend list).

Beryl was, if anything, an even more assiduous correspondent and at one point had to be reprimanded for writing too frequently: 'You seem to be going through a fortune on stamps,' her mother complained. 'Darling, you needn't write every day. How about writing about three times a week say, or perhaps twice and you could give me all the news in those letters just the same?'[15]

The lightness of tone of Richard's letters, written in the mock-Irish accent he had taken to using with her, seems to belie the harsh portrait Beryl would later paint of her father:

My Darling Berry,

Sure Im delighted ye got my little note & liked it. Its a very worried world I find meself [in] nowadays what with having no one to help me on Sunday morning & no one to shout at its terrible, terrible it is me child.

Ye can see from yer mother's letter that she's give you all the news & never a devil she cares about me but never mind me darlin I love you very very much. Are you in need of money, let me know, and let us know when we can come & see you.

With fondest love
Ye olde Daddy.[16]

In their contrasting styles, the letters Beryl received from her mother and father offer an insight into the influence that each had on her writing. While Winnie's are full of gossip, local news and the latest scandals, dissecting the subconscious motives behind people's actions, Richard's letters are more imaginative, driven by narrative and even fantasy. Beryl's departure from Goodacre prompted him to begin a series of fictional tales concerning Uncle Len and the pig he'd just acquired, which for the purposes of his stories he called Professor Hugo. The first instalment in January started out as a simple flight of fancy, but 'the latest doings of the LenHugo pair'[17] quickly became a weekly ritual and the saga continued off and on until the spring of 1949. Many of the stories ran to five, six or even eight pages of closely written foolscap and seem to have been written at a single sitting. A short extract suffices to give an idea of their tone and intended comic effect:

I understand yer dear Uncle Len has repented in his heart and granted a respite to his pig 'Hugo'. He has now made Hugo his personal attendant and friend. He insists upon Hugo accompanying him wherever he goes, which is very touching and sweet to see. Such devotion by these two to each other brings tears to the eyes of passersby. Picture to yourself yer Uncle in his upstanding manner clad in his Brown tweed plus four suit with 'Hugo' Black coat, old vest and striped trousers, walking along the main streets of Liverpool. I know to you it will not appear funny, understanding us as you do, but on Wednesday next both yer dear Mother and Auntie Lilian have objected very strongly against Hugo coming. Now for the life of us, neither yer Uncle or meself can understand the reason for such insulting behaviour to

Hugo, for both he and Uncle have promised not to get drunk so long as they are allowed to dance together.[18]

Nothing highlights the difference between Richard and Winnie's temperaments as starkly perhaps as the letters each wrote to their daughter at the end of February. While Richard was carried away by his story about the goings-on of Uncle Len and Professor Hugo the pig, Winnie clearly had no time for such fancies: 'Poor old Hugo was murdered yesterday and Uncle Len has lost his playmate. Nannie is now busy cooking the bits & pieces.'[19]

By February 1948, Beryl had begun to adapt to school life,[20] though she was still prone to bouts of insecurity about her parents, which Winnie tried to assuage: 'Darling, you haven't any need to worry about me. I am feeling loads better and Daddy has been marvellous since you went away. He misses you dreadfully and often says how he would love to have you here just to argue and fight with. His politics need airing and you are the only one who will argue with him.'[21]

According to Julie Andrews the regime at the school was pretty rigorous, with 'academic lessons in the morning and ballet, tap and character dancing in the afternoons'.[22] Beryl's view was the opposite: 'I'm at this new school,' she wrote to a friend, Billy Cousins, whom she'd met in Scotland the previous year, 'where we just dance or act or paint or do music, no school work whatever.'[23]

Ian suspected, not without some justification, that this was more a case of lack of application than lack of schoolwork: 'You don't strike me as working hard enough since you seem to be writing a lot of letters instead of working, and most of those seem to be done in class or prep.'[24] He pointed out the difference between their two approaches, though he hardly made his own sound appealing: 'You don't start work till the afternoon and you're finished by 8.30. By that time I'm only just about half-way through my work. I start at 10 in the morning and work until 11 at night. 13 hours a day.'[25]

No doubt the school expected pupils of Beryl's age to work by themselves in prep and study periods, which Beryl seems to have considered simply as free time. But it's also true that the emphasis at Tring was more on turning out quality dancers than academics – the school's founders 'shared one ultimate goal: to produce prima ballerinas'.[26] Even so, the educational part of the curriculum was taken seriously enough to the extent that Beryl's teachers had begun talking about exams. This immediately prompted sarcastic comments from Ian:

> Also emerging from odds and ends at dinner is a strange rumour concerning you. It relates that your oberlieutenants intend to put you in for your School Cert this next July (Prolonged Roars of Laughter). Some hopes. Your commanding officers must be either escaped lunatics or communists. Anyway they haven't the foggiest notion of what they're doing. As a sort of proof of their madness I quote from your last letter: '. . . and the term lasts 10 weeks, or 70 days, or 4,820 hours, or something near there.' There is not the faintest resemblance between your reckoning and the correct answer. In 70 days there are only 1,680 hours, that's more than 3,000 difference.[27]

A similarly incredulous tone was adopted by a former Merchant Taylors' schoolfriend, Annette Moore, which shows the lack of esteem in which Beryl's academic standing was held among her peers: 'I think its a hell of a lark! you taking School Cert in July!!! how funny – just how do you think your going to do it???? I hope you dont take Geography!! and MATHS!!! O Dear I'd love to see your face when you see the exam papers!!'[28]

It was perhaps inevitable that the pattern enacted at Merchant Taylors' would repeat itself at Tring: Beryl excelled in drama ('Well done, little girl,' Winnie wrote encouragingly. 'We are proud of you being top and I was very thrilled with the remarks passed by your drama mistress . . .'),[29] but her inability to concentrate on other subjects led to conflicts and a general disengagement with school life.

Unsurprisingly, her exams didn't go well. Ian went through her finished papers shortly afterwards to work out whether she'd passed and his conclusions weren't encouraging: 'I don't say anything about Biology, but you seem to have answered confidently, if not competently. I wish you success . . . Your French paper you can class as a complete failure. I've never seen such rot. "I was reading" you put as "Je etait lire" i.e. no accent on the "e", wrong time, completely senseless.'[30]

But the end of the exams meant Beryl was free to go back to Formby, back to her walks in the pine woods, and to her meetings with Lyn, who was counting the days till she saw her 'lickle girl' again: 'Come round on the 22nd of course you adorable stupe,' Lyn wrote excitedly. 'Don't oversleep kid or I'll brain you. I'm looking forward to seeing your teeth and everything (not forgetting your Adam's apple) so much I can hardly wait . . .'[31]

The seashore and pine woods at Formby were where Beryl could feel free and escape the emotionally cramped confines of Goodacre. She was more than a little concerned, therefore, when she read in the *Formby Times* that the council might approve plans for a bus service to the shore. In the event, the siting of a bus terminal proved too difficult and the idea was shelved. The matter might have rested there, but in the 'Formby Forum' section of the newspaper Beryl read a letter with the mawkish heading 'Beach Trek is Too Far For Tiny Feet', which registered a 'strong protest' against the council for postponing the bus service, complaining that 'countless families are prevented from using our own foreshore' and 'innumerable happy hours of sunshine, sand-play and sea-bathing are lost to young children just because the journey to and from the shore is too long for little feet'.[32] The letter's sanctimonious attempt to paint children as helpless victims was too much for Beryl. She took up her pen to defend her little patch of freedom and the result was her first piece of published writing:

> Sir – I should like to reply to the letter in Formby Forum (5th March) regarding the bus service to the shore to save those tired feet. This would involve the removal of overhanging branches to ensure complete safety and comply with the transport regulations.
>
> Ever since I could walk I can remember tramping down to the shore and sprawling in the sand at the side of the road, and eating the blackberries that grow on the lane to the sea.
>
> Every summer one sees groups of children of all ages, with their dogs, rambling along with their jam jars over their shoulders, to the tadpole pools.
>
> A bus service would cause inconvenience to the scores of cyclists and numerous dogs and children who like to go by other means than motor transport. Besides, the shore is always, and always has been all

the year round, more than empty of Formby folk, who seemingly have no interest in the sea or are too lazy.

Buses would be an abomination. They are utterly modern and completely out of keeping with the beauty of the shore.

Those who care sufficiently about the sea always will walk, and enjoy it into the bargain. I appeal to the citizens of Formby not to ask for buses to run them down. The quietness and tranquillity of Formby foreshore must not be disturbed.

BB, Ravenmeols Lane, Formby.[33]

The letter has all the hallmarks of Beryl's later writing on social issues, with its tirade against modernity and change, and its contempt for those who wanted everything to be made easier for them. The following week, Winnie gleefully wrote that her letter had prompted no fewer than two replies. One of the correspondents picked up on the logical weakness of Beryl's argument – her statement that the shore was empty of Formby folk 'all the year round' was more a point against her position than for it – and went on to describe her as 'a little behind the times' and her stance as 'a little unreal'.[34] It wouldn't be the last time such accusations were levelled at Beryl's public pronouncements.

Although technically Beryl had another year of school, by the time she returned to Tring in the autumn of 1948 even her parents considered there was little point.[35] Beryl was never going to catch up academically, and her focus was almost entirely on a future working in the theatre. At Christmas, Richard agreed that if she were to find a suitable job she could leave school in the spring.

Back at Tring, it didn't take long for the tedium to set back in: 'God I hate this crowd of louses,'[36] she noted, barely three weeks into the New Year. A month later she was even more blunt: 'I hate everybody here. They neither understand or like me . . . Ah! Bleeding fools.'[37] She was fed up with being treated like a child and, like many rebellious teenagers, had begun to adopt the outward signifiers of adulthood: smoking and drinking. 'I'm longing for a ciggarette,' she wrote in her diary shortly after her return, 'I am bad tempered. I need a still whiskey.'[38] Despite this, there were a few moments of respite – fencing lessons with a male master, Jamie Milligan, was a particular highlight: 'He really is rather sweet, noone likes him (so they pretend) but I do. His bottom is so energetic.'[39]

Nevertheless, the thought that 'this is going to be my last term'[40] cheered her up, as did her loss in weight ('I'm thinner, must stay that way too'). On her half-term break there was more good news. Utilizing some of his old business contacts, Richard arranged a meeting with Robert Hall, a Liverpool councillor and former lord mayor who had connections to the Playhouse. As a regular theatregoer Beryl would have known of Maud Carpenter, the Playhouse's general manager, by reputation if not in person, and she had been to the Playhouse so many times she was on speaking terms with those who worked there, including Fred Kearney who handled the theatre's publicity. But there was nothing like an official recommendation to open the right doors, as Beryl noted in her diary: 'Went with Daddy to see R. J. Hall. Ex Lord Mayor of Liverpool. He gave me a letter of intro to Maud Carpenter. She was so terribly sweet. Fred did look surprised.'[41]

This success buoyed her up for the next few days, though she must have been frustrated by the unadventurous caution of her relatives. After she had written enthusiastically to her grandparents about her possible future at the Playhouse, they urged her to be patient and concentrate on her schoolwork. But it was too late for that sort of advice. Beryl had her mind set on her future career ('I want the theatre, always the Theatre')[42] and she was more determined than ever to leave school ('I must leave school. I must').[43]

One of the few girls Beryl liked at Tring was Jean Aubrey, a dancer also looking to pursue a career in the theatre, and it was during a weekend spent with Jean at her parent's house in Nottinghamshire that the most immediately fruitful opportunity for gaining some theatrical experience arose. As the two girls passed the Olympia Theatre in Bulwell they saw an advertisement for a talent contest to take place during Easter week. On the spur of the moment they decided to enter, and after talking to the theatre's owner he booked them for the event there and then. 'Oh wonderful glorious life,'[44] Beryl noted excitedly.

The Olympia Theatre had in fact just opened less than a month previously, after having been closed for eleven years due to subsidence, and the talent show was part of its campaign to attract a new audience. The contest would intersperse performances by established theatre regulars with those of local amateur acts. Each night over the course of the week leading up to Easter one of the hopefuls would win a place in Friday's final, and the three most popular acts, judged by 'an applause-measuring machine',[45] stood to win cash prizes of £15, £10 and £5, plus the opportunity to perform in two shows on Saturday.

All this sounded ideal to Beryl and Jean, but less so to their parents, the reason being that the Olympia was a variety theatre, not a repertory theatre. As Winnie snootily put it: 'We weren't exactly thrilled when Jean's Daddy rang up because we are not anxious for you to try Variety. Ian was very indignant when he read what you intended doing because he said they are all too ancient . . .'[46]

It is easy to put Winnie's begrudging attitude down to snobbery, which to an extent it was, but there was a certain justification in it. Among the variety acts the Olympia had lined up for the week after the talent contest was Gus Brox and Myrna, 'musical clowns from Holland', Billy O'Sullivan 'the Rogue with a brogue', the 'cheeky and charming' Doris Clifton, and Koppa Goldwyn, 'a trick xylophonist'.[47] Winnie had not spent years encouraging and training her daughter, spending money on elocution lessons and ballet schools, in order for her turn into a variety performer. Nevertheless, Beryl and Jean set about applying pressure, in the form of letters and telephone calls, to persuade their parents to let them perform. Richard's response was suitably considered: 'I would sincerely counsel that caution and patience should be exercised,' he said, adding that he would give the matter his 'serious and undivided attention'.[48]

A week later, after discussions between the parents of the two girls, Richard was ready to concede, and somewhat improbably Beryl and Jean got their way.[49] During Easter week Beryl went back up to Nottingham. Sandwiched between Dave Kaye, a professional comedian, the Ten Wonder Starlets, a dancing and tumbling act performed by diminutive girls, and Viscount, 'the radio and film dog, who answers mathematical problems for members of the audience', Beryl and Jean tried out their hastily improvised routine. First was a joint rendition of Billy Cotton's 'Hang on the Bell, Nellie', a blackly comic song about a girl whose father, in attempting to protect his daughter's honour, kills her would-be seducer and is sentenced to be hanged. This was followed by a version of 'Abdul Abulbul Amir', Beryl's solo recitation of a monologue,[50] and a dance routine as a finale.[51]

Although the two girls didn't win, the experience confirmed their desire to work in the theatre. Years later, Beryl would nostalgically recall her first proper live performance on that stage in Bulwell: 'It was not that I found the applause gratifying or the experience ever less than terrifying, but there was a moment, just before the end of the monologue . . . when fear and embarrassment lifted and I was no longer trapped within myself. For that one moment I floated as free and as aimless as the specks of dust that shimmered like fire-flies above the footlights.'[52]

At the end of the spring term in April 1949, Beryl left Tring for good. In Formby she passed her time in trips down to the shore or meeting friends in Liverpool and hanging round the docks. It was either here or at a meeting of the Young Communist League (YCL) that she met Les Carr[53] (no. 16 on her boyfriend list), a twenty-two-year-old in the Merchant Navy. Carr was intelligent, impulsive and politically committed, and though he was clearly attracted to her he was sensitive enough not to force his attentions. After meeting her a few times he wrote to tell her: 'For the past few days I have thought of nothing or nobody but you . . . What I am really trying to say is that I miss you very much. This is the first weekend we have been apart since we first met. All my love, Les xxx.'[54]

But there was a problem: he was not exactly 'suitable'. He came from a Catholic, working-class family, one of ten children brought up in a small two-up two-down terraced house in Anfield. They both knew that Beryl's parents wouldn't agree to them seeing each other. It is easy to overlook the fact that Beryl had a privileged upbringing. The veneer of social respectability may have been thin – too thin for comfort in Winnie's mind – but it was undeniably there, and when the lines were drawn between 'us' and 'them', Beryl was clearly in the former camp.

Les felt that the distance between them was insurmountable, and in one of Beryl's school exercise books he wrote out his feelings of frustration, imagining what might have happened if she'd been born into another, less well-off, family: 'Wish she had been born as Andy Howard's daughter, things might have been different. I must be going nuts. She's not Andy Howard's daughter and things are no different. She's Berry

Bainbridge of Formby who has never had to worry her pretty little head about anything in her life, nice, kind, respectable pampered middle class, doesn't know what work, struggle, fight, love, and hate means.'[55]

On their next meeting they went to hear Paul Robeson sing and give a speech against racial discrimination outside St George's Hall. As if to justify her parents' fears, at the end of the rally there were scuffles and truncheon-wielding police waded in, during which Beryl was struck on the elbow. Beryl's pithy comment in her diary – 'Awful lot of trouble'[56] – referred not only to the melée itself but to the aftermath at home: when her father found out he banned her from attending any more meetings, putting a peremptory end to her political activism.

Despite the parental restrictions, Beryl continued to see Les several times over the next month or so, often down by the docks, where they took expeditions together out in boats. Almost imperceptibly, the relationship settled down into something more intimate, especially as far as Les was concerned, and he referred to her familiarly as 'Babs' and sent her mildly suggestive letters: 'It's two oclock in the afternoon. I'm lying on my bed naked – try it sometime – when I'm around . . . My centre piece is dead centre neither to the right nor the left but dead centre – if you know what I mean, just like the man on the cliffs.'[57]

As the summer progressed, Beryl began to realize she was becoming attached to him: 'I met Les this afternoon and he looked bitter, and when he lay back he looked uplifted. The sky was very blue and I didn't want it spoilt. He lay very close to me and put my nipple in his mouth. Funny tight burning sensation. He also asked me did I really feel anything for him. I said "Yes". When he was away I came the nearest I ever was to loving him.'[58]

But something held her back. Whether it was the perceived class differences between them, her own confused emotional state, or simply that navy life was not conducive to a proper relationship, the writing seemed to be on the wall: 'I think it all over now, and I begin to despise his speech and cheeky chappie Liverpool face. I'm such a contradictory muddle . . . Shall I tell him? Of course not.'

Adding to the muddle were her still not quite resolved feelings for Harry, to whom Beryl had recently written what he called 'a very affectionate letter'. His reply had given her another cause for anxiety: his plans to return to England seemed to be progressing and his desire for her appeared as ardent as ever: 'Now I begin to economize already for the train-journey to Hambourg and for the ship-journey then to Hull . . . What is for me Germany, though my parents are here and my relations and I have my job, if my love-roses bloom in England? . . . If it is possible, perhaps we can your seventeenth birthday celebrate together. That were a joy!'[59]

This letter and her responsibilities to Harry played on her mind and she wrote in her diary: 'He is coming to England and wants me to love him always. He says if I break from him, his life will be finished.'[60] When Beryl next saw Les she 'felt ashamed',[61] not just because Harry would be upset about her going out with someone else, but also because Les had declared his feelings for her, telling her that she was his whole world, and she knew that she would end up hurting him, too. Although she was 'fond of him . . . almost against my will',[62] she wasn't in love with him, and she began to feel increasingly guilty about having effectively led him on.

Shortly afterwards she wrote Les what amounted to a 'Dear John' letter. He protested that he wasn't hurt and that he understood: 'I don't think you would hurt me intentionally . . . besides there's no one knows better than I do that things will never work out the way I want them too in regard to our future.' In spite of his disappointment, he couldn't help being struck by her vivid style, like many of her correspondents: 'If ever in later life you get tired of the stage take up a pen – you can write, anyhow.'[63]

Although Beryl would never quite lose contact with him, Les and the events of that summer were quickly overshadowed by other developments. Her favourable meeting with Maud Carpenter at the Playhouse in February led to further interviews in May, and finally in the first week of June 1949 a definite decision was taken: 'Today I got a letter . . . and was told I was to start under Hugh Goldie on July 28th at the Playhouse . . . I don't know whether to be excited or not about the Playhouse, because I am very frightened.'[64]

Having to start work at such short notice meant there was little chance to take a proper family holiday. Instead, in July, she went with Winnie to Blackpool, and spent a week taking in all the big shows.

On her return Beryl began her long-anticipated life in the theatre.

SEVEN

The Playhouse

At sixteen I was again at home and went to work in the
repertory theatre, and met a great number of people who
profoundly influenced me. From one I became obsessed with
beauty of face and soul, so that life became an unending
search for harmony and suffering and sadness. From another
I achieved power because for the first time I realised in an
unbudded way I held a great many qualities deemed strange
and fine . . .[1]

T HE LIVERPOOL PLAYHOUSE IS situated in Williamson
Square, at the very heart of the city. It was established in 1911
when the recently incorporated Liverpool Repertory Theatre Ltd.
bought the struggling Star Theatre, raising capital for the venture
through a share issue, and in the process becoming the first Rep to
own the freehold of a theatre. Its subsequent reputation as one of the
most important provincial theatres was forged principally through the
combined effort of two people: William Armstrong, the director and
producer at the Playhouse from 1922 to 1944, and Maud Carpenter,
who served as its general manager for nearly forty years until her
retirement in 1962.

For such an influential figure, remarkably little has been written
about Maud Carpenter, who was born in 1892,[2] the daughter of a
bricklayer in Toxteth Park. She began her working career in her late
teens as a box office clerk at the Liverpool Rep prior to its takeover
of the Star Theatre,[3] and in the years that followed she worked her
way up to become a business manager and administrator par excel-
lence. It was Maud who looked after the day-to-day running of the
theatre, sorting out everything from hiring staff, setting salaries and

drawing up contracts, down to bar arrangements and the rights to sell refreshments.

The 1949 Playhouse season was directed by Gerald Cross, a handsome but temperamentally erratic actor looking to move into producing and directing. As an actor at Dundee Rep a few years before, he had directed some successful productions, and after joining Liverpool Playhouse in 1947 and working under the director John Fernald he had carried out directorial duties on a couple of occasions. When Fernald moved to London at the end of the 1948 season, Cross jumped at the chance to take over. Alongside Cross, the Playhouse company featured a number of actors who were well-known figures around Liverpool, such as Cyril Luckham, John Warner and Peggy Mount.

Beryl was still two months short of her seventeenth birthday[4] when she started as a student actress at the Playhouse. Perhaps unsurprisingly, she was completely swept up by the strange new world that opened out before her. She was immediately attracted by the cosmopolitanism of the theatre's personnel who, in comparison to herself, seemed exotic, cultured and experienced in the ways of life. Her desire to belong to this grown-up artistic company is reflected by the fact that when her name didn't appear in the programme she would write it in herself, adding her job title, 'Prompt' or 'Assistant Electrician and Call Boy', for good measure.

Initially her tasks were somewhat prosaic and included numerous jobs usually undertaken by an assistant stage manager, though she was never officially credited as an ASM in programmes.[5] Her first production – technically speaking the last production of the previous season, which ran from September 1948 to August 1949 – was George Bernard Shaw's *You Never Can Tell*, with stage direction by Hugh Goldie and sets designed and painted by Paul Mayo. Beryl's job seems to have been limited to that of prompt, though she may have had a minor walk-on part, or more precisely a dance-on part, as Jacques, her French penfriend, lamented the fact that he couldn't be in Liverpool to see her dance onstage, and assured her she must have looked pretty in her blue and red costume.[6] However menial or inconsequential such jobs might have seemed at the time, observing actors at first hand and learning the nuts and bolts of stagecraft was vital training for her subsequent career in the theatre.

But there were other things an actress as young – and attractive – as Beryl had to learn, foremost of which was to negotiate the attentions of male actors, and in this she wasn't always so successful. The Irish actor Tom St John Barry (later a broadcaster for ITN) would put her across his knee and spank her with a rolled-up newspaper whenever she came into his dressing room to call 'overture and beginners'.[7]

The emotional ferment of the theatre – a self-contained and pressurized environment that seems especially designed to produce short-lived and unstable unions – was an aspect that Beryl found compelling. Far from being immune to such emotional volatility she quickly and inevitably succumbed. After the successful first night of Eve Morgante's *Westward Journey*, which opened in the first week of September 1949, Beryl confided in her diary:

> I am nearly seventeen, and I think I am in love with Hugh Goldie. In years to come or perhaps even tomorrow this will sound schoolgirlish and very silly, and I shall want to laugh. But tonight I mean it. Afterwards Miss Eve Morgante came and thanked us, and Gerald Cross said 'Well done Children', to us. That to me was very happiness. We went into the room upstairs and had a sherry and Hugh made me sit by him.[8]

Beryl's crush on Goldie was understandable. Thirteen years her senior, Goldie cut a dashing figure: not just professionally – he was an actor who had made his debut as a director earlier in the year with a production of *Hobson's Choice* at the Sheffield Playhouse, starring Paul Eddington and Patrick McGoohan – but physically, too. Tall, thin, and with a shock of blond hair falling over his lean, angular face, he looked every inch the ex-RAF pilot he was; he had been decorated on several occasions for his war service.

Although the two hit it off immediately, Goldie had a serious drawback as a romantic possibility: he was married – to a Viennese refugee with whom he now had a two-year-old son. Consequently, Beryl took to her diary again shortly afterwards to record a change in her emotional attachments:

> I am no longer in love with Hugh. I am very fond of him and he is very fond of me, but I love Paul Mayo. Every night I pray 'Please God make Paul Mayo love me.' Everybody in this place is so unhappy and Nuroctic . . . with such a lost sick look in their eyes. Why does everything have to be so sad? I'm so lonely. I'm so desperately lonely.

Everyone is. They wander around, with their hands cold, and want something that only one in a thousand shall ever get. Must I get lost too?[9]

Although she'd had a lot of boyfriends, none of them had developed into a serious, lasting relationship – and given the combination of differences in age, nationality and social situation, none of them had much prospect of developing into one either. At seventeen Beryl had an idealized view of love, but had never met anyone who fulfilled that ideal. She liked the boys she had met, but apart from her youthful idealization of Harry Franz she had never actually fallen in love. Harry had discerned this, as Beryl noted in her diary after sending him a photograph of herself: 'Funny thing. I feel I know such an awful lot about men and love and yet Harry said my eyes in the photo held no experience of love.'[10]

Consequently, she wasn't prepared for the unsettling sensations that love provoked:

The very mention of the designer's name caused me to break into a fit of trembling, and if I actually came face to face with him, which I did four or five times a day, I had the curious feeling that my feet and my teeth and my nose had enlarged out of all proportion. When he spoke to me I could never hear what he said for the thudding of my heart and the chattering of my out-sized teeth. In spite of this I hung about the paint frame whenever I could, hoping to be noticed.[11]

But Mayo remained aloof and despite Beryl's undoubted physical attraction he seems to have regarded her not as a potential girlfriend but simply as another young, rather naive girl. Clearly ambitious, Mayo had other things on his mind, having already made his name as an innovative set designer. His sketches for two Playhouse productions in the 1949 season, along with those for *You Never Can Tell* and from a number of productions dating back to 1946, featured in an exhibition at the Bluecoat Chambers in Liverpool in October 1949, which Beryl visited and the programme of which she would religiously keep. But she soon realized he wasn't interested in her – his Christmas card that year was signed with the impersonal greeting 'from Paul Mayo'.

Beryl's intense desire to be loved, coupled with her insecurity about how attractive men found her, was a dangerous combination, leaving her susceptible to overtures by anyone who expressed an interest in her and emotionally troubled by those who didn't. As it was, she already had three men – Harry, and her two penfriends Jacques Delebassée and Paul Vigo – writing to say that they loved her and proposing to marry her. But these reassurances of her desirability did little to allay her anxieties.

The problem of Harry, especially, continued to exercise her. In August she wrote and attempted to tell him that his scheme to come to England and marry her was not realistic. She tried to let him down gently, suggesting that it was 'a very big thing to do, to come away from your home and country, all for a girl who was just fourteen when you left her and who did not know much of love'.[12] But whether led astray by his feelings, or by his poor grasp of English and his inability to read between the lines of Beryl's ambivalently worded hints, Harry brushed her doubts aside and ended with yet another outpouring of love:

> Darling . . . it is my only wish, that we us, as soon as only possible see again, that will be the more nice day of my life. Dearest, ever and ever again, I remember me on the nice hours in the summer 1947. If we us see again, we must have no fear more, you are not more fourteen years, and I am not more a prisoner. Then you will be not more shy anymore.
>
> <u>Darling</u>, believe me I miss you more as anything in the world. Please, keep on loving me as much as I love you, and think of me every minute of the day, then no doubts will us separate! K.T.M. means Keep true me.[13]

At the same time as she was confiding her passion for Hugh and for Paul in her journal, she was also writing to Harry saying she wished to see him again. This wasn't coquettishness, her feelings for him were genuine enough, and Harry's letters, importunate and demanding as they were, seemed to exhibit such genuine feeling that she found it impossible to put an end to his dreams once and for all.

In September she wrote to Harry again and at the start of October he replied, somewhat comforted ('Darling, I say thousend thanks for your confidence to our love!'), though still frustrated by the lack of news about jobs and travel permits: 'Did you get till now still no offer or anything? Have you written since your last letter to a factory and so on again?'[14] Nothing if not persistent, he had heard that couples who had been separated after the end of the war could get a royal permission to travel and he begged her to write to the Queen and petition her. She took Harry's plan to come over to England seriously enough to tell her close friends, and over the next few months they would keep asking for news: 'How's Harry? Has he come over yet?'[15]

One positive thing about three-weekly Rep was that the work was so intense it left little time for dwelling on such matters. For the next production, Somerset Maugham's *The Letter*, Beryl was given a proper walk-on part – as one of a group of 'Chinese Boys, Malay Servants, Etc' – and her name appeared in the programme for the first time.

Then, after having spent only three months at the Playhouse, her big chance came. Gerald Cross had scheduled the premiere of A. R. Whatmore's *The Sun and I*, a play that called for a child actor in the part of David, a young mathematical prodigy. Cross had originally chosen Bruce Moffat, an eleven-year-old boy from Crosby, to play the role, but the local education authority was unhappy with the arrangement. As a replacement, Whatmore suggested Edmunde Stewart, an eleven-year-old he had worked with at Dundee Rep, but four days before opening night the Scottish authorities refused him permission too. Despite the fact that Beryl was understudying the part, Cross continued to look for another boy, but time was against him. The day before the play opened he told Beryl she could have the part if she had her hair cropped. Half an hour later she made up her mind and was sent off to be given a short page-boy cut, the considerate hairdresser draping a towel over the mirror so as to lessen the shock of seeing her long hair being cut off. 'I don't know what mum and dad will say when they see me looking such a sight,'[16] she told a local newspaper reporter.

The play opened to enthusiastic applause, and immediately attracted good notices ('A notable success', *The Stage*;[17] 'The play has moments of great tenderness, irony and beauty', *Daily Post*[18]). Alongside the reviews there were also numerous 'human interest' pieces, revolving around the haircut and Beryl's transformation from girl to boy, complete with 'before-and-after' pictures. Although this certainly made good copy, Beryl didn't particularly enjoy the extra publicity. Already insecure about her appearance, it added insult to injury that it should be her passable resemblance to a boy and not her feminine beauty that had attracted attention, and significantly she never sported short hair again.

Nevertheless, the numerous plaudits she received for her performance must have been satisfying: 'The evening was in many ways a triumph for 17-year-old Beryl Bainbridge, who took the part of David at short notice and gave a remarkably faithful portrait of a schoolboy, complete with unruly hair specially shorn for the occasion and half hesitant, shuffling gait.'[19]

Winnie, too, could hardly have been more pleased by the coverage, and pieces such as that which ran under the heading 'That Boy David' hit all the right notes: 'Nobody watched the performance of B. M. Bainbridge as the boy David . . . more intently than did her mother, for though it was difficult to believe, David, with "his" closely cropped hair, untidily schoolboyish, is a dainty 17-year-old girl, Beryl Bainbridge . . . With the new play one wonders if a new "star" has been born.'[20]

The more or less constant schedule at the Playhouse of performances in the evening and rehearsals during the day perhaps accounts for the lack of entries in Beryl's diary. After her description of the first night of *The Sun and I* on 29 November 1949 there is nothing until a hurried admonition to herself six months later in June 1950: 'I really must learn to keep a diary properly. I get so behind hand.'[21]

The first half of 1950 had been taken up with a sequence of very minor performances. Her success in *The Sun and I* didn't lead, as she perhaps hoped, to an influx of larger roles. In the productions up to the end of the season, she was given only a series of non-speaking or small walk-on parts: a lady-in-waiting in *Richard II*, Sherah in *Tobias and the Angel* ('. . . a word of praise is due to [one] of the younger members, Beryl Bainbridge for her song sweetly sung . . .'),[22] and a tea-house girl in Alfred Klabund's *The Circle of Chalk*.[23] Low-key though such roles were, it was all part of the training process and over the next few months Beryl cemented her position as a staple within the company.

———

Beryl's brief crush on Hugh Goldie had given way to a close friendship that was warmly reciprocated. After he left the Playhouse to go to Sheffield in the spring of 1950, they corresponded regularly and kept up to date with each other's activities. During this period Beryl's sensitivity to her parents' arguments exacerbated, and in June she wrote anxiously in her diary: 'Things have been getting to a head between Mummy and Daddy. I'm so horribly miserable about it.'[24] She confided her worries to Hugh and though he provided a sympathetic ear for her complaints ('Are you on speaking terms at the moment or is there a current feud?!!'),[25] his replies show that even he unconsciously suspected she was prone to exaggeration: 'How are things at home, darling? Are your people really thinking of separating or were you only being unduly pessimistic?'[26]

Like Les Carr, Hugh was struck by Beryl's ability to write. He even compared her stream of consciousness style to that of James Joyce in *Ulysses*, albeit in a slightly tongue-in-cheek fashion, hinting that her misspelled and grammatically incorrect use of English was akin to Joyce's deliberately unconventional spelling and punctuation. Nevertheless, he was genuinely impressed by her writing ('you are by far the most interesting letter writer that ever writes to me . . .'),[27] and would later counsel her not to let her 'very real talent for writing blossom unseen'.[28]

After he moved to Oxford to produce a series of productions there, Hugh wrote a long, effusive letter, 'wondering what inspiration is eminating from the Fenomenon of Formby': 'What about Beryl – alternately looking a tramp and a sweetie, an angel and a little naughty funny cat? Have you learnt to draw yet – and can you speak and is your bottom measurement keeping where it should be? Do burn some midnight oil one night and curl up in bed and write to me and tell me all about life in Liverpool . . . Janet sends her love and so do I with a big kiss (big brotherly of course). Be good. Hugh.'[29]

Hugh remained an important figure in Beryl's life over the next few years, and would be instrumental in finding her theatrical work on a number of occasions. But their friendship wasn't without a more dangerous undercurrent: his attraction to her wasn't entirely as 'brotherly' as he implied, nor had she completely got over her initial crush on him. Their mutual attraction, amusing and diverting though it was when constrained within the bounds of friendship, always had the potential to develop into something more, and would nearly end with disastrous consequences.

Gerald Cross's penchant for European plays came to the fore at the start of the 1950–1 season, which opened with a translation of Alberto Colantuoni's *I Fratelli Castiglioni* (*The Brothers Castiglioni*), a black comedy in which four unscrupulous brothers compete against each other to find a winning lottery ticket, hidden by their uncle just before his death. For the production a young drama student from Bristol, Kenneth Ratcliffe, was drafted into the company, and it was during the first rehearsal, when Beryl was handing out scripts, that they met for the first time. They got on immediately: 'I really homed in on Beryl, I had a lot of rapport with her,'[30] Ken recalled, and over the weeks that followed he began to hope that their friendship might develop into something more.

Work in the theatre, like film work, is intensive, but also includes long periods of down-time, and Ken and Beryl had many hours to fill in which to talk about their lives, about art, literature and religion. In their spare time they would go to exhibitions at the Bluecoat Chambers or the Walker Art Gallery, and as Ken had an Equity card – Beryl never applied for hers – they could get into matinee performances in theatres and cinemas for free.

Beryl took up painting again. One of her ideas was to paint a portrait of Ken. In the back of her diary for 1950 she scribbled down the sizes of a couple of suitable canvases – one 18 x 14 and another 20 x 23 – which she bought for the job. With Ken posed, seated in his dressing room, Beryl painted a pale and wan figure in a dark jacket. This was the first proper portrait she had painted in oils, but at the time Ken thought it unflattering – 'it had the look of Hamlet seeing his Father's ghost'[31] – and, somewhat untactfully, decided against buying it.

It was around this time that Beryl's interest in Roman Catholicism began to be stimulated, and on Sundays she and Ken would go to a Catholic church such as St Peter's in Seel Street, a ten-minute walk from the Playhouse: 'At that time I had a religious streak and so did she. We often talked about religion, and she would often drag me to a Catholic church, which she really enjoyed being in, sitting at the back, listening to the service, smelling the incense, getting the atmosphere. The Catholic ritual appealed to her, it was theatrical.'[32]

They also shared similar tastes in literature, both being avid readers of D. H. Lawrence and Graham Greene. When *The End of the Affair* was published in 1951 they would read it out loud, each taking a chapter in turn. They also read T. S. Eliot's plays, *Murder in the Cathedral* being one of Beryl's favourites. Beryl was particularly taken with Eliot's post-conversion poetry: in her 1949 diary she had copied out part of Eliot's *The Rock*, and she would often quote the famous lines from *Little Gidding*: 'And the end of all our exploring/Will be to arrive where we started/And know the place for the first time.'

This interest in Catholicism was undoubtedly encouraged by the atmosphere of the Playhouse: Gerald Cross was a Catholic, as were several of the actors. 'There was a feeling of religion about the place',[33] as Ken Ratcliffe put it. In the autumn of 1950, during rehearsals for a production of Gerhart Hauptmann's *The Beaver Coat* ('Beryl Bainbridge cuts a quaint figure in flounced knickers . . .'),[34] Beryl met its charismatic translator, Eric Colledge, a senior lecturer in English at Liverpool University who specialized in medieval mysticism. His flamboyance (he wore bright yellow or red waistcoats and spats), his enthusiasm, and the fact that he was also a fervent Catholic (he would take religious vows and become a monk in the early 1960s), clearly made an impression on her. When she eventually took instruction about converting two years later in Dundee, Colledge wrote to her as 'an old chum'[35] to say how pleased he was at her decision.

After *The Brothers Castiglioni* the next production was George Bernard Shaw's *Caesar and Cleopatra*, with Peggy Mount playing Cleopatra's nurse and Cyril Luckham in the role of Caesar. Once again, Beryl was given a male part, that of Ptolemy the boy-king. The production opened to good reviews, and she gained several favourable notices ('Beryl Bainbridge deserves mention for her brief but effective performance as the young Ptolemy . . .'),[36] though not all critics were convinced by her cross-gendered performance. The *Liverpool Daily Post*, in a back-handed compliment that reveals the extent to which Beryl's name had already become familiar among theatre-going regulars, complained that it was 'an affront to realism to cast a girl as Cleopatra's young brother, even though she be Beryl Bainbridge'.[37]

EIGHT

Austin

A year later I had my first love affair, which irrevocably changed me for good. Strangely I became younger, I trusted and loved implicitly.[1]

Nothing shall be as sweet as the Liverpool days, nothing so hopeless as the time in Hope Street. And when if it happens I should be torn from the warmth and carried out into deepest death, my mouth would open and I would ~~shriek into~~ cry into eternity the name of Austin.[2]

T HE PRODUCTION OF *Caesar and Cleopatra* turned out to be more significant to Beryl for personal rather than theatrical reasons. In previous productions Paul Mayo had been assisted in painting sets and scenery by Betty Gow; for *Caesar and Cleopatra*, however, a local art student, Austin Davies, was drafted in to help with some of the more technical backdrops.

In later life Beryl gave a highly romanticized account of her meeting with Austin: dramatic elements such as coincidence, misunderstanding, and a love triangle in which everyone had fallen for the wrong person, played their part. At the time of her eventual marriage to him, however, three and a half years afterwards in April 1954, Beryl would give a more prosaic version of events to the local paper. In this account, printed under the headline 'A raffle won him a bride', Austin was busy painting scenery in the theatre workshop when she asked him an apparently simple question: 'Do you want a water set?' Confronted with his blank expression – he had no idea what a water set was – she explained that it was a prize in a raffle and sold him a ticket.[3]

It is difficult to overstate the impact Austin had on Beryl's life. In emotional terms he was her first experience of a fully committed sexual relationship – and, equally significantly, her first experience of the crushing humiliation that comes from rejection. But the relationship was also significant in that it influenced the course of her subsequent life and career. Austin not only inspired her to take up painting seriously, he also supported her financially during and after their marriage – thereby allowing her to write – and he was instrumental in her decision to leave Liverpool for London in the 1960s. He even bought the house she would live in until she died.

Tall and handsome with a gaunt bearded face, Austin Howard Davies looked every inch the bohemian artist in his chunky sweater and his black duffel coat. In fact, he came from a relatively affluent Liverpool family, a world away, socially and culturally, from that of Winnie Baines and Richard Bainbridge. His father Harold Hinchcliffe Davies was a renowned Liverpool architect, as was his father before him.

But if Austin's family was more financially comfortable than Beryl's, it was also more troubled. His parents had married young in 1917 – Harold was only seventeen at the time – and the decision doesn't seem to have been an entirely voluntary one. Not only did Harold lie and give his age as twenty-one on the marriage certificate, no relatives acted as witnesses, hinting that they married without parental approval. Suspicions about the reason for his hasty union with nineteen-year-old Nora Winifred Wood are confirmed by an entry in the register of births a few months afterwards – their child, Harold Jr, was born in early 1918.

By chance, Harold and Nora were immortalized through their connection to the Liverpool-based photographer Edward Chambré Hardman. While in Provence on holiday in 1926, Hardman took a picture of Harold, Nora and an architect friend Frank Jenkins sitting in a French *jardin*. Harold is depicted in a louche attitude, leaning back in his chair, legs crossed, a cigarette in his mouth and his hands in his pockets. The photo transcends the mundane reality of the experience it records. The sunlight dappling the trees in the background instils it with a romantic, nostalgic quality, presenting an idealized image of how those in the affluent middle class wanted to see themselves. Entitled

A Memory of Avignon it subsequently went on to sell in enormous quantities and is still available as a print today. But this idyllic scene belied the reality of life in the Davies household, and what is left out of the photograph is more telling than what is captured by the lens: the couple's children are conspicuous by their absence. After Harold Jr, a second son, Anthony, was born in 1923, and Austin followed at the beginning of 1926, just six months before the trip to Provence.

Nora, a cold, distant woman, according to Austin, didn't adapt well to the role of mother, something not made any easier by Harold's hands-off approach to fathering and his busy professional life. In August 1934 she took Anthony to Marseilles for three weeks, where she met the artist André Lhote and came to a realization that her enforced marriage and the subsequent demands of motherhood had stifled her own creative development.

Shortly afterwards the marriage fell apart. Harold met and fell in love with a woman of a very different character to Nora, Elizabeth Anne Parry, and Nora abandoned her children, leaving Liverpool for Paris to study painting at André Lhote's Académie de la Grande Chaumière in Montparnasse. Austin always blamed Elizabeth for breaking up the family and as a result never got on with her.

After the fall of Paris in June 1940, Nora returned to Liverpool. Harold took the opportunity not only to instigate divorce proceedings, allowing him to marry Elizabeth in 1942,[4] but also to urge Nora to take responsibility for Austin, who was seen as a disruptive influence. Nora encouraged Austin to prepare for art school,[5] and in the autumn of 1945 he enrolled at the Liverpool College of Art, where he would remain almost continuously – as student, postgraduate student and lecturer – until he left Liverpool for good in 1960.

By the late 1940s Austin had grown into an idealistic, ambitious young man, combining his mother's enthusiasm for art with his father's rigid commitment to hard work and discipline. Earnest and socially engaged, he believed passionately in art and in the power of culture to transform and enrich people's lives, but this positive outlook was undermined by psychological fault lines, his aloof family upbringing having left him reserved and wary of emotional attachment or commitment.

A turning point in Austin's life came when he met Dorothy and Gordon Green. They lived in a large Georgian house in Hope Street just opposite the art school where Austin was studying, and a short walk from the Philharmonic Hall where Gordon, a concert pianist and music teacher, was a member of the Liverpool Philharmonic Orchestra. Midway in age between Austin and his parents, the Greens played a huge part in his development, not just through their personal friendship but also through their influential position in the Liverpool cultural scene. Their house served as a meeting point for musicians and artists, as well as a convivial space in which political and social ideas could be discussed. Fritz Spiegl was a frequent guest, Sviatoslav Richter and Artur Rubinstein would drop by whenever they were performing at the Philharmonic, and the sculptor Herbert Tyson Smith was one of many visitors connected to the art world. A number of Austin's early commissions for portraits came through contacts made while at the Greens' Hope Street house, the basement of which they generously let him use rent free. For the next few years it would serve as Austin's studio and eventually as a living space, and he would sleep on a divan under the window, through which he could watch the female art students going into college.

Austin was always appreciative of what the Greens had done for him: 'Being so short of cash and the means to buy my materials, if it was not for the help of my greatest friends, the Greens, my position would be critical. Of these latter I could never say too much. Dorothy Green's constant encouragement and interests, her belief in my ability, and her untiring pursuit of sitters and patrons, means more to me than I could ever tell.'[6] Dorothy was also Austin's confidante as regards his emotional life, or what he referred to as 'my numerous girl friends'. On every matter of importance to him she proffered her advice and judgement, and he wrote in his journal that he had never yet known her to be wrong in her criticism or guidance, whether relating to art or affairs of the heart.

During the summer of 1950 Austin was at a loose end. To pass the time before starting his final year at college in September, he began looking for a job. Hearing that the Playhouse was advertising for student painters to work on set designs for their forthcoming production of Shaw's *Caesar and Cleopatra*, he decided to go along; he had nothing to lose and it might prove an interesting experience.

As she had with Hugh Goldie and Paul Mayo before him, Beryl fell for Austin immediately. She seemed to have no middle gear once her emotions were engaged, it was all or nothing. Austin was not like that; although he was undoubtedly attracted to her – publicity photographs at the time perfectly capture her distinctive wide-eyed look and her pouting expression – he also found her naive, not to say immature. He affectionately called her 'tatty-head' and 'sweetie', but his tone to her was frequently paternal and superior – something that could be, and often was, mistaken for condescension. Certainly Austin's innate caution, his emotional reserve, was at odds with Beryl's instinctive spontaneity.

Ken Ratcliffe found Beryl's infatuation with Austin somewhat disconcerting. Although Austin had succeeded where he had not, Ken still thought their difference in age and temperament gave him a chance if he bided his time: 'Austin was a mature man, he seemed to me a kind of father figure. I never thought they'd get married. Beryl was just another girl friend. My hope was that eventually she'd steer away from him and come to me. But it didn't happen that way.'[7]

Austin may have won Beryl's affection, but Ken was working closely with her for hours at a stretch under the pressure-cooker atmosphere of constant rehearsals and performances. This was not a healthy situation for any of them, and it quickly settled into the classic love triangle that would recur so many times in Beryl's life and in her fiction. Beryl was fixated on Austin; Ken was increasingly frustrated by his unrequited passion for Beryl; and Austin, though he was flattered by Beryl's attentions and enjoyed her company, refused to commit himself to a serious relationship, preferring to retain the freedom to embrace any experience, romantic or otherwise, that came his way – as he felt an artist should.

Austin would take Beryl out, picking her up at the stage door on occasional evenings after a performance had ended, but it was Ken who was invited to Sunday lunch with Beryl's family at Goodacre. Looking at the photographs of him in the back garden, tall and elegant in his pale double-breasted suit, handsome in a manly, distinguished way, it is hard to avoid the feeling that Winnie would have preferred Beryl to be seeing Ken, not Austin, whose bohemian appearance and attitudes were antipathetic to the values she held dear.

The first sign that Austin might be taking his relationship with Beryl more seriously was the Easter weekend of 1951, when he took her away to Wales. He'd become interested in sculpture and wanted to find some suitable stone. Beryl's account of the trip, written the following year, indicates that she saw it as marking a new phase: 'I loved him very much and he loved me . . . I had known him for almost a year, and yet that Friday it was like a tentative new meeting, a delicate interplay arose between us.' After walking through the snow that lay deeply over the hills and fields of the Welsh countryside, they went into a wayside inn to warm up, and the physical intimacy between them was clear for all the world to see: 'We sat on two chairs drawn very close to the fire and he pulled my head down on his knee so that my body was against him and his arm round me and his face on the top of my hair. And I held tight to his big firm hand and loved him so hard it went right through both our bodies, and the snow on the ground, to the brown earth beneath.'[8]

In July the Playhouse began rehearsals for its revival of *The Sun and I*, which was scheduled to open at the end of the month as part of the Festival of Britain celebrations. This time Beryl was to play the part of Grace Abbott, rather than reprising her original role as the boy David. It was around this period that Beryl made her first attempt to leave home. She would later recall renting a bedsit in Liverpool but that after three days her father 'dragged' her back home.[9] Tensions between Beryl and her parents had been mounting – understandably enough given her age and the fact that she and Austin had recently started sleeping together. This was not a step Beryl had taken lightly, as Austin put it shortly afterwards:

> She treated sex with the highest degree of respect believing it to be perhaps the most beautiful of all matters relating to human beings, she never could understand what it was that made men turn to prostitutes for mere gratification; believing that the sexual act was the highest form of human co-operation and communion, she could only envisage sexual union between two people who were very much in love and for whom it was the final contact of two souls.[10]

This 'final contact of two souls' seems to have taken place at a flat in 31 Falkner Square – at least Beryl used this address as the title of a semi-autobiographical account in which she describes her first sexual experience with Austin. The story, in which Austin's name is changed to Adam, is remarkable for its flat tone, betraying little of the emotion the event must have inspired in her:

When the Festival came I had a flat in Falkner Square, with the cathedral looming beyond the end of the road. Facing the door was a leafy barren enclosure with a splintered war damaged shelter. In the daytime the children swarmed and screamed all over it, and at night time couples nestled frantically together and the air was full of warm mutterings and secret things . . .

I was not happy because I had seen very little of Adam, he was working so hard on one of the many exhibitions, while I had opened in a new show a week earlier and had my days free . . . The day before the Festival began Adam came in the afternoon to see me. He was very dirty and pale and his skin was bad with too little sleep, and he took off his shoes and lay down on my bed under the coverlet. Then he said 'Come to me', and we both took off our clothes. Afterwards he went fast asleep, lying half on top of me, and I moved slowly away, and pulled the coverlet over him, and turned him on his back. And I lay beside him till it was time to go to the theatre, listening to his breathing, watching the afternoon sun struggle behind the brown drawn curtains. He did not move even when I got up and washed my face and dressed, even when I opened the door and went out. And when I came back in the evening, with the negroes lounging on the street corners, and slow cars drifting aimlessly up the roads, slight rain began to patter on the leaves, and trickle in the gutters. The room was practically in darkness and he still had not moved. I filled a glass with milk, got out some buiscuits, and set them on the table.

His left arm was lying heavily over the side of the bed, his large square hand heavily veined, and I held it lightly till he woke. When he drank the milk a film spread over his lip, and he wiped it away quickly with his arm.

Then he had to go back to the studio to finish final details and I stood under the leaves and watched him walk away up the street. As I turned to go into the house there was a half smothered scream from the shelter across the square, and the rain began in earnest to murmer in the trees.[11]

To Beryl such brief intimate moments were Pyrrhic victories. Austin's commitment to art and to his development as a human being seemed to be stronger than his commitment to her. This suspicion was only reinforced by his next decision. Now that his work helping to prepare art exhibitions for the Festival of Britain was over, Austin decided to embark on his own bohemian version of the Grand Tour, taking in the major capitals and art galleries of Europe – all on as little money as possible, hitchhiking whenever he could, walking whenever lifts weren't forthcoming, and relying on the kindness of strangers for bed and board.

In mid-August he went to London for a few days before setting off for Brussels. Significantly, despite the new development in his relationship with Beryl, his first letter to her dwelt almost solely on descriptions of the exhibitions he'd seen: 'I have been to practically everything there is to go to in London', including the Royal Academy Summer Exhibition which was 'too terrible to describe, a really horrifying experience'.[12]

Over the course of his tour, which in the event lasted until mid-October and included Brussels, Amsterdam, Frankfurt, Munich, Vienna, Venice, Florence, Avignon and Paris, Austin wrote to Beryl every few days, seventeen letters in total. While they were not exactly love letters – or not what Beryl would have considered love letters, being more concerned with recording his social and cultural experiences than the state of his feelings – they nevertheless conveyed a sense of his deep affection for her and an awareness of a growing attachment. 'I am beginning to feel somewhat lonely – an unusual feeling – not a general loneliness but a loneliness only for one person,' he told her before he set off. 'I have felt there was something missing during this stay in London and for a while I wouldn't admit that it was you.'[13]

Such hints, brief though they were, must have given Beryl a sense that her feelings for him were justified and that at least at some level he too saw a potential future together: 'Be good Sweetie, I think of you last thing at night and first thing in the morning and often in between whenever I see something that would have delighted you, why is it that a pleasure is not quite complete unless it is shared?'[14]

Absorbed as he was in his own experiences, Austin seemed to be unaware of Beryl's intense feelings of jealousy, and among his descriptions of towns and art galleries are numerous admiring references to passing girls who catch his eye. He was struck by the women in Brussels, 'tall slender delicate dark mysterious looking creatures who never speak',[15] while those in Munich were 'large and handsome with great deep pensive eyes, they wear no shoes and their legs are brown and inviting'.[16]

Austin undoubtedly found women sensually attractive, but his letters to Beryl also reveal someone who felt threatened by predatory sexual desire in others, male or female. He writes how uneasy he was in a gallery in Amsterdam when two men started talking to him, fearing that they might be homosexuals, and later, outside, he experienced a similar unease when confronted by the knowing glances of women in the streets:

> The women here, even the lovely looking ones, look at you in such a way as to leave no ambiguity, no doubt as to what they mean, even in the lonely poor quarters they lean against their front doors, smile blandly and with a nod of the head towards the interior, invite you to partake of what they offer. I walk with my eyes down, for I dare not look up straight because what I see makes me want to flee before the horror of the female sex . . . I cannot stop to stare at a building, a new or even a so-called 'ARTIST' painting in the street, without girls in front or behind giggling nudging or casting furtive glances, they do it to everything in trousers – how I detest it.[17]

A few days later, in a letter to Beryl from Amsterdam, he tried to capture both a sense of his feelings of despondency at missing her, and his excitement at experiencing so many new things:

> When I was in London I felt that at last I was free, free to roam, to wander, that is why I did not write to you. I said to myself I am free, I will be free but what did it mean, what is freedom? I soon felt the emptiness of your absence, I soon felt it when I had time on my hands. Really – though I am discontented about not having you here and the way people live – I am learning so much, so very much about my work that I am bursting with knowledge and the desire to work it all out in paint, and stone, and pencil, and charcoal, and ink. The stimulation is great, very great.

Inevitably Beryl saw in Austin's desire to be free only the implication that he wanted to be free from her, and in his enthusiasm for knowledge, for work and for contact with other people a proof that she wasn't enough for him. Misunderstandings on both sides were magnified by the unreliability of the post. Arriving in Vienna, Austin found there were no letters waiting for him and dashed off a peremptory postcard full of resentment, annoyed by what he assumed was Beryl's indifference.

He immediately regretted it and sent a letter of apology.[18] But Beryl's letters, when they did finally arrive, only made things worse. Upset at his references to being 'free', her tone was querulous and she questioned his motives for going. Austin, who valued the ideal of openness and honesty over a more tactful consideration of other people's feelings, didn't hold back in his response:

> Having not had any letters from you for over two weeks . . . I was overjoyed to find two waiting for me in the morning. But the tone of both was so despondent, so miserable that the joy was taken away. Why all these questionings, why take a phrase out of its context and quote it? I cannot and do not want to be free from you, the freedom I meant was the freedom from School, from the studio, from Liverpool, as you say the stimulation is the important thing, and here in Europe it is everywhere.
>
> Always I think of you and what it will be like to see you again, I visualise sitting opposite you in my studio or in a café and looking at your beautiful soft eyes and wide cheek bones and feeling so happy because of the love which between [us] we have built into something which is more beautiful, more great, than anything we could build separately . . .
>
> Of course we will go away for a weekend when I return, there is nothing I want more now than to be with you alone for a long time. How can you have so little faith? We have a great future before us, you must believe in it always, or you might destroy or undermine it by your doubtings. I love you, I always will, believe that and there is nothing to panic about, nothing to fear.
>
> Beryl, one must live, one must continually be experiencing life as fully as possible . . . Direct experience is far greater than indirect experience i.e. reading about it. It is because you show that you despise 'stupid people' that they do not invite you to a party or seek after your company.[19]

This mixture of earnestness, moralizing, and a genuine attempt to understand and explain was never going to work with Beryl. Temperamentally, she was too self-absorbed to devote herself to trying to understand people she didn't like or considered stupid. Nor was her overly romantic notion of the way things should be between lovers well adapted to survive real-world practicalities. To Beryl, Austin's notion of loving common humanity was all well and good, but it paled into insignificance beside the love of two people.

The rest of Austin's grand tour passed without any further major rows, but it was clear there were considerable differences between them in temperament and outlook. In personal and intellectual terms Austin felt that the tour had been an immense success, and after his return at the end of October he would write in his journal that it had broadened his attitude to painting and provided a 'terrific stimulus'[20] to his art. It had also confirmed him in his desire to be an artist and not to let anything stand in the way of his art. When he finally arrived back in Liverpool he had more or less made up his mind that it would be a mistake to tie himself down or let himself be distracted from his true calling: his art had to come first.

Beryl's expectation that once Austin returned their relationship would continue as it had before was not an unreasonable one. Even if his letters seemed to spend more time than she would have liked on the fascinations of European life and its culture – not to mention its women – there were enough declaratory statements to give her confidence in his attachment to her: 'It is essential that we should be together though, whether in Liverpool, with you working outside Liverpool somewhere in a rep, or whether in London, where we could work together,'[21] he wrote to her from Venice. 'Sweetie . . . don't stop thinking about me,' he urged a few days later from Florence, 'this waiting till I see you aches all over when I think about it, which is very often, very often. The Italian women are absolutely beautiful, but none in the way you are. I just have to think of you and they don't interest me in the least . . . everybody suffers when compared to you.'[22]

But if she had feared all along that Austin's desire for her, his love for her, was not enough, even she could not have anticipated the inflexibility with which Austin would pursue his goal once he had set his mind on it. After considering the situation, he saw no way in which to combine a romantic attachment with the discipline and dedication required of an artist, and shortly after his return he abruptly ended the relationship.

Beryl was shattered, the news bringing on a kind of emotional breakdown that was marked by physical symptoms. She was ill for months afterwards, and as if her body was attempting to express the loss symbolically her periods stopped for three months – initially prompting fears she might be pregnant: 'The psychological effect of our parting', Austin explained in his diary, 'has been very great, so great that this function has ceased.'[23] She confided in Ken that she was 'worried stiff' about the possibility, and there followed a whole week of waiting, with Beryl bursting into tears and crying, 'I'm late, I'm late.'[24]

Beryl's incomprehension at Austin's decision to break with her was, ironically, matched by his own:

> What came upon me that I had to finish all relationships with her? And after we had planned our whole life together? Every movement of her mind and body became so familiar and harmonious that now she is gone I feel the lack, a great hollow emptiness which finds expression and relief only in my drawing and painting, so that I must work and work. That such a thing should happen is beyond my comprehension, we were very much in love for nearly two years, for two years we were part of each other mentally and physically, she gave me everything, understanding, encouragement and herself. Then one day she asked 'Are you still in love with me?' and I could not answer 'yes'. Why! Why![25]

Austin's intellectual theorizing about his role as an artist, his feeling that he needed to be free of responsibilities in order to pursue his painting, was undoubtedly a screen for other less lofty, less palatable reasons for their break-up, a way of shifting blame from his own failings and weaknesses. In truth, maintaining a relationship with Beryl demanded too much of his emotional energy. It was easier to put the temperamental differences between them down to her immaturity:

> She was such a child, eighteen just when I met her, with all the wisdom of the mature and all the mannerisms and idealisms of the immature. She would start and grasp my arm to point out a beautiful face or a running child, she would brood deeply on the problems of life, and would rapidly become confused, frightened, even desperate, when confronted by the horrors people make of their lives.[26]

Austin undoubtedly felt a deep affection for her, loved her as a person even, but his upbringing had left him feeling insecure about emotional commitment and driven by an overriding need to prove himself, to succeed. Art took the place of a religion for him, and as such it mattered more than the feelings and the happiness of ordinary human beings – himself included.

For Beryl it was a psychological blow, something she never got over emotionally. His rejection of her undoubtedly fed into her subconscious feeling of rejection by her father, and would establish a seemingly inevitable pattern of failure that would play out in her subsequent relationships. Even towards the end of her life the memory of it left her feeling depressed: 'It's rejection that gets one down. Being rejected always. I felt that happened an awful lot to me. By men anyway. Always rejected by men.'[27]

Over the course of the 1951 season, tensions had been building up behind the scenes at the Playhouse. A number of the actors, including Ken, had become increasingly dissatisfied with Gerald Cross's behaviour and what they saw as his unprofessionalism. Distracted as he was by events in his private life, they felt he'd lost focus on his work at the Playhouse and they complained that he wasn't giving them sufficient direction, that rehearsals were lax. To make matters worse, he was going through one of his periodic bouts of heavy drinking. Hugh Goldie had been aware of the problem. After his departure from the Playhouse the previous year, he asked Beryl in an aside how Gerald was coping and whether he was 'off the booze'.[28] In October things came to a head. Gerald Cross resigned – 'to resume his acting career',[29] as the *Liverpool Daily Post* euphemistically put it – and Willard Stoker was appointed as the new director.

These changes at the Playhouse would, indirectly, lead to both Ken and Beryl leaving the company in the New Year. Although Ken regarded Stoker as a better director than Gerald Cross, he disliked working under him and was beginning to feel disillusioned with his roles at the Playhouse. One of the other actresses in the company, Sally Latimer, had recently joined Caryl Jenner's Mobile Theatre, and her suggestion that if Ken joined too he would have a chance to play some bigger parts sounded tempting. It would mean moving down to London before the company embarked on a tour of Strindberg's *Easter*.

The decisive factor, though, was Beryl. Following her break with Austin, Ken's feelings for her, held in abeyance for so long, had begun to resurface. Beryl, realizing he was falling in love with her, and not wanting him to raise his hopes or to get hurt, wrote Ken a long letter over the Christmas period, echoing what she had told him a number of times already – that though she loved him as a person she wasn't in love with him, and that despite Austin's rejection of her she was still attached to him.

Seeing little to keep him in Liverpool any longer, Ken decided to take up Caryl Jenner's offer and move to London. In the New Year he wrote to Beryl explaining his feelings for her as openly as she had hers about him:

> My darling girl, during the past month I have seen you every day, & at times virtually all the day, and it wasn't until today that I began to feel that you felt we were seeing just a little too much of one another, & that I should take the opportunity to have the evening to myself. But two hours away from you was more than I could bear, my whole being longed for you until eventually I could stand it no longer & hared off to Exchange Station. The rest you know – or do you know? I do love you Beryl, please believe me, as far as I'm concerned there is no one else but you.[30]

He understood that the 'fire' of her love for Austin hadn't 'quite gone out & continues to burn sometimes', but he was willing to give it time: 'I can do nothing except to wait with you for another season to pass. This will doubtless prove difficult since the future won't find me perpetually by your side as it does now. Yet I feel if there is anything at all between us – & please God I don't deceive myself in thinking there is – we will weather this storm as we have weathered others, & even yet may find a place in the sun . . . With all my love, Ken.'

Before he left for London at the end of the month, he met up with Beryl for a last concert together at the Philharmonic Hall. As chance would have it Austin was also there, and when she saw him it brought on an anxiety attack and she had to go and be sick in the Ladies. Her gloomy state of mind is reflected in her response to the music, which she scribbled on Ken's programme while the music was playing: 'The slow tinkling sound of the harpsichord, and the deep crucified chello, and the steady singing of the violins, and everyone here is listening with half their minds or all their minds, and outside it is very cold, oh so cold.'[31]

At some point over the New Year period, Beryl decided that she too should leave Liverpool. She was still suffering emotionally and physically from Austin's rejection, and being in such close proximity to him didn't help matters, as the incident at the Philharmonic painfully demonstrated. Not only that, living at home was becoming increasingly stressful. Beryl's fraught emotional state was hardly conducive to a harmonious domestic life. Confronted by her parents' disapproval not just of Austin but of her conduct with him – they'd probably gathered from the pregnancy scare, if not before, that she'd been sleeping with him – things went from bad to worse.

After talking with Ken about the possibility of coming down to London – an idea that he positively encouraged – Beryl decided to quit the Playhouse when the production she was currently working in, James Montgomery's comic romp *Nothing but the Truth*, came to an end.

In London, Ken fixed himself up in temporary accommodation with a fellow student from his days at Bristol theatre school, Peter Nichols. Nichols, who hadn't yet become a fully fledged playwright, was still trying to find work as an actor, but with only sporadic success. As Nichols was already sharing the flat with two other actors, Ken had to make do sleeping on a camp bed in the living room, though the flat itself in Cranley Gardens, South Kensington, was conveniently placed and gave him a base from which to work.

He wrote urging Beryl to come down as quickly as possible; he was longing to see her and he had already been making enquiries for possible flats. After asking about her work plans, he broached the subject that was really concerning him: 'Have you seen Austin since I left? Please make your goodbye to him brief B. I don't want you to come down here feeling unhappy & full of regrets.'[32]

In fact Beryl had gone to see Austin and unsurprisingly, given his contradictory feelings about her, things had got out of control again, as his account of her visit makes clear:

> She came to say goodbye as a friend, she was not upset, she had got over that long before, but we were talking when I felt a trembling desire to hold her. I asked if I might kiss her goodbye, of course that was fatal, for as soon as we touched the memory of all those nights together, of how we suited each other, of how we had delighted in caressing each other's body, came rushing back and we stood together overwhelmed by our desire, clutching each other with joyous panting breath.

It was inevitable after that, it was arranged that she should come to me the following night, for it was too late then and besides we had not the 'necessary'.

It was a delightful, wonderful evening that we spent together . . . nobody I think will ever be so pleasant, so harmonious to talk to, to make love to as my Beryl. I often think, when I allow the subject to arise in my mind, that I am still in love with her and that I might one day marry her, but then I think of the responsibilities and obligations that marriage implies, and I rejoyce that I am free to walk alone, to think alone, to be alone. Perhaps when I have worked for another ten or fifteen years and produced the quantity of work that I must produce, then perhaps I shall marry, it might easily be Beryl if she is still there.[33]

Needless to say, such fancies were completely unrealistic, and took little account of Beryl's feelings. In many respects Austin was indulging in the stereotypical male fantasy, wanting all the sensual benefits of a relationship, but none of the emotional complications or responsibilities. But Beryl, as she would so often be, was her own worst enemy. She knew how damaging Austin's indecisiveness was to her state of mind, but she couldn't stop herself from returning to see him the following night.

Answering Ken's letter, she disingenuously told him only that Austin had taken her back to his studio and 'tried to make love to her again'.[34] She didn't mention that Austin's supposed seduction attempt had in fact been a voluntary, prearranged meeting, necessitated by the lack of a condom. Ken was understandably hurt by Beryl's account, which 'cut like a knife', and he urged her not to delay her plans to come down to London: 'Why did he do this Beryl? Why did he want to go & open a wound which had almost healed? Your brief note leaves all my questions unanswered & when you say you are very unhappy, but not because of him, I know that you are wrong. Your whole life is not in a mess, love – obviously a part of it is at the moment – pray God you'll be happier when you come to London. Make speed down here. I want to see you more than ever now.'[35]

In the meantime Ken's flat-hunting had paid off. After hearing about a vacant bedsit a ten-minute walk from where he was staying in Cranley Gardens, he wrote to Beryl to tell her he'd found somewhere suitable.[36] This sparsely furnished bedsit at 18 Redcliffe Road, SW3, would be her home for the next four months.

NINE

London

During the last three years I have achieved almost nothing, I am inarticulate and intolerant and full of sin. I use sin because it is a catholic word, and my sins are catholic minded. I have been in several places living in a tiny room behind the Bolton studios, and working at a theatre in Leicester Square. I have been an usherette in a cinema in Tottenham Court Road, always waiting it seems, and very silently.[1]

WHEN SHE ARRIVED IN London at the beginning of February 1952, Beryl wrote an account of what it had been like to leave home,[2] seen off at Lime Street station by her parents, her brother and his girlfriend, and Dorothy Green. Austin was conspicuous by his absence:

In the station the whitefaced clock never falters. And I who stand in the shadow of the bookstall find calm to wonder at the fleetness of the time that goes. Dorothy stands talking clutching my arm with hasty fingers, and I watch her wet face with my eyes wide open. She tells me how I must be strong and not think too much and pushes me out to where my parents stand, sullen with waiting and unbelief.

My brother holds onto the hand of his girl who has a handbag secure beneath her arm with a gold clasp, and my father walks bitterly away to look at the platform, leaving me isolated with my mother, whose mouth is set with suffering. And her voice is distressed as she looks at me. She tells me with her eyes so blind and brown that I am raindrenched. There is a quiver of fear and pain about all her words. Only later shall I realise this. Now I only think – How dare you spoil the last hour with criticism of my appearance? Austin does not love me anymore. As always and he will not ever, my heart cries as my mother stands desperately beside me in the ladies room.

'Here comb your hair for goodness sake.' Miraculously by straightening my brown hair and powdering my nose I find I can earn love that way. So stupid I tell myself, looking half smiling at my reflection in the mirror. It does not show in my face, I think, the utter desolation I feel, this power of suffering, layer upon layer of it, mounting up over the last ten years and hurting me. But I am not allowed to cry yet, at least for him and the end again of belonging . . . Janet and Ian precede us in silence, hushed, lost in the train sounds. My father is nowhere to be seen, he is somewhere beyond us all, feeling the futility of having had children no doubt.

Then I get in a train carriage, very wet. I do not care how wet, or where my luggage goes, though my brother says I must. Then my father appears and cries out tenderly 'Oh how you hurt us, you wicked girl.' And I too cry out 'But you never understood . . . I love . . .' But mercifully I begin to cry because he is, and besides there is a deafening uprush of steam from the front of the engine.

Then my father gets out and I go to the window and say boldly, 'Good-bye Ian.' My mother and father are looking white faced at the rest of the train, until the train begins at last to move, then my mother turns and I cry out very brokenly 'Good-bye, good-bye . . .' and I cry deeply all the way in the empty carriage to Crewe, and the rain coming down the windows and nothing behind in the grey studio in Hope Street for me anymore. The wheels on the track say 'No hope, no hope, never no more no hope.'

Even at this stage I am not however without any hope.[3]

Even at nineteen, leaving home to live in London was no small affair, still less so for Beryl in her fragile emotional state. Her prospective bedsit in Redcliffe Road was at the top of a four-storey terrace, its back window overlooking a row of gardens and the Bolton Studios in neighbouring Gilston Road. At the time it was a largely run-down part of South Kensington, and many of its elegant terraces had been converted into small flats and bedsits.

On her arrival Beryl had a number of things to sort out, not the least of which was how to earn money. In the meantime she signed on, and her father agreed to give her £2.10s a week so she could buy food. Initially, she found living on her own difficult, but one of the benefits of unemployment and solitude was that it gave her time to write. One of her earliest pieces was a description of her surroundings:

> I can see many things from my window. There is a wall below me and beyond it the upright flat roofed studios. In the day-time an orange cat rolls heavily upon the blue slates and stares unresistingly all the way round. Now and then a thin young woman with very long tight green trousers will climb out of the fan light at the extreme end and stand perfectly still looking round . . .
>
> At night the lights never go out in the studios and sometimes a panio plays, and there are occassional outbursts of talking. Beyond the studios are three long lawns side by side in front of three tall crumbling yellow houses . . . Each house is divided into numerous flats like the one I live in and each window leval assumes a quality all its own. There are broken window boxes and tiny balconeys and none of the windows are curtained. There is a white haired man who lies always on his bed and a girl above who sits by the window, rolling grey clay between her hands, and a young man to the right on the balconey who sits and watches the sky and listens to the wireless and who smiles so gently at the clay girl . . .
>
> When it rains the gardens are all empty, the windows become misty and indistinct, and the yellow houses stain a brighter lemon. In the middle garden there is a stone statue, a face and neck. Its eyes are stone and grey and we stare back at one another silently across the city lonliness, till the rain brings slow tears down the grey cheeks.[4]

This, along with other pieces she was writing around the same time, became part of a collection that Beryl later entitled 'Fragments 1951–53'.[5] Unable to afford a proper notebook to write in, she utilized the same technique she had in the past, pasting blank sheets of paper onto the pages of an already printed volume, in this case a 1947 copy of *Points of Contact*, a large-format, illustrated collection of journalism. In a letter to Austin sent shortly after her arrival, Beryl mentioned that she was writing, and as he felt that artistic expression was vital to one's development as an individual, he tried to encourage her: 'You talked about starting a book – do you mean you are writing one – if so I think it's an excellent idea. It would be a good idea to write short stories and send them to a publisher as pot-boilers, you write so very beautifully that I am sure you could succeed. I should love to read a book written by your hand, for your letters give so much pleasure and the words flow smooth and kindly.'[6]

His comments were intended to be constructive, but he had an unintentional knack of saying the wrong thing. His reference to pot-boilers seems to betray a sense that he didn't take her writing seriously, and his closing comment, 'Do not eat <u>too</u> much, I would not like <u>you</u> to grow fat', was hardly the most sensitive thing to say to someone as obsessively concerned about her appearance as Beryl.

Not surprisingly, given the circumstances of her departure and her present situation, Beryl was prone to bouts of loneliness and depression. Her attempts to find work didn't help: visits to theatrical agents sometimes produced offers – but it was work at a price. As Austin noted in his journal: 'Apparently she visits a theatrical agent nearly every morning to ask for a job, they take her particulars and tell her to return on a particular date when they announce with solemnity that they have a job for her and before going to take it she can stay the weekend at such and such an address. There is no doubt as to the meaning of such a suggestion, thus she gets no job . . . it must be very depressing.'[7]

Even though he was staying only ten minutes away in Cranley Gardens, Ken could do little to alleviate her loneliness, his days now being occupied with rehearsals for the Mobile Theatre's Strindberg production. Although he'd long wanted to get Beryl away from Austin and have her to himself, he was frustratingly committed to going on tour: he was due to leave London in March and wouldn't be back for months.

Two weeks after Beryl moved to London, Austin wrote asking whether he could stay with her for a couple of days, framing it as a work, rather than a personal, visit: 'I am coming to London perhaps, on the bus Wednesday night, to do some research in the V & A Museum . . . Would you, and could you let me stay with you? You might have changed your mind since I last saw you – having received no letter it may be that you have decided never to see me or write to me again.'[8]

After this unemotional, matter-of-fact request, signed simply 'Austin' with no final term of endearment or expression of affection, he seems to have given way to a sudden burst of emotion and the rest of the page is filled with an outpouring of feeling: 'I cannot write just that, there is so much more I would write if it was not that I am afraid – afraid to know what I think – afraid to believe in the eternal or lasting things – everything to me is as temporal as the passing of the day or the dissapearing of a cloud . . .'

There followed a confused rationale of his past behaviour towards her, a mixture of justification and self-recrimination, which, in its attempt to express things he'd long been mulling over in his mind but that weren't easily expressible in such a brief space, Beryl would have made little sense of, though the final paragraph made it clear he felt he was to blame: 'I am guilty – guilty – guilty of not knowing what everyone should know, myself. Every day your photograph looks at me and says, "<u>You</u> . . . <u>are</u> . . . <u>guilty</u> the fault is yours – yours is the weakness, the immaturity, the abject fear – COWARD!!!!!!!! you have committed something that is far worse than murder." '9

Whether it was this reopening of old wounds that led to a renewed bout of anxiety, or whether she simply caught a chill in her draughty bedsit, Beryl fell ill almost immediately afterwards. A concerned Winnie came down to London to look after her, and Austin was forced to postpone his visit until the following week.

Dorothy Green, who clearly saw a link between Beryl's illness and her unhappiness over Austin, wrote advising her to break all contact with him: 'My dearest girl I am sorry you have been so worried about Austin – you know I really do feel the only thing to help you is not to see him or write to him and ask him not to write to you – you know it is quite impossible for you to get over this feeling for him, if you continue to see or write to him . . . if you want me to I will always send the news and let you know how he is and what he is doing.'10

When Lyn heard the news she, too, dashed off a distraught letter of enquiry: 'Bash darling my dearest, I've just met Austin and he's told me you're ill, sweetie dearest, I'm frantic, whatever's the matter – and he told me your allowance hasn't come off, what's the true position – let me know <u>please</u>, this is no time to be proud, you know I'll do anything I possibly <u>can</u> do to help you, please tell me truly how things are, you know I love you and nothing would make me happier than to be able to do something.'[11] She gave Beryl the number of her current boyfriend, Charles Robinson, who ran a confectionery shop ten miles away in South Woodford, and told her to ring him in case of an emergency

In need of Lyn's advice – and wanting some news about Austin – Beryl wrote back and asked her what she thought his motive for visiting her was and whether the rumour that he was now seeing one of Lyn's fellow students at the Art School, Anne Lindholm, was true. (By one of those curious coincidences that would strain the credibility of a work of fiction, Anne Lindholm would later become Beryl's editor at Duckworth, having married the future publisher Colin Haycraft in 1956.) Lyn did her best to calm her and reason out the situation: 'Lovie, how do I know why Austin's coming down – at a rough guess, which is all I can make, he wants to work and he wants to see you. You know if you've been like you and Aus have been, everything doesn't just go bang! (This is the way the world ends . . .) and you still like a person tremendously and genuinely want to see them and talk to them. This is all I can possibly say.'[12] As for Anne, Lyn assured her that she and Austin weren't 'going round' together.

———

Austin's journal for 1952 shows that his reason for coming to London wasn't entirely work-oriented: 'Next week I am going to London to study silver and gold work at the V & A for a few days . . . Beryl has promised to put me up! I was to go early this week but she wrote to say that for one her mother would still be there, and also that her period was beginning, so it should be all-clear by Thursday night of next week. It will be good to sleep with her after so long.'[13]

His account of his visit reveals at once how complex, not to say contradictory, his feelings were. Although he concedes that his relationship with Beryl offered a peace he could not find elsewhere, his determination to put art above personal happiness remained implacable. The issue of how fair it was to Beryl to string her along and prolong the sexual side of the relationship despite being conscious that he didn't want to commit himself to her, seems not to have entered his mind. He was more concerned about the dilemmas facing him as an artist:

> I stayed with Beryl in London three days and two nights, travelling by bus overnight. I was very tired and fatigued when I arrived and

had to rest all morning, before setting out with Beryl to the V & A museum. When I arrived she looked so attractive when she opened the door, with a pinny over her skirt and her hair tied on top of her head in a bun making it appear that she was taller, that I realised, not for the first time, how very beautiful was the structure of her face, and I knew then how much I had missed Beryl in Liverpool . . .

When we lay together that night, tired, quiet and peaceful it seemed to me that it was possible that we could live so together in complete coordination. It seemed to me that to struggle and slave as I had been doing was unnecessary, it seemed that all the pain, the tearing of ones very sinews trying to achieve an elusive infinite goal, was a waste of life and living.

And yet I knew that 'It must be so' there was no question of choice or happiness, what I must do is to paint and draw, to continue to create, and create things that would live after and beyond me to achieve something in my life. But there is no question of choice. I cannot stop, I cannot relax, I must exhaust myself, must squeeze every ounce of energy out of this body of mine . . .

Into all this where does Beryl fit? Is there room for such things, is it not better for me to be alone, to work alone, or would Beryl be an asset to my work or a hindrance? It would become a major tragedy if it turned out that she were to collide with my work – the risk is too difficult yet to even consider. One day I shall know but that day may be too late, she may be gone.

In London we walked about during the day looking at people and exhibitions and spent our two evenings alone in her little room, talking about our futures and where it was leading us, how long it would take and what the satisfaction, then we lay together in her bed feeling that ultimate fulfilment existed here, in lying together in the closest proximity, feeling that here at last is where our struggles, our pains, pass away and complete peace and quiet exists.

Coming away from London in the bus I was dozing and woke suddenly to see an illuminated sign flash past, the words were 'THIS IS THE END.' Strange is life.[14]

In a letter to Beryl explaining why he had to finish with her, Austin compared what he was doing to what she'd done to Ken – with this difference, that when Beryl told Ken there couldn't be a relationship between them she did so knowing she was in love with someone else, whereas he had pushed Beryl away despite his feelings for her, in order to spare her further unhappiness: 'I was driven by an inner force to do that which was unnatural for the sake of tomorrow's happiness, tomorrow's sake. I cannot <u>now</u> be happy for I have achieved nothing, thus I would make anybody closely connected to me intensely unhappy . . . I must first achieve that state of self-respect and wisdom that I now lack.'[15]

If Beryl was perplexed at these abstract equivocations, her confusion would only have been compounded by Austin's next letter a few days later, which opened with the words, 'It was like a dream to be with you in London.' His letter was almost certainly prompted by Beryl's question to him about why he had come to see her if he wanted to end the relationship. Again his response seemed to be inconsistent with his decision to break with her: 'Why did I come? I felt an emptiness, a hollowness which could only be alleviated by your presence, I felt a lack which only you could provide for. I think it will always be so!'[16] The rest of his letter was filled with mundane news about his work and general bits of news. It didn't sound like a man committed to continuing a relationship.

With Austin back in Liverpool, Beryl set about finding a job, organizing herself, as she would for the rest of her life, by making lists of things she had to do, such as writing to Willard Stoker at the Playhouse to see whether he could recommend her for any jobs; picking up some socks and a skirt she'd left at Ken's in Cranley Gardens; answering Dorothy's concerned letter about her health; getting a door key cut for the flat; writing to the Pitlochry theatre festival; and sending her mother a box of chocolates as a thank-you present for looking after her.

The following day she planned to write letters to a variety of prospective employers: to Robert Digby, the director of Colchester Theatre, to Guildford Theatre, and to the New Boltons Theatre Club in Kensington. However, it was the final task of the day that produced the most immediate results. Film-going had always been one of Beryl's pleasures, and at some point during her first weeks in London she met Robert Lawson, a film buff interested in foreign cinema who, like so many others, would fall in love with her only to be disappointed by her inability to requite it. With a view to finding her some part-time work as an usherette, Robert introduced her to one of the managers of a cinema on Tottenham Court Road, who in turn arranged an appointment on 13 March to see Mr Martin, at the Berkeley Cinema. In her diary she jotted down what to say at the interview: 'Ask for intro to Mr Rive, say Mr Colman sent me.'

Kenneth Rive was a well-known figure in film circles. Having started out as a projectionist, he now ran two cinemas in Tottenham Court Road, the Continentale and the Gala Berkeley, and was considered 'a leading influence in the development of post-war arthouse cinema'.[17] Beryl's meeting with him was successful and the following week she started as an usherette:

> I am going to work in a cinema, flashing a torch. I do it nine hours a day, in a fawn overall, and in the interval I sell icecreams, plain and chocolate. I feel happy then because it is half dark and no one can see my face is ugly with not knowing, and I say: 'Sixpence Sir, have you got any less I am short of change.' My coat is green, dark green, and I have red shoes on. Every morning I sew myself into my black dress, because it is too tight over my breasts, which makes me feel full and womanly.[18]

But there were other things on her mind besides her new job and Austin's ambivalence. The period she was expecting at the end of March didn't start, and despite the fact they had been irregular for months, she feared the worst and wrote a panicky letter to Lyn telling her she thought she was pregnant. Lyn tried to calm her, though even Beryl felt her attempt to make light of the matter went too far:

> My dear Miss Bainbridge, re yours of the 5th inst I am so happy for you darling, if you are too that is . . . Now of course, being presented with the facts of the other, it is absolutely absurd to suppose that you are enceinte . . . If it doesn't come within the next two days, go and see a doctor . . . I would be the first – no the second, person to get into a sweating flap if I really thought there was any possibility whatsoever, so take my advice and stop worrying, that's probably half your trouble – but if it makes you happy I'll write and tell Charles to sharpen up his old knitting needles . . .[19]

For the next few weeks Lyn would write making a series of comic allusions to Beryl's state, referring to 'Baby Austin',[20] and jokily telling her not to mess up their plan to meet in London or she would 'withdraw my offers as baby-sitter'.[21] However, Beryl's condition seems to have been just another bout of amenorrhoea, and by mid-April Lyn's references to pregnancy and babies ceased.[22]

At the end of March, Austin received the news that he was a runner-up in the Topham Trophy competition – the £8 prize money meant he could now afford to buy some clothes and some painting materials. But his elation didn't last long. The same day a parcel arrived from Beryl, along with a sealed letter that she told him he wasn't to open. Ignoring her injunction, he read it straight away and was shocked by its contents:

> On Tuesday night I rang you up at the Greens at about 10 minutes past midnight but I couldn't get an answer. Perhaps it is just as well, I wouldn't know how to say it.
>
> Coming out of the cinema Tuesday evening a man spoke to me and seemed so charming and kind. He was about 40 with such a beautifully modulated voice, and small white hands. I went for a coffee with him, and then we caught the bus and went into a little pub in Brompton for some cider. I hadn't had anything to eat since Monday, so I expect it made me a little hazy.
>
> We went back to his flat and when he opened the door of his room it had a small red lamp and no other light, and he turned the wireless full on. And he locked the door, Aus, and I heard the key turn behind me, and still I wasn't afraid. And like a fool I started my foolish creed . . . about talking things out of people, telling him he had a beautiful face and how lonely he must feel. And when he kissed me, I actually was surprised believe me, because it didn't fit in. And it began, the fear. And he knocked me down and I screamed and he tore my clothes off and hit me in the eye with his elbow, and jammed his knee into my mouth. And still I thought I could talk him out of it. I said all about people believing they got near through bodies and it wasn't true, and I could feel the wimpering futility of it all, because he didn't understand one word.

I shouted and shouted and he told me to carry on as no one could hear . . . He kept crooning at me that he was going to look after me for always and how much he wanted me to love him. He kept repeating over and over again, 'I'm not a liar darling, I've never been a liar.' I told him I did love him, I'd never leave him, but he just sprawled on me, trying to push it in. And finally he hit me again near the mouth and did get it in, but I pushed my knee up, and he cried out, and it went soft like a white worm.

I thought he was going to kill me, because he just lay on his side shaking and staring at me. So I said 'I do want you terribly but I must go to the lavatory first.' Finally he said he'd get me a basin, and he walked out of the door presumably into the kitchen. I grabbed my mac and reached the second landing and he flung the basin at me, and I slipped and the darkness was all broken up, and the thud of his body all over me and I screamed and screamed, and then I nearly went mad because I felt water falling down my thighs and I thought it was his urine. He pushed me into the room and tried to sooth me, but I just hit him, so he gave me my clothes and I pushed them into my pocket, but he wouldn't let me pass till I'd got calmer.

He kept repeating 'Now I haven't harmed you darling you came of your own free will.' Finally he let me go, and when I ran downstairs the front door was locked, and I couldn't find a key and he came behind me and opened it and threw my shoes out . . . and I ran down the street into the phone box . . .

And now I can't get clean and am afraid he had a disease. So in three days I'm going to have a check up just to make sure. I can't go to the police, because I did go of my own free will, and they'd get in touch with home and they'd bring me back, and I don't want that ever. I won't post this till I hear from you, perhaps you wont write for some time.

Everything seems to be so bad somehow, why dont you want me properly, why wont you come for me, and tell me you'll look after me, because I can't anymore, I can't, I won't. Why couldn't I talk to you on the phone, because I wanted to, I wanted to so much. I don't think I can ever talk to you again about that or me. Beryl[23]

Although Austin's initial reaction was one of sympathy – he wrote in his journal that while reading it he had been 'reduced to agonising tears' – his belief that as an artist he had to be independent of others and free of all emotional ties quickly reasserted itself. Indeed, he even saw the incident as a further validation of his decision to break with her:

> The whole of that day I walked in abject misery thinking of Beryl alone in London. Thinking of what she had described to me. Gradually it wore off, gradually I saw that it wasn't a major tragedy, just a thing that happens to lots of girls. I nearly went to London but cancelled my bus reservation at the last minute. I know that I must be free and alone, this thing interferes with that freedom, or would if taken to its logical end. Therefore I must end it all, I must write to say that she must live her own life, and stand on her own feet, as other people do. But it is so terribly sad, I can control what I feel, I can be objective. Beryl won't, and one day she must learn, and it's usually the hard way that one learns such things.[24]

He dashed off a short letter to her, but it could hardly have afforded Beryl much comfort. His tone was harsh and accusatory, even taking into account male attitudes to rape at the time, practically blaming her for what happened: 'The letter which you said I was not to open I opened and was horrified! Ashamed that you should have gone through such an ordeal, ashamed to admit to being the same sex as 'him'. I could not understand what you were doing to have gone back with him, you know men, you know what to expect, you know what "he" wanted – then why?? I suppose its simple really you were lonely, perhaps also hoping he might feed you, I know you are often lonely. I only wish you could make more genuine friends in London.'[25]

As if the rape had been nothing more than a trivial incident, the rest of the letter went on to give details of two painting commissions he'd received and the news that Fritz Spiegl had just got married, before ending insensitively with the words, 'things are not too bad', and signing off with an impersonal 'Austin'. He would not write to her again for over eight months.

———

Beryl rarely alluded to the assault in later life, though it is clear it had a profound impact on her feelings about herself, about sex, and about men.[26] Even fifty years later the memory of it was as fresh in her mind as if it had happened the day before, and in her final novel, *The Girl in the Polka Dot Dress*, Beryl's alter ego, Rose, is attacked in an almost identical way:

> Once, a man had bought her drinks in a pub in South Kensington and then taken her to his room near the Brompton Oratory. It was a posh area, so she didn't think anything could go wrong . . . The man had forced her onto his bed, knocking a tooth out in his struggle to hold her down. Bloody-mouthed, she said she'd do whatever he wanted if he'd just let her use the toilet first. As she fled down the stairs he'd emptied a cup of water over the landing bannisters, and she'd fancied he was weeing on her.[27]

Although she probably played down her physical injuries in her letter to Austin, the violence with which the man had tried to subdue her was considerable. His blow had dislodged a tooth, and for the next year or so she would be plagued with toothache and a bleeding gum ('Woke up with my mouth full of blood. My teeth are very painful').[28] She would eventually get a dental plate made, with a false tooth to replace the one that had been knocked out.

But the scars left by the assault were not just physical. Traumatic experiences such as rape can result in a loss of emotional engagement, feelings of depression, guilt and low self-esteem. In Beryl's case, she told Austin that in the wake of the attack she went through a period when she no longer cared who she got involved with and had 'slept with many men, seven or eight perhaps . . . because it didn't mean anything. I didn't even know the names of some of them, I didn't care whether I died.'[29] In later life Beryl would claim that she had often given in to men's sexual advances out of a perverse sense of politeness ('I could never say "No". First, I sort of felt they were doing me a favour; and second, it was impolite to refuse . . .').[30] Yet the lack of emotional engagement and low self-esteem this response betrays can be seen as part of the psychological fallout from the assault.

In an interview conducted in the wake of her success as a novelist in the 1970s, when Beryl was more open about this aspect of her life than she would later become, she admitted this was the case:

> For years and years, though not perhaps recently, I despised myself . . . I've never yet had a relationship with a man where

I thought anything a man did to me . . . was out of the ordinary.
I thought whatever they did to me was pretty well justified . . . I
used to be a terrible masochist. I used to make men treat me badly
and then one of two things happened: either I was doing it to them
before they could do it to me, or I actually enjoyed it.[31]

Beryl didn't tell Ken or her other close friends about the incident, but
she did mention it to Lyn. Her response was as flippant as her reaction
to the supposed pregnancy, though Beryl may have deliberately played
down the incident or hidden from her how traumatic it really was:
'Dearest Bash, Thank you for your letter. I shant comment on it, until
I see you to get the proper picture, because, put as baldly as it was, the
only comments are obvious, suffice to say you are a right bloodstained
clown and would Miss Addison think you were being quite nice?'[32]

––––––

At the end of March, Beryl wrote to Lyn, saying that she was thinking
of spending the Easter weekend at Formby. If she had any lingering
hopes that she might see Austin at Easter she was to be disappointed.
Despite Lyn's reassurance a month before that there was nothing
going on between Austin and Anne Lindholm, nothing could have
been further from the truth. Although Austin had initially seen Anne
as little more than a friend, despite 'a minor flirtation with her' when
she had first started college in the autumn of 1951, over the course
of the first few months of the year – during the same period he had
decided to break with Beryl – their relationship took a more complicated turn.

Things began in January, when Anne came to his studio ostensibly to borrow some paints, according to his record of their encounter
in his journal. Slightly annoyed by her lack of commitment, he took
her to task for her indiscipline, telling her that she should 'pull herself
together', accusing her of being more interested in films and parties
than facing up to her inability to work: 'You're either just plain stupid or
what is worse in love,' he told her, which led to a surprising confession
on her part:

She looked blankly into the distance with her great cow-eyes 'Yes, I
am in love.'

This surprised me for only two days before I had been round to her flat towards the evening, and had been amazed to find myself making love to her, for her charms are considerable, though I must admit without being allowed to take it to its ultimate conclusion – for she is very virtuous. So I asked her, 'How can you sit there and say that you are in love when only the other day you were kissing me, who is it? Do I know him, perhaps I could do something to help.'

Suddenly I thought, she can't be in love with me, that's not possible. I mean to say I've known her a long time, we were always good friends but no more.

'Just tell me one thing, it's not me is it?' She just looked sad but made no reply – I had had my answer! And this had existed for over a year without my knowing.

'Oh don't worry, I'm alright, I can control it. I've had plenty of practice, if you like I shall not see you, then perhaps it will go.'

She was very sad, and cried a little against me, but it was not only for me that she cried, she was very unhappy about her life. No plan, nothing particular to look forward to, I feel I must help her but how? She doesn't seem to have any particular interests. I can't imagine how she came to study art.[33]

Austin's relatively sympathetic attitude to her problems didn't last long. With Beryl in London, his feelings of sexual frustration were exacerbated by Anne's principled resistance to his advances:

That Anne, as Dorothy calls her, has been to see me here frequently and invited me to her flat. I have been several times, the last was at about 10.30 pm for a late meal. I spent from 11.30 to 4.30 bringing all my powers together in a storm upon her virginity. I made considerable progress, she returned the most intimate of caresses but would allow no entry. I am amazed at the girl's fortitude, or perhaps it is not fortitude, perhaps it would be more apt to call it middle class conservativeness of the worst sort. I returned to my virgin couch much exhausted, but am all the more determined to achieve my goal, it has become to my mind a challenge to my manhood.[34]

This account of his failure to progress sexually with Anne was written the same day as Austin's letter to Beryl suggesting he come to see her in London. Two weeks later, however, he changed his mind as regards

Anne, feeling that his physical attraction to her was getting in the way of his work and that it would be better not to take things any further:

> At present I hate women for they distract me from my work. Anne is not to be compared with Beryl, Anne is lazy, unstimulating, cowlike by nature, whereas Beryl is virile, full of energy, has an enquiring mind and a fine sensitive character. I have wasted too much time on Anne . . . I have allowed the physical to superimpose the aesthetic part of me . . . I feel that unclean animalism in me desires Anne, but there is nothing of the spirit or the soul about the relation and I begin to hate myself for thinking or writing as I have done . . . I make a vow now to finish any relation I have with her, better none than such a base sort.[35]

But after his visit to London and his renewed decision to break with Beryl, Austin changed his mind yet again. Whether this failure in resolve was due to Anne's persistence, or his inability to resist, isn't clear. Either way, she ended up posing for a portrait in his studio, a large three-quarter-length nude study of her sitting in a chair.[36]

While in Formby for Easter, Beryl learned the distressing news that, as if to add insult to injury, Austin had taken Anne to Wales for the weekend, just as he had taken her to Wales the preceding year. In her journal she wrote a bleak account of what she felt, her emotional anxiety bringing on another bout of illness: 'This Easter I am not well and have a cough and I have not seen him for some months, and there is no snow. And to know that he is working in his studio and becoming intense with another girl and striding out over the fields still using the map, sets my face white and hard because I am so lost and betrayed.'[37]

The choice of Wales as a destination was, in this instance, coincidental. Anne's parents lived in Penmaenmawr, Conway, a few miles from Austin's father's house, where he and Beryl had stayed in 1951. The visit to Conway may have marked a new stage in Austin's physical relationship with Anne, but as his brusque dismissal of this 'success' shows, it didn't signify any change in his views about the essentially ephemeral nature of the affair:

> I lay with Anne during the afternoon in a secluded croft overlooking the sea, we became amorous and she made no objection to my

pursuing such an activity to its ultimate end, indeed became an active participant despite her Catholic prejudices about the value of virginity and the evil of contraceptives. However this meant very little to me as my painting and drawing is at last beginning to progress again. I am beginning to feel a new surge of life, this I partly attribute to my new-found freedom from emotional ties . . .[38]

Understandably, given the emotional trauma of the night in Brompton and the breakdown in relations with Austin, Beryl sought consolation elsewhere and found it in Robert Lawson's company. Over the following weeks and months they developed a close friendship, so when Beryl's landlady gave her a month's notice to leave – ostensibly because of Austin's stay in March – Robert suggested she move in with him. Beryl wrote to Dorothy for advice and her reply was cautious: 'My love . . . do think very hard before you live with anybody – <u>please don't live with any man because you feel sorry for him</u> – I think the only time to live with anybody at all is when you cannot help doing so, life so easily becomes far too complicated and worrying . . . you know you will have many many men falling in love with you, because you are so beautiful to look at and so beautiful mentally. I do want you to think of yourself, please darling girl try.'[39]

The letter seemed to have an effect, but while Beryl didn't actually move in with him, Robert was still instrumental in finding her a new flat – 65 Parliament Hill, where he himself had lived a couple of years previously and which was just a few minutes from his present flat in South Hill Park. If neither of them was working they would walk together on Hampstead Heath, and Beryl would frequently spend her evenings with him: 'Shall I remember it poetically, the nights I mean in Robert's room, the 22/- a week room with the picture on the wall that says underneath 'Nothing to Fear' . . . Incredible the memories that come from Robert's mind, in his chair on the other side of the gas-fire. Very soon I tell myself I will get up with my thick sick head and creep down the hall, and run up to No. 65 and try to sleep . . . and I laugh to myself in the road in the early morning, and think how astonishing a life I am leading.'[40]

Beryl had told Lyn about 'Roberto the bird man', as she referred to him, and by mid-May Lyn was enthusiastically jumping the gun, hoping that this time Beryl had found someone she cared for: 'I'm glad Roberto loves you,' she wrote, asking whether she had any intention of marrying him.[41] But despite their easy companionability, feelings on Beryl's side remained platonic, though this didn't prevent Ken from feeling twinges of jealousy: 'Does Robert provide you with his company?' he asked her. 'As long as he gives you a little happiness. I was going to say I don't care, but I do and yet no matter . . . I am glad Robert has been able to cure you finally of A[ustin] – that was something I thought I could have done some time ago . . . Never mind. You say you are not in love with R[obert] & I still cherish the hope that in your peculiar way you are still in love with me.'[42]

Beryl's work prospects had also taken a turn for the better since her move to Hampstead. Hugh Goldie, who was now in London working as production manager for the Arts Theatre in Great Newport Street, told her that Roy Rich was looking to cast a production of Harold Brighouse's *Hobson's Choice*. Beryl went up for an audition in early May, choosing a scene from Jean Anouilh's *Point of Departure* as one of her pieces, and was drafted in to play the part of Ada Figgins, alongside a cast that included Donald Pleasance as William Mossop and Patrick McGoohan as Albert Prosser.

During the course of the production she began going out with Gareth Bogarde, Dirk Bogarde's younger brother, who was working as an assistant electrician. He quickly fell for her, recognizing in Beryl a fellow spirit who, like him, had suffered from an emotional rejection 'caused by someone that one loves very very much'.[43] As the production neared its end, he wrote her a frank declaration of love and outlined his hopes that things might work out between them.

But Gareth, like Ken and Robert, was another unfortunate whose heartfelt attraction to Beryl remained unrequited. Although a part of Beryl had put Austin behind her, there remained another part that continued to feel they were destined for each other, despite all that had happened. When Dorothy wrote at the start of June to say that things between Austin and Anne weren't working out, Beryl must have felt a tinge of satisfaction: 'He has taken Anne Lindholm out from time to time,' Dorothy confided, 'really because there is no one else and because she runs after him, but he is now getting to the screaming stage about her. Of course he has never pretended to me, and I hope not to Anne, that he was the slightest bit attracted to her except as a friend . . .'[44]

The Bainbridge family c.1898, shortly before the death of William Bainbridge in 1899. From left: John, George, Ellen, James, Richard (seated), Deborah, William.

Beryl's father, Richard 'Dick' Bainbridge, in Conway in 1926, around the time he first met Winnie Baines.

Beryl's mother, Winnie Baines, on holiday in July 1924.

Dick and Winnie on their
wedding day, 6 July 1927.

Ian and Beryl c.1933.

Winnie and Beryl c.1937.

Beryl and Ian c.1945.

Beryl, sporting her much loathed perm, with her dog Pedro, c.1947.

Beryl in a photograph taken by the Regent Studio, Liverpool, in 1948.

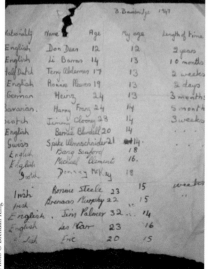

Beryl's list of boyfriends. It covers the period 1944 to 1949, and features 17 names.

Beryl on holiday in Greystones, Ireland, in July 1948.

Beryl with her hair cropped to play the role of young David Cartwright in A. R. Whatmore's *The Sun and I*, 1949.

Kenneth Ratcliffe, who joined the Playhouse company in 1950, with Beryl's dog Pedro in 1951.

Dick and Winnie in party mode in the 1950s. From left: Lily Baines, Leonard Baines ('Uncle Len'), Dick, Ruth Roche, unknown, Winnie.

Beryl leaning on the gate of 65 Parliament Hill in
Hampstead, during her first period in London, 1952–53.

Beryl and Austin's wedding day in Hightown, 24 April 1954. From left: Nora
Davies, Gordon Green, Lynda South, Austin, Beryl, Bill Bateman, Winnie, Richard.

Beryl and Austin on their wedding day in Hightown, 24 April 1954.

Aaron and Jo-Jo in the early 1960s. Austin's portrait of Beryl is hanging in the background.

Austin standing next to the Crossley, outside 45 Catharine Street, c. 1958. The car was later sold to Mick Green.

Beryl in a publicity photograph taken by John Sidney Bailie, c. 1959. Bailie lived at 15 Huskisson Street, a few doors down from Beryl and Austin.

Beryl at the wedding of her cousin, Hilary Baines, in 1959, shortly before her separation from Austin.

Donald Michael Green, the 'Wild Colonial Boy' of *A Weekend with Claud*.

Beryl with Cyril and Pat Taylor in Italy in August 1962. The Taylors had invited her out to stay with them as she was feeling very low at the time.

Beryl wrote to Lyn for confirmation and her reply assured her that Austin was 'not going out with anyone' and that 'Annie L and he are definitely parted'.[45]

This was technically true, but things were more complicated than that. If Austin had parted from Anne it was because he'd begun a relationship with another woman he had become obsessed with over the past few months, Fanchon Frohlich. Fanchon was in many ways Beryl's complete opposite: cultured, self-assured and ferociously intelligent, her academic prowess threw Beryl's educational failings into even sharper relief. Born Fanchon Aungst in 1928, she came from a wealthy German family who had emigrated to America in the late nineteenth century. A consistent winner in state-school debating competitions and editor of the school newspaper, at the age of seventeen Fanchon won four separate scholarships,[46] and went on to major in theoretical physics at Chicago University. When she switched to art in the early 1950s, she brought the same intellectual rigour to the discipline, uniting theories of aesthetics with those of the philosophy of science. Her heavily theoretical approach was expressed in a range of both representational and abstract work, and she would write articles for the *British Journal of Aesthetics* with titles such as 'The Function of Perceptual Asymmetry in Picture Space', and 'The Locations of Light in Art: From Rembrandt to Op Art and Light Environment'.

It was while Fanchon was at Chicago University that she met and fell in love with her professor, Herbert Frohlich, twenty-three years her senior.[47] When Herbert was appointed to the chair of theoretical physics at Liverpool University in 1948, Fanchon went with him. They were married in 1950.

At Liverpool, Fanchon and Herbert made a distinctive and slightly curious couple, he with his shock of white hair and his intense gaze, she young, pretty, Germanic and aloof. Austin found Fanchon's combination of personal beauty, intelligence and aesthetic sensibility captivating. Convinced there was an unspoken rapport between them, he went day after day to the same restaurant the Frohlichs frequented in the hope of seeing her. He discussed with Dorothy the possibility of an affair with Fanchon, but as she already disapproved of his treatment of Beryl and

Anne this new example of what she saw as his selfishness in relation to women exasperated her and she didn't hold back in giving her opinion: 'You know I think you are a rotten sod,' she told him. 'Just for your own pleasure you are prepared to risk a happy marriage being broken . . . the fact that you can discuss it so coldly and tell me that you have decided between you that neither will get hurt, and that you have no intention of changing what you call the status quo, indicates that you are both being extremely self indulgent and selfish.'[48]

Austin was taken aback, but it had little effect. Shortly after, with Herbert Frohlich away in Paris, he saw his chance and at last achieved his objective. But the affair left him unsatisfied, and he gradually came to a realization that his behaviour betrayed a psychological immaturity:

I am aware, self-conscious as I am, of a great inconsistency in my emotional make-up. I enthuse about Beryl . . . but it is probably only sentimentalism. I extoll Anne one moment and dismiss her contemptuously another. Fanchon, the latest about whom I have written so much and with such apparent sincerity, has ceased suddenly to have any meaning for me. I respect her. I still see her and Frohlich often, and I enjoy their company. But it seems as though, having enjoyed her company, having enjoyed her love, having slept with her, there is no more to be gained, I hate to think that this is the process, but the evidence is irrefutable. I must be emotionally shallow, though I would prefer to believe that all my feeling, all my interest, all the force of my emotional life goes into my art, there is little doubt really but that I am a callow raw youth.[49]

TEN

Dundee

My embracing of the church was to have given me an inner peace, a shield against temptation, but conditions were unfavourable to say the least . . .[1]

B EFORE HIS FIVE-YEAR STINT at the Liverpool Playhouse, Gerald Cross had been an actor, then producer, at Dundee Repertory theatre. After a string of popular and critical successes in both capacities he had left Dundee in 1946, with a gift from the directors and an expressed hope that he would one day return.[2]

So when, in June 1952, the then director of productions at Dundee, Geoffrey Edwards, dropped what the local paper termed 'a bombshell' and announced his resignation, the theatre wasted no time in inviting Cross to fill the vacant post. Cross immediately accepted, drafting in a number of people to rebuild the creative team at the theatre: Joan White, an actress who had ambitions to produce, was to assist him in production duties; Neville Usher, who had designed the set of Benjamin Britten's opera *The Rape of Lucretia* took over as scenic designer; and Freddie Payne, a RADA-trained actor, was hired as Cross's stage director, having already worked in that capacity for him in Liverpool. Payne's wife, Myrtle Rowe, a prize-winning RADA graduate, also joined the company.

Two more recruits were brought in from Cross's Liverpool days. The first was Noel Davis,[3] a camp, charismatic character actor, with a deserved reputation as a skilled raconteur: 'Quite the funniest man I have ever met,'[4] recalled Paul Bailey, who worked with him in the early 1950s. The second was Beryl. By chance, Cross had bumped into her in London shortly after hearing about the job offer at Dundee and asked her whether she wanted to join him. The work would not be too onerous: she could reprise her role as Adelheid in *The Beaver Coat*, and she was already familiar with *Young Madame Conti*, having understudied one of the parts.

Cross's offer sounded tempting and had the additional attraction of allowing her to escape the attentions of an actor connected to the Arts Theatre, André Belhomme.[5] A character actor with a colourful background, Belhomme pursued Beryl – or Tarbula as he nicknamed her – with an enthusiastic persistence that was hard to shake off. Whether Beryl kept any of the rendezvous he tried to arrange is unclear, but his unruly passion demanded a constant psychological agility in her dealings with him that was tiresome to say the least.

In late July she moved up to her digs in Dundee, ready to start rehearsals for the new production of *The Beaver Coat*: 'It was a lovely flat I had in a tenement. All grey stone, and a tram running down the length of the street, and I had a fire lit in my room by the landlady when I came home late at night.'[6]

When she arrived Beryl immediately bonded with the Liverpool contingent. She may have been in emotional turmoil over Austin, but Freddie and Noel – who Beryl nicknamed 'Noel, Noel' – were enlivening company and offered plenty of distraction. The only person Beryl didn't seem to get on with was Joan White, who she described as emotionally unstable and dramatically incompetent, always forgetting her lines. According to Beryl, Joan had an unrequited crush on Gerald, despite the fact that he was outwardly and incontrovertibly gay, and consequently she spent much of her time in an emotional state in the dressing room.[7]

The nucleus of the Liverpool set formed a potent and volatile mixture of temperaments: Noel was an outrageous and witty storyteller; Freddie was impulsive, neurotic and vaguely unstable; while Gerald was effusive, with a fondness for drink. The sudden arrival of this new group of actors, most of whom already knew each other from their Liverpool days, created a certain tension among the rest of the company. The assistant stage manger at Dundee, Maggie Dickie, remembered feeling initially piqued by the arrival of Beryl, who made more money than her even though she had less to do.

But it wasn't just the Liverpool group's tendency to stick together that caused problems. Cross's predilection for experimenting with European drama in translation – his season began with a version of

Hauptmann's *The Beaver Coat* in which German peasants spoke with Lancashire accents – ended up splitting audiences and critics alike, and undoubtedly contributed to his subsequent downfall.

One of the leading lights of the Dundee Repertory company was a twenty-six-year-old actor, Kevin Stoney. With his jowelly face and hooded eyes, Stoney was distinctive looking, though not necessarily in a classically handsome way. Even when young his looks were more suited to playing the villain, and he would go on to be cast as the baddie in numerous television series in the 1960s and 1970s, most notably in *The Avengers* and *Doctor Who*.

Even though he was engaged to another actress in the company, Rosalie Westwater, Beryl quickly began to develop a crush on him. After the run of *The Beaver Coat* had ended, Rosalie left for a short period to have an operation on her nose, and in her absence Stoney began to take Beryl out. Although they didn't have an affair as such, they 'meddled around a bit' as Maggie Dickie put it.[8] The relationship, such as it was, had little chance of success, but this didn't stop Beryl becoming emotionally involved.

In parallel with this semi-adulterous flirtation with Kevin, Beryl had started taking steps to become a Roman Catholic. She had long been fascinated by the aura of Catholicism – or rather she was captivated by the flamboyant behaviour of the charismatic Catholics she knew from the theatre, such as Noel and Tom St John Barry. No doubt there was also an element of rebellion in her attraction too – it was as good a way as any of distancing herself from her parents. This is not to say that she didn't have a strong desire to believe, or that there wasn't a genuine religious element to her impulse, just that she wasn't interested in Catholic theology or dogma per se. When she later had children, not only did she not bring them up as Catholics, as all Catholics are enjoined to do, she didn't even have them baptized.

There was one aspect of Catholic theology, however, that did appeal to her at this point: the notion of the forgiveness of sin. She had increasingly begun to see herself as a bad person – sinful, to use the vocabulary of Catholicism. Her desire to be loved had led her into affairs that were 'immoral', and which fed her feelings of guilt and unworthiness. She blamed herself, and saw herself as deserving, indeed as the cause of, her own misfortunes.[9]

The brutal assault in Brompton had confirmed this corrosive sense of herself as a sinful and impure person. Reaching a crisis point, she felt the need of something larger than herself to intervene, to absolve her of the feelings of unworthiness and self-loathing that plagued her.[10]

In order to become a Catholic in England you had to be of legal age. In Formby, Beryl had been too young, too much under her parents' control; to be able to do anything about her religious impulses. But the laws were different in Scotland, where the age of majority was lower. With this in mind she decided that while in Dundee she would begin the process of conversion.

In September, Beryl wrote to Father Vincent Wilkin SJ, the chaplain of Liverpool University, telling him about her decision and asking him what she should do. Father Wilkin put Beryl in touch with Father Campbell at St Joseph's Catholic Church in Wilkie's Lane, a short bus ride from the Dundee Rep. For her instruction proper, Father Campbell turned her over to Sister Mary Antony, one of the nuns at St Joseph's Convent. Beryl's instruction took the usual path: a course of study, followed by a formal baptism. Although by its very definition a conversion should be founded in the deepest openness with regard to matters of the heart and conscience, Beryl seems not to have talked with her confessor about Kevin or Austin, nor mentioned the traumatic assault earlier in the year.[11]

Beryl's conversion was scheduled for Friday, 10 October. On the Sunday before, she wrote in her notebook her impressions of attending Mass at the convent that morning:

> All the nuns stand like black-birds with wings folded as we begin the Novena. All my years go like a dancer beyond the kneeling birds to the tabernacle, and the autumn flowers fill me with yellow wonder. Oh I cannot write sufficiently what is in my heart. Sister Mary Anthoney is so good hailing Mary with her rosary, because she has no youth or womanhood spent, all her placcidity is for God, and behind the folded wings her eyes rest tiredly, murmuring comfort to herself, the steady outpouring of continual love. And I who am so unworthy sing between bruised lips 'Ora pro nobis, Ora pro nobis' wondering why Austin ceased to love me, why I am so unkind to my parents, and why I am so full of sin.[12]

After this there follows a description of the evening's events: first, a performance of *Young Madame Conti*, a courtroom melodrama in which Beryl played one of the witnesses; then an account of going back to her digs with Kevin (here referred to as K). Just as she is about to 'sin', she pulls back and experiences a brief moment where she feels she has been saved by God from the consequences of physical desire. Here the link between her desire to be a Catholic and her sense of unworthiness and guilt over her sexual relations with men is made explicit:

> Tonight I love K so greatly, and all my self goes melting in the theatre . . . And then I walk softly in the wind with K to here, and sit upon the bed and let my love unloose itself once more, quite gladly. And I tell him of my love and recieve the answer that I knew before the question, that he has never loved [me] or ever will. And I remember with clutched fists on Friday I will be a catholic, and move from his body, and the pain is great.
>
> And a short while goes and almost we have sinned, and then it is passed and he is left shaken with wonder, and me with a lightness behind my eyes, for God has made a miracle to save me. And I am so unworthy, so unworthy that I long to whip myself, to lie in pain never to move, because I love Him so.
>
> K walks with a grey head above his black overcoat, across the road in the wind and I stand at the window and wave to him. Oh that my heart could utter the thoughts that arise in me. Tonight I know that God would give me Austin if I prayed or K, but I do not pray. I want nothing more but to rest in this certainty of grace, but I want that my unworthiness shall go. What will be the words when I am received? All the angels in Heaven protect me to follow through the little that I feel. I can do good, but why . . . and where . . . and when. St Francis and St Bernadette, Blessed Gaberiel oh help me in my unbelief. Take away things like grey heads above black overcoats, and the lonely wanderings in railed church gardens. And the tooth-ache in my mouth, and the soul ache in K's heart take away and fill with knowledge. For ever and for ever Amen.[13]

As Beryl agonized over her feelings for Kevin and the preparations for her conversion, events at the theatre were spinning out of control. The audience response to Cross's productions had not been as enthusiastic as the theatre had hoped, and the decline in ticket sales began to affect the theatre's bottom line. The decision to follow up Robert Sherwood's *The Queen's Husband*, an obscure play that failed to convince either audiences or critics, with yet another translation, *Young Madame Conti*, sealed Cross's fate: it was the last production the director would oversee at Dundee Rep. On 4 October 1952 the *Dundee Courier* reported:

> REP DIRECTOR RESIGNS
>
> It was announced from Dundee Repertory Theatre yesterday that 'Mr Gerald Cross has, with great regret, resigned the position of director of productions, following on differences of opinion on matters of policy.' Mr Cross, who has been producer since June 30, would not make any further comment . . . Others leaving the company now are Joan White, who has been acting and assistant producer; Myrtle Rowe, who came north a few weeks ago for *The Hollow Crown*; Beryl Bainbridge and Noel Davis.[14]

The news of the resignation came as a shock and prompted something of a small backlash in the letters page of the local paper. In response, the directors were forced to justify the decision, claiming that the theatre had incurred losses of £1,716 since Cross took over, due to declining audiences and increasing expenses, and that the decision was necessary for the theatre to survive. The reasons for Cross's resignation were, however, more complicated than those given in the *Dundee Courier*, and the issue of artistic quality or the negative response of the audience may have been simply a pretext for Cross's removal. At the Liverpool Playhouse Cross's turbulent emotional life, coupled with bouts of drinking, had affected his ability to focus on his work. Everyone at the Playhouse knew that Cross was gay, but this had only become an issue when his messy emotional life spilled over into his professional work. At Dundee, it happened again.

The details are not exactly clear: Maggie Dickie believed that Cross's predatory attempt to seduce some of the other male members of the cast caused the problem, and the factions within the Company didn't help matters. Under a huge amount of emotional strain and reading Cross's persistent efforts to console him as homosexual advances, Freddie Payne – who was in a distraught state because his wife Myrtle had just left him and taken their nine-month-old child with her – made a half-baked attempt at suicide by lying on the tramlines.[15] Beryl claimed that he went temporarily insane and had to be restrained in a straightjacket.[16] Once the directors had got hold of the story, there was no way back, and it seems that Cross was forced to resign to prevent a public scandal.

Cross's own view was different: as far as he was concerned he had only been trying to help Freddie, who he admitted was a neurotic character. 'Nobody in this world, not even his own wife or family, has done more for him than I have. I gave him two quite handsome jobs, fought his battles for him . . . pleaded without cease with Myrtle for him . . . wept for him, guided & counselled him . . . devoted myself to his interests – all this I have done cheerfully & without complaint as if he were my own brother,'[17] he told Beryl, shortly after his return to London.

In any event, it was clear that the situation within the Company was untenable. Cross had initially attempted to bluff it out, telling the Liverpool contingent that if they were united the management would relent. Following his instructions, Beryl and Noel said that if Gerald went they would go too. Unsurprisingly, the directors didn't appreciate this attempt at blackmail and took measures to deal with the remaining members of the Company that Gerald had brought in, who were now seen as troublemakers. Beryl, Noel, Myrtle and Joan were all forced to leave, while Laurena Dewar resigned from her post as the producer's secretary.

Pending an inquiry by Equity into the circumstances surrounding the resignations, the wages of those concerned had been withheld. Consequently Gerald, Noel, Joan and Beryl, now broke, had to hole up in a derelict bungalow near the mud flats below the Tay Bridge. Eventually money was sent, and by the middle of October Beryl was back with her parents in Formby. What their immediate reaction was to the news of her conversion isn't known, though Beryl always maintained that her father detested Catholics.

Hardly had she got back to Liverpool, however, when another offer of work came in: Windsor Rep wanted her to step in at short notice for a series of comic plays starting in less than two weeks' time, in an engagement that would last until Christmas.

Beryl would retell the story of her time at Dundee Rep and of her conversion to Catholicism many times in later life, either in relation to her work as a drama critic or in articles on the subject of religion. But the humorous tone of these memoirs is misleading. Intended to entertain rather than reveal, they pass over in silence what she was really feeling at the time.

Shortly after she left Dundee an event occurred that she would not mention in public until the very end of her life, one that threw a black cloud over the whole period and which would have lasting repercussions on those involved for the rest of their lives. Despite Lyn's reassurances back in June that Austin wasn't going out with anyone and that his relationship with Anne Lindholm was over, Beryl's worst fears were confirmed when she got back to Liverpool. Lyn may have been right that Austin wasn't seriously committed to Anne, but she was wrong in thinking that their on-off relationship had run its course. In the early autumn of 1952 Anne discovered that she was pregnant.

Being unmarried and pregnant would have been a traumatic state of affairs for any woman at that time. Inevitably it had a devastating psychological impact on Anne. Robin Riley, a fellow art student in the year below her, recalls that she became very depressed and left the art course without taking her exams. The practical side of the situation was complicated enough: abortion wasn't legalized in the UK until 1967, so the decision to terminate involved finding a 'backstreet' abortionist, while the alternative meant having to face the social stigma of being a single mother and all the economic hardships that might entail. But on a personal level it put Anne in an impossible situation, one that challenged her religious beliefs and her sense of morality.

To Beryl, the news was shattering. 'I want to die more than anything,'[18] she wrote to Lyn at the time, feeling more solitary than ever because she couldn't talk to Austin about it, fearing 'he would not understand' – or didn't love her enough to try to understand – what she felt. She asked Lyn for more information, but Lyn had been ill in bed and had heard nothing. In any case there was no way she could have known quite how traumatic the sequence of events would turn out to be, events that Austin felt compelled to recount in painful detail in his journal:

Since I last wrote much has happened. Anne with whom I have been associated at intervals since I first mentioned her, conceived, and caused me to be considerably concerned about the consequences. In the beginning she tried quinine, but this made her sick for some days with no result. I went to a doctor who advised me about the use of a piece of wood called slippery elm, this I tried to obtain, but could not and gave up after a few sporadic attempts. Then June the model said she knew of someone in London. I told Anne this but she refused to have anything to do with the idea, she said 'Its wicked, sinful, going against nature. I want my child, I must have it.'

'But,' I replied, 'how do you propose to bring it up without a father, for whatever happens, I intend to remain single?'

'Oh I could go away and get a job.'

'Where do you propose to go, you who are so dependent upon your friends, you depend, in fact live, upon your friends, you are quite incapable of looking after yourself, never mind a child?'

'I could go home.'

'Yes and inflict your responsibilities upon your parents who are by no means in a position, financially, to support you <u>and</u> a child. Besides what do you think it would be like in such a small village as that when it "got about" that you were pregnant and unmarried?'

At this she broke down and cried hysterically. 'You must marry me, you can't leave me, what shall I do, what shall I do?' And she rushed round the room holding her head between her hands sobbing dramatically. As usual making the most of the situation emotionally in the hope of making me change my mind. She was determined to make me marry her and refused any other solution.

I was desperate, what could I do? She might tell her parents as a last resort and they could make things very awkward for me. She threatened suicide, threatened to tell the Principal, Mr Stevenson, at the College of Art here where I am teaching, and make me lose my job.

I left her completely alone when she refused to go to London, saying in a considerable rage, 'Well if you refuse to cooperate, if you refuse to see how impossible it would be for me to marry you, then you can damn-well stew in your own juice.' I then slammed the door after me, and returned to the studio, realising that there was no point in dwelling upon the situation. I must not neglect my painting no matter what happens.

Anne returned to my studio a few days later saying that she would agree to an operation in London. This was good news and I prepared to accompany her immediately. We stayed at first in Windsor at a place that my mother recommended, while we tried to establish contact by devious and intricate means with the appropriate people.

We eventually, after being in London a week, managed to arrange a time and a day. I spent a good deal of money upon entertainment to take her mind off the object of her visit, and upon accommodation, and was looking forward to a successful conclusion of our visit. But when we arrived at the doctor's surgery, she started a hysterical fit, weeping, sobbing, holding her head etc, as she had done so many times before when she was not getting her own way. So at the end of the second week we returned and there was still no solution.

It appeared to me that she was making a last determined bid for marriage. She did not think that I could possibly maintain my determined stand after having demonstrated how desperate she was, for while we had been in London and just before we were due to leave for the surgery she took 19 aspirin tablets, believing that I would presume she was attempting to kill herself. This of course is an almost harmless dose, nevertheless I called a doctor and she was taken in an ambulance to have her stomach syringed.

There is no doubt in my mind that this was to force me to change my mind, however it did not, for there are cases every week of people taking overdoses of aspirin and only when they take 40 or 50 do they ever prove fatal. Even then, if caught early enough a stomach wash is usually quite effective, and everybody knows this including Anne.

Now I was disgusted and sick of it all and when we returned to Liverpool, on the train and in the bus, I did not talk to her, for I was furious that I should have wasted 2 weeks and so much money and with no result.

More weeping, sobbing and platitudes about it being a mortal sin.[19]

Shortly before leaving, Austin had met Beryl briefly at Euston station. She was now back in London and preparing for her stint in Windsor. He told her that Anne had refused to have the operation and planned to keep the baby. The impact of this news was profound, leaving Beryl feeling confused and betrayed. In her 'Fragments' book she dashed off a poem expressing how she felt:

I cannot bear for you to make a child
Inside another when I am here

I feel as if I had been cruising round the world
Leaving you staying out too late at night
And now I cannot stop the womb from building
Or the body beautiful to swell
And they can talk for hours on worthlessness
And still I know I love thee far too well.[20]

The 'they' who talked about Austin's 'worthlessness' no doubt included Beryl's parents, though they were almost certainly unaware of Austin's relationship with Anne and the present crisis. But it was also an allusion to Dorothy Green, who in her desire to protect Beryl from what she increasingly saw as Austin's unreliable and cavalier attitude to women, spared no detail in her accounts of his misdeeds.

Dorothy had observed this painful drama unfolding in front of her very eyes, and even though she had no fondness for Anne, she couldn't help but be distressed by what she was going through. In a letter written shortly after a fearful scene between Austin and Anne, she filled Beryl in on the latest news:

I hardly know what to say about this appalling tragedy and of course the person who is going to suffer most is Anne and she is so stupid – I don't say that because she changed her mind at the last moment – but, she has changed it, well, perhaps twice since she came back to Liverpool. She has been to see Dr. Garvin, and told him of course, and says she wants to go away, and the last news is, he is writing to some Convent in Manchester where she can go till it is all over. I don't know what to say about her reasons, I think of course they are mixed up with religion and I think, but of course don't know, wanting to marry him, my goodness she doesn't know how lucky she is in one way that they are not marrying, she would be so unhappy with him it hardly bears a thought.[21]

The drama was not, however, over. Austin's unyielding stance achieved the desired result. A few days later Anne changed her mind again and went down to London, accompanied by her friend Margaret Evans, for the abortion. But as it turned out Margaret could only stay for two days and Anne would have to be in London for four, so Austin, feeling that he couldn't leave her to face the operation alone, went down to look after her. He was with her when she recovered from the anaesthetic and again recorded the traumatic experience in his journal:

> How can I say whether what she said after coming round was really delirium, or was she still acting.
>
> 'Oh Mary Mother of God forgive me for my mortal sin. Forgive – forgive – forgive – I know not what I do, Our Father which art in heaven, hallowed be thy name . . .'
>
> 'Anne! Anne! wake up, it's me, wake up.'
>
> 'My baby's gone, he's taken him away – and he was so little, so little, he was safe there in the warmth, but I betrayed him, now he's alone all by himself, alone with no one to look after him and he was so little – oh God give me my baby, where is he, where is he, so little and alone, so little by himself in the cold, God! Why? Why? I never did any wrong. Austin! Austin! he was your child, your child, give me another child, I want another, yours, yours. I want your child – I want your child – I want your child. I want, I want.'
>
> I cried, I could not stop myself, this was real, she meant this, poor child, poor child. 'Be quiet now, be quiet now,' I said softly, stroking her hair and the tears rolled down my cheeks and I was sick that I should be the cause of all this, but there was no other way. She is very unhappy, and I think that I have not heard the last of her.[22]

Beryl learned at least part of what had happened through Dorothy, who wrote again four days after her previous letter:

> Anne . . . came round last Sunday and had a tremendous hysterical fit and asked Austin if he would not marry her would he come and live with her, which he absolutely refused to do, and eventually she went home . . . Then on Monday she came around and said she was going to London Tuesday morning, she had apparently written to the Doctor, same one, asking him if he would see her, as she had changed her mind & wanted it 'doing'. So Tuesday morning she went to London – more money for Austin to find. Tuesday night Austin had a telephone call to go to London on Wednesday to bring her home on Thursday, so he went and is now home again. Anne is going to the Lake District tomorrow to take a job looking after children! I think perhaps the whole time she was hoping he would marry her – I don't know, anyway it is over, she is alright and the only thing we can do is to close the chapter, don't you think?[23]

Dorothy's assessment that Anne was 'alright' was some way short of the mark. She may have been trying to ease Beryl's feelings, but it is clear that Anne was anything but alright. The decision to have an abortion had been a painful one, and her unresolved feelings of guilt about it provoked what she herself later admitted was 'a nervous breakdown',[24] a total re-evaluation of her beliefs, her life and the kind of person she was. She gave up her art course and turned increasingly to religion, not necessarily for comfort, but for meaning, for absolution, and for a new way of structuring her life. Perhaps inevitably she came to feel that the emotional and moral trauma she had experienced was a logical consequence of the atheism and liberalism that Austin professed, his casual approach to human relationships. She felt she had been seduced down this path and didn't like what she had become: '. . . the experience was of hell. It was unremitting light with no shadows; the absence of God.'

Although the forgiveness of sins is a key element of Catholic faith, Anne never forgave herself for what she had done. Had Austin married anyone but Beryl, it is possible that in later life she might have been able to face telling the truth about what had happened. As it was, the whole episode was doomed to remain a dark secret, and when she met up with Beryl again twenty years later it became a subject that could never be mentioned in public. The web of deceit, humiliation and lying this engendered played on Anne's mind until the end of her life.

If the termination had brought the 'chapter' on Austin and Anne to a close, Dorothy still had a chapter to relate about Austin and another girl, Toni Butler, who he had met through the Frohlichs. Austin had started using her as a model, and rumours of some sort of romantic connection between them would periodically surface over the next year. In mid-November, Dorothy wrote to Beryl, giving her a lengthy account of Austin's activities following the affair with Anne. She must have sensed that Beryl would find it upsetting, and tried to emphasize how distressing she herself found Austin's behaviour: 'I have told him so many times how appalling is his attitude towards women.' She hinted that 'when he came back from London after this awful thing', she had done all she could to prevent more upsets by encouraging him to work and commissioning a picture from him.

But at the Greens' bonfire night party, when Toni Butler didn't appear, Austin had rushed off, telling Dorothy he'd forgotten to mention he was going to another party that night. Somewhat suspiciously, he stressed that he was going alone as he'd have a nicer time if he went by himself, and Dorothy agreed telling him it would be better not to 'get involved with any girl just yet'. But he had in fact taken Toni Butler to the party and later on 'he arrived home with his mouth covered in lipstick'. And this, Dorothy added in a scandalized tone, just 'one day after Anne had left Liverpool, four days after the job had been done'.[25]

What Austin himself called 'the female question' brought things to a head with Dorothy, and for the sake of their friendship they decided it would be better if he moved out. As he put it in his journal, at least then 'she wouldn't know what went on and [would] thus be spared the torment of tears and the sight of what she calls my selfish, heartless attitude to my girl friends'.[26]

With all this going on, it was fortunate Beryl was distracted by work, playing Hazel Nutt in Mabel Constanduros's domestic comedy *King of the Castle*, which opened on the 27 October. The play was well received and, given events, there was a certain unintended irony in the reviewer's summing up: 'Beryl Bainbridge, in a near-Cinderella role as the younger Nutt daughter, charmed us so that we were glad to see her get her reward in the "everybody's-happy-now" ending.'[27]

The next production, another domestic comedy entitled *For Better for Worse*, featured a strong cast – including Leslie Philips, Patrick Cargill and nineteen-year-old Geraldine McEwan – and enjoyed good reviews. Despite her relatively minor role Beryl's performance merited a mention: 'Beryl Bainbridge, as the ubiquitous and affected Sheila, aptly portrays the type of young woman who can be as amusing on stage as she is maddening in life.'[28]

Beryl's short season at Windsor was brought to a close in mid-December with R. F. Delderfield's *Worm's Eye View*. At the end of the two-week run Beryl returned to Hampstead before travelling up to Formby to spend Christmas with her parents. Her first year in London could hardly have been counted a happy one. Not only had the man she loved rejected her, he'd got one girl pregnant and by all accounts was now seeing another.

ELEVEN

Engagement

10 January 1953: Went to Liverpool with Austin to buy an
engagement ring. Am I happy?[1]

GIVEN THE EVENTS OF October and November 1952, Beryl
could scarcely have been looking forward to her return to Formby.
But if Anne's pregnancy had cast a dark shadow over Beryl's world, it
had also had a profound effect on Austin. He was, and felt himself to
be, essentially a morally minded man: he prided himself on his human-
itarian view of the world and everything he did was infused with a
moral determination to improve the lot of ordinary human beings. His
students would later testify to his engagement in their intellectual and
cultural development, and to his commitment to raise their political
consciousness. To have been the cause of wrecking Anne's life in such
a thoughtless and banal fashion shook Austin's sense of himself to the
core, prompting a radical change in his assessment of his own life: 'I
have for some time, since the affair of Anne, been disgusted with myself.
Was it that I had previously imagined the delights of a Don Juan to
be an ideal goal, or was it just that I preferred to be independent, to be
alone, to travel and to please only myself? Or was it that I shirked the
responsibility of any binding union?'[2]

With one life already blighted, as he saw it, through his inconsiderate
actions, he began to reconsider his behaviour in relation to Beryl. After
months, not to say years, of prevarication – his feeling that Beryl was
too young, his uncertainty as to how suited they were, his belief that his
work as an artist took precedence over purely personal romantic concerns
irrespective of the pain it might cause – he came to admit the possibility
that he'd been mistaken and that in Beryl he might find the one stable
element in his emotional life. She had stuck with him despite all that had

happened, she had proved she loved him whatever his faults, and surely that love would be able to sustain him, to restore his sense of himself as a worthwhile human being, to re-establish his lost sense of emotional integrity?

At the beginning of December, barely a month after returning with Anne from London, he decided to write to Beryl and bring matters to a head. He sent her a long, painstaking explanation of his change of attitude and concluded with a proposal of marriage. Then he sat back and waited for a reply. None came, and the doubts began again. Maybe things had gone too far: 'Perhaps she is beyond my reach already,' he speculated, 'she has a poor opinion, I think, of my weakness and I have hurt her enough already.'

Once again his mind fractured into opposing choices: if he remained alone, he could work, he would be free to drop everything, to do what he wanted without having to consider anybody. But alone he had no external stimulus to drive him forward, and when overwhelmed by depression he felt sick, weak and empty, without support or consolation. And what was the point of working selfishly, egotistically for oneself alone: 'Every joy to be complete must be shared. When I produce something good, there is nobody to talk to about it . . . It is so lonely, so wasted, so meaningless without the warmth of love.'

It seemed impossible to know what was the right direction to take. He couldn't even be sure that the qualities he saw and admired in Beryl weren't simply a reflection of the qualities he wanted to find in himself: 'Beryl is deep, introspective, enjoys the greater things in life, music, literature, painting, sculpture. Just like me. Oh, what conceit! I only love this reflection, the great flattering reflection of myself in her deep brown eyes. How can one even love sincerely when aware that it is this reflection that one loves?'

Amid all this doubt and self-questioning, he would come back to one secure position, his faith in art: 'I do not question the sincerity in my desire to paint, this gives greater joy, greater misery and dejection than anything.'

In London, Beryl too was waiting. Dorothy had warned her that Austin was going to write to her, but the days, and then the weeks, passed and still nothing arrived. She was plunged back into a state of anxiety, wondering what he had intended to say and why the letter had not arrived.

The answer was almost farcical in its banality: it had got lost in the post. After weeks of anxious waiting on both sides, Austin finally discovered what had happened by a chance telephone call to Dorothy, when she mentioned that Beryl had rung her:

'How is she?'

'Not, I believe, so well.'

'And the letter?'

'She did not receive it.'

And back came all this anxiety, this torment. What now? Ring her, tell her? But can I be sure, yes, yes, as sure as ever.

We had lunch New Year's day, a little embarrassed I feared reproaches, but how shall it be, will we, can we; to live together always is a long time and my wanderings, my empty heart, shall these cease to be? Logically it is perhaps unwise, but must all things be subject to logic. I do love as much as I ever can, and if this were all settled I could work and work and not succumb to all the smallest temptations.

'What did you put in your letter to me?'

'I wrote asking you to marry me.'

What reaction had I been expecting? She said nothing and looked at me in the half light of my basement studio.

'But you can't just say that, it doesn't mean anything.'

How could I explain?

'I have always felt it to be inevitable. Remember when we met in Euston and I told you Anne had refused categorically to go through with it? I felt then like almost an erring child returning to the fold to relate his relapses. I felt close then, almost as though I had not been away, that I had been out and got drunk, nothing more and was returning to where I belong, a little ashamed and so sorry.'

'Yes, yes it was like that. I felt it was inevitable that you should come back.'

'And now I feel I have the courage to face it and be with you always. I ran away from it, avoiding the responsibility of maturity. Now I can't run any more. I don't want to be alone, to work alone.'

But such a volte-face was not easy to take in. Beryl's mind was still full of the traumas of the past year, Austin's rejection of her, the rape, the succession of messy involvements with other men – with Robert, Gareth, André and Kevin. Would a relationship with Austin even be possible now, after all that had happened? 'How can I believe you or trust you?' she asked him. 'You said before once in London that you were as sure of this as you were of your work. Yet you wrote later that awful letter . . . and you made it so I didn't care and slept with many men, seven or eight perhaps, I don't know, because it didn't mean anything. I didn't even know the names of some of them, I didn't care whether I died, and you did this. Now you say you have courage. Oh Aus, you don't know, you don't realise.'[3]

Beryl accepted his proposal. What else could she do? This was, after all, what she had been hoping for, and fantasized about, for so long. But coming so soon after the disastrous affair with Anne, it was like a bolt out of the blue. There were also some conditions. This wasn't going to be a spontaneous, romantic sort of wedding, its date set by the calendar of love or desire. If Austin was going to marry her, it would be on his terms: they had to have separate working lives as well as a shared personal one. They needed to fulfil themselves as individuals in order to be fulfilled as a couple. For Austin this meant having the time and space to paint, for Beryl the freedom to further her career as an actress. They also had to have money. Before he and Beryl could afford to marry and live together, Austin wanted a secure job that would enable him to pay off his debts. Although he had started lecturing at the Liverpool College of Art in September, he still owed the Greens some £150, over half of which had been loaned to cover the cost of Anne's operation. This was a considerable sum given that the average salary at the time was around £600 a year. So Beryl would need to work too: there could be no question of having children right away, dragging them down into a pit of domesticity and debt.

It should have been a happy time and yet Beryl still felt ill at ease, suspecting that there was something other than love that was at the root of his decision. Her diary shows she was still troubled by doubts: 'Went to Liverpool to talk to Austin. Find it difficult sitting in the studio to connect what he says now, with what he said in the past.'[4]

Austin, too, was equally uncertain whether he was making the right decision. He was torn between contradictory feelings: his guilt about his past behaviour, his attraction to Beryl, and his fear of facing up to his responsibilities: 'I am ashamed of this last year, but I am sure there could be no-one like her, who so completely satisfies the loneliness, the wanting of someone . . . This year has just begun. Now it is not I singular, alone, but we, plural, together. But the knowledge of my weakness, my impressionability makes me a little afraid. What has 1953 to show?'[5]

Beryl returned to London on 14 January, and again set about trying to find work. That same evening Austin went round to see Richard and Winnie, to formally ask for Beryl's hand. Winnie especially had never taken to him: his appearance was too much that of the bohemian artist and she held him responsible for making Beryl ill the previous year through his callous treatment of her. Austin, aware that he was *persona non grata* in the house, was not looking forward to the visit, and his letter to Beryl describing the evening is strewn with military metaphors. His plan was to 'go into the field of battle', and 'creep upon the enemy quietly', using 'all the tactics of a cat stalking a mouse', delaying the pounce 'till the victim is assured'.[6]

But in the event, 'the supposed enemy' extended a hand of greeting with the disarming words: 'We have been expecting you, but we are surprised you took so long to arrive.' Richard then took Austin aside and confided his feelings about the whole situation, man to man, in a monologue that Austin later regaled to Beryl in comic fashion:

Well Austin! I mean to say, as I said to Beryl before she left, I'm quite sure that if I did have any objection to make, it would make absolutely no difference to your decision . . . if you take my advice, and it's the advice of an older man with more experience . . . you'll wait till you have got something behind you . . . She is very fond of you, desperately fond of you and if you feel that way about her all well and good, I am the last person to stand in your way, but Beryl's not domesticated you know . . . All I can say is don't take on any responsibility till you are in a position to do so, it's not worth it, you're young yet, 27 is it? Well I didn't marry till I was 37.

Much to Austin's surprise the evening passed off agreeably, and her parents 'seemed most affable about the whole thing . . . even faintly approving'. Nevertheless it is difficult to avoid the suspicion that Austin overplayed Richard's business-like caution, using it to bolster his own view of the need to take things slowly. 'They would prefer to wait at least till you are 21,' he told Beryl pointedly: 'From our point of view this would probably be better. I will have paid off my debt to the Greens . . . and for both of us our future prospects will surely be clearer.'

But while delaying the personal and financial responsibilities of marriage seemed attractive, deferring its more physical pleasures was not. Austin's argument that 'we both have so much to do that we will not notice the days, the weeks, the months, as they fly past' seemed to be more an attempt to convince himself than Beryl. A week later he was already feeling the tedium of inertia, and in his next letter he fantasized about the physical intimacy of their joint life together: 'I am so impatient to get to London to be with you all the time. How wonderful after a full day to come back late in the evening just before you and to have something all warm and savory for you to eat after the evening show, and then to talk (in bed) about all the happenings of that great long separated day.'[7]

Having started his new term at the College of Art, Austin's days were now fully occupied teaching and he would have no time off to see Beryl until Easter, in the first week of April. But he found the prospect of physical separation difficult, especially when he lay in bed at night opposite the photograph of Beryl he had hung on the wall and heard the couple in the house next door making love:

It is terrible to feel such tension and realize that I must read or write or do something for I cannot reach you. I cannot take you by the shoulders, look deep down into you, and see the pupils of your eyes go black and large.

Please dear Beryl don't be cross if I write like this. I fear you may think, as you have thought, that these things are becoming too dominant, it is not so, only tonight circumstances precipitate my feelings and I feel violent almost.

It seems awful to me that I cannot see you till Easter . . . Now that I have succumbed to, and admitted, my love for you, it burns like a great fire, there are no waters now to dampen it and it spreads wide and deep. I am yours now, it will not be long before we are together every night and every morning.

All my love, Austin[8]

The same day that Austin posted this outpouring of sexual frustration, doubt and insecurity, Beryl was confiding a very different set of emotions in her diary:

> Most nights I go to Roberts room and sit in the crowded messiness behind cheap curtains, always with my coat on and Roberts off. And the cigarrettes we smoke, till two in the morning. Without him I think perhaps I would go quite mad. I am so lost in a coma, no work, nothing and never any money. I eat potatoes, two a day, and six sausages last 3 days, and coffee, coffee, coffee. And of course the All-Bran. I am constantly disatisfied with myself, my size, my face, my body, I would like to eface myself. Of Aus I think but little. How can I? He had it all for so long, I do not need him anymore, though I believe I love him.[9]

It was not just these disturbing undercurrents that hinted at a breakdown in communication between them. Wanting to share Austin's enthusiasm for art, Beryl sent him some of her drawings. But Austin saw himself as a serious artist and took art seriously. He was incapable of making sentimental allowances in his critical judgement, and simply measured her work against an unbending standard of artistic competence, as he would with any other student. His comments about a self-portrait of Beryl's were hardly tactful: 'When I looked at your drawing of yourself thinking of me, I thought well?? If she finds it so painful she should think of something a little more cheerful – you look so agonised!!'[10]

Beryl's attempt at a more modern, more abstract style fared even less well. 'I didn't mention your drawings cause quite frankly I didn't understand them,' Austin told her in a condescending tone. 'I mean ter say, are they meant to be figures or are they not? If not, then they seem to have a vague resemblance to figures, no doubt this is accidental. It's all very well doing this modern futuristic stuff, what you want to do is to get down and learn to draw.'[11]

The distance between them is perhaps summed up by the single entry in Beryl's diary for February. Although it was written on Valentine's Day, it wasn't about Austin she was thinking: 'Birthday of mein liebchen Harry Franz. So long ago.'[12] Beryl was barely twenty and already she saw her past life with the bitter-sweet nostalgia of someone looking back over a lifetime of experience. As if to bring the point home, two weeks later there was another melancholy entry in the diary noting the death of Pedro. It seemed to sum up the passing of an era: 'And now the days of Harry and the sea are finally over.'[13]

In London, Beryl met up again with her Dundee confidants: Freddie Payne, still separated from Myrtle, was now renting a room in Camden – 'tiny and sordid and smelling of unwashed stockings'[14] – and Noel Davis was living just around the corner from her in Belsize Park. As in the past, their respective emotional entanglements and ongoing dramas became the subject of conversation.

On top of everything else Freddie was constantly short of money, and he would borrow from her even though she had little enough herself. Taking pity on him after she had collected her dole, she would treat him to coffee or egg and chips in a cafe in Camden. Noel was not much better; borrowing from her and then spending it rashly. One Sunday – Noel and Beryl would go to Brompton Oratory together – she lent him a pound, a considerable sum given that £2 10s was enough to cover food and rent for a week, and by Tuesday he had spent it all.

Aside from being a drain on Beryl's finances, Noel and Freddie were also a drain on her emotional energy, what with Freddie's worries about Myrtle and his sexual orientation, Noel's convoluted relationships, and Gerald's agitation over his split with his long-term partner. The constantly shifting allegiances and petty misunderstandings between the three of them were exhausting. But she felt a bond with them, and they were enlivening and entertaining company.

Beryl made the mistake of confiding some of this to Austin and revealing that she was short of money. To Austin's way of thinking he was doing the right and honourable thing: he was enduring the pain of separation in order to earn enough money to marry her. Out of the little he earned he would send Beryl money when he could. And now he found out she was giving it away! He was incensed, his righteous anger fuelled by a kind of moral outrage at the dissolute lifestyles he imagined Freddie, Noel and Gerald were living. After a long anecdote about how he had once been duped and taken advantage of himself when younger, he launched into a blistering attack:

> I burn with an inner anger at the thought of you wasting your soft heart upon an unworthy, disgusting subject. I am angry with you for the weakness which allows this . . . Don't sweetie, don't!! the idea of your being used in such a manner makes me indignant. You do

him, Freddie, more harm than good anyway, you encourage this weakness of character. When he is aware of the possibility of tears of lamentations, of recriminations, do you think for one minute he will hesitate when he finds this a good method of gaining his own ends? Do you suppose you are the only one at whose feet he cries – No! it is despicable you must not allow it!!! . . . I feel sick at your being associated with dregs like Freddie and Noel, at your being associated with them in any way, for people may judge you by the company you keep . . . I find it impossible even to talk to such people, perhaps I am intolerant. Oh! How I was revolted by Noel when I saw him with you, when you brought him here, I felt ashamed for you, even of you. What is it that so attracts you to people like this? They have a horrible veneer of sophistication which I am quite unable to counter, this too easy flow of mellifluous words.[15]

Almost immediately Austin repented of what he'd said, and attempted to forestall criticism in a letter of apology:

I am overcome with remorse on recollection of my last letter to you. That I should presume to criticise you, to censure as it were your friends, to interfere to such an extent into your private relationships, seems to be exceedingly presumptious, for have we not agreed that we must possess a separate life as well as a mutual one? What was the word I used – dregs? – sweetie please forgive me, I don't understand why I should be critical like this . . . but please understand that I become so indignant when I think you are being imposed upon, when I think people are taking advantage of your soft heart.[16]

But this row over money, over her friendship with Freddie and Noel, was only a symptom of broader differences between them, in temperament, in expectation, even in religion. Beryl had written to Gerald telling him about Austin, hinting at the trouble that might arise from the fact that he wasn't a Catholic, and even suggesting that if they had children she could bring them up as Catholics without him knowing. Gerald, who had occasionally written for the *Catholic Herald* on theological issues, immediately put an end to that line of thinking:

Now as to your marriage. You cannot bring these children up as secret Catholics & hope Austin won't notice. If you marry in the Church A[ustin] will have to sign a promise that they will be brought up as Catholics – if you marry outside the church you excommunicate yourself & cease to be a Catholic yourself. If you will take my advice you will speak to your confessor <u>at once</u> about all these possibilities & get the matter <u>straight</u> in your own mind. I know it's difficult for women to be <u>clear</u> & <u>factual</u>, but the difficulties are infinitely worse later on if you don't.[17]

Austin sensed Beryl's underlying unease but was unable to offer any consolation: 'Your letters are so full of a deadly despair now and I wish continually that I could do something to make you happy . . . Sweetie why do you say I am so cruel, I do not mean to be, I want you to be happy and at peace, but you are torn to pieces with your desperation, your frustration and I feel, at this moment, powerless to help in any way.'[18]

The one bright spot in the situation for Austin was the thought of the Easter break, when he could come up to London and see Beryl: 'Oh Sweetie! time passes slowly till Easter, and I ache for you continually. If only we could, by an effort of will, transpose our minds from one place to another we could lie in bed talking for hours each night about the day's happenings . . . Letters, mine especially, are so inadequate, how can one express in words the significance of a deep glance or the extreme gentleness of feeling that floods up like a tidal wave, without any reason? How can one put into words, what is far best expressed by a silent embrace?'

TWELVE

Break

A few months in Salisbury alarmed me because I lost control
of certain events . . .[1]

IN FEBRUARY 1953, HUGH Goldie, now at the Salisbury Arts
Theatre, contacted Beryl to see whether she was free for a run of
five productions, beginning in March and going through to the end
of April. The schedule was intensive: Salisbury was a weekly Rep,
and Beryl was due to work three weeks on, with a week off at Easter,
followed by a further two plays in two weeks. The first production was
Little Women, Marion de Forest's adaptation of the novel by Louisa
May Alcott, which opened on 16 March. Beryl began rehearsals on
the 10th.

Salisbury remains a relatively compact city dominated by its magnificent Gothic cathedral; in the 1950s it had the air of a small provincial
town. This had its advantages: the theatre was just a short stroll from
open countryside, and Beryl and the other members of the company
would spend some of the little time they had off taking walks, or going
to a country pub just outside the city borders.

After *Little Women* ('Beryl Bainbridge [plays] the invalid Bess,
whose fond farewell to Jo is certainly memorable . . .')[2] the next production was Elmer Harris's *Johnny Belinda*, about a neglected deaf and
dumb girl rescued by a doctor who teaches her sign language. Goldie,
who had championed Beryl since their early days in Liverpool, gave
her the leading role – albeit technically a non-speaking one – of the
mute Belinda. His confidence was amply rewarded and her 'outstanding performance'[3] was universally applauded: 'It is a most difficult
part for anyone to play, but Miss Bainbridge is wonderfully appealing,
conveying her feelings of sadness and joy, of fear and trust, and above

all of love, by her expressive eyes and clever facial expressions. It is a performance that tears at the heart-strings.'[4]

While Beryl was riding high on the success of *Johnny Belinda*, Austin was suffering from a series of disappointing setbacks: an exhibition committee had turned down all three of the portraits he'd been working on, and his entry for the Topham Trophy didn't even merit a mention ('Not a bloody sausage not even a runner-up . . .').[5] This was doubly frustrating, both as a rejection of his work and for the loss of prize money it represented. All his hopes now rested on a meeting at the start of April with Johannes Schmidt, owner of the Galerie Apollinaire in London, to discuss the possibility of a one-man show. He planned to meet Schmidt first, and then come on to Salisbury to see Beryl, booking a double room at a hotel to avoid causing problems at her digs.

They had been writing regularly to each other since the engagement, but the misunderstandings between them continued. After Austin had seen *The Road to Hope*, an Italian film about a group of miners forced to leave their village in Sicily to find work, he wrote enthusiastically about the film's portrayal of women, describing their 'great heavy eyes, high cheek bones and gorgeous mouths, smouldering, burning, with projected firm bosoms and long hair'.[6] He had meant to express how moving the film was as an account of human experience, but insecure as she was about her looks Beryl took his comments as an implied criticism, and wrote back saying she was ugly and that he seemed to find Italian women more beautiful than her. His attempt to set her mind at rest hardly improved matters: 'You are stupid saying you are not beautiful, you are! I have only to glance up at your large photograph hanging on the wall to reassure myself. I agree the photograph of you leaning over the garden gate is not particularly good, you look older and weary.'[7]

Beryl was disappointed that Austin wouldn't get time off work to see her in *Johnny Belinda*, and as the date of his visit approached he detected a further note of unease in her letters: 'You sound unhappy,' he told her, 'what are the difficulties of which you speak?'[8]

Beryl's 'difficulty' was the usual one of trying to work out what she felt. The proximity of Hugh Goldie was beginning to unsettle her. Hugh had always enjoyed Beryl's company, and though he had a happy home life, he was not immune to her attractions. At the Liverpool Playhouse and in subsequent encounters he had framed their friendship as that of brother and sister, mutually sympathetic and affectionate – but platonic. However, the experience of working so closely together had pushed things in a disturbing direction. Beryl's Playhouse crush on Hugh briefly revived and she seems to have told him about her feelings – and about her doubts regarding Austin. Matters came to a head when Austin arrived, and Beryl's diary charts the painful disintegration of their fragile bond:

> *2 April Thursday*: Austin came to stay at Salisbury. Rain everywhere and Hugh's white face, and the empty theatre and the cool dampness of A's cheek, and the immense distance between us from the awful begining.
>
> *4 April Saturday*: A dreadful scene with Austin . . . I realise he will not marry me. Once more it is over.
>
> *5 April Sunday*: Realise Austin and I are hopelessly out of sympathy with one another.
>
> *6 April Monday*: Went to Kate and Mortimers for a drink with Jim Paige Brown and Hugh and Austin. Looking up at the stars on the way home I suddenly turn to Austin but it is futile. He does not understand. It is better to let the tide go over us.
>
> *7 April Tuesday*: Said good-bye to Austin in more ways than one. Tore my lovely ring off when his train had departed and cried brokenly, but for what?[9]

Austin was also painfully aware that things weren't working out. Analysing the situation in his journal afterwards, he ruefully noted that at the start of the year he'd been optimistic, perfectly sure of his relationship with Beryl, but that his feelings had changed over the course of a few months: 'Strange how things can mean so much and then so little.' Although he enjoyed Beryl's company and the 'pleasure of complete knowledge', he felt an 'emotional and physical inadequacy' when he was with her; he realized that 'something more was required' but couldn't give it. At Salisbury he'd begun writing a long and affectionate letter, and when Beryl came across it and realized it was to Fanchon, not her, 'the pain she felt was evident' – she was horrified he could use such affectionate terms to another woman. His summing up of the Salisbury trip betrayed little hope of a joint future with Beryl: 'We parted friendly, yet separated, and both sad. She knew then that it was impossible and always had been. Perhaps it was the romantic element which made me believe, want to believe, so much in our association.

Perhaps because there was no fresh stimulation, no immediate surge of passionate interest, my feeling automatically died.'[10]

———

How much Austin guessed about Hugh's involvement in the break-down of his relationship with Beryl is difficult to determine, as neither his letters nor his journal mention him by name. But Hugh himself was certainly feeling the strain from the off-stage drama. Tired and emotionally fraught, he returned home to Portsmouth on 7 April – the same day Austin went back to Liverpool – his work at Salisbury now done. That night Hugh wrote Beryl a long letter, a mixture of exhilaration at the thought she returned his feelings, anxiety at what the future might hold, and guilt about what he'd been responsible for:

> Beryl Darling . . . I feel as if a bomb had exploded in my life. What will happen when the dust blows away and what will be left I no longer feel capable of assessing, all I know is that something drastic has happened in the last few weeks . . . The truth is I don't feel I have any right to offer words of wisdom to my little erstwhile 'sister', because I'm afraid I'm very largely responsible for the turmoil in your life at the moment . . . it seems awful to think that loving you as I do has been a destructive force, and not creative as love should be . . . but despite these feelings I can't honestly say that I wish it hadn't happened . . . Forgive me darling for loving you so much. God how I miss you, Hugh.[11]

Beryl spent the next week in a state of emotional confusion, and the following Saturday, perhaps hoping to get some answers, she went down to see Hugh in Portsmouth. To talk privately together they went out for a walk, wandering around the fairground at Southsea, where they went on a roller-coaster, an appropriate enough metaphor for Beryl's emotional life over the past few months.

But the trip to Portsmouth resolved nothing. Although she knew a relationship with Hugh had no future and risked breaking up his marriage, she couldn't stop imagining some romantic connection between them. The following day, after spending the afternoon with him, Beryl returned to Salisbury for the last week of her scheduled engagement, playing Aisla Crane in Edgar Wallace's classic whodunnit, *The Case of the Frightened Lady.* Back in her digs, she wrote a poem expressing her feeling of uncertain expectancy about a possible relationship:

> If I should come across you yet once more . . .
> Ernestly sweeping back the fair hair
> From your brow, and easing up your collars
> Sending soft arrows of unspoken energy
> From eye to eye, allowing here and there
> A slow message for the watching others.
> I shall not know how to conceal my worthless love . . .
> My inarticulate heart will suffer and dilate
> Watching my brothers, watching others
> Watching me wait, waiting to live.[12]

As if Beryl didn't have enough to cope with while she was at Salisbury, an obsessive fan had taken a fancy to her in her guise as Belinda. The man, Frank H. Gopsill,[13] was in his early sixties – two years older than Beryl's father – and had been a second lieutenant during the First World War. After being invalided out in 1918, probably as a result of shell shock, he subsequently became a patient at the Old Manor Mental Hospital on the outskirts of Salisbury and had been there ever since. He was considered harmless and allowed to go out, and having done this kind of thing before, no one at the theatre was particularly surprised when he fixed his attentions on Beryl.

Beryl's response was very different, however, from that of other actresses who had been stalked in this way. Rather than avoid him, she acquiesced in his fantasies and started going out for walks with him. Her openness to, and acceptance of, offbeat and eccentric people who others might have gone out of their way to avoid, would be a lifelong characteristic. It was partly a self-conscious act, designed, like her desire to be seen dancing in the street by her neighbours, to present a particular image to those around her, and throughout her life she would form friendships with individuals her other friends considered strange or even mad. As she put it at the time: 'I find I draw to me all kinds of weak unbalanced people, mostly a good deal older than myself, [who] rely on me and trust me and burden me with their sorrows.'[14] But it was also a consequence of her almost pathological inability to say no to anyone who asked something of her. In later life she would be plagued by visits from local drunks, social misfits and those with mental problems, who would knock at her door demanding money or attention. She might hide from them or pretend she was out when they called, but she found it almost impossible to tell them to go away.

Gopsill wasn't the first in this collection of exotic human specimens, and he wouldn't be the last. Such encounters weren't, however, without their pleasures, and they at least provided a distraction from Beryl's emotional upheavals. Their first excursion together was to the Old Mill, a country pub a short walk from the theatre:

> Mr Gopsill would pause, lean on his stick and say far too loudly 'My dear Miss B, breath deeply, relax, one two, three.' And I would do as he said laughing. But I was too full of wonder at my ability to attract such an interesting person to realise what exactly I had done . . . I would laugh and look wildly around me, singing inapropiately to myself 'Aye-O, here we go again Sister Anna.' Sometimes I said this aloud. It could not have been thought strange amid the shouts and threats and stick waving.[15]

But after a subsequent outing she gradually realized that it wasn't so much a case of her taking pity on him, of living up to her moral ideal of loving all mankind, as it was Mr Gopsill pitying *her* – he considered *her* the lonely one in need of friendship and sympathy. 'I decided not to see him again,' she wrote in her diary:

> and went out by back entrances, or road out of the theatre in a strange hat on the electrican's bicycle. Every morning Mr Gopsill took up his post outside the box office, way laying the company, asking them questions. Afternoons I lay in the fields about the town reading books beside the rushes, starting everytime a swan glided down the stream past me. When it came time for me to leave for London I relented and he came to say good-bye to me at the station, presenting me with a brown holdall containing a bowl of earth and cacti, a fountain pen and the book *Rob Roy*. Sedately we walked arm and arm, up and down the platform till it was time for my train to depart. He kissed my cruel hand and I bent from the window and touched his lips with my cheek.

Despite her gloom over Austin's visit and her anxieties about Hugh, Beryl managed to hide her feelings from the other members of the company. The final two days were a mix of high spirits and light relief, tinged with sad farewells. On the last day, she and fellow actress Prudence Clayton conspired to entice George Selway, another actor with a crush on Beryl, into the dressing room in order to kiss her. But in the middle of these antics she heard Hugh's voice in the corridor and she froze, struck by how stupid it all was.

When she arrived in London in late April, Robert Lawson met her off the train at Waterloo, and she struggled with her bags and her presents from Mr Gopsill, laughing uncontrollably whenever one or other of them fell out of her arms. At 5.20 she caught the train to Liverpool and was back in Formby that evening: 'I do not know what to think of the whole seven weeks that has gone so quickly and so strangely.'[16]

Before going home that night Beryl called in briefly to see Lyn, who told her she had now broken up with Charles ('Have dropped me pillar of virility with a bang',[17] as she put it) and joined an anarchist group, after falling for one of its charismatic members, a red-haired art student called Rufus Segar. In September she was going to live in Upper Parliament Street with him and some other politically active students. Lyn suggested meeting the next day at Rufus's flat, but Beryl didn't want to risk bumping into Austin in the quiet streets around the cathedral, especially as he might be with Fanchon, who had taken up art and attended Austin's composition classes.

The following evening she met Lyn and they walked to the pine woods in the half-rain. The wind was blowing wildly on the dunes behind St Luke's and they ran in and out among the trees, howling, the sand blowing into their eyes and ears. 'Several times I lay flat down in the wet sand and buried my face in it,' Beryl wrote, 'because it was so good to be there.'[18]

The next day she rang Austin and arranged to see him, and after dinner with Dorothy and Gordon Green she went round to his flat in Canning Street. It was clear that the relationship had reached an impasse: 'He said how he was utterly without feeling, so we decided to finish everything.' They tried to be mature about it, to talk about other things, but it didn't work, and Beryl couldn't restrain her emotion: 'I cannot stop crying, so that he shouts at me angrily "It isn't fair".'[19]

After a melancholy day spent painting, Beryl went round to see Dorothy and Gordon again, and the three of them sat and talked. They discussed Austin, and Dorothy said it was better the relationship between them had finished. When it was time to go, Austin, who had been working down in the studio, offered to accompany Beryl back to Lime Street, though it wasn't a convivial journey: 'On the bus to the station we do not talk, and on the platform he looked very hard at me. I am quite cold inside and impassive.'[20]

The next few days were spent in similar fashion, picking up news here and there and trying not to be swamped by the aftershocks of past events: 'Dorethey tells me that Anne Lindholme came to Liverpool about going into a convent, last week. She is going to be a nun, perhaps.'[21] At lunch with the Greens she saw Austin again, and again the atmosphere was strained: 'I could not speak to him. I looked out of the window and saw Fritz go by in tight black trousers. He smiled and said something like "Are you here for ever and ever?" And when I shouted back, "no, not for ever and ever", I meant it so many ways.'[22]

Even so, she still believed deep down that there was a connection between herself and Austin that went beyond the world of appearances. After attending a concert together one evening she tried to describe this somewhat paradoxical state of affairs: 'We sat side by side, Austin and I, holding each other's hand, but only a hopeless sense of something missing was between us. And yet it is as if we are already man and wife, all this withdrawing and the scenes seem make-believe, the invisible knot exists, no amount of pretending will untie it. So while Dorethey advises him, and Frau Freulïch feeds his mind, and Tonie Butler his body, it doesn't really matter.'[23]

———

At the start of May, Beryl's lethargic mood was broken by news about a job. Lionel Harris, who was directing televised productions for the BBC's *Sunday Night Theatre*, rang and asked her to come to London immediately to talk about a role in *Rookery Nook*, to be broadcast live later in the month. There followed a farcical rush to get to the station on time, involving attempts to contact her father for money, and Winnie throwing a fit of hysterics as she was going into hospital that afternoon to have her varicose veins removed. In the middle of it all, four letters, a telegram and a package containing a velvet duster and a book entitled *The Art of Marriage* arrived from Mr Gopsill, who had proposed to Beryl after her return and now sent her letters and presents on a regular basis. 'At 3.5. I get on the London train, rather weak in the sunlight. Daddy waves to me at Lime street with more money and a packet of cigarrettes. He is a little merry. At 9 oclock I call at Lionels who says the job is mine. At 9.45 I see Freddie, at 10 oclock Robbie. At midnight I finally find a hotel in Belsize Park and ring home. I am very weary.'[24]

In between rehearsals for *Rookery Nook*, in which she played Rhoda Marley, a part she had previously understudied at the Liverpool Playhouse, her life resumed its familiar round. On Sunday she went to Brompton Oratory, though arriving late meant she had to climb over the pews to sit next to Noel. She was too distracted about Austin to follow the service, and as the Host was being consecrated tears sprang to her eyes and she fantasized about seeing him: 'I wander again up Mount Street, thinking everything will be the same if only I tap softly enough on the studio window.'[25]

Freddie began calling again at all hours, and Beryl would meet up with Robert, spending her free time seeing films with him or walking on Hampstead Heath. Ken, now back from tour and looking 'very tall and elegant in his new black suit, like a raven walking up the street', also came to see her, though his jealousy of Robert sometimes led to awkward situations. The vacuum in her emotional life left by Austin was filled by anxiety, and she felt increasingly bleak about her prospects: 'I wish I could believe that as I grow older everything will be happy for me. Sometimes I am inarticulate with a misery that rises in me and threatens always to engulf me.'[26]

The days prior to the live performance were hectic: there were two full run-throughs of *Rookery Nook* in Paddington on Thursday, then long camera rehearsals on Friday. Beryl was intensely nervous, self-conscious that the green silk pyjamas she had to wear for the role were showing 'the too full curve' of her thighs. There were in fact two performances on Saturday, a matinee that effectively served as a full dress rehearsal, and the televised one in the evening. In the break between the two, Beryl went over to the Union Hotel to have a bath, expensive at five shillings but 'worth it, I was so hot and tired'.[27] The broadcast performance passed off well, despite her nerves and the heat of the lights, and looking out into the audience she saw some old Playhouse friends – Cyril Luckham, Maureen Quinney and Thomas St John Barry.

The production wasn't entirely a critical success: the *Daily Sketch* critic, Mark Johns, felt that some of the male actors 'weren't up to it' and that 'the whole thing creaked', though he conceded that farce was difficult to do on television. He did, however, single out Beryl's performance, swayed perhaps by her skimpy attire: 'I liked the doe-eyed Beryl Bainbridge as a damsel in distress – and pyjamas – run out of her home in the middle of the night for eating worts.'[28]

After *Rookery Nook*, Beryl returned to the seemingly endless round of signing on and looking for work that constitutes the life of a jobbing actor. She spent lazy days reading or sketching on Hampstead Heath with Robert, and to earn money she began working at Charles Robinson's shop in South Woodford, 'selling bars of chocolate to children and woodbines to men from lorries',[29] as she put it.

Unsurprisingly, she was soon bored by her job at the confectionery shop. The initial charm of Charles's idiosyncratic, somewhat cantankerous, personality was beginning to wear thin. Moreover, after Lyn had broken up with him, he had become more morose and would sit on his own in a back room drinking sherry. The late-night journeys from South Woodford to Hampstead were also tiring. Everything left Beryl feeling in a gloomy mood: 'I feel rather depressed today. I have been tossing at night and thinking of A. Hopelessly,'[30] she wrote at the start of June: 'I feel very depressed and lonely. I hate myself too.'[31]

The day after Winnie came down to see her in London, Beryl received a letter from Austin, or rather some invitations to his exhibition at the Galerie Apollinaire, due to start in a few days. There was no letter, only a short note reading: 'Please send these to any wealthy people you might know.' Its impersonality left her dejected, and the thought he would be in London and they wouldn't meet made her feel even further away from him: 'The streets become very empty, I seek him everywhere, I am torn with a sort of restless suffering, which my mother senses and cannot understand. Somewhere I knew A. was. I want to scream I am so nervous. If I was alone I would plunge into the crowd and try to find him.'[32]

On Winnie's last day, Beryl went to see her off at Euston station, her mind still fixated on Austin's invisible presence somewhere in London: 'A gulf of desolation begins to open in front of my eyes . . . I will be alone in London with him, only he will never know.' Afterwards she went to Westminster Cathedral and sat in a pew and cried:

> There is a que outside the confessional but nobody behind me. I said 'Father, I need help.' He was very quick and cool with me, to make me cease crying. He said 'Why haven't you come before? You know don't you what danger you have run. You could have been under a streetbus and gone to hell for all eternity.' And like a child I said 'Yes Father.' And for 3 hail Mary's I was absolved. 'God,' he said, 'had forgiven and forgotten'. But I still cried.[33]

Austin's exhibition opened on 19 June, but Beryl, unable to face meeting him, went three days later, after he'd returned to Liverpool. The visit was a painful one. She was particularly upset by a painting entitled *The Inevitability*, which represented herself and Austin, with Anne Lindholm on a bed. Johannes Schmidt did his best to calm her, but made matters worse with his indiscreet remarks about Austin:

> Johannes Shmidt came down the stairs of the other room and I sat still, very hopeless. And I was crying and he was saying 'Oh but yes, but he is not good enough for you. He will never be anything. You must now love someone fully and become loved fully yourself.' And he was very gentle, real sadness in his eyes . . . And then because I was really hopeless, his mood changed . . . and he was impatient for me to go. But I could not go gracefully, I felt at a loss, crying over this white haired man who was a stranger and who understood how I felt, and I wished I was <u>not</u> so inarticulate and always so untidy.[34]

But there was still the problem of what to do about Hugh: 'I would like to contact Hugh, but feel it is stupid too, I ought to be quiet and await [what] happens.'[35] Deep down she knew a relationship with him couldn't work and that whatever had started between them had to be formally ended:

> Tonight I went to meet Hugh in Golders Green and we caught a trolly up the hill and went a walk over the heath into Kenwood. He made me feel very old and responsible. It seems as if now for oh so long I have been the wise one in all my relationships, doing the worrying and thinking too many times. So that Hugh in his corduroy jacket seems part of a familiar pattern, there is nothing new to be said or inacted, only the form of saying good-bye, as I must. How can one love with a wife and children at home? I wish I could be alone, yet happy.[36]

She tried to convince herself of what she had to do ('I realised it would be better to ring Hugh and tell him I could see him no longer'),[37] but she was unable to take the initiative and do it. After dragging on for a further month and a half ('I feel so strained and worried about the whole thing concerning Hugh'),[38] the situation came to a head at the beginning of July. Hugh was directing his first London production, *Love's Labour's Lost* at the Regent's Park theatre, and he arranged to meet Beryl for tea in her Parliament Hill flat, after which they walked on Hampstead Heath, watching the young couples kissing and cuddling in the hollows.

The following day they went to the National Film Theatre to see *Men Are Such Rascals*, a film by the Italian actor and director Vittorio de Sica: 'Later Hugh and I talked ineffectually by the pond in Hampstead and I wish I were alone, or dead . . . In the light Hugh's face is strained. Why is it one has not the insight at the first to see why relationships begin? I do not see that Hugh longs and dreams at all possible times about desire and consumation. I interpretated it as love for me, but then one is always so full of pride.'[39]

They met again the next day, at a coffee place in Charing Cross where they sat holding hands very indiscreetly. Seeing Johannes Schmidt standing nearby, smiling in amusement at her, she went up to him and asked whether any of Austin's pictures had been sold, but this reminder of Austin just filled her with gloom: 'Going back to Hugh my heart sinks, I love Aus so. Walking down Piccadilly we saw the ruined church and the garden and sat on the bench under the cool trees and became unbearably tender. "How sweet you are. Oh my little love. How tenderly I care for you." And so on, and I think I am too unhappy to live.'[40]

Resistant as she was to confronting Hugh, things couldn't go on like this much longer and the next time she saw him she was more open about her doubts: 'Hugh called soon after lunch and we looked and sighed at each other. But I no longer desire him, and told him so. He became strange and said. "The truth is you don't love me." At that I protested but I am not even thinking of him.'[41]

A few days later it was Hugh's turn to try and dampen the fire, realizing that his infatuation for Beryl risked destroying his family life. The last time he'd been at her flat the landlady, Mrs Hannah, had dead-locked the front door while they were both inside. As Beryl had mislaid her key, Hugh had to climb out of the bathroom window and down the drainpipe, snagging his trousers in the process. It wasn't the sort of activity that became a theatre director of his standing, and not for the last time Beryl would have to listen as a married man tried to backtrack his way out of a relationship that had become too complicated for him: 'Hugh came round about eleven and we went shopping . . . He talked at great length about his life with Janet. How much he loved her, but how full her life was with the children and work for him, so that at night she was too tired to turn to him. Listening to him I know he is worrying whether to tell her about us. That way I am glad there is nothing to tell, for how should it be justified?'[42]

THIRTEEN

Paris

For a long while the Colonel and I had planned going to
Bordeux, for companionship.
'I am' he said, under the rain filled hedge, 30 inches round
the belly, no!'
And how shall it be, I thought, loving a man in the french dusk
who is keeping in his breath to hold his belly firm.[1]

IN JULY 1953, BERYL returned home to Formby for three weeks.
At some point during her stay a meeting took place that effectively
changed her life, in that it formed the inspiration for her first full-length
novel, a book that would relaunch her stalled literary career and propel
her to critical and popular success for the first time.

The meeting was with George Greggs, a fifty-five-year-old married
man whom Beryl and Lyn had nicknamed 'the Colonel'. He was a well-
known figure among the locals, and could frequently be seen strolling
up the lane arm in arm with his wife Edith (née Tebay), or 'Tibs' as he
called her. His distinctive house, with its Gothic-looking tower, was
situated on the corner of Ravenmeols Lane and Anthony Lane, five
minutes from Beryl's and a minute or so from Lyn's, and the two girls
would pass it each time they went to the pine woods.[2]

Consequently, 'the Colonel' became a minor character in their shared
fantasy world, along with figures such as 'Molotov', 'Lochinvar' and 'Old
Mr Redman'. On one of their encounters George unwisely confided
that his marriage to Edith was not entirely happy, and Beryl and Lyn
began inventing 'wicked stories' about him and became quite 'obsessed
about him',[3] though this had gone no further than the kind of teasing
many schoolgirls indulge in: testing boundaries with men their father's
age and making up private jokes about them.

The meeting in July, however, seemed to mark an abrupt change in George's relationship with Beryl, and in her diary she recorded a short cryptic account that at first reads like a fantasy sequence:

> The Colonel and I were married tonight in St Lukes. His gods in their thousands applauded but my God was silent, remembering other things. Gliding toward the isle end, hat in hand, not quite sober, 26 years ago, so he tells me, he married Tibs here . . . The Colonel's friend The Rev Stephen Henry Philomel performed the ceremony. Mr Fernly and George's mother were the only two in the church beside these three . . . Then they walked out . . . and began the night-mare journey of 30 years.[4]

Despite its dreamlike quality, the diary entry faithfully records the actual events of George's wedding day. The Greggs had indeed been married nearly thirty years previously in St Luke's, by Reverend Stephen Henry Phillimore. Reverend Fearnley, the parish priest of St Luke's at the time, had attended, but Phillimore conducted the service because he was George's parish priest in Seaforth and had baptized him as an adult two years prior to his wedding. George's mother was the only other witness because his father had died in 1917.

But what was the significance of Beryl's use of the word 'married' to describe her meeting with George? How had things come to the point where she could make even an ironic allusion to a marriage between them? The answer lies in a series of references to the Colonel in Lyn's letters over the previous year.

After Beryl left Formby for London in 1952, she and Lyn had renewed their fantasy scenario about Mr Greggs and began playing with the idea that they were rivals for his amorous attention. In one of her letters Lyn joked that the 'one faintly shining compensation for the fact that you are away' is 'that I now have sole sway over Mr Greggs',[5] and in another she told Beryl that she had 'just seduced Mr Greg (Gentleman Greg of the 49th)'.[6] As with Beryl's later 'marriage', this was not a literal seduction but simply an exaggeration, a wickedly funny joke that appealed to 'the peculiarly distorted South-Bainbridge sense of humour'.[7]

Over the next few months Lyn kept Beryl up to date about her meet-ings with the Colonel, some of which were no doubt real given the proximity of their houses, but which were recounted in a fantastical way that was meant to be taken with a pinch of salt. In another letter, after saying that she and the Colonel were 'still having a great time', she comically described how they had been 'riding pillion on a black stallion at 50 mph through the village on a Saturday morning'.[8] Beryl no doubt contributed to the joke in her letters to Lyn, unfortunately now lost.

Beryl's meeting with George in July 1953 and the subsequent 'marriage' was not, therefore, a singular event, but the culmination of the previous year's sequence of chance encounters and the semi-playful fantasies that had been constructed around them. Lyn gave no indication that she thought of her meetings with the Colonel as anything other than an amusing diversion while she was separated from Charles. Indeed, the distinction in Lyn's attitude to the two men is clear: while her references to the Colonel are tongue-in-cheek and ironically playful, her references to Charles are deadly serious, and on one occasion she earnestly begged Beryl not to steal him away from her: 'Glad you like Char – he's wonderful but please he's mine. I'm terribly jealous for him. He's mine.'[9]

But while Lyn and Beryl may have seen the whole thing as a joke, George didn't. By the time Beryl was at Salisbury things had developed to a dangerous point. In April 1953, Lyn told Beryl about meeting George down by the shore, and though her tone was one of ironic detachment, she noted his earnestness in telling her how beautiful her eyes were and how he'd held her hand in an affectionate way – as he would a few months later with Beryl. George's impulse to take things further with Beryl seems almost certainly to have been provoked by these rendezvous with Lyn, her mock-flirtation holding out in his mind the real possibility of an extramarital affair.

Beryl's first meeting with George that July was accidental, at least it is described as such in an early novel, 'The Summer of the Tsar' (later *Harriet Said*), where they both happen to visit the grave of 'old Mr Redman',[10] who had died the previous year. On the evening of 23 July they met up again, probably in the pine woods, as they subsequently went into St Luke's nearby, and it was while inside the dark, deserted church that George told Beryl the story of his life, and the two re-enacted his wedding at the altar.

It may have been a joke, but there was an undeniable symbolic element to it and afterwards they began to see each other in a different light. The day before she left Formby, Beryl met George again, while taking the new family dog, Laddie, out for a walk. The idea of some sort of relationship was now beginning to form in both their minds. It was still one on the borders of fantasy – they held hands and joked about Laddie being their 'deformed child'[11] – but given Beryl's emotional fragility after the break with Austin and George's professed dissatisfaction with his wife, it was a dangerous game to be playing.

After Beryl returned to London, George wrote suggesting he come down and see her, and she seemed at least to consider the possibility of an affair, though as with Hugh, his age and the fact that he was married made it more problematic: 'It will never work out, of that I am sure.'[12] Going through her mind were a whole series of contradictions and counter-arguments: she loved Austin, but he didn't seem to love her; they were meant for each other, but they couldn't get along; George was too old for her, but he was kind and affectionate. The dilemma was summed up in her diary: 'He's old, perhaps. But oh to salvage a little happiness for us both.'[13]

As the summer advanced, Beryl's feelings about Austin, George and Hugh remained unresolved, ebbing and flowing with events. The fact that Kevin Stoney, who she had fallen for in Dundee the previous year, was now in London after having married Rosalie a few weeks before, only added to her unsettled state of mind. The news from Dorothy Green that Austin was 'going around'[14] with Toni Butler again did little to put Beryl at her ease, pushing her closer to George, whose affection seemed simpler, more innocent by comparison.

On 27 August, George came down to London and they arranged to meet at four o'clock, in the lounge of the Pastoria Hotel in St Martin's Street: 'He sat in a dark suit trembling, and we drank tea and smoked cigarrettes. Strangely enough almost at once we are at one with the situation, it is natural to hold hands in the crowded streets and walk together up Frith Street.'[15]

Beryl had become adept at keeping the various parts of her emotional life in separate boxes: Ken had no idea that Beryl was flirting with the idea of an affair with Hugh or with George; George was in the dark about Hugh; Austin had been unaware of Beryl's crush on Kevin Stoney in Dundee and didn't know about her feelings for Robert or George. Inevitably, it became increasingly difficult to keep these compartments watertight, especially given the restricted social sphere that Beryl inhabited in London. As she sat with George having dinner at Fava's, an Italian restaurant in Frith Street, drinking sweet wine and watching a cat through the window, Kevin Stoney and Rosalie walked in: 'There was much confusion. Rosalie is guarded very friendly, I grow inchorent, Kevin stares hard, trying to visualise things, looking G. up and down.'[16]

The next morning she met up with George again, but the day was ruined by another chance encounter. After going to the Labour Exchange so Beryl could sign on, they bumped into June Furlong, an artist's model at the Slade who had known Beryl and Austin from her time as a model at the Liverpool Art School. As George stood admiring her form ('How the Colonel dwells on her breasts', Beryl jealously noted in her diary), the walls keeping the various parts of her life separate threatened to spring another leak:

> June says 'Oh yes Austin was dancing about on one leg, saying "I'm engaged isn't it lovely?"' And then she mentioned a young girl called Jane who adores him. And at once on the bus between June the model and George I feel sick, my heart lurches, and I am very frightened. I belong, I groan inwardly to him, why has he forsaken me?[17]

The following day Beryl was racked with indecision, a confused mix of guilt, jealousy, hope and anger: 'I cannot help thinking of Austin. I keep hearing what June Furlong said. Somehow and most illogically Austin and I are bound, however we may strain and part. But I am so full of anger. I should like to hit him for being so cruel and foolish. I have gone down so much since him. Even I think I love George, he is so strange and thin and nervous.'[18]

———

Since the beginning of August, George had been trying to persuade Beryl to fly to Paris for a weekend away together. Given recent experiences, he probably considered that an affair between them was as unlikely to start in London as it was in Formby. But Beryl, still two months short of her twenty-first birthday, didn't have her own passport, so the trip had to wait until all the paperwork was sorted. She went to Somerset House to get a copy of her birth certificate and five weeks later, on 23 September 1953, her passport was issued.[19]

Less than a week later, on 1 October, George and Beryl took the bus from Waterloo to Heathrow and flew to Le Bourget. Beryl was immediately enthralled by Paris, and she captured her impressions in lengthy diary entries:

> We were in Paris at lunch time. The city is breathtaking and beautiful. I know if my parents find out they will be upset for many reasons, but truthfully, truthfully I am not doing wrong, and it is worth it all. Perhaps not quite worth causing them unhappiness, nothing is worth that, but I would be wrong to myself not to go to Paris. We walk along the quay in the sun, with the Seine so clear, and the little book stalls . . . In the hotel Georges gets a room with a bidet. I sat on it at once and was very thrilled. We have to climb several flights to our room, at which the chamber maid calls to us . . . 'Courage' 'Vie la sport,' calls back Georgès.[20]

Their room was dark, but with large luminous windows; there was a fire in the grate, and a brass bed with a blue eiderdown on top and a white chamberpot underneath. A reproduction of Paul Gauguin's *Yellow Christ* hung over the door. The hotel was situated in the heart of the Left Bank, just off the Boulevard St Germain, so after Beryl had put away her clothes they took in the sights.

Beryl's image of Paris had been shaped by one of her favourite books, Elliot Paul's picaresque novel of bohemian life, *A Narrow Street*. Now here she was in the Paris of the 1950s, a Paris that would become the stuff of legend: the Left Bank really was the haunt of students and bearded existentialists, Jean-Paul Sartre could still be seen in Les Deux Magots, and for Beryl the reality of Paris lived up to her impossibly romantic image of it. In 1948 she had written to her French pen-friend for information about Sartre; now she was sitting in the very café he wrote in. She noted down a mass of details that caught her eye: the little courtyards and alleys, the statues, the musicians in the street, the Haussmannian boulevards flanked by tall stone buildings, and the stalls of the *bouquinistes* down by the river:

> We wander along the Rue la Hachette of the *Narrow Street*, and

gaze at the Hotel Normandie. Visit St Suplice, with pidgeons in the square. Also the museum of modern art . . . We sit in a park, among flowering trees watching the children in the sun, the little boys wearing pinyfores. A dusty little church near St Severin called St Julien le Pauvre. We see two more weddings, 1st and 2nd class. At each the guests wear mourning. Sat outside the Deux Maggots watching the students, the lovely women and the bearded men. Indescribably nostalgia everywhere. Later we went on the Metro to Montmartre which is so evil. Hundreds of drunk Americans lying about, and prostitutes and negroes, and great neon signs.[21]

On their last evening they dined again outside Les Deux Magots, eating steak and drinking Cinzano, 'I never want to leave',[22] she wrote later that night.

But Beryl's distinctive looks, and the incongruous discrepancy in age between herself and George, inevitably attracted attention, bringing to the fore the question of what exactly the relationship between them was. Although she found George kind and charming, and his obvious feelings of attraction to her were in stark contrast to Austin's frustrating reticence, she began to see that George was too old for her, incapable of the sort of romantic gestures and spontaneity she craved: 'I want suddenly for G to kiss me but he is not sure of him[self], and I become irritated. Firme t'a geule, I want to cry.'[23]

The final straw came when a student, mistaking George for Beryl's father, tried to pick her up in a café:

It was not till we began drinking coffee that the party of students came in and sat by us. I could only see the men wore jerseys and shorts and some had little fluffy beards and no moustaches, and that the women were firm and dark clothed with hair tied up with ribbons. The Colonel did not even glance up, he was too weary all at once, holding his cup with a tired white hand. And when the man with the red beard leant forward and spoke to me, he did not look up.

'You are very pretty', said the man quite loudly in English, smiling round at his companions. And then 'Won't your father go home soon?'

The Colonel looked at me while this was said, and I looked away at the door of the café, clothed in little spotted curtains. And all at once our friendship was like the dream you might have at a feast, of soft white bread, and looking down you find it crumbling greyly between your fingers.[24]

Their last night in the hotel room was a bit of an ordeal, inducing in Beryl a kind of existential panic about what she was doing with a man old enough to be her father:

> There was nothing more to talk about once we sat facing each other across the bed, drinking the wine, and as long as I looked straight at him I was not lost. Look away however from the familiar thin face with the cold eyes and I was utterly alone in a strange country with a perfect stranger . . . And so I grimaced at him and waited to be brave. Of course we were old friends, who shall deny it. And he was too tired of an old old habit and I too sick of an old old wound to spoil things by clumsiness and disregard.[25]

Back in London it didn't take long for reality to start creeping in: 'When I returned here a letter from Mummy sends me a cutting of one of A's exhibitions. I want to cry, but go out and meet George for dinner.'[26]

For the next few days, while George remained in London, they continued to see each other. He would either come to Parliament Hill or they would go out to the theatre or for dinner at Fava's, and her feelings for him intensified once more: 'I love him very much. Again I am unhappy.'[27] When George left to go back to Formby – and his wife – she went to see him off at the station: 'I felt so lost having to say good-bye and did not know what to do.'[28]

But despite her indecision things were moving to a close. On his return to Formby, George seems to have had second thoughts. He wrote saying that he thought Edith suspected something, a hint that they might need to cool things off. Beryl noted in her diary that the idea that she might make them unhappy made her feel 'a little sick', though she still loved him 'very much'.[29] For a few days after his departure she was wracked by conflicting emotions ('Oh my dear little George, where are you? Do you miss me? And Austin? Oh you too!'),[30] but without George's physical presence it was easier to separate herself from him. Coming so soon after her involvement with Hugh, the ease with which she had got herself mixed up with another married man, and the realization that deep down her need to be loved outweighed any moral or ethical considerations, scared her: 'A letter from George today, full of love, and I miss him. But I am such a bad bad girl, I frighten myself.'[31]

Whether it was Beryl or George who initiated the final break isn't clear: the entry in the diary about his letter is her last reference to George, and he effectively disappears from the scene. In any event she now had more immediate concerns to worry about: three days after her return from Paris, Robert Lawson had asked her to marry him – and the situation with Ronnie Harris was beginning to get out of hand.

Ronnie Harris was an antiques dealer who lived with his wife, Cheryl, just down the road, at 8 Parliament Hill. In an almost literal sense Ronnie was a self-made man: born Ronald L. Harris in 1916, after his marriage in 1946 he simply added his middle name to give himself the more distinguished-sounding double-barrelled surname of Lowther Harris.

In later life Ronnie would boast that Beryl had written a book about him and that they had a passionate affair, conducted 'on and off' over a number of years. According to Ronnie, after one night of passion Beryl had said to him 'I've never given you anything' and had written him a large cheque – only to send her accountant round the next day to retrieve it.[32] Much of this is wishful thinking, though it's true Ronnie figured as a character in her novel *A Weekend with Claud*, and on at least one occasion Beryl did lend him money.

What is more certain is that, from the very first, Ronnie was violently attracted to Beryl. At the time of her trip to Paris with George, Beryl knew Ronnie only slightly, having met him in passing the way people who live on the same street occasionally do. Nevertheless, Beryl was aware of his feelings towards her – a few weeks previously, as she was going past Ronnie's flat, he had invited her in to meet his wife, who was six months pregnant, and their three young children. As he showed Beryl out, he tried to kiss her in the hall. At the time, she had noted her sense of distrust about him ('There is something fake somewhere . . .'),[33] but despite this obvious warning sign and her own misgivings, she continued to see him in a series of cat-and-mouse meetings that were clearly intended, on his part at least, to offer the possibility of seduction: 'At about 1 a.m. there was a rattle on my window and Ronnie was there, in a muffler. The car was parked in South Hill Road, and we went a drive up beyond the pond. He is so nice, but I cannot place him as yet. He is a little infatuated with me, but I do not know what to make of him . . . Got home at 3 a.m. With what excuse I wonder?'[34]

Ronnie was a larger-than-life character,[35] and nothing if not persistent. Although he presented a somewhat comical image, 'clad in white trews and a sailor blazer and his beard in tiny tendrils', Beryl wasn't the only one to be seduced, metaphorically if not literally, by his patter and by his swaggering self-confidence. Even so, one can't help feeling that Beryl's passive acquiescence to his whims was as pathological as his need to constantly importune her. In one of those acts of rashness in relation to men that frequently exasperated her close friends, Beryl arranged to meet Ronnie, alone, in his shop in Chelsea: 'In the little back room he lit three candles on a bracket on the wall and we had ham and tea and grapes. Finally he told me he was in love with me, and how he only made love to Cherry three times a year, how she was cold, and how it was a barrier between them. As I listened I got more and more desolate. What on earth, I told myself, am I doing here, in an antique shop with a man with a beard and four children?'[36]

But there were limits even to Beryl's passivity. Despite her reluctant fascination, deep down she distrusted him and preferred the company of Robert or Freddie. Even so, rather than confront Ronnie she preferred to hide whenever he called, or huddle close to the wall when she passed his house in case he saw her. After a few more random and seemingly unsuccessful seduction attempts, he disappeared back into his own hectic concerns – for a while at least, though he would reappear in Beryl's life at sporadic intervals over the next twenty years.

The complicated relationships with Hugh, George, Robert, Freddie and Ronnie weren't the only ones that were drawing to an end in the autumn of 1953. Out of the blue, Lyn, for so long Beryl's confidante, co-conspirator, teacher, muse and role model, experienced for the first time what she had perhaps been looking for all along: true love. Ever since their schooldays together Lyn's letters to Beryl had included running commentaries on her passing fancies and passions, the boys and men who were drawn to her being cast off almost as soon as she had captivated them: Phil, Sandy, Geoff, Ralph, Rufus, Bill, Charles, all had their moment in the sun, but all had been found wanting. Then in August, while working as a bus conductress on the Isle of Wight, Lyn met Rik Medlik and fell completely and absolutely in love.

Unlike Lyn's previous passions this one didn't fade, and embarrassed now by her past life she began to distance herself from it. She and Beryl went to see Charles in order to retrieve the letters she'd written to him and put a final end to that whole episode. Beryl looked on, by turn cringing with embarrassment at Charles's humiliation and feeling elated at his final comeuppance.[37]

Whether Lyn was simply too taken up with Rik or felt that Beryl was inextricably linked to a past she wanted to forget, the result was the same: they began to drift apart. In a letter to Beryl in August, Lyn complained that her friends had reacted to the news of her unbounded happiness with Rik in a decidedly lukewarm fashion, and her pointed criticism seems also to have been directed at Beryl. Although she wouldn't have admitted it, least of all to Lyn, Beryl couldn't help but feel envious of her friend's new-found bliss, especially when she considered the current state of her own relationships.

Lyn also disapproved of Beryl's conduct with the Colonel. Flirting with him and constructing a joint fantasy about an affair was one thing – doing it in reality was another. There was a world of difference between Lyn's comical evocations of galloping through Formby on horseback and Beryl actually spending a weekend in Paris with him. Although she was rarely at a loss for words and not shy in giving her opinion, Lyn could barely bring herself to mention the Paris trip: 'I saw G[eorge] last night. I don't know what to make of it',[38] was all she would say. Although on the surface they remained friends, they saw one another less and less, and things would never be the same between them.

As autumn progressed Beryl's situation looked bleak. On the work front things had dried up completely. Apart from a week at Maidstone in July, reprising the role of Hazel Nutt in *King of the Castle*, she had

had no theatrical work since the live television performance in May and was beginning to get desperate. In lieu of proper work, she eked out small amounts of pocket money by babysitting for Ronnie and Cherry. Ronnie, still completely infatuated, would also take Beryl out and give her money from time to time.

She was also unsettled by Robert's proposal. Initially, she had wanted to laugh, but he was in deadly earnest and she had to spend the next few weeks trying to assuage his hurt feelings at her refusal. Inevitably talk of marriage prompted thoughts about Austin, and she would imagine him walking by her side, holding her hand: 'Oh God! how unhappy I am. I really am.'[39]

November started as desultorily as the previous month had ended. A seemingly endless round of overwrought meetings with Robert, strange encounters with Ronnie, and tearful regrets about her missed chance of happiness with Austin. Towards the end of the month, Beryl returned to Formby to spend her birthday with her parents. At some point she met Austin and there seems to have been another emotional scene between them – in any event two pages from her diary, covering her birthday and the following day, have been ripped out. Whatever it was that was recorded and subsequently destroyed, the next entry a week later said all that needed to be said: 'Austin and I have made it up again.'[40]

The following day, before Beryl returned to London, they talked about the future. Austin confessed he'd been unaware of the extent to which Beryl had misread his actions, and he now committed himself to break with his life in Liverpool and work towards creating a new life for them in London. A few days later he wrote to her, going over all they had talked about, trying to be positive in the face of negative thoughts about the past and the practical difficulties that lay in the future. Inevitably, his disastrous affair with Anne hung over the letter like a black cloud:

> My dear Beryl, if only, seems to be all I can say to myself, and even that seems to be an excuse. What a waste of time and money there has been. I think of what life is and then what it could be, or what we could make of it. I think of all I have written and the promises I have made, and I am reduced to nothing.
>
> The mixed feelings, mostly of despair and depression, which I feel when I know the profound misery I have caused, overcome me so that

I can see no solution to our problem, it seems too great for there to be any solution. Yet I know with my mind that things are not so bad . . . I can and will make enough money to afford a Chelsea studio and to afford to get married . . .

It would be an insult to ask you to believe anything after what has passed – it is even impossible for me to believe myself now. I can only hope, as do you, that what seems eventually inevitable is not also just another delusion. I can only reassure you that what we discussed when you were here has not become, because of the passage of time, a fantasy. It is real, or as real as anything feels now. But I feel so continually guilty. I wish to expiate, but am unable.[41]

But even with the engagement back on, their relationship seemed ominously precarious, each prone to doubts about themselves and about each other. Rumours about Austin's past girlfriends still played on Beryl's mind and she couldn't stop herself from asking him about them, provoking a peeved response: 'I have no engagement with Toni or any other girls! How could you even think that I could prefer another girl to you?'[42] He tried to convince her, and himself too, that he had changed, that she could trust her feelings with him: 'Beryl, I too am afraid of myself, afraid that again the separation will come, but believe me I will not change towards you, it is almost something over which I have no control this wandering of mine. Really I think I am ready now. I am sick, as you are, of playing at being in love, the word love has almost no meaning for me, I am sick of wandering about aimlessly, of living in the present.'[43]

They spent the weekend before Christmas in a charming cottage in North Wales, walking each day for miles and returning for meals. They listened to the wireless, read from Osbert Sitwell's autobiography *Left Hand Right Hand*, and went to bed. As Austin put it in his journal, it was 'uneventful but most pleasant'.[44] This was hardly a fulsome expression of passion.

Beryl returned to London in the New Year, but she had not been back long before she contracted an infection on her lungs.[45] A day or so later the young assistant stage manager she had met at Dundee Rep the previous year, Maggie Dickie, now working in London at the Prince of Wales Theatre, came round and noticed that Beryl was coughing up blood into her handkerchief. She consulted Mrs Hannah, the landlady, and they decided it was serious enough to call Winnie, who immediately took her back to Formby. Beryl was taken to hospital, where she lay racked by fits of coughing and groaning 'Christ!' over and over again during the night, until the woman in the next bed told her to shut up.[46] After repeated X-rays the chest specialist concluded that her symptoms – a chronic cough, shortness of breath, chest pain and coughing up blood – were suggestive of bronchiectasis, a condition in which the airways become damaged, probably caused by her bout of pneumonia in 1940.[47]

As the wedding approached, Austin continued to have serious doubts and seemed unable to convince himself he was making the right decision. His barely subconscious desire for flight was reflected in an impractical idea that he needed to live abroad to further his work as an artist. Fed up with what he saw as the provincialism of Liverpool, he applied for a travelling scholarship, though how Beryl fitted into these plans wasn't entirely clear in his mind: 'The fact that I am re-engaged to Beryl makes no difference to my desire to travel, could make no difference. I am bored by now with my vacillations with regard to Beryl. Now I regret – and only a month has passed since I last saw her – my re-engagement. I know very well I cannot marry her, nor I think anyone, but perhaps next year or even next week I shall feel and think differently. I am beginning to be rather weary of my indecisive nature.'[48]

FOURTEEN

Married Life

> I who have reached my destination and struggled with all my
> strength now have resigned myself. Now begins the dawning
> of placidity, the mature bloom on my mind. I am like an apple
> that has fallen heavy from the bough and is warm and yellow
> in the sunlight. But my husband is green and hard with the
> rain and his core is unformed and bitter to the taste, because
> he will not submitt.[1]

BERYL AND AUSTIN WERE married on 24 April 1954, in the
Catholic church of Our Lady of Victories, Hightown, a small
village on the coast a few miles south of Formby. Bill Bateman, Austin's
colleague at the College of Art who specialized in furniture design,
served as best man, and Lyn acted as bridesmaid.[2] Photographs show
a beaming Beryl, wearing an elegantly modern ballet-length dress of
cream Chantilly lace with bead embroidery and a coronet of lilies of
the valley. By contrast, Austin looks stiff and uncomfortable in his
three-piece suit, his jacket bunching up at the waist as if incorrectly
buttoned.

The wedding attracted more than usual attention in the press. Beryl's
connection to the Liverpool Playhouse and her appearance on television meant she was considered something of a minor celebrity, while
Austin was a local figure in his own right, not just as a lecturer and artist
but as the son of the city's most famous living architect. Significantly
Harold did not attend, though Nora did – the first time Beryl had met
Austin's errant mother.

After a reception for about seventy guests at the Hightown Hotel,
the newlyweds did not go on honeymoon as might have been expected.
Instead, they drove to New Brighton and took in a European film,

though whether the decision stemmed from Austin's refusal to spend money he did not have on something as indulgent and ephemeral as a honeymoon, or an equally determined refusal to bow to convention, isn't clear.

In many respects the wedding, supposedly the symbolic union of two individuals, served to highlight the differences between them. Austin, out of sympathy with what he saw as Beryl's overly sentimental and romantic streak, and unhappy at the idea of marrying in a Catholic church against his convictions as a committed atheist, looked back on it as a humiliating experience. The very recollection of it made him cringe with mortification. He had always hated formal occasions, and in any case he could never quite believe in Beryl's new-found Catholicism and all the theatricality that went with it.[3]

But there were other differences of opinion. Beryl wanted to have children immediately; Austin was adamant they should get themselves sorted out financially first – they simply didn't have enough money to start a family. He was trying to do the right thing, to be a responsible husband and provide a home and security for his wife and eventual family. Besides, in order for the relationship to work he felt they both needed to develop themselves as individuals, and that Beryl should continue to work as an actress for her own sake. While a lot of men of the period might have tried to prevent their wives from working, seeing a woman's economic independence as a challenge to their own power and authority, Austin insisted that Beryl should go out and work. As one of the local papers put it: 'She does not intend to leave the stage on her marriage.' A week before the wedding, on Good Friday, Beryl had even had an audition at the Liverpool Old Vic. But nothing came of it and here, as elsewhere, Austin's plans were frustrated. Beryl would only work twice in the theatre during the course of their marriage.

———

In common with the majority of newlyweds, the couple's first concern after the wedding was to find a place to live. As luck would have it one of Austin's fellow lecturers at the College of Art, Arthur Ballard, was moving out of his top-floor flat at 45 Catharine Street, a small but elegant Georgian terraced house with a decorative Ionic-pillared portico.

At the time such architectural flourishes were deemed old-fashioned, and when the house had been converted into flats the original period features inside, even the elegant banister rail, were cased in behind tongue-and-groove and plasterboard.

The next few months were taken up with the practical issues of settling in and decorating: Austin's taste was for more contemporary interior design, Bauhaus-style fittings that were simple and functional. One of the rooms was painted black – Beryl later wrote that her father wouldn't go in, saying it was nothing more than a funeral parlour[4] – and, as he had done in his studio in Hope Street, Austin covered over the old cast-iron fireplace with a piece of hardboard, drilled with little air holes and painted yellow. On the door at the top of the stairs leading to the flat he mounted a proprietorial brass plaque reading 'Mr and Mrs Austin Davies'.

The flat, situated conveniently close to the Art School in Hope Street, and a five-minute walk from the Greens' house and Austin's old studio, was a spacious one: kitchen with dining area, bathroom, bedroom, living room (the tiled fireplace surround of which Beryl decorated with painted flowers), studio, and a room that served as a store for Austin's paintings. A flea-infested cat, which they called Tolly – short for Ptolemy – and which featured in one of Austin's early portraits of Beryl, lived in the cupboard under the stairs. On a fine day you could see the Welsh mountains from the skylight in the attic, which was filled with paintings, an etching press, and other bits they didn't know what to do with.[5]

From the three sash windows on the top floor Beryl could look out over St Bride's church opposite and up to the magnificent, if slightly foreboding, central tower of Giles Gilbert Scott's Anglican cathedral, a monumental building even by cathedral standards. Beryl's church of choice, however, was the small Catholic church of St Philip Neri, three minutes down the road. Although it wasn't particularly old, having been designed around 1920, it had an ornate and pretty Byzantine-style brick exterior, and was decorated inside with mosaics, giving it something of a bright Mediterranean feel.

In 1954 Catharine Street and the area around Liverpool 8 was not what it is today, an enclave of re-gentrified and high-priced properties.[6] Although many of the houses had been built in the nineteenth century, at the height of Liverpool's economic power, since the turn of the century the city had been in a progressive decline: the wealthy had moved out from the centre to the more spacious suburbs, and the once-elegant terraces of Huskisson Street, Canning Street and Upper Parliament Street, together with the network of streets surrounding them, had been divided up into flats and bedsits. They had been taken over by Irish, Chinese and African immigrants, and by 'a colony of native artists, musicians, poets and layabouts', as George Melly put it, who were drawn to the area by cheap rents. 'Liverpool 8 had a seedy but decided style; its own pubs and meeting places; it was small enough to provide an enclosed stage for the cultivation of its own legend.'⁷ In short, this was Liverpool's bohemia.

At the Greens' dinner parties Austin and Beryl would mix with university types, artists and musicians. A flavour of these evenings, with the talk at table constantly revolving around artistic matters and which seemed to Beryl like a cultural sparring match, is fleetingly captured in a passage from *A Weekend with Claud*:

> And then the dinners for six or seven, wine with each course . . . 'Well, you see painting doesn't purely represent the visual aspect . . .' and . . . 'I thought Bernard played a little too fast . . .' and 'Maybe I should take up philosophy.'⁸

They would go to concerts at the Liverpool Philharmonic, where they heard Holst's *The Planets* and Andrés Segovia playing a guitar concerto conducted by Hugo Rignold (who sat for one of Austin's portraits, described by the *Manchester Guardian* as being 'of great refinement and sensibility').⁹ But such evenings always had the potential for conflict: Austin took music seriously, appreciating it as an intellectual experience, whereas Beryl's more emotional, physical response, her habit of whistling and tapping to music that moved her, and fidgeting during any that didn't, distracted and annoyed him. Going to the cinema was no better. Austin preferred realistic dramas that dealt with serious issues, whereas Beryl's taste ran to a different order. When she and Austin went to see *A Song to Remember*, a romanticized biopic about Chopin, he dismissed it as rubbish and the subsequent argument ended with Beryl bursting into tears.

Although there don't seem to have been many public squabbles, the temperamental differences between them remained a source of potential irritation. Bubbling away under the surface, these tensions would crystallize around certain issues and suddenly erupt: religion was one ('Last night in bed Austin stubbed his foot against the metal hot water bottle and screamed out "Christ". Why should this be so hurtful to me?');[10] personal grooming was another. Austin admired Beryl for her beauty and he couldn't understand why she wouldn't take more care over her appearance or became so defensive and prickly whenever he suggested she comb her hair before they went out.[11] To Beryl his attitude seemed just like her mother's, worrying too much about what other people might think. She didn't want to be told what she should wear or how she should look: she no longer took it from her mother and she wasn't going to take it from her husband either.

Housekeeping was another issue that generated conflict. Much as Austin wanted to focus on the significant things in life – his art, philosophical ideas, social engagement – he couldn't help regretting the little home comforts that, as a man, he'd come to expect. But Beryl had not been trained by her mother in the traditionally feminine domestic accomplishments of cleaning, washing and cooking. Austin was in some ways more advanced in his attitudes than many men of his generation, but he still saw the division of labour within the household in conventional terms: if he was out working all day earning money, surely the least Beryl could do was cook a decent meal and keep the house tidy?

Life in Catharine Street marked a sharp contrast with Beryl's previous existence in London. Although the constant to-ing and fro-ing of life in Hampstead and the fraught emotional dramas involving Freddie and Noel, Ken and Robert, Ronnie and Hugh had been detrimental to her emotional stability, they had at least provided a distraction. Now she was married and out of the capital, this network of male friendships dissolved overnight. With Austin either at the Art School or closeted in his studio doggedly pursuing his work as an artist, Beryl had to find new friends, new amusements and new activities to fill the void.

In London, Beryl's circle of friends had mostly been actors or those involved in the theatrical world. Now that she was back in Liverpool not only did her correspondence with Ken, Hugh, Noel and Gerald cease, she seems to have deliberately avoided socializing with her former Playhouse colleagues, despite the expectation that she would return to the theatre.

Instead, in the early years of her marriage, Beryl's social world revolved around Austin and his close friends. Aside from the gatherings and dinner parties at the Greens', there were parties at the Frohlichs' huge house on Greenheys Road. There were also evenings down at the pub. They would usually either be at The Philharmonic on Hope Street, an ornate wood-panelled dining room-cum-saloon with art deco fittings, which, as its name suggests, was practically opposite the Philharmonic Hall and was the haunt of musicians and university types; or at Ye Cracke, a more intimate, less grandiose pub in Rice Street, which had been colonized by artists, art college lecturers and students.

There were numerous exhibition openings to attend, shows in which Austin or his colleagues had paintings, including private views for the annual Liverpool Academy show at the Walker Art Gallery, or smaller shows at the Bluecoat Chambers and the Sandon Studios Society. Through Austin, Beryl met many of the pivotal figures in the post-war Liverpool art scene over the next few years. They included Arthur Ballard, Nicholas Horsfield, Bill Stevenson, and the Hungarian-born emigré Georg Mayer-Marton, who had trained at the Academy of Fine Arts in Vienna in the 1920s.[12]

Another of Austin's close friends was the painter Don McKinlay, who had been a student with him in 1949. Don, described as 'direct, occasionally abusive, naturally talented in the basics of his chosen craft and uncompromising',[13] had studied under Arthur Ballard, and like Austin before him, was working as a scenery painter at the Liverpool Playhouse. He and his wife Helen would be regular visitors to Catharine Street over the next few years.

Beryl gradually began to form new friendships of her own. At one of the Frohlichs' parties she met Robert Shackleton, a geology professor at Liverpool University and a nephew of the Polar explorer. Shackleton was a highly respected geologist with the ability to illuminate his subject in conversation with others, but he was also unconventional in both dress and manner. His habit of quizzically raising both eyebrows as he listened to his interlocutors could be off-putting. One of his colleagues recalled that during a field trip to Connemara he would 'progressively strip off layers of clothing' while driving back to the hotel, and that when he pulled into the forecourt he ran in naked so as to be the first in the bath.[14]

It was Robert's second wife, Judith, who would become one of Beryl's closest friends during this period. Judith was an artist and equally unconventional in matters of clothing, wearing floaty dresses and no bra.[15] Born in 1915, Judith was, if not exactly a mother figure to Beryl ('Judith was never maternal towards anybody, including her children',[16] as her daughter put it), at least more sympathetic to her problems than Winnie. Their friendship served many of the same functions as that with Lyn had done, and over the next twenty-five years Beryl would write long letters to Judith, keeping her up to date on the vicissitudes of her fraught and complex emotional life.

The Shackletons hosted a number of parties at their home: they lived in a converted stables at the back of a massive Victorian house about a mile and a half from Austin and Beryl's flat in Catharine Street. Less intimate and formal than evenings at the Greens', which tended to focus on conversation about political and artistic matters, and less intellectually high-powered than gatherings at the Frohlichs' (Robin Riley recalled meeting the quantum physicist and Nobel prize winner Erwin Shrödinger there one evening),[17] the Shackletons' parties were frequently described as 'wild' affairs. They provided an opportunity for students, lecturers and professors from a whole range of disciplines – geology, philosophy, medicine, art, music and physics – to mix with one another.

Another significant acquaintance was Dr Cyril Taylor, who became Beryl's doctor shortly after her marriage. Born to Orthodox Jewish parents in 1921, Taylor trained as a medical student during the war, but it was as much for his political activism as for his talents as a doctor that he became such a respected figure in Liverpool 8.[18] Taylor's house in Sefton Drive, where he lived with his wife Pat and their two children, was an important locus of activity for those on the political left, as well as for actors with the Unity Theatre, who would rehearse in the garden.[19]

Over the next decade Beryl would come to rely on Cyril for emotional support, as well as for medical advice, and always looked on him with affection: 'Cyril nice in his black moustache,' she wrote during one particularly traumatic period, 'if I won a fortune would give him and Pat some.'[20]

During his Easter break from the Art School in 1955, Austin took Beryl to Bardsey Island, off the Aberdaron coast of Wales. The facilities at the rented cottage, shared with Austin's brother Tony and his wife Zena, were fairly basic: when Beryl went outside to relieve herself, she noted how the searchlight from the lighthouse strayed over the grey stone wall in the garden and turned her shoes white.

The holiday was ostensibly to mark Austin and Beryl's first wedding anniversary, but neither seemed to be in celebratory mood. The windswept spot – there were no trees on the island – brought back memories of Beryl's wanderings in the Formby dunes, but the present seemed to pale in comparison to the past, provoking a wave of bleak nostalgia: 'Perhaps never again though will it be enough or ever the same joy just to lie in the grass, as it was years ago at home. The sky seems more limited somehow, yet as vast, but infinitely colder.'[21]

Austin was reflecting on the past, too, and still seemed to be uncertain as to whether he'd made the right decision: 'I was married a year ago April 24,' he noted in his journal, 'I do not yet know whether I shall regret this.'[22] Since the wedding he had been working hard on his painting, though his output always seemed to fall short of his unrealistic targets: 'I think that during the past year my average must have been about 3 every two weeks, this seems to be rather a small number considering I have four whole days freedom from teaching.' Equally 'depressing' was the fact that the money he made from the sales of his paintings was not commensurate with the amount of time he spent on them – his total sales for the previous year amounted to £500, a reasonable sum in those days, but nowhere near enough to allow him to give up his job.

Had he been content to continue working as a portrait painter he would no doubt have established a solid reputation for himself over the course of time. His work in the Liverpool Academy exhibition nearly always attracted favourable critical attention, and he had already made some important sales to art institutions. His portrait of Beryl, begun shortly after their wedding, was shown at the Liverpool Corporation's autumn exhibition under the title *Portrait of the Artist's Wife*. It was later bought by Manchester City Council for its permanent collection.

But like many artists of the period Austin was growing tired of representational art. He wanted his painting to be part of the modern consciousness, to be challenging, to be new. Aesthetically, he was drawn towards a kind of abstract expressionism, but he was continually being dragged back into portraiture as a means of making money.

Austin's exhibition at the prestigious Piccadilly Gallery in Cork Street, a month before the anniversary trip to Bardsey Island, was a perfect illustration of his artistic dilemma. Although the exhibition had gone well – he received a glowing notice in the *Daily Post* which described him as a 'painter of original and striking vision' and compared the effect of his 'strange and powerful'[23] paintings to the work of El Greco – most of the paintings that sold were figurative works, not those in his new abstract style.

Interestingly, and uniquely, Beryl had also exhibited alongside Austin at the Piccadilly Gallery – her first public appearance as an artist. In fact her work for the show consisted not of paintings, but of decorative painted plates, their craft feel presumably appealing to the gallery's owner, Godfrey Pilkington. How well the plates sold isn't mentioned, though significantly the experiment wasn't tried again.

Austin's frustration at his lack of commercial success undoubtedly contributed to the tensions between himself and Beryl. His dissatisfaction with the Liverpool art scene, which he felt was too provincial, too 'narrow and restricted', was reflected in what he saw as his 'ultimate aim' – that he and Beryl should move to London in the near future: 'Whenever I think of how we (I am even becoming accustomed to this collective term) could live in London. I become almost sick with suppressed excitement to live in a house in Hampstead with a studio overlooking the Heath, to be right in the middle of all that I value most.'[24]

But such plans would have to wait. Since the wedding, Beryl had hardly worked at all. She had gone back to the *Children's Hour* studios for a couple of small roles on radio – as Hilda in Grizelda Hervey's *Princess of Northumberland*, which was broadcast in 1954 and reunited her with Billie Whitelaw, and as Trudie, a lady-in-waiting, in Nan McDonald's adaptation of the Grimms' fairy tale *The Giant with the Three Golden Hairs* a year later. There was also a week-long engagement in *Jane Eyre* at Warrington in August 1955. But this did little to take the financial pressure off Austin. By the time she was offered some serious theatre work – an engagement for two plays at Windsor Rep, where Hugh Goldie was now resident director – Beryl had to turn the work down. As if to confirm Austin's fears, in the early summer of 1956, Beryl found she was pregnant.

FIFTEEN

The Summer of the Tsar

Put into words the sense of loss of you and I together
The firelight shining, and the children sleeping
The books never read
The valleys undiscovered, and
If I had the power I would fill you with enough love
Enough love for you and I together . . .[1]

H AVING A CHILD WAS something Beryl had longed for for years, a tangible proof of her bond with Austin. A year before they were married she had mused in her diary about having children, and had already come up with a list of names: 'When, if ever I have a girl-child I would wish it to be called Francesca. The boy-child of course Paul Aaron, and maybe Simon Peter.'[2] A story in her 'Fragments' book written in late 1953 abruptly breaks off and devolves into a series of doodles in which Austin's surname is combined with possible names for children: Paul Hinchcliffe Davies, Manuala Davies, Paul Aaron Davies and Paul Simon Bolivia Davies – showing that Beryl was attracted to the myth of the romantic revolutionary even if she couldn't spell his name.

When it finally happened, the pregnancy was not without its anxieties and difficulties, and Beryl's doctor friend, Cyril Taylor, suspected she might have a weak or 'incompetent cervix', as it was commonly termed. As a result, he wouldn't let her go on holiday – Austin had planned to take her to stay with the Greens at their cottage in Nefyn, North Wales – fearing she might lose the baby: 'He could not understand how I had even concieved as my stomach is funny,' she told Judith, 'and he did not think I could hold it . . . I must stay near a hospital.'[3]

Instead, she and Austin spent three weeks in London. The choice may have been dictated by medical reasons, but Austin saw it as an opportunity to visit galleries and to try to arrange an exhibition. In the event it was a less than satisfying holiday. Long-standing causes of tension, such as money and Austin's exacting expectations, were exacerbated by the physical and psychological complications of Beryl's condition. As she explained to Judith afterwards:

London for us was in so few ways suxcessful. I don't know why, just that it cost so much to get anywhere, it was a bit wet and stormy, things happened. To go for the day into town meant putting on nice clothes, blue and high shoes to feel more dressy and tall, and white gloves in the sunshine, mainly because one was a little spotty and not so nice in the face, an off-day, and A. does like me a little elegant which is never possible: Result – swollen feet within one hour, dirty gloves in 10 minuets, enormous sums of money for the privilage of travelling on a bus and eating even the smallest lunch, and because I caught a glimpse maybe of myself in a store window looking dreadful, or just a small look on A's face . . . not of distaste but dissappointment in me.[4]

The second week was even worse: Beryl spent the whole of it in hospital, 'with little Willie threatening to move to pastures new'. The final week dragged on, with Beryl, now out of hospital, lying on the couch feeling dreadful and attacking Austin, calling him a coward because he got cold feet at the thought of hawking his pictures around galleries.

On their return to Liverpool, Beryl made a final attempt to get some acting work. She had read in the *Manchester Guardian* that Otto Preminger was looking to cast an unknown actress in the role of Joan of Arc for his forthcoming film adaptation of Shaw's play, *Saint Joan*. Having already seen countless young actresses in America without success, Preminger had now come to England to hold an open audition, and so on 4 October Beryl sat among other would-be hopefuls in the anteroom of the Midland Hotel in Manchester. It was hardly a realistic plan – already four months pregnant she had to wear a corset to hide the bulge. Unsurprisingly she didn't get the part, which eventually went to Jean Seberg.

Now that acting work was ruled out and her condition precluded physical activity, Beryl passed the time at home in writing, using a typewriter for the first time. Prompted by the prospect of imminent motherhood, she began a projected series of children's stories, the first of which was entitled 'Ceedy Man and the Bellringers'. The stories, aimed at children of nursery or pre-school age, recount the amusing adventures of the eponymous Ceedy Man as he conducts his group of bellringers at various social events.

Although Beryl was never an ardent advocate of technology, she decided to submit a tape-recorded version of her story to the BBC. The idea had originated in an evening she and Austin spent at the Greens' a few years before, after Gordon had acquired a Baird reel-to-reel tape recorder and Beryl was able to listen to her own voice: 'When it was played back I sounded very clear and well-spoken and a trifle hesitant, most surprising.'[5] Austin had been taken with the machine and subsequently bought a Grundig, which Beryl used to record her stories.[6]

The first story was submitted to the head of *Children's Hour* at BBC Manchester. In August Denness Roylance wrote back saying she wanted to include it in the *Nursery Sing Song* programme for September and asked whether Beryl could come over and read it herself.[7]

'Ceedy Man and the Bellringers' is not, it is fair to say, a classic piece of children's literature. The stories were aimed at too young an audience to allow for any depth of characterization or narrative substance that might give them a broader or lasting appeal. One would have to look long and hard to find anything that might be considered an allusion, however distant, to a meaningful event or experience in Beryl's own life. Almost any passage from the stories gives as good a flavour of the whole as any other. This is the opening of the title story:

> Ceedy Man and the Bellringers lived in a very nice little house next door to the farm. Ceedy Man wore blue trousers and a little red jacket with gold buttons down the front, and on his head a jolly little straw hat with a curly brim. The Bellringers wore blue trousers too, and little red jackets with gold buttons down the front, but on their heads they wore little round, yellow caps. Because Ceedy Man wasn't actually a Bellringer himself. No, he was the conductor and wrote all the music while the others did what he told them.

There were five Bellringers. There was Mrs H. who rang the very tiny bell because her hands were so small, and Maison Dixey who was very fat and rang the biggest bell. And there was Mr Ta-Ta who played the next to largest bell, and William Henry and Bluebell who played the duets and had their names on the programme in a special kind of print because they were different from the others. They all played every where on all the great occasions in the village. At weddings and birthdays and christenings, and sometimes when any important visitor arrived at the station and was met by the Mayor.[8]

Although the BBC recordings have long since been wiped, Beryl's distinctive reading style undoubtedly gave the stories a quality that is lacking on the printed page. The BBC seemed happy with the result, and a follow-up story, 'Ceedy Man and the Christening', was broadcast at the end of November. Six months later another story was commissioned, and in June 1957 Beryl returned to the studios in Manchester to read 'Ceedy Man and the Mysterious Visitor'.[9] Despite their relatively insubstantial nature, the stories provided Beryl with her first positive experience of writing, showing that it was possible to earn money with her pen: for writing and reading each story she received £7.7s (this was when the BBC still paid fees in guineas), as well as her ten-shilling return fare to Manchester.

At the same time as she was producing these anodyne stories Beryl conceived another writing project that was a truer reflection of her personal and creative interests. The catalyst was a report in a two-year-old newspaper, about the New Zealand murder case in which Honorah Parker was killed by her teenage daughter and her best friend. The trial, referred to as the Parker-Hulme case after the names of the two girls involved, was the subject of considerable coverage in the *Liverpool Echo*, after the news broke on 8 August 1954. Beryl was probably drawn to the story not just because one of the girls, Juliet Hulme, was originally from Southport, but because there were a number of parallels between the obsessional friendship of the two murderers and her own intense friendship with Lynda South. Parker and Hulme both kept diaries, and they also wrote letters to each other using adopted personas, not unlike Beryl and Lyn who had written themselves into their own fictional stories and whose letters often blended fact and fantasy. In much the same way that Parker and Hulme's parents were unhappy at the closeness of the two girls' friendship, Beryl's and Lyn's parents each suspected their daughter's friend of being an unhealthy influence.

The Parker-Hulme case may have been the inspiration for 'The Summer of the Tsar', as Beryl called the resulting novel, but it is in no way a fictional version of it. In fact Beryl used a procedure that served as a template for a number of her later books, incorporating elements of her own experience or those of people she knew into a plot structure taken from a newspaper story. In later life, Beryl would repeatedly describe the novels that resulted from this process of blending real life and fiction as 'autobiographical',[10] though they are not autobiographical in any strict sense of the term.

This is clear even from a casual reading of the text. Leaving aside the murder itself, the book is full of incidents that have no correlation to the actual events of Beryl's life: she was not locked in the church with George Greggs; she and Lyn did not spy on him and his wife having sex in their living room; nor did George ply her with drink as a child in an attempt to seduce her. Added to which, as Beryl's diaries show, 'The Summer of the Tsar' is not based on her experiences as a thirteen-year-old, but on her and Lyn's semi-playful, but ethically dubious, flirtation with George in 1953 when she was almost twenty-one.[11]

Although a complete manuscript from this period no longer exists, a number of handwritten drafts do, along with some pages from what looks to be a typescript that was sent to publishers. From these it is clear that 'The Summer of the Tsar' would have been a stunning debut novel. Although obviously in need of serious copy-editing, the text is in many places almost identical to the book Beryl published under the title *Harriet Said* in 1972.

The manuscript of 'The Summer of the Tsar' also reveals something of Beryl's working methods. Despite having a typewriter, Beryl preferred to write out sections in long hand, which she would read through again and amend. This draft would then be typed out, in the course of which it would undergo more revisions. Later, when she had children, Beryl would say that she wrote at night because that was when the children were asleep, but this habit seems to have formed early on, as one of the pages of the manuscript contains a note to Austin written late at night and left for him to see in the morning.

In a somewhat symbolic piece of timing, Beryl finished the manuscript of 'The Summer of the Tsar' and gave birth to her first child at around the same time – February 1957 – though it would not be until the end of May that she had a clean typed copy to send out to publishers.

The first publisher Beryl approached, Hodder & Stoughton, turned it down. Hodder must have returned the manuscript sometime in the autumn, as John McDougall at Chapman & Hall, the next publisher on Beryl's list, wrote to reject it in December, though he at least offered some encouragement: 'We have read with some interest, and some distress, the typescript of your first novel, THE SUMMER OF THE TSAR. We found much in it to praise and consider it a very creditable effort as a first attempt from an author of your age.'[12]

The ambivalence of the letter piqued Beryl – if they thought it praiseworthy and creditable, why did they turn it down? She wrote back, asking them to explain in what way it was distressing and why they thought it an 'unfortunate subject' for a novel given the wide exposure in the press that the New Zealand murder case had received. McDougall replied:

> I quite understand that the newspaper case only served to set your imagination on its way, and I suppose that your picture of two girls looking in a sort of existentialist way for experience is a logical development of the theme. But what repulsive little creatures you have made them, repulsive almost beyond belief! And I think the scene in which the two men and the two girls meet in the Tsar's house is too indecent and unpleasant even for these lax days. What is more, I fear, that even now a respectable printer would not print it!
>
> If you don't get someone else to show interest in this book I shall of course be glad to see your next. But you shouldn't take my word on this one; why not try it on some other house?[13]

A few months later she took McDougall's advice, sending off the manuscript to Anthony Brett-Jones at Chatto & Windus. Despite praising the novel even more fully – he was perceptive enough to pick up on its black humour – and offering some positive encouragement, he too refused it:

> Although we have decided with regret that we cannot make you an offer of publication, we have been distinctly impressed with your novel, which is freshly and audaciously written, has a personal flavour, and contains some effective comic passages . . . We feel that the

book hovers rather uneasily between the lighthearted and the grave, between near-farce action and near-tragic, and it would . . . be rather a difficult novel to sell . . . However, we admire the talent you display in this work and should be keenly interested to see anything else you may write in the future.[14]

At the time Beryl was too insecure to take anything positive from these comments and became very discouraged about her writing.[15] Consequently, it would be a number of years before she tried fiction again and instead she turned to painting as a more immediate creative outlet, though this decision was probably also a result of the difficulty of trying to write while looking after a young baby.

———

On 5 February 1957 Beryl gave birth by forceps delivery to a boy. Although registered as Paul Aaron, the baby's first name was quickly dropped as Beryl had always liked the sound of Aaron, which had been inspired by D. H. Lawrence's 1922 novel, *Aaron's Rod*. This didn't go down well with her father. His objection was in no way anti-Semitic – Beryl always adduced her own empathy for Jews to her father's influence – but rather stemmed from a feeling that Beryl was being deliberately unconventional in her decision to spurn traditional Bainbridge family names. He felt it was pretentious, another example of her showing off.

Richard nevertheless idolized his grandson, though he persisted in calling him Paul: 'Come on little chickie, sit on Grandpa's knee, little Paul. I love you . . . Kiss your old Grandpa, Paul.'[16] Despite Cyril Taylor's concerns during the pregnancy, Aaron was a healthy baby, almost too healthy: 'He threatens to weigh 3 stone before his 5 month,' as Beryl informed Judith. 'His legs are monuments of pillargetic art. Not that he stands squarely on them by any means. You could hold a cigarette in the folds of his knees. Nothing fits him, he has grown out of his 2nd year vests.'[17]

In July, Austin took the family on holiday to Barcenaciones, a small village near Santander in Spain. Somewhat rashly, he decided to go by car. The previous year he had bought a pre-war Austin London taxi that must have looked extravagantly antiquated even in the 1950s, and thereby joined a growing band of vintage motor-car enthusiasts in the neighbourhood, such as Fritz Spiegl who had a 1924 Rolls Royce, and Mike Pugh Thomas who had a Bull-nose Morris. In a letter to Judith Shackleton four days after acquiring their taxi, Beryl excitedly drew a picture and described it: 'This is ours. It is a 1935 Taxi, huge with a John Peel horn, and a hood that lets down, and in beautiful condition. It holds about 10 people and is lovely. No more hiring taxi's, this will carry the Walker Art Gallery. It cost £40, and so far it is running beautifully. Austin is very much the proud Papa, and leans out of the window all day to admire it.'[18]

But the taxi, christened 'Leocardia' by Beryl,[19] had its drawbacks. There were no locks, it was awkward to drive, and the driver had to sit in his own compartment separated off from passengers in the rear, the space next to him being used to store luggage. The idea of driving it – with a five-month-old child on board – on a journey of over 800 miles across France and into Spain was adventurous to say the least, but despite a number of scary moments along the way, against all odds the car made it, as Beryl later recounted to the Shackletons:

I do not know how to begin. The sleeping out at night was awful. Such a diving of mosquitos and a crawling of wee and untimerous beasties I have never known. I feel I am scarred for life. My screams and sudden alarms have been heard across France. In France Austin remembered we were in Emile Zola country, 'Earth, do you know it? Very sensual and bad and sensational.' One early morning being fast in a ditch in a field I walked to a farm for help, saying over my shoulder to Austin I wondered if they had heard of Emile Zola. Came a big exasperated row, because he thought I wanted to discuss books and he was still in the ditch. We did not speak for a day and a half. We ate loaves and cheese and lemonade for four days, while Leocardia steamed steadily on . . . The villa was horrid, like a brown box with a hat on, and no furniture or carpets, and that is all. Then Donna Catalina arrived to bid us welcome to Spain. She is 79, Irish and delightfully incoherent. She lives in a Palazio across the way, an immense building with a tower of pink stone, and wodern galliries running all the way round the four stories. When we said we thought the villa a little bare she thoughtfully hammered in three nails to hang our somberos on.

We have a bath of spiders, and sort of hot water. The lavabo does not work, and there is a bidet, also broken. We share electric light, which means tonight we have it, tomorrow we don't . . . Two days ago a lady with a bosem strung with pearls and a pair of tortoishell glasses arrived and sat in our hall for 6 hours. We could think of nothing to say. The next day she returned. Donna C. informed us she was a prostitute and would stay a day and a night for 100 piasetas.

The car, a rare enough sight in rural Spain, caused disruption and amazement wherever they went: 'The beach we go to is hot and mostly deserted. All the way there we have a triumphant ride. Donkeys race ahead, their riders screaming out a warning to the villagers, children are snatched up, cattle beaten frantically into the ditch, a harsh cry of wonderment and awe. Austin grinning like a fiend honks the horn and doffs his sombero. An old man on seeing us suddenly jumped [into] a hedge and his wife waved her fist at us. Leocardia being covered with a fine white dust is looking superb.'

But even without the car they were objects of curiosity in this pre-mass-tourism era:

Twice we have been approached by civil gaurd carrying bren guns. We have been once to a biggish town Torre la Vega, but the people stood silently in a ring round us and followed us from stall to stall. There is something unnerving about a fleet figure running down a side street and reappearing with several others to stand silently and with disbelieving eyes, to watch us go by. Also there were sheep tied by their feet, lying in the street on their backs, giving cries like desperate hungry children stricken with croup. And a hen with a crushed leg, quite mute, with its face to the kerb. I did try to be aloof and unbritish, but all me instincts were to write a letter to the Times.[20]

At the start of 1958 Beryl got an offer of a two-week stint in a production of *Jeannie*, due to open at the Liverpool Playhouse in February. It was a play she had studied ten years previously with Mrs Ackerley in order to practise her Scottish accent. But Austin's hopes that this signalled a more permanent return to work in the theatre were dashed again. By the time the play opened, Beryl discovered she was two months pregnant.

She received a mention for her 'neat cameo' in the part of Maggie, acting alongside the future *Coronation Street* star Thelma Barlow, but it would be the last time Beryl appeared on a theatre stage.

Realizing that the top-floor flat at Catharine Street was unsuitable for his growing family, Austin began looking round for somewhere larger with its own garden. In June he took on a leasehold mortgage for £900 and purchased a terraced house, 22 Huskisson Street, just round the corner from Catharine Street. The new house represented a step up from a flat, with its extra space and garden. On the ground floor was a large living room with a fireplace, its walls covered in Sanderson wallpaper with a Sicilian lion motif, a studio at the back, in which Austin could paint, and the kitchen; upstairs was the bedroom with its large brass bed, the children's nursery and the bathroom.

There were, however, some idiosyncrasies that took a bit of getting used to. The bathroom contained a tub rather than a proper bath, and the large copper boiler that bulged from the wall was notoriously difficult to light. It made a deafening retort when it finally caught, and the rest of the time it produced a slight but constant smell of gas. The bathroom and boiler would feature in one of Beryl's paintings of the time, which shows the children playing in the tub. Beryl herself made do with washing in the sink.

Something else that took some getting used to was the fact there was a sitting tenant in a self-contained flat on the second floor, Nellie Zealandia Liddiard, who owned the Liddiard clinic in Bold Street specializing in hair removal through electrolysis. Nellie's increasingly eccentric attitude – Beryl claimed she had a phobia about electricity and wore rubber gloves to switch the lights on – began to get bothersome and one night she was found in the children's bedroom waving a torch. Eventually, in an attempt to force her out, Beryl would organize GRON (Get Rid of Nellie) parties, and these finally resulted in her moving out in 1961.

There were other eccentric characters on the street as well. Just down the road was Dr Kefalas, who lived on the corner at number 14. Beryl referred to him as 'the mad doctor'. In his late fifties, Dr Kefalas would come round unannounced and in the course of his visits give her graphic details of things he'd seen during his time in practice, such as when a man had stuck his fingers up a woman's nostrils and tore them apart.[21]

Huskisson Street was still in the process of gentrification, and it was partly the resulting social mix, the poor living side by side with the newly affluent, that gave the area its dynamic. Brenda Powell, one of Austin's art students who became a friend of Beryl's, recalls that in the late 1950s prostitution was still rife in the neighbourhood. On summer evenings she and Beryl would sit with their legs sticking out of the first-floor window and resting on the small balcony, and watch the nightly ballet of policemen trying to chase prostitutes off their beat.[22]

On one side, her neighbours were the Wenton family, Beryl's published recollections of whom were a typical mix of misinformation and exaggeration: 'I lived . . . next door to an albino lady from Scotland who was married to a Portuguese West African. They had 19 children.'[23] Beryl was fascinated by their seemingly unruly lifestyle, and her diary for 1959 records an incident in which the Wenton's oldest son Ritchie met her by chance and proceeded to tell her he'd got into a little bother over an unwanted preganancy: 'This morning Ritchie ruined my reputation with the butcher . . . We discussed at some length, while I chose the joint, the last paternity order. Said he told the girl's brother he'd pull a flick knife on her if she bothered him. Butcher fairly goggled at this and charged me half as much again as usual for the modest lump of pork. Ritchie left by saying he was dodging "that coloured bastard me Dad".'[24]

By a happy coincidence, Beryl discovered that she already knew her new neighbour on the other side, Maggie Gilby, having met her in September 1956. Beryl had been sitting in the back of the St Philip Neri church, watching Robin McGhie paint a mural, when Maggie happened to come in. The two women started talking and discovered they had friends in common. Maggie had moved into 20 Huskisson Street six months prior to Beryl's arrival, and the fact that they were both young mothers – Maggie's son had been born shortly after Aaron – sealed their friendship.

For Austin, the move to Huskisson Street was also part of a larger scheme to make money. Attracted by the large sums that were being made in property development, his plan was to use the house to generate income, renting it out as flats when he and Beryl eventually moved to London. In the meantime he was increasingly involving himself in other redevelopment plans. At the College of Art, Austin had met Sam

Wanamaker, who, as the recently appointed director of the Shakespeare Theatre in Liverpool, had come up with the innovation of adding a dining club to the theatre. This idea inspired Austin to set up the Picasso Club, a casual, artist-friendly space in a derelict building in Upper Duke Street, where art students and lecturers could drink coffee and listen to music.

The Picasso Club was short-lived, but another venture soon afterwards offered the prospect of making some real money: Dorothy Green's 23 Club. Like the Sandon Club, a popular meeting place for the artistic and intellectual community located in Liverpool's Bluecoat Chambers, the 23 Club had aspirations of catering to a cultured clientele of artists and musicians, as it was located at 23 Hope Street, close to both the College of Art and the Philharmonic Hall. Dorothy turned for help to Austin, who, in turn, readily threw himself into the work, hoping to make enough money from the project to enable him to quit his teaching job and work full-time as a painter. In this, however, he would again be disappointed.

On 19 September 1958, Beryl gave birth to her second child, a daughter called Johanna Harriet, who soon acquired the nickname Jo-Jo. Beryl would later recall that winter 'with nappies by the fire and Jo-Jo on my knee, breast dripping milk, faces flushed, everything warm and protective'.[25] It was a wholesome, homely image, one that belied the growing tensions between herself and Austin. Within a year their marriage would come apart at the seams.

SIXTEEN

Separation

> This year has been . . . a mad summer. So much happening.
> Bren and Fritz, me and Mick, Aus and I splitting, Pugh and
> Julie, Wendy and Terry Moran seperating, Stevenson divorcing.
> The whole structure disintegrating. And I so sure we were not
> like the others.[1]

THE DEMANDS OF SETTING up the 23 Club were considerable. Austin was still teaching at the Art College, so the work ate
into his free time at weekends, when, in search of items to decorate
the Club, he would go to Paddy's market to buy up antique frames,
pictures and small bits of furniture. Time spent at the Club meant
time away from Beryl and the children, and inevitably there were
conflicts.

In Austin's defence, his view was that it was only by earning
money that he and Beryl could have the lifestyle they wanted – and
a successful and lucrative venture was even more imperative now
they had a family. Well-intentioned as it may have been, Austin's
relentless work ethic didn't make the demands of coping with two
young children any easier. Brenda Powell, who helped Beryl out with
baby-minding and shopping, felt that work on the 23 Club interfered with Austin's home life: 'Austin would come home and want
to play with the kids, and then the phone would go, and it would be
Dorothy Green: "We've been here since 5 o'clock, where are you?"
Austin would go off again.'[2]

But while the heavy workload didn't help, it wasn't the cause of the
problem. In later life, Beryl would give various reasons for the breakdown of her marriage. Sometimes she would lay the blame, half-jokingly,
on Colin Wilson's *The Outsider*, claiming that after reading it Austin

211

had gone off to live the life of an artist.[3] At others she would say it was the result of Austin's infidelity, that on returning from hospital after the birth of Jo-Jo, she'd found the remains of a breakfast for two on the kitchen table.[4] Variants of this account included Beryl peremptorily ordering him out of the house,[5] and the notion that their break-up led to her becoming a novelist: Austin had abandoned her with two children, 'So I started writing.'[6]

In reality the reasons for the breakdown were both more simple and more complicated than these neat, dramatic narratives allow, being the result of temperamental differences that had afflicted their relationship since its beginning. As far as Austin was concerned, Beryl was incapable of engaging with his interests on a rational, intellectual level: she was too emotional, making discussion impossible and arguments inevitable. He blamed himself for his inability to respond to what he saw as her neediness, but he found her impracticality, her irrationality, and her irresponsibility with money impossible to live with.[7] For Beryl, the fact that Austin felt his relationship with her wasn't enough was a personal reproach, a failure of love.

By the end of 1958 they were effectively leading separate lives, with Austin sleeping in the back studio. Things didn't improve over the next few months and in July 1959, taking advantage of his extended summer break from college, Austin went to Paris in order to think about how Beryl and the children would fit into his future.

From the Hôtel de la Place de l'Odéon, close to the Jardin de Luxembourg, he wrote to Beryl, telling her he wanted to 'improve matters and arrive at some understanding of myself. I must, you see, do something to attempt a solution.'[8] As in his letters of the past, Austin's references to beautiful and apparently predatory women seemed unconsciously designed to play on Beryl's jealousy and confirm her suspicions about his fidelity: 'Everybody keeps very much to themselves,' he told her shortly after his arrival, 'except for a very young and quite attractive American widow who keeps telling me in a most delightful southern accent that she sees no reason whatever for not going to bed with a man she likes the look of. All frightfully dull but think how the Frohlichs would approve!'

A week later he wrote again, telling her that he was having an 'otherwise idyllic existence' and hinting he was optimistic that things might work out: 'I do nothing all day but loll about, write, draw and occasionally think . . . I feel much quieter and more at peace and all those problems, which at one time appeared insuperable and infinitely depressing, seem now to be at least within range of solution.'[9]

This was all very well, but while Austin was in Paris indulging, as Beryl saw it, in abstract speculation about what it meant to be an artist, she was having to look after two young children. Irked by his complacent tone, she couldn't resist the temptation to hit out, and in her reply she made a pointed comparison to Nora, Austin's mother, likening his flight to Paris to her abandonment of her children in the name of art. The comment stung: 'Reference to my parent could with sensitivity have been omitted,' he responded, 'this does you know, of course you know, torment me.'[10] He attempted to justify himself, saying that like Henry Miller – he'd just been reading *Tropic of Cancer* – he was striving for the 'quality of loneliness' essential to him as an artist, even if it caused him 'to suffer' in his personal relationships.

As Austin walked the streets of Paris trying to find a 'solution', it must have seemed to both of them that things were reaching a point of no return.

———

Earlier in the year, when Austin was looking to sell the open-topped Crossley he'd acquired to replace the taxi 'Leocardia' on their return from Spain in 1957, he didn't have far to look for a buyer. Hearing that the extravagantly stylish car he'd so often admired was for sale, Michael Green, a solicitor who lived further up the road at 36 Huskisson Street, immediately offered to buy it.

Mick, as he was more familiarly known, must have noticed that things were not going well between Austin and Beryl, and he was not insensible to Beryl's attractions. He made his move one day in St James's cemetery, while Beryl was taking Jo-Jo out for a walk. Beryl recalled the scene in an early draft of one of her novels:

> The very first contrived meeting . . . baby girl in her pram, a pink outfit, a wooley hat on the bald pale head . . . 'Hallow,' the bowler is lifted not quite comfortably, the black shoes splay out as they walk. 'She's very white,' looking down at the sleeping infanta . . . 'I think you're wonderful . . .' boyishness oozes from him.[11]

Mick was not handsome by conventional standards. One photograph shows him looking pasty-faced, slightly overweight and prematurely balding. Most of those who knew Beryl were surprised, even slightly shocked, that she should have fallen for him, though this may have been partly because, as a bowler-hatted and be-suited solicitor in the Town Clerk's office, he didn't seem to belong to the same bohemian world of artists, students and university types. But to Beryl, feeling neglected by Austin, Mick had something of the charm of the overgrown schoolboy; he was her 'little boy lost' with his 'spoilt beauty boy face', and she was captivated by 'his kindness and his generosity and his emotion and his wide wide mind'.[12] She had never known, or liked, a man before 'who went in pubs, who smelt of beer, who smoked tobacco, who went to football matches, who drove fast cars and had men friends'.[13]

Born in Hull in 1932, Mick didn't come from a privileged background like Austin. His working-class father had worked his way up from office boy to a partner in a firm of solicitors, and both were Yorkshiremen through and through. Generous and open, Mick had a lively sense of humour, and Beryl enjoyed his company. His one fatal flaw was his inability to settle, to commit. 'He was absolutely terrified of commitment,' his wife would later recall, 'there was this wild streak in him, he was absolutely terrified by it.'[14]

Beryl fell in love with him almost immediately. The turning point came one evening when she returned home after visiting the Shackletons. Mick and Austin had been discussing, amicably, what to do about the ongoing situation. Hearing her come in, both ran downstairs, Mick telling her 'It's alright, we'll be together now', before rushing off, bowler hat in hand, saying he'd be back once Austin had talked to her. Austin reassured her he was fine about Mick: 'I understand sweetie, it will be alright.' When Mick came back an hour later there were further discussions, Beryl sitting in the big brass bed with Mick on one side, Austin on the other. A couple of years later she would tell Mick: 'When I think of it I must have been on the fringe of lunacy, the whole thing, and all of us involved. Looking back from this distance it was too civilized and improbable to be true. Had Austin socked you on the jaw, or I pocessed any normal feelings at all, or you any experience of such ridiculous people, how different life might have been. Austin would have gone, I would have altered, but the damage and the destruction might have been less.'[15]

Despite the surface harmony, by August Beryl was already writing to Judith, anxious that Mick seemed to be hesitant about their relationship: 'I am now so mis[erable] over M. who fluctuates so alarmingly between doubts and certainties. I am torn between the lovely tolerant acceptance of A, whom I no longer love as I did, but whom I increasingly admire, and the soaring normalness of M. whom I don't admire but whom I love. An awful lot of whomes . . . Nothing is any different but nothing is said, because it is all so complicated.'[16]

The word 'complicated' aptly described Beryl's personal life, even if the complications were at least partly self-generated. One complication was Ronnie Lowther Harris. Even from her earliest dealings with him, she'd felt uncomfortable in his presence, sensing there was something vaguely dislikeable or untrustworthy about him. But her vague feeling of distrust was matched by fascination, and however annoyingly, or even appallingly, he behaved, she couldn't quite bring herself to shake him off.

Despite now having six children, Ronnie was still obsessed with Beryl, and his desire to consummate their relationship was only whetted when he learned of the way things stood with Austin. Now based in Tring, where he had opened a huge antiques emporium called Corner Cupboards, Ronnie decided to take advantage of Austin's temporary absence and pay her a visit. But his badly timed arrival clashed with one of Mick's departures, leading to frantic efforts on Beryl's part to keep the two men from meeting. In a letter to Judith, Beryl recounted the events of the evening, during which Ronnie's attempts to seduce her after a meal at the Adelphi Hotel were thwarted by Brenda Powell:

At the risk of seemingly being inexhaustably dramatic as always, there have been great doings on here. The antique dealer with the six children arrived last week for five days. M. was going home for the weekend and brought me a street lamp for the back yard. As he went for it Ronnie arrived and I told him to go away for an hour. Mrs Taylor was terrifically valliant and stood in Aaron's room fiercly waving his car on and on round the block . . . Anyway one went and the other came and was so monstrous and terrible and this all I wanted to flat him with the street lamp. We had a huge chicken effort at the Adelphi, me lady-like in me verulant blue that you despise, and all a glitter with jewels and those extra trimmings that appear to draw men, and so fasinating I was and lilting . . .

Once home the scene began. Great rememberances of ruby days in Hampstead and the old old magic like a magnet drawing us together. (This I hope you understand are his original phrases, not mine) 'Oh the clap clap of the hearts, the only true ones in Europe who understand love, who KNOW. Maybe we have eight children between us, does it count when tomorrow we die and our eyes close as the world stops spinning . . . Little Brenda returns and stays on my bed till four. At intevals the radiogram stops and Beau Geste clatters down from the attic, only to find all lights on and Pompeii Bren on the old golden bed. Finally Bren discovers a lock and practically nails me inside, and nothing remembered till the morning when I am let out. He came down at four . . . and battered at my door, went into the studio, pawed the walls, tore upstairs, packed, and went back to London at 4.30.[17]

Austin returned from Paris in the first week of September, and Beryl now had to negotiate a path between living with him during their ongoing period of separation and carrying on her relationship with Mick. It was not exactly a conventional situation, but some days there was even an illusion of normality: 'It is Thursday and the children have moaned and snivelled all day. At five A. came in and went to bed with flue. I bought cough sweets and paper nose wipers and things and had Bren carry up a tray of gentle eggs and Tizer the Appetizer and chocolate. And very comfortable and beneficial too, in the cool studio with the huge global lamp hanging by his John the Baptiste head . . . I left at seven feeling I had been kind and wifely.'[18] Except that after her 'wifely' ministrations to Austin, she went down the road to be with Mick.

For Mick, as for Austin, the way Beryl expressed her love came to feel like a test he was destined to lose. There were moments, certainly, of pleasant, almost homely, relaxation: 'Mike and I sat by a large fire and listened to the radio. He was very buisness man and hard day at the office and so darling in his big black suit, and the guitar clutched to him. I was very happy just to be with him in the firelight.' But Beryl was so acutely sensitive to perceived slights, to apparent differences in their appreciation of the moment, that evenings together would run a complicated gamut of emotions in which they passed from a state of blissful content to frustrated irritation to sheer depression faster than the blink of an eye. When a tune caught his fancy and he got up to play his guitar, she felt it as a rejection, and when he returned, assuming she'd be waiting for him, she in her turn pushed him away:

> And then he said: 'Its no use, I must face facts, I can never live up to what you want,' and all the fear and panic came back and I thought, Oh for once a man, a real man to say I am strong, damn hell the world and take me in sure arms and straddle everything. And because he couldn't do it I got up and ran. And Mike, so weak in resolve became so fierce in action and twisted my arm and called me spoilt and sat me down again . . . I sat in his lap and he kissed me and I could feel all my bones and desolation everywhere. Something he said about perhaps I ran too hard or chased him too much. And I thought of the love poured out sickeningly over Austin, how many years of it, and dreams like flowers opening, and poppy-coated gaurdsmen keeping watch over my dreams and everything growing darker all the time and a funny swooping feeling as the earth dropped away and no heart left.[19]

She knew her love for him 'was oppressive and possessive and too swift and overwhelming', but she couldn't help herself: 'Either I love and can show it till I'm blown king-sized heavenfull, or I don't love. Its no good pretending.' Giving herself up so spontaneously to her feelings was what made love so exhilarating: 'The glory in the love one feels, the nearness and dearness and closeness one feels. The transformation of me, one individual, into a superbeing, a thing of beauty and wonder, a being to cherish and to be truthful with.'

But Mick's blunt admission that her effusive affection struck him as neediness, his cautious insistence that he had to feel free to be able to love, seemed to Beryl like a lack of commitment – or worse still a rejection: 'By hurting my stupid pride and making me feel so unloved he's shrunken my love for him. Its so sad. You can't be truthful or you lose the love. And I've lost mine, not altogether, but the miracle tip of it, made of pure joy and softest leaves . . . Austin made me lose it and now Mike. Such a waste. I could have made Mike so much younger and gayer and more happy. And he would have made me so much better. So much more cared for and blossoming and worthwhile.'

It was a paradoxical situation: she needed Mick to sustain her feelings of self-worth, but the more she tried to express her love for him, the more it drove him away. She was overwhelmed by feelings of insecurity and abandonment, foreseeing that she would end up losing everything: 'Austin is talking about moving. If it was not so tragic it would be funny. He is moving out when he can, and I will be here alone, so that me and Mike can eventually be together. Only thing is, Mike won't want me when it happens.'[20]

Such a fraught state of affairs could not go on. During previous periods of extreme emotional agitation and depression, she had expressed the desire to die or to be dead. This latest crisis differed from those of the past only in that this time, after what she felt was another rejection ('Tried to tell Mike, but he could not or would not comfort me . . .'), she decided to act on her self-destructive urge:

> Came home and pushed newspapers under the kitchen doors and put on gas in the oven. Waves of overwhelming self pity. Huddled near the oven, head on knees breathing it in. Colour blue. Kept hearing my Mother. Your fault, your fault. Did not make the best of yourself. Tried to tell her it was only the arrogance of my love, the belief I had in me and Austin. Mike saying I was stubborn, chased him too much, ran too much. Felt weak and shabby. Thought I heard Austin and tried to get up, dreading the failure, of him coming too soon. Fell over and began to laugh. Lit the gas. Fat sizzling in the oven, because had left the roasting tin in. Half hoped the oven would blow up. Turned off the gas feeling shabbier than ever. Quite stupid, ludicrous and unwholesome, like everything I attempt.[21]

The noise she had heard was indeed Austin and a few moments later he walked in, along with Don and Helen McKinlay and David Blond, son of the Liverpool entrepreneur, Leslie Blond. Although Austin remarked on the smell of gas, no one seemed to suspect anything. Beryl caught a smell of turpentine on Austin's jumper and immediately had a flashback of past times together, 'memories of unbearable tenderness in the basement in Hope Street'. She remembered, too, Dorothy's advice against getting involved with Austin, and thinking of her two babies downstairs, 'Why, oh why . . . did I not listen?'

After the aborted suicide attempt life returned to normal, or at least what constituted normal life at Huskisson Street. Although the intense feelings of insecurity, doubt and anguish that Beryl recorded in her diary during this period were real enough, the atmosphere of the house was not one of depressive gloom. She was adept at presenting an upbeat face to the world. There was an almost daily influx of visitors and many of those who called round for coffee, gossip, or to pass the time, would have been staggered to learn that Beryl could even have contemplated putting her head in a gas oven. Depressed as she was in private, in company she could still have what she called 'a laff'.

The day after the oven incident she was amused enough by Ronnie Armstrong's 'helpful advice' about her domestic situation to record it verbatim in her journal. Ronnie, an architect who lived nearby in Mount Street, had come round to see Austin as the two were planning to go into business. While he was there, he outlined a solution to their problems that he thought would be acceptable to them both. Austin could continue to have his affairs, but be more discreet about it. He'd have his studio and the 'odd girl elsewhere'. He'd come home once or twice a week, but otherwise be free to do as he pleased. As for Beryl, she would teach the children to be polite, prepare beautiful meals, and keep the house spotless in the hope of his eventual return, but she and Austin need never sleep together again. After Ronnie finished they were both stunned:

I say: 'But what do I do Ronnie?'

'Sublimate yourself in the children.'

'But what about sex?' Awful silence. Aussie giggled. Ronnie said I didn't need it. Said I did with some heat. Ronnie so moved as to get up from his chair and say in shocked tones: 'I've knocked around a bit and in 32 years I've never heard a woman say that.'

Felt like a nyphomaniac and told him that probably when he seduced a girl she had thought of it first. Horrified Ronnie. Drove home in his car going over the last seduction no doubt.[22]

Beryl still hadn't told her parents about their decision to separate. Now, however, with Austin looking for a house so he could move out, she sensed that the situation was irreversible and arranged to see her father to break the news: 'Had coffee in town with Daddy. Cried when I told him about Austin and me. Told him to look at me and see I wasn't unhappy.'[23]

That Beryl could tell her father she 'wasn't unhappy' less than a week after she'd tried to kill herself shows how confused she was about what she felt. Her moods veered wildly between extremes. After seeing Mick, she would feel happy and 'wanted to beg him not to go away'.[24] A few days later she would feel 'abandoned'[25] by him, knowing deep down that they wouldn't be together and almost wishing it was already 'finished'.[26] Her life, as she put it in her diary, was 'unbearable in its contradictions'.[27]

In October events forced matters to a head. The catalyst was a party at Huskisson Street, which coincided with Brenda Powell's twenty-first birthday on 3 October[28] and would become part of Beryl's public myth – as well as a minor footnote in the history of The Beatles. One of Brenda's fellow students at the art school was Stuart Sutcliffe and they often used to hang around together. They would occasionally babysit for Beryl, taking Jo-Jo out in the pram, pretending she was their baby. Aside from art, Stuart's other main interest was music and, drawn by a mutual love of Elvis Presley, he'd become friends with John Lennon, one of Austin's pupils in the year below Brenda. John, Stu, Paul McCartney and a young George Harrison had recently started playing together under the name Johnny and the Moondogs. As Stu shared a flat with Rod Murray just round the corner in Percy Street, Brenda asked him whether he wanted to come to the party and bring the rest of the boys.

The party seemed to split naturally into two factions: Austin had invited Fritz Spiegl and a number of musicians from the Philharmonic, and they gravitated upstairs, while the younger students and art school crowd colonized the downstairs rooms. Tony Carricker remembers playing both sides of Ray Charles's recent single, 'What'd I Say', in a seemingly endless loop. A lot of alcohol was drunk, and an inebriated sixteen-year-old George Harrison raised tensions when – without realizing he was talking to the principal flautist of the Philharmonic – he asked Fritz, 'Hey Geraldo, got any Elvis?'[29] By 11 o'clock the party was in full swing, and guitars were being played very loudly. With all the noise Aaron and Jo were unable to sleep, so Beryl took them down the road to Mick's.

According to her divorce petition, the next morning when she tried to get into her bedroom to collect some things, she found the door locked and was told that Austin was inside, in bed with a woman who had been at the party. It was after this that Beryl formally asked for separation, with a view to an eventual divorce. It is possible that elements of this account were fabricated for the purposes of the divorce – in the 1960s adultery had to be proved rather than simply asserted – and that Brenda Turner,[30] the woman cited in the petition, simply agreed to be named. But the fact that Beryl also claimed Austin was the father of one of Brenda Turner's children – an accusation he vigorously denied and demanded be struck out – shows that she believed they were having an affair at the time.

However closely the official version matched actual events, the party marked a symbolic end to their relationship. Up to this point Beryl still went through periodic fits of believing that she and Austin had a future together ('Feel perhaps I must stay with Austin . . .'),[31] even though she knew he was seeing other women and she herself was contemplating the possibility of marrying Mick.

But after the party in October, Austin, who had bought the freehold of a house in Prince's Avenue, left for good. Beryl's next-door neighbour Maggie Gilby recalled: 'I'd been out and when I came back Beryl was in the yard, screaming, "Maggie, Maggie, come round, he's gone, he's left." And I went down, and he'd gone. She was distraught, absolutely distraught.'[32]

Beryl had imagined that when Austin moved out, 'me and Mike can eventually be together',[33] but in this she was to be disappointed. At the beginning of 1960 Mick told her he had a new job and was moving to London. He said he would drive up to Liverpool on weekends to see her, but the move inevitably unsettled her, something made worse by the fact that her period was late.

In the New Year she wrote to Austin to discuss the possibility of marrying Mick, but her necessarily vague letter struck him as hopelessly impractical. He told her the more he thought about her plans, 'the more I am convinced that I should prevent this unrealistic alliance, which of course I could . . . Before I will free you to re-marry you must convince me that you are not just clutching wildly at a straw and in the end going down with both children.'[34]

Shortly afterwards she told Mick that she was pregnant. His response was hardly effusive, though he tried to reassure her he was prepared to do the right thing: 'You must become official so to speak with no more furtiveness at home . . . In the meantime I want you to cease worrying and, despite all that has happened, begin to believe that I love you and am to be trusted.'[35]

But she continued to feel 'incredibly panic stricken at the thought of the future'.[36] What would happen to her if she went through with the pregnancy and Mick abandoned her? She already feared Austin's reaction to finding out she was pregnant when her relationship with Mick was so precarious. How would she cope if Austin withdrew his financial support?

Overwhelmed with anxiety, at the end of January 1960 she took matters into her own hands, as Maggie recalled: 'One morning Mrs Taylor, the Irish woman who used to come and help Beryl, was screaming in the street that she couldn't get in. Eventually she got in and the children were in their bedroom, and Beryl must have been lying in the other room, pretty out of it: she tried to abort, and Mrs Taylor was quite, quite het up, quite frantic, so she rang Beryl's doctor and she was taken to hospital.'[37]

In her diary Beryl wrote about the incident in muted terms: 'I have been in hospital with a 16-week miscarriage, and felt very ill.'[38] The miscarriage was most probably brought on by the same method Austin had tried to procure for Anne Lindholm: 'slippery elm'. This is a type of elm bark that is inserted into the cervix, where it absorbs water and expands (and becomes slippery, hence the name), dilating the cervix and triggering contractions. Before abortion was legalized it was commonly used to terminate unwanted pregnancies, but it was a risky procedure to say the least, and infections could be life-threatening. In Beryl's case she haemorrhaged and required a blood transfusion.[39] Cyril Taylor took her to Liverpool Stanley Hospital where 'an incomplete abortion was cleared out for her in the theatre',[40] after which she made a good recovery and was discharged.

While Beryl was in hospital Brenda moved into the house on Huskisson Street to look after the children. She remembered Mick coming round one night and asking where Beryl was, but she refused to tell him. Winnie, too, wanted to know where Beryl was – she seems to have sensed something was going on but didn't know what. Brenda, aware that Beryl didn't want her mother to find out, fobbed her off whenever she rang by telling her: 'Oh she's just gone out for ciggies . . .'[41]

But the end of the pregnancy didn't mean an end to Beryl's worries, and the process involved in instigating a divorce did little to help matters. Once solicitors were hired,[42] she had to prepare a Petition of Divorce, which meant going over everything that had happened in fine detail. Meetings with Austin to talk about it not only stirred up bitterness and resentment, they also brought to mind memories of the person she'd fallen in love with:

> Austin came at four to discuss divorce. Wanted to shout and break things. He looks at me as if he actually dislikes me. Such distaste in me. The love I held deep in me for him. The warmth in the long nights. As if it never happened. Oh God why does anyone get born? His worn face when he said he had a girl now who would do for hotel evidence. The lines on his forehead. The gentleness when he held Jo-Jo on his lap. The invisible wall between us. The cancellation of beauty, truth, such a young love, since I was sixteen. Oh Austin, Austin, where are you?[43]

Beryl began to wonder whether she'd made a mistake, and friends told her things that seemed to hint that Austin regretted the break-up. Ronnie Armstrong said he knew Austin still cared for her, but that 'his pride would not let him admit it', and he had been 'shattered' by Beryl's interest in Mike.[44] She started to see their relationship through the nostalgic lens of the past, and mourn for what she'd lost:

> If one could pretend that time was returnable, that all these years could be got back. The time we went the Good Friday walk . . . 'I need you Beryl, don't ever let go'. The running through the streets in the rain with his birthday book, the crying in the basement, the beauty of him. Darling Austin, so much of one is you, and you find me so hateful now. All the talking we did, the future in the taxi, the two unborn children, the house for us and the Greens, my heart will break. For all love lost, all dreams gone, all hope spilled away . . . I wish I was someone else. Someone less born to be made miserable. I wave my tiny fists

helplessly, hitting out so futilely against destiney . . . But the pain of it all. Oh god deliver us. Never to know any peace. Austin sleep please. Children grow up, me grow old, die quickly. Stop all this nonsense.[45]

Despite the ongoing divorce proceedings, as Beryl had foreseen months before, Mick got cold feet on the question of marriage. He confessed as much to her during a long weekend away in Cemaes, a small village on the north coast of Anglesey. Beryl would refer to the incident a few years later in her novel *A Weekend with Claud*:

> Four days on a windy beach, a drink of coffee in a shop at night, some drinks in a garden. 'I can't, after all, marry you,' and up the road goes my love with thirty shillings of mine and the bowler on his head . . .[46]

By this point, though, Beryl, had come to a similar conclusion herself: 'I don't feel I should marry again. It seems a little foolish. Like being caught in a thunderstorm and jumping into the sea for safety. And me not able to swim.'[47]

But Mick's next decision came out of the blue. He told her he'd been offered a job as a legal consultant to a mining firm near Mount Isa in Australia and had decided to accept. He tried to sugar-coat the pill, saying that he was going in order to earn enough money so they could afford to set up house. But he could hardly have chosen anywhere further away, and the distance he was putting between them seemed symbolic as well as literal. At the end of the summer Beryl accompanied him to Manchester airport, and he stepped onto a plane bound for Sydney. It would be nearly three years before she saw him again.

SEVENTEEN

I'm Not Criticising . . . I'm Remembering

To be frank it would have been almost impossible to find a time when Maggie would not be placing herself in a position of unfaithfulness, her affairs came so thick and fast. Any breathing space between lovers was in the matter of days, and those ritualistically taken up with grief and sobbing, and such pronouncements as 'God, I'll never go through that again Norman. If you knew how it hurt . . .'[1]

There is nothing like a night shore under flying stars in a flying world to make one ask questions out loud to oneself. One in particular keeps cropping up. Who are you, Beryl Bainbridge?[2]

WITH MICK AWAY INDEFINITELY in Australia, Beryl was effectively living as a single woman for the first time for as long as she could remember. In some senses the period between his departure and his eventual return in 1963 was one of relative calm – if only in comparison to the fraught two years that had preceded it. This was partly due to the social support network that Huskisson Street provided, a diverse group of friends, lodgers and neighbours who would call in at all hours, gathering round the kitchen table with its blue oilcloth 'stained by the ringed indentures of dozens of mugs of tea', drinking and 'endlessly talking . . . talking'.[3]

One of these Huskisson Street regulars was Leah Davis, a Jewish woman in her sixties who, despite her abrasive qualities and eccentricities, Beryl befriended in the late 1950s.[4] They had probably met through Cyril Taylor, whose family, like Leah's, came from Russia; and like Cyril, Leah had ties to the Unity Theatre and the Communist movement. In an unpublished television play Beryl wrote during this period, 'I'm Not Criticising . . . I'm Remembering', she drew a portrait of Leah under the name Esther: 'Jewish. Very. Heavy spectacles. Grey hair with a bit of a pigtail under a black beret. Stout. She keeps her coat on and has several heavy bangles on her wrists, and scarves about her throat. She has a big handbag full of letters, cuttings of newspapers. Her voice is cultured, even theatrical.'⁵

Leah was an acquired taste. There were many who, finding her too loud or too confrontational, couldn't get on with her and actively avoided her – which only increased her already overdeveloped sense of paranoia. She was given to vituperative outbursts, both in person and in her letters: 'I wish I never saw a living creature again,' she once complained to Beryl. 'Everywhere I turn, disillusionment & hypocracy. How I hate them all.'⁶

Nevertheless, Beryl was fascinated by her, feeling that Leah was like a version of herself 'taken to extremes of Jewish disintegration forty years hence'.⁷ 'She has such a lovely way with words,' Beryl would say, even if her habitual expressions were typically doom-laden and full of resignation: 'There is a moment when everything is too late' or 'Sometimes the book closes for ever.'⁸

Another Huskisson Street regular was Stanley Haddon, the bass clarinettist of the Liverpool Philharmonic. Fifteen years older than Beryl, he had been married twice and was in the process of divorcing his second wife. He had something of a reputation as a womanizer, so when he and Brenda started seeing each other Beryl would keep Judith informed of the state of their fractious relationship in her sporadic round-up of local gossip: 'Brenda and Stanley are still together in shingle nail biting harmoney, which is no harmoney at all,' she wrote at one point; and again a few months later, 'Brenda and Stanley still bickering.'⁹

By mid-1961 Austin's money problems had necessitated a number of changes in the living arrangements of the house, with Beryl vacating the first floor, which was now let out to Austin's stepbrother and his wife, Bruce and Edna Parry. Whether as a result of the GRON parties or not, Nellie the sitting tenant on the second floor had also left ('Nellie, not cherished, but gone, leaving a table and one light bulb'),¹⁰ to be replaced by a more sedate couple who paid a proper rent. In order to maximize the rental income, it was decided that the back studio should be let and Beryl set about finding a suitable candidate.

Someone mentioned a man they knew who was 'quiet and clean and did not like meeting people', so she arranged for him to come round:

> When I opened the door he was small and Victorian, and straight down trousers without a turn-up when everyone else had turn-ups, and a high collar with round edges like my Father wore, and under the flat peaked cap a face like Harry had, eyes turned down at the corners and a nose with wide nostrils and a long thin lip . . .
>
> There was a fire in the living room, which was a nice room . . . and I felt very like a landlady, which I was, and very formal. I started to say that I did like to be quiet, but he did not stop at a distance to listen but advanced closer and closer, neck stuck out like a tortoise above the wing collar, head inclined slightly, till we were nose to nose and he squinted at my mouth . . .[11]

When the prospective lodger started smacking her on the bottom with his cap she at first thought it was some kind of sexual advance, before realizing that she'd been standing too close to the fire and he was beating out her burning skirt. Or at least that is the version of events given in *A Weekend with Claud*.

The new lodger's name was Harry Mohin,[12] a thirty-one-year-old compositor who worked on the *Daily Post*. Born in Liverpool but of Irish extraction, Harry lived and breathed politics. He had early on been drawn to the Communist Party and was active in the trade union movement. He seemed to have a knack for getting on with people instantly, to connect even with those holding opposing viewpoints to his own. Harry was also very particular in the matter of clothes, frequenting a gentleman's tailor at the back of Lord Street, where he would go to have his suits made to measure in real Harris Tweed.[13]

Harry and Beryl got on immediately, and they would sit up late, talking into the early hours. She would confide in him about her feelings, about the 'unbearable meloncholy sadness of her supposed world, a private globe in which she lies impossibly mangled with unending imagined conflicts'.[14] Although the issue of sex was taken out of the equation early on and she refused him 'the solace of her bed',[15] she would embark on long and detailed discussions about the state of her love life and about her current lover, 'his minute perversions, his vast inhibitions'.[16] Like Leah, Harry would feature in *A Weekend with Claud*, where he appears as 'Victorian Norman', one of the novel's three narrators.

It was on one of the evenings drinking and talking round the kitchen table with Harry, Leah and Stanley that a telephone call came through from Winnie, ringing to tell her that Richard had just had a coronary thrombosis and was being rushed off to hospital. The prognosis didn't look good – 'He's going, Beryl' – and indeed he died in the ambulance on the way to Southport infirmary.

Her father's death evoked a confusion of feelings in Beryl, varying from the sentimental 'my little Dad . . .'[17] to the bitter 'Oh the hate I bore for him so many years ago.'[18] During his final years her relationship with him had deteriorated again, probably the result of her separation from Austin: Richard considered it unseemly for both Austin and Beryl to be carrying on with other people while they were technically still married. Years later, in an article recalling the year 1959, Beryl wrote that when he and Winnie came to visit her father wouldn't come into the house and stayed in the car, and that he was patently uncomfortable meeting Mick when she brought him to a Christmas party.

The funeral was held at St Peter's in Formby on 20 December 1961. When the priest recalled how 'cheerful he always was' and how he had 'a zest for life', Beryl's immediate reaction was a bitter one: 'God forgive those years and years of never speaking, take all that unhappiness away . . . did they think his eyes looked like that because he was a cheerful man, a merry man?'[19] But as the funeral cortege left the church the image of her father as a child onstage about to sing 'Lily of Laguna' provoked a more tender response: 'One foot after the other we track the vanishing body . . . going now my Lily of Laguna, out of the door, O he's my lily and my rose, gone, carried by four strangers towards a millennium of sleep.'[20]

Frustrated by the latest failure of 'The Summer of the Tsar' to find a publisher ('Very sorry to have to tell you that it is not quite right for Weidenfeld and Nicolson'),[21] Beryl began to take her painting more seriously. With Austin in London she could paint more freely, without feeling her work was being constantly inspected or criticized. Painting during the day when the children were at nursery school,[22] she began to develop her own style, using thick layers of paint and dark ochrish colours. She concentrated on domestic scenes – the back yard of the house, the children playing on the sofa, in the bath – or on portraits of the people around her, including Leah, Harry, Stanley and the children. A group portrait from this period, entitled *Three Friends*, features Leah, Beryl and Harry seated at the kitchen table in Huskisson Street.

Beryl may have made a small amount of money from selling her paintings, but for the most part she seems to have given them away. Acting was more profitable, even if with two young children it was difficult to commit to the demands of theatre work. Instead, she took small roles or walk-on parts for television, which paid well and wasn't too time-consuming. Her first job was a small part in the Granada television series *Biggles*, in an episode entitled *Biggles on Mystery Island*, which aired on 22 July 1960.

This led to a part in the long-running television series *Knight Errant Limited*. The episode, in which she played Elspeth Walker, was entitled 'Baker's Dozen' and broadcast on 22 December 1960, though it was later wiped, as were all but two of the others. Even the series producer, Denis Forman, seems to have been embarrassed by it: 'the memory of it still makes me shudder'.[23]

Shortly afterwards Beryl got what would become her most famous television part, playing Ginnie, one of Ken Barlow's girl friends (rather than his girlfriend), in an early episode of *Coronation Street*, then in its first season. The creator of the series, Tony Warren, had, like Beryl, been a child actor on *Children's Hour*, though this doesn't seem to have been a factor in her getting the part, and she featured in only one episode. In it, Beryl is ostensibly helping to prepare posters for a 'Ban the Bomb' march, though in practice she spends most of her time lounging on a sofa doing her make-up. It wasn't a great performance – being more experienced at projecting her voice to theatre audiences, she wasn't used to the more intimate, natural delivery needed for the television camera – but she looked the part, with her tight slacks, bobbed hair, pouting expression and rebellious attitude.

Her next television part was in the Granada Television series *Family Solicitor*, which starred Robert Fleming and Geoffrey Palmer. In an hour-long episode called 'Slander', broadcast on 14 September 1961, Beryl played the role of Linda Baxter: 'Quite a nice little bit, small but eloquent with repressed meaning', as she told Judith.[24] This would, however, be her last television work for nearly ten years. Although Beryl succeeded in getting into a series in which she featured as a returning character, her briefly raised hopes of earning some serious money collapsed when Sidney Bernstein, the head of Granada Television, pulled the plug: 'My TV job, like so much else, has dissolved like so much milk on the cloth, spilt . . . I did five, and was paid well, but then they scrapped the whole series. It cost Mr Bernstein 20,000 pounds, so I suppose he may be suffering more than me.'[25]

Although Beryl would later come to realize that her affair with Mick had effectively ended when he bought his plane ticket to Sydney, they had not broken up formally and for the moment she still retained a hope that the relationship would resume once he returned, or even that she might go out to Australia to join him. The latter option was hardly realistic and when she mentioned it to Austin, now working as an art lecturer at East Ham Technical College, it immediately provoked a scathing response. To him it seemed as if Beryl's emotional over-dependence on men was leading her to make unwise decisions that threatened to take his children out of his reach: 'Perhaps if you can understand more,' he told her:

> you may not be so frightened of the future and would be less likely to clutch impetuously at the nearest straw, which in the present case from my point of view is more likely to produce an intolerable situation in the future . . . I'm sorry now we ever started this divorce business, since it also implies (amongst all those other problems specific only to Mick Green) it will inevitably lead sometime to your living out of touch, so that I can no longer see Aaron & Jo-Jo when I would wish. I suppose I can't persuade you to just accept a separation (although I can see how intolerably lonely you must perpetually feel)?[26]

Loneliness was certainly an issue, and it is a word that recurs in Beryl's diaries and letters. She was still an attractive woman in her late twenties. Her uncertain status – separated but not divorced – and the fact that she was practically housebound with two young children to look after, made her if anything more of a tempting proposition for predatory men looking for a casual relationship. As Brenda put it, she became 'a sitting duck'.[27]

On one level, there was no reason why she should not get involved with any man she chose, but her tendency to indulge in casual relationships, as she later admitted, to 'give myself a game to play, a delicious will-he-won't-he, does-he-doesn't-he obsession to take care of my life',[28] made things more complicated. The anomalous situation between herself and Mick didn't help: she loved him, was even committed to him in a way, but he'd moved to the other end of the world and she had no idea when or if he would return. In the meantime she needed affection, and she took it whenever the occasion arose.

In the year or so that followed Mick's departure she became involved in a string of relationships that, with one exception, were generally short-lived. Although they provided a distraction, and were less fraught than her messily complicated involvements with Austin and Mick, they did little to resolve her conflicted feelings about herself. Even at the time, a number of close friends found it distressing that she allowed herself to get entangled in relationships with men who seemed to be patently unsuitable. Brenda disapproved and Judith found it difficult to restrain her exasperation at the succession of calamitous romantic adventures that Beryl got herself into.

But one must be careful not to take Beryl's fictionalized portrait of herself too literally. Maggie's affairs in *A Weekend with Claud* may have come 'thick and fast', but in real life things moved at a slower pace. There were enough men to give the impression that Beryl was involved in a succession of affairs, but a number of these were in fact partial flirtations or attempted seductions, one-sided relationships in which men projected a romantic connection where little or none existed. These mini 'affairs' may have provoked temporary dramas that were dissected in late-night talks with Harry, Leah and Stanley, or with Brenda, or in letters to Judith, but deep down Beryl wasn't really affected by them, her emotions not having been fully engaged.

One such 'affair' was with the actor Derek Waring, who would go on to marry Dorothy Tutin a few years later. Beryl met him on the set of the television series *Biggles*, and he was captivated by her, nicknaming her 'Aztec', probably because the episode was set on a strange island in the Pacific and she was playing one of the natives. Beryl ended the relationship, such as it was, shortly afterwards, and he reluctantly acceded to her wishes: 'I would like to have had more than your body,' he told her, but 'I can and will withhold my bodily demands since you wish it.'[29]

Another would-be suitor was Gerhard Voll, a German-born lecturer in the Geology Department at Liverpool University.[30] He had first met

Beryl at a social event organized by the Shackletons, and on the pretext of wanting to talk to her about her 'unpublishable' novel, 'The Summer of the Tsar', asked Judith for her address. Gerhard wanted a serious relationship, but he was another of those earnest and well-intentioned men Beryl enjoyed talking to but was not physically attracted by. Nevertheless she seemed to be giving him mixed messages – she counselled him to 'grab' girls he fancied, but when he took her at her word she turned him down: 'You say, you are fed up with being grabbed,' he complained in a long letter trying to explain how he felt, 'and yet I feel it is largely your own fault. To encourage it seems to have become a sort of habit for you, even if at the same time it leaves you empty and bitter.'[31]

Already annoyed at Beryl's indiscretion – she had sent Judith copies of his private letters – Gerhard's suspicion that they both treated men in a cavalier fashion would have been amply confirmed if he had known about Judith's decision to set Beryl up with Jim Cassels, a professor in experimental physics at Liverpool University. Judith felt it would be good for Cassels to have a fling to spice up his marriage, and although Beryl was not attracted to him – she would later depict him in a novel as 'that professor all fourteen stone of chasmy fat'[32] – she agreed to do it. Unsurprisingly, when his wife Jane found out it caused a lot of bad feeling: 'The Cassels and I are all to pot. I won't even write what has happened but I am way out of my depth and hope to God it all blows over, as of course it will. Jim is behaving oddly and making statements that I presume are not serious and I cannot get at Jane because he won't let me and because I am working.'[33]

This doomed liaison resulted in a lingering feeling of resentment, and over a decade later Beryl would still reproach Judith for her role in it: 'That awful buisness with Jim Cassels that you and Bobby encouraged me into, saying he needed more experience. I loathed him physically but I pretended because I thought it was expected of me.'[34]

There were others who temporarily shared the 'solace of her bed', their names listed in the back of her diary, such as Charles White (who she would later portray as Lionel in her novel *Another Part of the Wood*), Stanley Haddon and an architectural student she nicknamed 'Oscar'. But none of these affairs had a lasting impact. It was while a frustrated Gerhard was trying to convince Beryl that his feelings for her were genuine, however, that she met Edward L. Lohman[35] and began the most serious relationship she'd had since Mick's departure. Lohman, a third-year medical student from New York, had come to Liverpool on a study-abroad scheme during the summer of 1961, in order to research pulmonary disease in the city.

It is likely that Beryl and 'Prince Edward, the prince of Light', as she referred to him, initially met at one of the Shackletons' parties, which always attracted students and teachers from various disciplines within the university. Beryl was immediately smitten, and hastily wrote to tell Judith: 'Of course the most important thing is Edward and either I am bewitched or rather round the twist, or it is real, and I am 16 again, before Austin (you see what I mean) and all like a flower with dew on, all hushed and fragile and on the brink of something beautiful and not at all to be explained, because it is all motiveless. And I dread what will happen when I am left again for the 3rd time in two years (ghastly thought).'[36]

Three years younger than Beryl, Edward looked unmistakeably American. He had closely cropped hair and a slightly jowly face, and his dark eyes gave him a curiously intense expression. The mugshot-like photograph he gave her is recognizable in the thinly veiled description of him in *A Weekend with Claud*, where he appears as 'the American with his stony face'[37] and 'the American statue of liberty, who gazed coldly at us out of sloe-shaped eyes, dry as prunes'.[38]

Given the three-month limit to Edward's study period, the relationship was necessarily brief. Even so, it had serious implications. Having married in 1955, Edward had a wife waiting for him in New York. He told Beryl his marriage was unhappy, and assured her that he loved her, that he wanted to have children with her, and they began to make plans for the future. He talked about coming back to Liverpool after his divorce, or alternatively that she and the children should join him in America.

Beryl considered the idea and, after some of the Manchester actors she'd met while working on *Family Solicitor* invited her to join their new company, asked Judith for advice about what to do: 'Shall I go to New York or play the panio in Manchester. Which will lead to happiness?'[39]

After Edward's return to America in September 1961, an intense correspondence began. Beryl sent an initial letter accompanied by a number of items: a book, a record they used to listen to, a tie, a scrap of torn envelope with the words 'I love you' on it, which she had once left on his bed, some drawings by the children, a photograph of herself and a brief note:

The record so you won't ever forget,
The tie for an English gentleman's suit

The book for pleasure
All with love from me.[40]

She had also given Edward some letters on the train when he was leaving. These were more fraught, full of fears that he wouldn't come back, that he looked down on her, that he didn't treat her seriously. After reading them on the flight, he had rung her on his return, but finding her out he began to panic, sensing the depths of her emotional volatility: 'I was afraid you had done something foolish to yourself, either because I left or because you may be pregnant. Please don't ever do anything like that, it would kill me.'

Towards the end of September she wrote again, telling him that she had been 'hurt' by his departure, that he had 'betrayed' her, that her relationships were a repetitive 'circle' of men leaving her. She also said she thought she might be pregnant,[41] and that if either of them felt they were no longer in love they should tell the other. Edward interpreted this mixture of desire for reassurance and avowals that she would understand if he left her as an expression of her own reservations and simply renewed his protestations of devotion: 'I can come back, I will come back, I will come back because I love Beryl. I will take Beryl and her two or maybe three children to the US . . . with some luck and perseverance this may be accomplished in about two years.'[42]

In the New Year, Edward sent the letter Beryl had been expecting all along, the classic married man's attempt at self-justification in the face of his broken promises. After asking for forgiveness at the long delay, he went on to say that it had become increasingly obvious to him over the months that he could never leave his wife. He hoped she would believe that all the errors, the difficulties and the problems lay solely with him, that she was not to blame for his failure to return. He ended by thanking her for all the 'love, kindness and understanding'[43] she had given him and told her he loved her and always would.

Edward's final rejection didn't provoke the uncontrollable wave of despair that others had in the past. Deep down she realized that it would never work out, that she would come out second best, that the wife would always win: 'The only thing I knew that he did'nt, was that he would not return. He had a wife whom he thought would divorce him. And when he rang from New York and said she had tried to kill herself and that he loved me but would never see me or contact me again, I blessedly accepted and believed both statements.'[44]

EIGHTEEN

The Return of the Wild Colonial Boy

My own Darling,
So many things I would like to say, so little I will say, except
the physical love we knew is such a rare, such a thing to be
treasured, that it hurts to think about it.[1]

All I can say, albeit friskily, [is] that I can think of nothing
more lovely than a woodern bungalow and you in the middle
of the desert. And think how our ping-pong would improve.[2]

In July 1962 Cyril and Pat Taylor, feeling that Beryl needed a
break, suggested she leave the children and join them on holiday in
San Bartolomeo, a coastal resort on the Italian Riviera fifty miles east of
Genoa. Harry encouraged her to go, but there were some small matters
to sort out first, such as who would look after the children and where
she'd get the money from. Her mother, Mrs Taylor and Maggie Gilby
agreed to take care of the children, and a hasty note to Ronnie Harris –
'Forgive me . . . I need £24' – was replied to by return of post with a
cheque and the words, 'I understand, Nothing to forgive.'[3]

A fortnight later, 'clutching me bathing drawers, me underarm
deoderant, and little else', she set off. The Channel crossing was an
adventure in itself ('On the boat I ended up in the waiters cabin drinking whiskey . . .'), but was as nothing compared to the rest of the
journey, which Beryl recounted to Mick in typically dramatic fashion
on her return:

I went to Paris first, then I missed my train and a gentleman with a
monacle who had served my country for thirty years picked up my
case and took me to another train and I clung, stella marino wise

to the outside of it. Then I became involved with 6 Belgian railway workers bound for Nice. We drank all night and sang songs and vowed eternal friendship. Of course the one who like me most had a dead wife and a daughter Bernadetto in a chair with polio. At Monte Carlo or somewhere they half carried me onto another train. By the time I reached the Italian frontier I was almost but not quite sober. I sang to an old lady and she left the carriage abruptly. Then another train and yet another, and then the Taylor family with car and warm greetings. They were so kind to me.[4]

The place itself, the Villa Laura, was idyllic: 'A yellow room with a big black bed, a religous picture on the wall, a balconey overlooking blue blue water . . . A lovely flat with a bidet. Oh the cold swoosh of perfection in the warm still nights.' Nearby was the beautiful ancient hill town of Cervo, 'built on the rocks, the sea beneath, olive groves clinging to the slopes', and the weather was perfect: 'It was so hot and the oranges grew in the gardens and I swam underwater, with water wings on of course, and I drank wine, and I was really happy.'

The holiday was a welcome break from the day-to-day anxieties of real life: 'On the verander some Germans played guitars, we lay all day in the sun and I leant to swim, well almost. We went to two Communist rallies and were cheered, and I danced to a funeral march with the Presidente of the party . . . I am a new woman.'[5] The final night was suitably nostalgic and emotional: 'It was all luvely. We laffed most of the time, unless I was crying, which happened at a farewell party given by the germans. Oh the strains of "Lili Marlene", the heart rendereng essence of the pines at Formby all those light years ago, the stout Bainbridge that is so more, the vain egotistical goosegirl that will forever be.'

Back at Huskisson Street ('I have a tan like a golden doughnut, and am if anything even more irristable'),[6] there was a belated note from Mick, offering her some holiday money: 'Darling Mike thank you for your legal note about the money. I will frame it. It was a lovely thought.'

Despite the various short-term affairs Beryl had indulged in since Mick's departure for Australia, she still felt an emotional attachment to him and hoped in a vague way they would get back together. They continued to write to each other during his prolonged absence – 'A million words written on paper [that] tangled us together, and flung us apart as if we had never met in the flesh'[7] – though a brief postcard is all that remains of Mick's side of the correspondence. Whether the letters were destroyed or simply lost isn't clear, but if the snatches of them contained in various drafts of *A Weekend with Claud* are anything to go by, they encouraged Beryl to believe that she and Mick still had a future together: 'I think of you constantly, if I said come out here to me with the children, would you? I sit on my balconey over the harbour, the Sydney harbour and watch the lights and think of you. I drove in the bush last night, the gum trees sprawl in the dust, we shot a kangeroo later, when it was skinned there was a naked baby in the pouch, glistening, not quite breathing. I thought of you. How you would revel in this heat, how it would suit your unconventional ideas of summer dress.'[8]

A handful of Beryl's letters written during this period do still exist, however, the earliest dating from September 1961, a year after Mick left for Australia. On the surface, it seems to be a simple love letter, giving him news of what was happening at Huskisson Street and expressing a heartfelt longing for him to come back: 'Sweetie why are'nt you here? Forget your dreams of independance and self fullfillment. Swallow your dreams and fly home next week and let us for gods sweet sake be happy. Resign yourself to a life of uneatable meals, and hot arguments, and so very much real love in and out of bed, summer and winter till death or indigestion us do part. Is it unnesscessary to repeat I love you. Always Beryl Bainbridge.'[9]

But Beryl's emotional life was rarely so straightforward, and a quick comparison of dates shows that her letter to Mick coincided with the end of her affair with Edward Lohman and his return to New York. Edward, too, received a love letter from Beryl in September, similarly urging his return, though he sensed an ambivalence in her tone and suspected that her apparent concern about him falling out of love with her was disingenuous: 'Are you fishing for unneeded reassurance,' he asked pointedly, '[or] do you already contemplate not loving me, or slipping sexually on an impulse, or finding someone else?'[10]

The five remaining letters to Mick date from the following year, and cover the period from Beryl's Italian trip to his return. Mick had written to her in the summer of 1962 to say that he was planning to come back in a few months' time, as he was growing bored with his job and getting itchy feet. His intention seems to have been to sound Beryl out, to find out what he could expect on his return, as his friend, Geoff Minshull, had told him she'd been seeing various men since his absence. As Beryl's previous letters had given little indication of any change in her feelings for him, he accused her of not being entirely straight with him, and, as if to emphasize his commitment to her, told her he'd remained chaste.

Beryl responded with a long letter in which she tried to justify herself, saying she had no intention of misleading him ('If you feel there have been hints or half truths it was unintentional . . .'), and that if it seemed like she had a lot of suitors it sprang from her compulsion to be liked: 'I still find it difficult not to make people feel they are the most interesting people in the world. I still find a half hour talk with either male or female will make them feel we are soul mates for ever. I still charm almost all of them to distraction.'[11] She did admit to certain 'associations' with men during his absence ('I have had four proposals of marriage since you left . . .'), but they were ephemeral and didn't concern him. She exempted Edward Lohman from this, saying that she had genuinely felt something for him, though 'it was so short that I do not know if it were love'.

As Mick's letter had questioned her on her 'need for affection', her 'longing to be worthily loved', and her 'sexual needs', she tried to answer him openly, telling him that she had changed in the two years since his departure and that she no longer confused physical desire with true love:

My need for affection is not so pronounced. I receive it amply from my children and from the few real friends. My longing to be loved is no longer there at all. How shall I explain it to you . . . the longing to be loved was a great barrier to finding love that would last . . . Conditions before trapped me into believing that the only way to find release was through emotions . . . I presumably did this because of rejection in childhood. I suffered a very early rejection from Austin, the pattern was unbelievably repeated with you. As for me sexual needs, they are exactly as before. I think it is more difficult for me than you, my sexual needs are stronger . . . My parents' misguided view that the whole thing was nasty created in me an artificial barrier, so that I could only believe I was in love with those I went to bed with. That is, that having gone to bed I covered my guilt by believing I was in love. The change in me is that I can no longer believe that it is real love, so I leave bed alone, till such time as love strikes me blind . . . amen. This probably sounds smug. I have more likely grown up, or like Pavlov's dog in reverse, conditioned myself to run like hell when the bell rings.

Regarding her feelings for Mick, or whether she still loved him, she tried to sound non-committal: 'I did love you. I say I still do, but till we meet I do not know what I mean by it. Almost two years of being alone, and the divorce and your departure, and bringing up the kids and the trouble with Austin after the divorce, have at last made me realise how well I can fend for myself. Austin was right after all when he said I was practically indestructable.'

Feeling relaxed after her holiday with the Taylors ('I have come back so clearer for being away from house, children and people for the first time in almost nine years . . .'), Beryl's confident mood was bolstered by the news of Austin's latest plan. He had seen a house for sale in Earls Court for £11,000 and proposed to buy it for Beryl and the children. The picture he painted of her future was a rosy one: 'He offers me permanent financial securitity and a fuller life than I have now,' she told Mick a month later:

So you see my darling you need never feel guilty about me or my possible future, because being divorced from Austin is more secure than being married to him. So I beg you not to get any guilt complexes in advance or fears, because I am fine and dandy and feel somewhat smugly I can deal with you and Austin without blinking. I hope for my own sake that when you return I will see you and feel nothing, except maybe astonishment. Though in other moments I would wish for both of us a moment of truth, a lifetime of happiness.[12]

But this sense of security didn't last long. In the first place Beryl was affected by the drama surrounding the Bay of Pigs invasion and the Cuban Missile crisis of October 1962. With America threatening to attack Russia if it didn't withdraw its missiles, Beryl took to the streets to protest outside the American Embassy in Liverpool: 'I marched around Liverpool in a 200-strong procession, chanting stop this madness.'[13] The very real threat of global nuclear war unsettled her and she envisioned the possibility that Mick might never return – or that if he did there would be 'nothing to get back to'. 'This in a half serious way could be a farewell letter,' she wrote to him at the height of the crisis, and she closed on an almost desperate note: 'Oh I hope you will love me and me you.'

In the event, fears of a nuclear conflagration subsided almost as quickly as they had risen, but they were replaced by other causes of anxiety closer to home. Austin was 'busy being sued and summonsed',[14] she told Judith in October, his business dealings with Ronnie Armstrong having turned sour. Armstrong was now demanding the repayment of a loan, and Austin didn't have the money to pay him back:[15] 'How Austin is going to buy property in Earls Court from gaol I don't pretend to know.'[16] Her update on the situation a month later was even more gloom-laden. Austin's legal wrangle with Ronnie had ended badly, and there was now a possibility he might lose Huskisson Street as a result:

> Austin has finally landed himself in a real mess. He lost the case, got
> a lot of nasty publicity ('The affectionate friendship between the 2
> men cooled') and has just had a bankruptcy suite slapped on him. He
> arrived some days ago, low with nervous asthma and whatnot . . . The
> unsettling thing is he had not put this house in my name, and was
> told it was too late to do so . . . Anyway it will be one way of moving
> me from here.[17]

As the year drew to a close, Beryl was torn between contradictory emotions: hope that Mick's love for her would blossom again, and fear of another rejection. 'I am sitting dreading Mick's return,' she told Judith, 'I wish it would not happen. He comes in about 11 weeks time.'[18] Everything seemed uncertain, she didn't know whether he would even come back. Mick had already put off his return once before, so when he wrote to say he was delaying it again her reply to him was – unsurprisingly – a fraught one:

> And this morning an unhappy letter from you, and one that sends me
> all bitter and twisted because you wrote home last week and said you
> would not return till March, two more months longer. And maybe if
> you persist in wanting to throw up your job, or gambling it or send-
> ing it here, you will postpone it till the Summer and then the next
> Christmas. If you do I shall stop writing, stop waiting, even though

you have never asked me to, and cast you far back into the past, and to hell with you. You said some weeks ago you had bought your ticket for January 9th . . . please, please don't put it off much beyond the original date. Either that or write and tell me you are not coming back, or do not know when, and I can make my plans. I don't mean that I want to know what you feel about us, because I don't know about you at all, and I prefer my life as it is, but conciously or not all these letters have attempted to keep alive something that truely ended when you bought your ticket to Sydney. It did end then, because there was no reason why you should not stay had you cared enough . . . Its not what I feel for you that makes me tend to wait for your return, its merely the sentimental belief that if there is any way of atoning for past mistakes it is through you. That and a kind of curiosity to know what it will be like meeting you again after a lifetime of disaster.

What are you coming home for? What did you go for? . . . Am I being very harsh, very stupid, very ungrateful? I do love you, I care what happens . . . Oh dear dear love, try to reach me. Hold my hand we're half way there . . . Always B.[19]

Just before Christmas she wrote to him again. Anticipating his need for warmer clothes when he returned to England, she sent Mick a jumper, along with an incantatory note, the humorous tone of which only slightly masked the emotion she felt:

Dear Michael Green,
I hope you have a happy Xmas on your balconey, with the sun going down behind the ships, We will in our own humble ways here raise our glasses in homage to absent and seafaring friends. Long live the Empire, the Commonwealth and all our yesterdays.

May this fit you, become you, adorn you and warm you in the coming hard times. May the ship cast off quickly, the homecoming be gentle. May the arms that stretch out to greet you be the ones you anticipate,

With blessings and love and a kiss on your colonial mouth and more love and truth and sincerity

Your ever own Mrs Davies (lately)[20]

Mick's homecoming in February 1963 was every bit as anxiety-inducing as Beryl had feared. Mick was very different both in appearance and in temperament to Austin, but there was one sense in which the two men resembled each other: their conventional notion that a woman be house-proud and know how to cook. Her carelessness in relation to these domestic virtues had long been a sticking point and a cause of friction with both of them. Before his departure, Beryl had described how an evening with Mick, during which there had been 'much joy in the fire-light', had turned sour when he raised the question of 'the importance of well-cooked meals and made-up beds in marriage'. This immediately provoked feelings of self-doubt: 'Know he is right but all the time feel he is thinking "No wonder Austin no longer loves her." Feel the half-cooked food and the unmade bed a gigantic reproach. Want to say how I tried, how I truely tried, how I will try, how I can cook, but feel sad.'[21]

Knowing how particular Mick – or 'Billie' as she sometimes referred to him – was about little home comforts, Beryl tried to make sure that 'everything was just so for Mick coming home'. She tidied up the kitchen and bought some pork chops especially for him. Brenda recalled: 'We all kept away from her because Mick was coming back.' The night before his arrival she had sat up with Harry and talked about his impending visit. She could feel Harry's unease, sensing that he wanted her to be happy but that he knew it was going to be a disappointment. An early draft of *A Weekend with Claud*, in which the whole episode is recounted, sets the scene: 'I went to bed without washing properly and before I turned the light out I kissed the photograph face of Billie. And truely I did feel different, I did feel safe and happy and hopeful and clean and almost innocent, and I lay my head on the pillow and closed my eyes and was in no doubt that I loved and was loved.'[22]

Not for the first time Beryl used the iconic image of the Romantic soldier, the Black Brunswicker (as she would later do with Napoleon), to contrast her idealized conception of the lover and the flesh-and-blood reality:

On the 25th of February the Black Brunswick returned. At six the children went to bed, at six thirty I was washed, combed and perfumed; a fire burnt in the grate beneath the Syclian lions, the brass bed under white cover spun golden in the firelight. At the blue table in the kitchen I arched my brows and thought beautiful thoughts to make my face tender, and folded hands together on the lap of the dark plaid skirt, watching the shadow of the lampshade twist round and back again above the blue oil cloth . . .

A knock on cue shatters the house, throws echoes down the hall, through the keyhole, the wild Colonial Boy, a blurred outline behind glass, raises an arm to smooth his hair. Cold air as the door opens, a voice the ear refuses to recognise, a face the eye fails to photograph, only a coat, a check coat, clean and beautiful, alien, comes into the house.[23]

But after everything she'd done, all Mick noticed was the disorder. Beryl would later tell Brenda that in spite of the fact 'she'd really made an effort', his first words to her when he came in were, 'Oh Beryl, you were always so messy.'[24]

She had been half expecting him to propose to her: 'I'd built up in my head . . . how we'd be a proper family.'[25] In an unintentionally cruel parody of a proposal, he told her he had a present for her – and handed her an old-fashioned ring box, saying 'Open it.' When she lifted up the lid, she saw inside not a ring, but a sweet. Then, as if to add insult to injury, he told her he had to leave early to find somewhere to stay. She'd taken it for granted he would want to spend the night with her. His decision to leave felt to her like a humiliating rejection.

Brenda remembers calling in to see her the next day. Beryl had been absolutely devastated and told her hopelessly, 'He's gone.' With Aaron at school, she told Brenda to take Jo-Jo to the doctor because she had an ear infection. Alone, the thought of Mick's rejection sent Beryl into a desperate state and she began drinking the bottle of gin he had brought the previous day. Everything culminated in a thought she had expressed many times before, a wish to die. As she had in her failed attempt two years before, she sealed up the window and doors with newspaper, placed a cushion in the oven as a headrest, then turned on the gas.

By chance, Harry rang a moment or two later, and, automatically, she tried to answer, but almost unconscious from the fumes she couldn't speak. Realizing something was wrong, he immediately rang Cyril to tell him he thought Beryl was ill. Shortly afterwards, Brenda came back with Jo-Jo:

As soon as I opened the door . . . I could smell gas. So I put Jo-Jo in the nursery and I said: 'You stay in the nursery and don't you dare come out.' I went in and Beryl – she was usually so disorganised – had turned the boiler off, she'd packed the window, the one that Austin had put in, all round with newspaper, and the back door and the kitchen door. I just went in and dragged her out into the yard. She was unconscious. Smacked her face to try and bring her round. Got the duvet, the eiderdown, and put it round her and opened all the windows.[26]

By this time both Harry and Cyril had arrived. Harry sternly rebuked her, telling Beryl she had two children to think of. 'I'm deeply ashamed of it,' she would later recall, 'deeply ashamed that I had two small children, and at the time it never occurred to me for a moment what would happen to my children . . . To have attempted to do that to them . . .'[27] Cyril, realizing that attempted suicide was a crime, took her off to his house to recover. Brenda tried to reassure Bruce and Edna upstairs there was nothing wrong, that Beryl had been trying to light the gas but couldn't find a match. Unaware of the events going on below, they were concerned that the smell of gas was making their baby sick.

In the kitchen was an empty bottle of gin, the one that Mick had brought the night before. 'It was a dreadful thing to do,' Beryl would later say. 'I have no idea whether I intended it, or whether I thought somebody would come in, I don't know.'[28] But whether this second suicide attempt was planned or a desperate act carried out under the influence of drink, it showed a dangerous emotional fault line running through her conception of herself.

NINETEEN

A Knight in Tarnished Armour

I don't have the guts to say it to you, to shout at you that you're a brutal ugly boy, that you hurt me for no better reason than that you're a little person, a phony, both emotionally and logically, that you are so insecure that you try to be God and don't care about people or children or money or truth or beauty, nothing but the small piece somewhere thats called Alan. And what that is God alone knows. Don't you know what you do? You take people as if they were nothing, pieces of dust, you distort them and use them and blow them anywhere you choose.[1]

I N   T H E   S P R I N G   O F   1963, Austin finally realized his plan of establishing Beryl and the children in London. It was something of a comedown from his initial scheme, the £11,000 property in Earls Court being abandoned in favour of a lease on a modest top-floor flat at 27 Arkwright Road, a short walk up from the Finchley Road.

It was a big move for Beryl in all senses: physically, emotionally and symbolically. Coming so soon after the disastrous end to her relationship with Mick, it represented a chance to start again, to put that painful part of her past behind her, perhaps even to reinvent herself. After she had settled into the flat in April, she wrote to Judith breathless with excitement:

Oh great guns. Wait till you see. A long low living room with deep wide casement windows looking over green lawns and huge trees . . . All sloping ceilings and alcoves and warmth and the moose up and the new friendly stuffed life-sized fox half way up the sofa. Then a white white kitchen, all with deep sills and more sloping ceilings, and no distraction by picture or ships clock . . . And a pink bedroom for me with my brass bed, and a white rug on the floor, and a lilac room for the children and their furniture all painted white. The house is big and clean and faintly posh with garlic overtones.'[2]

With one child at school and another at nursery during the day – Aaron at Hampstead Parochial School just behind the Everyman Cinema and Jo-Jo at a nursery nearby – and with little space to paint, Beryl began to think about writing again. She had decided to write a novel about her relationship with Mick, and was already finding Arkwright Road, devoid as it was of the numerous social distractions of her life in Liverpool, a conducive place to work: 'In the morning I write my epic . . . This and the purity of my kitchen and the knives and forks and the utter stillness all through the day while I type away gives me a certain sense of unreality. No Edna or Leah or Bren or Stanley or Harry or the phone going or Mrs T or Sherpa or Billie or Val or Anna etc etc . . . I feel as if I am convelesing and am being given peace in abundance.'[3]

Occasionally, sitting in the deep casement window at night, she would think of Mick, now working for the Law Society in London, imagining him 'somewhere out there among all the lights and the bustle . . . with his dam soft car and his loveliness'. As in the past, one way of getting over a failed relationship had been to start another, and she confided to Judith that she had met someone shortly before moving: 'More to the point is the Young Man. A week before I left for London the young man rang me from London . . . So we went out and he was kind and so gentlemanly and then I said I was moving and now he is here constantly.'[4]

The 'Young Man' was Kenneth Doggett, a former student in Urban Planning and Civic Design at the Liverpool School of Architecture, now working at James Cubitt's architectural practice in London. On one of his trips to Liverpool, Ken had spotted Beryl walking across the floor of the Hope Hall Cinema and was immediately smitten. He started talking to her and to his surprise she agreed to go out with him. The following night he took her, somewhat ironically, to the 23 Club, which he considered 'the fanciest restaurant in Liverpool'.[5] He gave her his number in London, and after her arrival at Arkwright Road they met up again.

Initially, with his disconcerting combination of attentiveness and reticence, she wasn't sure how he felt: 'I cannot make him out, he is so gentlemanly, and flowers and the theatre twice this week and supplies the babysitters, and goes straight home afterwards after a chaste kiss on the brow.'[6] But Ken wanted a serious relationship, not a casual affair: 'Do you remember when I first met you,' he later reminded her, 'I wouldn't sleep with you. I wanted permanence. Not just sex. I wanted love.'[7]

Even so, Ken found certain aspects of Beryl's life difficult to deal with. There was Austin's continuing involvement – and then there was Ronnie. Beryl had told Ken about his ongoing obsession with her, but even forewarned Ken could hardly have expected what would happen when she took him down to Tring to meet Ronnie in person. 'He was a jolly sort of guy,' Ken recalled:

> had this tall, reasonably attractive woman who obviously idolised him. We were in the house, with the antiques and everything, and we stayed the night. Ronnie must have been insanely jealous of us being in bed; at two in the morning he began shouting and singing outside the door . . . The next morning we were sitting in the garden on the bench, when I suddenly heard this noise, like heavy flies hitting a window. I said to Beryl, 'What's that?' and she said, 'It's Ronnie, he's shooting at you. He doesn't like you.' It was probably an air rifle; it could have blinded me. It was a couple of feet above my head.[8]

But despite these occasional bumpy moments, the relationship grew more serious. Hampstead Heath was an appropriately romantic setting, and it was there, under the trees, that Ken told Beryl he loved her and she said she felt the same. Over the summer, after being offered a job in America, he proposed to her and she accepted.

Ken, like Austin before him, was not someone who found it easy to commit to marriage without a certain level of financial security. He needed to establish himself in a reputable job first. When he was offered a post at Virginia Tech, teaching graduate students in Urban Planning, he saw it as a step towards marriage with Beryl, something that would bring them together not force them apart. In September 1963 he moved out to Virginia for the start of the Fall semester, telling Beryl he would let her know when he'd found somewhere to live. She and the children could then fly out in the New Year.

It was inevitable that spending time apart would affect them both: Ken went through bouts of feeling 'lonely & depressed',[9] but the separation unsettled Beryl in a more complex way, going well beyond mere loneliness. Even though Ken's letters left little doubt as to his feelings, she couldn't accept what he said, not because she felt he was untrustworthy – if anything the opposite was true – but because her fear of rejection was stronger than any reassurance he could give. A hint of things to come can be seen in a letter to Judith written shortly after Ken's departure, in which her anxieties begin to distort her perception of the situation:

> What to say? Ken is gone. Owing to a terrible quirk of personality or perversity or something god knows what, the mere fact that he is gone, has gone, has catapulted me into deep darkest african despair. Why? Please why? Am I really mad? . . . I don't know if I love him or not. It doesn't really matter . . . Some half promise, some vague future. I cannot stand it. He went to New York two weeks ago. I presumably join him after Xmas. I say presumably because I only half believe it . . . The letters that say I want to marry you, I love you, but do <u>not</u> say when, how, where. It's the uncertainty . . . My Mother (ill in hospital) Austin (looking like death) his various friends, all say when are you going? And the awful truth is, <u>he</u> never told me, I don't know.[10]

The break with Mick was still on Beryl's mind and the possibility of another rejection threatened to overwhelm her:

> I wish I could just evaporate, Judith, don't think me daft, but if you <u>do</u> love me, please pray, not God, just hope this time it will be alright. Maybe I don't love him, maybe I'm incapable of love, but its like the golden thread that leads to paradise – if this snaps I'm through, god almighty that's it . . . Since last February I've felt nothing, nothing, and now a little I feel something, and its like believing in something. Its self preservation. If this too proves to be an illusion, if he writes and says no, what then? I feel sick. Basically sick that is. As if I need real help. I'm too subtle, too clever somehow to go the whole hog, but I do know I am ill mentally. I'm not normal.[11]

Although Ken sensed the confusion in Beryl's mind, he still felt it could be dealt with on a rational level. He simply needed to reassure her. But he could have had little idea just how deeply ingrained, or how extreme, Beryl's anxieties were. In a long letter to Judith she blamed herself for the emotional mess she was in:

> My worry is not that I love him, or whether I'm doing the right thing, but whether he loves me. The stupidity is that after the last little upheaval, a mere 5 months ago, I should have avoided any emotional involvements for a good year or so . . . I'm just not fit to be involved. I have for some reason twisted all this to be like Mick and Austin etc. He went (Ken) quite sure, I think, that everything was settled, that . . . he would send for me. He told my Mother this, he told Austin this, he told his parents and his friends. Its my lunacy that says he's telling lies, doesn't mean it. OK he might have married me, but he didn't. His reasons were quite logical. They were wrong reasons in that it was me he was dealing with. Wrong only because of me. After all why can't I wait 3 months? The fact that Ken didn't marry me . . . is felt by me as a great injustice . . . But its my fault not his . . . I am constantly obcessed with thoughts. The kids, this flat, Ken, are all like shadows. Nothing is real at all, only these fantasies of am I loved? There is no reason to doubt Ken, or his motives (unless he is as twisted as I am). There is every reason to suspect me.[12]

Confused about whether Ken loved her, about whether she should or shouldn't go to America, Beryl's state of mind seemed fraught enough as it was. It was about to get worse.

In October 1963, Hampstead Parochial School held its annual Harvest Festival. It was there that Beryl met Alan Sharp, a Scottish writer living in London, whose two daughters, like Aaron, attended the school. She had arrived slightly late and as she entered the school hall she took in the scene, the stage 'piled with apples and oranges and packets of cornflakes, and rows of children sitting cross-legged'. It reminded her of her childhood: 'Whilst I was smiling nostalgically at the stage I became aware out of the corner of my eye that someone was beckoning to me. I have always been very obedient. I went, still smiling, towards a vacant chair on the second row. I said thank you to the young man and sat down beside him.'[13]

After the service was over, the two went for coffee. Beryl was struck by Alan's appearance: his torn jumper, his 'wide mongolian face'[14] (likened by one journalist to that of 'an anxious boxer'),[15] and his hair, 'a shag of dull blond curls' that gave him 'the look of a slightly underfed lion'.[16] Beryl's account of their conversation, hinting at the sexual tension between them, appears in an early draft of a novel called 'William at the Harvest Festival':

> 'You've a very erotic face,' he said. He was looking at me searching.
> I really did feel ill. I was hot and my hands were shaking and I went feeling very cold and then very warm. Under the tablecloth my feet trembled on the carpet. He didn't smoke, but he lit my cigarettes.
> 'This fella of yours,' he said. 'Its really love is it?' He was crumbling half a bun between his broad fingers.
> I looked at the disintegrating pastry. 'He's my fiance.'
> 'Quite apart from that,' he said, 'is he love divine, all love excelling.'
> Outside in the high street there were people going shopping. I wish he hadn't said it. Put like that I felt disloyal. I felt very jelous suddenly of his wife, the mother of those flaxon-haired children sat behind the apples and tins of soup.[17]

This first meeting was followed by an invitation to Arkwright Road and from there 'straight down the primrose path to intimacy, passion and the chaos that was to follow', as Alan would later put it. 'There does not seem to me looking back that there was any place along that very short arc when things might have been different, no crossroad where either of us pondered which road to take.'[18]

Alan's confidence, his verbal exuberance and inventiveness, his spontaneity and his unmistakable desire for her made him irresistible to Beryl. One of his letters, written in the first flush of their affair, gives a glimpse of his seductive and romantic intensity, induced through a self-consciously literary swirl of words:

> My dearest love, I know nothing I might say that would hone my meaning keen enough to cut through all the swaddle of amazed believing disbelief in you and my love for you and your precious, homecoming, dawn falling love for me. To say I never expected is to say no more than the blatant; no sane man could expect, such would be a most monstrous conceit. That 'I hoped' is also un-necessary, had

I not always hoped for it then I would not have known it when it came.

No, what I did before, if I did anything before, does not concern, it is the now which matters, the enormous molten seminal aching now . . . You are my present, my gifted now, my cherish, my wish, my tender true treasure. My Beryl. And of you and now, nothing can I say that does not crumble gritty, into the merest articles of speech. Save perhaps the monotonous chaunt 'I love you. I love you, I love you,' that indestructible mantra, 'I' linked to 'you' by love, evol, our bridge across the abyss, making adjacency closest togetherness . . . I know nothing I say will match the calm murmur of my blood as you turn in my arms. Give hush its heed, we are alive and beautiful. I love you my dearest Beryl and in doing so am the more completely, your Alan.[19]

But there was a catch. The messy complexity of Alan's emotional life matched, even outdid, Beryl's own. Alan had fallen in love at first sight, but for him that fact overrode any other consideration, personal, practical or ethical:

I saw this hauntingly beautiful face with its hollowed cheeks, the mouth like a wound that could only be healed by kissing and a mind through which the light came at a distinct, inimitable angle and I wanted to know her. That I was presently married, for a second time, had no bearing on this, that I was, and remained for some very considerable time, pathologically promiscuous, did not deter me from falling in love, obviously in love, and acting out the implications of that condition. Beryl, I have to assume, also disregarded the sanity of getting so involved . . . I mean when you fall in love with a married man who had a recently divorced wife in the frame you are disregarding some fairly well-known warning signs.[20]

With hindsight it is easy to feel that Beryl could have or should have heeded those signs, but at the time she was too preoccupied with her own drama over Ken to worry whether Alan was sincere in his expressions of love, or what a relationship with him would actually entail. She had no way of knowing the depth or extent of Alan's duplicity, she was unaware that women drawn into his orbit risked being dragged down into an emotionally destructive black hole. As Beryl would shortly discover, his first wife's summing up of him as 'an accomplished liar and a great womaniser'[21] wasn't abuse, just a simple description.

Born Alan Foote on 12 January 1934 in Alyth, a small village twenty miles north of Dundee, Alan Sharp was the unintended consequence of a brief encounter between Ethel Foote[22] – an unmarried grocer's daughter from a Presbyterian background – and Peter Craig, a working-class labourer and Communist Party activist. Craig was born in conditions of dire social and economic deprivation and had negotiated an uncomfortable path to adulthood via drink and petty crime. Like his father, Craig was no stranger to the police cell.[23]

Six weeks after Alan was born, his mother gave him up for adoption. He was taken in by Joseph and Margaret Sharp, a working-class couple living in Greenock, twenty-five miles west of Glasgow. A joiner on the shipyards, Joe Sharp was 'a profoundly religious man',[24] and both he and Meg were active members of the Salvation Army church. It was these two, often conflicting, influences – the strictures of Protestantism and the harsh realities of working-class life – that shaped Alan's personality as he grew up.

In 1952 he entered the army for a two-year spell of National Service, and on leaving found himself back in Greenock, working as a plater's helper at the shipyards. Shortly afterwards Alan met Margaret Donachie, nine years his senior, and married her in 1955; their first daughter, Louise, was born in 1956 and their second, Nola, two years later. In 1959 he applied for a teacher-training scheme and received a £500 grant from Glasgow University. But if 'yooni' gave him ideas about literature and 'a realisation of his own talents as a writer', it was also a reminder that there was a whole world of experience out there that wasn't to be got from reading books. He wanted to travel, to go to Spain like Hemingway. He gave Margaret his grant money and left, ending up in Germany. She filed for divorce.

By October 1961 his divorce had come through and Alan was living in Belsize Park, where he met Sally Travers, a character actress thirteen years his senior. Less than a year later they were married, though it wasn't long before he realized he'd made a mistake with Sally too.

On his return from Germany, Alan had started writing seriously and found he had a natural talent for it. His early successes were in drama, first on radio in 1962 with *The Long Distance Piano Player*,[25] and subsequently on television with *Funny Noises with their Mouths* in October 1963, which formed part of the BBC's 'First Night' series and starred Michael Caine. In a typical act of generosity that wasn't without a self-consciously theatrical element, Alan bought Beryl a television set so that she could watch it.

Around the time he met Beryl, Alan finished the novel he'd been working on for nearly four years. Even before publication its exotic, vibrant mix of Scottish vernacular and sexual explicitness had created a buzz in the literary world. By the time Michael Joseph finally brought out *A Green Tree in Gedde* in 1965, Alan was already being compared to Joyce and Lawrence. No small part in the book's success was the frank way it dealt with sex: 'It's been called pornographic and excessively sexual,' he admitted. 'I'm an obsessive writer about sex. It concerns me the way damnation concerned Kafka. The only real thing to me today is relationships. Sex is something you have to get over with, or integrate, to get on with the relationship.'[26]

In October 1963, Beryl wrote to Ken and mentioned in passing that she'd met a 'playwright'. Although Ken had no idea who she was referring to, he sensed in her tone that she wasn't telling him the whole story, and in his reply he asked her why she'd used the word 'guiltily' in relation to her meeting with him.

His next letter expressed a growing anxiety: 'Darling Beryl, Five full days without a letter from you. What are you doing & what is up with you?' Unconsciously picking up on the cause of the problem, in addition to the usual questions about the well-being of Beryl's children and her mother, he asked her 'How is Mr Playwright?'[27]

Beryl responded with what she later described to Judith as 'a candid letter about having doubts'.[28] She didn't mention her ongoing affair with Alan, but instead tried to blame Ken, telling him that his decision to go to America was an unconscious expression of his lack of commitment to her. This provoked an anguished reply justifying his actions: 'Darling there <u>was</u> or rather <u>is</u> one difference in our decision-making attitude. I never queried marrying you, I merely wanted a firm base for our marriage . . . I left with you & me as the end product in mind. I felt then as I feel now – I don't mind Austin (not too much anyway) supporting the children, but I must be in the position of doing so if the occasion presented itself. I can't understand that you can't understand this. I love you & want to marry you in a complete sense. Are you being completely open? Have you told me all – have you made up your mind already?'[29]

In one sense she had. As she'd done with Ken a few months before, Beryl took Alan to meet Ronnie, almost as a kind of litmus test. There was no repeat of the shooting episode this time and in the face-off between the two men it was Alan who came out on top: 'We went to Tring in a taxi the other day for an hour,' she told Judith. 'Ron was a bit subdued I thought. He tried to be himself but Alan won hands down. "Cleave to the great glory man," said Alan, taking Ron's thunder. Ron rang last night and said very very seriously he was coming up to have a serious chat with me. Austin seems quite cheerful in all this. Apparently Alan has had a word with him. Maybe Alan's agreed to buy me. I do love him, O I do.'[30]

Letters from Ken now began arriving almost every day, and Beryl kept Judith up to date with a running commentary: 'He says he was wrong not to marry me before, that he's been mean, he should have given me money for food, he should have taken me home etc, that he didn't realise but he does now, and that I must come etc etc. He is trying to get a loan and wants me to fly out.'[31]

Torn between Ken's pragmatism and Alan's impulsiveness, Beryl constantly wavered between the two. A sudden panic that she might be pregnant served to put things in perspective and she told Judith, 'I must go to America. I won't say that my mind is as firm as all that, but I think I must be sensible.' A few days later, however, the panic subsided and with it her conviction: 'I feel so very cheery because I got a period two days ago, 10 days early, so I can afford to laff as they say. Strangely enough once that worry went the resolve to go to Ken diminished in proportion.'[32] But so indecisive was she that by the end of the letter her mind had changed again: 'I will go to Ken . . . I may even do it, though I love, love Alan.'[33]

By now the easy confident tone of Ken's earlier letters had disappeared: 'I thought there was no risk with you because I love you,' he wrote, 'can't you believe in me? I don't want a half-loving wife . . . Please Darling say you want to marry me . . . Please answer directly & without any ambiguity . . . Have I failed you? Answer honestly.'[34]

But honesty was out of the question. In fact it would be another two and a half months before she would admit that she had met someone else. In the meantime she told Ken, somewhat disingenuously, only that she was having 'doubts', which just prompted more protestations of love on his part.

Just before Christmas, Ken wrote to tell her that the 'down & up emotions' of her letters over the past few weeks had not been doing much for his 'peace of mind',[35] and in the New Year, seeing that his letters had clearly failed to clear up her doubts, he proposed coming back to London. It was this that finally induced her to tell him the truth, though she still didn't mention Alan by name.

The news of the 'new boyfriend' came as a shock, but Ken continued to believe their relationship was strong enough to overcome even this hurdle. For the next year or so he would repeat his offer that she should come to America, and in proportion to how well – or badly – things were going with Alan, her determination to go ebbed and flowed in her mind.

———

In the first few months of her relationship with Alan, Beryl hadn't been unduly worried about his wife and ex-wife. The fact that he was married was an inconvenience, but there was no reason why that should be the case once he was divorced from Sally. Beryl couldn't doubt Alan's passion for her, either in word or deed. The former was his speciality and his declarations of love approached the lyrical in their intensity: 'You are all delights to me my dearest, all things and all parts, I want no woman and I want no man while I am yours, the pleasures of this life are bounty in excess of my needs if you are mine. I love you with all of me that has the wit to sit up and scratch. I approach you in awe, and in the nights, when furled in sleep you lie, I wake and praise, with all the passion of the godless, the simple fleshly fact of nearness, that most prosaic of raptures.'[36]

Alan's actions were characterized by a spontaneity that could be intoxicating, but also unsettling. Just how chaotic life could be with

Alan can be gauged by one of Beryl's letters to Judith from this period, written with typical self-deprecating humour:

> I am so exhausted I do not know if I am happy or no. A typical timetable. Alan arrives at 6.30. A hearty discussion on Anglo Saxon dictionerys. At eight a meal. Bed. Then chat on the novel in English life. Then Salvation Army Lore, then a whole two hours of Scottish singing. Then tea. Then Bed. Then a sermon on Oliver Cromwell and his approach to God. Then tea. Then Bed. Of course I am refering to it in its carnal sense. About dawn I fall exhausted onto the couch, whilst Alan sings the Greenoak tree to me. At eight he goes out and pinches a pint of milk from a few doors away and rings the bell so that the kids can let him in. The children go off to school. A few hectic rides in a taxi round London for some script writer or some agent or the tele man and then bed. Then community singing. Then I go for the children and he goes home for a few hours. Presumably to sleep, the lucky devil.[37]

Exhilarating as all this might be, Beryl gradually became aware that Alan's unusual marital set-up – he rented a flat with Sally in Parliament Hill Fields, and his ex-wife and children lived literally around the corner – was more complicated than it first appeared. Rather than being the primary focus of Alan's attention, she realized she was just one stop on his bewildering and ceaseless itinerary, and that there was 'a daily running back and forth' between herself, Margaret and Sally. 'Will we always be shuttling like this: me, Margaret, Sal?' she asked in her diary, 'all with different bonds, all being held together by Alan, dispensing money and wisdom daily? But I want to be on our own, just together. Having been so ruthless as to cut free twice, two wives, then why cannot he let go?'[38]

The more time Beryl spent with Alan, the more his convoluted and emotionally messy involvement with his wives leaked into her life: 'Now, another crisis . . . his first wife has stopped working because she says Alan should support her . . . and now Sal has just been and cried really broken-heartedly and said "I am begging you to let me have him back". Alan arrived too and there was a lot of talk and if I could I would vanish. I don't want to break up their marriage, but Alan does, and I do love him.'[39]

Quite how Beryl imagined she could continue her relationship with Alan and not break up his marriage isn't clear, but what was clear was that the situation was having a destabilizing effect on her state of mind: 'My inferiority complex remains as bad as ever,' she concluded after yet another occasion when she returned home only to find he'd gone again. 'More and more I just know its not going to be alright,' she wrote, 'it hurts so much, it does hurt so much, it so does hurt. We're not even near each other. A hundred little actions and lies and compromises grow and push all the good things away and apart . . . I wish I was old and dead, and if that is wicked I'm not even sorry. I just feel frightened and there's noone, noone anywhere to tell or to hope for help. Only me, and I'm hopeless.'[40]

Beryl's insecurities had always left her prone to feelings of jealousy and suspicion, so to fall in love with a self-confessed philanderer amounted to an act of emotional self-sabotage. Although they both considered sex a vital component of the relationship, there was a fundamental difference in their conception of its function, as Alan would later point out: 'Throughout, the bedrock was, well, bed. If you harboured the exalted notion I did of sexual congress being the essential metaphorical experience, when mind, emotion, body and imagination had some chance of making common cause, then Beryl was a dream come true. In my case though, the dream did not contain the concept of monogamy and so inevitably we disintegrated on the rock of that reality.'[41]

Increasingly suspicious that Alan's 'lies and double-talk'[42] were attempts to cover some form of infidelity, Beryl had even begun to suspect his interest in one of her friends from Liverpool, Liz Thomas, who had recently come down to live in London. What made it worse was that she herself had introduced Liz to Alan and now he was showing a more than normal concern over her welfare. When Beryl discovered he'd paid one of Liz's medical bills, her suspicions seemed to be confirmed.

The previous November, when Beryl thought she might be pregnant, Alan had conceived a plan for them both to go to Greece until his divorce came through. The idea was to rent a house big enough for Austin and his new girlfriend to come too. As Beryl told Judith, Alan had been working on some well-paid television commercials and could 'well afford to keep us all'.[43]

This increasing reliance on Alan's money led to its own tensions, especially when Austin began to get into financial difficulties: 'Austin stopped my Alimoney 6 weeks ago . . . I have no income. I am entirely dependant on Alan. The arch-muddler finally mixed up with an equally strong arch-muddler. I should of course have gone to America.'[44]

When Winnie came down to stay with Beryl at Arkwright Road in the spring of 1964 she quickly picked up on the situation, and Beryl's attempt to justify herself led to a row that marked the lowest ebb of their relationship. 'She called me nothing but a prostitute,' she told Judith, 'I said he didn't pay me and finally she said she was going home, and now the usual guilt feelings and where do we go from here? Anyway I said I was living with Alan and I loved him and we want a baby, so at last I am learning to tell the truth.'[45]

Initially, the plan to go to Greece had seemed like a confirmation of Alan's desire to be with her; after all if he was going away with her, he was leaving the others behind. But in talking to Liz over the phone in May she discovered that Alan had bought a ticket for her too. When challenged about it, Alan's solution was to pay for Liz to go to Spain instead, as if that made it alright. Beryl found it doubly distressing, not just because of what it implied about her relationship with Alan, but because it meant losing Liz as a friend: 'I don't think I'll ever see her again, both because she's upset and so am I . . . I just feel I know I'm right, but I can't articulate, I can only appear jealous and adolescent. But thats what love is. I don't see how you can love and not be jealous. I am jealous . . . I didn't want it like this. I just wanted to be with him. I just wanted to love and be loved in return.'[46]

In April 1964, Beryl's writing suffered another setback. Through Alan's influence she'd been taken on a few months before by Nina Froud at the Harvey Unna literary agency, and met a script editor for whom she'd written a radio drama for possible inclusion in the BBC's 'First Night' series.[47] She had also made good progress on her novel: 'The ideas keep tumbling out and Alan has a very good effect on me',[48] as she told Judith just after New Year.

But in the event these projects came to nothing: 'The play's series ended without doing mine,' she complained to Judith a few months later, 'and the agent sent me a long letter saying she could not touch the book as it was just bad. According to Alan she doesn't count and all I do is re-type it and send it off to Heinmann, but I am througherly depressed, deflated, and utterly sad.'[49]

Nina Froud's assessment of the novel, now called *A Weekend with Claud*, pulled no punches, and her criticisms were devastatingly brutal compared to the generally complimentary rejection letters Beryl had received in the past:

> I honestly don't think it is a publishable proposition . . . [it] doesn't really begin to be a novel . . . I think publishers would also object to there being no chapter divisions, the multitude of mis-spellings, and the fact that a great many words can only exist in your own imagination. Thinking about it dispassionately, and forgetting that we are friends, I cannot help feeling that the book doesn't have much to say at all. My greatest quarrel however is with the quality of the writing, which lacks the imagery and force necessary to lift it out of the rut.[50]

Alan's seemingly unstoppable success only served to emphasize Beryl's failure, and she couldn't help but feel jealous: 'Its a little depressing to be living with someone who is winning every prize in sight and commissions daily, and never really appearing to write a line. 5 countries and America have now bought his book and a man in the West End wants a West End Play. So I make cups of tea, and fight huge endless battles with myself on the Heath and weep when he's out.'[51]

———

As the summer of 1964 approached, the arrangements for Greece continued. Tickets were booked and the flat in Arkwright Road was rented out to a newly-married Jewish couple: Cecil Todes, a South African-born psychoanalyst, and his German-born wife Lili, who was working as a journalist for *Newsweek*.

Prior to departure Beryl and the children had gone to stay with Austin in Richmond, but almost inevitably there were last-minute problems with Alan:

> Things could not get much worse. Everything like a see-saw. Alan and his stories, and Sal his wife now maybe going into hospital. First

she wrote and told me that 2 years ago in Ireland he stole £400 and that if she couldn't have him, I could'nt either and that she was going to the police. He has just come back and said he has no money. And that he can't go to Greece on Wednesday as planned because the doctor says Sal will break down completely, and even though I am definately pregnant, which I <u>am, was</u>, no am glad about, he is going to look after her.[52]

Shortly before she left, Beryl wrote to Ken to tell him that she was pregnant by Alan. He was taken aback, but held firm to his promise, reserving his blame for Alan:

When I said I loved you completely & for always, I meant it. You have been stupid – singularly stupid, but nothing harsher. If the <u>Alan</u> is a fair-haired man who hangs around the Cruel Sea & The Flask with a wife something like Margaret then you are unbelievably silly. You must get out of this sordid mess – for your own sake & for the children. The man is a complete phony – his actions are the most selfish that I've ever heard of. Do you really imagine this is love? My view is still unchanged. In short I want to marry you.[53]

With characteristic generosity, Ken sent her £200 to cover her holiday costs and so, on 15 July, Beryl, the children, Austin and his new girl-friend, set off for Skopelos, travelling via Paris, Yugoslavia and Idomeni, a marathon journey that took three days. Unsurprisingly, the atmos-phere was occasionally strained. Austin, brooding over the news that Beryl was pregnant, seemed in a fraught mood: 'His temper, which I never knew in our married salad days, is diabolic. A bit like my dear dead Father, as Jane Austin might say.' Alan finally turned up a month later: 'I met him on the harbour,' she wrote to Judith:

He bought me a gingham bikini and shampoo's and the typewriter and three boxes of pills for unmarried mother's to be . . . So much has happened to him too in the absence that it is more like a year or an age than four weeks. There was the final break with Sal, the parting with his children, the almost nightmare search for money and then two days before he was due to come the American paper-back company paid £10,000 for the rights of the paper backed book. The publishers get £5,000 and it is the biggest amount ever paid for a Penguin type. Nabakov was paid £900 for *Lolita* . . . now he is a bit drained and I feel a bit detached, but then I am nuroctic as a devil. He is so delighted about the baby. I would hate however for him to feel he had to be with me. Though I'm sure he loves me. Why are we all so sure we are unlovable in the last resort? We sit here in the sun, married 20 years, all troubles past, and something like an electric current of hope and panic flickering through my putrid little brain. I do not dare mention being made an honest woman of . . . Its all too bohemian, but if I could first consume one plate of Walls' sausages – life would be a bowl of cider and roses. If you ever had the energy or inclination could you send a bottle of H.P. sauce and a packet of tea.[54]

Alan's opportunities for indulging in mysterious disappearing acts and rounds of bed-hopping on Skopelos were severely reduced. Consequently, there were elements of the holiday that were almost idyllic, a hint of how simple life might have been if Alan's pathological promiscuity could have been curbed or restrained. This feeling was reinforced by the fact that in the pre-tourist-boom Greece of the 1960s they were living in an almost prelapsarian state of nature: 'To go to the toilet we strip. It is lovely to see Alan run by purposefully in just his black leather cap to pee among the fig trees. From the rafters we hang our sodden and sordid clothes. On the straw matresses the children roll naked, and clouds of smoke from the charcole fire billow out into the room, so that we all look like Rhonda valley miners, red eyes and sooty mouths.'[55]

But Skopelos was not real life, and underneath the surface the old problems lay unresolved: 'Nothing has been said about what happened in England and about Sal,' Beryl explained to Judith:

so that for the last two weeks I have woken crying and wondering what on earth I am to do. [Alan] told Austin's girlfriend that he would never leave his wife, that he could not ask for a divorce. He is so like me and lives in such a fantasey that I suppose I am recieiving what I deserve. But he tells me how he will never leave me, how he adores me, and then the letters from Sal come in answer to his and I read them guiltily in the bushes whilst he swims and it is a hot haze of horror, because he is telling her how he will return and how he loves her, and she is saying 'O my darling break from her now.' I asked him if she knew about the baby and he said no he could not tell her, and that he tells Sal he cannot return, and I know he is lying. And he knows I know he is, and what can I do? And I beg him to tell me now if he intends to leave me, and he says, 'How can you think such a thing?' etc.

Worn down by Alan's duplicity, Beryl tried to resign herself to a future that, if it included Alan at all, would have to be on his terms:

So after weeks of misery and inward despair I am now going to try to accept it all, because I do want the baby and he won't leave me I know that, its just he has to pretend to Sal that he will return. But he is so slippery. You see the book [*A Green Tree in Gedde*] is due out March with a hell of publicity. And the baby is due then, and I think he intends to pretend he is still with Sal, and maybe take her to America and I will stay in the country, which I suppose I won't mind. I shall lick my wounds and maybe write something.

At the end of September, Alan and Beryl left Skopelos for Athens, and then on to Paris before arriving in the UK. As the flat in Arkwright Road was still being leased, Alan had rented a cottage at Crews Mess in Devon, but once there he soon resumed his 'slippery' behaviour and disappeared. Left on her own, feeling 'yet again shattered', Beryl wrote to Judith to explain what had happened:

We got back and got to a cottage in Devon. On the Sunday before he said he would go to Sal, ask for a divorce, tell about the baby etc etc. 'How will I believe you?' I said. 'Well,' says Alan, 'you must see Sal after me and confirm it.' . . . We were to leave here on the Friday. Thursday morning he vanishes. All night I waited, not wanting to admit it, but so sick with fright. In the night I rang Sal. She told me that Alan had been telling her for months that he would soon get rid of me, that the baby was a shock, how if he played his cards right I would go to the States . . . he even dictated the two letters she wrote to me. Letters pleading with me to give him up . . . All his friends he's told I'm mad and evil and am ruining him. That I trapped him by getting pregnant. Well, he came back nine oclock the next morning with stuff all over his fly and still a bit drunk. I think he'de been with Liz. I rang Sal and she came and we tried to talk but he was so strange. He just sat, and I went numb and Sal just cried. Finally she said, 'Do you want a divorce Alan, you can have one,' and he said, 'No, I don't.' Then she went and he said, 'Give in Beryl, submitt, come with me. I won't tell you any more lies.' And we never mentioned anything again . . . Then we got here – the most beautiful cottage – truely – so lovely. A day later I got the kids into school and when I came back he had gone. He left a note saying he'de gone to a football match in Scotland. That was 3 days ago . . .

Last night Alan phoned. 'Back Friday – I love you.' And now what? I don't have to say I feel sick. I feel broken. The whole thing is just too fantastic. Its too complicated, nuroctic and sick. Its quite beyond me. For Gods sake write to me. I think my mind is going.[56]

In the solitude of the cottage at Crews Mess, feeling unloved and abandoned, Beryl's mind regressed to childhood, to the vanished past when she'd felt secure in her mother's love. She wrote to Judith: 'And in all this one thing keeps recurring. Not the baby, not the lies, not the mess, only why arn't I loved? And beyond that the next thought process is Mummy, Mummy, Mummy . . . When it gets too painful and it hurts so much I just say Mummy over and over, without the slightest desire to see her, and appallingly concious I am past thirty, and Jo and Aaron call out the same word.'[57]

With nothing to do all day she would write long, anguished letters to Alan, full of recriminations, trying to find the right combination of words that would bring home the damage he was doing to her:

I've got our baby in me. Do you know what that means truely? Thats reality. You and I made a baby and you said you loved me . . . Make it real. Only you won't. I know that. It will come. One day you'll go up to London and I'll pack and buy the ticket and turn the key and then I'll go . . . The heart doesn't break unless someone snaps it . . . I hate not sleeping, I hate not laughing. I'm half dead and I've got 2½ children to be alive for, and it means sweet fuck all . . . I wish I was dead. Truely so. I don't want to go on living in this sort of world . . . I'm sick too at what I'm doing to Aaron and Jo . . . Its become that I don't love them anymore, I only love you . . . but unlike Sal I want love back too, and I don't believe you can give love . . . So go to hell and just don't try to pretend about all this later. You did this deliberately. You almost enjoy it . . . And the awful thing is I do love you.[58]

Realizing now that she would have to cope with the baby on her own, her anxieties began to mount: 'I feel so sad about the baby. You see

I'm actually frightened of having it. Before it was sort of an offering, a this-is-me-and-you and it was all for you. I wanted to show you how beautiful the baby would be and how well I would look after your baby for you, and now there's noone to show it to. It makes Austin sick, my mother hopes it will die before birth.'

As she had in the past, Beryl sought to express what she felt in a poem, one of the bleakest she would write:

Its only words isn't it.
Its only words that make me remember
that you were going to say one day to our child that
he, she, was conceived in love, held in love,
grew in love. Which will not be true.
I won't be with you. I'll be alone and
crying and the baby will know only
me. Poor little baby. Poor little me.
Who is not poor, but a monster of
self-pity and self-deception.
Oh please God step in. Or
a miracle or a disease or a
holocaust or a bomb.
Just something to stop the pain.
I love you.[59]

TWENTY

Basher's Progress

> And now I feel so big, so full of something you cannot even
> begin to know about – My little love. And I think all the
> time how I shall tell him or her about you, and one day, one
> day that will mean little to you, he or she will come like
> you did, and say, 'I'm your daughter, your son.' Alan, why,
> what is it that stops all the love like a flower bursting right
> over you?[1]

A S THE BIRTH APPROACHED – the estimated date of confine-
ment had been calculated as 22 February 1965 – Beryl gave herself
up to the inevitable flow of events. By now her relationship with Alan
had effectively come apart at the seams, though it dragged on painfully
through a kind of emotional inertia, her residual feelings of love for
him persisting despite his infidelities and his frustratingly contradictory
behaviour.

Having recently discovered who his birth mother was, Alan was
spending Christmas with her in Dundee. Although Beryl was expecting him back in January, she was resigned to the fact that he wouldn't
show up, or that if he did the same round of excuses and disappearances
would start all over again: 'Soon you'll ring and say you're not after all
coming back tomorrow. You'll feel guilty and sad but you'll have to do
it. Because your Mother needs you and your wife needs you and you
couldn't say No.'

Away from Beryl, Alan's letters, in which he would protest his love,
his guilt, his willingness to change, took on an obsessive, almost masochistic quality that matched Beryl's own: 'What am I doing so far from
you Beryl,' he wrote from Dundee, 'I love you so much, so much more
than anyone else, how do I come to be here? . . . I know it is my fault and

still I am amazed and sick at the thought of it. It hurts and wrenches so much inside me and I have to clench my teeth not to cry out . . . Being with you is agony, being away from you is worse . . .'[2]

Unsurprisingly, given the ambivalent messages Alan was sending her, not to mention the hormonal imbalances usually associated with pregnancy, Beryl was subject to extreme mood swings in the months before the birth. There were moments of black despair and she even hinted at thoughts again of suicide: 'Each day it hurts so that but for Aaron and Jo-Jo I would do something. This is the dark night of the soul one reads about.'[3]

But despite these bouts of depression, and her unhealthy tendency to blame herself for Alan's rejection ('I suppose I'm not very loveable . . .'),[4] Beryl nevertheless had moments where she felt the baby constituted some form of genuine connection between them and she began to feel more positive: 'I'm even getting excited about the future. There comes a time when you have to settle for what you are, and then be more that than you were before. No regrets. Whats the sense of being inconsolable about anything. I had more love from you than I'll ever have in my life, or ever had before. I'm glad.'[5]

By the start of March the baby still showed no sign of movement, and thinking she was two weeks late Beryl began to get worried. As it turned out, she was not overdue – the due-date calculation was a month out, no doubt as a consequence of her long-standing problem with erratic periods.[6] Alan was due to go to America at the start of April to promote *A Green Tree in Gedde*, but in the meantime he was back in Arkwright Road:

> Alan is his usual exhuberent self. Flying here there and moved in again to be near me when 'our' child is born and sharing his nights between Sal, me and Liz. Liz and he sail for the land of honey in 2 weeks time, and noone has any money. None at all. However all is not lost. My sense of humour is returning. I crawl around behind my far flung stomach and have long dreams each night that are terryfying and intense and I write them down and think 'My God, this is life after all' and through it all get all Formby and pink and tender at the thought of the new baby. Lovely baby.[7]

The baby, Ruth Emmanuella, or Rudi as she soon came to be called, was delivered on 24 March by the midwife, a district nurse called Johanna

Bormann, a suitably inappropriate name given Beryl's fascination with the Holocaust. Lacking a suitable bowl to bath the newborn baby in, a casserole dish[8] was borrowed from the downstairs tenants, Philip and Psiche Hughes.

In the weeks that followed, Beryl wrote to Judith to say that she felt 'very fit and very gutsy. Ready to face all that life offers', and that the baby had put on nine ounces in a week ('Its the whisky and the Woodies that do it . . .').[9] Beryl's previous letter to her had flippantly mentioned not only that Alan was talking about taking her away to Malta, but that Ken had told her he was coming over in seven weeks' time. Judith, irritated that Beryl seemed to be taking her situation too lightly and colluding in her own misfortune, was unable to refrain from lecturing her, prompting a sharp retort: 'Please do not "go" at me anymore. I am too frail. Either you attack my financial immorality and suggest I actually work or you call me a sex maniac or say the children are unstable. Stop being my conciounce. One day I may redeem myself. No comments or criticisms please. Just like me a little. Love you. B.'[10]

A month after the birth Alan flew back from America, arriving at Arkwright Road with just a carrier bag. He had a new set of plans for the future, but after what Beryl described as 'an idillic 3 days', it all blew up again when she discovered he had really come back for Liz, who had returned without him due to illness, and that they were due to fly back to New York the following week. The result was a definitive parting – of sorts. If it wasn't exactly the first and wouldn't be the last, it did have a kind of symbolic quality to it, with both getting rid of the rings they'd exchanged, albeit in their own different ways:

> So I said goodbye and he in a grand gesture tore up his passport and the air-tickets into fragments, and Austin told him to get out and he went and they are all grounded somewhere.
>
> The roses still come. I feel quite exhausted and a bit off centre, only not depressed. Also Ken <u>says</u> he is coming in 3 weeks, I suppose he won't.
>
> Alan said (he came back in the middle of the night for his bits of passport) that he was now free of me, that he was cutting from Sal, and was going to try to be a good man and reach god.

'One day', he said, picking up his passport pieces, 'I will phone and say "Come to me", and you must just say yes or no, and if its yes we'll grow old together.' And with a last convulsive sob he touched the baby's cheek and went. He left his ring on her toe and I threw mine in the pond.[11]

In the period of limbo waiting for the baby to be born, Beryl had continued working on *A Weekend with Claud*, and by March it was all but finished. Alan's influence on Beryl's writing career went beyond his undoubted practical assistance – finding her an agent and suggesting publishers. He also actively encouraged her to write, and his example showed that it was possible to break into publishing by perseverance and self-belief.

There was one area, however, in which Alan's influence turned out to be less positive: Beryl's writing style. Having received so many rejections for 'The Summer of the Tsar', which was written in her distinctively spare and relatively unadorned style, Beryl couldn't help comparing her literary style to his, which was linguistically self-conscious, full of complicated sentences and obscure words. If it worked for him, why not for her?

Consequently, during the writing of *A Weekend with Claud* she made a deliberate attempt to inject a more 'literary' element into her style. The pages of the manuscript are littered with lists of obscure words, together with their definitions, ready to be inserted wherever necessary: '*hyaline*, glassy transparent; *imputrescible*, not corruptable; *banaustic*, merely mechanical; *avenous*, without veins; *atomy*, a tiny being'.[12] This, coupled with the radical formal device of recounting the action of the novel three times, each time through the eyes of a different narrator, made the book much denser, much closer to the kind of formal experimentation practised by contemporary novelists such as B. S. Johnson and John Fowles, both of whom used changes in authorial perspective as a way of achieving certain literary effects.[13]

After Nina Froud's damning appraisal, Alan had counselled Beryl to try elsewhere and so she applied to John Smith at Christy & Moore's. Smith, who had signed Muriel Spark in 1953, was a literary agent with a solid track record. He was impressed enough to submit the novel to Graham Nicol at New Authors, a Hutchinson imprint that was designed to showcase new talent and had already featured the work of first-time novelists such as Maureen Duffy, Alex Hamilton and J. G. Farrell. At the beginning of August, two months after submitting the completed manuscript, Nicol wrote asking Beryl to contact him, telling her that two of the three readers' reports had been good, though he warned her not to take this as a form of commitment.[14]

In the midst of this exciting development, Beryl had to deal with more emotional dramas with Alan, as she explained to Judith:

> Things here are much as usual, except I have begun painting again and my Mother has been <u>yet again</u> and gone and Alan arrived complete with baggage to start afresh forever with presents and money and I would'nt let him in. My choicest memory is of Mama at 3 in the morning vast in a blue nylon nightie on hands and knees crawling into the kids room where I lay sleeping on the floor (having got rid of Alan 2 hours previously) and her hissing into my ear 'That devil is on the landing moaning.'
>
> He lay out there all night moaning 'Beryl, Beryl,' and at 5 I let him in and he wept and I put him out again. Only thing was he hid in the basement all day and at one point added his suit to his baggage in the hall which sent my Mother into hysteric's and me floating up and downstairs shouting bravely 'Now be off Alan, pull yourself together or I'll call the police.' So about 11 the next night he goes and rings to say he has a room down the next street and the Americans are now giving him 50,000 dollars for the next two books etc. and could he take his child for a walk, and everyday, cap on and crew cut bristling, he wheels Ruth off and returns her with a fresh rose in her shawl, and at night he rings several times and mutters brokenly 'I love you'. Only thing is he is undoubtedly raving mad and I am truely over him and sick sick sick of his twisted carryings on. Sal has also thrown him out, and Liz and he are just 'friends' and the 1st wife rings me now in tears and says he had been going to bed with her too and its all a terrible frantic mess.[15]

Perhaps thinking to get away, she had spent the August Bank Holiday in North Wales, along with Austin and the children, staying in some huts at Coed Nant Gain, a wooded piece of land near Mold owned by

Iliff Simey, the conspicuously tall son of Tom and Margaret Simey, who Beryl had known from her Playhouse days. But while she was away, Alan broke into the flat at Arkwright Road and began sending her 'a series of insane telegrams' until she returned. Things resumed their former course, until his equally sudden and dramatic departure. As she told Judith:

> Two weeks later in the middle of a supper party with the people downstairs he upped and went. Really violent this time. Me I mean. Shattered and 6stone in weight, and lost me voice. Two days later both I and the woman downstairs got letters from him [in] Scotland. Mine said he did not love me but could he have Ruth every Monday and take her to Scotland for the week. Hers said he passionately loved me but I was too strong and he would never see me again. A day after I came in from shopping and found him doing the dishes. He said he was going to kill himself and we had cheese on toast and off he went again. He climbed up the drain-pipe and came through the window.
>
> Throughout all this madness I am unbearably sustained by the dreadful fact that New Authors to whom I sent the book about three months ago, wrote and asked to see me. He was very nice and enthusiastic and he thinks they will do it. I am just praying and praying that I will hear something deffinite soon.[16]

Nicol's letter had also included extracts from the readers' reports, which had many positive things to say about the novel:

> It is the work of a brilliant talker (the book's strength is its dialogue).

> One of the most skilful things about the book, apart from its great intelligence, is the emergence of the rather sinister character of Claud through the thoughts of the others and the linking passages which are very well written indeed.

> This is a wonderful book and I recommend it whole-heartedly for publication. Its chief value is the depth in which the author reveals her characters and makes them living people in spite of their coldness and eccentricity. Above all, she has a wonderfully fertile imagination for detail and incident.[17]

Even the most favourable of the reports, though, couldn't overlook one glaring feature of Beryl's manuscript: 'The author writes beautifully, though her spelling is terrible . . .' But the other criticisms were more pertinent if the real qualities of the novel were to be brought out:

> Though intelligible, her narrative is not coherent . . . the novel is little more than a series of monologues; and these bore because they are related to very little action . . . it grows clear that the author has not the stamina either to be committed enough, or else detached enough, to see her world whole . . . Her talent appears too volatile and unstable to be capable of submission to the extended discipline which a novel needs.

> I found parts of this book too chaotically overpowering and near-incoherent especially Maggie's narration . . . new authors who want to be original, as this one does, should be wary of a once-experimental style which has now been played out and over-used.

Part of Nicol's reasons for including such negative comments was as feedback for the revisions that he felt were necessary before the book could be published. Beryl was not unreceptive to constructive criticism and she took the suggestions on board, happy to agree with the changes Nicol wanted when she felt they were justified: 'I rang Nicol last Friday and said I would gladly rewrite the Claud pieces to make the 3 bits more clear, but I couldn't touch the 3 narritives at all. He told me he is putting it up this week anyway. By that he means he wants to do it but Hutchinsons have to veto it. I bet you it all falls through.'[18]

A short while later Hutchinson agreed to take the book, and Nicol sent her a contract. The New Authors imprint was unique in a number of ways: not only did its list consist of first-time novelists, it also had a standard contract for all its authors. There was an initial advance of £150, and royalties of 10 per cent on the first 5,000 copies sold, rising to 15 per cent after 7,500. Technically the company was run on a profit-sharing basis, and after the costs of publication and a fee of 25 per cent to cover overheads, the profits would be 'divided among the contributing authors in the proportion of their individual total sales in the relevant year'.[19] This sounded very equitable in theory, though in practice few authors benefited financially from the deal: Beryl's book did not sell enough for the profit-sharing arrangement to kick in.

Nevertheless this acceptance had a positive effect on her, giving Beryl some much-needed confidence. Alan's behaviour, particularly over the past few months, had driven her to distraction, but as she had noted to Judith, the process of dealing with literary matters had taken her mind off things and helped sustain her through the madness. She might still be 'bloody obcessed with emotional problems'[20] but at least she was going to be a published writer.

She was aware of the novel's failings, but had already started work on her next book, loosely based on the weekend at Coed Nant Gain, which would eventually be entitled *Another Part of the Wood*. The novel culminates in the accidental death by overdose of a young boy called Roland – modelled on Aaron, who was six at the time. Some writers might have had qualms about killing off a character based on their own son, but if Beryl was aware of the psychological implications she doesn't seem to have mentioned it. The inspiration for this plot twist came from a typically generous act by Austin, who had recently taken a young student with emotional problems into his home in order to look after him. This was mirrored in the novel by Joseph's decision to take care of a disturbed adolescent called Kidney, who is indirectly the cause of Roland's death. Beryl's would-be *inamorato*, Charles White, was concerned enough about the potential threat to Aaron and Jo-Jo's safety to warn her: 'Don't quite understand Austin sharing his flat (his new flat) with a 17-year-old schizophrenic . . . Do you think it a proper risk to leave him to look after the children until you know him better??'[21]

This combination of circumstances, the dramatic irony inherent in benign intentions leading to tragic consequences, all unfolding within the self-contained setting of the idyllically rustic Coed Nant Gain, appealed to Beryl's sensibility. Initially, she was pleased about the way the new novel was shaping up: 'The next one is good, about Wales,' she told Judith, 'not subjective or obscure or self-pitying like the last one, but a story. I will send you bits as I finish it. There is noone else I want to read it, or tell me what they think.'[22]

Despite the drama of Alan's last appearance, Beryl wrote to Judith shortly after he'd gone and told her that 'next month I may go to Germany with him'.[23] After everything that had happened, the idea of going away with him must have seemed wilfully bizarre to her friends.

There was, however, a kind of logic to the decision: Alan was going to the Frankfurt Book Fair, the foremost publishing market in Europe, so it made sense, given the recent acceptance of her book by Hutchinson, to go too. But in reality her motive for the trip, aside from a faint lingering hope of a reconciliation with Alan, was to visit the sites of the concentration camps ('I want to go to Belsen . . .').[24]

Alan's time at the Book Fair seems to have been productive, and Italian, French and Spanish editions of *A Green Tree in Gedde* appeared over the next year or so. Foreign publishers had no doubt been encouraged by the *succès de scandale* provoked on publication in April, and the book's frank treatment of sex had ensured sales and a healthy helping of outrage: 'Mustard should not be served without beef,' wrote one contemporary reviewer, 'but that is precisely what Mr Sharp has done . . . *A Green Tree in Gedde* is spread so thick with sex that it is hard to find the "meat".'[25]

For Beryl, the trip was less successful. Although her flight and accommodation had been arranged by Alan's German publishers – she was travelling as his 'wife'[26] – she doesn't seem to have attended the Book Fair itself.[27] Nor did she get to see the camps. This was in part due to her lack of geographical awareness, in that Bergen-Belsen was too far north of Frankfurt and Auschwitz was in Poland: 'I cannot find the camps,' she complained to Judith. 'Noone knows, not here, never heard of them, not anywhere, 360 miles already and still noone knows. Tomorrow I go to Munich, to Dachau, they must know there.'[28]

Judith disapproved of Beryl's decision to go to Germany, feeling that she was complicit in Alan's abusive treatment of her and was being corrupted by his money. Beryl sensed this and in her letters tried to forestall criticism by acknowledging it and taking the blame on herself:

I am somewhere in the Black Forest, but as usual I do not see the trees for the tears. Mainly of self pity – but mixed with self disgust. I have been bought up. A £100 worth of clothes, flying here there and everywhere, rich hotels, everything around me as corrupt as I am myself. This much I know to be true. He does not love me and I know it, and yet I am here and I indulge in the most dreadful suffering . . . This man is my devil and all I do is submitt. If in some few days I do not fight I shall really go under.

Wherever we stop he writes his bloody letters – to Liz – to Sal – to Margaret. If I had the guts or enough madness I would kill him, God help me I mean it. I am in an intense subjective world, the exit I know about, but he seems stronger than me. I have decided to go home, I mean back to Liverpool. I will die otherwise, and then what about the children?[29]

In some ways Germany was the last straw, a final proof, if further proof were needed, that she and Alan were bad for one another. Whether it was that reason prevailed, that Alan had broken her spirit, or that she'd simply had enough, when she got back she tried to get him out of her system, writing to tell Judith that with his departure she already felt a weight off her mind:

O dear I do feel such a fool because I am not in such chaos really, not to deserve such kindness and love in your letter, both written and between the lines. I mean I do deserve it, but I mean I'm not so miserable. The reason for the quick change of attitude is that maybe, barely breathing, I have seen the last, positively the last of Alan and because of this I am enormously much better and less sorry for myself and whatnot. Germany was dreadful, awful, like Greece only not so hot and so much more covered and oiled and besmirched with money and all that. We came back a few days ago and parted in the night, him to Liz I presume and me to Austin seated in the brass bed in his red satin underpants, twitching his head and making faces at the baby.[30]

Of course it was not quite as simple as that. A few days after writing that she had seen 'positively the last' of Alan, he was back, breaking into Arkwright Road again: 'I really wanted to kill him. My head starts to thump or is it my heart?'[31]

———

Two years before, Beryl had felt so overwhelmed by these emotional dramas she had considered writing to Cyril Taylor to ask him 'to put me in some rest home for a time. There was one he thought about once before, and I can't go on like this.'[32] She ultimately abandoned the idea, feeling that with the children to look after it wasn't practical.

Nevertheless, she was aware that her emotional instability was some-thing she had to deal with sooner or later: 'At this rate it can only get worse. Everything is sliding away. Useless to tell anyone what it feels like, because unless you feel like this, you can easily dismiss it as sheer hysteria. I feel so ashamed, and the strain of being normally chatty and everything is awful.'[33]

A month before Rudi was born Beryl told Judith she was still haunted by thoughts of suicide, and that she felt there was something psycho-logically wrong with her: 'Sometimes I believe I am sick. I write down unbelievable filth, fantasys of sexual torture done to me by elderly and balding buisness men. My head gets hot and I throw the pages in the fire, and want to vomit and wonder what is wrong with me. Somewhere I went badly astray.'[34]

Things didn't improve after the birth and she reached a point where she felt she needed professional help. Her doctor referred her to Charles Rycroft, then a consultant psychotherapist at the Tavistock Clinic and an influential figure in British psychiatry who had been R. D. Laing's training analyst. Rycroft diagnosed her as a 'hysteric with psychopathic tendencies',[35] but as she refused group therapy he put her on a waiting list for one-to-one psychotherapy. Eventually her first appointment with Dr Lawrence Kotkas, a member of the South Place Ethical Society, was arranged for 18 January 1966.

Kotkas picked up on her fascination with Jews, seeing it as a form of identification, and that their presumed passivity during the Holocaust was a metaphor for her own acquiescence in suffering. 'All my life I've been wanting to be persecuted,' she told Judith by way of explanation, 'asking to be punished because I feel unworthy of something or other. So I turn very easily to the Jew thing not because they were persecuted but more because they were so willing to be slaughtered. They went so meekly to die . . . He said I should study the reasons why the Jews so easily marched to their deaths and perhaps find out why I insist on being hurt.'[36]

After about six months the sessions ended as Dr Kotkas had to return to Canada. Whether it had anything to do with her therapy or not, the early months of 1966 marked a change in Beryl's attitude to Alan, and she no longer felt quite so in thrall to her feelings about him. Alan, who was now living in Greenock, having moved out of the flat he shared with Sally in London, sensed this shift in power between them: 'You are on the edge of freedom from me and my tearing into your life,' he wrote to her, 'the only thing you want is certainty and you are sure that it doesn't lie in Greenock with me. All of this I see and accept. It can't be denied.'[37]

His last attempt at a reconciliation between them took place in May, after he sent her air tickets to spend the weekend with him in Greenock. She came, but it was not a success. The relationship was past the point where it could be retrieved. In an undated letter to her, Alan summed up the emotional balance sheet of their mutual incompatibility:

We may argue about who is most to blame, but that doesn't matter. What matters now is that it stops. You are destroying me as much as I am you, and I want so much to be free of you and the reproaches you plant into me, the relentless tears and the way you cut Ruth off like she was a tap. We each have our own versions now of what it was all about and nothing will bring them together. I had hoped of this time we were together that we might not play the same cruel games, but we have and once more we're strangers in a foreign country and have nothing to say.

You are not for me Beryl. You are too much of too many things. I will never be able to name my list because in the end I always shrink from the truth. So I hover around the soft lie, the would-be kindly lie. I am in my nature an evader of reality and so I need someone who will not ask the same questions or who will leaven the asking with some compassion for my failings. That at least is something no one can accuse you of suffering from.

In your eyes I will always be what I am now, and I will always see myself through your eyes as long as I have you in my heart. I do have you there and sometimes I fear I wont get you out. But I will. I thought for a little time that you were going to look at me differently, and while I loved you I would be able to look at myself differently. But that is not your way, you are just as incapable of letting me off as I have been until now of tearing myself free. Now we are hooked into each other and nothing results but pain. We are terrible people, consuming so much of life in order to be unhappy.[38]

In August, Beryl went to stay again at the Simeys' place in Coed Nant Gain. As she had the previous year, she returned to more bad news. Not only had the television play she had written failed to be selected for production (there was small comfort in the fact that it was the runner-up), Graham Nicol had put back the publication date of her novel to the following March. More pressing, however, was her dire financial situation: 'Came back to 3 court summonses and one baliff order.'[39]

Fortunately, a round of letters asking for help produced results: Judith sent her some money, as did Harry and Ken Ratcliffe, Austin gave her £15 and Alan sent £10 (which Beryl disdainfully dismissed as 'sweetie money'). She had also written to her agent in desperation ('I was near to crying,' she told Judith) to see whether there was any way he could hurry an advance. He couldn't. Although the catastrophe was averted and the bailiffs placated, it nevertheless left her in low spirits: 'I carn't say I feel cheerful – its not the money or the Alan thing or anything concrete – it's a steady rising lump of mess.'[40]

She was, however, still writing, though her initial enthusiasm for *Another Part of the Wood* had now settled into the less joyous task of actually writing it, with all the doubts, difficulties and hesitations this involved. Despite her mood, the book progressed steadily: she had mapped out the characters, and by November she had worked out the dynamics of the book's tragic final scene:

> At the very end Kidney takes Roland up mountain. Balfour falls for Dotty. Doris tells Lionel how she hates him. Coming down mountain Roland takes pills to make himself as fat as Kidney. Dies in coma. Everyone goes in to see him during final game of monopoly. Balfour enters. Last sentances –
> Joseph: How is he?
> Balfour: D–dead.[41]

It was, as she put it, 'All phychological stuff.'

By the beginning of 1967 things had picked up on a number of fronts. Panther had agreed to bring out *A Weekend with Claud* in paperback, offering a £300 advance. As her agent explained, this was 'very good indeed for a first novel',[42] even if it was split with the hardback publisher. The novel was now finally and officially scheduled to come out in June and had even aroused interest in America.

Beryl had also finished *Another Part of the Wood*. Her agent had 'enjoyed it very much', despite feeling that the end 'was very abrupt'.[43] However, it would not actually be published for another year and a half due to the delayed publication date of *A Weekend with Claud*.

In a new, positive frame of mind, Beryl could even regard Alan's periodic reappearances with a certain equanimity. His life had not become any less complicated since their definitive parting the previous year and, as Beryl told Judith, Liz now seemed to be suffering a fate similar to that which she had endured: 'Lizzie had a boy last month and has gone back home and Alan now has a 17 year old debutante type in her place. He chases me and Ru along Finchley Road most days begging to see her and she says "Hallo man", and I laff. Not nastily, I don't mind anymore and he does look funny, with that funny phoney expression and all his ex-demented wives and mistresses in ruins all over points South and North.'[44]

Despite the awkward position Liz was in, Beryl felt none of the *schadenfreude* she thought she might: 'I feel very sorry now – its not much fun having an illigitimate baby at the best of times, but certainly not the first time – and she must be unhappy if she's at all normal after being with Mr Sharp.'[45]

There was more good news in April: Austin had completed the purchase of a house in Albert Street, Camden Town, and his long-held hopes of providing a home for Beryl and the children were at last a reality. His plan was to convert the basement into a self-contained flat, which he could live in while doing the work himself. Then, once Beryl and the children were installed and the work on the house was finished, the flat could either be rented for income or sold to release enough capital for himself.

The timing was perfect: Austin would move in on 1 May and Beryl would follow three weeks later, just in time for the launch of her novel on 21 June. The scale of the building work required may not have been what she had in mind, but for the moment the disruption and the lack of money paled into insignificance. As if the fates were conspiring to engineer a fresh start in life, by the summer of 1967 Beryl not only had a new place to live, she also had a new occupation: writer.

TWENTY-ONE

Albert Street

> I am alright now. A bit miserable but beginning to bounce
> again. I miss you. You are a fool rushing away. Think of the
> glories of wet and storm tossed Albert St.[1]

THE HOUSE AT NO. 42 was one of a short line of terraced houses
at the lower end of Albert Street, built for railway workers in the
mid-nineteenth century. It would be Beryl's home until she died, and
came to be seen as an expression of her personality, its eccentricities of
decor a reflection of her own.

When Beryl first moved in, many of the street's terraced houses
had been divided up into flats or bedsits. 'It was a very run-down area,'
remembered Penny Jones, Beryl's next-door neighbour who had lived
there since 1962, 'multi-occupational, mainly Irish and Greek-Cypriot
immigrants; there were rooming houses, with people in every room and
sinks on the landing.'[2]

But the process of gentrification had already started. A number of
houses that were previously multi-family occupiers were being converted
back to single-occupier properties, and an increasing number of middle-
class families or those in upper-income professions were moving in.
By the time Beryl arrived, there was already a solid core of middle-
class incomers: the barrister Barbara Mills (later Director of Public
Prosecutions) lived up the road, as did the architect Beeban Morris,
while the innovative designer and engineer Sigur Max Fordham moved
in two doors down in 1963.

In the short term the conversion of No. 42 meant a drain on the
finances, not to mention disruption, inconvenience, dust and delays:

> Last week we might have moved in quite reasonably but this week
> it is uninhabitable by virtue of Aussie and his mania for posh doing

overs and taking out all the wires and the pipes and all the fireplaces, so we now have a litter of bricks and debris. After 3 days of this he collapsed and I threw a hard boiled egg at him. We finished up with £1,987 on the Friday and -£15 on the Sat. During the hours from riches to rags he hired a lorry, a plumber, and an architect, as the basement wall he had started to remove was holding up the rest of the house. I reckon we will be in debt for another 25 years . . . I sometimes think he does it just to have something to worry about. Whereas all I want to do is put up me pictures, arrange the plants, and write me next book. Still, it will be alright. For one thing me suite – me middle floor – is beautiful, long windows, an iron balconey and double doors à la Noel Coward flourishing into the bedroom.[3]

Short of money, and with the bailiff incident still on her mind, Beryl wrote again to her agent John Smith, asking whether he could speed up payment of the second half of her advance. He couldn't, but instead he offered to advance her the money himself, 'just to keep the wolf from the door'.[4] This may have been intended as an act of kindness, but it established something of a bad precedent: before her first book was published she was already in debt to her agent.

The actual publication of *A Weekend with Claud* was something of an anticlimax. It had been so long in production that anything short of an overwhelming success would have seemed like a poor reward for so much time and effort. In the lead-up to publication, things looked promising. Beryl was featured in two profiles, the first of which appeared in *The Sun* alongside what the paper called the 'most unusual literary photograph of the year', a picture of Beryl and the children posing in front of some of her paintings:

Her startling first novel, one of the most personal I have ever read, is not only a novel. For this Liverpool-born writer it was also a piece of emotional therapy. Miss Bainbridge who is divorced and lives with her three children in Hampstead, told me this week: 'Almost from the moment of writing the thing down, the relief was tremendous. It's rather like my diary, as though I crammed in what actually happened. It was therapy – I was writing something out. The thing that does worry me now is that in a few years it could seem a neurotic carry-on, it could look too self-pitying. It was meant to be comedy.'[5]

In February Beryl had given her play 'I'm Not Criticising . . . I'm Remembering' to John Smith to see whether he could place it, and he had sought the opinion of the famous theatrical agent, Peggy Ramsay. In something of a bad omen, a month before *A Weekend with Claud* was published, Beryl received news that the play had been turned down again. Ramsay had sent Smith a blunt analysis of its failings, which was all very well, but his decision to copy out a passage of this damning assessment and send it to Beryl wasn't very diplomatic. 'I honestly don't know what to say about the play,' Ramsay began, before demolishing it, 'Miss Bainbridge is obviously not without talent, but this is not a TV play one could show to anyone, because Miss Bainbridge hasn't grasped TV technique. She seems to organise a series of film shots all over the place, and then sits down to interminable duologues which wouldn't hold on TV.'[6]

Shortly after this setback, the initial reviews of the novel started appearing, and they weren't overly complimentary either. They picked up on the book's complicated literary structure, its dense writing style, and what they saw as its concentration on a group of characters who were too self-obsessed and self-absorbed to be interesting to anyone else. The *Observer* was harsh in its criticism: 'Perhaps the prose intermittently has something, but generally this novel spectacularly fails to convince that there is hard imaginative currency supporting its considerable literary pretension. Interior monologue is one thing: character another.'[7] If anything, the *Sunday Telegraph* was even harsher: 'No amount of mannered writing – and there is quite a lot of it – can conceal that Miss Bainbridge hasn't much to say.'[8]

It wasn't very encouraging. As she told the *Hampstead and Highgate Express* twelve days later: 'I've got some really terrible reviews, so I've just given up reading them.'[9] Despite these initial setbacks, the novel did attract some positive attention. There was a very enthusiastic profile-cum-review in *Books & Bookmen* written by the assistant editor of the magazine, Alex Hamilton, another writer from the New Authors stable: 'I am a plot person, thinking that self-indulgence is the reader's rather than the writer's prerogative, but reading this book I felt for once 'The hell with the plot', in the pleasure of seeing a brilliant writer emerging.

It seems to me likely that in the books which follow this one we may see Beryl Bainbridge writing rings round many established names.'[10]

But it wasn't just critical assessments in newspapers, whether positive or negative, that Beryl had to deal with. There was also the response of her friends. *A Weekend with Claud* was openly autobiographical – perhaps the most truly autobiographical book she would write – and it featured portraits that were both indiscreet and not particularly flattering. Many of those closest to her appeared in only the very thinnest of disguises: Harry was 'Victorian Norman', Ken was Edward, Mick was Billie, Ronnie was Claud, Austin was Joseph, and Leah was Shebah. When the book first arrived from the publisher, Beryl immediately realized that the standard legal disclaimer was missing, technically leaving her open to claims of libel: 'To my horror there is no mention in the front of the book of "All characters are fictitious etc." That scares me, but its too late now.'[11]

But no legal disclaimer could prevent individuals from being hurt or offended by what she had written. The reactions of those depicted in the book varied: Ronnie seemed to be unperturbed, actually even flattered by his inclusion, despite his portrayal as a somewhat seedy character, while Austin passed the book over in silence, by now taking it for granted that Beryl's view of things was a distorted one. However, Leah and Harry don't seem to have been so forbearing. Initially, Leah wrote to wish Beryl 'All the MITZVAH (Good luck!) in the world in your new home & your "creation"'. She enthusiastically looked forward to reading the book, a copy of which she had seen at a mutual friend's house. Leah hoped that its publication would mark a new beginning for Beryl: 'Perhaps it will all change now & things will turn out well for you. You, too, have suffered so much. And also, I think, martyred (like me) here.'[12] What Leah thought after she read it is less clear. There are no further letters from her and Beryl doesn't mention her again in any of her letters or diaries. There was a similarly abrupt silence from Harry, hinting that he too may have felt she'd overstepped the mark and betrayed their friendship by revealing things he'd talked to her about in confidence.

———

As if moving house and the publication of her first book weren't enough to keep Beryl occupied during the summer of 1967, she also fell in love. And as was often the case, things weren't entirely straightforward.

Harold Retler was an American computer programmer on a three-month visit to the UK. He had come over in pursuit of Judith Gleeson, an ex-work colleague who had been persuaded to take up a computing job in London by Beryl's former neighbour, Philip Hughes, an IT consultant who had met her in the United States the previous year. But Harold's somewhat extravagant romantic gesture – he had given up his job in Washington and sold his house and car before coming over – was in vain. By the time he arrived in the spring of 1967, Judith's affections were elsewhere and she was already engaged.

At one of the Hughes' dinner parties, Philip's wife Psiche introduced Judith Gleeson to Beryl, with the view to getting her to commission a painting, and the two women had become friends. Consequently, when she heard that Beryl was about to move from Arkwright Road to Albert Street, Judith roped in Harold to lend a hand carrying the numerous boxes of 'junk' – Beryl's own word for her assemblage of Victoriana, stuffed animals, paintings, books and furniture.

After this hands-on introduction they began to see each other. On one level, they made an unlikely couple, and not just because Harold, bearded and balding, stood a head taller. They were completely different personality types: Harold, two years younger than Beryl, was an only child and more emotionally reserved. Nor, on the surface, did they seem to share the same interests – after studying mathematics at Lawrence University, Harold had gone into computer programming, still a relatively new field, first at Westinghouse Electric, then at Rand Corp. This led to a job in Washington, where he bought a house in the historic Georgetown district. As if to emphasize the cerebral nature of his interests, he gained admission to the Washington chapter of Mensa, which demands an IQ score of 130 or above. It was this connection to the US capital that inspired the nickname by which Beryl would always refer to him: 'Washington Harold'.

But underneath the surface they had a number of passions and enthusiasms in common. One was literature, Beryl urging Harold to read D. H. Lawrence and he pressing her to read Thomas Wolfe. Another was music, especially old 78s, such as Al Bowlly's touchingly sentimental rendition of 'There's Something in Your Eyes', and the comical 'Cicely Courtneidge Plonks her Guitar'.

They also shared an interest in art. As she had with Judith, Psiche prompted Harold to commission a painting, and impressed by the portraits Beryl had done of Judith and her sons he followed suit. Consequently he sat for his portrait, posed in the large rocking chair in her bedroom, which served as her studio at the time. When the picture was finished she didn't want to charge him and gave it to him as a gift. To ensure she wouldn't lose out financially he bought another painting – the double portrait of Claud and Shebah that happened to be propped up on the sofa in the publicity shot taken for the book – and a self-portrait she had done in pen.

Beryl had initially been drawn to Harold by empathy, wanting to console him over Judith's recent engagement, but her feelings quickly – and as usual too quickly – developed into something more serious. At the start of July she wrote to Judith Shackleton, ostensibly to tell her about her daughter Chloë's visit, and admitted she was 'in love with Washington Harold'.[13]

But Harold's time in England was already coming to an end. Shortly before he returned to the States he took Beryl to Ronnie Scott's to hear Blossom Dearie, the American jazz singer and pianist. Aware of the impracticalities of continuing the affair, and perhaps uncertain of Beryl's commitment, he tried to rationalize the situation and explain why things wouldn't work between them. He listed the drawbacks – she had too many children, she was too closely connected to Austin, he didn't want to hurt her. But of course he already had. In an attempt to alleviate her feelings of rejection, Beryl proceeded to get drunk and almost passed out. Harold had to take her out of the club to revive her.[14] She had the feeling of history repeating itself and in a letter to Judith she resigned herself to events: 'I shall no doubt survive . . . I just wish Washington Harold would like me.'[15]

On the eve of Harold's departure for America, Beryl wrote him a letter, trying to put into words some of the things she felt but which she hadn't been able to say to him in person. Just before he left, she handed it to him:

> Dear Washington Harold. I am not tight so I can do this without too many mistakes and seeing I won't see your face and you won't turn away or look trapped as is your wont, I can tell you that I love you and wish you could have felt the same. Howevere this is an ego

building letter for you maybe to look at when the wounds Judith inflicted get too much to bear again, and though its never quite the same, it should make you a bit happy, whatever that is. I think you are the goodest person and the most beautiful because you are not slick or climbing or any of the usual things. It might have been better more for me had you been a bit more inclined to believe in emotions. I wanted to talk to you so many times but I feared you thinking I was being a drag on you, you are lovely out of bed and lovely in bed, which in a way is more important, though maybe I don't mean what you think. I just mean its easier to get closer in bed and the way you are then makes it not matter how distant you are in the day. Lots of people appear to be close night and day, but its phony. Anyway take care and be happy and miss me a little.[16]

Along with the letter she also enclosed a token: the First World War medal belonging to George Ripon Towers, the husband of her Aunt Sarah, which Harold had worn while she was painting her portrait of him: 'I really do cherish it and its the most deaerest thing I had to give you. You can wish on it or pray or cry all over it. The name on the back is my Uncle's who died from gassing in the war. One day when we are very old you could send a telegram from G. R. Towers saying you were coming to England and I'd know it was you. I love you.'

Harold was deeply moved by the letter's contents, though his doubts remained and he reiterated his reasons for breaking things off while it was still possible to do so without causing too much distress on either side:

Dearest Beryl
It is a long way from Miami Beach to the house in Albert St and the big brass bed, a long way no matter how you measure it – I just read your letter five minutes ago, the first time since I read it many times the night you gave it to me, and I cried as I did that night and I haven't read it again til now, because I'm hardly ever alone and I didn't want anyone to see me cry because they would never understand, never – and if I pick it up again the tears will flow, because it is so beautiful, so very beautiful, the most beautiful letter I've ever received, and because I've hurt you, as I knew I would, but I needed you and you have meant as much to me as any person ever has. You said 'I love you and wish you could have felt the same' and you were

right that I did not feel the same, but I did, do, will, love you, but not with the intensity you felt for me and maybe this was the reason I had to run, because I knew I could never make you happy (or me?) and maybe I was afraid of this intense love.

Someone once said if life could be summed up in one word it would have to be goodbye – so goodbye Beryl, please write if you want to, goodbye, love Harold.[17]

In her reply Beryl tried to take up the role of friend-not-lover:

All this is a good chatty letter to a casual friend, dear heart Washington, as I have not been drinking, only staring at your empty bottles in the bookcase. It is just as well because I might say too much and make life like fiction which it undoubtedly is, and regret my impulses. I will say some things about your letter. It was a beautiful letter. I have read it over and over. One, you did not hurt me, I hurt myself – only because I wanted you to stay, whilst you were here you made me happy, caused me no hurt . . . I love you. I don't know what else to say to you. There is something I could say but the distance is too great and your complexity too vast and my own duplicity too monumental.[18]

Now that Harold had gone she found it hard to picture him, not having been to America or seen where he lived. 'I visualise nothing,' she told him, 'save you with your eyes sliding about and getting your glass of water at night. I put the photogarpah on the wall above my desk. I am looking at it now. I am looking at you now. Ru is in my bed, Aussie is asleep in the basement, the children are above. The lamps shine in the street. I hate goodbye's, O parting, always parting, whoever invented you.'[19]

Three weeks later she again wrote to him, this time on a potentially more serious issue – her period was late. She had tried calling him, but had only managed to get through to the friend he was staying with, Senter Stuart. As she was worried Senter might have told Harold and that he would be anxious about it, she wrote to tell him it had turned out to be a false alarm: 'Harold flower: This is not a proper letter . . . I thought I was pregnant but its all alright now. I am very relieved but also rather sad, because I love children and it would have been a nice baby. I didn't really want you to know, as maybe you would have felt I was asking for money or something, but beyond that I think maybe you would have felt badly guilty and there was no need to.'[20]

In a hasty postscript she added: 'I was going to call the baby Thomas Wolfe Davies. Pity.'

———

Somewhat belatedly, in mid-July *The Sunday Times* had published a glowing review by Julian Symons of *A Weekend with Claud*. Symons appreciated the book's formal complexity and praised the author's subtle handling of the material before concluding: 'There is no doubt that the book is the product of a lively, wayward, constantly enlivening and amusing mind, or that Miss Bainbridge writes with delicacy, wit and an assurance remarkable in a first novelist.'[21]

The favourable notice produced immediate results. Beryl received a letter the next day from Jilly Cooper, then fiction editor of *Intro*, a newly founded magazine aimed at 'teenagers and young twenties'. Cooper asked her to contribute a short story, saying that she was anxious to 'break away from the normal woman's magazine routine' and publish things that were really well written. Her brief was a broad one: 'they can be sexy, zany, romantic, realistic, suspense, etc', the only proviso being that 'they relate in some way to young people today'.[22]

As it happened, the commission coincided with a visit by Judith Shackleton's sixteen-year-old daughter, Chloë, who had come down to London to see her brother. As she certainly classified as a 'young person', Beryl took the opportunity to turn the visit into the subject of her story, setting it against the backdrop of her recent fling with Washington Harold.

The finished story, published in the September issue of *Intro* under the title 'You Could Talk to Someone', featured a character called Moona, roughly based on Beryl, giving advice on romantic matters to her friend's daughter, Katie, the story's narrator. Harold appeared anonymously as Moona's current love interest, being described simply as an 'odd man'. Beryl took a number of liberties in order to turn actual events into a more dramatic narrative: when Moona's 'odd man' calls round, she sends Katie to the basement where the lodger, Bernard, sexually assaults her in a vaguely indeterminate way. Although Chloë recognized herself in the basic outline of the story, even at the time she was aware there was a certain amount of fictional embellishment going on. She wasn't anywhere near 'as sophisticated or cynical'[23] as Beryl had made Katie and the lodger's predatory assault was entirely invented. Nevertheless, it is interesting to note the affinities between Beryl and her fictional alter ego in this early short story. Certainly Judith would have immediately recognized Beryl in Katie's description of Moona, and Moona's words are an echo of Beryl's own:

> Every time I've ever seen her she's been in a crisis. Always about men, yet she keeps laughing when she's telling you how awful it is, and then she almost cries, but not quite. She's fantastically naive.
>
> 'I just don't know what to do,' she told me, 'I've fallen in love with this odd man. I mean I am mad about him, but he is odd.' All her men have been odd.[24]

Despite the relatively high sum she had been paid – £40 – Beryl wasn't happy with the result. When the published copy of *Intro* arrived she discovered that the story had been cut. She sent a copy of it to Harold, along with a note: 'Dearest Flower: After all I send the crappy magazine. The story is altered and changed in places, phrases etc, not to make space but I think they thought I had made genuine grammatical errors. Peasants!!'[25]

Nevertheless, published stories paid well and Beryl was encouraged to try again. She began a story called 'A Walk in the Park', about a young married woman called Ann. Unlike the story for *Intro*, it wasn't based on a contemporary real-life incident, but drew on Beryl's early married life with Austin. Ann is presented as having an ideal relationship with her husband, but after a chance meeting with an older woman, whose disillusion about her married life seems to mirror that of Winnie's, Ann begins to feel a deep 'sense of depression',[26] and as she walks away, she realizes 'that this first depression in marriage would re-occur again and again'.

If Beryl had imagined that writing short stories would be a quick and easy way to earn a living – the story for *Intro* had been 'money for old rope',[27] as she told Harold – it was not so simple in practice. She submitted the story to *Woman's Own*, but on 21 November, Beryl's thirty-fifth birthday, Jean Bowden the assistant fiction editor wrote to turn it down. Bowden gilded her criticism with a little praise: 'You write very well,' she told her, but the story was more of a 'mood piece' and she knew 'from bitter experience' that the magazine's readers 'don't much like mood pieces; they prefer something with more plot, more progression'.[28] Two weeks later, Camilla Shaw at *Woman* also rejected it. 'It is not our sort of thing,' she explained, 'it is rather too downbeat and inconclusive for us, and the idea that the two alternatives now are total domesticity or running away from it all gives the story a slightly old-fashioned air.'[29]

It would be nearly ten years before Beryl had another short story published.

With all the 'comings and going's . . . and the house still in chaos',[30] as Beryl put it, it was surprising she could write at all. She might have been referring to the purely physical chaos created by Austin's alterations to the house, but the description was equally applicable to her day-to-day life. A case in point was the arrival of one of Robert Shackleton's former students, Ian Pringle, otherwise known as Sherpa, an account of which Beryl recounted to Judith with characteristic relish:

> Oh yes – what about Sherpa! Came at midnight with a man called Ivan the Terrible and persued me relentlessly till dawn. Quite unabashed. I didn't know whether to laugh or cry. I just wanted to be left alone and he just kept coming at me. And then Ru slept walked and him running round in a blanket. It was absurd . . . I think he must have been deranged. He's always seemed so quiet. I never fail to be surprised by men – I always pick the wrong ones. Sherpa's normal I think, whereas Washington Harold just runs away and weeps in corners and buys me paintings as a substitute. I can't go on. I'm so tired. I love you. Boozey me![31]

Over the next few months the state of the house hardly improved, and despite the onset of winter the heating arrangements still hadn't been sorted:

> Harold Flower: It is three in the morning. I am very dirty and covered in paint and life is hazadous. You would not know the house now – the central heating is half in – there are floor boards up and ladders (thats not unusual) and pipes everywhere and I am so god damned tired and grey, spattered with peach coral paint, my teeth under a fine coating of nicotine, my nails all broken, my-self in ruins. Until – next Wednesday, when God and the gas-board being good the heat will be on, the hot water going, the new bath working etc etc. Then – oh then.[32]

Freezing up in the top bedroom Beryl stared moodily at Harold's photo and mulled over his last letter, which she had received weeks ago but still hadn't answered. He had suspected she was unhappy. 'I can more than understand you're feeling low & depressed,' he wrote. Although he was sorry for any 'actions (or inactions) on my part that were contributory to blame', the distance between them meant there was 'very little that I can do or say in a positive vein, except that you mean very much to me and always will'.[33] In her reply Beryl sought to reassure Harold that his effect on her had been a positive one: 'No I'm not unhappy. I feel fit again and the book is going well and despite the little upset you did restore me to life, my flower. Its always a blessing to know that one is still capable of feeling intensely. Also you did another thing. I am at last, after 15 or more years of immaturity, able to say no if I really don't want to. I never wanted to seem impolite if I was pushed, you know – a refusal always offends – but now I feel more safe, more me.'[34]

Christmas passed uneventfully despite the presence of Beryl's mother and her mother-in-law, Nora, who kept 'asking if the children had their bowels moved regularly'. There was a 'flaming pudding and a huge turkey and the stockings filled and everything organised'. In the evening there was a party: songs were sung at the piano and Beryl played 'There's Something in Your Eyes' on the gramophone and thought of Harold. He had sent some books over as Christmas presents, including a deluxe copy of *Alice in Wonderland* for Jo, and *The Essential Lenny Bruce* and a work of philosophy for Beryl. In his accompanying card he had raised the possibility of her coming over to America at some point in the future, and so in the New Year she wrote to him, nostalgically reflecting on the short time they'd spent together and thinking it had represented a missed opportunity: 'I wish so many times you were here. I think you were so much more relaxed toward your departure, and I now am so less obsessed that had we come together at the right momento I would have made you laugh.'[35]

It was in this positive mood, tempted by the idea of a visit to America, that she closed her letter to him with a tentative agreement: 'Dear heart, have a good new year and year. Yes, one day I will come to America, I have an impulsive idea to save up the fare and come for a weekend. Its the thing to do. It sounds so extravagant and swinging.'

TWENTY-TWO

America

Have you ever had a book written about you? Or for you?
Or to you?[1]

THE NOTION THAT BERYL could find the time or the money to go off on a trip to America sounded far-fetched. She was, after all, a single mother with three children to look after and a source of income that was precarious at best. But at the end of January 1968 she returned to the idea: 'It is only half one in the afternoon but I am half seas over owing to an unaccustomed amount of people calling as if it was a birthday or the like, all with booze. I want to come to San Fransico, I don't know how to arrange it . . . I can't leave the kids for very long, but I have a desire to run, to sling me beads in Hate Ashford or whatever it is and to make love with you. I think the latter is more important than the beads but still.'[2]

After giving Harold some advice about a short story he had sent her – 'I think you write beautifully . . . you should experiment more and let go. Get drunk a bit' – she closed her letter with an account of a dinner party she had just attended. She had found it amusing – so much gin had been consumed that the ageing hostess, who was usually inhibited, became 'more and more indiscreet about the dirty soldiers during the war trying to get her to handle their tools'. All in all, it had been a boozy, convivial day – 'I have not had a day and an evening of such drinking for a long time' – all it lacked was someone to share it with: 'The logical ending would be for you to be here like in a dream of sweetness, and then it would all be alright. But you are not. Can I really come and see you? I will try to work something out, but it will take time to think about. To you in Baltimore which is exotic to me, from me in Alberto strasser . . . I do miss you, I send you real love flower.'[3]

The New Year had seen changes at New Authors, with Graham Nicol giving way to 'a young whizz-kid editor',[4] Michael Dempsey. Dempsey, a brilliant, impulsive, hard-drinking Irishman, was an editor with attitude: 'He wanted to put out books that upset people and was a natural magnet for trouble.'[5] He would become legendary in publishing circles for his various whisky-fuelled excesses over the next decade or so, until he died in 1981 after falling down the stairs in his flat, trying to change a lightbulb while drunk.

Dempsey was keen to speak to his authors, so at the end of January he wrote to arrange a meeting with Beryl in order to discuss publication plans for *Another Part of the Wood*,[6] now scheduled for October. If he was looking for unconventional authors, he can hardly have been disappointed, though Beryl herself felt somewhat embarrassed by the day's turn of events:

> The new editor came to lunch, barely 24 years old and I thought, just once Bainbridge be your age, don't mention Ru, your ex, your past etc, be adult, formal, retiring. All went well for one hour and then the rat man came and behind him Alan, the first face-to-face encounter for a year or more and Ru saying 'Oh my other daddy, come and meet Ethel' (her doll). Upstairs they went and me like jelly, out comes the whisky for the cup of tea, and the editor tells his dreadful secret life and I tell mine and we cuddle in the kitchen and Ru and Alan romp up and down. Alan goes and then the editor – who pauses on the step, breathes deeply and cries 'This is what its all about' and goes off unsteadidly to the tube. So again I have failed.[7]

But the chaotic, drink-fuelled introduction appeared to do the trick. Shortly after the meeting Beryl's agent John Smith wrote to her, noting that 'Michael Dempsey seems to be a lively wire' and adding that 'he is very keen on your work, so things may from now on speed full steam ahead; anyway let us hope so.'[8] But even though everyone at Hutchinson seemed pleased, a sense of ominous dejection was creeping into Beryl's mind about the book: 'the long months from acceptance to publication leave me very distant and hardly bothered,'[9] she told Judith.

Part of this was probably a feeling of disappointment that writing was not producing the kind of financial rewards she might have hoped. Just the opposite. Not for the last time, Beryl got into an enormously complicated situation over the monies she had received from her publisher. She hadn't entirely taken on board the somewhat two-edged nature of an advance – that it is in fact a loan from the publisher to be paid back out of future earnings. Constantly short of money and spending it when she had it, Beryl was now in the invidious position of being nearly £160 in debt to her agent, six months before the publication of her second novel. The convoluted mathematical paths by which these sums were arrived at left her head reeling: 'We sent you the full Panther advance on *Weekend with Claud*,' her agent tried to explain, 'though in fact we have so far only received £75 of that from the publisher (that is we have received half of the half of the advance that is due to you) this means that we are still owed £67.10.0d on that and we also of course paid you £90 which was £100 less our commission on the first part of the advance on *Another Part of the Wood*.'[10] It is little wonder that when Beryl came to making financial arrangements with her future publisher, Duckworth, she had an inbuilt aversion to advances.

More bad news came from Anglia Television, who had turned down 'I'm Not Criticising . . . I'm Remembering', as it 'did not appeal to the Drama Committee'.[11] Beryl's frustrations at these various setbacks to her writing career were reflected in her reading of a book Harold had sent her, *Editor to Author*, a series of letters Maxwell Perkins had written to authors he edited at Scribner's, including Thomas Wolfe, Ernest Hemingway and Scott Fitzgerald. She was struck by Perkins' frequent laudatory references to female novelists and the fact that their names 'might be in Chinese for all we know, so unsung, unremembered the writers are'. She couldn't help but see a similar fate for herself: 'I stamp the floor at night with rage at being neither talented enough or the right sex or single-minded enough to do what I really want to do, and so much of my energy goes into the children and washing the dishes and washing the clothes. And what about Wolfe travelling round like a demented being and Graham Green in Tahiti or whatever and me firmly in the soot of Albert Street?'[12]

This feeling of being trapped in her domestic environment fuelled a corresponding desire to escape. One suitably literal expression of this was an attempt to learn to drive, with Judith Gleeson giving her lessons in Austin's car: 'She is very brave and the brake does not work, the licence is out of date and the tyres are flat,' Beryl told Harold. 'I have had three lessons and drove to Hampstead and that hotel you lived in and back and felt like a jelly.'[13] Another was the increasing seriousness with which she treated the idea of going to America, and in this she was encouraged by Judith, who was herself going out to the States the following month. By April what was once a nebulous, somewhat fanciful notion was turning into a practical reality and a date was set: 'Washington Harold, flower: I want to come. May 27th – without Ru, Austin being aggreeable. But it depends on my Ma and fixing things up here for the kids. I do so want to come. I've been with the kids now for 11 years. I'm a bit frightened. It seems such a huge mountain to shift to get to you for a month. But I've begun.'[14]

Harold sent her a letter full of practical details and travel advice, but then he mentioned the possibility that in the autumn he might come to London again to enrol at an art college. Beryl was completely thrown. Was this an indirect way of saying he was coming over to be with her? After having rejected her the year before, was he backtracking and thinking the relationship would start up again where it had left off? The notion that he might now be seeing the visit in romantic terms sent her into a panic. Taking a swig of whisky, she started writing Harold a letter, attempting to explain her state of mind and questioning him as to his:

It is such a long time ago since I saw you. What do you expect? Am I chatty, will I amuse, can I give you something beyond the American dream? I feel inadiquate at this distance and scared to commit myself . . . When I asked you to stay when you were last here, I repeated an old old formula I have performed on many occasions. I wanted you to stay . . . I needed you, and you went away. I missed you for a long long time. But then I breathed again and I came up alive and resilient, as I always do and life goes on, and then you write and ask me to come and . . . after I come to you, you will come back here to England. This frightens me, in so many ways. I am committed to Austin. He has given me a home and taken Ru as his and he is so very good and lovely, and are you saying can you come here to live with me perhaps . . . because Austin would not like it. Or am I being presumptious and do you mean simply what you put . . . we will be good good friends and if there is time and aptitude for love then that too? Or are you saying nothing of this . . . I want to come to America . . . but you must tell me what you want. If you have changed your mind that is o.k. too, but I would like to be free just for once after all these years and look at things and laugh and drink and not worry about the washing or the children needing me. And I could make you laugh, as well as make you feel that something was happening inside you.

Tje ball as you sso tennisingly said is now in your lap or court or appartment. Do you want me to come? It is very sudden, is it not? Blessings, B.[15]

The conflicted tone of her letter didn't bode well for the trip, but there were other, more practical hurdles that had to be crossed before it could begin. Ten days before she was due to fly out, Harold received a desperate telegram: 'Visa refused stop require urgent letter from your bank sponsoring me for one month stop contact direct visa unit american embassy london love Beryl'.[16]

Harold immediately got in touch with the visa section at the American Embassy and told them he was 'able & willing' to provide the financial guarantees they were looking for. But as if the fates were reluctant to let her go, even this wasn't the end of the legal wrangling. With three days to go, Beryl sent him a hastily scribbled note:

Dearest W. Harold: They withdrew my visa and asked me all sorts of funny questions about who was I leaving the children with and why (4 times this). Why did you want to pay for me to go to the States. So in the end I rang Hutchinsons, the publishers and they threatened all sorts of press and TV action and they came with me to the Embassy and they apologized etc etc. My smallpox has made me delirious. I fall about and my arm has gone septic, also I went on the pill and that has blown me up. I feel so awful about all the money involved. One day I will pay it all back to you . . .

I will cable you exact time of plane etc. I can't do this till the last minuet because of my arm and the children. Sometime either 27th, 28th or 29th, but not later, probably 28th. Dear Harold when I arrive with my new knickers I will be the spotty (smallpox) fat (pill) one with the frightened face. I really am a bit frightened. Not of you, just all the moving. I am bringing £2. 4½ sterling in pocket money. Not quite, but almost.[17]

Finally, on 28 May, she flew out from Heathrow, landing at Baltimore airport seven hours later where Washington Harold was waiting for her.

There had been something else that had prompted Beryl's panicked letter to Harold a month before she landed on American soil. He had no way of knowing, but her passing reference to 'a friend' who was helping Austin to put in the bathroom was less innocuous than it sounded. The friend was Don McKinlay, who in April had arrived back in England from India, where he had spent a two-semester sabbatical lecturing at the School of Architecture in Ahmedabad. The last time Beryl had seen him was almost a year before in July, when, as if marking out his future territory, he had 'peed in the next doors garden on route to India'.[18]

Having stopped off to see Austin, Don decided to stay for a couple of weeks and help him with the conversion work. He already had experience of renovating property. A few years before, he had bought and restored an old, derelict farmhouse, Eaves Farm near Ramsbottom, where he had lived with his wife and young daughter prior to his trip to India. Together, Don and Austin had put in a bathroom on the ground floor so that the existing stairs to the basement could be sealed off and the lower floor turned into a self-contained flat.

Beryl and Don had known each other as friends for many years, but this time things were different. As Beryl would later tell him: 'I fell in love with you one afternoon in the kitchen in Albert Street when you were very brown and wore white Indian trousers. To be honest I have an ability to fall in love. I have a need to. But you talked so much about India and about animals and I thought you so beautiful.'[19] Don, too, could recall the precise moment that things changed: 'We were drinking a bottle of vodka together. We felt exactly the same about each other. I thought she was a beautiful woman.'[20] A photograph taken on the front steps of Albert Street at the time captures the moment perfectly: Beryl, her arms slung round Don's neck, stares straight into the camera in proud possession, while Don, bearded and glowing with ruddy health, his shirt casually open, stands in his denim jacket and white trousers, supporting her against his body, his right arm nonchalantly round her waist. They look like a model couple, made for each other.

But the timing could not have been worse. Beryl was due to go to America and spend three weeks with a man who gave every sign of expecting to restart their relationship of the previous year. Moreover, Harold was hardly to be blamed given that Beryl had been telling him she loved him for the last nine months. All the arrangements had been made, so there was no backing out of it now. With a feeling of anxiety about how she would cope over the next three weeks, Beryl left Albert Street, her children and Don behind.

Since his return to America the previous year, Harold had been at something of a loose end. After spending some time in Florida with his parents, he purchased a VW Beetle and headed back to Washington. His plan was to pass the autumn and winter in Baltimore with friends, and then head out to San Francisco in the spring of 1968 to meet up with his former Westinghouse colleague and flatmate, Don Wilson. In the meantime he found an inexpensive furnished room near Johns Hopkins University and moved in, not even bothering to install a phone as he'd only be there a few months. When he left Baltimore, it would be for good.

As the idea of Beryl coming to America took shape, the notion of combining her visit with his intended move to San Francisco seemed a logical step, and Harold continued his preparations. In the early spring of 1968 he saw an advertisement for a grey 1965 VW Microbus, factory outfitted as a camper ('wood panelling, ice box, sink, fold-down table, & seats that unfolded into beds . . .'),[21] and made a straight trade for it with his Beetle. With its modern combination of living space, affordability and manoeuvrability, the VW camper was the vehicle which, more than any other, would come to symbolize the counterculture, the hippy lifestyle of the 1960s. In slightly different circumstances, this freewheeling, communal mode of travelling across America would have seemed idyllic, but the first thing that struck Beryl when she saw the camper was the cramped sleeping arrangements, and she immediately felt uneasy about what this implied.

The itinerary Harold had planned was an intensive one, covering over 5,000 miles, from Maryland on the East Coast to Los Angeles on the West. When he'd offered to show Beryl America he meant it literally. The trip would take in some of the country's most iconic sights – the White House, Manhattan Island, Yellowstone National Park, Haight-Ashbury, the Golden Gate Bridge, Alcatraz – but it also included a mini-tour of Harold's own life, his birthplace in White Plains, his university campus at St Lawrence, and where he had worked in Washington.

After picking Beryl up from Baltimore airport, they went back to his apartment, driving down to Washington DC the following day so Harold could say goodbye to friends. The next day the trip began in earnest, and they drove up through Philadelphia to New York and Manhattan, where they stopped to have dinner with a computer programmer Harold knew, Larry Levine, in his Greenwich Village apartment. As they listened to a Fran Landesman and Bob Dorough LP, Beryl was so struck by the nostalgia-infused lyrics of a song about lost love – 'When Love Disappears' sung by Blossom Dearie – she copied them out in her journal: 'The memories will fade/Just like your tears/But where do you go/When love disappears?'[22]

Heading north from Manhattan, they drove up New York state, through Harold's home town of White Plains, and joined the State Thruway: 'Torrential rain, 8 lines of traffic. Radio playing "You'll never know just how much I love you". Spumes of water. Pontiacs, Cheverlot's, Buic's, Oldsmobile, Porches, Ford, Cadillac, Mustang, Lincoln, Mercury, Plymouth, Dodge.' Then it was on to Poughkeepsie, where they followed the line of the Hudson River up through Saratoga Falls and Albany until they reached Wanakena, a small hamlet in the Adirondacks twenty miles from the Canadian border, where Judith Gleeson and her sons were currently holidaying.

While there, Judith took a photograph of Beryl standing next to Harold, which makes a pointed contrast to the one of her and Don. Here the body language tells a completely different story. Beryl's arm rests on Harold's shoulders, but her head is hanging down, her eyes averted as if slightly embarrassed by the presence of the camera, while he leans slightly away from her and seems unsure what to do with his hands: one is stuffed into his trouser pocket, the other hovers at her shoulder, as if he is uncertain whether to touch her.

Unaware as he was of the change in Beryl's affections, Harold put her reserve down to shyness or embarrassment. In a letter written shortly after they left Wanakena, Judith told Psiche she thought Harold was enjoying the trip, so on the surface at least there didn't seem to be any obvious tension between them. But Beryl had also written to Psiche, telling her how uncomfortable she was finding it, how anxious the situation was making her feel. Guilty at having encouraged Beryl to go in the first place, Psiche apologized, saying she'd thought it would be a distraction from the complicated state of affairs with Don. She tried to console Beryl with the thought that even if it wasn't pleasant it would be 'an interesting experience'[23] from a literary point of view.

Knowing that Wanakena was a stop on Beryl's itinerary, Don had sent a letter to coincide with her arrival. The fact that it was delivered successfully, despite being addressed simply 'c/o Judith Gleeson, Wanakena', gives an indication of how small the town was: 'I love you and we must do something about it. The kids are fine, Austin working hard, and I love you. See you in 2 weeks.'[24] Uncertain as to whether this would arrive and wanting to make sure Beryl got the message, he also sent a telegram: 'I love you see you soon, Don.'[25]

The journal Beryl kept throughout the trip enabled her to deal with her conflicting emotions – and help pass the time. As well as reflections on what she was feeling that day, Beryl noted down her impressions of the landscape, snatches of conversation, names of towns they passed through, snippets of facts, and anything else that might be useful for a later writing project. She thus captured one of the most significant events of that troubled year just a few hours after it occurred – the assassination of Robert Kennedy:

> June 5th. 2.20 Just crossed into Canada. News comes over car radio that they've shot Robert Kennedy, right thru the brain. Condition critical. Feel sick. Hearty bluff man in tourist information centre – 'What? Oh yes they shot Bobby. Now where did you want to go, Sir?'

On the next page she hurriedly scribbled down the words of the news reporter who had been broadcasting at the moment the shots were fired, and whose running commentary of the unfolding tragedy was no doubt replayed constantly over the radio:

> Newscast. 'My God, my God they can't have. They've shot Senator Kennedy. Get him, get him. The assassin is standing right in front of me at this moment, He's still pointing the gun. Get that gun. Get that gun. His hand's frozen. Break his thumb if you have to. Get that gun. Get that gun. This is terrible, Senator Kennedy is on the floor,

shot in the head. Someone else is shot too. Now they've got the gun. Keep back. Keep back. Hold him. Don't lets have another Oswald for God's sake – not another Oswald. Hold him.'

Pressing on into Canada – the aim was to skirt Lake Huron and then cut back into America between Lake Superior and Lake Michigan – they camped by the shore of Lake Nipissing. With the sound of the water lapping, and the sun going down across the lake behind the ridge of mountains, they seemed a world away from the political turmoil of America. The next day seemed equally tranquil: Harold stopped off to swim in a river and in the evening, with the sound of a guitar coming from one of the other campers in the distance, they talked about their childhoods. Things seemed peaceful enough, but the tone of her post-card to Brenda and Stanley Haddon suggests that under the surface Beryl's mood was far from benign: 'Passed thru here on way to some-where or other. Acres of black desolation. Like me. O the jolly camp fires at night, the blood-sucking mosquitoes.'[26]

After crossing back into America at Sault St Marie, they ran along the length of the lower shore of Lake Superior, a distance of over 250 miles. Constantly camping by open water exacerbated the mosquito problem: 'I am great bites all over – under my hair, my elbow twice its normal size, between my toes. One eye closing. I want to come home.'[27]

As they passed through Jacobson, where they crossed the Mississippi, and headed through Chippewa National Forest, the relentlessness of the journey began to take its toll: 'The Indian reservation we went through was just trees, miles and miles. We drove 370 miles today and saw few people and only about 2 cars on the road.' The monotony of the seem-ingly endless driving added to Beryl's physical discomfort and fuelled tensions. Entries in her journal become increasingly critical of Harold's behaviour, the expressions of irritation more frequent. She began to see his urge to show her America, to be her guide, as an attempt to coerce and control her; she felt she wasn't free to do what she wanted: 'The only things we do are what Harold wants. He never asks if I would like to do anything. If I do ask he says no. Its a bit miserable, as I feel a bit far from home and I refuse to beg. I long to go into a café and drink coffee and talk to people. To see a picture or even just walk round a village or town. All we do is drive like hell and that makes me want to go to sleep.'

After travelling for over 150 miles, driving through the Badlands National Park into Wyoming, they finally stopped at a post office in the town of Cody, which was full of 'real westerners' with 'narrow suspicious faces, yellow under their stetson hats'. On the wall Beryl saw a wanted poster for James Earl Ray, the man suspected of killing Martin Luther King, and felt the urge to steal it, but her nerve failed at the last moment.

They spent the night in Yellowstone National Park, and Beryl noted down her impressions, though apart from a brief mention of bears coming up to the truck, it was the human beings not the landscape that she found interesting:

> How clean are the Americans, as they sit and strain forward, peering thru binoculars, their underpants gleam, their shoes shine, the pink skin on their skulls glow through the crew cut hair. When they are small and slim they are very small, tiny wrist bones, anxious elderly youthful faces, when they are big and overweight they are enormous, great guts and forearms and jaws, and the women wear Bermuda shorts strained tight at the crotch. On most wrists bright big wristwatches, or name bracelets, huge camera, binoculars, transistors, fraternity rings, graduation badges . . .
>
> At night in the bigger camps they turn on the generators in their trucks, their Komfy Kampers, Rest-U-Easy's, and the engines steadily hum, and they cook their hygenic steaks and drink diet cococola's, and calory low beer, and calory free sugar and low content bread. The meat is always perfect, fat trimmed off, you don't need to chew it at all.

By now they were two weeks into the trip, and still had almost two thousand miles to go. From the Yellowstone National Park they pushed on into Idaho, through the volcanic formations of the 'Craters of the Moon', through Bliss and Boise. Beryl had given up trying to help clean the van, noticing that Harold, dissatisfied with her standard of cleanliness, would go over what she did a second time. So while he tidied up the camper, she wrote 'copious notes for my new book', though as she admitted to Austin 'an awful lot would be unprintable'.[28]

By the third week, her irritation with Harold was almost palpable, and to avoid overt confrontation she made increasingly wounding attacks on him in her journal, some of the unkindest things she had ever committed to paper. She lambasted him for being 'inhibited' and 'immature', resenting him for the sense of obligation she felt over the fact that he had paid for her ticket: 'How many times have I walked and sat beside him and wished him dead.'

His attempts at humour made things worse. She became irritated by what she saw as his constant reference to her knickers: 'Whenever I washed out my pants and put them on a tree to dry he would giggle and touch them and ask about them – Gee! Knickers, he would say, over and over.' But in her irritation she had forgotten that it was she herself who had started the joke, with the repeated allusion to her knickers in the letters she sent him before she arrived.

In truth it wasn't so much Harold's words or actions that had prompted these outbursts as her own sense of guilt, the uncomfortable knowledge that she had led him on and then dropped him when Don had come along. Beryl knew she was being unfair, but rather than acknowledge the reason, she attempted to justify it through her feelings for Don: 'This is vindictive but it helps to take away the HATRED. I want to be with DON.'

As the journey neared its end, her mind kept reverting to Don. She worried that she hadn't expressed her feelings to him strongly enough before leaving, and resolved to be more forthright when she returned: 'If I ever get back alive and if I ever see him again I'll tell him everything. Not be shy. Tell him what I felt. Tell him. One should. I should. Its important. Because we go out so quick like little lights.'

The trip's itinerary, which roughly followed that taken by Humbert Humbert in *Lolita*, gave her an idea for a novel: 'Theme of the new book should be a journey but in what form? Lie in the truck all day and think of that. Be nice to write a simple story about living in the woods 100 years ago and being attacked by Indians. Or something called the Idyll. All about Don and tenderness. Something beautiful and without any analysis, at least not the sort I usually indulge in. Away with analysis.'

With less than a week to go before they hit Los Angeles, they spent the night on the slopes of Mount Shasta in northern California. At this altitude it was very cold with snow on the ground; they kept a big log fire blazing and Harold thought he saw a UFO. The following day they descended to a camp in Humboldt State Park – the drive took nearly five hours and Beryl despaired of ever reaching it – from where they could look out over the North Pacific. This time the camp had showers, something of a relief as she was feeling distinctly 'mucky'. Catching sight of her reflection in the bathroom mirror she experienced one of those existential jolts, a disconnect between her mental image of herself and physical reality: 'We passed a party of Y.M.C.A. girls in the wood. All yellow and orange and bold. A shower and a hair wash amid a bevy of young and tanned maidens. Forthright, loud, polite, sexless young American girls. When I saw my own face in the mirror I got a shock. I'm not young and yet I feel it.'

From Humboldt, they drove down through the Sacramento Valley to Mendocino Bay, and while stopping off to get supplies, Beryl was again thwarted in her attempt to get the elusive James Earl Ray wanted poster:

We came to a tiny village right on the cliffs. A store and a post-office. The post office was terrific – stuffed deer head, squirrels, all round the walls, and queer metal lockers with numbers on and wooden raftered ceiling and all the wanted notices. For murder, for arson, for rape, for the suspected assassination of Martin Luther King. I could have taken the lot but I had to ask and she said, No, they were federal property and she had no right. I said, but they've caught Charles [sic] Ray in London. Is that so, she says, I couldn't say, I've had no no-tif-ic-ation. Out I go.

That night they camped on Manchester Beach, looking out over the Pacific and Mendocino Bay. After collecting some driftwood to make a fire, Harold set about cooking a frozen chicken, while Beryl, with thoughts of Don in the back of her mind and assailed by an assortment of sensations – the fog drifting in from the sea, the sound of the warning bell offshore, the smoke and sizzle of the chicken spitting on the grill – jotted down impressions in her journal.

The next morning, as she went to the water tap to wash, she was still in a reflective mood and conceded that this 'drift wood life' wasn't entirely unpleasant: 'It has taken all this time to be released from the other way of life, I can see that even in such a way as this I could begin to think more creatively . . . there is so much time to let the brain think, no distractions of the children – no house-work . . . If I were at this point alone, maybe I could write poetry.'

The journey was now reaching its end. At one of the stops along the way she achieved a minor victory, noting in her diary: 'Pinched wanted poster Ray – Martin Luther King.' Finally, on 21 June, they drove across the Golden Gate Bridge, 'red like old rust', past Alcatraz and into San Francisco. Although the Summer of Love of 1967 was well and truly over, and 1968 had already seen its share of political assassinations and violent protest, the tide of hippie culture in Haight-Ashbury was still high, so to speak, and Beryl took in her first sight of a whole new counter-culture:

> Little shops, posters, peace signs, a word like leaves sighing – acid – acid – a man in a sheepskin rug, nothing else. Hippie kids – 3 on a side-walk – very happy – a man saying hallo to everyone – a negro gives a boy on the pavement a dollar and he says 'Why thanks man, gee thanks'. He squints up happily into the sunshine. 'Forget it,' says the negro, swelling with delight and swaggers away. Lovely girls, all clean and friendly and all the men looking like Don with brown faces, and bare feet in sandals and lying on the pavement in the sunshine. No babies, no one pregnant, that was a bit sad.

This glimpse of such a different way of life made her uneasy about her own: 'On a hill in San Francisco. Looking out over the city, wondering what the hell I am doing and who I am.'

Then they met up with Don Wilson, another computer programmer Harold knew from his Westinghouse days. Harold had spent a month in San Francisco with Don in 1962, during the course of a visit to the Seattle World's Fair, and had been determined to go back ever since. Waiting for Beryl at Wilson's apartment was a letter from the other Don: 'On Sunday night just lying in bed & loving you . . . why the fuck is it so hard to be with you.'[29] Don had also included a drawing incorporating two small photographs of Beryl cut from a contact sheet and covered in gold leaf, on which he had written the unambiguous message: 'Its impossible for me to write what I'm feeling. I just love you. THIS IS A LOVE LETTER. I love you.'

The following day, after lunching at Fisherman's Wharf, they headed out to Berkeley University, where Don Wilson worked in the engineering department, running the computers and teaching students how to programme them. As he was showing them the computer facilities, he asked Beryl to write a message, which he input via a punched computer card – or 'coded and recorded on the huge dictation machine', as Beryl put it. She had wanted to write a poem for

Don back in Albert Street, but felt Harold 'breathing over my shoulder' and thought better of it.

In the evening, they went to Hertz Hall on the Berkeley campus for a concert by Danny Rey, known as 'Big Black', whose sextet were playing as part of the university's extension programme: 'Africa: Its Music and Related Arts'. Rey was an exceptional conga player and percussionist, and Beryl thought the sextet's blend of Afro-Cuban jazz was 'sensational'.

It was an exhilarating end to a fraught three weeks. Had it been undertaken at any other time it would have been an unforgettable trip, but driven by her insecurities over her relationship with Don, and goaded by her guilty conscience about how she had treated Harold, Beryl exhibited a rare lack of generosity in her summing up of the experience, one that was distinctly unfair to the person who had made it possible: 'If I see him again in 1000 years it will be once too often.'

To get back to London from San Francisco meant taking two flights, as Beryl had explained to the children: 'It takes 5 hours to fly from S. Frisco to New York and then 7 to London. So I loose a day.'[30] At the airport, petrified by the thought of flying, she asked Harold for a dollar and bought a fifty-cent miniature of gin to take the edge off her nerves. It had the desired effect. Once on board her head began to spin, and she scribbled a long note for Don to read when she got back:

> At high altitudes one gin for 50 cents should by authority send one higher than the clouds we fly thru. The truth of this I have not yet wholly proved as the thought of seeing you has made my head already light . . . How does love grow? It is embarrassing at this age and this time to use the word . . . I should prefix it by if thats what its called, well sort of, kind of, something like it, but I cannot truthfully do so, being fully hung up, overboard, delirious, foxy, beyond myself, thru and under and over you with the emotion labelled by that word.
>
> Its a lovely feeling, being made free by happiness, wanting to shout, though it may not last long or at best be painful at termination. But having for 2 hours watched the hippies in Haight Ashbury, and read

their poetry for perhaps 30 minutes, I am fully in accord with the notion of love fucking love fucking forever, joy, light, and warm pink glow fuck, and it does not matter about the past or the future, only the now.

Of course it is the altitude and the 50 cents gin.

The dollar I asked Harold for at the last moment. Give it me, I said and he gave. I spent ½ of it so as to verbalise the sweetness of thinking of you. Thus we use other people, and are used by others, a rose is a rose, is a rose etc. But a fuck has to be <u>the</u> fuck, <u>the</u> fuck, <u>the</u> fuck. Nothing else will do. This is for you Don-Don, if by chance without booze or extreme tiredness I cannot show or tell you my feelings when I see you. But this is what I feel. Amen . . .

When I see you I will be thinking I love you but maybe I won't say it. When I see you I will want to embrace you but I won't because of the children. When I see you I will want to cry and I may, but you will think its because of the children. Dear golden boy, if I don't have the courage to tell you when we lie down at night, I you love. Amen. Amen. Amen.

TWENTY-THREE

Eaves Farm

I remember at Maggie's and in the pub and in our room and
in the bath. How I loved you, how you loved me.[1]

BERYL'S SUDDEN REALIZATION THAT she loved Don may have
felt spontaneous and natural, but in practical terms things were not
so simple. She was tied emotionally and financially to London and Albert
Street, whereas Don was obliged to live over 200 miles away, within
commuting distance of his job at Manchester Art College. He also had
his wife and their twelve-year-old daughter, Sheenagh, to consider.

Don's marriage with Helen had clearly been going through a difficult patch. He had been away for almost a year in India, during which
time he had sublet his farmhouse near Ramsbottom, and Helen and
Sheenagh had been living in Spain.[2] Whatever Don and Helen's
respective plans and intentions for the future were, Sheenagh at least
was anticipating that on her father's return they would all go back to
living at Eaves Farm as before. Don falling in love with Beryl just
before she left for America had changed all that.

Once Beryl was back in London at the end of June events moved fast,
and she dashed off a hurried note to Judith informing her of the latest
developments: 'Don and I are living together in happy ever after, he sent
for Helen told her, and left. Austin is pleased and the children. So am I.
Are you? It was all very sudden but then the best things always are. Feel
this time its alright. We are very alike I think.'[3]

The next few months were lived in an ad hoc fashion: over the
summer Beryl took the children up to Eaves Farm but, much to her
annoyance, Austin seized the opportunity to rent her part of the house
in her absence. In any case, there was the children's schooling to think
about, so by September Beryl was back in Albert Street. The situation

was far from ideal: Don's work commitments in Manchester kept him at Eaves Farm during the week, and although he would come down to London on free weekends it wasn't enough.

A new plan was decided: schooling was arranged in Holcombe, and Beryl and the children would join Don at Eaves Farm after Christmas. In the short term the children now included Sheenagh. While her parents decided whether she was ultimately going to live with Don and Beryl at Eaves Farm or with her mother in Spain, Sheenagh was installed at Albert Street.

There was, perhaps, no completely satisfactory solution, but inevitably this rapidly evolving situation was difficult for a young girl to deal with. It wasn't that Sheenagh was entering an entirely strange household. She remembered Beryl, Austin, Aaron and Jo from her childhood in Liverpool, and had gone to the same nursery as Aaron. Even so, the day Don first took her to Albert Street, after her parents told her they were separating and that she was going to live with Beryl, she found it difficult to understand 'why I was there rather than with my mum'.[4]

An only child, Sheenagh was now thrust into a communal life with three other children, sharing a bedroom with ten-year-old Jo-Jo and three-year-old Ru. And there were all sorts of other peculiarities to get used to in the new house: 'We weren't allowed to go into Beryl's sitting room, she would put the television on the landing and we sat on the stairs to watch it.' There was also the cooking: 'My first coherent memory is of how absolutely awful the food was. Beryl had made a special meal to greet us, a roast, and it was dreadful.'

Nevertheless, despite the potential conflicts or emotional problems that a situation like this might engender, Beryl's children and Sheenagh adapted relatively well: it was the adults who found this new life and living arrangements more problematic. As if things weren't stressful enough with the uncertainty over Don and an expanded family, she kept bumping into Alan. He and Liz were now married and lived in Belsize Park with their year-old son. Alan persisted in calling round to see Rudi, or contrived to meet Beryl when she was out with her. On the back of one of the manuscript pages of *Another Part of the Wood*, she sketched out a letter to him, addressed to 'Poor Sharp', in an attempt to sever contact with him entirely: 'You can't see Ru, ever. I don't want her to know you. It angers me that I should have to give reasons. I am living with someone and she regards Austin as her Father. It is not possible for you to call. You will only cause trouble if you persist. Her name has been changed by deed pole and there is no point now or ever in her knowing you. Take that as final. If we meet in the street again please keep away.'[5]

In spite of the decision she had made and the drastic turn her life had taken since her return from America, Beryl still couldn't face telling Harold about Don. The whole trip had been an act of generosity on his part, but so emotionally fraught had she been during the course of it that she was too embarrassed even to write a courtesy thank-you note. The silence struck Harold as odd, and two weeks after her departure he had dropped her a short, semi-playful postcard that had a hint of anxious reproach to it: 'You owe me a letter!'[6]

She felt she had to respond, but not wanting or daring to admit what had happened, she wrote a brief reply in which she tried to explain why the American trip hadn't been quite what he might have wished, though without mentioning anything about Don: 'I don't know what you mean about the trip not being so good. I will never never forget it, all my life. You were most generous and most patient with me and I worry about all that money and I don't know how to thank you or how to write to you properly. I think for now I will just send this so that you will know I am alive and well and then write you when I feel real and tell you all my impressions. Take care, forgive the silence. My love, B.'[7]

This carefully worded dissimulation forms a stark contrast to the blunt version of events she gave to Judith: 'Dearest Ju. America was a nightmare of misunderstandings. I would have to tell you not write. I had no money so could neither escape or write for the stamps cost money. Washington Harold was a madman.'[8] But this, in its own way, was as much a piece of dissembling as her letter to Harold. She knew Judith saw her frequently chaotic, not to say disastrous, relationships with men as dramas of her own making, and she knew too that Judith disapproved. Consequently, in her account of her affair with Harold she had confided neither the extent to which she'd been emotionally involved, nor the degree to which she'd encouraged him to believe her feelings for him were so strong. Beryl may have found the situation in America difficult, but she didn't want Judith to think she was responsible for yet another drama, so she tried to shift the blame solely onto Harold.

Judith, however, had known Beryl too long to be taken in so easily. Shortly afterwards, during a visit to Albert Street, she had confronted Beryl when they were talking about the subject and told her bluntly: 'Oh you never tell the truth, you're dreadfully dishonest.'9 It would be six years before Beryl wrote to her again.

Even taking this into account, Beryl's attitude towards Harold is still difficult to fathom. While she could be scathing about him in her letters to others – and she obviously felt frustrated and irritated by him on occasion – this was clearly not the whole picture. If her intimate and effusive letters to Harold were simply attempts to string him along, or to take the path of least resistance, then she spent an inordinate amount of time and ink in maintaining the subterfuge. Between August 1967 and June 1969 she wrote him nearly twenty letters, amounting to almost 10,000 words, full of details about her ideas, her reading, what she was doing and her thoughts on life. If the expressions of affection they contain weren't genuine, they can only be seen as shockingly manipulative.

The truth is she wasn't sure how she felt; she found Harold engaging and stimulating, but she couldn't understand him on an emotional level, seeing his hesitations and his lack of confidence towards her as a form of rejection. Although she felt embarrassed – and guilty – at how she had treated him in America, she genuinely wanted to clear the air and be friends. Accordingly, a month or two after her initial non-committal letter to him, she braced herself to break things to him in as kindly a fashion as she could:

Harold: I ought to tell you all the truth and then I will feel better though I fear you will be angry. I met someone 2 weeks before I came to America. I wasn't involved, at least not badly and he was going off to join his wife, from whom he'd been parted for a year, and his child, aged 13. When I got back he was at the airport with Aussie and he said he and Aussie had talked it over and he could live upstairs with me, and he would go off and tell his wife. You know me. I honestly didn't know how to say no – I wanted to, I wanted to paint America, and write it all down and be me. And I thought its all talk, he can't do it, tell the wife I mean – but he did, the same week and she went off to a love in Spain and the daughter stayed with us. Only she was hostile naturally and gradually so was Aussie, and he went to Spain and we went off to this man's farm in the frozen North, and Aus came back and <u>rented off my lovely</u> rooms without telling me . . . But I came back . . . I've got the choice of loosing the man or leaving here, uprooting the 3 kids and taking on another one. This man works at the Art College in Manchester and comes at weekends and I am miserable, and its all my own fault . . . You really are to be envied in one way, finding it difficult to become involved. I do effortlessly and endlessly and always with such complications. Its not sex and its not true deep love, its just not wanting to be alone anymore.[10]

Amid all this emotional upheaval, Hutchinson had finally published *Another Part of the Wood* on 14 October. As the manuscript had actually been finished in December 1966, it was hard for Beryl to avoid the feeling that the delay reflected a lack of confidence on Hutchinson's part. By the start of 1968 she had already hinted to Harold that she might be changing her publisher and that this would be her last book for Hutchinson.[11]

The considerable time lag also made it difficult to feel as enthusiastic as she might otherwise have done. Even so, the critical reaction to the novel, or rather the almost complete lack of it, was still disappointing: 'I am a bit depressed over the book,' she complained to Harold. 'It came out 2 weeks ago and not one review.'[12]

When a review finally appeared, it was perhaps all the more damning for the careful and considered manner in which it picked the book apart. Under the headline 'Cold Comfort', the reviewer in *The Times Literary Supplement* criticized not just the novel's structural weaknesses but the leading character's unpleasant air of self-absorption, a charge that had also been levelled at her first novel. This latter barb must have especially stung, given that in both books Beryl had been trying to depict herself and her emotional dilemmas seriously:

Miss Bainbridge's formula for her second novel is almost exactly the same as for her first . . . namely, to collect together for a few traumatic days a handful of very odd, lost and lonely people, each of whom is obsessed by his own problems, and see how much damage they do to each other . . . Her often intelligent search for the private motives and inadequacies of each character blinds her, perhaps, to the need to relate them to a more normal, less dismally self-engrossed and occasionally entertaining world, and the tragic end of their weekend would appear less abrupt and more significant if it had not been so obvious and gloomily predictable.[13]

Coming on top of the relatively poor commercial performance of *A Weekend with Claud*, the lack of any real critical coverage and lacklustre sales of *Another Part of the Wood* did not bode well for Beryl's future at Hutchinson. Michael Dempsey still kept an eye on her work, but even so she must have suspected that her literary career was all but over. Beryl's relationship with her agent was also coming under strain. Continually pressed for money, she had written him a complaining letter asking where her cheque for the second part of the advance was. She got a tactful but clearly irritated reply from John Smith, who set about explaining that it had been sent to her, first class, the day after he received it from Hutchinson, and that she was being a trifle unreasonable: 'I really don't think anyone could be expected to do things quicker than this. After all the cheque has not yet even cleared our own bank, and we are paying it out before paying it in.'[14]

Three weeks into January 1969, Beryl and the children arrived at Eaves Farm, Austin driving them up in a hired van loaded with various plants and bits of furniture.

Eaves Farm was a stone-built Pennine long house, tucked against a hillside and surrounded by fields and a meadow. If it wasn't the only house on the back road between Holcombe and Helmshore, it nevertheless felt remote, and the nearest village, Ramsbottom, was a thirty-minute walk away. The house was reached via a track that ran down from the road, where milk and the post were left in a box by the cattle grid. Aside from the house, there was a barn, a stone-built pig-pen, a stable and some outbuildings that housed chickens. In the bottom right-hand corner of the yard there was a tall mountain ash with a swing on it, and a gate that led out into a field that sloped down the valley and to the reservoir beyond.

When Don bought the farm in 1963 it had been practically derelict, lacking basic amenities such as electricity. He had done much of the conversion and restoration work himself, and the living space was now effectively composed of two parts: the main farmhouse and a converted cattle-shed, or shippon, attached to it. The shippon was on two levels: the upper floor was Don and Beryl's bedroom, while the lower floor served as his studio. The farmhouse was similarly divided: the upper floor comprised the children's bedrooms and a bathroom, while the lower floor included the kitchen, complete with Aga, a living area with a wood-burning stove, and a central dining room with an enormous tabletop made out of old oak beams. It was, to say the least, a change from life in Albert Street.

February 1969 was not perhaps the ideal moment to introduce oneself into this rural environment: a cold snap plunged temperatures down to -13C, and by the end of the first week there were three-foot drifts of snow that didn't clear until March. Although Don had recently installed central heating especially for Beryl, there weren't any radiators upstairs, so the bedrooms remained as cold as they always had been. When the wind was in the wrong direction the heating would blow out and the house would fill with fumes billowing up from the cellar.

Despite the potential of Eaves Farm to serve as a romantic rural retreat in which Don and Beryl could build a new life together, initially at least, reality fell short of the ideal. With Don at the Art College in Manchester, and Jo, Aaron and Sheenagh at school, Beryl was stuck inside on her own for the greater part of the day with Rudi. Although Jo had quickly settled in – Holcombe village primary was a good school run by an inventive and kindly headmaster – Aaron and Sheenagh, both at Haslingdon Grammar, didn't have it quite so easy. As newcomers, they were picked on and had to deal with bullying. Coming from the South with his London fashion and attitude, Aaron particularly stood out and there were fights. Concerned about the bullying, Beryl would let him stay at home if he wanted to, perhaps not the most tactful solution since Sheenagh still had to go to school.

Adding to these worries was the fact that Austin had just got married. The 'new girlfriend' whom Beryl had casually mentioned in her letter to

Harold a few months before Christmas turned out to be a more serious prospect than any of Austin's previous relationships. On his way back to Albert Street one evening in September, in the lift at Mornington Crescent tube, he had met Belinda Bond, a twenty-six-year-old New Zealander working as a schoolteacher in London. Struck by her looks, Austin had asked her if she fancied a drink. Although she declined the offer – and his follow-up suggestion that he accompany her to the party she was going to – she gave him her phone number. A few days later he invited her round for coffee in the Albert Street basement, and over the following months a close relationship developed. Belinda moved in with Austin in February, and on 3 March they were married in St Pancras registry office.

Although Beryl was well past the stage where she imagined, or even wanted, a reconciliation with Austin, the news of his wedding, which she heard about only after the event, undoubtedly had a psychological effect. Not only did it throw the seriousness of her own relationship with Don into the spotlight, it had possible implications regarding Austin's continuing financial support, not to mention the status of Albert Street, the mortgage of which was still in Austin's name.

With these anxieties coursing through her mind, it was little wonder Beryl started to doubt herself and her relationship with Don, and as so often before she began to see past events through a more nostalgic lens. After Harold sent her a copy of Emily Dickinson's love poems ('To Beryl, the flower of Albert Street, with much love . . .'), and feeling sorry for herself and guilty about her treatment of him, she wrote and tried to explain the situation she now found herself in:

Dear Washington Harold, I have always expected too much, give too much [at the] start, and ended up by being given nothing. I am in a field now in the snow in a 16th century farm-house with this painter man whom I do not understand and four children and no money and only a wish to get near and no hope of it. The book of poems was beautiful. I loved it.

You are kind and lost and hopeless like me too . . . I wish I could write poetry. I am a third way thru a book of you and me in the truck, for which the publisher rings weekly to try and get. I cannot do it because I need love, don't we all, and love is not gotten by chance.

To hell wuth all this.

Even if I don't wrote or have not written I think of you each day, chaque jour, the lost chances are the gardest to bear. Austin is married. I am not. Goodnight sweet prince. B.[15]

With the melting of the snow and the arrival of spring, however, things improved. Eaves Farm was a beautiful, secluded space in which to conduct a love affair and it was hard not to be seduced by the simple way of life it imposed. The positive side of the long periods Beryl spent on her own included a burst of artistic activity. In April she had received a postcard from a mutual friend (addressed to 'Mr & Mrs McKinlay'), which jokingly described the portrait on the front – an image of Napoleon in profile staring moodily into the distance, right hand stuffed into his waistcoat – as 'Napoleon out of his element i.e. Ramsbottom'.[16] Beryl picked up on this idea, and began to produce a series of pictures that played on the incongruous idea of the Romantic figure of Napoleon in the prosaic landscape of Ramsbottom. *Napoleon viewing the field*, for example, pictured Napoleon standing in military uniform by a living-room window, surveying the fields around Eaves Farm, while behind him a naked woman sits in an armchair, a hen perched on the backrest. The more explicit *Napoleon's campaign in Ramsbottom* featured Napoleon sitting in an armchair in the backyard of the farm, surrounded by sheep and hens, and indulging in foreplay with a naked woman on his lap.

What is striking about many of these drawings is their frankness – *Rustic Pleasures* shows a man taking a woman from behind on the flagstones of the Eaves Farm courtyard – though they were also characteristically witty. *Down on the Farm* features a thinly disguised Don and Beryl indulging in naked calisthenics in the farmyard, surrounded by chickens. Inspired by the intensity of her physical relationship with Don, this would be the first – and the last – time that she would produce such openly erotic drawings. The pages of the journal she was keeping at the time were also interspersed with sketches of herself and Don making love. Significantly, the only exception was a naked self-portrait in which, in a kind of artistic wish-fulfilment, Beryl portrayed herself as heavily pregnant.

Art was not the only means of passing the time while Don was away. Since her return from America, Beryl had been toying with the idea of using her experiences as the basis for a novel, though she remained uncertain 'what form to put the bloody thing in'.[17] She had started the novel shortly before Christmas, but her assertion that she was a third of the way through was perhaps something of an exaggeration, though she had written at least twenty pages in first-draft form. Although she would ultimately abandon the book, these pages would find a new life when she came to write *The Girl in the Polka Dot Dress* over thirty years later.

What the unfinished book would eventually have been called is less clear. On the inside page of her American journal Beryl wrote, 'This was meant to be turned into a novel, "I Was Doctor Wheeler's Intended"', and indeed that line appears in one of the existing 1969 drafts. But the note was added sometime around 2004, when Beryl was preparing material to go to the British Library, and it's unlikely this was the title she had in mind at the time.[18] In the journal itself, written contemporaneously with her American trip, is the title 'He's the Captain of the Team', with a list of the people whom characters would be based on underneath, including Washington Harold, Beryl and Austin. That this was the working title is confirmed by an interview she gave shortly after the publication of *Harriet Said* in 1972, in which she mentioned 'He's the Captain of the Team' as the book she was currently working on.[19]

Although there is a certain surface similarity in the prose and the setting of 'He's the Captain of the Team', in which Heine Melman is waiting at Baltimore airport for the arrival of Alma Bickerton from England, who has come in search of her ex-lover Dr Wheeler, and that of *The Girl in the Polka Dot Dress*, the two novels would have been very different. In the first place, the relationship between Heine and Alma is unlike that of Harold and Rose, and more closely reflects Beryl's ambivalent feelings towards the real-life Harold at the time.

On the first night of her arrival in America, for example, Alma goes to bed in Heine's apartment and wakes to find him beside her. Although this also happens to Rose in *Polka Dot*, the difference here is that unlike Rose, Alma is expecting Heine to make love to her, and takes his shy inability to instigate the first move as an insult, a proof of his lack of attraction to her:

She turned to him and against her belly she could feel him and he wore nothing. Still he made no move. It was uncomfortable for them both. He was waiting for her to be generous, to fulfill all that Doc Wheeler had promised of her, she was quite a woman and he was in bed with her.

And she was waiting for him to kiss her if that was what he wanted. He couldn't be that shy, he could not expect her to make the advances. Why that would make her no better than a tart.[20]

The fact that Alma wants Heine to make love to her is given further emphasis when, shortly afterwards, he starts to touch her: Alma tells him to stop and he takes his hand away. This irritates her in the same way as his inability to make the first move had, for Heine fails to realize that when Alma says 'No' she doesn't mean 'No':

'Why do you stop, go on, tell me?'

'Stop what?'

'Oh Christ.' She flounced upright and crossed her legs and stared out at the trees. He dare not look at her face, only the stretched whiteness of her inner thighs.

'I guess I'm just shy,' he said muffled, but she was not listening to him anymore.

Although in later life Beryl downplayed the extent of her emotional involvement with Harold, and indeed in *The Girl in the Polka Dot Dress* portrayed their relationship as one in which she was the unwilling partner, forced into close proximity – and even sex – with him, this was not how she experienced it at the time. Beryl's attitude to Harold both before and after the American trip was more complicated than the black-and-white picture she later presented. This is certainly reflected in the draft of 'He's the Captain of the Team', where Alma actively encourages Heine to make love to her: when she rouses from an erotic dream of Dr Wheeler to feel 'the heavy indenture of Heine's fingers pressing into her', she does not stop him but leads him on: 'She takes hold of his wrist and feels the cold curve of his watch and kneels upright, guiding him, holding his middle finger like a teacher helping a child to write its alphabet, tracing the capital of her cunt with him until he finds trembling the clung looseness of her labia . . .'[21]

One of the few people to read this early draft of the new novel was Beryl's editor at Hutchinson, Michael Dempsey, who visited her while she was at Eaves Farm. Although her writing was still not quite as polished and economical as it would later become, and the sex scenes would have been something of a publishing challenge in 1969, he was encouraging, advising her to 'try and work and then come back, organise it and then try for some grant to go abroad'.[22]

Dempsey also suggested she might be able to make some money teaching, and that meeting other writers would be helpful for her career. But with memories of Alan still in her mind, this didn't have quite the appeal Dempsey had intended: 'I don't want to meet any writers,' she wrote in her journal. 'They're probably all like me or Alan or Alex Hamilton and who the hell wants that. I would like Don's baby. I dream about that.'

———

This went to the heart of the matter. Drawing and writing were all very well, but there were more important things in life. 'I came to have a baby,' she would write in the journal she kept at Eaves Farm and which was part extended love letter to Don, part *De Profundis*-style self-justification: 'I came to have a baby, to love you, to be beside you every night, to grow fat on love and being loved.'[23] As in the past, she turned to poetry in moments of high emotion as a means of expressing her deepest feelings:

> There are sheep in the field
> A hen in the yard
> Six plates on the table
> Yellow flowers in a jug
> Butter in the fridge
> Bread in the bin
> A big brass bed golden enough
> To make a baby in

The problem was that such romantic fantasies always seemed to dissolve on contact with reality. In America, she had longed to return to Don and Albert Street, but once back in London the reality meant looking after four children, with Don visiting only on occasional weekends. The point of moving to Eaves Farm was 'to be alone with Don',[24] but now she was here the reality was she was spending large parts of the day alone looking after Rudi, and when Don did return in the evening he would often want to paint. To Don, teaching was a necessary job but being an artist was what he was, and being an artist required time on your own, time to think and to work. Don, like Austin before him, had an overriding commitment to art, but was hamstrung by the practical need to earn money, meaning he had to combine his teaching schedule with the full-time vocation of being an artist. It was hardly surprising that this didn't leave much time or emotional energy left over, and that Beryl felt short-changed.

Beryl had always demanded a total emotional engagement, and her insecurities being what they were, she perceived any falling away from this as a failure of love, an implicit rejection. She may have been aware that this was unrealistic, that she was being too demanding, and even that this was at the root of the repeated failures of her relationships, but if she was conscious of it she appeared to be psychologically unable to do anything about it.

By June 1969 she seemed to have reached an uneasy acceptance of the situation, and that rather than being 'alone with Don', she would have to make do with being 'alone, with Don'. Given her emotional volatility, it was hard to believe that this state could last for long. Harold had recently sent her the photograph Judith Gleeson had taken while they were in Wanakena, and in her reply Beryl painted a gloomy picture of herself as someone leading a solitary life, alienated and detached from the world and the relationships around her. Significantly, she broached the idea of returning to Albert Street for the first time:

Dearest Washington Harold,
The photohraphs of you were beautiful. Surprisingly of late you are much clearer, so that looking at the photo, I saw you in the shadows of the sunlight and remembered your freckles and the way you droop your head. I think your last letter was sad. I am not in Albert Street but I may go back. I miss it and yet I need a good life, a so called one with another existance. Unlike you I am lost when alone.

I think I have found something. I don't go out, I read, lie in the rain, hitch hike for food, have got fatter, I don't talk much anymore, I don't know the man I am living with, he is inward and an artist and you trust noone, but in a fashion we have understanding and maybe that is the best we should hope for, and far more than most have anyway.[25]

There was still a strong bond between herself and Don, and their passion for each other was undeniable. But on a practical level nothing had really been solved by the move to Eaves Farm, and indeed the problems seemed insurmountable. Don didn't like London, and though he had been content to travel down for the occasional weekend to see her, he certainly wasn't going to settle there full-time. But to Beryl, the alternative – uprooting herself and the children and leaving London for good – seemed equally unthinkable. In the first place it meant the loss of the independence and security she had with the house in Albert Street. It was fine for Don, who could drive and who had a job in Manchester, to live in the wild remoteness of Holcombe, but to Beryl, being stuck there everyday with no job and no means of escape, it would be like being in prison – a beautiful, open prison admittedly – but a prison nonetheless. Not only that, she had to deal with Austin's annoyance at the children being taken away – and what about the children themselves? Was it fair on them to disrupt their education, their contact with their father, their friends, the life they had previously known in London?

To these general anxieties were added the increasing tensions of day-to-day living. She began to brood on the unfairness of her situation, her solitary isolation during the day, and the fact that Don had a social life outside of his relationship with her and didn't always feel the need to include her in it. As in the past, she became increasingly prone to bouts of suspicion and jealousy, seeing in Don's actions and behaviour – even a visit to his family – a proof that he didn't love her enough: 'Don went to see his mother and Father today with Sheenagh. He is supposedly going to tell his mother about me. But when they came back later he did not mention it . . . All his friends who he never takes me to see. We could have all gone but he didn't ask me.'

She would focus on the smallest incident, magnifying it in her mind into a full-blown proof of his indifference to her. She began to see treachery where there was none. It was a recipe for disaster: not saying anything herself, not wanting to ask him what he felt, she instead interpreted events through the prism of her insecure paranoia, she saw signs of underhand behaviour and betrayal everywhere. When the annual Liverpool Academy exhibition came round, she wanted him to want her to come: 'I would have loved to go, to go to a party, I would have wished him to want me with him. To hell with that too. At night he wanted to draw me. I snapped at that too. Only because I have no confidence left in myself, no belief that he gives a shit about me.'[26]

To Don, such suspicions and paranoia seemed unreasonable, and inevitably they began to argue, which, like a vicious circle, fuelled the very insecurity she feared:

> I hate the feeling when we quarrel. It leaves me feeling bitter and Don feeling confused. He says I talk rubbish. All his eyes grow hard and he blinks a lot. I weep and feel unloved. I just want proof. I want the words.
>
> I've been told by others, and look what happened. If he doesn't say he loves me, does it mean he does not love me? It feels that way.
>
> I want more than anything to be beautiful for him. I spend ages combing my hair and changing my clothes, even though I freeze with the cold.
>
> Sometimes, he does not notice me.[27]

The problem was that nothing would serve as sufficient proof for her insecurities – when the words were offered, she didn't believe them. The sad thing was she knew that her fears were self-destructive, that they would end up destroying the very thing she desired. As the weeks passed, she became fixated on the fact that Don had stopped saying 'I love you', and her obsession, exacerbated by her insecurities and her loneliness, began to get out of control:

> He would think me fucking mad, all this. I used to be able to tell him, before he stopped saying it, before he stopped ringing me in the day. I used to say it in his ear. Now at night when he starts the clicking noise in his throat which means he is asleep, I lean over and say Don, Don I love you, beauty boy, dear lovely Don, over and over, very soft. It makes me relax and I curl into him and he turns over violently and says 'Jesus, the folder', and I say 'alright alright'.
>
> I watch everything he does.
>
> I am obsessed, bloody mad.[28]

Clearly things could not continue like this. The idea of returning to London gained in her mind, and Beryl would talk it over endlessly with

Austin, though even this led to more tension, with Don 'going on about the phone bill' because she had been on the telephone for hours. She tried to explain it all, to reason it out with herself:

> If its all gone, why am I still here? The furniture, the kids, the money, where to go? Where did it all go? Endless fucking questions.
>
> All the poems, the love songs, the half waking dreams of being in love and loved in return. Is it just an illusion? Cling tight to the illusions . . .
>
> All these days are very bad. I think too much about Don and I pity myself and I don't know where to go. I think Austin will let me return but I'll have to get a job to pay the rent. The thing is not that I want to go, but that I have to go. I love the house, these fields. I love Don, but he doesn't seem to want to know anymore.
>
> I try so hard to be cheerful when he comes in. Outside the sheep graze, big black crows come down into the field. The cars go up the road to Holcombe. I look out of the window and the children watch television and then the door slams and they shout – Don's here.
>
> He looks at me coolly. He goes off to draw then and I don't follow because I don't want to bother him.
>
> Its so ironic. Don's not drinking, not staying out, not spending, the children are settled in school, the bills are being slowly paid, I keep everywhere clean, manage on very little, and yet its all fucked up to hell. What happened?[29]

Trying to answer that question Beryl flipped between two equally unhelpful, emotionally damaging positions: first she would blame herself, then she would turn her anger and resentment on Don:

> He wasn't like this in London. Why when I got here? What do I do wrong? Too gloomy, not very pretty, too probing, too wanting words, too much analysing . . . If he doesn't want me thats his business. Too hell with him . . . If necessary I shall crawl to Austin and beg him to let me come back. I shall pretend its the schools, for the children's sake. I will sacrifice all for the children . . . If I hadn't been so vain as to think that Don would always love me I wouldn't have come. If I hadn't been so self-centred I would have worried more about the children. Here I am past 3 in the morning half cut on vodka, and all alone in a strange house and Don gone volentarily to a party because

he wanted to . . . and he didn't want me with him. So finally for ever, to hell with it.

Perhaps the last straw was when Aaron went to London to see Austin and didn't come back. At the time, Sheenagh, seeing how much Beryl missed Aaron, thought this was the reason she decided to leave Eaves Farm. But Beryl's journal shows just how strained her relationship with Don had become by this stage, and though she goes over the causes of the breakdown of that relationship in agonizing detail, Aaron's departure isn't even mentioned. In any event, by now Don himself had had enough. Living with Beryl when she was in this emotionally paranoid state wasn't easy: 'Don said that it was all over and done with',[30] as Jo-Jo wrote in her diary on 26 August, after overhearing one of their arguments.

The family who had rented Albert Street in Beryl's absence were given notice to leave, and at the end of September Austin drove the van up to Eaves Farm again. The plants, the bits of furniture and the stuffed owl were loaded up again, and just before they set off Don, who had been unaware that Beryl had decided to leave, returned home from work. It was a sad parting. Beryl stood in the field crying and smoking, not saying anything. Sheenagh recalls being absolutely devastated as she waved goodbye to Jo and Rudi, whom she had grown to love. 'Sheenagh's eyes were watering, and she was crying,' Jo noted in her diary, 'I felt sorry for her.'[31]

As she left, Beryl gave Don the journal she had been keeping. A note pasted into the front tried to sum things up:

I don't think this is really for you, more like for me. When communication goes there has to be some way to reach out, to record. When I have been happy it is because of you, when I have been unhappy that is because of you also.

Here on the Farm, in the North, the six of us, the four growing beautiful children, and you and I, not really grown.

I came here because I loved you and there was no way of not being with you, no way that is without being sad at losing you, for I would have lost you and indeed I did lose you.

For a long time I ran round trying to have you and safety and London and everything else, but that came to an end, as it had to, the long days, just you and I, trembling at each other . . .

TWENTY-FOUR

Bottle Factory

On Christmas Eve, somewhat the worse for party spirit, I
was trundled home in a pram. My neglectful nurse-maid,
summoned by a neighbour to more festivities, parked me by
the hedge and went inside. I woke at dawn, rained upon and
doubled up, without even a woolly blanket for comfort.[1]

B ACK IN ALBERT STREET there were a number of practical
issues that needed sorting out, such as organizing schools and
redecorating the house. The children of the American family who
had rented it for the last six months had left finger paintings all over
the walls, or as Jo-Jo put it: 'Dam tennents just walked out leaving a
stinking mess.'[2]

Another pressing subject was that of earning money. For some time
past Austin had been living in the basement, but now he and Belinda
were married and expecting their first child they had moved into a
run-down terraced house in Islington. Austin couldn't support two
households indefinitely, so Beryl would have to find work to help make
ends meet.

Although Belinda always got on well with Beryl, there were inevitable tensions over what she saw as Beryl's over-reliance, both emotionally
and financially, on Austin. She found Beryl particularly exasperating
when she played on Austin's guilt feelings about leaving the children.
After Austin and Belinda moved out, Beryl would often phone them
in the evening, wanting Austin to come over to Albert Street and sort
out some 'crisis' to do with the children, or what would appear to most
people to be a quite trivial practical matter regarding the house. Beryl's
impracticality when it came to money and household expenses was
another cause of friction, as Belinda recalled:

Money was always extremely tight, and we lived very frugally, so when we visited Beryl in the depths of winter to find her wafting about in very thin clothes while the central heating blazed away it was a bit galling, since we were paying the bills. On a number of occasions we found the front door wide open and all the heat escaping. She also refused to let us do a supermarket shop for her to stock up the fridge for the growing children – she said they would just descend like a plague of locusts and it would all be gone. She preferred to pay more at the small shop round the corner.[3]

The subject of money was therefore a touchy one. 'How dare she tell me to get a job?' Beryl would complain to Austin if ever Belinda questioned her on the issue. Nevertheless, Beryl did find work, though most of the jobs were of a temporary or short-lived nature. One of these was a series of uncredited performances in the television series *Doomwatch*. The programme, which featured John Paul, Simon Oates and Robert Powell as a team of quasi-autonomous investigators, examining threats from aberrant or misguided scientific research, would become a minor cult classic. It was a kind of proto *X-Files*, but with hammier, less convincing plot lines and frequently stilted acting, especially from John Paul as Dr Spencer Quist.

It's not clear how Beryl became involved, but it may have been through Kevin Stoney, the actor she'd had a crush on in Dundee nearly twenty years before, who starred in the first episode. In any case, these were not acting roles as such, simply extra work: in the surviving recordings Beryl can be seen in the background, as part of a group of customers standing at a bar or as a seated diner in a restaurant. In one episode she appears as a nurse, and in another as a WRAF officer. In all she appeared in seven episodes (two of which were wiped): the first, 'Tomorrow the Rat', was filmed on 20 December 1969 and broadcast on 2 March 1970, and the last, 'Flight into Yesterday', filmed over a year later on 19 January 1971 and broadcast on 1 February.[4] The schedule roughly consisted of a day's shooting, with the episode being broadcast a month or so later. Although the work was sporadic, it didn't take up too much time and it was relatively well paid, Beryl receiving five guineas for each day's shooting.

It was around this time that Beryl met Pauline Mani, who lived round the corner on Mornington Street and who ran one of the local playgroups. Her son, Johnny, was the same age as Rudi and went to the same school. Pauline was certainly a character, a larger-than-life figure in many senses. A Scot by birth, she was almost six feet tall and blonde: many people found her an imposing presence. 'She was large, and she was overpowering,'[5] recalled the filmmaker James Scott, who lived further up Albert Street. As one of the organizers of the Albert Street carnival he and his wife had got to know Pauline well and remembered her with affection. To Scott she was 'Paula', but to Beryl, fascinated by her abrasive personality and the extravagant stories she told about her life, she was familiarly referred to as 'Fat Pauline'.

Pauline was, like Beryl, a single mother and her dealings with men had been, if anything, even more fraught than Beryl's. Johnny's Nigerian father had left her and returned to his native country when his son was still an infant, and her subsequent marriage to Moshe Mani in 1967 was short-lived. Her experiences with men had left her embittered: 'My mother was a very angry woman,' Johnny told the *Camden Journal*, and her heavy drinking, which eventually led to her death in 2003, made her a dangerous woman to get too close to. Don's blunt comment, 'What the fuck are you doing with Pauline, keep away from her'[6] probably represented the feelings of more than one of Beryl's acquaintances.

In the early months of 1970, after coming across an advertisement in the local post office,[7] Beryl and Pauline started part-time work at Belloni's, a wine warehouse situated on the corner of Albert Street and Parkway. Although they would only work there for a short time, it was a suitably bizarre experience and Beryl would later turn it to good account in her novel *The Bottle Factory Outing*.

Beryl's job was to stick labels onto wine bottles by hand – this was in a pre-automated era – and most of her fellow workers were Italian immigrants who didn't speak much English. Although they were congenial enough, the factory itself wasn't an ideal workplace. For a start it was a large building, difficult and uneconomic to heat during winter. Beryl was so cold she used to wrap herself in sheets of newspaper beneath her jumper to keep warm. Hearing of this, her friend Lili Todes gave her a white woollen coat. The next time Lili saw it, the sleeves were stained in red up to the elbow.[8]

The work wasn't very well paid, but one of the dubious compensations was that you could drink as much as you liked. This aspect of the job was one that Beryl tended to play up in interviews and she would frequently claim that she had to be 'wheeled home every afternoon on a trolley',[9] or that they 'had to carry me home by 10.30'[10] in the morning. In private, however, whenever Rudi challenged her and said she remembered coming back to Albert Street after school to find her drunk, that she was moody or aggressive, and sometimes even unconscious on the sofa, Beryl would vigorously deny it. Either way, even if it was only a sporadic occurrence, having to deal with a drunken parent would have been a scary and unsettling experience for a six-year-old child, and over the years to come Beryl's immoderate drinking would be the catalyst for many family arguments.

Towards the end of 1971 Beryl and Pauline got involved in another temporary job together, this time on one of James Scott's film projects. Scott had previously made short documentaries on subjects such as Richard Hamilton and R. B. Kitaj, but was now looking to experiment with a longer, less restrictive, format. Shot for the most part in a friend's flat during November and December 1971, the result was *Adult Fun*, Scott's first feature-length film, which he later described as 'a semi-documentary thriller set in the world of industrial espionage'. Although the main characters were played by professional actors, such as Peter Marinker, Deborah Norton and Michael Elphick, most of the cast were non-professionals and much of the dialogue was improvised on the spot. Scott knew that Beryl had been doing some acting work to earn extra money, so when he was looking round for people to fill the film's minor roles he asked her and Pauline if they wanted to take part, which they did, despite the modest fee.

Beryl appeared in a scene playing opposite Bruce Lacey, the experimental performance artist who had featured as George Harrison's gardener in the film *Help!*, along with Lacey's wife Jill and Ken Garland, another Albert Street resident. Pauline played a prostitute. When the film was released in 1972, *Time Out* compared its parodic combination of genres to Jean-Luc Godard, though *Sight and Sound* was more ambivalent, its reviewer feeling that despite 'moments of acute observation', the film's satire of the British class system was 'too heavy handed', and that its 'metaphysical speculations . . . ultimately founder in a sea of contradictions and imprecision'.[11]

As might be gathered from the title, the film dealt with adult themes, and there is some nudity in it. Beryl later claimed she didn't know it was going to be 'a bit mucky', and that the first she heard about it was when she was talking with the director over lunch and he asked her, 'Oh by the way, you don't mind taking your clothes off?' Always self-conscious about her physical appearance, she hid in the bathroom, petrified, wondering how she could get out of the situation. In the end she did the scene but kept her bra on, though the other actress agreed to go topless. While they were shooting the scene – it involved a struggle between Bruce Lacey's character and the two women – Jill Lacey's naked breasts brushed Beryl on the arm, and Beryl screamed involuntarily.[12] She was hyper-anxious about physical contact with women and any imputation of lesbianism, which she put down to having to share her bed as a child with her mother.

Beryl found the film fun, but like television extra work, it didn't really lead anywhere. The next time she appeared in front of a camera it would be not as an actress reciting someone else's words, but as a writer reading her own.

————

The retreat from Eaves Farm had left Beryl feeling depressed and unable to eat. She went to see her doctor and burst into tears in the surgery, blaming herself for what had happened and telling him that she was responsible for breaking up with Don. He prescribed her amitryptyline, an anti-depressant.[13] But if the return to Albert Street was a blow to Beryl's hope of a lasting relationship with Don, it didn't mark the end of the affair completely. Absence and distance helped to heal the wounds left by the abortive attempt to live together. By Christmas, Don was once again coming down to London whenever he had a free weekend, and his passion and commitment seemed unabated, even if the practical difficulties of their situation remained unchanged.

Don felt partly responsible for the way things had turned out, and in January 1970 he wrote an impassioned letter to Beryl to reassure her he was still committed to her and that he would try and move things on regarding a divorce from Helen: 'I know I could have done a lot more and saved some money & done more with the solicitor & when I get some money I will do it. I love you, I want to marry you and have a baby, I love you. Without you its horrible. This house could be beautiful.'[14]

Don often had Fridays free, which made long weekends in London possible, and for the first few months of 1970 he'd drive down the M1, breathlessly eager to see Beryl again after a week's work: 'Coming down on Friday, marvellous thinking of you, we will have a nice little talk in the Mornington Arms, I will look at you and think you are beautiful, and mine, make you love me, kiss and love you.'[15]

But passionate though they were, long weekends were not enough. The time passed 'too fast', it was 'over too soon', there was 'no time to even talk'. No sooner had Friday arrived, 'then bang its Sunday. Beryl, mince and spuds, and away up the M1'.[16] Added to which, the 200 miles between Manchester and London was a wearisome hurdle to have to keep jumping over.

As the months passed, Don's trips to London began to get more erratic. Jo-Jo remembered how excited Beryl would be, anticipating these weekends, recalling how she would do her hair and prepare a curry especially for him. And then he wouldn't turn up: 'She'd go to all this trouble and he just didn't come.'[17] Something of this is expressed in a note she sent to Don around this time: 'Why aren't you here? And you don't ring and you don't write. Stuff you. I love you very much. U should be here to stuff me. Your adoring best friend and lover B.'[18]

Beryl's sense that the relationship was not working out intensified as the year progressed, and was reflected in the drawings she was doing at the time, most of which used the Eaves Farm setting as a back-drop. One, dated 'Winter 1970', shows a naked female figure watching Napoleon on television, while a sombre-faced Napoleon stands in the foreground, staring blankly out into space. The drawing is ominously entitled *A quiet evening at Eaves Farm or Hope does not spring eternal*. Another drawing from the same period depicts a bleak, post-coital scene: a naked female figure is lying on the floor, with tears rolling down her face while a naked man stands head bowed, eyes averted, avoiding both the naked woman and the gaze of the spectator. On the television set in the corner of the room are the words 'Do not adjust your set. The fault is permanent', and the title of the picture reads *There is no hope for the future . . . I'm off to the pub*. Other pictures in the series feature the same set of figures – Napoleon, a naked man and a naked woman – only this time the overtly erotic motif of the previous year has been replaced by that of death and murder, the naked female figure typically lying dead, sprawled on the floor, impaled on a knife.

Perhaps the best picture from this period is a large oil showing Don as Napoleon riding a horse, with a naked female figure behind him. The snowy landscape behind them is as cold and bleak as their expressions, and the grimly ironic title leaves little room for doubt as to the picture's meaning: *Napoleon and friend retreating from Ramsbottom.*

It was during the relatively brief 'bottle factory' period that an incident occurred which would achieve mythic status in later newspaper accounts of Beryl's life: her former mother-in-law's attempt to shoot her. Beryl often had to work a half day on Saturday, and one weekend early in 1970, as she was about to go to Belloni's, there was a knock at the door:

> My mother-in-law stood on the step, dressed in a grey coat and hat and clutching a handbag . . . She had come she said to get pictures of her children when young; would I please fetch them. I left her in the hall went up one flight of stairs to my living room and hurriedly searched through my photo albums . . . When I came out of the room she was standing one flight down, a little matronly figure digging something out of her handbag. Just in time I realised she was taking out a gun and . . . I jumped forward, jerked her elbow and ducked as a shot was fired at the ceiling. A shower of newly applied plaster fell on us like snow.[19]

Luckily Don happened to be up in London, and at the time of the shooting he was upstairs doing some decorating, painting the walls of the stairwell white. As if to give an added air of farce to the situation, he had stripped off and was wearing nothing but a raincoat – he didn't want to ruin his clothes and had no overalls. Hearing the commotion, he rushed down and managed to get the gun off Nora on the first flight of stairs. Together, he and Beryl tried to calm Nora down with a cup of tea, but she ran out of the house.

Not wanting to be late for work, Beryl headed off to the bottle factory, but a short time later the foreman came up and said she should go home immediately because the police were waiting for her. The police had picked Nora up – or rather she had flagged them down and told them she had shot someone. There then followed a comic scene, worthy of one of Beryl's novels, in which the shooting was re-enacted with Don still in his raincoat and a policeman playing the part of Nora, holding one of Beryl's handbags.

Although the incident was sufficiently bizarre and unusual in itself, neither Beryl nor the journalists who took every opportunity of recounting it could resist embellishing their account still further. The story appeared under sensational headlines such as 'The Day I Was Nearly Shot Dead by My Mother-in-Law',[20] and otherwise reputable journalists let their imaginations run riot, asserting that Beryl's mother-in-law had fired 'a shotgun at her, blasting holes in the wall', or that she had been 'blazing away with a revolver'.[21] Beryl herself would later claim that the deflected gunshot had 'brought down the ceiling'[22] in the hallway.

All of this was patent nonsense. The gun wasn't a shotgun or even a revolver, but an air pistol. It wasn't a bullet that was fired, but a pellet.[23] It did not bring Beryl's ceiling down and it would not have killed her, though it might, as they say, have taken her eye out. But despite retelling the story numerous times in the press, Beryl only once mentioned this fact, in 1989. But by then it was too late, the myth had taken hold. The idea of a gun-toting mother-in-law, and of Beryl's narrow escape from a bizarre death, was too firmly established as a part of the legend.

Although it spoiled the story somewhat to say so, Beryl not only knew what type of gun it was, she also knew that Nora, who by this stage was already having mental problems, wanted to shoot her. A month after the publication of *A Weekend with Claud* in June 1967, Beryl had received an unsettling letter from her, as she told Judith: 'Nora read the book and wrote at once saying she knew where she could get an automatic and she was coming to kill me. I don't know whether to feel flattered or not. It obviously affected her.'[24]

The timing of the letter was not coincidental: in the novel Beryl had painted a searingly frank portrait of herself, and alluded plainly to the collapse of her marriage and the string of affairs she had had in its wake. Although Nora's reaction was extreme, it is not difficult to see why she wanted to punish Beryl for having separated from Austin and to stop her making her infidelities public. Indeed, as the novel features its own shooting incident – Claud in a fit of jealousy tries to shoot Maggie's boyfriend Edward with an air rifle – Nora may even have got the idea from reading the book. Beryl took the threat quite seriously: six months later she wrote to Harold and told him that Nora had come round to the house but, fortunately, hadn't tried to shoot her.[25]

While the incident had few emotional repercussions for Beryl herself, it did serve as a useful plot device in *The Bottle Factory Outing*. Ironically, the fictionalized version is both less dramatic than the newspaper accounts Beryl would later give, and in some senses more truthful: not only is it an air pistol that was used, the reason for the shooting in the book is that Brenda's mother-in-law wanted to punish Brenda for leaving her husband. She felt that 'Brenda talked too much' and intended to silence her by shooting her in the vocal chords. Nora would certainly have felt that Beryl's public account of her failed marriage to Austin in *A Weekend with Claud* was an example of Beryl talking too much.

The shooting also formed the subject of one of Beryl's most striking paintings, entitled *Did you think I would leave you dying when there's room on my horse for two*, in which she represented both herself and Don as naked on the stairwell, with Nora coming up from below holding her gun.

Using one's own life experiences as the raw material for artistic creation is far from unusual, and one shouldn't expect artists or writers to behave as mental-health professionals sorting out the problems of the people they observe. Nevertheless, the Nora incident provides a clear example of the way Beryl appropriated the traumatic experiences of others and used them either as comic relief or as colourful cameos to illustrate her own life. She knew of Nora's mental instability, but made no attempt to find out what she was suffering from, where she lived, or whether there was anything that could be done to help her.

On 6 September 1974, Nora was killed after being struck by a train at St David's station in Exeter. Nora's mental instability was almost certainly a factor in her death, precluding her from a rational judgement of what she was doing, a fact reflected in the open verdict that was given in the inquest after her death. Whenever Beryl recounted the incident, however, it would not be as a tragic aspect of Nora's life, but as another proof of the comical bizarreness of her own.

At the beginning of the new academic year in September 1970, Jo-Jo started at Hampstead Comprehensive, the same school Aaron had been attending since their return from Eaves Farm. This circumstance wouldn't have been particularly worth noting if it weren't for some entries that appeared in Jo's diary over the next few months, though at the time the fact that Aaron had struck up a friendship with a boy in his year called William Haycraft, or that Jo had added a new name to her list of boyfriends, that of William's younger brother, Joshua, would have meant nothing to Beryl. She certainly couldn't have imagined that her children's new friends would have such a dramatic impact on the course of her own life.

A few months later, in early 1971, William was round at Albert Street playing upstairs with Aaron when the phone rang. It was William's mother, Anna Haycraft, wondering what time her son would be home. The two women began to talk and after a moment Anna asked, 'I recognize your voice, what's your name?' When Beryl told her that her maiden name was Bainbridge, Anna replied, 'I've read your two books; they are pretty awful. Have you got anything else?' She then told her she was the fiction editor of Gerald Duckworth Ltd., a publishing house run by her husband Colin Haycraft.

That at least was the public version of events, as recounted by Beryl many years later.[26] What was missing from her account – for understandable reasons – is the fact that the last time Beryl had heard anything about Anna was in May 1953. Then her name had been Anne Lindholm, the girl whose affair with Austin had led to such traumatic consequences. Even after so many years, Beryl's realization that she was speaking to the woman who had caused her so much anguish in the past must have been difficult to take in. Anna, too, must have been in an unimaginable state of trepidation: in order to ring the house she would have seen the number listed under the name Austin Davies in the directory. Maybe she had hoped it was a coincidence of names when she made the call, but she could have been in little doubt who she was speaking to the moment Beryl started to talk.

The situation was worse for Anna than it was for Beryl. The affair with Austin had been disastrous on so many levels and the abortion was something she never came to terms with emotionally. She had never admitted to it or talked about it in public, and its corrosive impact on her psyche was compounded by her public espousal of the Catholic faith. It had become a profound source of guilt, a shameful incident from her past that had to be kept secret at all costs. Later, when she became a public figure in her own right, Anna must have been acutely aware of the incongruity of being asked to talk openly about her Catholic faith and about Catholicism as a moral force, and repeatedly having to lie and give a false version of her own past. Catholicism was a religion founded on the notion of the forgiveness of sins, but ironically she could never forgive her own.

For most people, friendships are founded on a sense of openness based on mutual trust – the notion that one can talk to a friend about anything without fear of ridicule or embarrassment. With Beryl and Anna, the situation was almost entirely the opposite. From the very start, it was a friendship at the centre of which was a kind of mutual, unspoken pact: that both would never reveal the traumatic event that had linked their destinies. It was never openly spoken about between them, and each expected the other to keep quiet about it in public. So deeply ingrained was this feeling of secrecy that Beryl did not allude to the abortion even under the guise of fiction, and only referred to it in public once, several years after Anna's death, in a series of interviews conducted by the British Library.[27]

The gravitational force of that unspoken secret inevitably skewed the relationship between them, and their friendship was conducted almost entirely on Anna's terms. It was always Beryl who would go round to the Haycrafts' house in Gloucester Crescent: Anna would have found it unthinkable to go to Albert Street, where there was a possibility of a chance encounter with Austin. 'I don't remember ever seeing Anna in Albert Street,'[28] Rudi would later recall.

As it happened, Beryl *did* have 'something else' to show Anna. Her former agent, John Smith, had recently given up his position as managing director of Christy & Moore and he had returned the manuscript of 'The Summer of the Tsar', which had lain in a cupboard ever since Graham Nicol turned it down in 1965.[29] Not having heard anything about it for years, Beryl had assumed it was lost. She wondered whether Anna might be interested in it.

She was.

TWENTY-FIVE

Harriet Said

At that time my wife (who is the brains of the firm and edits the fiction, while I do the business and the punctuation) happened to meet Beryl Bainbridge and was shown the manuscript. To her eternal credit, and to the much-needed credit of the firm's bank account, she not only saw that it was a brilliant book (alas, not at all obscene), but knew at once that here was a real writer and one with a future.

Colin Haycraft[1]

G ERALD DUCKWORTH & CO. Ltd. had been a well-respected publishing house during the first half of the twentieth century. Established by Gerald Duckworth in 1898, the firm had a distinguished list, including works by Virginia Woolf – Gerald's half-sister – John Galsworthy, D. H. Lawrence, Ronald Firbank, Evelyn Waugh and the Sitwells. After the Second World War, however, when Mervyn Horder became the company's chairman, the firm began to lose direction. Horder, who became Lord Horder in 1955 when he succeeded to his father's title, was not business-minded, being more interested in pursuing his own literary passions than in developing the company as a commercially viable publishing concern. By the mid-1960s the Duckworth list contained some worthy titles, but with so little connection to the main current of contemporary literature the firm seemed old-fashioned and irrelevant. In 1968 Horder finally conceded that he was better suited to writing his own books than publishing other people's and began looking around to find a buyer.

At about the same time Tim Simon, who had worked at both the Curwen Press and the Pall Mall Press, sounded out an old friend from Oxford, Colin Haycraft, on the idea of their setting up a publishing house together. Colin mentioned that Mervyn Horder was looking to sell Duckworth and asked Simon whether he was interested, the only problem as far as he was concerned being one of money: 'Colin had no cash, but Tim was able to put up half the price, which enabled Colin to borrow the other half. So they acquired Duckworth and moved into its long-time premises in Henrietta Street where they inherited a languishing firm with a staff of fourteen people and a turnover of under £100,000 a year.'[2]

But almost immediately tragedy struck. In the summer of 1970, Tim Simon caught pneumonia during a trip to New York and died. As Colin had an option on his shares, he consulted Clive de Pass, an old school friend who was also his solicitor; in exchange for 10 per cent of the shares, de Pass lent him the money to buy control of the firm from Simon's widow. At the age of forty-one, Colin became sole owner of Gerald Duckworth & Co. – 'All on borrowed money,' he would later recall, 'I've always been strapped for cash.'[3]

If Colin Berry Haycraft was arguably the most influential independent publisher of the 1970s, he was certainly the most flamboyant and the most contrarian. Born in Quetta, on the borders of Pakistan in 1929, he was brought back to England by his mother when he was three months old, along with his older brother John, after their father, a major in the Punjab regiment, was killed on the parade ground by a Sikh sepoy resentful at having been passed over for promotion.[4] Colin was sent to Wellington College, and then went up to Queen's College, Oxford, where he gained a double first in Mods and Greats. He remained an enthusiastic classicist for the rest of his life, composing Greek verse and Latin epigrams – often in the bath, so it was said – and relishing any opportunity of displaying his almost flawless knowledge of the works of literary heroes such as Horace, Gibbon and Dr Johnson.

Colin's appearance later in life belied his physical abilities. Of modest stature and with the complexion and waist measurement of a seasoned claret drinker, he sported a bow tie, thick-rimmed glasses, and the kind of tweed jacket that denoted a desk-bound literary man. Yet he had been an accomplished rackets player and had not only won blues in lawn tennis, rackets and squash, but had played squash rackets for England. Michael Holroyd remembered watching him play in the 1960s: 'He was very good, very clever. He didn't bother to try too much or to run. To run after the ball was sort of undignified. So he did some marvellous shots – and would lose, but in such a way that you'd think "He's the better player".[5]

In the early 1950s Colin moved to London and began working for the *Daily Mirror*, as personal assistant to Cecil Harmsworth King, who was the paper's chairman and also happened to be his cousin. After meeting, and then swiftly marrying, Anne Lindholm in 1956 – 'I was sexually attracted to her and I liked her company. We got engaged within a week or so, married six months later'[6] – Colin moved into publishing, first at Bodley Head, and then at Weidenfeld & Nicolson. George Weidenfeld, who described Colin as a 'stubborn perfectionist when it came to quality' and 'merciless in his criticism', would later recall the seven years he spent working with him as belonging to the most 'exciting and gratifying' period of his life.[7]

In 1962 the Haycrafts moved their rapidly expanding family – William was born in 1957, Joshua in 1959, Tom in 1960 and Oliver in 1962 – from Belsize Crescent to 22 Gloucester Crescent, a large, rambling house located in a quiet backwater of Camden that seemed to act as a magnet for literary and artistic types: Jonathan Miller, David Gentleman and Ursula Vaughan Williams had houses further up the street, and Alan Bennett lived next door.[8] Distinctive and inconspicuous at the same time – the trees in its small front garden shaded it from the street and gave it an almost perpetually dark and gloomy aspect – 22 Gloucester Crescent would become the setting for innumerable book launches, social gatherings and literary parties.

There was one final piece in the jigsaw: in the autumn of 1971, Colin bought the lease on The Old Piano Factory, a twenty-two-sided building at the top of the Crescent, literally a minute's walk from his home. In the first few months of 1972, Duckworth moved out of the Henrietta Street offices it had occupied since the founding of the company and into the grand open space of the Piano Factory's middle floor: the eccentricity of the building was a symbol of the firm's unconventional and idiosyncratic approach to publishing.

At the same time, Colin set about reinvigorating the firm's list, commissioning a range of works of classical scholarship and philosophy from respected academics such as Hugh Lloyd-Jones, Alasdair MacIntyre, Mary Lefkowitz, Kenneth Dover and Jasper Griffin. As Barry Baldwin, Emeritus Professor of Classics at the University of

Calgary, put it, Colin 'transformed a publishing house whose former quiet ways had been the object of some affectionate satire in Anthony Powell's early novel *What's Become of Waring?* into a classical power-house that reflected his own dynamism'.[9]

Colin also appointed Anna as the commissioning editor for fiction, despite the fact that she had no formal qualifications for the post and had no prior experience in publishing or writing. Nevertheless, she was a keen reader and knew the market – or at least the fiction market – better than Colin, and her intuitive gamble on Beryl's talent paid off. Beryl's critical success was to give Anna immediate credibility in her role as editor, and over the next decade or so the firm built up a distinctive fiction list: by the end of the 1970s it boasted an impressive roster of names. After Beryl came Caroline Blackwood in 1973, Patrice Chaplin in 1975, and Penelope Fitzgerald in 1977 – the same year that Anna made her own debut as a novelist with *The Sin Eater*, published under the pseudonym of Alice Thomas Ellis.

The predominance of women on the fiction list – the first significant male novelist would be Jonathan Coe in 1987 – led to Colin's famous quips about novels belonging to the 'distaff side of the business', that fiction was 'a branch of gynaecology', and that he would unhesitatingly turn down any work of fiction by a man – and any work of non-fiction by a woman.[10] These comments have frequently been used to attack his reputation as a publisher, though anyone taking such deliberately provocative statements seriously is missing the point. Colin loved to provoke, and politically correct views – or what he would have called 'cant' – were a prime target for his wit.

In fact, as Beryl could testify and as the manuscripts of her novels show, Colin was an assiduous editor of fiction, whether written by a woman or not. It was he, not Anna, who copy-edited Beryl's novels, and he did so with a subtlety and sensitivity that belied his public dismissal of the form.[11] But it would be pointless to pretend that one can be neutral about Colin, or that opinions about him weren't sharply divided. Although his wit and enormous erudition made him many friends, the arrogance with which he dismissed the pretentions of others and asserted his own intellectual superiority made him as many enemies. For every person who respected the way he continued to publish quality academic books in the face of relentless commercialism and the pressure to dumb down, there was someone else ready to point out that his business model was unsustainable and that he dragged the firm to the verge of bankruptcy. There were those who loved him and those who hated him, and both camps could adduce their own personal experience to make their arguments.

Once Colin and Anna had seen the manuscript of 'The Summer of the Tsar', they agreed to publish the novel. Colin required some initial persuading, feeling that Anna was always trying to foist people she knew on him as authors, but after showing some of Beryl's writing to a friend who assured him it was worth publishing, he was quickly convinced.[12] From one of Beryl's letters to Don it is clear that by the summer of 1971 she had abandoned 'He's the Captain of the Team' and was revising 'The Summer of the Tsar' with a view to its publication: 'I have started the book, not the American one, but redoing another one that was lost. Colin is buying an old paino factory for an office. He keeps asking me to read manuscripts. Anna and I drool over beer and leave the brandy alone.'[13]

Although the agreement to publish was made in 1971, a contract wasn't signed until 2 June 1972, just three months before actual publication, when the revision was complete. This anomalous way of doing things established a precedent and the majority of Beryl's books would subsequently follow this pattern: the writing would come first, then a contract would be drawn up and signed shortly before publication. The reason for this was partly Beryl's peculiar attitude to 'borrowing' money. Although she needed money to live on while she wrote, she was never happy with the idea of an advance, feeling that it created too much pressure and that what she wrote might not be considered worth it. It was also a combination of her naivety in publishing matters – she didn't have an agent for the first three Duckworth books so she let Colin negotiate rights for her – and Colin's caution over money: as the firm had yet to prove itself commercially, not paying her an advance helped ease the cash flow.[14]

Instead of an advance, in the months leading up to the publication of the book, Beryl began working part-time at the offices of Duckworth itself. She had her own desk, and with Rudi now at school she could spend her mornings there, helping to deal with orders and invoices,[15] or revising the manuscript of 'The Summer of the Tsar', which was given a new title just two months before publication: *Harriet Said*.[16]

Because of the contrast between the two Hutchinson novels and the later Duckworth novels, with their sparer, more economical style, some people have speculated that it was Colin or Anna who shaped Beryl's prose into its newer, leaner incarnation. This was not the case: it was the wordy, self-consciously literary style of *A Weekend with Claud* – written under the influence of Alan Sharp's inventive and almost poetic use of language – that was the exception and which represented a departure from Beryl's earlier writing. In fact with *Another Part of the Wood* Beryl had already begun to move back to a simpler mode of writing, and when she sent some draft pages to Judith for criticism she specifically asked her to comment on whether the 'style and form' were 'more lucid'.[17] What would come to be seen as the distinctive style of her Duckworth period novels was in fact her natural style, and *Harriet Said* marked a return to it, not a radical departure from it.

The evidence for this can be seen not just in the draft pages of the abandoned American novel, paragraphs of which remained substantially unchanged when Beryl inserted them into *The Girl in the Polka Dot Dress*, but also through a comparison of the manuscript pages of 'The Summer of the Tsar' sent to publishers in 1957 with the version published by Duckworth in 1972. There are, obviously, some significant differences between the two, both in terms of the novel's structure – it was Anna who suggested the idea of the 'flash forward' opening chapter – and in the writing itself. Beryl was now a more experienced writer and it was inevitable she would want to rewrite sections during the process of revision. Nevertheless it is evident that the style so admired by reviewers in 1972 was essentially the same as that of 1957. This was something Anna immediately recognized: 'It was she who told me to abandon the flowery and obscure style of my two later books and return to the simple structure of the first.'[18]

What is also clear from the manuscript, and from Beryl's disappointed reaction to its repeated rejection, is that what she needed as a writer was a good copy-editor, and lots of encouragement. At Duckworth, this is precisely what she got: the former from Colin, the latter from Anna.

Beryl herself was clear about Colin and Anna's respective roles, and about how important both were in relation to her development as a novelist. Observing Colin's meticulous correction of her lax grammatical constructions and erratic punctuation served as an invaluable course of instruction, as she told *The Times* in 1981: 'Colin dislikes such things as hanging nominatives, sentences without verbs and the historic present. In the beginning I used split infinitives. I didn't know how to stop it because . . . I didn't know what a split infinitive was. In ancient Greek, he said, the split infinitive is the height of idiomatic elegance, but in English it is plain barbarism.'

As for Anna, she was not a copy-editor and didn't interfere with Beryl's text, rather she provided support and general editorial advice: 'In the initial stages I need to talk about what I am doing, to be told that I am on the right path (if I am). In other words, I need constant encouragement. This I receive fully from my editor.'

The impact that Colin and Anna had on Beryl's career is obvious, but the impact Beryl had on Duckworth's fortunes should not be overlooked. The relationship between author and publisher was a symbiotic one: without Duckworth, Beryl might never have become the writer she did nor enjoyed the success she did; but without Beryl, Duckworth's literary reputation would not have been so high, and its financial situation would have been significantly worse. It is also a moot point whether Anna would have begun writing novels, or at least writing the kind of novels she did, without Beryl's example.

Well before *Harriet Said* was published, Colin was already making plans to promote it. In April, having received a circular from the National Book League about the 1972 Booker Prize, he entered two novels: *Harriet Said* and John Symond's *Prophecy and the Parasites*, even though neither had been printed at that stage, telling the NBL that he would get proofs to them by 1 July. There was a lot riding on these new productions. They were, as Colin pointed out in his covering letter to the submission, 'the first new novels that Duckworth will have published in 4 years'.[19]

In the event, *Harriet Said* didn't get on the shortlist, but its critical and commercial success was hugely important for Duckworth. This was brought into sharper focus in comparison with the fate of the other would-be Booker nomination. When it was eventually published in 1973, *Prophecy and the Parasites* received almost universally unfavourable notices – Auberon Waugh demolished it in *The Spectator* – and it sank without trace, leaving Beryl as the *ipso facto* face of Duckworth's new fiction list.

Although Duckworth didn't have a publicity department as such, an astute marketing plan was devised. Almost all the original letters from those editors who had turned down 'The Summer of the Tsar' had praised Beryl's style, and said that they would be interested in seeing anything else she wrote. But such bland encouragement hardly made exciting publicity material, so Colin decided to ratchet up the supposed abuse heaped on the book and the controversial nature of its subject matter by carefully extracting the most damning sentences from the single critical response Beryl had received. This gave the book a whiff of scandal and a suitably alluring air of lasciviousness:

> *Harriet Said* has a curious publishing history. When it was submit-
> ted to various publishers in the late 'fifties they all turned it down.
> 'Your writing shows considerable promise,' wrote the head of one
> firm, '. . . but what repulsive little creatures you have made the
> two central characters, repulsive almost beyond belief! And I think
> the scene in which the two men and the two girls meet in the
> Tsar's house is too indecent and unpleasant even for these lax days.
> What is more, I fear that even now a respectable printer would not
> print it!'[20]

It was certainly effective. Almost every review and interview quoted the 'indecent' tag, and, as Colin knew, since nothing sells like sex the book was guaranteed healthy sales.

Although reviews were relatively few, those who liked the book were not only very positive, they would become enthusiastic advocates of Beryl's subsequent work. A brief, but positive unsigned review in *The Times Literary Supplement* was most probably by Arthur Crook, who became a champion of Beryl's work. Following the book's publication in America, Karl Miller, subsequently editor of the *London Review of Books*, championed her work in a similar way, calling her 'the least known of the contemporary English novelists who are worth knowing'.[21] During the latter part of the 1970s and early 1980s, Miller would give her work extensive and vital exposure in America.

Beryl's revision of *Harriet Said* during the autumn of 1971 provided at least some distraction from thoughts about Don. If his visits to Albert Street hadn't entirely ceased, they had tailed off considerably, so much so that at the start of the year Beryl began seeing someone closer to home. Graham Betts wasn't Beryl's usual type: several years her junior, he sported long frizzy hair, wore flares and tie-dyed tops, and drove a Mini.

Graham became infatuated by Beryl, almost excessively so, and his dog-like devotion eventually got on her nerves. He didn't exactly displace Don in Beryl's affections, but he was near to hand, and for a period his reliably constant affection provided a level of emotional stability that Don's long-distance and necessarily erratic passions couldn't. Don would still turn up sporadically at Albert Street, but when he did his presence had an unsettling effect on Beryl's state of mind. As Jo-Jo noted in her diary on one occasion in May after he spent the night at Albert Street: 'Mum will be upset when he leaves.' Not only that, his visits provoked Graham to rages of jealousy: 'Graham came in and said he would bash Don's fucking face in. And almost strangled mum.'[22]

Although Beryl and Don would remain friends until her death – she would always refer to him as 'Lovely Don' – by 1972 their relationship had effectively petered out. Shortly afterwards, Don met the painter Janina Cebertowicz and this time the relationship lasted.

In many ways Don was Beryl's last great love. Although she would continue to have affairs over the following years, the character of these relationships changed dramatically. After Don, she no longer allowed herself to be swept away by the idea of a fully committed romantic love affair. There were none of those desperate, pain-racked relationships, the ultimate break-up of which left her on the borders of despair: 'That doesn't happen any more,' she told Molly Parkin in 1974, 'I really believe that all that's finished for me.'[23]

It was perhaps no accident that this stepping back from the disruptive world of emotional intimacy should have coincided with her new-found creative activity at Duckworth and the rise of her literary career. Beryl herself recognized the connection between the two: 'I don't need to get frighteningly emotionally involved any more. I'll never do that again because if I did I'd never work again.'[24] For Beryl, the enemy of art wasn't so much Cyril Connolly's famous 'pram in the hall' as 'the gentleman's suit in the wardrobe'.[25]

From now on she would have affairs with men she memorably referred to as 'my Gentlemen Callers'.[26] For the most part these would be conducted on her terms: men would be fitted around her life as a writer, rather than her writing taking second place to her emotional infatuations with men. Significantly, the two longest-lasting relationships she had after Don were both with married men, as if she had accepted that her relationships should have strictly defined limits – and no ultimate future. This change was not without its benefits, at least initially, as she told her friend Judith Kirk: 'For twenty years (before writing) I was unhappy. Now I am happy because I'm doing what I want and because it's being published and making money.'[27] But if creative work offered a more tangible fulfilment than the tenuous fantasies of romantic love, the process was not without its downside: 'I do get lonely, not having someone special,'[28] she admitted. It was a lack that would increasingly weigh on her mind as she got older, to such an extent she later claimed that for all her success as a novelist, 'I'd pretty much swop the lot for a settled domestic life. I'd probably get bored with it in ten minutes flat, but I think I would.'[29]

By the spring of 1972, Beryl had finished the revision work on *Harriet Said*. Even before publication the Australian film director and producer, Peter Sykes, wanted to turn it into a film, and Colin, who was effectively acting as Beryl's literary agent at this point, arranged a joint meeting with Beryl to discuss the writing of the script. As Anna was in Wales, Beryl wrote to her to keep her up to date, both on developments with the film project and on Peter's attempts to seduce her:

> Anna Flower: You should be here, holding me hand or head or something, I can't make much sense of it. He came the night before you went. Graham was there and about 15 dissolute teen-agers, also Austin and 3 neighbours, so we were'nt exactly au pair or de trop of whatever. All Graham's shackles!! rose. He was most awkward. Other laddie knocked at door, seized me and came in. Face fell at music and bottles all over. Talked incoherently about book-film etc. Everytime we got rid of Graham for seconds he clutched me. All very dramatic. Oh yes he rang me at the panio factory again and when I got back this

morning he rang. Would Colin and I on Friday meet some producer.

I am trembling at the knees because he's so like all the ones I really know – if you follow me. I do feel he is proceeding without caution. He <u>seems</u> to be <u>keen</u> on the book. Or me. Or both. I do feel cheery though. Rosy cheeks and all.[30]

A week later, she sent Anna a follow-up to tell her about the meeting: 'We went to Peter's agent, and he asked Colin to discuss an option on the book for Peter for a film etc. I was bemused. Colin was terribly efficient and buisnesslike. We then went drinking and for a meal and talked about nothing but erections. Colin was so spot on.'

When they got back to Albert Street at midnight – minus Colin – she and Peter began talking, and much to her discomfort he told her he'd just read *A Weekend with Claud* and concluded she was only interested in transient relationships, that she 'play-acted' at love. 'Very much put me in my place,' Beryl told Anna:

> Made me feel I had all the faults in the kingdom and that I was hanging on to him with a ball and chain. I was very depressed. I don't know how to feel. He's certainly very keen on the book. Ses he will do it. Wants to work with me. Ses I'm brilliant. I think he's a very good man. So you see there is no need to worry. I just wish you were [here] to talk to as I am <u>very</u> low. Bit shattered. I just felt happy with him. I didn't even want an affair. Someone jumped the gun, me in action, him in thought. I don't know.[31]

Despite these emotional complications, a contract was drawn up, and Peter was given a free option for a year to get the project off the ground, with Beryl being paid £4,000 for the script if the project went ahead.[32] There were more meetings to discuss the script, though as Beryl confided to Anna, she wasn't entirely sure how things were going:

> As I have never yet seen 'our' man without being pissed within seconds I feel it may be <u>me</u> attacking him not him me. It is a bit of a blur. Main points last time I saw him. I am brilliant, the biggest thing to the film industry, I will be a sensation. Now I don't know <u>if</u> I'm going to be an elderly starlet or what? He says he is fascinated but I don't know by what – I think its me writing. I did ask him his intentions but I don't <u>remember</u> what he said. He said we must be friends – him and me.[33]

Perhaps inevitably, mixing business and personal matters in this way wasn't a good recipe for success, and in the end the project came to grief. Although Beryl wrote the film script, Peter had discussed it with her on several occasions, to the extent that he saw himself as a collaborator in the writing process. A short while later Beryl discovered that a version of the script was going round with Peter's name listed on the front page alongside hers. Colin immediately wrote to his agent demanding that this be removed, and stating that the copyright of the script belonged to Beryl and Beryl alone.

Peter responded that owing to all the preliminary work he'd done with Beryl on the script and the way he'd guided her through the rewrites, the only fair reflection of his input would be an 'in collaboration' credit and a 25 per cent share of the price of the £4,000 screenplay.[34] Neither side would budge. Colin wrote back to say that Beryl retained full copyright in the script, and that unless there was an agreement to that effect all copies of the script should be returned as soon as possible.[35] And with that, Beryl's first film project was at an end.

Since her return from Eaves Farm, Beryl had continued to paint and draw, even doing some etching after taking a local evening class. For the next few months she would ring Don for advice on hard ground etching, aquatint and other artistic techniques. Among her first experiments with etching was a reproduction of George Washington Wilson's famous photograph of John Brown leading Queen Victoria's horse – though in Beryl's version, while Brown is depicted relatively faithfully, sporran and all, the lady on the horse is naked save for a large hat. The image stuck in Beryl's mind, and twenty years later she would use it in the closing pages of *The Birthday Boys*, as Captain Oates's final hallucination as he walked to his death.

In 1971 Beryl got a chance to exhibit some of her pictures, and – more importantly to her mind – to sell them. Philip Hughes had been taking part in the annual exhibitions organized by the Medical Aid for Vietnam Committee since 1968. Thinking it would be a good way for Beryl to make some money, he encouraged her to do the same. The idea behind the exhibition was a simple one, to marry the commercial self-interest of well-intentioned art lovers to the political agenda of the organizers. The exhibitions offered a chance for collectors to buy reason-ably priced works by well-known or up-and-coming artists – such as Eduardo Paolozzi, R. B. Kitaj, Victor Passmore and Jim Dine – with the artists then donating up to half of what they earned to the Medical Aid Committee.[36]

Over the next few years, Beryl would contribute a number of paintings and drawings to these annual exhibitions. Perhaps the most commer-cially beneficial was that in 1971, held at Hampstead Town Hall: 'I sent 15 paintings and sold the lot at prices ranging from £30 to £70, accord-ing to size', as she told a *Guardian* journalist the following year.[37] This was a slight exaggeration, but she did make £400 from the sale of her work, a quarter of which she donated to the Medical Aid Committee.

Many of the paintings and drawings she sold at the show featured a character whom Beryl named Captain Dalhousie. He was represented in a series of scenes which, like the earlier Napoleon series, combined naked and clothed figures in a way that was both comic and slightly unsettling. Where the theme of the Napoleon drawings was predom-inantly sex or death – and sometimes sex and death – the Captain Dalhousie series seemed at first glance to be lighter in mood, featuring wedding groups or incongruous images of a naked Captain Dalhousie in the act of riding a penny-farthing bicycle, such as *Captain Dalhousie preparing to mount*. Playful though these watercolours and drawings were, there was often a darker undercurrent running just beneath the surface, which seemed to reflect the sadness Beryl felt that any hopes she had of marrying Don were over. In *Wedding group in field with hen*, for example, the bride has a blank expression on her face and a tear is rolling down her cheek.

In the summer of 1972 Psiche and Philip again tried to give Beryl's career as an artist another push, this time introducing her to Nigel and Sue Mackenzie, who ran a restaurant called The Hungry Monk in Jevington, East Sussex. The Mackenzies were painters and collectors themselves, and were very taken with Beryl's work: 'Her pictures were witty, beautifully painted, in a slightly sketchy style, which gave them a freshness and contemporary feel. In many ways they were like Beryl herself – irreverent, funny and highly original.'[38]

Having set up the Monk's Gallery alongside the restaurant, they invited Philip and Beryl to show jointly in an exhibition running from 10 September to 12 October, coinciding with the publication of *Harriet*

Said. A few days before the exhibition was due to open, the Mackenzies telephoned Beryl to inquire whether the paintings would be suitable, not just the kind of thing that would go down well in London. As many of her pictures featured naked men and women, Beryl assumed they were worried that her work was too risqué and spent the night cutting out plastic fig-leaves: 'I thought they might have wanted to dot one or two around in the appropriate places, but they didn't.'[39]

In fact the Mackenzies had no such qualms and the exhibition was a success: 'The combination of affluent restaurant customers and a private view before Sunday lunch was a pretty potent sales cocktail.'[40] Beryl sold around a dozen pictures, varying in price from £20 to £45, giving her a £250 profit after the gallery's percentage. Following the exhibition Nigel wrote her a note: 'I do hope we can do the same again next year.'[41] But by 1973 Beryl's writing career had already taken off and the experiment was not repeated.

The Mackenzies weren't the only gallery owners to be interested in Beryl's work, nor were they the only ones to be frustrated by her success as a writer. Around the same time Penny Jones had given a dinner party and alongside Beryl one of the other guests was Eric Lister, the co-owner of the Portal gallery. The two had got on well and as Lister was intrigued to learn she was a painter, she took him next door to show him her paintings. He liked what he saw and asked her to bring some examples to the gallery the following week, which she did.[42] However, like the Mackenzies, Lister was too late: Beryl was already committed to writing her next book for Duckworth.

———

With the critical success of *Harriet Said* having boosted her confidence, Beryl began to think about what to write next. Initially she had thought about continuing work on 'He's the Captain of the Team', the American novel begun at Eaves Farm. She had even told the *Liverpool Echo* in September that her new book would throw a few knock-out punches at Women's Lib: 'I'm getting really enthusiastic about it. Women's Lib is rubbish; they're defeating their own ends.'[43]

From the draft pages that remain, it is fairly clear why the novel would not have gone down well with feminists. The novel's heroine, Alma Bickerton, makes a number of ambivalent references to women submitting to sex against their will, and she is herself subjected to what appears to be a forced act of oral sex. At one point a nurse questions Alma about the violence inflicted on her in her relationship with Dr Wheeler, and Alma's response reveals a decidedly masochistic streak:

'You look today pale today Alma . . . you'll just have to put up with me poking my nose into your business . . . I can't stand by and see the change getting worse in Doctor Wheeler. He's like a man pocessed by the devil. I'm not a narrow woman, at least I don't think I am but last nights carry on almost finished me. All that banging about and shouting and him roaring like some animal. And the chairs broken, the one by the door, and you look bruised all over . . .'

I lean back against the settee so that she will see his teeth marks on my throat. 'Its all right, really it is. Its just he keeps tormenting himself.'

'But he was so tender with you before . . . now its all brutality . . . its not healthy.' Worriedly she strokes her own untouched throat and wonders what is happening.

'I don't mind,' I tell her. Its true, I can take the violence projected at me by Dr. Wheeler. It both satisfied me and reassures me.[44]

In one half-dream, half-fantasy sequence, typed out in red in the manuscript, Dr Wheeler tries to kill Alma out of sexual jealousy, by giving her a lethal injection. Again, Alma's response is entirely passive:

Dr. Wheeler was standing over her, face grave and freshly shaved. He was wearing a white coat with cloth buttons, there were shadows under his eyes. His cool fingers unbuttoned the front of her gown. Lie still, he bade her, lie still. Her breasts were splayed out under his hands, they burned against his chill palms, the nipples rose erect. Oh, she sighed. Nurse, he called in a low voice, fetch me a syringe. He was murmuring in her ear that she was not to be afraid, that he alone would be in charge. Its unprofeesional I know, he told her, the dark lashes of his eyes trembling with emotion, but I've got to be the one. I cannot bear the thought of another man touching you, do you hear my darling? The nurse returned with the cruel hypodermic. He took it from her and holding Alma's arm bent it at the elbow and slipped in the needle, deep into the vein. Her eyes widen with shock, he soothes her, careless of the fast dissolving nurse, telling her she is his younger than spring-time love, his true sweetheart, his till death us do part. Death, she murmers and her lips cease to move because he has withdrawn the syringe and with the rubbing of cool disinfectant on her skin, her mind ends and her lids close.

Alma's sexual masochism, her notion that the punishment handed out to her by men was justified and satisfied her feelings of guilt, seems to reflect Beryl's own masochistic feelings engendered after the violent sexual assault in London in 1953.

Whether she felt that the thinly disguised self-portrait in 'He's the Captain of the Team' was too revealing or not, Beryl decided to abandon the book and began looking round for another subject. Although at first glance there seems to be little to connect the contemporary themes of 'He's the Captain of the Team' to the wartime setting of *The Dressmaker*, there was a tenuous link. Bickerton, the surname of Beryl's alter ego Alma, was also that of her dressmaking aunt, the one who had been left a widow after the First World War. It took only a small leap of the imagination to see in the story of herself as a girl on the brink of puberty and that of her two aunts, one a frustrated widow, the other an embittered spinster, a psychodrama in which the themes of sexual awakening and sexual frustration, of jealousy and retribution, could be explored. With its mixture of nostalgia and loss, *The Dressmaker* was a powerful evocation of the war years, and the tensions between repression and liberation of British society is subtly mirrored in the individual dramas of Nellie and Rita.

It needed only a murder at the end to tie up the loose threads and as she had with *Harriet Said*, Beryl turned to old newspapers for inspiration in the library at Colindale: 'I found one report of a Yank who had disappeared. Just disappeared. And I used that. Figuring in the book that who on earth would trace something like that back to an old dressmaker and her sister?'[45]

The speed with which Beryl wrote *The Dressmaker* amazed even herself: 'It took me no time at all to write because it just flowed on and on, almost of its own accord. I couldn't believe I'd written it so quickly.'[46] Although she would subsequently maintain an output of a novel a year until the end of the decade, she never again achieved this enviable fluidity. Writing the novel also established something of a precedent as regards her working method: 'I take two months of thinking and three months of actual non-stop writing, from 11 o'clock at night till 4 in the morning.'[47]

If *Harriet Said* had laid the groundwork for Beryl's success as a novelist, *The Dressmaker* represented the harvest. It gained almost unanimously good reviews: Karl Miller described it as 'a triumphant success'[48] in *The New York Review of Books*, and *The Times Literary Supplement* hailed it as 'a remarkable achievement'.[49] In the autumn of 1973 the news came through that the book had made it onto the Booker Prize shortlist.

Winnie came down to London for the Booker Prize night, bringing a ball gown with her in the expectation that she would be invited to what was after all an important event in her daughter's life. But Beryl was too embarrassed: 'I told her that you weren't allowed to take guests,' she confessed to Anthony Clare twenty years later. 'I was ashamed of her. I felt bad about that, that was wicked.'[50]

The book didn't win, but even so the publicity value of the Booker was almost worth the prize money alone, and it had a significant impact on both Beryl's reputation and that of Duckworth. As George Yeatman suggested in his official interview with Beryl as a Booker nominee, the success of *The Dressmaker* constituted a 'necessary renaissance' for the firm.[51] Added to this was the bonus news that George Braziller had sold the American paperback rights for *Harriet Said* for what must have seemed to Beryl like a staggering sum: $35,000, or £14,400. However, as it turned out, this had to be split 50-50 between George Braziller and Duckworth, before she herself received her share.

After her low-key career at Hutchinson and her subsequent descent into obscurity, she now found herself, at forty years of age, a critically acclaimed novelist. Not only that, for the first time in her life she was financially independent: 'I've earned a lot of money on the book,' she told Judith, '1st money I've ever had . . .'[52]

TWENTY-SIX

Success

> I've just at last, late after 20 years of jittering about, found
> who I was, or at least what I wanted to do. So I write me
> books, and go to work and clean the house, never answer the
> phone or go out at all socially, lock the door, threaten
> the children with dire doom if they let anyone in to me.
> I don't even open letters except just sometimes. This is all
> whilst I am writing a book, as I am now. I have a couple
> of gentleman callers on alternate Wednesday afternoons
> and I go to bed at four a.m. every night (or dawn) of the
> week and get up at seven. I look about 130. When I am not
> writing a book I sleep a lot, do a bit of painting, see just a
> few people and try to fall in love. But only briefly – no more
> terrible heartbreaks and pangs.[1]

AFTER THE SUCCESSES OF the previous year, 1974 began
somewhat inauspiciously. In the midst of her busy social schedule of bridge parties and trips to the theatre, Winnie died suddenly
on 1 February after a heart attack. One of the last entries in her
diary was a note about Beryl, or more precisely about the English
paperback rights to *The Dressmaker*, which had just been bought
for £1,000.

The funeral was held at Holy Trinity church in Formby, and Beryl
duly went up with the children. She had already started writing early
drafts of what would become *The Bottle Factory Outing* in a notebook,
and perhaps thinking to use the time on the long train journey up to
Liverpool to write, she brought it along. Whether she was too distracted
to think about the novel or too involved with the proceedings of the
day, she instead scribbled down a hasty précis of events, perhaps as an

aide-memoire that might come in useful at a later date: 'Riding in train through rotting Liverpool. Puddles of rain. Bomb sites still there, craters of refuse and water. Broken cars. Train from London. The snow – the sun – Runcorn Bridge – the dirty yellow light, the whirling patterns of the bridge over the water.'[2]

When she arrived at Formby station, she walked to Ravenmeols Lane, where her brother Ian was waiting for her and where Winnie was laid out in an open coffin:

> There was the walk up a dark, childhood street, the night ballooning with the sounds of a brass band rehearsing in the hut on the corner, followed by the pushing open of a gate and a light coming on in the round window beneath the porch, I did think then of all the times we'd been scolded, my brother and I, for daring to enter through the front door.
>
> I took my shoes off when he let me in, so as not to mess the carpet, even though my mother wasn't there to shout, 'Hello stranger . . . the back door not good enough for you?' That night my brother slept in the lounge and I dossed down among the snuffling velvet cushions of the settee in the dining room, although none of us, except on Boxing Day, had ever lounged or dined in either.
>
> We didn't admit it, but both of us were scared stiff of sleeping upstairs. There was no one there; my father was long since dead and my mother laid out, cold as marble, the hard centre of an Easter egg, in a coffin frilled at the edges with white paper. All the same, the house was full of ghosts, not least of ourselves when young.[3]

When they arrived at the church the next day there was a group of mourners outside, among whom Beryl noted four ladies in flat hats and tweed coats, and her Uncle Len, his tinted glasses giving him a 'flavour of the American'. With the wind blowing the cellophane-wrapped flowers laid in tribute, they formed up behind the coffin and went inside: 'Jo sniffs. Aaron sings. Some confusion about kneeling. Man behind sings beautifully. Responsibility of being chief mourner. Follow coffin. Back into car. Long slow drive.'[4]

Winnie, like Richard, died at the age of seventy (five weeks short of her seventy-first birthday to be precise), leaving Beryl an orphan at forty-one, a relatively young age to lose both parents. Despite the closeness she had felt to Winnie as a child, she had grown emotionally detached over the years. Winnie's censorious attitude irritated her, and their relationship had reached a low point in the debacle over Alan and her jibe that Beryl was 'nothing but a prostitute'.[5] There were bitter feelings on both sides and neither was able, or willing, to bridge the gap:

> Such was the unfinished business between us, my mother and I, the unresolved, ambiguous love, the resentment – she seemingly disappointed in me, naggingly expecting something I couldn't give, I equally aggrieved, waiting for that one sentence, that all-embracing hug that would make everything okey dokey – that I had imagined her death would fill me with terror and guilt. I didn't feel guilty when she died; I simply grieved, mourned that we were so close that touching we bruised.[6]

Right up to the time of her death, Winnie had visited London every few months, and indeed had planned to see Beryl in March. A flavour of these frequently strained encounters is given in a story Beryl wrote the following year, which captures the tone of condescension and disapproval always lurking below the surface of Winnie's attitude towards her:

> At two o'clock the taxi arrived with my Mum. She stood on the pavement, nylon wig motionless, fox fur quivering in the sunlight. She laughed shrilly like some animal caught in a trap when I embraced her. I touched her frozen curls and buried my mouth in the soft fur at her neck. How we hugged each other, how we began sentences and never finished them, what a noise she made; how she teetered between the cracks in the flagstones of the tiny garden. She had painted her nails scarlet and she wore her serpent brooch and her pearls and her second-best watch. I carried her two suitcases inside and left them in the hall alongside the hat box in which she kept her Joyce Grenfell wig.
>
> 'Don't leave my cases there, dear,' she said. 'If you don't mind.'[7]

Winnie's death clearly prompted reflections about Beryl's own shortcomings as a mother: one of the things that haunted her, especially during the latter period of her life, was the idea that she had let her children down, that they had suffered as a result of her failed relationships and the subsequent emotional fallout they had to go through. She blamed herself particularly with regard to Aaron, who as the eldest had borne the brunt of her emotional distress: 'He's had a rotten adolescence . . . a bawling screaming Mum,' she told Judith, 'but I guess he will come out of it.'[8]

In the short term, however, Winnie's death acted as a psychological release from what Beryl called 'the scenes and demands and whatnot'[9] of an emotional relationship that she had come to consider 'so harmful'[10] to her own state of mind. Significantly, it also freed her from the image of herself that Winnie constantly projected onto her, allowing Beryl to reinvent herself and her own past. Or as she put it: 'And then she was dead, so I could do what I liked.'[11]

For her next novel, Beryl returned to a more contemporary setting, taking her part-time job at Belloni's warehouse and her friendship with Pauline as the starting point. Although this was also the traumatic period of her break-up with Don, Beryl decided not to deal with that part of her life head-on. In the novel, the breakdown in Brenda's marriage to Stanley, who lives on a farm in Ramsbottom, occurs before the action starts and is alluded to only incidentally: 'She . . . had left him because she couldn't stand him coming home drunk every night from the Little Legion and peeing on the front step.'[12]

The shift to a more comic tone for *The Bottle Factory Outing* was deliberate: 'After *The Dressmaker* I wanted to write – well, not a light book, but a lighter one. The true story could have been a much deeper book. Duckworth said I should do a black comedy.'[13] That Beryl so readily adopted the suggestion shows how close the creative partnership with her publisher had become. Her earnings from *Harriet Said* and *The Dressmaker* now freed her from the stop-gap necessity of working as a clerk, but she asked to be able to keep her desk at the office, 'a small, rough table that stands amidst pillars of cardboard rolls and stacked boxes of paper',[14] so she could come in and write during the day: 'I love it at Duckworths',[15] as she told Molly Parkin.

Beryl's involvement with the production of her novels extended to the cover design. For *Harriet Said* she had used a photograph of herself and Ian as children and drawn pigtails on him so as to make him look like a girl, while the cover of *The Dressmaker* featured an old photograph she had 'found in a barrow somewhere in London of a rather sinister lady standing in an allottment'.[16] For *Bottle Factory* she went a step further, mocking up a shot of the wine warehouse and its workers. In the resulting photograph, taken on the steps of the Old Piano Factory, Colin and another Duckworth employee pose as pseudo-Italians in Mafioso-style sharp suits and hats, while Beryl and Pauline stand in the foreground, Pauline dwarfing Beryl both in height and girth.

The success of her previous two books had already created an expectation, and as publication day approached Beryl felt increasingly anxious that she had made a mistake in opting for a more lightweight comedy than the serious themes of her previous two books. 'The book comes out on Thursday,' she told Edward Pearson, Penny Jones's father, who was himself a novelist, 'so there may be reviews on Sunday. This is the worst moment. The most depressing I find. I feel absolutely awful and down and wish I had never written the dam thing. I think its fairly trivial, but I did intend it to be lighter than the last one, but not so light as to be completely dismissed.'[17]

She need not have worried. If anything the critical response was even more enthusiastic than before. The distinguished author Ronald Blythe made comparisons with Graham Greene[18] and almost ran out of superlatives in his review:

> After turning the final page of *The Bottle Factory Outing*, one can only gasp and grope for the right phrase. What a talent, if that is not too mild a word. Such an atmosphere of impending doom has not been created since *Brighton Rock* – except that Beryl Bainbridge is mercilessly comic instead of being mercilessly vicious . . . she is so in control of her marvellous little story that one hangs on her words from first to last. What originality, what pleasure.[19]

The news that *The Bottle Factory Outing* had also made the Booker shortlist marked another high point – the last writer to have achieved back-to-back Booker nominations having been Iris Murdoch – and the novel became Beryl's most commercially successful to date. Although she would again be disappointed (the papers were already talking about her as a Booker 'bridesmaid'), the book was awarded the *Guardian* Fiction Prize, which provided some compensation in critical, if not in financial terms, the prize money being a relatively restrained 200 guineas.

As Beryl's star rose, Austin's fell, and at the point where he could least afford to look after her and the children – as he done for so many years – she became financially independent.

By the late 1960s Austin had become dissatisfied with his job at East Ham Technical College. Using his knowledge of interior design and his practical building skills, he began converting run-down terraced houses in Islington, near where he now lived, into modern flats. At first, he was so successful he felt confident enough to resign from his job in the art department and set up his own property-development company: Shrowcroft Properties Limited, which was incorporated in March 1972. Austin was not the only one to be attracted by the profits to be made in house conversions, and as the number of property developers active in London in the early 1970s expanded, so the market swiftly turned into an unsustainable bubble. The collapse in 1973 of the London and County Securities Bank, which was heavily committed to the property sector, marked the start of the crash. Banks called in loans to property companies, causing a domino effect of defaults. Many companies were forced to sell their properties for whatever they could get, often at a loss, and house prices plummeted.

Austin lost almost everything; he had to sell his house in Islington and a property he was converting into flats in Arundel Square, and as the mortgage of Albert Street was still in his name, for a time Beryl feared he was 'about to crash in pieces taking this house with him'.[20] In order to deal with the situation, the plan was for Belinda and their children to go back to New Zealand, where Austin would join them after he'd sorted out his business affairs and finished work on the Albert Street basement conversion. He was determined to pay off his creditors rather than opt for what he considered the less honourable route of bankruptcy, and his plan was to sell the basement for £14,000, while Beryl would purchase the rest of the house for £12,000.

In addition to this, Austin was also carrying out renovation work on an old stone cottage in the Brecon Beacons National Park in Wales. He had originally intended it as a holiday home – Beryl and the children had in fact spent some time there despite its lack of electricity and basic amenities – but now he had to finish the building work almost single-handedly so it could be sold. A family photograph shows him digging the septic tank with snow falling around him.

Graham's offer of assistance to work on both Albert Street and the cottage in Wales was a big help to Austin, but it didn't go down so well with Beryl, as she and Graham had now split up. The previous year Graham had joined the family holiday to Corfu, but early on he and Beryl had a massive falling out, after Beryl had locked him out of their villa when he had gone to a bar on his own. On his return he couldn't get in, and in trying to clamber up the walls he'd injured himself and bloodied his face. He had to sleep in the garden and spent the rest of the holiday sulking on the beach.

Not surprisingly, this added tension didn't help the situation – nor did the fact that Austin had now moved back into the basement at Albert Street, as Beryl complained to Belinda in New Zealand:

> Aussie. Things between him and I are very bad at the moment. This 6 months for him has been dreadful and he is all twisted up in conse-quence. I'm sure I don't help, but I cannot understand why he is so bloody bossy all the time. Graham (who never speaks to me) in the house for months and Aus making the most terrible mess. Weekends as well. Never tells you when he is going to do a job so you end up with no loo one minit and no water the next. Gives his phone number to everyone, so constant phone calls. Has a front door key and is on the landing morning, noon and night. When I asked for my key back he refused: 'My bloody house' etc.[21]

Austin saw things differently, and in his letters to Belinda he vented *his* frustration with Beryl: 'She's cutting up ruf 'bout her privacy – wont have anyone in house before 11 am and must be out by 4 pm. So we've stopped working on her part till she stops behaving like a vestal virgin.'[22] From the basement he could hear her taking it out on Aaron, Jo and Rudi: 'I have to suffer Beryl screeching at the chil-dren morning and night. Noon – and it seems most of the day – she sleeps.'[23]

Despite the frayed tempers, the building work progressed: 'The basement is dam near finished,' Beryl wrote to Belinda just before Christmas, and six months later, in June 1975, work on the cottage was also completed. Austin could now begin to make plans to emigrate: 'If I leave for NZ within a month I'll be lucky. But if I can, Beryl says like she'll look after the house in Wales and show people round till it's sold to some other capitalist pig.'[24]

With the sale of both the Albert Street basement and the cottage Austin finally managed to pay off the company's debts (though it would take until 1980 before Shrowcroft Properties was eventually released from the liquidator), and in October he left to start his new life in New Zealand. After all he'd been through, it was little wonder he should be so incensed by Beryl's casual reference to him twenty years later, in a national newspaper, as a 'bankrupt'.[25]

With the prospect of Austin's eventual departure for New Zealand, there were a number of legal matters that needed to be sorted out. Not only did Beryl have to take over the legal ownership of 42 Albert Street, which entailed applying for a mortgage for the first time, but a range of other issues had to be dealt with, at Austin's prompting, such as getting a will drawn up so that the children would be looked after in the case of Beryl's death, and changing Rudi's name legally from Sharp to Davies. These issues would be dealt with by Clive de Pass, whom Beryl had got to know a year or so before during her period working at the Duckworth offices.

Clive, like Colin, had been educated at Wellington College. He had spent the 1960s working at the staid and respectable firm of Gilbert Samuel & Co. in the City of London, and was now looking to join the Duckworth board as a way of engaging with something more fulfilling than his current legal work. A father of five with another child on the way, Clive had been married for over twenty years to the painter and printmaker Jenifer Green.

Clive seemed to have a successful and comfortable life; he had a pied-à-terre in Hampstead, and had recently moved to a large country house in Suffolk that not only contained an artist's studio which had belonged to the painter Josef Herman, but was also sufficiently spacious to keep a couple of ponies for his daughters.

But despite all this he had become disillusioned, both at work and at home, where he felt he had become surplus to Jenifer's needs, or as Beryl would put it, using the standard justification in these situations, 'his wife doesn't understand him'.[26]

Meeting Beryl was like a breath of fresh air: she was spontaneous, funny, unconventional, unlike any woman he knew. But Clive, who described himself as a 'cold blooded fish',[27] was not the sort of person to rush into an affair that could break up his family. However dissatisfied he may have been in his marriage, he would feel 'a selfish horrible shit'[28] if he deserted his children. For her part, although Beryl enjoyed his company and found him amusing, initially at least she couldn't take him seriously and the idea of an affair seemed faintly ridiculous.

Nevertheless Clive persisted in his hesitant fashion, urged on by desire but held back by thoughts of the serious repercussions an affair could cause. Unable to make up his mind whether to 'take the plunge', he spent months 'teetering ludicrously on the brink'.[29] To Beryl, the situation seemed irresistibly comic, and she kept Anna up to date on the latest developments:

> Saw Clive last night. I am still laffing. Pauline called him Cyril so I decided a stroll on Hampstead Heath. He kept protesting. So there we were at 1 in the morning with a bottle of scotch with Clive running after me – begging me to put me clothes on . . . he was terribly upset – said he was a respectable solicitor and an officer and a gentleman and I must come home and I fell over a bench and he bundled me into the car, only he did'nt know where we were. We kept driving up and down King Henry's road with him getting crosser and crosser.
>
> Anyway that's the last I remember. I woke at 5 with me clothes in the hall – I was in bed – and a bloody big bruise on me back – serve me right. And not deflowered. I must ring him to find out where he was – he may still be among the dust bins in Primrose Hill.
>
> I do wish you were [here] because I've left out all the funny bits – the exact desperation in his voice floating up Hampstead Heath – 'Do please pull yourself together, I'm a respectable solicitor'.[30]

Eventually, Clive overcame his scruples. He wrote to tell her that he hated the thought of not seeing her, that there wasn't anyone he'd rather be with: 'Can't I see you on your terms?'[31] And so, much to the surprise and vague amusement of her friends, who considered Clive too proper for such a carry-on, he and Beryl started seeing each other, as she confided to Belinda: 'I am going out proper with Clive now, who is very sweet and a bit Father like and takes Aaron for driving lessons and hands Jo pocket money. Unfortunately he has a wife and SIX kids, but he is very rich and doing all the house manipulations for me.'[32]

This wasn't the first time Beryl had had an affair with a married man. There had been her short infatuation with George, though a long-term relationship with him had never really been a practical possibility. There had been Edward, but again the fact that he lived in America and was a temporary resident in the UK made any long-term commitment unlikely. There had been the one-night stand with Jim Cassels, though this didn't really count, as she had been more or less pushed into it against her will. There had been Hugh, though Hugh was really a friend who sometimes let his emotions get the better of him; in any case his visits were so sporadic it hardly counted. There had been Alan, though to be fair, when she began her relationship with him she didn't know he had only married his second wife the year before. And there had been Don, though he had made it clear, almost from the start, that his marriage was already over. With Clive, however, it was the first time she had embarked on a relationship conscious of the fact that it could result in the break-up of a marriage, with all the correspondingly messy consequences for his family this would entail.

In order to keep Clive's identity secret Beryl began referring to him, if ever she had to tell people she was seeing someone, as 'Jimmy Boots', a name derived from his being an old Wellingtonian. This air of secrecy gave the relationship a certain frisson of excitement, and for a short while at least Beryl recaptured with Clive the exhilarating feeling of being in love that she had experienced in the past:

> Writing this in an absolute sweat between pages of new epic about Alan Sharp. Helped by the fact that I am besotted about Clive . . . I have known him for four years and thought him a joke and silly etc. He persisted and has been so dam nice to me and now I am head over heels, which is nice but painful. I don't know what will happen. He is public school, my solicitor, Duckworth director, big tummy, boyish forelock, Jewish, though he denies it . . . We play rummy and do crosswords and hide from the children.[33]

But Clive's situation, his unwillingness to take any decisive step in relation to their future, made conflict inevitable, and after this honeymoon period the relationship devolved into a fractious and argumentative game of emotional chess. Beryl tried to get Clive to commit and attacked him for his reluctance to make an open break with his wife. But at the same time she was herself defensive, unwilling to commit to him unconditionally in case things didn't work out. As for Clive, he prevaricated. He tried to get Beryl to be more reasonable, to see that the emotional and financial disruptions a break with his wife involved could not to be taken lightly, while at the same time somewhat paradoxically attempting to convince her that he was committed to her.

The result was a continual series of tactical advances and retreats, fuelled by frustrated emotions on both sides. Nevertheless, despite their seeming incompatibility, despite the endless irritations and the perpetual bickering, the relationship continued in this erratic way for several years, each feeling a peculiar blend of fondness for yet exasperation with the other.

The 'new epic' Beryl was writing during this period was the novel that would become *Sweet William*. She had considered writing about Alan and her early years in London as far back as 1967, but had eventually decided against it: 'I am too close to it,' she told a journalist. 'This is a much more ruthless place than the North, I couldn't be funny about it yet.'[34] She tried again in late 1973, sketching out the opening of a novel based on her experiences with Alan, provisionally entitled 'William at the Harvest Festival'. But again she had put it off, finding it easier to write about a subject with more comic potential, such as her time at the bottle factory.

Now she took up the idea again. After working on it for a month and a half, and giving the novel a new title, 'Just William', she showed the opening pages to Anna, but this time the response was not so positive: 'She criticised this, said that's wrong, that's weak, and I went home and reread them and found she was dead right . . . So I had to start again, thinking about who was telling this story.'[35]

Although Beryl made light of the incident in the newspapers, at the time the criticism had stung and she wrote to tell Edward Pearson how much it had affected her: 'I too have had an awful setback. I took my first quarter draft in and it was torn to shreds and thrown out as cliche ridden and like the last one and no good etc etc. I smarted for several days and now am laboriously starting again, but my pride is hurt and I feel foolish.'[36]

Nevertheless, she took the criticisms on board and began to restructure the novel. But the pressure to match the novels that had gone before was undoubtedly beginning to tell. 'I'm frightened now of embarking on my next novel. That's what a reputation does for you,'[37] she had told a Canadian journalist earlier in the year. Consequently, her writing process was now coming to resemble a kind of neurotic obsession: 'I work in a very concentrated way: once I start writing I never go out, or very rarely indeed . . . I re-write and re-write endlessly, or re-type rather, since my handwriting is fairly awful . . . I do one page and don't do the next page till I get the first one right: and that may take another eleven pages. That goes on and on. Every morning I re-read the final draft again and possibly change something yet again.'[38]

Her uncertainty about the novel was reflected in her indecision over what it should be called. She had told a newspaper reporter that she was at work on an anti-hero comedy called 'Unjust William',[39] but by the time she had finished, this had been dropped and a definitive title still seemed elusive, the manuscript's first page simply listing five alternatives: 'The Trick Cyclist', 'Michaelmas Daisies', 'Sweet William', 'A Travelling Man', 'The Man on the Bike'. Anna preferred 'Sweet William', so that was the one which was chosen.

As if picking up on Beryl's hesitations about the novel, reviewers hinted at a slight feeling of dissatisfaction. *The Times Literary Supplement*, while still generally positive in its praise, felt obliged to state 'this is not Beryl Bainbridge's best book'.[40] Peter Ackroyd in *The Spectator* went a step further, and although he appreciated parts of it he concluded that it made 'no real advance upon her earlier novels'. Ackroyd divined that in this instance Beryl seemed to have had problems transmuting her lived experience into an autonomous fictional narrative, and that her inability to be emotionally detached from the story had impacted on her telling of it: 'It may be that Beryl Bainbridge is too close to the experience to give it those hard edges and that strain of wilful comedy which generally mark her work.'[41]

Alan himself felt the novel's weakness lay in the fact that 'the anodyne Ann is nothing like Beryl', that Beryl had in effect 'left herself out of the story'. It also seemed to him she had made no 'attempt at understanding or depicting the roots of [William's] behaviour', and to his mind this refusal to engage seriously with the psychological complexity of the two main characters added up to 'a complete avoidance of the reality we both inhabited'. But then, as he admitted, Beryl hadn't set out 'to render a portrait of a relationship, but to write a comic novel'.[42]

The success of *The Dressmaker* and *The Bottle Factory Outing* had brought Beryl to the attention of the arts establishment. At the start of 1975 she was invited to participate in 'Writers on Tour', a six-day literary tour of Northumberland and Tyneside, jointly arranged by Northern Arts and the Arts Council. The four other writers involved were Michael Holroyd, who had recently been commissioned to write a biography of George Bernard Shaw; Ronald Harwood, the author of a number of screenplays and four novels, the most recent of which was *Articles of Faith*; David Harsent, the youngest of the five, who had already established a reputation as a promising poet; and Joseph Hansen, an American who had made his name with a series of cultish noir thrillers featuring a gay insurance inspector called Dave Brandstetter.

The tour itself, billed as a chance to 'discuss the satisfactions and problems of creative writing with internationally known writers', ran through the first week of March and took in Bellingham, Berwick-upon-Tweed, Morpeth, Wooler, Walbottle and Killingworth – an itinerary that involved travelling around 200 miles between events.

None of the writers had met before – and most were unfamiliar with each other's work – but in this instance the mix of different person-alities and the pressure-cooker environment of touring and travelling was conducive to an almost immediate sense of camaraderie between them. Joe Hansen and Beryl immediately hit it off. He found it easy to talk to her and on the train up confided in her about his emotional problems.[43]

Beryl struck the others as quite unlike anyone they had ever met. Ronald Harwood's first impression was that she was 'as mad as a hatter. I didn't think she could write a proper book, she seemed crazy to me.' Later, he came to realize that there was an element of pose in her scatty forgetfulness: 'She seemed to take pleasure in being daffy.' When he told her his latest novel was called *Articles of Faith*, she made as if she had never heard the word 'articles' used in this context and joked, 'You mean, like articles of clothing, like knickers?' After which the book was habitually referred to as 'Knickers of Faith'.[44]

David Harsent, who had already read some of her novels and was aware of her reputation for eccentricity, had a similar feeling:

> On one occasion we were crossing the road in Newcastle and Beryl was searching in her handbag for a letter she'd had from Jimmy Boots, which she'd misplaced or couldn't find. She was so distracted by this and so determined to find it she sat down in the middle of the road, fishing about in her bag for this letter. There was a bit of a wind and things were whipping off down the road, like money and other bits and pieces from her handbag. I suppose it would have been pound notes in those days, I can't imagine Beryl had a fiver on her. Eventually she was encouraged to get off the white line and go to the pavement, but the letter from Jimmy Boots did seem crucial.

Although he felt her 'scatter-brained attitude and eccentricities were absolutely genuine', Harsent also recognized that she was 'bloody good at projecting this image of herself', and that somewhere within her 'there was a steel core'.[45]

Beryl got on well with the others, but it was with Michael Holroyd that she was particularly taken. The connection between them was immediately apparent: 'Anyone who was involved in the tour was aware of it,' Ronnie recalled. 'Neither were very good concealers.' Consequently, there was a certain amount of 'toing and froing between the bedrooms'. Even so, Ronnie didn't think the affair would last, feeling that deep down they weren't well suited: 'They were both complex personalities, but complex in different ways. I didn't think the ways were compatible.'

The tour was a memorable one, but the successive days of drinking with Joe ('He got very pissed all the time, he drank like a fish . . .')[46] had taken its toll. Back in London, Beryl wrote to tell Ronnie: 'Children pleased to see me but thought I looked raddled with the drink.'[47] The drinking did not stop with the end of the tour, however, as Joe was currently working in London on a Fellowship grant from the National Endowment for the Arts. 'Joe and me are dipsomanic in Soho',[48] she informed Ronnie in another letter a fortnight later.

Beryl had also been seeing Michael, but any hopes she had that things between them might develop further were quickly dashed. In order to be close to the research material he needed for his life of Shaw, Holroyd had taken a house on the outskirts of Dublin and was due to move there at the end of March. As Beryl mournfully told Ronnie: 'I love the boy Holroyd and he loves me, but he is going away.'

Although she knew that Michael found her fascinating and enjoyed her company, Beryl also sensed that her affections were more engaged than his. After he had left for Dublin, she sent him a long letter telling him her news ('An exhausting day with Joe – crying and things . . .'), at the end of which she couldn't help referring to what was uppermost in her mind, blurting out in a postscript: 'None of this is what I meant to write. I did write another one but I tore it up. It's snowing here – I love you but it doesn't matter.'[49]

Over the next month or so Beryl lost herself in trying to finish *Sweet William*. Although the book was nominally based on her experiences with Alan, her feelings for Michael were beginning to distort her portrayal of William: 'The book is very disjointed. All about you and Samuel Palmer, I keep thinking you're him under the moon. Its a rotten book. Disjointed. The main character has moved from Rudi's Da to J. Boots, to you. I have another 30 pages to do and am staying up all night mostly. I will send you the proof or whatever those lavatory pages are, with pages of you duely marked.'[50]

Beryl's American publisher, George Braziller,[51] who had bought the rights of all her novels up to this point, was trying to get her to come to America in April to promote the launch of *The Bottle Factory Outing*.[52] This wasn't practical as she was still writing *Sweet William*, so he suggested a tentative date of August instead. As Michael had told her he too had to go to America, she thought they might be able to synchronize her trip with his and maybe even travel together. Arranging it was not so easy, however. Not having heard anything from Beryl for a few weeks – during the opening of an exhibition at the National Portrait Gallery she had got drunk and lost her address book – he somewhat rashly and extravagantly booked a double cabin: 'I am going on the QE2 at <u>immense</u> expense – 1st CLASS, one way, on 19 August.'[53] It would be, he said, trying to persuade her, a 'unique' experience, and '<u>of course</u>, intensely romantic'.[54]

But this wasn't practical for Beryl, as Aaron and Jo, now old enough to travel on their own, were going to Greece for the whole of August, leaving her with ten-year-old Rudi to look after. To Michael this left only one alternative: 'I think it'll <u>have</u> to be aeroplane: we can swallow each other's tablets, hold each other's hands (no difficulty there).'[55] But Beryl hated flying, and in any case if they went in August there would still be the problem of Rudi, so she now had to consider the possibility of taking her with her.

She had recently had lunch with the poet and critic Dennis Enright, during the course of which she had told him about her predicament, and in a letter shortly afterwards she alluded to her uncertainties about Michael and her frustration at the situation:

> I don't know about Mr X. From a shy retiring sort of fella he is turn-ing out to be a Mr Bluebeard. He says we must fly now. But even if I got up, to get to him I have to go down again at Dublin and get up again (how rude it sounds) and I would die of shock I fear. And I may have to take my smallest one with me and she is dreadfully poces-sive. Also I fear he may be a TORY. How can one love a TORY? Its an Oxymoron – like a family holiday etc. I am a bit down at the moment.[56]

By now, Joe had returned to America. He had travelled by way of a Russian ship, the *MS Mikhail Lermontov*, which gave Beryl the idea of an alternative to flying. Its September departure date meant that Aaron and Jo would be back in time to look after Rudi. She wrote to Michael to explain why she couldn't fly and to tell him her new plan:

> Now flower . . . I wonder if you will be in the States in Sept, or will you have gone on to famous research centres? Because on Sept 7 the Russian boat goes to New York. Even if I could get on a plane it will go up and down won't it? I mean to get [to] you. And I don't suppose they stop anyway at Dublin. Even if I got on one I can't possibly land and go up again in one day. The shock would kill me. And we can't do anything on an areoplane. Not after I'm drugged up to the eyeballs.
>
> But can you come back to New York or would you want to in Sept? I mean if you were not proud I could pay the hotel . . . You are a bit difficult Michael Holyroyd. I mean I think I know who you are but as you are so polite and I am too . . . it is akward to know what you are thinking. I mean I would like to be just friends and gallop over New York with you, I am sure we could have a lovely time, but I don't know if you want that. But I would be happy being with you in a foreign land.

I want to meet you in New York about Sept 16 or so. Do you not want that? It would only be for a week to 10 days as I have to get back for the children. When are you going? Oh do write and tell me what to do?[57]

But Beryl sensed that Michael was not really interested romantically. In June she wrote to tell Joe how the plans for America were going and added: 'I realise now never never go with a Virgo. He's a darlin' boy but obviously regrets jumping in with both feet. I am jolly sober and sleep a lot and wait quietly for the next disaster to hit me.'[58] Nevertheless, whatever Michael's feelings towards her were, it looked like Beryl would have to follow through with her plans to go to America, and a few weeks later she wrote to Joe again, still feeling deflated by it: 'The children leave for Greece this week for the summer and then I am going to take Rudi to Venice, and then later, get on the boat. I am scared to book as I do not know what to do when I get there if Michael is not about. He is so beastly vague . . . Apart from a broadcast next month sometime, I am doing nothing at all, and for the first time in my life I am actually begining to feel lonely. I think I shall have to look for someone else with eyes as soft but true etc etc.'[59]

But despite the months of complicated arrangements, the American trip had still not been arranged by the end of that summer. George Braziller had fallen unaccountably silent, so Michael flew out alone. 'The boy Holroyd rang to say he was off on the 28th,' she wrote to tell Joe, 'I still think he is beautiful but as a memory. Maybe I am fickle or maybe I see him clearly, and we are as Ronnie said, disasterous together.'[60]

At the start of September copies of *Sweet William* arrived and Beryl sent one to Michael, along with a note saying that a visit to America looked unlikely: 'Dearest Boy – For what its worth – book. Due out 2nd Oct. Book, not me. Doubt if we shall ever meet again – at least in this life . . . Your loving friend. Beryl.'[61]

This vague feeling of disillusion leaked over into a general weariness with the whole process of writing, and when Joe wrote to tell her that he was blocked, that his head was empty and he didn't know what to write,[62] she replied: 'I cannot think how to cheer you up, as I am not in the highest spirits myself. Gloomy about me book, I suppose. I think for people like us, fulfillment only comes out of more work, and the gaps in between are hell and the times doing it are hell as well – so where's the fun?'[63] Another reason for her lack of high spirits which she didn't mention, was the thought she might be pregnant. But the test in January proved negative, and once again it turned out to be amenorrhoea.

As if fated to be continually out of step, by the time Beryl's visit to America was arranged at the end of February 1976, Michael had returned to Dublin. He wrote and invited her to come over, but she wasn't sure about the idea, telling Joe: 'Its too long ago and I should be shy I think.'[64] What with her work and having got used to an independent life, maybe relationships of that kind were just too complicated. She still had Clive, and for the moment Clive would have to do.

Beryl's next novel was to be 'the story of a family living in Lancashire thirty years ago'.[65] She had originally intended it to be called 'Semi-Detached', but during the writing process it acquired the more evocative title *A Quiet Life*. One of her motives for writing the book – described by *The Spectator* as 'a tragic, comic study of what has been called "the psychosocial interior of the family"'[66] – was to make amends for the misleading impression she'd given of her parents elsewhere. Having made her mother a comic figure in *Sweet William* and in *Tiptoe Through the Tulips*, a television play broadcast earlier in the year, she had begun to feel guilty about having caricatured her for the sake of 'cheap laughs'. 'I would dearly like to stop being so comical,' she told Joe, 'and be more heavy-weight.'[67] As a consequence, she wanted to treat her parents seriously in *A Quiet Life*, telling a reporter from the *Radio Times* that the book would be 'an attempt to do them justice, to portray them sympathetically, as they were'.[68]

In the event, however, the novel ended up reinforcing the distorted portrait of her parents she had initially said she wanted to avoid. As she admitted in an interview shortly after publication, space constraints meant the book tended to present a one-sided view of family life: 'Since I write to a very short time limit, I had to leave out so many of the nice things, the fact that they were good parents whom I liked. So one only sees the gloomy parts.'[69]

As domestic conflict is inherently more dramatic than domestic harmony, her emphasis on the more confrontational side of life was perhaps inevitable. In any case, as Alan had noted in respect of *Sweet*

William, Beryl was writing fiction, not autobiography. She was not bound to strict factual accuracy or even fidelity of experience, but to the dramatic exigencies of telling a story.

One of the ways this heightened sense of drama was achieved in *A Quiet Life* was through Beryl's decision to write the book from the perspective of her brother. This allowed the reader to take a more nuanced view of Madge than if she had been presented through a first-person narrator, one of the conventions of autobiographical fiction. In interviews Beryl would frequently assert that 'all the facts were true' in *A Quiet Life*, but this categorical assertion is undercut by the novel itself, in which 'facts' seem to be infinitely interpretable, each character having their own version of a reality that is at odds with everyone else's.

By now, glowing reviews had become such a fixture that she told a *Newsday* reporter: 'I think if I got a bad review, I'd get a hell of a shock.'[70] Although there had been some slight quibbles over the issue of whether Beryl's style was achieved at the expense of characterization, the reviews for *A Quiet Life* did not disappoint: Hugo Williams in the *New Statesman* described it as 'a near perfect book',[71] and Francis Wyndham in *The Times Literary Supplement* called it 'a truly remarkable insight'.[72] But while the subtle black comedy and the bleak, generally downbeat tone of Beryl's novels went down well with newspaper critics, these were not characteristics that tended to endear them to the larger buying public.

The *Newsday* piece had been tellingly entitled 'A writer whose public consists of critics', hinting that in America, as in the UK, Beryl was still considered something of a niche writer. What was troubling – for Colin if not for Beryl – was that her resounding critical success was not being translated into commercial sales. Over the last five years she had produced a string of novels that had made her name and given her a reputation as one of the country's leading novelists. But the sales figures betrayed a disturbing tendency: while print runs had progressively increased – from *Harriet Said*, with a modest 2,600 copies, to *Sweet William* and *A Quiet Life* with 8,000 copies apiece – sales had stalled, and those of the last two novels had even declined after the high point reached by *The Bottle Factory Outing*. For the moment it didn't seem too much of a problem. Paperback sales were healthy and the sale of American rights and translations helped make up any immediate shortfall in revenue. But for a publisher working on small margins it was a worrying trend.

TWENTY-SEVEN

The Writing Life

My face aches with the effort of smiling and answering formally yet one more speech of welcome. I have had a wonderful time though, with immense hospitality and lots of drink and food which I can't appreciate because I am so busy attempting to be charming, interesting and amusing all at the same time. I have had press conferences, slittered about on the ice being photographed, been on Tele, climbed near a ski jump, gone 12 hours in a train through the frozen wastes and now lie dying in bed after yet another party. I am friends again with Clive, though the love is now friendship on my part, and I am trying to start writing Hitler.[1]

A LTHOUGH BERYL HAD FREQUENTLY drawn on her experiences with men in her fiction, it was invariably only after the relationship had ended: she and Austin had divorced by the time she portrayed him as Joseph in *Another Part of the Wood*, her affair with Mick was already over when she depicted him as the Wild Colonial Boy in *A Weekend with Claud*, and Alan had long since disappeared from the scene before she attempted to write about him in *Sweet William*. For her new novel *Injury Time*, however, she not only began using her ongoing relationship with Clive as material, she also began to mention him in interviews: 'We lie awake at night talking about Trust Funds,'[2] she told one journalist, caricaturing him as a man obsessed by finance.

Originally, the intention was to base the novel on the events of her previous year's holiday in Crete, which she had thought 'might make rather a good setting for the passions and tensions in the relationships of three middle aged couples'.[3] But in the end she decided on the more familiar setting of Albert Street. As in *Harriet Said* and *The Dressmaker*, the domestic backdrop was framed by an external plot device, this time based on the Balcombe Street Siege, a stand-off in December 1975 between the Metropolitan Police and four members of the Provisional IRA, who had taken two people hostage in their own home. The six-day siege was widely covered in the media and its dramatic, and peaceful, conclusion was relayed on a television news broadcast that was watched by millions.

In the novel the terrorists were replaced by bank robbers on the run, but the central idea remained the same, the sudden elevation of private life into the public arena: 'What was going to be this quiet dinner party is suddenly on nationwide telly.'⁴ Consciously or unconsciously, Beryl's fascination with the notion of the private suddenly becoming public went well beyond its attraction as a dramatic or novelistic conceit. At some level she must have been aware that she was upping the ante on Clive's commitment – or lack thereof – and Clive must have felt that not only were her references to their affair in public unwise, but that the novel was in some senses a wish-fulfilment for a public exposure of their relationship.

If *Injury Time*, like most of Beryl's novels, was a finely crafted fictional narrative rather than a slice of autobiography, it nevertheless captured something of Beryl's frustration with Clive, her feeling that their relationship wasn't really going anywhere. Significantly, at the end of the book, Edward is jettisoned from the robbers' speeding getaway car, a fate that symbolically prefigured Clive's own.

For the last couple of years she and Clive had continued to see each other in their affectionate if fractious way. The constant friction between them, rooted in their different personalities and their shifting levels of commitment to each other, meant there was rarely a dull moment and Beryl was not above using the resulting dramas as comic material for her fiction. A rare dinner party, to which Clive was invited, became the inspiration for that depicted in *Injury Time* – and then there was the time she persuaded Clive to join her on holiday in Corfu. In order to get away he told his wife he was going on a fishing trip to Ireland, and then had to spend a week in the sweltering Mediterranean heat hiding from the sun, so as not to acquire an alibi-breaking suntan. The dramatic and comic potential of this incident was such that Beryl used it not only in *Winter Garden* but also in her short story 'The Man who Blew Away'.

By the summer of 1976 the relationship was already showing signs of unravelling. Clive's constant hesitancy, his continual projection of a future in which he would leave his wife for Beryl though never quite having the nerve to do so, began to wear thin, and the arguments between them became more bitter. When the contentious issue was raised during a particularly drunken evening, Clive walked out, as Beryl explained to Penny in a note she typed immediately afterwards, her spelling even more erratic than usual as a result of the drink:

I have had a violent argument. Suprise – he takes off his bliddy golishes and lies down. Alright if he's paying the bills, but wot a romantic set up, if he is my sooter. I have sed his hair cut is losey . . . andd I will neffer wash his underdrawers, not if he is paralised. He ses I have holes in my jumpers. But I sed I am an orther, and they have holes. Silence. Then he said he is telling the butler to go. I said why did you not tell the butler you were leaving your wife? Confusion. He has gorn orf.[5]

Although Clive didn't want to break with her, he couldn't bring himself to leave his wife and children either; he was, as he put it himself, 'utterly snookered'.[6] He was aware that Beryl found his prevarication humiliating, and that he couldn't keep repeating the same scenario over and over again: 'I can't promise again and fail again.'

Yet part of Clive's failure to commit to Beryl was his feeling that she wasn't absolutely committed to him, that she didn't really want him: 'If only you'd whisper in my ear you love me,' he told her. In this he was at least partially justified. While Beryl frequently castigated Clive for his lack of courage, shouting at him and calling him a cheat and a fraud, for the past few years she had nevertheless been content to accept his vague assurances of a shared future because she herself was unsure she wanted to change the status quo.

Now she decided to force the issue, though the oblique way in which Beryl told Clive she was emotionally committed to him seems to betray her own lack of resolve:

During the last six months you have talked possibly unwisely about your committment to me. You have on one occasion got rotten drunk and tripped repeatedly over your braces. Nasty words were said. I beleive the term was 'ugly old bitch'. However when I saw you the following day I think I forgave you rather prettily and more or less instantly. I did not lecture you. Practically every time I have seen you in the last six months or legal session, you have thrown at me the desire to be with me more permanently and added, 'But you won't have me will you? You won't tell me.' Out of a mature sense of the rightness of things I held my tongue even if I did not cross my legs. Finally on the 19th I was carried away enough, before Vodka mind you, to tell you that I did want you. In the past I had implied that I didn't want you and that it was impossible anyway. On the 19th I thought I implied that I wanted you but it was impossible. This should have transported you to whatever heights there are, but it seemed to me you were appalled by my protestations.[7]

Clive sought advice from Anna Haycraft, who tried to reassure him, telling him he should have no fear that Beryl would be anything other than an 'utterly faithful companion'.[8] But this didn't persuade him either. Perhaps part of the reason for this was that he suspected he wasn't the only person sharing Beryl's bed. 'If you hadn't been sleeping around,' he told her by way of excuse, 'I would have come. I think in time I should have had to have made the break.'

In the event, the relationship dragged on for another two years. By 1978 they were both getting to the stage where they'd had enough. 'The last two years have been misery,'[9] as Clive bluntly put it in a letter that served as a post-mortem on the failed relationship. 'I don't know whether it matters to you now,' he wrote, explaining how he felt, 'but it was the rows, the hassle, the dark thoughts and not answering back, the fear of being humiliated if I had, the trying to get away, if only for your sake, and not being able to . . . all mixed up together in an indigestible mess, sitting on my chest, suffocating me for months and months.'[10]

There was a last-ditch attempt to save the relationship, with Clive flying out to Corfu to be with Beryl on holiday, but it was to no avail. Two days after his arrival he felt ill and was already looking to return: 'Clive may or may not be going home. He's very undecided',[11] as a friend of the family staying with Beryl at the time put it. When he got back, Clive wrote a long letter effectively drawing things to a close. He conceded that perhaps Beryl was right in thinking they were 'bad for one another',[12] but felt they should have been gentler, less impatient with each other – by the end they'd both been 'hacking away at the mental bond so that it hardly exists'. There were faults on both sides: he knew his prevarications had humiliated her and made her suffer, but he also felt that she was too controlling and too quick to attack him. If anything Corfu had made things worse. At least in London when she got drunk and shouted at him he could walk out and it would be alright in the morning. But in Greece he couldn't, and in front of other people he found her treatment of him too much to take: 'You're not always right and just for once you should have kept your mouth shut if you couldn't keep off the booze!'

'Let's call a truce,' he concluded, which they did. Despite the insults that had frequently been exchanged over the years, both in person and in letters, they would remain friends long after the affair was over.

———

One of the consequences of Beryl's literary success was that she started to take on the role of a professional writer, with all that this entailed. She was now regularly being interviewed and profiled in the press, and would often be asked to write articles on issues related to family life or her childhood experiences. She also began to be invited to give public readings and take part in literary events, both at home and abroad, as her international reputation grew. From the mid-1970s onwards these engagements would form an integral part of her life: between 1977 and 1979 alone her foreign itinerary included Budapest, Israel, Yugoslavia, the Netherlands, Norway, Sweden, America and Russia. It was, as she wrote to Judith, a full-time occupation, but one that had its drawbacks:

> I really do work very hard. I have been to America, to Scotland, to Greece, to Belgrade, to Suffolk, to Yorkshire, yes for a split second, to Liverpool, in the last 8 months, plus two tele scripts, and one novel and the children and the house. Not to mention my gentleman caller. I get anything from 50 to 75 letters a week and I refuse to go mad and have secretaries or cleaners or anything, and mostly I just work and work (though I don't call it work) and things like friendship seem not to be part of my life anymore. I see the children, the next door neighbour, Clive and that's it. I don't go out to dinner or lunch's or party's. At first it was exciting but now it also a very real race to earn the mortgage and everything.[13]

Beryl's theatrical background inevitably contributed to her success as a performer onstage. The openness with which she talked about her life experiences and her work enthralled audiences, and she was an accomplished reader of her own prose, her incantatory reading style echoing the manner in which she would compose sentences and recite them in her head in order to get the rhythm right. A. N. Wilson, who as literary editor of the *Evening Standard* invited her to be a guest speaker on a number of occasions, recalled that 'she held the audience like a diva. She had a particularly actressy voice, but it was actually a very beautiful and euphonious voice.'[14]

In 1976 Beryl sufficiently overcame her fear of flying to go to New York to see George Braziller and promote the American edition of *Sweet William*. Although she failed to meet up with Joseph Hansen, as they had tentatively planned, because she couldn't work out the American phone codes, she wrote to him from the Royalton hotel to tell him what she'd been doing: 'I had a most beautiful time. I had a suite in the hotel opposite the Algonquin – and lunch everyday in the Algonquin. I had interviews and photies every 45 mins for 4 days – plus theatres and concerts and a party for me and radio – saw *Newsweek, Sat Daily Post, Newsday, Publishers Weekly, New York Times* and some others. Then I flew to Chicago to the *Tribune* and on something called Bob Cromie's *Bookbeat* on tele.'[15]

She was on her best behaviour – 'I didn't dare drink in case I disgraced myself' – and the only embarrassing moment of the trip came when she let her guard down and went to a Japanese restaurant after drinking with some English friends from *Newsweek* and fainted four times: 'They called a doctor and he said I was anemic. I wasn't – I was drunk. I was a pale silver colour and bright blue lips. Three glasses of bourbon and a bucket of salted raw fish in a Japanese restaurant. I think I was highly controlled not to throw up all over the kimono's.'

The following year the Israeli cultural attaché in London, Moshe Don, invited Beryl to take part in a tour of Israel. Other writers on the trip included John Bayley, Melvyn Bragg, Iris Murdoch, Bernice Rubens, William Trevor, Fay Weldon and Ted Willis – 'as alluring a panel of British writers as has ever collected on one platform',[16] as the *Jerusalem Post* noted in its report of one event.

Like the Northern writers' tour of 1975, the trip to Israel introduced Beryl to writers who would become lifelong friends, most notably Melvyn Bragg and Bernice Rubens. Bernice's first encounter with Beryl at the airport was indicative of things to come. Their flight had been delayed, and the party was shunted into a hospitality lounge and drinking ensued: 'I don't remember much about the very moment I met Bernice,' Beryl later recalled, 'because I disgraced myself . . . I was wheeled to the aircraft on a luggage trolley and slept on a small bed at the back.'[17] Bernice was not, however, unduly put out by Beryl's unconventional behaviour: 'I warmed to her because it was pretty apparent she was cuckoo.' When she had sobered up, Beryl found out that she actually knew Bernice's brother, Cyril, a musician in the Liverpool Philharmonic; Austin had met him through the Greens and painted his portrait in the late 1950s.[18] Bernice, too, was a skilled musician, playing the cello, or, as Beryl would refer to it, 'the banjo'.[19]

After their arrival at Ben-Gurion international airport and their first night at the Plaza hotel in Jerusalem, the delegation got straight into their impressive – and impressively thorough – itinerary. The ten-day trip was meticulously planned down to the last detail, a punishing schedule that could not have been more structured if it had been organized by the Politburo. Most days, the schedule of events began at 8.30 in the morning, though 7.30 was not unusual, and almost all involved a full twelve-hour programme.

Visits to places of cultural or political significance – the Israel Museum to see the Dead Sea scrolls, a refugee camp in Gaza, Yad Vashem holocaust museum, the Golan Heights, the Jordan Valley, a tour of the holy sites and the Sea of Galilee – were usually followed by a formal dinner in the company of some functionary, followed by a visit to the home of a local notable or worthy.

'The trip was a great laugh,' as Beryl would later recall, but it was not without its awkward moments, at least initially. Beryl saw herself as the 'new girl' and she felt rather nervous and in awe of the rest of the group. Nor did she and Bernice hit it off straight away ('It wasn't like we got on amazingly at first . . .'),[20] and had Bernice been less accommodating she might have taken offence at Beryl's somewhat enthusiastic, tourist-like insistence she come with her to see the Yad Vashem holocaust museum. In the event, Bernice refused and Beryl went on her own. At the time Beryl couldn't understand her attitude: 'She told me afterwards, that she couldn't because it was too much, too brutal for her', that while it was 'comparatively easy for a non-Jew to feel emotion at man's inhumanity to man . . . for Jews tears are not enough and can never lessen the pain'.

Despite their differences in temperament, after returning to London Bernice and Beryl would remain friends until Bernice's death in 2004. Beryl was a frequent guest at Bernice's dinner parties in her flat in Belsize Park, and it would be at Bernice's that she first came into contact with a range of new writers outside the Duckworth circle, including Howard Jacobson and Paul Bailey, who would become a close friend.

The visit to Israel was undoubtedly a factor in the choice of subject for Beryl's next novel, *Young Adolf*, published the following year in 1978. The catalyst was a book she read shortly after her return, Robert Payne's *The Life and Death of Adolf Hitler*, which contained 'a paragraph . . . about Hitler coming to Liverpool'.[21] This struck her as a great idea for a novel: 'I couldn't really miss a chance like that. It had all the ingredients, it had Adolf, and my father's time and my own city.'[22] Payne was the first biographer to publish the information, which he had come across in a diary purportedly written by Bridget Hitler, née Dowling, who had married Adolf's half-brother Alois Hitler in 1910, and who claimed Adolf had visited them in Liverpool in 1912.[23] There is no evidence to back up her version of events and most historians now regard it as bogus, though this does nothing to detract from the novel's brilliant evocation of Edwardian Liverpool, which was informed by the stories Beryl's father had told her when she was a child.

Young Adolf took longer to write than usual. Not only was Beryl tackling a subject outside her immediate experience for the first time, the moral and ethical dimension of depicting Hitler was also causing her difficulties. 'It's a very difficult problem when you think of it,' she later told an interviewer who asked about how she arrived at her portrayal of Hitler in the book, 'the world thinks of a monster, and you've got to make a character out of a younger man who is not yet a monster. That was a great difficulty. In the end I think I bypassed it, I failed there.'[24] She had initially thought to use her father as a model for Hitler, but in practice she couldn't do it: 'I love my father so I would have been too sympathetic to Adolf.'[25] As a result she had to take a step back and rewrite it: 'I had to decide . . . that my Adolf Hitler was going to be a much more cardboard figure, almost a clown.'[26]

In January 1978 she had written to tell Colin: 'I am battling away at Adolf and its alright as far as it goes. I hope to let you have it in about two weeks time and I'm sorry I'm late on delivery. Its been tough this time – I don't seem to know any sentances.'[27] In fact it would be another six months before the book was completed, by which time she was feeling exhausted and ill: 'All today and yesterday I was trying desperately to finish *Young Adolf*. I have conjunctivitis & laringitis and feel lousey.'[28] When she handed in the manuscript she was still slightly uncertain about it and included a hesitant covering note to Anna: 'Hope you like it. Please ring when you've read it. I won't ring you in case you don't like it.'[29]

Another sign of Beryl's success as a writer was the increasing number of commissions for television work she received. The first of these, in June 1974, was for a sixty-minute television play to be entitled 'These Foolish Things', as part of the BBC's 'Play for Today' series. Beryl couldn't meet the intended September deadline, but as she had already been paid the £850 fee, she was given an extension. She delivered the script the following year, by which time she had given it a new title, *Tiptoe Through the Tulips*.

Directed by Claude Whatham, and featuring Rosemary Leach and Michael Gambon as its two principals, *Tiptoe Through the Tulips* was broadcast on 16 March 1976. In many ways it is a precursor to *Injury Time*, featuring a similar set of characters and a similar backdrop, that of an evening dinner party. One of the striking features of the play is the extraordinary performance by Rosemary Leach as Rita, the contrarian divorcée with a tendency to drink. Rita is perhaps a more accurate self-portrait of Beryl in middle age than any contained in her novels, and Leach perfectly captures the complex and often contradictory elements of her personality – her flirtatiousness when tipsy, her vulnerability, and the devil-may-care, unconventional front she presented to the world, behind which lay a mass of anxieties and an inner sense of desperation and loneliness.

Following the success of *Tiptoe Through the Tulips* the BBC contacted Beryl when they were planning *The Velvet Glove*, a series of six dramas exploring the lives of influential women. Through her talks with Michael Holroyd and his work on Shaw, Beryl had become interested in Annie Besant, the social reformer turned Theosophist and Indian activist, and chose her as the subject of the fifth play in the series. The resulting script, *The Warrior's Return*, which aired on 23 February 1977, was directed by Philip Saville (who had also directed Alan Sharp's 'Play for Today', *The Long Distance Piano Player* in 1970) and starred Rosemary Leach as Besant, Denholm Elliott as Charles W. Leadbetter, an adherent of Madame Blavatsky's Theosophical Society, and Ben Kingsley as Gyanendra Chakravarti, the Hindu nationalist and mystic. Saville was very taken with the play when Beryl showed it to him: 'I loved the script, because it was all about social injustice, about Besant's dabbling in politics and her subsequent slither into metaphysics and the mystic world of the East. I was thrilled at the casting; Rosemary Leach was absolutely amazing. I must admit it's one of the best things I ever did. This was such a beautiful piece.'[30]

Shortly afterwards they met up again and Beryl happened to mention she had just read Payne's book about Hitler and the alleged visit to Liverpool. Saville in his turn mentioned the idea to Anne Head, the producer of *The Velvet Glove*, and she commissioned the two of them to write a dramatized version of events. To work on the script, Saville would go round to Albert Street: 'We'd meet regularly and have a mug of tea, she'd make a nice piece of toast and jam. Then she'd say, "I'll just write this down . . ." We worked like that for about 10 days.'

But it was in the shooting of *The Journal of Bridget Hitler* that things started to get really interesting and the result was unlike anything the BBC had produced before. In a dramatic spectacle just short of two hours long and broadcast on 6 February 1981, Saville employed Brechtian alienation techniques, the latest Quantel videographic technology, Chroma key or 'green screen'-type special effects, projections of archival footage, and dramatic reconstructions that featured live actors. Perhaps the most famous scene was that in which a group of skinheads come into the BBC canteen where actors in costume and members of the crew, including Philip and Beryl, are eating, and start to smash the place up, as a kind of simulation of, or allusion to, the violence of the Brownshirts. 'I had about 30 or 40 people,' Saville recalled, 'and Anne Head said, "I hope you won't do anything too mad." I told the floor manager to tell them to go for it, to throw things at each other – not bottles – and that they could smash things. Anyway they went for it.' It was certainly dramatically effective, though it didn't go down too well at the BBC: 'I was told not to show my face around the place for weeks afterwards.'

Beryl had the luck to fall in with another director sensitive to her work, Tristram Powell, when it came to making *Words Fail Me*, a dramatized version of scenes from *A Quiet Life* in which interviews with Beryl talking about her family were interspersed with dramatized recreations. *Words Fail Me* was broadcast on 22 February 1979 as part of BBC2's *Omnibus* series. With a script by Powell, and helped by strong central performances by Joanne Whalley in the role of the young Beryl, and Peter Jeffrey as her father Richard, the film presented a more tender and nuanced portrait of family life than that which Beryl would recount in later interviews. Here her father's temper is given a partial justification in the provocation offered by Beryl's precocious behaviour and her frustrating habit of lying. As her fictional brother Alan puts it: 'She was always making things out to be different than they were. She called the tree in the back garden a willow, when everyone could see it was a sycamore. She needed a blithering good hiding.' In this view of family life, Beryl's, or at least Madge's, habitual lies and deceptions are as much a factor in the family dynamic as her father's moods and her mother's snobbery.

Some of the exterior scenes were filmed on the Formby dunes, and it was during one of her visits to Liverpool for these location shoots that Beryl acquired what would become a literally lifesize expression of her eccentricity in the public mind: the stuffed water buffalo she would call Eric: 'We happened to pass the Rialto cinema . . . and there was Eric.' Tristram jokingly said to her, 'I wonder how you've managed to live without him . . .', and the sheer ludicrousness and impracticality of the idea appealed to her. The next day she went back and bought him. When he was delivered to Albert Street it became immediately apparent that his seven-foot-long body, mounted on a wooden plinth, not to mention horns that spanned almost three feet, presented a logistical problem: 'He came up on a van with only one driver, nobody to get him in. Originally I wanted him in my sitting room. I was going to put him on rockers – he was going to be a rocking buffalo. But you couldn't move him. We had to go to the local Irish pub, and get a whole pile of Irishmen. We got him into the hall, but we couldn't get him into the kitchen. So he stayed there.'[31]

The only exception to the string of critical successes was *Blue Skies From Now On*, which was broadcast on 20 November 1977 as part of ITV's *Sunday Night Drama* season. The play was an adaptation of *Another Part of the Wood*, but in transferring it to the small screen much of the book's subtlety was lost, and its bleakly depressing ending seemed too arbitrary for an hour-long drama. The *Observer* was damning in its summing up: 'Old-fashioned and over-written, it's further over-directed by Graham Evans, changing shot every two seconds, rushing his cameras about like things possessed.'[32] Richard Ingrams, then television critic for *The Spectator*, also picked out *Blue Skies From Now On* for special abuse, naming it one of the runners-up in his 'Worst Play of 1977 Competition'.[33]

In April 1977, Kendon Films took out an option on *Sweet William*, and offered a deal that involved £2,000 for Beryl to write the screenplay, with a further £5,000 due on the first day of shooting. The film featured a high-profile cast, with Jenny Agutter taking the role of Ann and Sam Waterston as William, and there was strong support from Arthur Lowe as Ann's father, Anna Massey as William's wife, and Geraldine James as Pamela. Melvyn Bragg played himself as an arts presenter.

Sweet William turned out to be 'a tight little gem', as a review in *Films & Filming* put it, partly due to director Claude Whatham, who was sensitive to the script's tragi-comic subtleties having previously worked on *Tiptoe Through the Tulips*. (In fact Beryl would be fortunate in her dealings with the film business, and the two subsequent adaptations of her novels, *The Dressmaker* in 1988, with Joan Plowright as Nellie and Billie Whitelaw as Margo, and *An Awfully Big Adventure* in 1995, with Hugh Grant as Meredith Potter and Georgina Cates as Stella, were both remarkably faithful to the originals.)

To tie in with the release of the *Sweet William* film, Fontana produced a new cover for the paperback edition featuring a naked Jenny Agutter draping herself over the naked torso of Sam Waterston. Underneath, a strap line read: 'No one can say no to the bastard!' Colin was appalled and wrote back to Simon King at Fontana who had solicited his opinion on the design: 'What an awful jacket. I thought you'd improved with the jacket for *A Quiet Life*, but this in my view is very retrograde! And what a silly subtitle!'[34]

There was one insidious downside to Beryl's newly acquired success, one that would have an increasing impact on her personal and professional life as the years passed: drink, or more specifically in Beryl's case, whisky. During the 1960s Beryl had drunk and sometimes been drunk, but her limited financial means meant that on the whole drinking tended to be kept within moderate bounds. Now, for the first time, she was in a situation where she not only had the money to buy alcohol whenever she wanted, she also had open entry to a world that actively encouraged drinking and where alcohol was in plentiful supply. Consequently, the number of occasions when Beryl passed out – euphemistically described as being 'under the table' – and the number of times this would lead to potentially dangerous or socially humiliating experiences increased as Beryl's resistance to alcohol, both psychologically and physiologically, decreased.

Literary parties and book launches were just one manifestation of this. Events at Duckworth were renowned for what became known as 'Colin's Killers' – a sugar cube covered by a shot of Cointreau topped up with sparkling wine and a maraschino cherry – a heady mix that loosened tongues and lowered inhibitions. After one such party, Beryl had gone on to the opening of an exhibition of photographs by Augustus John at the National Portrait Gallery. Once there, the effects of the drink took hold and she passed out: 'I woke on a woolsak . . . at the time I did not know it was a portrait gallery. I did note the photos of a bearded gent but I was a bit sleepy. I also remember someone wanting to examine my bag – at the precise moment I thought it a bit cheeky – I tipped me bag out. The next morning my bag was half empty, and my address book had gone.'[35]

Drink was also de rigueur during the evenings at Gloucester Crescent. As Anna told a reporter from the *Guardian*, she and Beryl 'got drunk all the time, but a lot of drinking went on in those days . . . Beryl was very shy and I think that's why she got so drunk. I'd got this teddy bear and she'd go to sleep with it under the table. But she's so skinny I've seen a glass of wine go straight to her head.'[36]

The stories of Beryl's whisky-drinking exploits, regaled as they were as amusing expressions of her high spirits, created a myth of her as a drinker impervious to alcohol's downsides. But what such public myths often hide is a private world of feelings of shame and humiliation, of depression and inadequacy, not to mention the tensions and arguments within the family that a reliance on alcohol can cause.

Beryl was aware of the effect that alcohol was having on her life. She admitted to one journalist that getting drunk all the time interfered with her writing,[37] and the self-portrait she painted of herself as Rita in *Tiptoe Through the Tulips* gives some indication of the way drink was affecting her personal life, its pervasiveness in her social interactions. Part of the problem was that she found it hard to resist both the social pressure, and her own desire, to drink – and once she began drinking it became difficult, if not impossible, to stop. As she said herself, if her parents had been rich and she had inherited money when they died, she would have become an alcoholic at an early age: 'It's like leaving a bomb behind.'[38]

In March 1979 Beryl travelled to America again, this time on a more extended tour, taking in New York, where she had tea with Robert Payne in the Algonquin ('He was lovely . . .'); Pennsylvania, where people were still being evacuated after the accident at Three Mile Island ('apart from clouds of smoke at Harrisburg, felt nothing . . .'); Boston, where she went to Harvard University ('a fair amount of drink and everyone looking like Auden with dandruff . . .'); Los Angeles, where she gave a reading at UCLA; and San Francisco: 'I am so exhausted that I can't write this letter properly . . . If I get home I'll never do this again. Went on a phone-in show. Somewhat alarming as a lady said she was going to kill herself and another man asked me if Mrs Thatcher was religious. The same day, I was on Tele with a man called the Chip Cookie King, and he threw biscuits all round the room and a sign came on to say laugh and scream and people did. I suppose it was a more light-hearted book show and the *South Bank* could learn from it.'[39]

Beryl had also brought Rudi, now fourteen, with her. The reason for this was that Alan, who hadn't seen Rudi since his departure for America several years before, had asked Beryl to be allowed to see her. Beryl was reluctant but had agreed to meet up in Los Angeles where Alan worked as a screenwriter. In a letter of thanks after the visit, Alan regretted he hadn't spoken to Beryl more, 'but on reflection that was probably not on the cards nor really advisable'.[40] Despite the fact it had been over ten years since they had split up, she still found the meeting unsettling, not least because she discovered that even her wildest suspicions and jealousies about Alan during their relationship had fallen short of reality. Beryl now found out that Alan also had a son by a woman she had never heard of before – and as he was the same age as Liz's first child, he must have been conceived at the same time Alan was urging Beryl to marry him: 'A farce going on here,' she wrote to Don McKinlay, 'met Alan Sharp plus his wife and 2 kids, plus a woman from Scotland and her son, plus me and Ru. Some of the children are the same age. Its all most odd, and in an odd way, upsetting.'[41]

Six months later, Beryl embarked on a literary tour of the USSR alongside the veteran novelist Harry Hoff, more popularly known as William Cooper. Harry found her a congenial travelling companion: 'She's irrepressible. She sees things differently to me. She transmogrifies events in her own way.'[42] The trip had been organized by John Roberts, under the auspices of the British Council, and included talks, meetings with other writers and artists, and visits to sites of cultural – or political – interest, such as Stalin's birthplace in Gori: 'There was a mud hut arrangement comprising one room and a cellar, the whole obviously reinforced with something stronger than mud because they'd built a Greek temple on top of it. There was a stove pipe coming out of the roof, and a photograph of Stalin, when young, looking like Omar Sharif without the moustache.'[43]

To begin with, Beryl and Harry would alternate the toasts they were required to give at official functions, so that the other could drink the vodka that was invariably provided, but after a while she couldn't think of anything to say and made him do them all. Hoff's orations were often tongue-in-cheek, playing up to the stereotype of the romantic Russian sensibility: 'How nice it would be if our voices still existed floating around somewhere after we were dead and that perhaps the echo of Pushkin's voice is still in this room . . .'[44]

Although they met few fellow novelists, they did meet a number of Soviet poets, including Yevgeny Yevtushenko, to whom they talked about literature and art. Beryl would later recall that he would ring her up at the hotel, late at night, shouting down the phone, 'I am your brother!'[45]

Beryl was fascinated by the bizarre manifestations of Russian officiousness. On one occasion, as they were being chauffeur-driven to an official function, they passed a shop in the window of which was a dress that Beryl liked the look of. She casually said, 'Ooh that's nice', whereupon the car stopped, policemen appeared, wooden barriers were set up and the shop was cleared. Beryl and Harry were then led into the now-empty shop to look around.

After Beryl's return home she set about turning her experiences into a novel. The idea behind it came from an incident in Moscow that occurred when she was taken to the house of an illustrator of children's books: 'It was a two roomed flat with parquet floors,' Beryl recalled a few years later. 'By the door was a fluffy white rug. When I entered I scuffed the rug and there was an irregular piece of flooring. I asked what it was, and after a lot of dithering, was told that someone had been murdered in the flat 3 years ago. The pieces of flooring had been taken away for examination.'[46] This chance discovery of a death in mysterious circumstances, one that seemed to have been officially covered up in such a slipshod manner, inspired a plot in which the boundaries between reality and paranoia about Russian state bureaucracy seem blurred.

Winter Garden, unlike *Young Adolf*, 'just wrote itself. I kept a small diary with me. But the whole thing was so vivid, like a dream, all I had to do was just write it down.' Part of the reason for the hallucinatory quality of her recollections, apart from the vodka – 'the Russians give you so much to drink, so we were very tired and very disorientated . . .'[47] – was that during the visit she had fallen ill. The weather in October had been colder than average – at one point it spiked to minus 14°C – and Beryl arrived ill-prepared: 'I had no socks, because I never wear socks, but I also hadn't got a hat or anything. Someone had lent me a fur-coat, but they kept on saying: "You'll be really ill, it's terribly cold." I literally didn't notice it. I thought they were fussing.' However, while she was in Tbilisi she came down with what she later described as 'pleurisy' and went to a doctor, who gave her a pill, 'just one . . .', which made her high for about six hours. 'I was walking on air. I saw Rasputin looking over a hedge, among other things.'[48] The fact that the surgery was on the roof of the building – she could see the official car below her – and there was a goat tethered to the wall, only added to the dreamlike impression.

When it was published in October 1980, the book received mixed reviews. A frequent criticism was that it was confusing and opaque. 'Lots of people said they didn't know what happened at the end,' Beryl admitted. 'My publisher didn't understand what happened at the end.'[49] Some of this was deliberate, the reader's uncertainty about what is real or imagined reflecting the Kafkaesque convolutions of life in the USSR, but it was nevertheless demanding. As Frank Kermode put it: 'Nothing is straight-forward . . . piecing this world together is a formidable, perhaps impossible task.'[50]

Having come off second best again in her encounter with a married man, one might have assumed that Beryl would be wary of entering into another relationship along the same lines. But that kind of prudence, that kind of emotional restraint, was not in Beryl's nature. With a kind of fatalistic recklessness, shortly after her final break with Clive, she allowed herself to become emotionally entangled with Colin. It was an affair that would have a profound effect on her personal and professional life, not to mention its impact on her children and the Haycraft family. Untangling the complicated web of personal and emotional factors that led up to it is not easy – in such situations no one comes out entirely unscathed, sides are taken, judgements made, stones cast.

When a marriage breaks down it is a moot point whether an extra-marital affair by one of the partners is a cause, or merely a symptom, of the problem. Which side of the argument one comes down on will often depend on whose perspective one takes. Beryl's view was that Colin and Anna's marriage had broken down well before the start of her affair: she had witnessed bitter arguments between them and it seemed to her that Anna had withdrawn herself emotionally and sexually from Colin.

That Colin and Anna had once loved each other – and there were those who believed they continued to do so even after the affair with Beryl had begun – is undoubtedly the case. But Anna's own public pronouncements about love and marriage are hard to reconcile with that of a happy union, and if they represented a genuine expression of her feelings it is not difficult to see why Colin might have felt under-appreciated: 'The marriage was unimportant to me because the children were everything', Anna would write after Colin's death. 'I was very fond of him and I suppose as far as I was capable, I was in love with him. But I was never the sort who yearned to be in love. Some are the marrying kind, some are maternal. I know women who seem to love their husbands more than they love their children, which I find extraordinary.'[51] In her 'Home Life' column for *The Spectator* during the mid-1980s, she would refer to Colin dismissively as 'Someone', and even though it was meant as a joke, it was also a symbolic act of depersonalization, one that effectively reduced his role as her husband to that of a cipher.

The public expression of such sentiments could, of course, be explained as a post-rationalization in the face of Colin's infidelity, a way to strike back at him and assuage the pain and humiliation of his betrayal by diminishing his significance. Nevertheless, on the surface at least, they hint at a breakdown in empathy between them.

But there were other factors that may have contributed to Colin's need to look outside of marriage for some kind of solace, whether emotional or physical. Anna was prone to bouts of depression and an earlier tragedy had undoubtedly left its mark on her. In the autumn of 1970, around the time of her renewed meeting with Beryl, Anna had been pregnant with her sixth child. This would have been her first daughter, but the baby was born two months premature at the start of November and died of an infection two days afterwards.

This painful event would be overshadowed a few years later when Colin and Anna's second son, Joshua, fell through the roof of a railway shed and died in May 1978 after spending nine months in a coma. Anna found the fatal accident impossible to come to terms with: 'The death of a child is like the end of your life.'[52] In her own analysis, the effect on the family was profound and profoundly isolating: 'The family fragmented, everyone retreating into their own bit; you can't share grief.' Anna's rigorously insular view of personal trauma meant that there was no therapy, nor any kind of engagement with others, that could relieve the pain: 'You either hang yourself or you live it, endure it, get through it alone.'

The psychological impact of these personal tragedies reverberated through Anna's subsequent writing, both in her fiction and in her journalism, and death would become a dominant preoccupation: 'The place on earth where I come closest to peace is in the graveyard amongst all the quiet dead', she wrote in her autobiography. 'I seem to have thought, all my life, of little but death'.[53] Anna's feelings of guilt about the events of November 1952, though they would remain unspoken,[54] undoubtedly contributed to this obsession with death. In Colin's view, Anna had never recovered emotionally from the abortion and he blamed Austin for the psychological damage it had done to her.[55]

On one level it is easy to see how Colin's affair with Beryl started. Colin felt he had been spurned by Anna, a situation reflected in the fact that he now slept on a small bed in his own book-lined study. There were the quantities of drink that were consumed at Gloucester Crescent whenever Beryl was around, not to mention Anna's retreat from the scene both figuratively and literally. She would spend much of her time in the small recessed kitchen and would frequently retire to bed before nine. And then there was the fact that Beryl's house was only ten minutes away and it was natural that Colin should walk her home.

All these factors played their part, but the roots of the affair went back much further than the particular conditions affecting Colin and Anna's marriage at the time. Beryl had been captivated by Colin's wit and erudition from the moment she had met him. As early as 1973 she had confided to her next-door neighbour Penny that she had feelings for 'himself', as she would refer to Colin. It may be that she never considered it something that could actually happen, but it was a dangerous desire to entertain even in a semi-playful fashion, especially as with drink inside her the boundaries of what were or were not acceptable dissolved.

Beryl would often contact a friend after a particularly heavy bout of drinking to ask them what she had done the night before. On this occasion – an evening round at Gloucester Crescent – the subject of her suspected drunken *faux pas* was a little more serious than the usual embarrassment at having passed out or made a fool of herself in front of other people. She recalled having talked to someone about her feelings for Colin. The next morning she wrote a note to Penny to ask whether she remembered who it was or what had happened:

Pen-Pen: Please could you give me a brief ring at work and just tell me if I did. I mean I have a recollection of telling someone I was madly in love with him. You know who. Did I imagine it or did I tell you – worse still did I vanish anywhere with Anna and tell her? Did I tell him – himself? It is 5 oclock in the morning – I am going for a walk as I can't stop laughing.

Thank you also for putting me to rest. There is a note here from Graham. Did he call or was he at Anna's? I just hope I never said anything to <u>him</u>. I told someone I know, but who was it? Did you see me wrapped round him or anything awful. I shall have to leave my job.

On second thoughts I daren't go into work without knowing.

Your friend, Ethel[56]

In the event it turned out to be a false alarm, and anyway her relationship with Clive, which began shortly afterwards, put an end to her thoughts about Colin, at least for a while. In the intervening period she came to know him more closely as a friend, on one level perhaps better than she knew Anna. This was partly a result of the dinner parties given by Derwent May, the literary editor of *The Listener*, and his wife Yolanta, at which both Colin and Beryl were regular guests. Derwent had invited Colin and Anna on numerous occasions, but Anna would invariably decline, as she didn't like these semi-formal social occasions where she was obliged to meet and talk with people she didn't know. Eventually Derwent would simply telephone Colin at the office and invite him on his own. As Derwent and Yola had both come to know Beryl at around the same time, it seemed natural to invite her, too. The Mays' house in Albany Street provided a neutral space in which Colin and Beryl could meet and talk outside the confines of Gloucester Crescent, and as they both lived only five minutes away, it allowed Colin to leave with Beryl and walk her home without arousing undue suspicions among the other guests.

In order to prevent her children finding out, Beryl began renting a room on Parkway, next to the Regent Bookshop in Camden Town. Nominally it was a place where she could work, and she did indeed work there, having installed a desk and a typewriter. There was no toilet – 'I have to pee in a bucket'[57] – but there was a bed, allowing her to keep her assignations with Colin private. She would continue to rent the room for a number of years until Rudi, who as the youngest was the last to leave home, moved out of Albert Street in the mid-1980s.

In the early days the affair was kept secret from all but Beryl's closest friends. Inevitably it divided opinion. There were those, like the Mays, who saw it in a positive light: 'She adored Colin. He was the great love of her life',[58] as Yolanta put it. Others, such as Michael Holroyd, who had never warmed to Colin's peremptory manner, felt it was an 'unfortunate arrangement'[59] and feared that the relationship would ultimately end up harming Beryl in some way.

The question is often asked, and Beryl herself would continue to ask it even into the late 1980s: did Anna know? Of course she knew. It was inconceivable she didn't know. Yet she never alluded to it or hinted at it in public, nor did she seem to let it affect her attitude to Beryl – until much later when their friendship began to break down. Ironically, despite Anna's obsession about keeping her private life out of the public sphere (she would later describe herself as 'having spent a lifetime keeping private life <u>private</u>'),[60] the affair, at least in symbolic or figurative terms, would resurface in her novels, in which infidelity seems to be a recurring motif.[61]

Obviously Beryl's decision to begin an affair with Colin has to be seen at some level as an attack on Anna. This would be a truism even if there had been no history between them, but given the events of 1952, the affair represented – subconsciously at least – an act of revenge for Anna having 'stolen' Austin from her all those years ago. In any event, Beryl was certainly conscious of the emotional impact that what she was doing would have on Anna: 'I think the only victim is the woman, either wife or friend,' she wrote in an article about marital infidelity, 'sexual betrayal doesn't do a great deal for a woman's sense of adequacy.'[62]

The affair with Colin was the last major relationship of Beryl's life, and though it is the latest in date it is also, due to its necessarily secretive nature, the least well documented. There are no open declarations, no letters between them that hint at the relationship's development, its ebbs and flows. Colin's private communications with Beryl were brief. A telephone call or a jotted note on a postcard would prompt a meeting or confirm an arrangement.

What his feelings for her were cannot be truly known. That the relationship was something deeper than the purely physical affair more cynical observers took it to be seems clear given its duration and the number of trying circumstances it survived. It may not have been perfect, it may not even have been love, but at the very least it allowed two emotionally damaged people to find a degree of companionship and affection that was otherwise lacking in their lives.

TWENTY-EIGHT

Fact and Friction

As any kind of discussion on these matters seems to cause you extreme irritation, and as my letters to you, and yours to me are unintelligible (though mine are a little more consistant than yours, as yours go from me owing you over £4000 to you owing me £5000 in the space of a few days) I would prefer that you didn't reply, even supposing you would actually find the time to do so.[1]

I T WAS BECOMING CLEAR that Beryl's prodigious rate of working could not continue indefinitely. The toll of writing a book every year, not to mention the television plays and film scripts, was starting to have an effect. Before the publication of *Winter Garden* she was asked whether she could maintain her 'rapid writing pace' and her answer had been slightly guarded: 'I think I can keep it up. I'm not afraid of producing a failure. If I try very hard I know it should be all right.'[2]

Suspicions that Beryl was finding it hard to 'keep it up' were borne out by the fact that two of her last three novels had been revised editions of those she had published with Hutchinson during the 1960s. This exercise in recycling, in paring down the older books to match the sparer style and format of her Duckworth novels, may have saved time and allowed her to maintain her schedule of a novel a year for ten consecutive years, but she would pay a price for the decision: neither of the revised editions, *Another Part of the Wood* in 1979 and *A Weekend with Claude* in 1981, were as critically or commercially successful as she or Colin had hoped, and the lack of critical momentum dragged down sales of *Winter Garden*.

It is always debatable whether revising a creative piece of work, even when carried out by the artist, can produce a better version than the original, whatever its faults were perceived to be. This doubt lingers over the Duckworth editions of *Another Part of the Wood* and *A Weekend with Claude*. Beryl had excised phrases she now deemed to be too flowery, cut out extraneous characters and simplified the plot lines, but though she expressed satisfaction with the results, the two books seemed to lack the vital spark that animated her other novels.

Reviewers of *Another Part of the Wood* were lukewarm about the changes, preferring the 'more intense and lush early Bainbridge'.[3] Julian Symons, himself a Duckworth author who had praised Beryl's earlier books, called it the least successful of her novels and wrote that it had 'an air of contrivance uncharacteristic of her best work'.[4] The critical response to *A Weekend with Claude* was even worse. Gloria Valverde, in her exhaustive study of the textual differences between the original and the revised editions, noted that critics almost unanimously agreed that the narrative 'lacked the crispness and clarity of Bainbridge's other Duckworth novels'.[5]

It wasn't just reviewers who felt that she needed to find a new direction 'and risk the drastic re-think that all creative writers should undergo at some time in their careers'.[6] Even while she was working on the revised edition of *A Weekend with Claude*, Beryl was planning a departure from the slim, semi-autobiographical novels on which she'd made her name. In an interview with her local newspaper, she revealed that she had started work on a novel that would tell the story of the nineteenth-century headmaster and classical scholar, the Reverend John Selby Watson, who had murdered his wife in 1871: 'It won't be what they call "faction", it will be more historical than that. I've done a lot of research into the case and the period.'[7] The result, *Watson's Apology*, was clearly a forerunner of her later work, a novel in which an intimate personal drama was set against the backdrop of a larger historical event or period, but it was also a novel that sparked off a personal drama of its own, one that almost saw Beryl breaking with Colin and Duckworth for good.

———

Beryl's affair with Colin had inevitably had consequences for her personal and social life, but it would also have a considerable impact on her work as a writer. In the first instance the secrecy that necessarily surrounded the relationship meant that a whole area of her emotional life which she had previously mined for her fiction, and which she would frequently assert was the wellspring of the creative impulse, was now practically out of bounds, or at the very least had to be treated in an oblique and opaque manner. However much the real-life Alan differed from his fictional representation in *Sweet William*, or however many liberties Beryl might have taken with Clive's personality in her depiction of him as Edward in *Injury Time*, they remained distinctly recognizable to those who knew them. Such an act of literary representation could not be considered in a relationship with as potentially explosive consequences as her affair with Colin. In the short term, Beryl's decision to revise *A Weekend with Claude* obviated the difficulty of trying to write a contemporary novel along the lines of *Injury Time* or *Winter Garden* that might allude to her personal life, but over the longer term this form of self-censorship would present a problem that somehow had to be overcome.

In the meantime she found another solution. When writing *Young Adolf* she had used her recollections of her father and the things he had told her about the Liverpool of his youth as a framework for her depiction of the proto-Führer. She realized that the same technique might apply when it came to writing about John Selby Watson: 'The interesting thing I've found is that the more you think about history, the more you realise that things are not so different after all. In this kind of book I'll still use people I know as bases for the characters, but I'll just move them back in time a bit. It's interesting to see how well they fit into another time.'[8]

The idea of writing about Watson had not originally been Beryl's. In the April/May issue of the *London Magazine* for 1979, Mervyn Horder had published an article about the Watson case, covering his conviction for murder, his sentence to be hanged, the subsequent press campaign for clemency, and his eventual death in prison in 1884. Colin was so taken with the story,[9] which seemed to provide ample scope for an ironic treatment of the battle of the sexes, that he not only encouraged Beryl to write a novel about it, he also assisted her in her research, enquiring in libraries or archives for relevant material.

Although Beryl never saw things from an academic perspective, her enthusiasm for the subject allowed her to share Colin's literary passions in a way that Anna clearly didn't. Beryl even persuaded him to accompany her in some hands-on research:

In pursuit of Watson's past we tracked down the resting place of his butchered wife in Tooting Bec cemetery. At no time did Colin have any sympathy for the battered Mrs W. Ever the publisher, he would groan, 'What a tragedy! All the poor devil wanted to do was get on with his *Life of the Popes.*' The gates were locked when we arrived . . . but I managed to jump over the railings and find a ladder for Colin to ascend. Athletic though he was, being a chap he was sensibly anxious of hurdling spikes . . . We didn't know that we'd been spotted by a caretaker/gravedigger who had promptly rung the police.[10]

The incident was picked up by the gossip column in the *Evening Standard*, though Colin's participation was tactfully airbrushed out:

Difficult moment for Beryl Bainbridge. She was just leaping over the railings into Lambeth Cemetery at around seven one evening when she was spotted by a passing security man. She assures me she utterly charmed the man by explaining that she was a novelist in search of background for her next book about a Victorian clergyman who murdered his wife.

'I've only just started this research and got carried away tramping around looking at this man's house and combing the libraries for information. In the evening I tootled off to find the cemetery closed so I legged it over the railings.'[11]

In hindsight, Anna's response to the escapade was extraordinary, seeming to hint at a knowledge of the affair and a simultaneous desire to turn a blind eye to it: 'There was the occasion when she and my husband were apprehended trespassing in a cemetery. I think they were researching epitaphs but I'm not clear about the details, for when they tried to tell me about it I closed my ears. I have the same reaction when my children try to explain their various misdemeanours. On the whole I prefer to be left in ignorance. Life is difficult enough already.'[12]

Beryl had been thinking about and planning the novel since the autumn of 1980. Writing it, however, turned out to be harder than she imagined. While Colin's close involvement had been beneficial and even fun at the start, as the novel progressed she felt daunted by his expectations, and increasingly worried that her portrayal of Watson and his wife had too much of Colin and Anna in it.

When, in 1983, Beryl was invited to take part in Anthony Clare's series of televised interviews, *Motives*, an early incarnation of his subsequent radio programme *In the Psychiatrist's Chair*, one of the first things she admitted was that she was finding the novel difficult to write: 'Actually to be honest, I've got a kind of a small writing block at the moment.'[13]

As she approached the end of the book her confidence in it seemed to sag:

Dear Colin,
I've done a lot of work on Watson and I think its stronger. I'm a bit confused about chapters. You did say you'd ring on Tuesday, but I expect you forgot – so I've done the chapters as best I can.
    Love, Beryl xx[14]

It was around this time that Michael Holroyd happened to call round to Albert Street and, noticing the manuscript lying on the table, he asked what it was. 'That's my new novel,' she replied, 'for what it's worth.' He asked whether he could take it home. After reading it he immediately rang to say it was the best thing she had done. Following the book's publication Beryl would say that if it hadn't been for him she would never have finished it.

Finally, on 6 June 1984, nearly four years after she had first started working on the project, she scribbled in her diary: 'Finished Watson.' But this wasn't the end of her problems with the book. A meeting round at Gloucester Crescent to discuss the manuscript degenerated into a slanging match. Colin's initial response to the book had not been positive, and Beryl was annoyed by his seemingly intrusive and pedantic editing – he had crossed out lines of dialogue and changed occurrences of 'he' to 'Watson' and 'Watson' to 'he' – and she told him he had no right to alter what she had written. Colin, seeing in Beryl's depiction of the pathetic, emotionally stunted Watson a veiled critique of himself, lost his temper. He accused her of turning Watson into a caricature[15] and began kicking the manuscript around the room. Picking it up, Beryl told him: 'If that's what you think then you can just fuck off.'[16]

Shortly afterwards she flew to New York on a publicity tour of America. Still angry, she wrote to Michael Holroyd to tell him what had happened the day before she left. The disagreement over *Watson's*

Apology was the first serious rift she'd had with Colin, and it upset her so much she even considered the possibility of leaving Duckworth:

> I was called round on the Wed to see to a semi-colon and he was grouchy etc. Also the manuscript wasn't available. He said I could'nt see it. I sent the au pair to get it (while he was at lunch) and she had a fight with the office. It was something of a misunderstanding but I lost my temper yet again and stormed out . . . but I stopped at the pub on the way, then rang [him] an hour later and said I hadn't signed any contract and was withdrawing the book. He said, 'Fine,' and slammed the phone down. When I had sobered up I waited till 9 at night and spoke first to Anna who was like whipped cream and then to himself who said he'd sent it off and when he saw it in proof he was sure he would like it and that he was sorry etc. He would ring me in the morning to say good-bye. Needless to say he didn't. He said the proofs would be ready in 10 days. So that's that . . . I don't think I've ever spent one day in such a bad temper in the whole of my life, let alone 5 days, and I must say it was an eye-opener, and had the effect of making me sleep without seditives from the time I got on the plane till I got off 9 hours later.
>
> I don't know what to do when I come back. I have got to fix up my life in some way. In many ways I wish I had quit Duckworths. I find the whole buisness rather alarming and had'nt (until now) seen the extent of the game between the 2 of them. I always knew I coluded etc, but I had'nt quite grasped the depth of it. Still don't, really.[17]

By the time she returned from America *Watson's Apology* was already in proof, and things began to calm down between them. Despite the flare-up and Colin's initial hostility, Beryl recognized that his input and enthusiasm, his assistance in areas such as classical references where her knowledge was weak, and his careful copy-editing of the text, had helped to improve the book. On the top page of her final proof, beneath one or two last-minute corrections, she held out an olive branch of sorts: 'Thank you for getting it ready so well and so quickly. Everything seems fine except for above. Pity you don't like it. Love, Beryl.' On 2 October, just two days before the book's official publication date, a contract was finally signed.

Colin may have had his reasons for feeling disappointed with the book, but other friends saw it as a striking achievement. Michael Holroyd thought it extraordinary, full of sadness and tragedy, and it became his favourite of all her novels.[18] Brian Masters, who was then working on a biography of the serial killer Dennis Nilsen, read it with such terror and amazement at her perception of the human condition that he felt weak: 'You paint a dark, true picture, but you do it with the heart. One learns more from *Watson's Apology* than from any chapter on philosophy.'[19]

The press response to *Watson's Apology* was also overwhelmingly positive. In *The Spectator* Harriet Waugh evoked comparisons with Muriel Spark and concluded: '*Watson's Apology* is Beryl Bainbridge on top form and no other novel has given me as much pleasure in the last six months.'[20] Humphrey Carpenter was equally enthusiastic: 'The result is that old cliché "a small masterpiece" – small-scale in that Bainbridge presents the story for what it is and doesn't try to enlarge on its tragic possibilities, masterly by virtue of the credibility of her reconstruction of the contradictory emotions that accompany the case.' Carpenter was particularly struck by the presentation of Watson's relationship with his wife: 'The marriage was in many ways a failure from the start. Neither partner was capable of achieving love, though both wanted affection. What the book succeeds in showing is the element of failure in all relationships.'[21]

Aside from her 'small writing block', there was another reason for Beryl's delay in finishing *Watson's Apology*: work on the television series *English Journey*. With the fiftieth anniversary of J. B. Priestley's book drawing near – *English Journey* had originally been published in 1934 – the BBC had approached Beryl in 1983 about presenting a documentary series that would retrace his route around Britain. The plan was for eight forty-minute programmes, together with a book tie-in, which would be a co-production between Duckworth and BBC Publications.

The project necessitated a considerable amount of time-consuming travel. Between August and the end of October 1983 Beryl's hectic filming schedule included Southampton, Salisbury, Milton Keynes, Birmingham, Bradford, Liverpool, Manchester and Newcastle. Presenting a television programme was a fresh departure for Beryl. It would introduce her to a new, much larger audience, most of whom were unfamiliar with the tragi-comic novels by which she was known among the London literary set.

Beryl faced a number of challenges in writing and presenting the series, not least of which was dealing with Jimmy Dewar, the executive producer. For one thing she found his physical resemblance to Colin distracting. Dewar had chosen her because he thought she was an admirable eccentric, and initially at least he treated her in a high-handed and condescending manner. When Beryl said she wanted to end the journey in a field above a nuclear bunker in Thetford, he dismissed her suggestion with the words, 'Yes, yes, dear, what a cheap idea.' To make matters worse, Dewar's marriage seemed to be on the point of breaking up and his wife was finding it difficult to cope. The emotional fallout from this tension-inducing situation seeped over into work meetings. Beryl described one particularly fraught occasion to Michael:

> Things are getting v. interesting here. Imagine the scene – me, the camera man, director, assistant, sound man, PA etc, plus the head of TV in Bristol, the immortal <u>Jimmy</u>. A man <u>so</u> like he who shall be nameless as to defy description. And tonight he arrives back with his wife who is having a nervous breakdown, and it becomes obvious why – he has caused it, even she can't speak as she's so cut-up, and he attacks me because I disagree with him. His wife starts to cry. The crew tip-toe out. Me and the director are left. It is a very rum do. If only you had been here to witness the scene. I cannot write it down as I am totally incoherent.
>
> I have been on the road now for months, still covered in mud. I come home on the 1st Nov to write the bleeding thing. He who shall be nameless seems alright – though the novel [*Watson's Apology*] has never been mentioned again. I don't think this is a good year. Some upheaval is happening in me. I am in Lincoln I think, or maybe Hull. Tomorrow I'm up a tower, bellringing, and then to Norwich to Malcolm Bradbury or maybe thats in Milton Keynes. Two days ago I was on a beach somewhere picking coal, and discussing the cod war somewhere. I can hear the wife sobbing through the wall. Dear God.[22]

The early months of 1984 were interspersed with frequent trips to the BBC studios in Bristol, to assist with editing and dubbing, and writing the text for the book. After handing in the manuscript, Beryl told Colin: 'I'm glad you are pleased with the book and I hope it does well for both of us. I think we deserve it – you for being a good publisher, and me for having the sense to know it.'[23]

Before the series aired, Beryl had lunch with the ageing Priestley and his wife, Jacquetta Hawkes. It wasn't an entirely satisfactory occasion – Priestley's deafness and his bluff manner made conversation difficult and misunderstandings frequent:

> When we were alone for a few minutes, I said to him: 'It's confusing, isn't it . . . this television business?' He said, 'What?' a shade tetchily, and beckoned me to sit closer to him. 'What are you on about?'
> I didn't want to shout, so I wrote on the back of my chequebook, 'I'm a bit in the dark, too,' and showed it to him. He looked down at it, baffled, and at that moment people came back into the room, and I snatched the chequebook away. God knows what he made of it.[24]

The programmes, which ran from 26 March to 21 May 1984 on BBC2, divided public opinion and the letters page of the *Radio Times* was initially swamped by a storm of protest: 'Beryl Bainbridge shows neither the verbal technique of an interviewer nor any descriptive ability,' one viewer complained, while another felt she 'lacked both personality and enthusiasm'. A third took her to task for the unreliability of her information: 'After her visit to Salisbury I began to wonder how long she spent there; I am now rather sceptical about the accuracy of the rest of her journey.'[25]

Those who doubted Beryl's suitability as a presenter of such a programme had a certain point. In the same way that she was not an academic, she was not adept at serious political or social analysis. One of her ideas for solving unemployment, which she put forward in all seriousness to a slightly dumbfounded Terry Waite a few years later, was to reopen the shipyards of Liverpool and Newcastle and start building ships again – not for use, but as a job-creation scheme: 'You could build a ship one year and take it apart the next year and start all over again.'[26]

Such an approach to the economic problems facing Mrs Thatcher's Britain at the time – unemployment was running at over three million – was hardly likely to satisfy anyone looking for a politically astute commentary: 'Good writers are not necessarily competent reporters', as the literary editor of *The New York Times* Anatole Broyard put it in a withering review, 'there's something intrinsically absurd about a highly regarded author of 10 novels describing a machine that makes cigarettes, or a chocolate factory.'[27]

But if political analysis wasn't Beryl's strong point, people, their relationships and how they lived their lives, were. She had an easy familiarity with people across all classes, and her sympathetic tone, the fact that she never came across as condescending, endeared her to her interviewees. Perhaps the most telling moment of the whole series was in Liverpool, when she went back to her old house in Huskisson Street, which was now a boarded-up crumbling ruin. Visibly moved, her voice cracking with emotion, she picked her way through the backyard and found one of her old dining chairs rotting among the rubble.

As the series progressed, the number of her supporters soon outweighed that of her detractors, and also drew praise from those within the BBC. The controller of BBC2 wrote to tell Dewar that it had been a 'totally rewarding series' and Roger Mills, the executive producer of *Forty Minutes*, considered the programmes to be 'witty, intelligent and perceptive . . . the best networked documentary series ever to come out of the regions'.[28]

The following year Dewar proposed a companion series to *English Journey*, again with Beryl as presenter, and they met to discuss ideas. During the course of *English Journey* Beryl had been struck by the differences she saw between the north and the south. In her outline for the project, provisionally entitled 'Living with Ourselves', she recalled Harold Macmillan's warning from 1962 about Britain becoming two nations, 'a poor north and a rich and overcrowded south', and decided to make this the focus of the series: 'I want to find out through the medium of television what the differences are, if any, between the people of the north and the south . . . in an attempt to confirm or refute the suppositions of Macmillan's speech.'[29] The idea was to do this almost literally, in a series of programmes that would concentrate on six families, three in the north and three in the south.

Once again the schedule was intensive, and between August and October principal shooting was completed in the six locations, Hastings, Barnsley, Liverpool, Birmingham, Northumberland and Hampshire. 'I have no idea where you are,' she wrote from Barnsley to her friend Psiche, 'and even less where I am. I'm among brass bands and miners, being frightfully militant on film and defending Arthur Scargill. You'd be proud. I've been in Oxford, Liverpool and now here, among some lovely families. I come home in another week or so and then go to Hastings or Northumberland or both.'[30]

Working with Dewar had not got any easier since the previous year, and his behaviour seemed to be a reaction to the death of his wife. Two weeks into the run of *English Journey*, she had committed suicide by throwing herself off Clifton suspension bridge. Jimmy was now drinking heavily and had developed something of a crush on Beryl. Consequently, she had to spend her time in between shooting trying to fend him off, as she reported to Anna midway through the filming:

> Darling Anna: Went for a walk at six this morning because I had a hangover from last night. Bit difficult being with Jimmy. He's very proper and all that, but its like being perpetually bathed in a sweat of adoration – jolly boring. He's nervous of me till opening time (mid-day) then maudlin till opening time in the evening, then over the top with excitement until midnight . . . Still, for some reason he's scared of me, so its all right.
>
> Thinking of death a lot at the moment because I'm always in a car with our Jim and he's usually pissed out of his mind.[31]

Unlike words, which Beryl could endlessly move around and manipulate to achieve the dramatic effect she wanted, the raw material of her documentaries – people – were not so compliant:

> It's so frustrating – you do an interview with some total nonentity who can't get a word out, and then as soon as you're off the air they tell you the story of their real life and its stuffed with drama and intrigue. One lady says she's visited at night by a ghost in a raincoat, a sort of spiritual flasher. She's very serious about it, and her husband says its causing a rift between them, but I mustn't mention it on the tele, because her boss wouldn't like it. I'm off in a minuet to go a walk with the accountant whose wife has had cancer. We're to talk about the differences between north and south but he only says things like 'I've nowt to say, Beryl', so I'm not hopeful.

Both the series, now titled *Forever England*, which ran from 7 May to 18 June 1986, and the book, published in April the following year, elicited a more muted, less partisan response than *English Journey*. 'It's a modest book,' as Bea Campbell noted in her review, picking up on the strengths and weaknesses of this kind of reportage: 'It doesn't pretend to engage with the problems of power, or economics, or politics. And it's forever forgiving. You might not share her pessimism or her nostalgia, but as an anthology of "common-sense" it makes strangers seem familiar. And that's what Beryl Bainbridge is good at.'[32]

Colin's handling of *Watson's Apology* wasn't Beryl's only cause of discontent. For the last few years she had been paying what she considered 'huge sums' in tax, and despite the high amounts she was earning on paper, she still seemed to be having money troubles. Following the publication of *Watson's Apology*, she complained about the situation to Colin: 'After twelve books I still can't pay my bills,' she told him. 'I'm not blaming you, I'm simply saying I need help or advice or something, to stop me feeling so worried.'[33]

In some senses the problem could be said to go back to Beryl's time at Hutchinson. Her inability to cope with the irregular payments involved in being an author during this period had left her feeling hard done by, resentful of publisher and agent alike. This residue of distrust over money matters had influenced her financial arrangements with Duckworth from the very beginning.

When Beryl first started at Duckworth the firm was in the process of re-establishing itself in its new incarnation, and money, including that for advances, was tight. As *Harriet Said* was the first new novel Duckworth had published in years and as Beryl was an unknown commercial quantity, the idea for her to work as a clerk in the company while she prepared the book for publication, rather than pay her an advance, had seemed a reasonable compromise.

After the publication of *Harriet Said* this evolved into a mutual agreement run on similar lines. In lieu of the more usual form of financial arrangement between publisher and author – an advance before publication which was then paid back from royalties on sales – Colin and Beryl agreed that Duckworth would pay her a standing order for a fixed amount every month, giving her a secure income, rather than the variable uncertainties of the advance system. All she had to do was produce a novel a year. This suited Beryl and for the first few years it seemed to work: the regular income provided a level of stability that enabled her to write, and her critical and commercial success repaid Duckworth for their original outlay in the system. 'It was a marvellous idea,' Beryl said. 'It stopped me getting too euphoric over royalty cheques and spending all I had.'[34]

During this early period Colin had also effectively acted as a literary agent for Beryl's novels (while Jenne Casarotto at Douglas Rae Management handled television and film rights). Despite the conflict of interest this presented, he had been efficacious in promoting her work internationally and pushing for higher advances for translations and paperback rights. Indeed, it was in his interest to get the best deal he could, as paperback advances were shared between Duckworth and the author.

As Beryl became more successful her financial arrangements grew more complex and more difficult to keep tabs on. In 1978 she wrote to Colin with a list of petty grievances: she couldn't understand the Duckworth statements, some of the sales figures seemed to be missing, and she hadn't received an amended contract that was due: 'I am also worried about VAT, whatever the bleeding thing is, and though I know its my problem I just feel its all too much to bother about. I must get everything put straight. Clive doesn't seem to be able to, and you and I have these turgid discussions which never amount to anything.' Feeling she needed someone outside of Duckworth to handle her literary affairs, she told Colin: 'I've decided to move everything to Jenne Casarotto in the hopes that she will sort it out.'[35]

But this didn't produce quite the results Beryl was hoping for: relations between Colin and Jenne don't seem to have been particularly warm and a repeated theme of the correspondence between them was Colin's tardy responses to her letters. In April 1979 Jenne had written to him about Beryl's earnings, demanding information that needed clarifying so that Beryl could be registered for VAT and her accountant could determine what was eligible for which tax year.[36] Six months later, after several letters urging him to respond, she still hadn't received a reply: 'I am now extremely perturbed about the lack of communication from you on various matters. Despite letters from me, promises from you to rectify the situation, and now untaken telephone calls from me, nothing has happened. We simply cannot continue to operate this way.'[37] Although such delays probably had little effect on the Inland Revenue they gave Beryl the impression that Colin was being uncooperative or inefficient in dealing with the situation.

Between 1978 and 1979 Beryl's income nearly doubled, as it did the following year. But with the ongoing confusion over Duckworth's financial statements Beryl found it difficult to work out how much she was earning and, equally importantly, how much she should put aside to cover her tax bills. These turned out to be much higher than she expected and she struggled to find the money to pay them.

In 1982 she moved to a new accountant, Malcolm Gunn, who gradually began sorting out her finances and found that she now owed over £8,500 in tax, including nearly £2,000 in interest charges for late payment. Beryl had to use most of the money she earned from presenting *English Journey* to pay this off in December 1983 and July 1984, but by then she was due to pay another £8,000 in tax for the current tax year, money that she no longer had. In September 1984 she was obliged to borrow £5,000 from Philip and Psiche Hughes in order to help clear her outstanding debt.[38]

Desperate about the financial mess she was in, she wrote to Michael Holroyd for advice, hinting that her inability to deal with it effectively was linked to her feelings for Colin: 'I do wish I could get my life sorted out satisfactorily – a lot of the time it all seems absolutely senseless. I shall sort this tax business out and maybe in doing so I shall sort the other, more pressing problem out once and for all. I feel totally imprisoned in something of my own making, a web of intrigue and fantasy and obcession. I despise myself for it but feel powerless. I don't know where to turn when I feel like this.'[39]

Yet there was no need for things to have reached this state, at least as far as money was concerned. Throughout the 1980s Beryl's income averaged over £30,000 a year, three times the national average. So why were her finances in such poor shape? Confusion and inefficiencies in the Duckworth accounting department didn't help matters, but in truth the situation was the result of two factors, the first being the informal and non-standard arrangements by which Beryl was paid and which she herself had agreed to.

The advance for *English Journey* was a case in point. In December 1984 Beryl asked Jenne to press Duckworth for a supposedly outstanding advance, but Colin had to remind her that she'd agreed to a convoluted scheme to get more money out of the BBC:

Jenne has been on to us about the remainder of the advance 'due' for *English Journey*. You have so far been paid £6,666.66 for this book, of which £5,000 was contributed by BBC Publications and £1,666.66 by us. The contract stipulated a total advance of £10,000, but the reason we didn't pay you the remaining £3,333.33 was that you and I had agreed that we needn't. As it was a joint publication, the only way we had been able to get the BBC to stump up a large advance was for us to appear to be paying a large amount ourselves. I managed to get the overall figure to £10,000 (after Jenne had failed to do so) and as the BBC had to see the author's contract that figure had to be in it.[40]

Even if carried out with the ostensible intention of helping the author, such ethically dubious arrangements were counter-productive and made accounting difficult: what figure would be used on royalty statements, for example: the amount listed in the contract or the amount she'd actually been paid? In the end Colin conceded to her agent that 'in view of the complexity of Beryl's contracts'[41] it would perhaps be simpler if he paid the outstanding £3,333 after all.

The non-standard system of standing orders that had worked so well at the beginning also became a major part of the problem, as it was not well adapted to large swings in earnings. In the early days Duckworth had effectively subsidized Beryl to write, the standing orders being paid out before receipts from book sales and paperback rights came in. But as Beryl's commercial standing grew, the pendulum swung the other way: at one point in 1981 she had been told she was owed £18,000.[42] Duckworth had simply held on to the money, like a bank, paying out her standing orders as agreed and seeing any excess as a reserve out of which she would be paid in the future. Over time, the standing orders were increased to compensate and continued even after Beryl's yearly output of novels stopped in 1981, with the result that by the end of 1983 she was in the ridiculous situation of actually owing her publisher something in the region of £6,000.[43]

The second major factor in the increasingly volatile state of Beryl's finances was her own inexperience in dealing with money. During the 1970s and 1980s she had spent money as it came in rather than putting aside sufficient to cover her income tax, which at the time was levied at a rate of around 30 per cent. 'As I never knew what I was earning, and was in any case in receipt from Duckworth of more money than I had ever had in my life, it never bothered me,'[44] she told her agent.

Had things been less tense between Beryl and Colin in the wake of the furore over *Watson's Apology*, Beryl's financial affairs might have been resolved more amicably. As it was, her long-simmering resentments about money and what she regarded – not always fairly – as poor treatment by Duckworth, boiled over.

On 9 January 1985 Beryl's accountant told her she would be facing another large tax bill, and by coincidence Colin's letter responding to her query about the *English Journey* advance arrived the same day. Colin made the mistake of telling Beryl that her novels were hard to sell: 'Concerning *Watson* I have heard from the Little Brown agent that he does not think that the book is commercial in USA', he explained and added that 'translation offers haven't been good'.[45] Anxious about her tax and irritated by Colin's seemingly unconcerned attitude to her problem and his high-handed tone – 'Your calculation seems to offer confusion worse confounded', his letter began – she hastily arranged a meeting to discuss the matter with him at the Duckworth offices the next day.

The meeting, in which Colin again told her that her books were selling poorly, did not go well and ended in an argument. Beryl took his comments not just as a slight on the quality of her novels but also as a personal attack. Back in Albert Street – and almost certainly after a swig of whisky – she vented her anger to Colin in a letter that she had 'thrown'[46] through his window:

> You mentioned that *Sweet William* was something of a flop, as indeed were most of the others, and that the sheets piling up in the warehouse are costing you money in storage, so I suggest you pulp them. Nor should you bother to do another reprint of *Harriet*. As you also say that Fontana are disatisfied with the books and nobody wants to buy them, and as I know by George's statements that he too makes a loss, I begin to wonder if I shouldn't take up a different career, one which wouldn't cause so much aggravation and hardship to publishers in general. Unfortunately the contract has been signed with Fontana, and unfortunately I can't afford to return the money, otherwise in the mood I'm in I would certainly tell them I didn't want *Watson* to go into paperback or any of the other five titles. My heart bleeds for them when I think of the effort and cost that will go into their selling of them and how poor the returns will be . . .[47]

The follow-up to *English Journey* had just being mooted by the BBC and Beryl concluded her letter by hinting that if Colin didn't want it, she would take it elsewhere: 'If this new BBC series gets off the ground, plus book to go with it, then I will get in touch nearer the time to find out whether you might be interested in publishing it. Having told me to fuck off twice yesterday, something which I have had the feeling you've been actually saying, though not verbally, for some time, I shall do so, though I cannot pretend that I don't love you and Anna very much and that the whole thing saddens me greatly.'

Despite this peevish outburst, relations between them quickly returned to normal, and over the course of the next few months her financial situation was gradually straightened out. Part of this was the result of having moved to a new agent, Andrew Hewson of the John Johnson literary agency. Beryl had met him previously at a party a few years before for another of the authors he represented, Joseph Hansen, but Andrew had been particularly recommended to her by Leon Garfield. Beryl had come to the conclusion that Jenne wasn't dealing effectively enough with Colin, so after a meeting with Andrew on 22 January 1985, accompanied by Michael Holroyd for emotional support, she decided to leave Douglas Rae Management.

However, Beryl's habitual inability to confront awkward situations meant that while she had unofficially moved to Andrew in January, and had already begun sending him her correspondence with Duckworth, marked up with her spider-crawl handwriting to explain anomalies and errors, it would be nearly six months before she informed Jenne of her decision. 'I still haven't the nerve to tell her I've gone to you,' she confessed to Andrew in February, 'but will tell her next month when I've said I'll have lunch with her.'[48] At the end of the month she drafted a letter to Jenne citing a long list of grievances, and concluded by admitting that she wasn't an easy client:

> I went to you simply because I found it too embarrasing to ask Duckworth for money when I needed it. I always thought, and still do, that I was lucky to be published and particularly by them, and I hoped you would take over the odious buisness of asking for money. But after the first year or two you too forgot to ask for the royalty statements, and as I didn't know any money was due I took on more and more outside work to cover paying my bills.

To be fair to you I have always balked at you trying to get advances from Duckworth or from a publisher in the States other than George Braziller. It cannot have been very satisfying for you, and I think perhaps that is why you became a bit dispirited on my behalf. Also I don't think many people could ever deal with Colin unless with a sledge hammer when it comes to the Royalty statements.[49]

But at the last minute Beryl lost her nerve and didn't send the letter, perhaps feeling it was too critical. Only at the end of July did she gather up her courage to write again, though the reason she gave for moving to Andrew was hardly likely to have endeared her to Jenne: 'He seems to be able to handle Duckworth,' she told her, 'perhaps its because he's a fella.'[50]

Despite the move to the new agency, and the reasons behind it, Beryl limited Andrew's freedom to act on her behalf as far as Duckworth and her American publisher were concerned: 'I don't want advances from them (they can't afford it) unless I get absolutely broke. Nor do I really want to leave George [Braziller] ever. I do think one should be loyal, and I hate having given Jenne the push. I really do have a funny thing about money – I never think I deserve it, and what I want is someone to think ahead for me and persuade me that I do deserve it and that noone is being exploited.'[51]

Beryl's attitude to Duckworth and money would remain a contradictory one. After the standing orders were cancelled at the start of 1985 so that all amounts outstanding could be paid off, Colin offered to return to the standard set-up of advance and royalty: 'For future books you will be paid all subsidiary money when it comes in and we can also pay you advances if you want them,'[52] he told her. But Beryl declined and a few months later she returned to the system of standing orders, now set at £700 a month.

The resentment she felt over her treatment by Duckworth during this period would remain at the back of her mind, and would flare up again whenever she suspected the company, or rather Colin, of not acting fairly with her. After Colin's death Duckworth's poor treatment of her would become an accepted myth, in large part due to her repeated assertions in the press that Colin never printed more than 3,000 copies of her books and never paid her more than £2,000 for a novel – both of which were demonstrably untrue.[53] Beryl was incapable of realizing the damage she could do to other people's reputations by unguarded and inaccurate statements that were offered off the top of her head in order to make a dramatic point about herself.

Colin had justifiable reasons for feeling irritated by Beryl's complaints about lack of money. As the 1980s progressed it became increasingly clear that Duckworth was having financial problems of its own.

When Colin had told Beryl that her novels weren't selling particularly well he wasn't making a personal attack, but stating a simple, if inexplicable, fact. For Duckworth, the turning point was the decision to produce revised editions of Beryl's earlier work. Up to 1977 Beryl was Duckworth's leading commercial asset: her reputation in both critical and commercial terms had been growing year by year, and sales had been correspondingly marked by a steady increase.

With the increase in sales, the print run of her books had also increased: 2,600 in 1972 for *Harriet Said*, 4,000 in 1973 for *The Dressmaker*, 5,000 in 1974 for *The Bottle Factory Outing*, and 8,000 in 1975 for *Sweet William*. The initial print run for *Harriet Said* may seem laughably small in hindsight, considering the reception it received, but it was on such small margins that Duckworth had managed to survive. Prudence in not printing more than it could sell ensured that debts didn't spiral out of control.

Given the progressive momentum in Beryl's sales, Colin's decision in 1978 to increase the print run for *Young Adolf* to 10,000 was not a rash one. But despite healthy critical notices, the book didn't sell quite as well as it should have, leaving Duckworth with just under 5,000 unsold copies after the first year. This was a warning shot across the bows, yet it would not have been a problem if Beryl's next novel had continued on an upward curve. But the decision to follow up *Young Adolf* with a revised edition of *Another Part of the Wood*, as a quick way of producing a novel and allowing Beryl to concentrate on television work and on the film script of *Sweet William*, turned out to be a costly one.

Taking a gamble on *Another Part of the Wood*, Colin stuck with a print run of 10,000 copies. This time it was a more serious mistake: with sales of just over 2,300 copies in its first year, it not only left a considerable hole in his budget, it started to create problems in terms of storage.

Although Colin attempted to remedy the situation with subsequent books – *Winter Garden* was scaled back to 7,100 copies in 1980 – it still wasn't enough. Sales of *Winter Garden* were not even up to *Injury Time* levels, and the even poorer figures for *A Weekend with Claude*, despite a reduced print run of 5,400 copies, exacerbated what was now becoming a snowballing problem.

Reducing the print run of *Watson's Apology* to 4,000, the lowest since *The Bottle Factory Outing* in 1974, did little to help, and in any case such measures are always self-defeating: by definition the lower the print run, the more expensive each book becomes to produce, and profit margins are accordingly reduced. As if to rub salt into the wound, *Watson's Apology* actually did sell out of its initial print run, with the result that Colin was forced to print an extra 1,600 copies, but this simply incurred extra costs without any meaningful profit. Despite Beryl's high critical standing, her commercial stock seemed to have fallen. Inconceivably, by the early 1980s she had become a money loser rather than the spectacular moneymaker she had previously been.

The seriousness of the situation was compounded in no uncertain terms when Duckworth went into collaboration with the BBC to produce the books of her two television series, *English Journey* in 1984 and *Forever England* in 1986. Once again, despite the critical success of the series and the anticipated publicity that television exposure should bring, sales were disappointing. Worse still, the BBC had insisted on a print run of 15,000. It was hardly a surprise a few years later to find that both *English Journey* and *Forever England* had been remaindered, the only time Beryl's books had suffered such an indignity.

For many publishers, and for most people looking from outside, the deal with the BBC seemed like a good one – exposure on national television would surely guarantee higher sales. But despite the quality of the books they were producing, Duckworth was still a small operation, and it simply didn't have the marketing and distribution channels to reach the wider audiences generated by BBC publicity. Instead, the BBC joint productions became a millstone around its neck.

Duckworth made a loss on *English Journey*, which was compounded by a similar loss on another BBC joint production, *Orwell: The War Broadcasts*. By 1986 Duckworth owed the BBC so much that it was forced to use the advance on another joint edition – based on the forthcoming *Forever England* series – to pay off the outstanding debts it had already contracted.[54] Although there were many other factors that led to Duckworth's decline over the next five years, such losses were indicative of the difficulties small independent firms faced in a market that was increasingly coming to be dominated by aggressively commercial multinationals. By the end of the decade Colin was embroiled in what would become a disastrous sequence of financial deals aimed at keeping the firm afloat. But these would eventually, and almost inexorably, lead to Duckworth's demise and his own death, brought on by stress and anxiety.

If Beryl had hoped a session with Anthony Clare might cure her of writer's block, she was to be disappointed – at least as far as novels were concerned. There had been a four-year gap between her last two original novels, *Winter Garden* of 1980 and *Watson's Apology* of 1984, and as the decade wore on there was no sign of another novel, or even a desire to write one. Instead, it seemed as if Beryl preferred to turn her hand to any other literary form. Aside from her two non-fiction documentaries, she prepared a collection of previously published short stories, *Mum & Mr Armitage* – despite her dismissive contention that short stories were 'a waste of a good idea'[55] – and tidied up a piece of juvenilia, 'The Tragedy of Andrew Ledwistle and Martin Andromiky', which was published as *Filthy Lucre*. Neither did much to restore the critical momentum – and perhaps more crucially for Duckworth, the sales – of her best work of the 1970s.

This drift away from fiction looked set to continue. In June 1986 Andy McKillop, who had published Beryl's first novel in paperback while at Panther and was now the commissioning editor at William Collins, asked her whether she would be interested in writing a book on Liverpool, as part of a forthcoming series in which established authors would write about a city they had a close connection to. The book would be part history, part observation and part reminiscence, McKillop told her, offering a £15,000 advance.[56]

Worried that Colin might feel she was being poached by another publisher, Beryl asked Andrew what she should do, and he reassured her that it didn't compromise her option to write novels for Duckworth in the future. In any case, the money was too good to turn down and

Duckworth was hardly in a position to make a counter-offer 'given the precariousness of their finances'.[57] On 19 December 1986, therefore, she signed a contract for a book of around 100,000 words, provisionally entitled 'Liverpool', the manuscript of which was to be delivered by September the following year.

At the time it seemed like a good idea, but her enthusiasm for the book never took off. She began some initial research – reading James Picton's *Memorials of Liverpool* and Grace Wyndham Goldie's history of the Liverpool Repertory Theatre – but as the months passed Beryl still hadn't written anything and became increasingly anxious about the approaching deadline. She told Graham Greene about her dilemma and he wrote back with the admirably simple advice: 'Do give up Liverpool & write another novel.'[58]

TWENTY-NINE

Goodbye Mr Chips

> My thing about ageing was brought on by the realisation that
> it's now all over, and that I still 'love' you know who and that
> its still hopeless, also that we've damaged our children. Our
> parents harmed us . . . and we pass it on. I've started another
> novel. I go out a bit, I drink a lot. I live in the past – but then,
> I always did.[1]

ACTING ON GRAHAM GREENE'S advice was not as easy as it
sounded. Beryl had already taken the first third of Andy McKillop's
advance – amounting to £5,000 – and she wasn't in a position to pay
it back. The sense of financial obligation, on top of her already real, if
slightly neurotic, aversion to letting people down, made it seem impossible to get out of the contract, with the result that the book about
Liverpool, or rather her inability to write it, hung over her for the next
two years.

After the original September deadline had come and gone, Beryl
admitted to Andy McKillop that she was having difficulty – though in
typical fashion she told him, as a kind of token of good faith, she'd written fifty pages when in fact she hadn't written a word – and he agreed
to a year's extension. But it did no good. Lacking the desire to write it,
Beryl was plagued by writer's block and towards the end of 1988 she
backed out of the project and paid back the money.[2]

However, Beryl's research, particularly on the history of the Liverpool
Rep, had prompted the idea of a novel, or rather the return to an idea
she'd had two years previously. 'What I really want to do is write a novel
about Peter Pan and James Barrie, on whom I've gone nuts,' she had
told the *Literary Review* in 1986. 'It could be called something like
An Awfully Big Adventure – The Lost Boys has already been used. I love

the bit where Peter brings down a Mummy to the boys and one of them shoots her and says something like "Oh, Peter I've always wanted a Mummy, and now when you've brought one, I've shot her, Peter!", although God knows how I'm going to write a book that I can get that into. Perhaps I could set it in a rep company.'[3]

But while the idea for the novel gradually took shape in early 1988, there were other factors that got in the way of writing it. The deteriorating financial situation at Duckworth had led to an increasingly desperate search for books that might have a commercial appeal, and another non-fiction project was put forward. One of the packers at Duckworth had met a man who said he was the illegitimate son of the painter Walter Sickert, and had brought him round to Gloucester Crescent to see Colin. Joseph Sickert, as he called himself, had been the source for Stephen Knight's best-selling book *Jack the Ripper: The Final Solution*, in which the Ripper murders were alleged to have been carried out to cover up a secret marriage between Queen Victoria's grandson, then second in line to the throne, and a working-class Catholic girl. Sickert had subsequently retracted the story, saying it was a hoax, but now he said he wanted to reveal the truth behind the Ripper's identity and that he had documentary proof to back it up.

From the start the project had a dubious air about it: not only were there doubts whether Joseph Sickert was who he said he was – his real name was actually Joseph Gorman – but his far-fetched conspiracy theory involving Lord Randolph Churchill, Winston's father, seemed equally suspect. Nevertheless when Colin told Beryl about the story she became enthusiastic and it was suggested she should write a kind of biography: Sickert would recount his life story onto a tape-recorder, and she would then turn it into serviceable prose. Sickert accordingly turned up at Albert Street looking very much the bohemian, dressed in a fawn corduroy jacket, waistcoast and cravat, and with his moustaches twirled up at the end in flamboyant dandy fashion. The only thing that detracted from his striking appearance was the fact that he didn't have any teeth, which gave his speech the flabby tone of the dentureless. After the first recording session it quickly became apparent that it was a bad idea – Sickert had no ability to create a scene or invoke a sense of place and he seemed to have no memories of his own. Nor could he provide the documentation – a diary written by one of the police inspectors investigating the original Ripper murders – which he claimed proved his story. After a few sessions the whole idea was dropped.[4]

Since the beginning of 1987, Beryl had been writing a weekly column for the London *Evening Standard*. Coming on top of the increased exposure she'd received from the two BBC series, it would cement Beryl's new identity as a media personality, transforming her from a well-known figure within the narrow confines of the Camden Town literary set, to a writer with an audience of over a million Londoners.

The column for the *Standard* was well paid and not particularly onerous – Beryl could write it in a morning – giving her both a sense of financial security and the time to work on her novel. If her money anxieties didn't entirely go away – by now Duckworth had stopped paying her their standing order of £700 per month, effectively halving her income – journalism nevertheless allowed her to focus more on writing than on trying to earn a living through Duckworth.

By the end of January 1988 the overall structure of the novel was all but worked out, after an accident prompted the idea that would give the novel its original plot twist. According to one version of the story, Beryl had tripped over some books while drunk and banged her head. Slightly concussed, she had tried to use the phone but had kept getting through to the Speaking Clock.[5] This gave her the idea to make the novel's central character, Stella, the daughter of the woman behind the voice of the Speaking Clock.

But if finding a plot was relatively quick and easy, writing the novel wasn't, and during the course of 1988 she was plagued by writer's block. Beryl struggled to get the right tone, complaining that she'd written the opening page eleven times. Part of the problem was her decision to go back to a past she found it increasingly difficult to remember, as she told Tony Wilson in an interview the following year: 'I must be mad, I've gone back to Liverpool again. It's the most ridiculous thing to do. I can't remember who I was.'[6] Her mood was hardly improved when Colin sent a contract for the new novel, offering an advance of £100, which, as she angrily put it, 'wasn't worth the paper it was written on'.[7]

Nevertheless, *An Awfully Big Adventure* was well received by reviewers when it was published at the end of 1989, and importantly for

Duckworth, it also sold well. Many critics were impressed by how convincing its portrait of theatrical life was, but also by the economy and subtlety with which the various strands of the novel's plot and the psychology of its characters were woven together, like 'an intricate piece of emotional clockwork'.[8]

The success of the novel was sealed when it made the short list for the Booker Prize – the first of Beryl's books to be selected for over fifteen years. Welcome though the announcement was, at the time Beryl was more concerned about the row she'd had with Colin the night before, after he'd commented on her being drunk when he called round to Albert Street: 'I don't know what happened last night,' she told me, 'you should see the kitchen, it's a real mess. I think I must have been throwing things at him. There are shoes and papers all over the floor. I think I told him to piss off.'[9]

———

As Duckworth's financial situation worsened, Colin embarked on a series of what would prove to be disastrous business deals and partnerships in an attempt to save the firm from collapse. To give a full account of these complex financial arrangements, which invariably ended in either legal disputes or personal acrimony – or both – would take up too much space here. But the sequence of events has to be covered, as Beryl was an active participant in much of what went on, and it profoundly affected her personal and professional life at the time.

The beginning of the long and painful slide into the firm's eventual demise was Colin's meeting with Roger Shashoua, at the beginning of 1988. Shashoua was an Egyptian-born businessman from a well-to-do Jewish family who had 'made a fortune out of buying, developing and selling inventions and patents'[10] in America during the 1960s and 1970s. By the late 1980s, however, he was looking for a new business opportunity after being 'frozen out', as he put it, from the exhibition management group he had set up. Shashoua was captivated by Colin and saw in Duckworth not just an opportunity to publish a book he had written about himself, but, more damagingly, a chance to get a foothold in the publishing market. When Colin told him Duckworth was short of money, Shashoua seized his opportunity and offered to purchase a 45 per cent stake in the firm.

Beryl with Alan Sharp, c.1964.

Beryl and Rudi in 1966, with Iliff Simey (standing on left) and his wife and their son, at Coed Nant Gain, near Mold in North Wales, the setting for *Another Part of the Wood*. Austin is taking the photograph.

Beryl with Aaron, Jo-Jo and two-year-old Rudi in 1967. The painting in the background is of Stanley Haddon and Aaron. The portrait in the foreground is of Leah Davis.

Beryl with Austin, Jo-Jo and Rudi at 42 Albert Street in 1968.

Beryl with Harold Retler in Wanakena,
June 1968, during their trip across
America in a VW camper.

Beryl with Don McKinlay,
on the doorstep at Albert Street,
c. September 1968.

Graham Betts, Beryl, Jo-Jo, Pagan
Davies and Austin in the front garden
at Albert Street, c.1972.

Beryl with Michael Holroyd, who
she met on an Arts Council writers'
tour in March 1975.

LEFT: Beryl with
Joseph Hansen c.1975.

BELOW: Beryl with
Clive de Pass, c.1977.

Beryl with Neville the shop dummy in the study-cum-bedroom that occupied
the middle floor of 42 Albert Street. Neville was often seated in the window
to make it look as if there was a man in the house.

Colin Haycraft in the Duckworth offices at the Old Piano Factory, 1989.

Beryl in 1988, during the writing of *An Awfully Big Adventure*.

Beryl and Anna Haycraft at 22 Gloucester Crescent c. 1996.

Photo © Brendan King

Family group gathered outside 42 Albert Street to celebrate Beryl's birthday in 1989. From left: Charlie Russell, Jo-Jo, Aaron, Julie Gallagher, Beryl, Rebecca Hussey, Bertie Russell, Rudi, Mick Ford, Abby Ford, Rachel Ford.

Beryl and Brian Masters at a
Duckworth party in the Old Piano
Factory, Camden Town, 1990.

Bernice Rubens in the garden
of her Belsize Park flat in 1989.
Beryl was a frequent guest.

Beryl in 'The Laboratory', the room at the top of the house where she wrote, seated
at a child's desk. The word processor is a Logica VTS 2200 with twin 5½ inch
floppy disk drives, which she used from the early 1980s until 2005.

ABOVE: Beryl and the author during one of their weekly meetings to deal with the post, c. 2000.

BELOW: Beryl's gravestone at Highgate Cemetery. The statue of the little girl had featured in her garden.

ABOVE: A self-portrait which Beryl drew at the request of the owner of Books & Co, during a trip to New York.

BELOW: Beryl in June 2009 holding a dummy cigarette to stave off cravings, after being told to give up smoking.

At the time it seemed like a mutually beneficial partnership, with each playing to their own strengths, as Colin himself described it: 'I should stick to the publishing side, of which I had total control, and he would do the finances, which he would control. He knew nothing about books and I knew nothing about money, so there would be a perfect division of labour.'[11] But Shashoua's knowledge of business law far outstripped Colin's, and when he drew up an agreement proposing to increase the share capital Colin realized he had been outmanoeuvred. In a fatal move on Colin's part – he later admitted that he signed the agreement without consulting his solicitors – he sold sufficient shares to Shashoua to effectively give him a controlling interest in the company. Although Colin's financial difficulties were such that desperate remedies were called for in order to pay off his mounting debts, and technically he had Shashoua's assurance that the partnership could be dissolved if he became dissatisfied with the arrangement, it was still a risky move and proved to be a costly one.

From the start Beryl distrusted Shashoua, or 'Roger the Lodger' as she would call him, and was antipathetic to the ostentatious marketing schemes he tried to introduce at Duckworth, which he vaunted as a means of saving the firm but which in reality dragged it further into debt. She refused to interview Shashoua for the *Independent* or give him any publicity when Colin published his book, *The Paper Millionaire*. When, at the launch of Anna's novel *The Fly in the Ointment*, he took Beryl aside and tried to reassure her there would be sufficient money for her next novel, she told him bluntly: 'I don't want your dirty money.'[12]

Shashoua returned the feeling. When Colin brought him to Albert Street to discuss the situation at Duckworth, his first words to her were: 'I don't know why I'm wasting my time coming round to talk to you . . .'[13] He most probably had no idea who Beryl was and in any case would have regarded her, not without a certain justification, as completely unbusinesslike and unprofessional. Years later, when he came to write about his experiences in publishing, Beryl's name was not even mentioned.

Shashoua's penchant for flashy promotional events and marketing hype was the very antithesis of everything Colin and Duckworth stood for, and over the following year the relationship between them became increasingly strained. Things came to a head in September 1989, following the launch of one of Shashoua's new initiatives, held at great expense at the Hammersmith Palais, during the course of which Roger told Beryl: 'Colin doesn't pull his weight, he doesn't do anything, and if he doesn't knuckle down that's it, he's out.'[14]

A few days later a report of the event appeared in the *Evening Standard* which, rather than swallowing the line about Duckworth's rosy future, pointed out the fact that the firm was in 'financial straits'. A letter was fired off by Shashoua's ally, Jonathan Reuvid, threatening legal action if the comments weren't withdrawn. Reuvid went on to state that what he called the 'Duckworth Group' – Shashoua had registered variants of the company's name to give the appearance that the firm was expanding – now had five subsidiaries: alongside Gerald Duckworth itself there was Duckworth Production Ltd., Duckworth Investment Division, a Euro-Distribution division, and even a supposed Italian subsidiary, Editione Duckworth Italiana SRL.[15] All this fooled no one and in *The Times* Ned Sherrin ridiculed Shashoua's hubris: 'Today Duckworth – Tomorrow the World.'[16]

Colin, too, was unimpressed by Shashoua's costly and ineffective schemes to make money, and at a board meeting a week later on 21 September, he told Shashoua he was unhappy about his methods. Shashoua angrily called his bluff: 'That's it – if you want to take the company back then just give me the money. You've got seven days.'[17] The meeting was a fractious one: Shashoua's wife wrote to Colin that he had humiliated her husband in front of the other directors,[18] and Reuvid complained about the distasteful manner in which Colin had conducted proceedings.[19]

Shashoua's subsequent claim, published many years after Colin's death, that in his first year in charge Duckworth had made 'several hundred thousand pounds profit'[20] and that Colin told him this would ruin the company as authors would now ask for back royalties, is patently ludicrous. Several hundred thousand would have immediately cleared Duckworth's overdraft with enough left over to pay whatever royalties were outstanding several times over.

Colin now began to negotiate with Michael Estorick, the son of a wealthy art dealer, whose first novel he had published a few years earlier. Estorick was interested in getting more involved in the editorial side of publishing, so the opportunity to buy into Duckworth seemed a good one, and a deal was put forward in which Estorick would take over Roger's shares for a cash input of £500,000. There was a lot of to-ing and fro-ing over the next few days, with Colin unsure whether to trust Estorick or stick with Shashoua.

During these negotiations Beryl frequently acted as a go-between, fielding telephone calls from both: Estorick relayed messages to Colin through her, and Colin confided in her about his uncertainties regarding Estorick. Late one night after a bout of drinking, and wanting to offer Colin her support, she wrote him a simple statement saying she trusted him and that whatever he did she was behind him, and posted it through the door of the Duckworth offices.[21]

At the beginning of November a deal was done: 'Roger has given in – he's backing out. Of course Colin is still worried about Michael, but it's terrific news, isn't it?'[22] A new contract for *An Awfully Big Adventure* was produced and this time Colin offered a more respectable £10,000 advance.

In the first year of the new partnership Estorick's second novel *What Are Friends For* was published, a somewhat ironic title in the light of how quickly things turned sour and what would follow. One sticking point was Estorick's desire to have a larger editorial role on the fiction list, something that didn't go down well with Anna and was hardly improved by their mutual antipathy. Another investor in the firm, the Joseph Rowntree Reform Trust, a charitable organization set up by the Halifax-based confectionery giant, became equally dissatisfied with Colin, though for different reasons: Duckworth's financial situation didn't seem to be improving and profits were slow to materialize. In what inevitably seemed like a symbolic move, the firm, no longer able to afford the high business rates of Camden Town, was forced to exchange its iconic home for more prosaic premises in Hoxton Square in the East End.[23]

Unhappy at the return on its investment the Rowntree board sided with Estorick in blaming Colin's attitude and business methods. As John Jolliffe subsequently put it in his history of Duckworth: 'Relations between the two factions were almost as bad as could be, and at a board meeting on 26 November 1991 Estorick is minuted as having thrown a file at Colin and then having left the room in anger.'[24] A few months later Colin was unceremoniously fired and locked out of his own office.[25] Beryl hurriedly scribbled a note to her agent Andrew Hewson to tell him the news: 'C was sacked yesterday and given 48 hours to clear desk! I feel sick.'[26]

But Colin had factored in a safety clause when Estorick had bought Shashoua's shares, inserting an option to buy them back within a period of eighteen months from the date they were sold. Colin now took the gamble of exercising his option, and on informing Estorick's solicitors of this he was reinstated as ipso facto head of the firm.[27] The only problem was that with the deadline rapidly approaching, Colin had no money with which to buy back the shares.

———

It was around this period that Colin started giving extracurricular Latin lessons to Jo's two sons, Bertie and Charlie, and in order to encourage them Beryl decided to sit in too. In a notebook she used for writing out her Latin homework, its inside cover appropriately enough giving the complete conjugation of *amare* (*to love*), the ongoing drama with the Rowntree Trust was reflected in her exercises. Alongside the traditional phrases about Cato and Gaul that Beryl wrote out and tried to translate, there were others of her own invention, the import of which no doubt went over her grandsons' heads: 'The writer thinks of the publisher with love (*Scriba publicatori amorem multum*). Colin, you will defeat the Barbarians of Halifax (*Coline, Halifaxis barbaros superabis*). You will save the day by a stratagem (*Diem consilio servabis*).'[28]

All of which may have been bad Latin, but as a piece of fortune-telling it would turn out to be worse. One 'stratagem' that was considered was for Beryl to move to another publisher for what would amount to a 'transfer fee', the money being used to ease Duckworth's financial situation. (Anna had already left Duckworth for similar reasons, moving to Viking in 1990.) It was something Beryl discussed with Colin and which she asked her agent to make discreet enquiries about, even though she wasn't very enthusiastic: 'I don't really want to leave Duckworth – I have a gut feeling my creative whatsit depends on the sort of way they've always treated me. Perhaps I'm a masochist. I don't know. O dear.'[29]

Another 'stratagem' – the idea of using Beryl's house as security for a loan – would become one of the most contentious issues surrounding her financial dealings with Duckworth, with Beryl being portrayed as the victim and Colin as ruthlessly exploiting his emotional hold over her in an attempt to save his own skin. Needless to say, this is a gross distortion of what occurred.

The collateral idea was probably initiated by Stephen Hill, an investment banker who became involved with Duckworth around the time Colin was looking for an investor to replace Michael Estorick. Colin had initially asked Malcolm Hill to invest in the firm but he declined and suggested his brother Stephen instead, though he gave Colin a piece of warning advice: 'Take the money and say goodbye; things can become nasty.'[30] In any event, the idea arose shortly after Colin and Stephen met and it would be Stephen, not Colin, who would be the chief architect of the plan, which involved a consortium of guarantors and properties, including Colin and Anna, Colin's brother John, Beryl and Stephen Hill himself.

One of the main difficulties Colin faced was that the bank wouldn't lend him or the business any more money without further guarantees, and if Colin defaulted on the existing overdraft, which amounted to around £200,000, he stood to lose everything, house and business. The idea was therefore put forward that John and Beryl could use their secure financial positions to 'guarantee' a further loan to Duckworth until Stephen came up with the money to buy out Estorick and the Rowntree Trust. Everyone agreed that this was a good idea in theory, and Stephen set about putting the plan into action.

This was not the first time a bank loan, guaranteed by property, had been considered in order to keep Duckworth afloat. In April 1989 Roger Shashoua had told Colin that he needed some security for the money he was putting into the firm, but as there was already a large mortgage on Gloucester Crescent, a move was made to use the Haycrafts' cottage in Trefechan in Wales – or the 'Taj Mahal' as Beryl referred to it – as collateral instead. Roger drew up a form to this effect, but Colin, fearing it would mean losing everything if he defaulted, lost his nerve when it came to signing the form. He later told Beryl he ran out of the back exit and into the nearby pub, The Good Mixer. He started talking to a man at the bar but then burst into tears. At the time he thought he was having a nervous breakdown.[31]

When Beryl agreed to act as a guarantor she had no idea about the legal implications of such an arrangement, and that if Duckworth went bust she might be liable for their debts. Somewhat naively, she thought that guaranteeing a loan was like being a character witness – and who wouldn't be a character witness for a friend? When solicitors became involved and an agreement was drawn up, however, she was soon apprised of the dangers of what she'd innocently agreed to. In her Latin notebook she sketched out a number of questions to ask Colin the next time she saw him: 'Loan on houses. Would bank give money on it? or the full amount? For how long? What safe-guards?'[32]

Shortly afterwards, Beryl's solicitor, Tony Ellis, wrote to Stephen Hill to clarify the situation: 'When the matter of her property being offered as collateral was first discussed it was on the basis that her guarantee would be for a short term only and that she would then be released from it.'[33] But six months later the issue was still dragging on, only now Stephen seemed to be asking Beryl to invest directly in the company, and her solicitor wrote to Duckworth in no uncertain terms to disabuse them of the idea: 'Beryl Bainbridge has always made it clear from the outset that she would be prepared to be involved in an arrangement which would involve her house being used as collateral security for a short-term bridging loan . . . She is, I know, horrified that her offer to help with security for a bridging loan appears to have been interpreted as an offer to support an open-ended loan. I, as you know, have on several occasions both spoken to Stephen Hill and written to him to make Beryl's position clear.'[34]

Undaunted, Stephen wrote back to say that the Haycrafts were putting up 22 Gloucester Crescent as the first security (despite the fact that it was heavily mortgaged), together with their share in Duckworth, and that he and Beryl would commit to approximately £200,000 each. In addition, Anna and John Haycraft would be signing joint-and-several guarantees for £75,000 each. Stephen tried to sweeten the pill by saying that Beryl would be the first to be repaid.[35]

Aside from Stephen's seeming inability to take on board the plain statements that Beryl's solicitor was making about her involvement, there were worrying discrepancies in what was being stated to the various participants: Stephen told Beryl and her solicitor that the bank had agreed to a 'facility' for £400,000, but a letter to Stephen from the Bank of Ireland shows that he was negotiating a loan of £600,000, and despite Ellis's repeated insistence that Beryl's guarantee should last no more than three months, the bank was told it would be five years.[36]

Whether Ellis knew about the Bank of Ireland letter at the time isn't clear, but in any case he wasn't happy with the terms of the loan as Stephen had outlined them, and even less so by the fact that Stephen hadn't told him that the Rowntree Trust had applied for a court order preventing the transfer of Estorick's shares to Colin. His reply was brusque: 'It seems to me you are asking Beryl to pledge her property to secure borrowing by Colin Haycraft to purchase shares in Duckworth (shares probably substantially overpriced) the transfer of which, maybe, could not be registered into Colin Haycraft's name and which in turn he would therefore be unable to transfer to an investor. Unless Colin Haycraft made a lot of money (and I understand he has other substantial and pressing debts) Beryl would be locked into this arrangement for ever . . . It is not what she had in mind.'[37]

This should have been the end of it, and had Beryl left the matter in her solicitor's hands as everyone around her, including her agent and close friends, was urging her to do, it would have been. But now she unaccountably told Stephen that she might be able to raise £100,000 cash – perhaps thinking that it would get her out of committing her house. When Stephen wrote back to welcome this proposal she immediately took umbrage again:

> Dear Stephen,
> Re your letter of the 16th, and your delight at my suggestion that I could raise £100,000 privately. Naturally you're delighted – notwithstanding the fact that it would place me under a considerable financial burden. You mention something called a Convertible Loan Stock and a Current Yield, and though you rightly state I'm 'not into shares and those capitalistic thingies' there would be no necessity to convert my loan into shares, but my debt would be recorded in this fashion!!! You say 'don't worry about this aspect of things – it only means that my resultant debt would be a real debt payable by the company'. As a little woman, who should not worry her head about such abstruse matters, I'm sure you're in the right. As a fully solvent member of the human race (regrettably no thanks to Duckworth) I'm worried about this disreputable matter of a Convertible Loan Stock. With all due respect – bugger off![38]

Aside from her innate suspicion of financial deals, her animus was also fuelled by the vaguely insulting notion that her assets were more important to Duckworth than her reputation as a writer: 'Do you realise how this affects me!' she complained to Stephen in another letter, 'I've stuck by Duckworth thru thick and thin and in the end, when the chips are down, my house is of more value than my books . . . if Duckworth is really now into surviving and becoming a responsible company, I would have thought it might have valued the author.'[39]

The idea of the guaranteed loan was eventually dropped, but for Beryl the damage had been done. Although Stephen had been doing much of the pressuring – Beryl later referred to him as an 'awful bloke'[40] – she was justifiably angry with Colin for mixing up their personal relationship in what appeared to her to be a murky scheme in which she could potentially lose her house. Coming on top of her still-simmering resentment over the royalties and payments issue, it was hardly surprising that she gave free rein to her criticisms in outbursts suggesting that Colin had tried to get her to sign over her house.

When A. N. Wilson stated this in print in a portrait of Beryl written after her death, he was doing little more than repeating her own words, however partial or misleading they may have been. But his implication of actual financial impropriety on Colin's part was less well founded. Wilson's assertion that Beryl 'saw almost none' of the money Duckworth earned from her books is flatly contradicted by the figures she gave to her accountant of her Duckworth earnings. Nor did the 'house issue' spell the end of her relationship with Colin. Whatever she may have told Bernice Rubens, who urged her to break with him over the matter, Colin's visits to Albert Street, as evidenced by Beryl's diary, resumed shortly afterwards.

In private, Beryl's own assessment of the 'house issue' was slightly more nuanced. 'That buisness of the fall of Duckworth and my house being involved upset me terribly. Nobody, apart from my children, who . . . took the full force of drunken scenes and muttered threats that I wanted to die, realised quite how it affected me . . . I'm well aware that whatever it was that upset me had more to do with my own temprement – a need for approval – rather than outside forces, but the fact remains I was knocked sideways.'[41]

The anxiety that Beryl was feeling over financial matters at the time was undoubtedly compounded by a letter she received in August 1992 from an embarrassed Genevieve Cooper at the *Evening Standard*. It had been Cooper who had introduced Beryl as a columnist at the

Standard and now she had to tell her that the paper's new editor, Stewart Steven, was dropping her, and that the column she was currently writing would be her last.

On the bottom of the letter Beryl scribbled, for posterity's sake: 'Last column 2 days later. Bit of a shock seeing its my only source of income.'[42] This, like almost everything Beryl said about her finances, should not be taken literally. According to her tax form for that year, money from the *Evening Standard* articles actually represented less than a third of her total earnings, which amounted to nearly six times the national average.[43] As much of this figure was made up of advances and royalties on books, it was stretching the point considerably to accuse Duckworth of not contributing significantly to her income. If anything highlighted the difference between Beryl's perception of things and factual reality, it is her tax returns, which refute the derisory figures she would repeatedly claim to have earned from Duckworth, whether she was talking to close friends such as A. N. Wilson or to journalists. In these matters Beryl seemed to follow Mark Twain's advice to never let the facts get in the way of a good story.

After the collapse of the loan scheme, Stephen came up with the money by other means and at the last minute Estorick and the Rowntree Trust were ousted in what became known as the 'Boardroom Coup'. A press release was put out through Peter Carter-Ruck & Partners: 'Colin Haycraft, Chairman and Managing Director of Duckworth . . . announced shortly before 4.00pm on Monday 7 December 1992 that he had completed the purchase of the 38% shareholding formerly held in Duckworth by Mr Michael Estorick . . . Colin Haycraft now owns 72% of Duckworth.'[44] The event was marked by celebratory photographs taken on the roof of Hoxton Square. Ominously, John Jolliffe noted that on the day of the share transfer, described by one of the lawyers involved as 'a life shortening experience', Colin suffered a mild stroke.[45]

Whether by this stage anything could have really saved Duckworth is a moot point. It certainly seemed that nothing could save Colin. As if his financial situation wasn't bad enough, a few months earlier he had been careless enough to voice his thoughts about Rowntree in public, and was subsequently sued for libel. The damages awarded against him were considerable and coming on top of a Capital Gains tax bill his personal problems continued to mount. Two years later the legal bill was still hanging over his head, and he told his solicitor 'there seems to be little alternative to my going bankrupt'.[46]

The financial problems threatening to overtake Duckworth had consequences that went well beyond the world of publishing. If the firm went bankrupt it would be a disaster for the Haycrafts as a family, entailing the loss not only of the house in Camden that had become symbolic of a whole way of life, but also the cottage in Wales, which Anna increasingly used as a physical and psychological retreat from the more unpalatable realities of life in London.

Given the situation it was little wonder that tensions between Colin and Anna occasionally erupted into outright confrontation. Beryl recalled one evening at the Crescent during this period when Anna called Colin down from upstairs and began insulting him in front of her, telling him he was useless as a father and that the sooner he dropped dead the better.[47]

On another occasion shortly afterwards, she and Anna happened to meet Yolanta May, who suggested going for a meal. Thinking that if she got out of it she could see Colin instead, Beryl declined saying she felt ill; at which Yola said to Anna that they should go to the Crescent and pick up Colin, unwittingly undoing Beryl's plan and leaving her with no option but to go back to Albert Street on her own. The meal had not, however, been a success, and Yola rang Beryl the next day to tell her that Anna and Colin had had a blazing row in the middle of the restaurant: 'I thought they were going to kill each other.'[48]

This state of heightened tension also affected relations between Beryl and Anna. Beryl found Anna's attitude unsettling. She was unsure of the extent to which Anna knew about her affair with Colin or was colluding in it, and suspected she harboured lofty feelings of contempt for her. The fact that their friendship, underpinned as it was by a whole network of secrecy and lies, had to be conducted in public and was frequently the object of scrutiny by the media, only exacerbated the problem.

Some of these tensions surfaced when Beryl and Anna were invited to lecture on a British Council tour of Poland in May 1991, organized by Stoddard Martin, a friend of the Haycrafts who had taken a post as a lecturer at Lodz University. As Beryl refused to fly, they went by train, a punishing journey that took them to Warsaw, via the Hook of Holland, Berlin and Frankfurt: 'It was ghastly and it was my fault because I hate flying. Dehydrated, hungry and without matches, we travelled 30 hours by train and arrived looking worse than our passport photos.'[49]

Despite this, things began well enough. Anna and Beryl seemed like two naughty girls, and at a British Council reception that evening they got very drunk, Beryl especially, and started telling indelicate stories that were somewhat more shocking than the assembled dignitaries were used to.[50]

After Warsaw, they were driven to Gdansk, where they stayed at the Grand Hotel in Sopot, a huge building on the shore of the Baltic Sea that could count Adolf Hitler, Greta Garbo and Omar Sharif among its previous guests. Beryl and Anna were intrigued by the prostitutes who worked the hotel corridors and hoped – without much success – to be mistaken for one. When not involved in official lectures or functions they would spend time at the bohemian Actors' Club not far from the hotel, after which they returned to Krakow for the final leg, where they met up with Peter Conradi, a British Council-sponsored professor at Jagiellonian University.

Beryl and Anna spent their last evening in Conradi's tiny flat downing a litre of whisky he had been given by a friend, and having an uninterruptible row. As the whisky kicked in, Beryl started a systematic attack on Anna, ostensibly about her not pulling her weight as a speaker, but becoming more personal as it went on. 'I've never seen drinking on that scale, Homeric,' Conradi recalled, 'I had never witnessed an attack of that ferocity, or that went on so long. It felt like the harangue went on for an hour or longer . . . Anna bore the whole thing with an astonishing courage and stoicism.'[51]

The following day, sensing that Conradi had found the evening deeply uncomfortable, Anna tried to play it down, suggesting it was just an aspect of Beryl's rich and complex personality, or that it had been the result of the drink. But even at the time, Conradi sensed there was something deeper to it than that: 'I was certainly aware there was a complicated three-way relationship, how much that played into the situation I don't know. I've never quite witnessed this sort of sustained aggression between friends.'

In the course of her researches on James Barrie and *Peter Pan* for *An Awfully Big Adventure*, Beryl had been struck by a curious piece of information she found in Andrew Birkin's biography, *J. M. Barrie and the Lost Boys*. When the bodies of Captain Scott and his men were found frozen to death in the Antarctic in 1913, one of the last letters Scott wrote had been to Barrie. She began to wonder what it was that could have drawn an adventurer like Scott to Barrie, and this led to the idea of writing a novel that would tell the real story of the man behind the myth. The South Pole may have seemed like a big leap from the Playhouse in Liverpool, but Scott and his men had been on her mind for a number of years and during the 1980s Beryl had written that her favourite book was *The Worst Journey in the World* by Apsley Cherry-Garrard, 'the man who went with Scott to the Pole and brought back the eggs of the Emperor Penguin'.[52] After borrowing books on Captain Oates and Scott from the London Library, the new novel, which she initially called 'Poor Tom's Cold', began to take shape.[53]

There followed trips to the Royal Geographical Society and the Scott Polar Research Institute in Cambridge ('Full of hoary explorers with frost-bitten noses . . .'),[54] though her research wasn't always conducted along such conventional lines. For New Year 1991 she spent a few days by the sea at the house of a friend in Shingle Street, Suffolk, where, as she told Mervyn Horder, she indulged in a little imaginative role play:

> Last week I spent in a hut on a beach in Gt Yarmouth. The idea was to plod up and down the shore in me nightie clutching a digestive biscuit, but I gave up in thirty seconds flat. The cold was horrendous. The excursion was in the nature of research, as the new book is about me being Oates at the South Pole. My Dad (of course) is Captain Scott. Last night I dreamt the whole book, sort of, and woke thinking I need'nt do any more writing as it was already finished. What a disappointment.[55]

In fact at a very early stage she had already visualized the book's final scene. When Oates delivered his immortal line about 'just going outside', the others in the tent were surprised he could walk at all, as his feet were so badly frostbitten. Yet his body was never found, and to account for this Beryl imagined Oates had been led to his death by a vision of Queen Victoria and John Brown – she on her horse and he holding the bridle, as in the famous photograph – and that in his mind he had clung on to the tail of the horse and been dragged across the ice.[56]

The novel would take over a year and a half to complete. The reason for this was partly the practical difficulty of writing it, the fact that the five narrators were all men from different classes and spheres of life, not to mention the large amount of technical and historical material that needed to be assimilated.

Another reason was that Beryl had also begun working on a theatrical adaptation of *An Awfully Big Adventure*. After the book's publication, Ian Kellgren of the Liverpool Playhouse had contacted Beryl about the possibility of turning the book into a play. The idea seemed a good one to both sides: the Playhouse, which was itself going through a difficult period financially, saw it as a means of capitalizing on the novel's success, and Beryl had long wanted to write a stage play. During the early months of 1990 she went to Liverpool a number of times to discuss the changes that would be required to adapt the action of the novel to the stage, and by the autumn the script was finished.

The play was originally scheduled to open in March 1991, but in January the Playhouse, now facing bankruptcy, was granted an Administration Order and the production was cancelled, pending some financial workaround. After the administrators negotiated a grant from the Arts Council, the play opened a year later than planned on 11 March 1992, with a cast that featured Rodney Bewes as Uncle Vernon, Tim Woodward as O'Hara, David Allister as Potter, and Rudi, now twenty-six, in the role of Stella.

Beryl had immediately thought of Rudi for the role as she had been working as an actress for a number of years. However, the idea of playing her mother was not one that appealed to Rudi and initially she turned it down: 'I think she did so on the grounds that she didn't want to be linked to me,' as Beryl put it. But she encouraged Rudi to read through the part again after the play's deferment and eventually she agreed: 'If it had not been my mother, I might well have gone on saying no,' she explained at the time. 'But now, the more I read it, the more layered and deep and sad and funny I think it is; this is Beryl writing about herself as she thought she was then. But she's writing about it now, so it might not be her at all when she was that age, but the child inside her now.'[57]

After finishing the play, Beryl's work on the novel, now called *The Birthday Boys*, began again in earnest. When it was published in

September 1991, it became one of Beryl's most commercially successful novels to date, perhaps because it appealed to an audience already familiar with the Scott legend. To many, Beryl's most impressive feat had been the way she had so convincingly managed to get inside the heads of the men on the expedition, or as the reviewer in *The Tablet* put it: 'It is a man's book written by a woman.'[58] It was this aspect that particularly struck the former Regius Professor of Greek at Oxford, Hugh Lloyd-Jones, who wrote to Colin to tell him how much he enjoyed the book: 'I really think she has a touch of genius. How can a woman have understood those chaps – and all the things they had to do – so perfectly?'[59]

In hindsight, there was a certain inevitability about Colin's death. He had been exhibiting signs of stress for quite some time, and he and those around him were worried about the effects on his health. His first stroke in 1992 was a clear warning sign. But it was one he seemed unable to heed and a short time later Beryl described his agitated state after an argument with Stephen Hill: 'Last night he was in the sort of mood guaranteed to kill him (C, I mean) he was shouting his head off and going red in the face. I thought he'd have another stroke.'[60]

In February 1993 Colin complained of having difficulty breathing and Beryl paid for him to see a private doctor, who gave him an ECG and a capnograph, a diagnostic test to detect certain respiratory problems. But with no solution in sight to his financial problems, things looked ominous. A few months later, in August 1993, a second, more serious stroke followed, which led to him being admitted to University College Hospital, and for a time he had difficulty speaking.

For almost a year after Colin's release from hospital the ceaseless round of negotiations to stave off bankruptcy continued, though without much success. In June 1994 Colin told Stephen he was 'sinking fast' and a month later he wrote to Beryl telling her that Carter-Ruck had rejected his accountant's financial restructuring plan and that his debt over the libel action still stood.[61] In the midst of all this, to mark his election as president of the Classical Association, he devoted the early months of 1994 to writing an address, which he successfully delivered on 6 April at the University of Exeter, though a slight hint of the previous year's stroke was still detectable in his speech.

Despite the furore over the house issue, Beryl had continued seeing him throughout 1993 and 1994. According to her diary, in which she recorded her rendezvous with Colin using a secret code – a large asterisk above the date – their final meeting was on Tuesday 20 September 1994. On the Friday she went to the King's Lynn Festival, and it was there, the following day, that she received a telephone call to say Colin had just had another stroke and died. In a cruel piece of timing, a letter from him arrived on the Monday, which he had posted the day before he died, in which he sent her a copy of his speech to the Classical Association: 'Darling Beryl, here is the printed version of that dread address – expanded to ridiculous proportions. What do you think? It may be mad, but I hope not silly. Love Colin xxx'[62]

After the news of Colin's death broke, a number of close friends who knew about the affair wrote to Beryl to express their shock and to offer their sympathy. For Beryl it was doubly hard having to grieve in secret, her connection to him being unrecognized by the outside world. She was contacted by the *Independent* to write an obituary, but what she initially sent in was too overly emotional to be used:

Colin Haycraft . . . was abrasive, bloody minded, his own man, whatever that means. I find this extra-difficult to write, because I went to say goodbye to him this morning in the mortuary, and somehow he's standing over me, less icy cold than he was in that horrible little room in the bowels of UCH and he's telling me, get it right, that I can't use that word, that my sentance is clumsy, that my whole syntax is wrong. How do you tell other people who didn't know him, and for that matter, those who did, how important he was? He really was much loved, for his vunerability, heavily disguised, his formidable scholaship and his devastating wit.[63]

Despite the tensions and disagreements that had marked the last years of their relationship, Colin's death had a profound impact on Beryl's sense of her self. She saw it as marking the end of her sexual life and any hope she might have of long-term romantic companionship. When the affair began she had been in her forties – young enough that love affairs seemed neither ridiculous nor undignified to her. But at sixty-two she felt she was too old to expect or even hope for a physical relationship of that kind. If anyone tried to broach the topic she would close down the discussion with a brusque 'Oh I'm too old for all that now.'

A year after Colin's death Stoddard Martin put together a collection of reminiscences and recollections in his honour, including pieces by some of those who had known him best: George Weidenfeld, Francis King, Richard Brain, Brian McGuinness and Hugh Lloyd-Jones. Beryl's own piece was entitled 'Mr Chips', an allusion to James Hilton's 1934 sentimental novella *Goodbye, Mr Chips*, about a schoolteacher whose passion for Greek and Latin seems out of sync with his times, but who becomes a great educator after falling in love. In it, Beryl made the point that Colin was 'first and foremost a teacher of considerable power', not necessarily in the narrow formal sense of the Latin lessons, but through his example as a person, the fact that he 'never spoke down to those less educated than himself'. She described her early days round at the Crescent, sitting cross-legged on the floor, almost literally at his feet, and how he had served as her mentor in matters of language and literature. Although she could not, of course, admit to the true nature of their relationship, she nevertheless expressed what she felt, and her short tribute ended with an unequivocal declaration, hidden in plain sight, as it were: 'I loved him.'[64]

THIRTY

Celebrity

Dear Judith, I think life is just another cock-up, heroic but unplanned, much like poor old Scott going off with such hopes, such bravery, such stupendous, awful stubbornness in search of a mythical pole. All sorts of things have come from writing about him – inside me and from outside. Something to do with unfinished buisness. Did I ever talk about J. W. Dunne in the old days – that chap who thought that time was <u>always</u> – life going on forever, and always the same, that that one particular night in your kitchen in Liverpool is still happening. We are still sitting there, and you are still meeting Bobby for the first time, and we are all still sitting in the Frolich's sitting room eating that bloody awful german cake, and Aussie is still standing in the hall in Huskisson Street telling me he doesn't love me anymore.[1]

A FTER COLIN'S DEATH THERE seemed to be no reason to stay at Duckworth any longer. Beryl owed no debt of allegiance to Stephen Hill and so she told her agent Andrew Hewson to sound out some other publishers and try to get the best deal he could. During the brief period when she had considered leaving Duckworth in order to get a large enough advance to help pay off Colin's debts, she had come up with the idea of a series of three novels, one set during the Crimean War, one on the sinking of the *Titanic*, and another about Dr Johnson and Mrs Thrale, which she hoped would convince publishers to come up with some money.[2] It was this 'three-book deal' that Andrew now began to offer round, albeit secretly, as Beryl didn't want to attract publicity.

Not long after this, at the beginning of November 1994, Beryl received a letter from Robin Baird-Smith at Constable. Robin told her he'd been in discussions with Colin before his death and that their conversation had ranged from the idea of a merger between Duckworth and Constable, to Robin taking over from Colin at some point in the future. Hinting that 'various things are happening at Constable' and that he was considering a move to Duckworth, Robin asked whether they could meet up to 'talk about all this'.[3]

Two weeks later, Robin confided in her that he was planning to leave Constable and take over Colin's position at Duckworth, but he urged her to secrecy as negotiations were still ongoing. Having been Muriel Spark's editor at Constable, Robin had a considerable track record and to his mind a major part of the attraction of coming to Duckworth was the chance to work with Beryl, a writer he had long admired. That Beryl also represented a significant commercial factor in Duckworth's future survival was something Stephen Hill was only too aware of. His last words to Robin before giving him the job of managing director of Duckworth were 'Now make damn sure you do not lose Beryl Bainbridge.'[4]

When in due course Duckworth announced Robin's appointment everything seemed to him to be going to plan. But unbeknown to Robin, Andrew Hewson was in the final stages of negotiating a lucrative deal for Beryl to move to Viking. It was something of a shock for Robin, therefore, when Andrew wrote to him at the end of February 1995 to say that Beryl was leaving Duckworth. Andrew explained that both he and Beryl felt 'a clean break would be best for everyone',[5] and stressed that this was not a reflection on Robin's appointment. He regretted that Duckworth's announcement hadn't been made earlier, but the decision had now been taken. Beryl, too, regretted the way things had turned out, and she hastily sent Robin an embarrassed letter to explain her apparently deceptive behaviour:

Dearest Robin,
I expect by now Andrew H. has written to you. I don't have to tell you that our decision has nothing to do with you and everything to do with Stephen Hill.
    When Colin died and it looked as though Anna might loose her house, I asked Andrew to hold off until we knew which way Hill was going to jump. We then met, but I couldn't tell you what Andrew was

planning anymore than I could tell him about you, as I had promised both of you that I would not betray confidences. Now, however, it seems that the firm and Anna's house are saved. With you in charge I don't see how Duckworth can fail.

It is sad that I won't be with you at Duckworths, but Andrew has held off for years because of my affection for Colin and I trust absolutely in his judgement as to what is best for my future. I think he has also explained that my move will be very low-key. Noone needs to know for ages and even then it will be done without fuss.

Be confident and happy at Duckworths. You've made the right choice and whatever private feelings I may have about Hill, he does seem to be behaving very well. I wish you all the luck in the world.[6]

As a postscript, she gave an appraisal of the existing Duckworth staff – Deborah Blake, Ray Davies, William Haycraft (Colin and Anna's eldest son), Christine Halsey, and Colin's former secretary, Nicky – all of whom she recommended unreservedly. The only exceptions were her comments on Anna and Stephen Hill, though as Beryl was not in the habit of bad-mouthing people behind their backs, her doubts about them had to be read between the lines. Anna, she said, had 'a real genius for spotting and nurturing talent', but was 'not a copy editor'. In a hint at what she saw as Anna's lackadaisical approach to work, Beryl explained that she was 'deeply depressed at the moment and will need pushing if she's to get down to the buisness of reading manuscripts'.

As for Stephen, she alluded to his sense of his own self-importance ('Wants to be thought a heavyweight in the Colin Haycraft sense'), and described him as 'a maniac'. Beryl had always distrusted the ethics of the very wealthy. The fact that the company Stephen was a director of, LICA Development Capital, made its money out of offering tax-avoidance schemes to the rich, and dealt with engineering firms that included military hardware among their products, was not something that endeared him to her: 'Personally, I find it hard to trust anyone who has apparantly made a fortune out of "nice" tanks, even if the money has saved Duckworth.'

But Robin wasn't going to let Beryl slip through his fingers without a fight. He wrote to Andrew to say that Beryl was key to Duckworth's plans for the future and reassured him that the new Duckworth would be 'something so different' it would satisfy Beryl's desire for a break with the past. He added that he had previously negotiated a direct deal with Penguin for Muriel Spark's paperback rights and envisioned the same kind of lucrative deal for Beryl, one which would cut out the share Duckworth had previously taken.[7]

He also wrote to Beryl: 'I am going to do everything in my power to persuade you to stay with us.' As if to hammer the point home about his own independence, Robin stressed that he was 'the managing director and publisher of Duckworth (not I repeat not Stephen Hill)'.[8]

Negotiations continued, however, until October, when Andrew wrote to tell Beryl that Clare Alexander of Viking had now upped her offer to £35,000 per book, but that a decision had to be taken soon in order to meet the printing deadline for the catalogue. What happened next was typical of Beryl. Embarrassed at the idea of letting Robin down, she arranged to meet him in a pub off St Martin's Lane, and when he told her he would match the Viking offer she agreed to stay at Duckworth.[9]

At the beginning of January 1996 a contract was prepared and Robin wrote hopefully to Beryl: 'Happy New Year. For both you and me, this is going to be our *annus mirabilis*.'[10]

With the birth of Jo-Jo's first son, Charlie, in December 1980, Beryl had become a grandmother at the relatively early age of forty-eight. During the late 1980s and early 1990s her public image consequently underwent something of a transformation.

Readers of her column in the *Evening Standard* were regaled with anecdotes about her escapades with Charlie and 'Darling Bertie', his younger brother, and vicariously enjoyed her unconventional attitude to childcare. In a conscious act of rebellion against the normal routines and practices of their parents, Beryl would let her grandchildren play with toy guns, watch television, eat sweets and stay up late. This approach did have its downsides, as Beryl confessed to Michael Holroyd on one occasion when it turned out that giving lockable metal handcuffs to a young child – in this instance Rudi's four-year-old son, August – wasn't such a good idea: 'Yesterday, phone goes. "Mum, mum, this is serious." August, four, chained to chair by handcuffs. (I gave him them.) Can't call the police in case he's taken into care. Friend rushes round with cutting tools. Prisoner released. Me in "Coventry".'[11]

Nevertheless, Beryl involved herself in her grandchildren's education in a way that she hadn't done with her own children. Now she was not only unencumbered by romantic attachments and obsessions, she could also afford to take her grandchildren out regularly to museums, exhibitions and plays. As Kate Kellaway put it in an *Observer* profile, 'The relationships which now most occupy her are with her grandchildren.'[12]

Beryl's role as drama critic for *The Oldie*,[13] a magazine set up in 1992 by Richard Ingrams to cater for the over-fifties as a corrective to what he saw as the youth-oriented obsession of the media, also had an impact on her public image. She was now increasingly seen as one of a group of celebrity figures who took a generally anti-PC stance on social issues and who embraced the caricature of themselves as being out of sync with, and antipathetic to, the modern world.

In truth, Beryl wasn't really part of this vogue for what came to be known as 'grumpy old men' (and women). She didn't consider her comments as being knowingly ironic, as many of the other celebrities did, with the result that her unguarded remarks about certain social issues led her into controversies that, for the most part, others managed to avoid.

One of the most public of these was the furore over regional accents and 'the importance of talking properly', controversial statements that she made during the course of a dinner, in 1999, to celebrate winning the W. H. Smith Literary Award. 'Have you ever listened to the kids on *Brookside*? They don't speak the English language,'[14] she had complained. But it was her comment that 'uneducated regional accents' such as Scouse should be 'wiped out' that provoked the most anger.

Some of these controversies were simply storms in a media teacup, such as when a reporter asked her what she thought of 'Chick Lit': Beryl had never read anything that might be considered Chick Lit, but it didn't stop her dismissing the whole genre as 'froth'. On other occasions, however, her off-the-cuff pronouncements came across as crass or ill-considered rather than refreshingly contrarian, and were more damaging to her reputation. Into this category fell her views on what constituted rape and child abuse, which betrayed a serious lack of understanding of the issues involved and a curious lack of empathy with those affected.

With Colin's death Beryl lost the centre of her emotional life, and the whole web of social interaction that revolved around Duckworth began to dissolve too, including her friendship with Anna. Inevitably, they now saw less of each other. Anna already spent several months of each year in Wales, and when the house in Gloucester Crescent was sold in 2001 the distance between them became literal as well as figurative.

Instead, as the 1990s progressed Beryl developed a compartmentalized network of friends whom she would see on a semi-regular basis, usually in the course of evening dinner parties: Mike and Parvin Laurence; Derwent and Yola May; David Swift and his wife Paula Jacobs, who had acted with Beryl at the Liverpool Playhouse back in 1951; Michael Holroyd and Margaret Drabble; Melvyn Bragg and his wife, Cate Haste; Robin Baird-Smith and Mark Bostridge, whose guests frequently included other writers, such as Blake Morrison, John Bayley, Francis King and Penelope Lively; and Brodie Taylor, a theatrical agent whose soirées included actors such as Ian McKellen.

Beryl's increased public profile and the numerous invitations she received to attend lunches, dinners and other media events brought her into contact with a large number of celebrities, film stars and politicians, including David Tomlinson, Dirk Bogarde, Woodrow Wyatt – the pools boss otherwise known as Lord Wyatt of Weeford – Timothy Renton, Neil Kinnock, Mo Mowlam and the union leader Rodney Bickerstaff.

It was during this period that Beryl got to know Terry Waite, who she had first met in 1986 as a guest on his short-lived interview show, *Terry Waite Takes a Different View*. Shortly afterwards, in January 1987, Waite had been taken hostage in Beirut, where he was held for nearly five years. On his release, he began writing a book about his experiences and rang Beryl for advice, often late at night, leaving long messages on her answer machine. He would later testify to her willingness to spare the time to talk and offer suggestions.

Although she was not a huge reader of contemporary fiction, Beryl was always amenable to those who solicited her opinion about their manuscripts. However, as A. N. Wilson recalled, this was sometimes the result of embarrassment rather than any conviction as to literary quality: 'She was the worst person in the world to do that to, because she would always say "yes". There are various people who used to do it to her all the time, and she'd then get into terrible stews by lying to them, saying that she'd really liked the book.'[15]

The number of books that carry ringing endorsements from Beryl on their covers testifies to her unwillingness to let people down. However, this seemingly positive response was belied by Beryl's habitual practice of telling the author – or in some cases the marketing department that had solicited the quote – that they should simply write what they wanted and put her name to it, the implication being that she had neither read the book nor agreed with the opinions attributed to her.[16]

Shortly after completing *An Awfully Big Adventure*, Beryl had begun another novel, originally intended to be called 'Kiss Me Hardy', which opened with the words: 'At half-past ten on the morning of 29 September – the weather was mild and the leaves still stuck to the trees – a madman died in Hardy's arms.'[17] After writing the first chapter, however, the story ran out of steam and she abandoned it,[18] though she would later reuse this image of a man dying in a stranger's arms for the opening of her book about the *Titanic*.

Originally, the first novel in the three-book deal was going to be about the Crimean War, but Beryl quickly realized she 'didn't know enough about it'[19] and the subject would need more time to research. The sinking of the *Titanic*, by contrast, seemed to be on more familiar territory: not only was the disaster contemporaneous with Scott's expedition, she also felt an affinity with the subject because of her father's connection to the sea and to the White Star Line, the ship's owners.

Furthermore, the idea of writing about the *Titanic* was partly inspired by Beryl's experiences as a babysitter to a growing band of grandchildren: one of the videos she would watch with them to keep them amused was *A Night to Remember*, the classic 1958 film of Walter Lord's book about the sinking of the ship.[20] In 1990, four years before she started *Every Man for Himself*, as the novel was called, Beryl had written a Christmas playlet for her grandchildren to perform. Directed by ten-year-old Charlie and with special effects by seven-year-old Bertie, 'The Last Battle' was based around the *Titanic*, although with a cast that included Winston Churchill and Prince Albert, and scenes involving helicopters, Nazis and 'scoober divers', it had scant regard for historical accuracy: 'It was the worst of days, it was the best of days. The *S.S. Titanic*, pride of the British passenger fleet was cruising close by the clifts of Dover. At three oclock on a wintery afternoon the German Navy made a dastardly attack on this noble ship . . . (Noise of seagulls).'[21]

Writing a novel about the *Titanic* was obviously another matter altogether, but even here the grandchildren were occasionally roped in. Bertie assembled a model-kit replica of the ship that was over two feet in length and which helped in visualizing its physical layout.

Many of those who had known Colin recognized him in the character of Scurra. Beryl had originally got the name from a textbook acquired during the course of her Latin lessons – Philip Corbett's study *The Scurra*, about a stock figure who appears in a number of classical satires. Kirk Freudenberg's description of the *scurra* shows why Beryl was drawn to the name: 'The *scurra* is associated with the city (Corbett calls him a "Townie"), and he seems to specialise in upbraiding those who fall short of community standards. His wit may earn him a place at the table of those who are better off; but his sharp tongue causes unease among his potential targets . . . The *scurra* is thus the close counterpart of the satirist, especially the convivial satirist.'[22]

Every Man for Himself effectively marked the end of Anna's editorial input into Beryl's novels. Although for many years her role had been limited to providing initial encouragement, confirming that a book was going in the right direction, and rubber-stamping the novel once it was finished, Beryl still nominally considered Anna her editor, and always went out of her way to credit her as such in interviews. But now – perhaps because this was Beryl's first book since Colin's death – Anna didn't simply offer general comments about shape and tone. Instead, when Beryl sent her the first ten pages, Anna sent them back marked up with numerous minor textual amendments, changing Beryl's carefully phrased and balanced sentences into something that more resembled her own idea of 'correct' English. Significantly, Beryl ignored her changes and suggestions completely, indeed the final manuscript was published with very few editorial changes at all.[23]

Shortly after finishing the novel, Beryl went to New York to meet Kent Carroll of Carroll & Graf, her American publisher since *The Birthday Boys*.[24] In the course of her visit she was introduced to Robert Ballard, the man who had spent years searching for the wreck of the *Titanic* and was instrumental in finding it.

Every Man for Himself received extremely positive reviews when it was published, making it onto the Booker Prize shortlist and winning the Whitbread Novel of the Year. Ironically, the first novel Beryl published after Colin's death would be the one that sold the most and made her the most money. This was not just a reflection of the book's quality. Its success also owed something to chance and to Robin Baird-Smith's marketing, as its publication in hardback coincided with numerous media reports about an attempt to raise the *Titanic*, and a month after it appeared in paperback James Cameron's hugely successful film opened. Whether it was a result of the sudden increase in popularity of the subject, or whether, as Beryl suspected, that some people actually thought the book was connected to the film, the paperback sold over 100,000 copies, the first time one of her books had reached such a dizzying figure: 'Popularity is such a shock at my age,' she told one interviewer. 'For years I had a kind of cult following, but my books didn't actually sell. I think it's only because of *Titanic* that things have gone a bit mad – even a rotten book about the *Titanic* would sell . . .'²⁵

In the 1970s there were already signs that Beryl's drinking was becoming a problem, but its more serious effects were mitigated during this period by other counterbalancing factors. Not only was she still relatively young and her tolerance for alcohol higher, her children were still living at home, so the opportunities for drinking alone were minimized. Her rapid critical and commercial success as a writer had also, perhaps for the first time in her life, given her a sense of self-worth, and consequently she was less prone to the feelings of negativity that give rise to the desire to drink.

But by the 1980s these restraining factors had begun to evaporate. Jo and Aaron had already left home, and when Rudi followed suit in 1985 it became harder for Beryl to resist the temptation to drink on her own. Her relationship with Colin went through a number of crises during this period, provoking in her a pervasive sense of emotional insecurity, and the subsequent bouts of loneliness and depression fuelled her desire to drink. Not only that, the illicit nature of the affair gave rise to feelings of guilt and betrayal which she sought to assuage through drink. Nor did fiction provide the same sense of creative satisfaction it once had. Indeed the act of writing had become a struggle in itself, and the alcohol provided an easy short-term solution, albeit an illusory one. Paradoxically, the older Beryl got and the more she drank, the lower her tolerance to alcohol seemed to be and this began to have increasingly negative consequences when she drank in public.

The potential for Beryl's social drinking to get out of hand was often exacerbated by her urge to drink before she went out. Part of the reason for this was her feeling that alcohol helped her get through the ordeal of socializing, as she explained to an old friend in Liverpool: 'I am about to go off to a posh do at a posh hotel and I loathe going out. In order to function I have been at the vodka.'[26] But even when she was meeting friends, the temptation to drink beforehand was often too strong: 'She was quite nervous before coming out to dinner,' Derwent May recalled, 'and she would drink quite a bit before she came.'[27] This was a habit that A. N. Wilson also noticed: 'Quite often, if she was feeling depressed, or if I called on her before a party, she'd get through half a bottle of whisky before going out.'[28]

In certain situations, where hosts were sensitive or congenial, such as with Derwent and Yola May in their Albany Street home, the effects of an excess of alcohol were minimized, though even here it could lead to potentially dangerous situations. After a dinner party at the Mays' in 1993, Beryl and Colin left together as they tended to do, but as Colin was feeling ill Beryl insisted he return straight to Gloucester Crescent. As she drunkenly made her way to Albert Street alone she got into an altercation: 'Have got a black eye – man hit me on way home,'[29] as she later told Derwent. A contrite Colin apologized to Beryl the next day: 'So sorry to hear about your contretemps after Yola's do. You're right, I should have walked you home. I wasn't well, but no excuse.'[30] On another occasion, again after an evening round at Albany Street, Beryl insisted on walking home despite being obviously very drunk. Shortly after she left the house, she sat down on the kerb in Park Village West and passed out, only waking up several hours later.

But even when she was in the company of friends, her drinking would occasionally result in aggressive or antisocial behaviour. A. N. Wilson recalled one dinner party he had attended with Beryl at Bernice Rubens' flat, which provoked such embarrassment that he subsequently resolved to meet Beryl only in alcohol-free situations. Beryl had already been drinking before she came out and at the table she became confrontational:

> She started showing off, and the more she did it the less attention anybody paid, because she was already being incredibly silly. She went

on hands and knees to the front door and came back with two or three wellington boots [it had been snowing earlier and guests had left them at the door to prevent dirtying Bernice's pristine carpet]. She plonked them onto the neat little dinner table, and started scooping first her food and then other people's food into them. People did get jolly cross actually.

The next thing she did, when she was made to put the boots down, was to crawl over to Bernice's cello – which was Bernice's most prized possession – and knock it over. There was this great crash . . . it was just awful. After that, I said: 'I think you're behaving so badly I'm going to take you home.' I just thought it was so cruel to Bernice.[31]

One problem was that Beryl found it hard to stop drinking once she started, and as she wasn't physically able to handle drink, these bouts led to lapses of memory and occasionally even to blackouts. She found these experiences humiliating to recollect, especially when they happened in public, such as the time she interviewed Julian Barnes at the King's Lynn Literary Festival in 2004: 'The Julian Barnes thingie is a closed book. I was so nervous I bought a half of whisky ½ an hour before, and have no recollection of the interview.'[32] Although the organizer tried to reassure Beryl that those who witnessed it 'agreed they had never laffed so much since the war ended', it didn't stop her feeling deeply ashamed of these losses of self-control.

Consequently, she would continually resolve not to drink in public, but this resolve was easily overcome by the persuasion of those around her. Things were made more difficult by the fact that Beryl's reputation preceded her, and she had to face the situation many public figures with a weakness for drink find themselves in: having alcohol forced on them by people who expect them to live up to their hard-drinking reputation. She grew to dread public occasions such as lectures, where she might be given a drink before the event had even begun, and literary festivals, where well-intentioned hosts would welcome her with a bottle of whisky – as if she was a connoisseur who drank for pleasure rather than as a psychological aid to help her through difficult social situations.

Those who gave Beryl drink were rarely the ones who had to deal with the emotional (and sometimes physical) fallout. On one occasion in 1988 Beryl was invited, along with the actress Beryl Reid, to take part in a BBC *Review* programme discussing Beryl Cook's paintings. Beryl arrived on time, but as Reid was late the producer asked her whether she wanted a drink. She put it off for as long as she could, but then gave in. By the time Reid arrived fifteen minutes later, Beryl was already tiddly. They were then both given more drink: brandy for Beryl Reid, and whisky for Beryl. On the way home after the programme she was so drunk she fell over in the street and bruised herself – she had a vague recollection of passing out on the Tube, but couldn't remember how she got back.[33]

Beryl's drinking was one of the principal causes of arguments with her children, most particularly with Rudi, whose experiences as a child had left her with a lifelong aversion to seeing her mother drunk. Beryl was acutely aware of Rudi's disapproval: 'She goes on and on about my drinking. She can't stand it. She'll snatch my glass out of my hand and pour it down the sink. And she always knows when I've had one secretly, she can spot it a mile off. And I don't mean getting drunk, I mean having a drink. There've been times when I've been walking down the street, not staggering or anything, and she'd go "Muuuum!" and come running towards me and then stop dead, toss her head and flounce off. And she was always right.'[34]

Drinking is often a way of alleviating bouts of loneliness and depression, feelings that Beryl was increasingly subject to in the years following Colin's death, so much so that she was sometimes overwhelmed by thoughts of suicide. One evening, while working for Beryl, I returned home to find a message from her on my answer machine – when she was writing she would frequently call about changes she wanted making to her text – but this time it wasn't about work. Instead she sounded depressed and clearly inebriated: 'I'm just . . . I'm not sure that I can go on,' she began, before pulling herself together and adding, 'No . . . forget this, I'll be perfectly alright in the morning.'[35] It was close to midnight, but she seemed so desperate I immediately went round to Albert Street. The lights were out and there was no sign of life, so, apprehensively, fearing I might find her stretched out on the floor in the hall, I let myself in, bypassing the security chain on the door that was so long you could reach in and unhook it. I called her name softly, in case she was awake and thought I was a burglar, and went upstairs. She was asleep in bed: I listened to her breathing for a few minutes to make sure she was all right and left. Although this turned out to be a false alarm, it was a reminder of the fragility of Beryl's emotional state.

In an interview with Melvyn Bragg around this time, Beryl alluded to these gloomy feelings: 'Sometimes I even think it would be preferable to die, because more and more as one gets older, one knows about the terrible things that happen, the sudden accidents, the dreadful calamities, the diseases that befall one – and that has one in a state of permanent worry.'[36]

At first glance, the idea of Beryl writing about the Crimea seemed a strange one – apparently even to herself: 'I don't know how the blinking Crimean War cropped up,'[37] she told one journalist shortly before *Master Georgie* was published. A few years before, however, in 1992, she had claimed that her fascination was of much longer standing: 'I've always been interested in the Crimean War', and she included Michael Barthorp's *Heroes of the Crimea* among her favourite books of that year.[38]

Beryl's initial interest in the subject may have been stimulated by her fascination with medical books – *George Lawson: Surgeon in the Crimea*, a series of letters written from Sebastopol and Balaclava between 1854 and 1855, featured in her library – but the catalyst for the novel was the work of the Victorian photographer Roger Fenton. She had been struck by Fenton's images of the Crimean battlefields, particularly one that depicted the 'Valley of the Shadow of Death', void of all life and scattered with hundreds of cannonballs. It was Fenton's static, carefully posed photographs – exposure times in those days required subjects to be perfectly immobile – that would inspire the idea of structuring the novel around a series of still images.

It was also after seeing Fenton's photographs that she decided to make the novel's central character, George Hardy, an amateur photographer. Beryl wrote to Pamela Roberts, curator of the Royal Photographical Society in Bath where a major collection of Fenton's work was housed, for more information: 'I am about to start a new novel on the Crimean War and have decided to include a fictional assistant to Roger Fenton. I would be most grateful if you could recommend to me the most helpful book on the technical and chemical processes of the time – and where I might borrow one. If that is not possible, would I be able to come to Bath and take notes?'[39]

A photographic image was also the inspiration for the novel's other main figure, Myrtle. During a trip to the Isle of Wight with Mike and Parvin Laurence (to whom *Master Georgie* would later be dedicated), Beryl went to Dimbola Lodge in Freshwater, which displayed a collection of photographs by Julia Margaret Cameron. 'There was this amazing portrait, a black-and-white portrait of a girl. On the back of the photograph, it explained about her: She had been married three times . . . She had finally run away to sea, and then she died of typhoid, all by the time she was 27. So I bought a postcard of it, and that was Myrtle. That was one way of getting a character.'[40]

Interestingly, despite the fact that most people would be hard pushed to detect in *Master Georgie* any trace of autobiography, or any hint that her own life experiences formed any meaningful parallel with those in the novel, Beryl would continue to insist that what she was writing wasn't fiction. To understand what she meant by this one has to try and make sense of her idea about imagination and the role it plays in the creative act. Beryl claimed not to 'believe' in the imagination. Imagination to her was synonymous with 'the person you were from the past'. It was 'sort of like a bucket' that gets 'filled up with memories and impressions and stuff', and it was from this well of experience that writers drew; they didn't simply 'make things up'.[41] At one level this was a truism – we are all the product of our experience and all writers and artists create, directly or indirectly, from that experience – and to that degree all art is autobiographical. This is perhaps little comfort for anyone looking to read Beryl's fiction as disguised autobiography, as by definition there is no direct relationship between the lived experience and its fictional representation.

At the end of 1997, with the book almost completed, the *South Bank Show* invited Beryl to the Crimea and filmed her visiting the battlefields of Sebastopol, Balaclava and Inkerman, as part of a programme about her forthcoming novel and her writing process. There, in the freezing sub-zero temperatures of a Ukrainian winter, as she struggled to finish the book, she got the chance to compare reality with the fictional landscapes she had created in her head. On her return, she handed the 132-page manuscript, now complete, to Robin.[42]

When it was published in April 1998, the book was overwhelmingly well received, with some reviewers regarding it as her best yet.[43] More good news came in September when it was announced that *Master*

Georgie had made it onto the Booker Prize shortlist, the fifth time Beryl had been nominated. As one of the judges was Valentine Cunningham, who had given *Harriet Said* a good review back in 1972, and another was the former Duckworth author Penelope Fitzgerald, Beryl considered that this time she had a good chance of winning: 'I've been lying down. I get terribly excited the day they announce the shortlist. It's always between 3.30pm and 6.30pm. You can't bear to be away from the phone. So I attacked the vodka. Then I had to go out to dinner. Now I'm feeling very groggy, but cheerful.'[44]

For *Master Georgie* the level of expectation was raised higher than usual, not just because no one had been nominated five times before and it was assumed Beryl would get the Prize as a kind of lifetime achievement award, but because she was also being touted as the people's – and the bookie's – favourite. Julian Barnes was sufficiently convinced of the result to put £40 on Beryl to win.[45] But she was denied again, this time by Ian McEwan's *Amsterdam*. Although McEwan was considered a worthy winner in many people's eyes, there was nevertheless a faint whiff of scores being settled behind the scenes about the verdict, with a finger being pointed at Penelope Fitzgerald as the culprit. Fitzgerald had herself been nominated for the Booker in 1978, for her novel *The Bookshop*. In a review in *The Times Literary Supplement*, Cunningham had somewhat unfortunately described the book as an example of 'the Beryl Bainbridge school of anguished women's fiction',[46] a description Fitzgerald didn't find flattering: 'I'm said to be of the Beryl Bainbridge school,' she remarked cattily, 'which is a good corrective to vanity, I expect.'[47] It seemed an unfortunate coincidence, therefore, that Cunningham and Fitzgerald should be on the same judging panel, as it gave the latter a chance to show the former she was nobody's pupil, least of all Beryl's. Whether Fitzgerald's vote was decisive or not – the chairman, Douglas Hurd, confessed his preference was for *Master Georgie* – the prize went to McEwan.[48]

Although both of Beryl's novels published under his tenure at Duckworth had been critical and commercial successes, there were increasing signs that Robin Baird-Smith's vision and objectives for the company were out of step with those of Stephen Hill.

This was made abundantly clear in an event organized by Stephen to mark Duckworth's centenary at the end of 1998. The fact that it was a glitzy celebrity function held at the Dorchester Hotel perhaps gives some indication of the disconnect between what most people considered to be Duckworth's literary heritage and core values, and the kind of image of the company that Stephen wanted to project. He seemed to believe that if Duckworth simply acted like a big-shot media company it would be seen as a serious player in the media business, a pretension that was cruelly lampooned in the press:

> Duckworth this week celebrated its centenary with a dinner for 300 at the Dorchester. It also marked the launch of Duckworth Literary Entertainments, a film division headed by Tom Hedley of *Flashdance* fame. MD Robin Baird-Smith looked embarrassed to be there, Anna Haycraft (novelist Alice Thomas Ellis, widow of Colin Haycraft who ran the company for 30 glorious years) was visibly disapproving, while star author Beryl Bainbridge seemed to find it eccentric even by her standards . . . Many of the guests appeared to be B-list celebs – among them punk svengali Malcolm McLaren. Heaven knows what he made of the specially-written grace by Jasper Griffin, Public Orator at Oxford, which was delivered in Greek.[49]

Over the next few months the situation worsened and Robin confided to Beryl his growing dissatisfaction with the way things were going: 'Sometimes I feel I am being torn apart here – a slow crucifixion.'[50] Matters came to a head the following year and in a move that seemed like history repeating itself Stephen unceremoniously sacked Robin, as the book page of the *Guardian* reported:

> Beryl Bainbridge's publisher, Robin Baird-Smith, has been ousted as managing director of Duckworth, apparently having failed to move the company forward fast enough – or to be infected by the funky vibe of the new Duck Editions imprint. Duck is certainly taking the genteel publishing house in new directions – highlights from its Spring 2000 programme include *Tramp L'Oeil: Memoirs of a Door Bitch* (a revealing tale of 'glamour's underbelly' at Tramp nightclub) and the latest masterpiece from yoof style goddess, Bidisha, which, Lord help us all, is billed as 'a Tarantino-esque reinterpretation of the Arthurian legends set in contemporary London.' Offerings like these

are not obviously to Baird-Smith's taste – and the prospect of bedding down with such stable-mates might not appeal to Bainbridge either, especially as her contract only extends to her next novel.[51]

The subsequent history of Duckworth Literary Entertainments and Duck Editions proved that Baird-Smith's scepticism about these ventures was justified: as of 2014 the former had no assets and liabilities of over £188,000,[52] while the latter has published only two books since 2004 – both by Stephen Hill. As for Duckworth itself, the firm went into liquidation in March 2003 and was bought from the administrators by Peter Mayer a few months later.

With Robin gone, Beryl was back in the situation she had originally sought to avoid and once again began sounding out ways to leave Duckworth. She asked Andrew Hewson to write to Stephen and tell him that her new novel about Dr Johnson and Mrs Thrale – the last in the projected three-book deal – would be considerably delayed, as Robin's departure had brought on writer's block. Stephen didn't 'buy' this line for a moment and curtly reminded Andrew that 'Beryl is contracted to us' and that Tom Hedley, who Stephen had appointed as Chief Executive, would only consider releasing her from her contractual obligation to Duckworth for a 'large cheque'.[53]

The breakdown in relations between the two sides was epitomized the following year when the Duckworth catalogue not only misspelled the title of Beryl's novel, but also described its eponymous character – Mrs Thrale's daughter, Queeney – as a servant girl. In a bad-tempered exchange of letters, Andrew Hewson's wife Margaret, who was now working full-time at the agency, complained to Stephen about 'the incompetent blurb writers at Duckworth', and he countered with the accusation that her firm was 'unilaterally seeking to break a solemn contract in writing with Beryl'.[54]

By this time Andrew Hewson was in discussions with Richard Beswick at Little, Brown, who were interested in taking Beryl on, and negotiations on a suitable 'transfer fee' were opened. Beswick eventually came up with sufficient money to satisfy Stephen, and it would be Little, Brown, not Duckworth, who published the book.

While all this in-fighting was going on, Beryl had been trying to write her novel. It had initially been entitled 'Dearest Sweeting', from Johnson's habitual manner of addressing Mrs Thrale's daughter in his letters. After the first chapter was completed, however, it acquired a new title, *According to Queeney*, which more aptly reflected one of the underlying themes of the novel: the subjectivity of experience, particularly in the matter of relationships.

In the same way that both *The Birthday Boys* and *Master Georgie* had required an organizing principle around which the narrative could be structured – the birthdays of the five men in the case of the former, and a sequence of photographic images in the latter – the breakthrough with the novel came with the idea to structure it around a series of definitions from Johnson's *Dictionary*. They would serve as a kind of commentary on the events of each section.

After the debacle over the original Duckworth blurb, Beryl decided to write her own for the Little, Brown catalogue. Although it wasn't used, her synopsis – which she found 'far more difficult than writing the dam book'[55] – shows what Beryl herself felt the novel was about:

> The comically cruel candour of this story of unrequited love, passion, rejection and possession, explores the sexual tensions that lie beneath the ordered surface of everyday life. The widower, Dr Johnson, shuttling between his own household of bickering dependents and the comforts of the Thrale establishment, deceives himself into thinking he and Mrs Thrale will never be parted. The narrative leads us on a dance of thwarted relationships interrupted at intervals by the wittingly misleading letters of Mrs Thrale's daughter, the aggrieved Queeney.[56]

As Beryl herself later admitted, writing a book about Dr Johnson wouldn't have been possible if Colin had still been alive. To have attempted it would have risked a repeat of the acrimonious bickering over *Watson's Apology*: 'I'd have felt I didn't know enough. Or he would have told me I didn't know enough!'[57] Colin was nevertheless the presiding spirit behind the novel and served as a model for its central character: 'With his acerbity and his intellectual sharpness, he was really rather like Johnson. I still miss him and I'd have loved him to have read *According to Queeney*.'[58]

Beryl had worried that Colin's death might irreparably damage her ability to write: 'I was scared that I wouldn't know what to write or who I was writing for.' She had seen the end of her relationship with Colin as the end of herself as an active sexual being, and in her mind sex and creativity were closely connected: 'I think all creativity comes from the sexual urge . . . I was quite frightened that when I got older, and all that was over and done with, I'd not be able to do anything.'[59]

According to Queeney was the last of the three books Beryl had projected while Colin was still alive. Finishing it therefore represented a symbolic conclusion to her relationship with him, as well as to the whole Duckworth period. This sense that a vital part of her life was now over contributed to her subsequent struggle to find the motivation and energy to write. Beryl was approaching her seventieth birthday; she had long found the mental and physical effort of writing a strain, but in the last decade of her life this would be exacerbated by other, more pervasive problems that frequently come with old age – loneliness, feelings of depression and ill-health.

In August 2001, as part of the publicity campaign surrounding the publication of *According to Queeney*, Beryl agreed to an interview with Graham Turner of the *Daily Telegraph*. When it appeared, however, it provoked a furious reaction from Anna, and she wrote an accusatory letter to Beryl that effectively marked the end of their friendship.

It is not difficult to see why Anna was so incensed by the tone of the article in general, and by Beryl's comments in particular. The interview began innocuously enough, covering the familiar tropes concerning Colin, Duckworth and Beryl – that he had been a kind of Svengali figure in her career, and that the firm had treated her badly in financial terms – but then, whether the subject was prompted by Turner or whether Beryl was simply caught off-guard, she began to talk about Colin and Anna's domestic life, their disagreements and the breakdown of their marriage, and even alluded to the effect on them of their son's death: 'I was often piggy in the middle when they were having tremendous rows – either about religion (Colin disapproved of the whole damn thing) or who was to blame for the tragic death of their son Joshua, who fell through a roof after going for a walk at three in the morning. I never said anything because they'd have told me to shut up. Their marriage was never quite the same after Josh's death.'[60]

Turner then put it to Beryl that she had been Colin's mistress. Although she vehemently denied it in print, and later claimed she hadn't initiated the topic and that she had been misquoted, the damage had been done, at least in Anna's eyes.

Anna wrote to the *Daily Telegraph*, saying she had been 'sickened by the grossly impertinent' reference to her son, before going on to refute the points made in the article and denying that Colin had had any influence on Beryl's career: 'Colin is now being described as a Svengali figure,' she wrote, 'which is odd since he took little interest in individuals and did not care for fiction.' The letter ended with a backhanded swipe at Beryl's loyalty to Colin and the firm, saying that Colin had alienated most of his authors and that Beryl was 'almost the only novelist sufficiently docile to put up with what could be described, I suppose, as his scholarly approach'.[61]

Although the published version of the letter was heavily edited, Anna sent an uncut version to Beryl, along with a letter telling her in no uncertain terms to shut up. It opened with a harshly worded assault on Colin (referred to as 'Horace' because of his near-infatuation with the Latin poet), Beryl's literary agent and Beryl herself: 'Was it your idea to go on about poor Horace or did the P.R. girl suggest it? Your agents wrote to D'worth when they wanted a reason to flog you to someone else saying he'd "guided your career" – which is twaddle. He didn't give a toss for careers or novels, yours or anyone's. Particularly not in the last years which were devoted to the meticulous pursuit of self-destruction.'

Adducing Colin's erratic behaviour to a series of strokes that had left him 'pretty mad', Anna added, 'I really don't want him talked about any more.' The letter ended with a piece of haughty advice for Beryl: 'So be a duck and natter about something else. Any mention of Col must turn some light on the family and having spent a lifetime (despite the home lifes and all the publicity) keeping private life <u>private</u>, it makes me not best pleased.'[62]

Stung by Anna's scathing tone and the implication in her letter to the *Telegraph* (actually cut from the published version) that it had been Beryl who had brought up the subject of Joshua's death, Beryl typed out a reply fuelled by her own barely suppressed resentments:

> Dearest Anna, I guess I should have ignored your letter, in that I'm the sinner, and you have every right to chastise me. But there was

something about your letter that made me cross. There were so many things that you got wrong. I know you were hurt by that fucking article, and quite rightly, but your letter didn't mention the thing that most upset me – the bit about Joshua . . . You seem to think I've encouraged these personal interviews. Stop nattering, you say. I have never yet given an interview without giving full credit to your part in my literary suxcess. You must admit this. If they don't care to print your part in my career, that is not my fault . . . In your letter you say something about my agents 'trying to flog me somewhere else.' The reverse is the truth . . . It was not my agents who 'flogged me' but Duckworths. I am now with Little Brown because Duckworth sold me to them. Neither my agents or me received a penny for this transaction. When I told you that Duckworths (Stephen) was after my house, you said that was never serious. I have all the letters from my bank and my solicitor to prove it.

Money was a sore point with Beryl, and she couldn't stop herself bringing up Duckworth's slackness in paying her while at the same time finding money to fund expenses incurred by Anna's house in Wales:

When you write that, yes, Colin was bad about money as regards me, but that he treated everyone the same, you seem to forget that the majority of the other authors were acedemics receiving Univervisty saleries. I was supporting three children, and while the Welsh house was being given money to rebuild it – Clive was on the board and told me of the sums side-lined to this enterprise[63] – I was being denied royalties. I don't mind any of this. I don't care – not until you try to suggest that my 'nattering' is upsetting you and is somehow linked to a 'silliness of mind.'

In the end Beryl wisely decided not to send the letter, realizing that her counter-accusation about Anna's behaviour towards Colin – that she had encouraged their children to be 'appallingly disrespectful' to him and that this had so upset him Beryl had seen him weep as a result – overstepped the mark and would only aggravate the situation. Rereading the letter in the cold light of day, she may also have noticed that it closed with an incongruous attempt at self-justification, one that was plainly untenable given her relation to Colin: 'I have never knowingly betrayed you, and would never.'[64]

THIRTY-ONE

Illness

Dear God! it is no joke getting old, but I often wonder why we want to go on living when all the bits that made life sparkle – sex, ciggies, drink – are all banned or else no longer have appeal.[1]

A FTER THE PUBLICATION OF *According to Queeney*, Beryl settled down to a spell of painting, an activity she had sporadically indulged in after completing a novel, at least since *The Birthday Boys*. Both the race to the Pole and the sinking of the *Titanic* had provided plenty of scope for reworking the iconic images associated with them: one of the paintings for the Antarctic series was based on Herbert Ponting's famous photograph of an ice sheet, for example, while one of those for the *Titanic* series, *The Sinking*, was based on an illustration of the upended ship disappearing into the water that had featured on the cover of the video of *A Night to Remember*.

On the face of it, Dr Johnson offered less in the way of familiar iconography, and perhaps as a result the paintings based around *According to Queeney* were less purely illustrative of the novel itself and had a more personal, autobiographical element to them. *Dr Samuel Johnson in Albert St with his cat hodge* features the habitually gregarious Johnson sitting alone at Beryl's table in her front room, looking decidedly gloomy. The whole painting is surrounded by black, an almost physical representation of the encroaching depression and thoughts of death that haunted Johnson and – increasingly – Beryl herself. Another, *Colin Haycraft, Dr Samuel Johnson and me, learning Latin in Gloucester Crescent*, shows Beryl seated across a table from Colin, a bottle of Bells whisky (Beryl's usual brand) between them, while the figure of Johnson, holding a cameo of Mrs Thrale over his heart, stands next to Colin.

The parallel between the two couples seems intentional, but whether the painting is meant to express an equivalence – that Beryl is to Colin what Mrs Thrale was to Johnson – or a difference – that she and Colin remained separate with only a bottle of whisky to unite them – is open to interpretation.

The themes expressed in these paintings, of lost love and of the imminent approach of death, were indicative of feelings that had been building over recent years. Even before she began writing *According to Queeney*, Beryl had confessed to Melvyn Bragg her sense that her life was reaching its inevitable conclusion: 'The struggle's over, the struggle money-wise, partially, and life-wise is over. One is going towards the edge of the cliff. I mean there's not much ahead.'[2]

There were objective signs, too, that her career as a writer was reaching its apogee. In the late 1990s Michael Holroyd, in his capacity as President of the Royal Society of Literature, had submitted Beryl's name to the honours committee, and encouraged other influential figures – including her agent – to write to the Central Appointments Unit and offer their support. The campaign bore fruit in 2000 when Beryl was made a DBE. Although she was slightly embarrassed by the formality and vague pomposity of the title 'Dame', she was nevertheless proud of the award.

Another sign that her career was drawing to a close – in the eyes of others at least – was winning the David Cohen Prize for Literature in 2003, a biennial literary award given to writers in recognition of an entire body of work. The prestige of this was slightly diminished by having to share it – and the prize money – with the poet Thom Gunn.[3] Not that Gunn wasn't equally worthy of the award, just that both deserved to win it outright. In any case such 'lifetime achievement' awards are always double edged, the implication being that its recipient's productive life is to all intents and purposes over – and indeed Thom Gunn would die a year later in 2004.

After finishing *According to Queeney*, Beryl was now in the situation – for the first time in many years – of not having anything to write about, a problem she hadn't had to consider since coming up with the plan of the three-book deal nearly a decade before.

To give herself more time to think of a suitable subject, she reverted to an idea that had long been in the back of her mind, that of turning *Injury Time* into a stage play. With its small cast of characters, its unities of time and place, and its farcical set pieces it seemed ideal. Beryl hoped that a theatrical adaptation might even be commercially worthwhile, especially given the recent success of a revival of Michael Frayn's *Noises Off*, which had been running since October 2000 and showed no signs of flagging in popularity. Initially, the idea was to offer the adaptation to Alan Ayckbourn to produce at his theatre in Scarborough, and, if it was successful there, move the play to the West End. But the completed script provoked little in the way of a positive response. Whether the play's 1970s setting now seemed too out of date, or it was felt that the drama of the novel didn't translate into a piece of theatre, nothing came of it.

Another theatrical project begun around this time did, however, have more appeal. It was initiated by Richard Ingrams, who had the idea of creating an evening's entertainment on the theme of Dr Johnson and Mrs Thrale. A former president of the Johnson Society, Ingrams had edited a book of Mrs Thrale's anecdotes about Johnson over a decade before the publication of *According to Queeney*, so it seemed logical that he and Beryl should write something together. The intriguing part of the whole enterprise was that they would act in it themselves.

In April, Richard visited Albert Street to discuss the project and Beryl was struck by his somewhat abstracted air: 'He didn't notice the buffalo or the new wallpaper, or anything. I do think the upper classes are very unobservant, or are they just withdrawn?'[4] Shortly afterwards a script was hastily put together, with Beryl cutting and pasting Richard's suggested photocopies from his book and adding linking bits of dialogue. Music was to be provided by Raymond Banning, a piano teacher and friend of Richard's. An inaugural performance was set up by Clive Conway and on 15 August 2002 the unlikely trio stepped out onto the stage in front of an audience of 350. Beryl later gave an account of the night's events to her agent:

Performance of 'Dr J and Mrs T' at the New Vic Theatre, Stoke-on-Trent, went surprisingly well, seeing that there had been no rehersals and I wasn't sure what I was meant to do. I wrote the script, to

Richard's confused guidance, and then this nice chap who does music turned up to play Hydn, Bach etc in between.

Richard (shirt hanging out and hoisting trousers): 'The programme ses this is *The Tragedy and Triumph of Dr Johnson* . . .' (pause to consult notes and hitch trousers, also clearing of nose) '. . . but it isn't. It's to do with the friendship between Mrs T and Dr J.'

(Music): A lot of it.

Me: 'But for James Boswell etc who would have heard of Samuel Johnson.' And so on.

Interval came after journey to France. Huge applause (God knows why) and we bowed. On our return more music to introduce death of Henry Thrale. Then introduction of Piozzi, then marriage of Mrs T to Piozzi. Johnson's death, more music. Then questions, and they were numerous: 'Did Johnson f . . . Mrs T?' 'Was Boswell a drunkard?'

Then Richard, trousers really in a bad way, rose to announce he and Raymundo would play a duet. At the end applause was tremendous. Talk about achieving something by the seat of one's pants.[5]

For a short period there was talk of staging a series of performances, but despite the relative success of the evening it was an experiment that wasn't repeated.

By now thoughts about a new novel were beginning to take shape. In conversation with Susan Hill at the Hay-on-Wye Literary Festival, Beryl admitted that she had an idea for a book, but that it was 'complicated', being about 'parallel universes, that sort of thing'.[6] This was an allusion not to the parallel worlds of science fiction but to J. W. Dunne's theories about the 'serial' nature of time. Dunne had proposed that time wasn't linear, it was just perceived that way by consciousness, and that in 'reality' all moments in our lives, past, present and future, existed simultaneously. The most famous proponent of Dunne's theory was J. B. Priestley, who had used his ideas as a plot device in 'Time plays' such as *Time and the Conways* and *Dangerous Corner*. Beryl's own 'particular preoccupation'[7] with Dunne's ideas had been rekindled when writing about her youthful theatrical experiences in *An Awfully Big Adventure*, as she had learned parts of *Time and the Conways* in 1944 for her drama exams and served as prompt for *Dangerous Corner* while at the Playhouse.

Another play that Beryl had performed in during this period, *Dear Brutus*, provided the title of the new novel. This was a fantasy by James Barrie in which the characters are given a brief chance to experience the life they might have had if they'd made different decisions. Beryl had played the role of Margaret, the 'dream daughter' imagined by an unhappy artist after his estranged wife hints that things between them might have been different if they'd had children. Later, when it dawns on Margaret that she is a figment of the artist's imagination and that on his return to the real world she will cease to exist, she exclaims: 'Daddy, come back; I don't want to be a might-have-been.' The line had struck Beryl as particularly poignant when she delivered it in 1951 and had stayed in her mind ever since.

For the moment the question of how all this would fit into a novel was one she couldn't answer. In truth Beryl would rather have been tackling a less abstract, less philosophically complicated subject. 'Wish I could do Colin and Anna and me,'[8] she confided to Margaret Hewson, but her self-imposed proscription about dealing with the contemporary events of her private life meant this was effectively off-limits.

Another element of 'Dear Brutus', in which Beryl loosely portrayed herself as a girl called Rose, was her trip to Paris in 1953 with George Greggs, the 'Tsar' of *Harriet Said*. But the catalyst for the novel, the event that tied various disparate ideas together and gave it its structure, was an unwelcome – and literal – accident. On 11 March 2003 the taxi Beryl was in was rammed by another car just yards from her house in Albert Street. As she wasn't wearing a seat belt Beryl was propelled forward into the glass partition between driver and passenger, which shattered on impact. She was left with 'multiple facial lacerations',[9] a black eye, a swollen nose, and a deep cut requiring several stitches over her top lip, which ballooned up to twice its size: 'I don't have a mouth anymore, more of a pig's snout.'[10]

As if this wasn't bad enough, a subsequent X-ray revealed that there was still a fragment of glass in her lip and she had to undergo an operation at the end of May to remove the shard, leaving her with a small but permanent scar. Although this was not, for obvious reasons, stated in the novel, it was the origin of Rose's self-conscious habit of touching her lip.

At some point in the course of the following months ideas about her 1953 trip to Paris, her car accident, and her recent visit to Paris with

Psiche Hughes, during which she'd been to the site of the car crash that killed Diana, Princess of Wales, and Dodi Fayed in 1997, all merged in Beryl's mind. The Paris of the past and the present could be linked in parallel fashion, the slippage from one to the other triggered by passing through the Parisian underpass. At the time, it seemed like a good idea for a plot: 'I've just had a shot of genius,' she told a friend, 'anyway, I think it's brilliant. Hope I don't go off the idea.'[11]

Over the course of the next six months an opening chapter was written, worked on and refined. It traced the development of the relationship between a girl called Rose, a version of Beryl as she had been in 1953, and an older man, Mr Williamson, based on George Greggs. It also included a short 'flashforward' section at the beginning, a technique she had utilized before, most notably in *Harriet Said*, in which Rose and Mr Williamson sat and talked in the Paris Ritz, prior to leaving in a taxi; and the accident that would combine the two disparate time elements of the novel:

> They had crossed the second bridge when the taxi hit an obstruction in the road and slewed sideways. Mr. Williamson bounced to the roof; his hat came off. The girl tumbled forwards and fell with her face against the door.
>
> She didn't cry out or make a fuss. Mr. Williamson pulled her upright and clumsily patted her back. 'I do care for you,' he said, 'I really do,' and added that in time she might believe him.
>
> 'In time,' she murmured. A star of blood, delicate as a snowflake, melted upon her upper lip . . .[12]

But if the idea of incorporating the deaths of Diana and Dodi, via some theory of parallel realities, into a tenuously autobiographical narrative sounded complicated, that's because it was. Beryl herself had difficulty explaining the novel's plot: 'It's something like – I'm 17, and having supper at the Ritz (which I never did) . . . and then I go back with a group of people in 1997 and dine at the Ritz the night it all happened. And it's either my fault or that of the chap who's driving me. I don't know.'[13]

Despite being scheduled for publication in September 2004 and announced in Little, Brown's catalogue,[14] the novel's progress stalled and Beryl asked her agent to break the news to Richard Beswick, her publisher. 'I'm still doing it, but it's slow. I would be grateful (relieved) if you could hint to Richard B that it won't be ready this year. It may be – there's another five months, but I'm just finding it so hard – my breathing, the hot weather, the deadening of words in my head. I will do it, but not on schedule.'[15]

Ironically, though the novel was based on the notion of eternal recurrence, when it came to it Beryl could no longer remember the person she had been. It was this as much as the sheer technical difficulty of combining the different elements of the plot that led to the abandonment of 'Dear Brutus' in its incarnation as a novel about time at the end of 2004.

The fact that Beryl had cited a difficulty breathing as one of the reasons she found it hard to write marked a worrying development as regards the state of her health. Although she had been afflicted with bouts of breathlessness during the past ten years, which had necessitated the periodic use of a salbutamol inhaler – a drug that helps to dilate the airways during asthma attacks and in cases of chronic obstructive pulmonary disease (COPD) – this had not seriously affected her ability to work.

She had first been diagnosed with COPD in 1994,[16] after complaining to her doctor of periods of breathlessness that sometimes lasted 'up to six weeks'. Beryl described how she was often short of breath and coughed up phlegm, and on one occasion even had a spell of spitting up blood.[17] Bad though these symptoms were, the doctor still considered her problems reversible and, not for the first time, counselled her to give up cigarettes.

But Beryl had had respiratory and bronchial problems since childhood, and she had become somewhat blasé about such warnings. Physically uncomfortable though her cough was, she almost considered it normal. Despite repeated warnings to give up, Beryl's smoking actually increased during this period, going up from thirty a day in 1995 to thirty-five a day in 1999, and forty a day in 2002.[18] The consequences were entirely predictable.

Anyone who witnessed Beryl's cough in her later years will not forget it in a hurry. It seemed incredible that anyone as small as she was could produce a cough as loud and physically strenuous without doing themselves an injury. Her grandson Charlie captured one of her morning bouts of breathlessness while filming a documentary about her: 'This is how I spend half my night,' she explained to camera, doubled up in bed in between a fit of coughing and gasps for breath, 'bent over my knees like this because it's easier to breathe.'[19]

Breathlessness and coughing were one thing, but the progressive damage to her arteries that prolonged smoking and a high-fat diet were causing was something else altogether. While out shopping on Christmas Eve, 2003, she started to get a violent pain in her left leg that made it difficult to walk. She was taken to hospital and the doctor diagnosed 'a superficial femoral artery occlusion'[20] – in other words narrowing of the arteries. His blunt warning that if she didn't give up smoking altogether she risked damaging the arteries in her leg so much it could lead to amputation, shocked her into taking the problem more seriously than the usual exhortations to cut down for the sake of her cough.

'I've given up smoking', she wrote to Mary Thorne, an old friend from Liverpool. 'Not in order to live, just to avoid having one leg to stand on.'[21] But having been a smoker for so long, Beryl found it more difficult to give up than she imagined. For a short period she succeeded in cutting down, and other techniques, such as holding a dummy cigarette, also had limited success. But as with drink, she never succeeded in giving up entirely and the habit would gradually reassert itself: two cigarettes a day in 2006, nine a day in 2007, and ten a day by the end of 2009.[22] Like drinking, smoking became a bone of contention with her children. She instinctively balked at their appeals to give up for the sake of her health. 'I'm not proud of my lack of willpower,' she said of her relapse in 2007, 'but feel it's important to live one's declining years in comfort.'[23] Rather than risk open confrontation, she took to smoking in secret, though the results were about as successful – and as conducive to family harmony – as her attempts to hide her drinking.

Beryl's difficulty in breathing brought home to her in a frighteningly literal way how fine the line was between life and death. But it wasn't just illness that served as a reminder of her own mortality. In common with many people who reach their seventies she couldn't but be aware that her contemporaries were beginning to die off around her.

As the decade progressed, names that had meant so much to her in the past began to disappear with what seemed like increasing regularity: her former doctor, Cyril Taylor, died in 2000, as did her one-time confidante, Judith Shackleton; Noel Davis died in 2002, the same year as Harry Hoff, with whom she'd toured Russia in 1979; Fritz Spiegl died in 2003, as did Pauline Mani, the model for Freda in *The Bottle Factory Outing*. Pauline's death, which the local newspaper described as 'tragic and squalid',[24] was particularly shocking to those who knew her. Suffering from depression, she had lapsed into alcoholism and died alone, her body only being discovered when neighbours called the emergency services to complain about a foul smell coming from her flat. 'I saw her once or twice on the street and spoke and we were always going to meet,' Beryl told a reporter, perhaps feeling slightly guilty that she had not done more to help, 'but it was obvious by then that she was in a pretty bad way and not herself.' Tellingly, she chose to recall Pauline as her own fictional creation, rather than a person in her own right: 'I prefer to think of Freda, cloak billowing in the wind, forever galloping across Windsor Park.'

One death that affected Beryl especially deeply was that of Margaret Hewson. Since the late-1980s, Andrew Hewson's wife had been working full-time at the John Johnson agency and had come to take a leading role in Beryl's literary affairs. Beryl appreciated the ebullience and pugnacity with which Margaret fought her corner, but it was her sense of humour, her generosity and her unfailing positivity that cemented their friendship. In 1998, when the *South Bank Show* offered to take Beryl to the Crimea in the depths of winter, it was Margaret who had accompanied her for support – 'holding my frozen hand'[25] as Beryl put it. As Lynn Barber noted, Margaret was not only Beryl's agent, but her 'friend, confidante, travelling companion, research assistant and counsellor'.[26]

It was a shock, therefore, when in early 2002 Margaret was diagnosed with liver cancer and given only a matter of months to live. The speed with which the disease took hold was disturbing enough, but the debilitating physical effects of chemotherapy seemed doubly distressing in someone as habitually elegant and as vivacious as Margaret. Beryl felt her own quality of life had been diminished by Margaret's death – her wide range of cultural interests and enthusiasms helped keep Beryl's engagement with contemporary culture alive – and in her obituary tribute she wrote of feeling 'bereft that she has left this world before me'.[27]

The death of Bernice Rubens in October 2004 was another sad loss that touched Beryl particularly closely, though it was perhaps that of Anna Haycraft, six months later in March 2005, which more than any other symbolized the end of an era. Since their spat over the *Daily Telegraph* interview in 2001, Anna and Beryl had rarely seen each other. Anna now lived permanently in Wales.

In 2003 Anna had been diagnosed with lung cancer, and though an operation at the time had apparently been successful she suspected she might not have long to live: 'Cancer is a strange disease and I am aware that it may be lurking around, biding its time.'[28] In late 2004 Anna published an article that seemed designed to provoke, headlined 'I didn't miss Colin at all when he died'. This was not the sensationalizing misquotation of a sub-editor, but a deliberate attempt on Anna's part to minimize Colin's role in her life: 'I forget now when it was that Colin died of a stroke. We had been married some 40 years but I didn't miss him at all. The marriage was unimportant to me because the children were everything.'[29]

Anna had also retold her story about failing to become a nun, and once again she made no reference to Austin, the abortion, or Beryl. Beryl's reaction to the article was predictable. It annoyed her that Anna was trying to belittle Colin the way she had when he was alive, and she couldn't help but feel there was a hypocritical element in Anna's claim that being a Catholic 'is my most serious thing', given her refusal to acknowledge the truth about her past.

In early 2005 Anna's cancer returned and in March she was admitted to Meadow House Hospice in Ealing. But when Beryl enquired about coming to see her as she lay dying, Anna told those with her that she didn't want her to visit: Anna may have refused to acknowledge publicly what had happened in the past, but in private she no longer felt the need to hide her feelings. It was perhaps understandable. Beryl had been the cause of two irreparable humiliations in Anna's life: unintentionally in the case of Austin's betrayal and rejection of her, and deliberately in the case of the affair with Colin. To have Beryl look down on her now, while she was on her deathbed, was too much to take. Understandable though her decision was, it was also a deliberate snub, a final renunciation of their friendship.

Of course when Beryl was inevitably asked to write a tribute to Anna for the newspapers, none of this could be talked about. The piece she did write, published under the heading 'Kindred Spirits' in the *Guardian* a few days after Anna's funeral, must have seemed curiously bland and distant to anyone expecting to read about the painful loss of a close friend. Beryl's article was more about Duckworth than Anna, and ended on Anna's departure for Wales several years before: 'Sometimes we wrote each other letters and sometimes we spoke on the telephone. We didn't talk about writing, hers or mine, but then, we never had.'[30] A curious summing up of someone who had nominally been her editor.

One of the results of this heightened sense of mortality was that Beryl began to make preparations for her own death. She wrote letters to those close to her, not to be sent but to be given after her death. Some of these were notes containing bequests of books or money, others a final message, almost as a kind of leave-taking, a summation of what the recipient's friendship had meant to her.[31]

More practically she also decided to sort out her literary estate. Upstairs in the 'laboratory' was a large tin trunk in which were stored old manuscripts, folders stuffed full of letters, and various other documents relating to her literary career. The idea of selling these archives to a library or institution took hold after she'd seen the large sums that the sale of certain other writers' archives had made.

With this in mind, her papers were now sorted roughly into those related to her work, which could be sold, and those that were more personal, which could be kept.[32] In October 2004 a valuer from Bernard Quaritch, the firm acting as agents for the sale, came to inspect the material, returning a couple of weeks later to take away a large cache of documents so that they could be inventoried. The valuer considered it 'a rich and fascinating archive' and admitted to Beryl that she had 'never come across anything to compare with your dealings with Duckworth!' In 2005 this sizeable bulk of material was acquired by the British Library for a sum in the region of £70,000.[33]

Beryl's persistent problems with breathlessness, and the threat that continued smoking might lead to the amputation of a leg, were serious enough, but there was another, potentially even more worrying, threat to her health. Towards the end of 2003, after an initial examination for abnormal bleeding during her periods, Beryl's GP became concerned about the possible side effects of her prolonged use of hormone replacement therapy, and expressed her worries to a specialist at the Elizabeth Garrett Anderson hospital: 'This lady has been on HRT and does not wish to come off it. Incidentally, she doesn't do breast examination [*sic*] and is aware of breast cancer risks.'[34]

Beryl had been on HRT since 1983, and despite the fact that its link to breast cancer had long been established, she repeatedly declined medical advice to undergo a regular breast examination because she was 'not keen on mammograms',[35] as her doctor put it back in 1995. In the spring of 2006 Beryl noticed a lump in her left breast; initially, she did nothing about it: 'I don't think about such things,'[36] she later explained to her doctor. However, after talking to Parvin Laurence, she was finally persuaded to have the lump checked. A mammogram in August revealed an irregular mass, tests on which came back positive for cancer.[37] The doctor was in no doubt that Beryl's prolonged use of HRT had been a contributory factor and was surprised that she had continued using it after having been told of the risks in 2003.[38]

The tumour was excised in September, but it was much larger than it had appeared on the ultrasound scan. Shortly afterwards, following tests that suggested the tumour had spread, a mastectomy was recommended and carried out in November. Beryl herself was remarkably serene about the whole procedure: 'I can't say I felt ill afterwards – I was home in 24 hours, and who needs two bosoms once the nurture of children and the excitement of sex has diminished?'[39]

As she was considered to be at high risk, Beryl was initially scheduled to have post-operative chemotherapy and radiotherapy, but on further inspection the consensus of opinion was that it was a late diagnosis of an indolent tumour, rather than an aggressive one, and she was fortunately spared chemotherapy. By the beginning of 2007 she had completed her course of radiotherapy, and her doctors were pleased with the response. Her tests came back clear and her specialist reported that 'she feels extremely fit and is hard at work again on a new book'.[40]

In September 2008, during one of A. N. Wilson's regular breakfasts with Beryl at a cafe on Parkway she referred to as 'El Sordido's', he noticed a large purple bruise on her arm. As she tucked into her plate of sausage, bacon, egg and fried bread, he asked her what had caused it: 'Oh, lamb,' she replied, 'I had a heart attack.'[41]

The week before their breakfast meeting, Beryl had suffered a bout of breathlessness and an ambulance was called to take her to A & E. There, after an examination, she had what doctors called a percutaneous coronary intervention, in other words a stent was non-surgically inserted into one of her arteries through a catheter in her arm (hence the bruising). This is a fairly common practice in cases of ischemic heart disease as a way of dilating clogged arteries and aiding blood flow.

Again, smoking was most likely a contributory factor in this deterioration in her condition. The previous year Beryl admitted to her doctor that she'd been unable to give up smoking completely. She began having recurring fits of breathlessness, and one attack in May 2008 was so severe she was taken to A & E in an ambulance and spent the night in hospital. She was given a course of steroids to ease her breathing, but as the specialist noted, she had 'a problem with breathlessness even on slightest exertion'.[42] She was given a new inhaler, but still struggled for breath during the night,[43] something that was not only worrying in itself, but left her feeling tired during the day.

These increasingly frequent, and increasingly serious, bouts of illness severely curtailed her ability to carry out the kind of physically intensive literary activities she had previously been able to manage, even a few years before. She now rarely attended literary festivals or gave book readings, agreeing only to those she felt obliged to support out of a sense of loyalty, such as the King's Lynn Festival. Although she still went to the theatre and wrote her column for *The Oldie* (as well as articles for other newspapers), and attended the occasional lunch or book launch, for the most part her diary now contained more references to doctor's appointments and evenings spent babysitting than to literary events.

There was yet another unsettling development at the end of the year. During an evening round at Mike and Parvin Laurence's a week after Christmas, Beryl suffered an 'episode' in which she experienced a 'loss of consciousness and seizure'. As a doctor, Mike must have been extremely disturbed by what he saw, reporting to her GP what he described as 'a possible myoclonic jerk of one arm and left-sided facial droop',[44] symptoms of a lack of oxygen to the brain or a stroke.

One of the last literary events Beryl agreed to attend was in March 2009, when she went up to Leeds to take part in the Headingley LitFest. After the event she had been due to catch a train back to London at 6.10 p.m., but an hour or so beforehand she was taken out for a meal by the organizers and by the time she arrived at the station the train had left, leaving her with a wait of two and a half hours before the next one. Unfortunately the organizers had also given Beryl a bottle of whisky, which was opened as they sat waiting with her in the cafe: 'All I can remember was . . . they'd each hold their tea and I'd pour some whisky in, and then I got on the train. I can remember the first stop after Leeds and that was about twenty-five past eight. The next thing I remember was sitting on the sofa in my kitchen in pyjamas of some sort, with two police.'[45]

Beryl had been met off the train at King's Cross by police officers and taken to A & E. Her admissions form included the abbreviation ETOH++, a hospital code for very drunk.[46] Sometime during the journey a gang of drunken football supporters got on and invaded the first-class carriage. One of them suggested to Beryl they should 'go into the bog for sex', and her recollection of what happened next is somewhat hazy: 'I thought to myself, they must have been terribly hard up, I mean good God what's the matter with them? And I said to one of them, "Oh go away, you're only a little boy", or something like that.'

A woman sitting nearby overheard the exchange and, worried that some sort of assault was going to take place, reported the incident to the conductor who called the police: 'It was awful, awful,' Beryl recalled two weeks afterwards. 'They [the football supporters] got off at Milton Keynes and then I suppose the police met me at the other end, removed my clothes for forensic. I only got my clothes back two days ago. I was in these peculiar pyjamas from prisons . . . awful. But I can't remember any of it . . . I remember nothing. My mind's a complete blank.'[47]

Beryl's own view was that it was the mixture of alcohol and the pills she was taking that was to blame, though this was not the first time she had suffered from memory loss – or an acute sense of embarrassment and shame – as a result of her inability to stop drinking once she had started. The fact was that she was now so physically weak that drinking alcohol, especially in public, almost inevitably exposed her to situations that were potentially catastrophic.

Shortly after this, Beryl began suffering a new symptom: acute abdominal pain. This would get progressively worse until, at the end of November, she had to spend a week in University College Hospital (UCH). She was diagnosed with ischemic colitis, in layman's terms an inadequate blood supply to the intestines, exacerbated – like so many of Beryl's health problems – by the build-up of plaque in her arteries as a result of smoking. This was the longest she had spent in hospital, and she was again advised to stop smoking. That Beryl was aware her life was now hanging precariously in the balance is clear from her blunt response to an interviewer who asked what the future held in store: 'Death. Death and a full stop, that's it.'[48]

Clearing out the manuscripts in the 'laboratory' had one unexpectedly positive consequence: Beryl came across the journal she had kept during her trip across America in 1968 with Washington Harold. Not only that, she also found some thirty pages of a draft of 'He's the Captain of the Team', initially begun in 1969 and sporadically worked on during the early 1970s. Together they constituted a firm base from which to start her novel afresh.

The discovery brought on a renewed burst of energy, and the next few months were spent reworking and combining the draft of the abandoned novel with the already completed pages of 'Dear Brutus'. The Lady Diana and Dodi timeslip theme was dropped altogether and, instead, the most dramatic political event of the American trip – the assassination of Robert Kennedy – became the central plot element around which the new novel would develop. After reading about the unidentified woman seen running away from the scene of the shooting, who was described by witnesses as wearing a polka-dot dress, she also gave the novel a new title: *The Girl in the Polka Dot Dress*.

The original opening chapter of 'He's the Captain of the Team', in which Heine Melman meets Alma Bickerton at Baltimore airport in his new VW campervan, was substantially reused and is still recognizable as the opening chapter of the published version of *Polka Dot*. Although a lot has been added and reworked, and the names have been updated to Harold and Rose, many phrases from 1969 were carried over to the new version.

As for the opening chapter of 'Dear Brutus', the 'flashforward' section set in a Paris hotel between Mr Williamson and Rose now formed the basis of the scene between Harold and Rose in the Ambassador Hotel. Meanwhile the extended passage tracing the developing relationship between Mr Williamson and Rose was chopped up and incorporated as a series of flashback sequences in which Rose recalled her childhood meetings with the mysterious and vaguely menacing figure of Dr Wheeler.

After Beryl had used up all this 'new' old material, the novel again stalled. Her self-imposed view that as a writer her only interest was herself when young began to reveal itself as the creative straitjacket it was. Although she had updated the book's setting from Paris in the 1950s to America in 1968, she kept the character of Rose essentially unchanged, preferring to try and portray herself as single and childless – as she had been when she went to Paris with George Greggs – rather than as a divorcee with three children, as she had been in reality in 1968. But this presented enormous difficulties: 'For the life of me, I can't remember who I was in 1955, not really . . . I was married but hadn't got any children and who the person was who didn't have children I can't imagine.'[49]

Aside from finding it hard to imagine the person she'd been fifty years before, there were other factors that made writing the novel particularly difficult during this period. Recurrent bouts of illness and trying to give up smoking (or at least radically cut down) had disrupted Beryl's routine and made it hard to concentrate, while feelings of loneliness and an acute awareness of her own mortality, provoked by the deaths of close friends and her own precarious state of health, left her feeling depressed.

On 17 August 2005, two days after she was interviewed for a Radio 4 programme about creativity, she visited a hypnotist in Bayham Street to see whether there was anything he could do about her writer's block.

In an unsent letter to her agent Andrew Hewson around this time, she outlined her troubled state of mind:

> Dearest Andrew: I don't want you to reply to this letter, or to refer to it on the telephone. I just think I ought to tell you that I'm going through some sort of depression. It began a year ago, but has got worse. I've been to a doctor and a hypnotist – the latter (though I think its rubbish) has had some effect – the doctor finds nothing wrong.
>
> My problem is, I don't [know] who I am anymore. The me of 2 years ago seems to have evaporated. I write a page and find it's rubbish. I'm not giving up, just wanting to confide in a dear friend what's going on. I haven't told the children, but they suspect something. Some of it has to do with age. I do keep thinking about the end, not in a bad way, or scary, just that it can't be far off.
>
> So one wonders what the point is. The point used to be the plot, meaning writing, but I now find that so difficult to steer into – rather not the plot but the correct way to construct the sentance. I enclose some pages, some of which are not so bad, but it's such a struggle.[50]

For the next few years, her writing would ebb and flow with the state of her health, almost stopping completely during her diagnosis of and treatment for breast cancer. The doctor's decision to take her off HRT had a particularly negative effect. She had been taking it for so long that she experienced the equivalent of withdrawal symptoms – she couldn't concentrate, she felt lethargic, and she became tired very quickly. 'To keep me alive,' she later explained to Derwent May, 'I was taken off HRT which I'd been on for 20 odd years. Six months on from then, my writing dried up.'[51]

In June 2008 she went to her GP to talk about the problems she was having, saying that she was frequently miserable and tearful, that she felt apathetic and had no urge to go out, preferring to stay at home rather than attend social engagements. Beryl was also having persistent sleeping problems, finding it difficult to fall asleep and then often waking up at four in the morning. She enquired about whether she could be prescribed beta-blockers to relieve her anxiety, but they weren't recommended for patients with arterial problems and COPD. Instead, she was given advice about managing her depression and some sleeping tablets to help with her insomnia.

She now found living on her own 'more lonely than I thought it was'. She began to feel a sense of detachment from life, boredom even, her illness making it more difficult to distract herself, either through work or social interaction: 'Before, when I wasn't ill, I used to work and work and work. Well now I can't. There's long stretches of time when I'm not doing very much, so I listen to the flaming television . . . which annoys me . . . it's so boring, just watching telly.'[52]

For the first time Beryl also admitted to her doctor that she was having a problem with alcohol, and that she would sometimes drink a bottle of whisky in the space of a few days. Admittedly this was not exactly drinking on the scale of an Oliver Reed or a George Best, but Beryl was physically small and her tolerance was low, and it indicated an underlying sense of her unhappiness. The fact that she would even go to her doctor about the problem at all is an indication of how serious she felt it was. In his covering letter to her consultant Beryl's GP described her as 'a completely uncomplaining woman who only accesses help when she is very much in need'.[53]

The following year, in 2009, after tests showed that her cancer had not metastasized, she requested to go back on HRT as she was still convinced she couldn't write without it. Her doctors were not exactly keen, admitting that 'the decision to re-introduce HRT may seem controversial to say the least', but on balance it was considered that Beryl would probably feel a great deal better taking HRT and that it would help her to work. 'A week ago I asked my cancer surgeon if I could go back on HRT,' she told Derwent. 'God Bless him, he said "Yes". Hopefully, I will be more myself again in a couple of months.'[54]

Over the next few months Beryl's cancer specialist noted that the reintroduction of HRT had made 'a really dramatic improvement to the quality of her life' and that she was 'now able to work with more concentration than before'.[55] She began sending off regular, if sporadic, packages containing draft pages of the novel:

Dearest Bren: Some more pages. Could you type them quite soon and send them to me? Seeing it typed properly spurs me on, that and the increasing page numbers. I'm doing it every day, but I don't find it flows. The amount of crossed out pages is huge.[56]

This was no exaggeration: my own copy of the working manuscript, including reworked, variant or abandoned passages, comprised at least

500 pages, of which the edited 'clean' version amounted to some 150 pages, tantalizingly close to the restrained page count of around 170–180 pages that Beryl normally considered a complete novel. More packages followed in September ('These few pages are at last right – I think'),[57] and by November she had got Harold and Rose as far as Santa Ana, less than an hour's drive from the Ambassador Hotel on Wilshire Boulevard where the novel would reach its climax.

———

At the start of 2010 Beryl wrote to Dr Sackville-West to say that she wasn't feeling well: 'I am still tired, lacking energy and unable to eat without forcing myself.'[58] She mentioned that she knew a doctor – in fact Mike and Parvin Laurence's son Ari, who had recently become a consultant haematologist at UCH – and she wondered whether it could be arranged for her to see him professionally.

Dr Sackville-West's letter to Ari Laurence mentioned the bout of ischemic colitis a few months before, and added that she was suffering from gastrointestinal bleeding, as a result of which she was showing signs of mild anaemia. Sackville-West expressed concern that Beryl was 'very weak and easily exhausted', and that although she looked well, she was 'very frail' and 'slightly pale'.[59]

Beryl's list of medical complaints and diagnoses was now beginning to pile up – chronic obstructive pulmonary disease, breast cancer, bronchitis, ischemic heart disease, ischemic colitis, anaemia – and her medications on prescription ran to an impressive three pages: Ramipril, Simvastatin, Anastrozole, Premarin, Omeprazole and Aspirin (all to be taken once a day), Diltiazem capsules (twice a day), Cyclizine tablets (three times a day), and Tramadol and Paracetamol (four times a day). On top of this she also had three types of inhaler to help with her breathing: a Beclometasone aerosol inhaler (two puffs twice a day), a Serevent Accuhaler (one puff twice a day), and a Salbutamol aerosol inhaler (two puffs four times a day as required).

Unsurprisingly, given how weak she was feeling, she was finding it difficult to get down to writing: 'I am still having difficulty in finishing my new (and probably the last) novel,' she wrote to Derwent and Yola May in February, 'but I struggle most days in an attempt.'[60] Nevertheless, she continued to work and would sporadically send off pages to be typed and edited: 'I enclose 6 new or newish pages . . . I'm getting on – if slowly. Please return in folder, so that I can send you next lot – if there is a next lot. At least I'm trying.'[61]

Worryingly, Beryl was now beginning to lose weight, not just from a loss of appetite, but because of her anxiety over the adverse physical reactions she experienced when she did eat. By April her weight had dropped to 46kg, from 51kg the previous year, and she would lose another 2kg over the next month. Friends couldn't help but notice the effect that her problem with eating was starting to have. Mark Bostridge noted his concerns in his diary after an evening with Beryl and Robin Baird-Smith: 'Beryl says she's writing every day and hopes to finish in July . . . She looked terribly thin, and told Robin during dinner that she feared the cancer might have returned. I had to lend her a cardigan as she felt so cold in the dining room. She looked on, a bit pathetically, at the edge of the proceedings.'[62]

Throughout March and April she suffered from intermittent abdominal pains, but as the gastrointestinal bleeding had stopped there seemed to be little doctors could do to remedy the problem. Essentially Beryl's problem lay in the word that was affixed to the problems affecting her lungs, heart and intestines: ischemic, a medical term for a restriction in the blood supply to a part of the body. Beryl's long years of smoking, coupled with her high-fat diet of fried foods, was reducing the ability of her body to deliver blood and oxygen where it was needed. As the specialist bluntly remarked in trying to sum up what could be done in her case, Beryl 'would need to modify her risk factors to gain control over this problem. In particular she needs to stop smoking.'[63]

Given the severity and frequency of her problems, it is difficult to believe that even had Beryl given up smoking completely at this stage it would have had much impact. Shortly afterwards, at the beginning of June, she had several recurrences of the abdominal pain she had been experiencing and was given an appointment to see a specialist on 18 June.

But the pain continued to get worse. A few days before her consultation she went to see her local doctor, and by the following morning it was so severe she had to be taken by ambulance to the A & E department at University College London. An examination suggested there might be a partial obstruction of the intestine and after an X-ray and an intravenous blood test she was discharged. The abdominal pain persisted, however, and shortly afterwards Beryl was readmitted to hospital. Over the next few days it became increasingly clear that the compacted bowel was more problematic than had initially been thought, and she was put on a morphine drip to help ease the pain. Even so she continued to think about her novel: 'I've got to finish the book. It's worrying me,' she told her children, adding that she wanted to be moved to a bed that would allow her to sit up and write. Even though the morphine made it difficult to concentrate, she would read pages through – or have them read to her – while Jo and Rudi took it in turns to take notes.

Worse news was soon to follow. Blood tests now showed that her cancer had metastasized and spread. Despite her worsening condition – at times the pain became so severe she had to have injections of morphine in addition to the intravenous drip – she was adamant that it was 'utterly impossible' for anyone else to finish the book and clung to the idea that, with help, she could still get it done. The fate of her characters now merged in her mind with that of her own: 'I know that both the characters and myself are going to die.'[64]

On 28 June, Rudi had phoned me to say that the latest prognosis wasn't good: Beryl had hardly been able to speak that day and it was feared she would drift into a coma – she might have only a matter of days to live. The following morning, fearing the worst, I went to see her at the hospital, calling in at Albert Street beforehand to pick up the last few pages she had written before being admitted.

When I got to the ward I happened to meet Rudi, who had been visiting her mother and was just leaving. She said that amazingly Beryl had revived, that she was the most alert she had been for days – even the doctors were taking it as a positive sign. It was still a shock to see her in bed, as it always is when you first see someone who is seriously ill, but after a few minutes talking with her it almost seemed possible that she would pull through again. She sat up in bed, and we talked about the effects the drugs were having and the hallucinatory dreams they inspired, one of which involved dancing with Colin.

There was still the matter of the novel to consider, so we spread out the pages that had been printed so far. After the talk with Rudi the night before I had begun to think about what could be done to reduce the amount of writing Beryl might need to do in order to finish, and suggested she move an earlier flashback sequence to the end. This would continue the narrative on from the point it had now reached and bring it to the brink of completion, leaving only a handful of pages to write.

But as it turned out these speculations were academic. The next morning she had a relapse, falling into a state that bordered on unconsciousness. For years, despite her shortness of breath and her cough, despite her smoking and drinking too much and eating too little, despite even her cancer, Beryl had seemed indestructible. Now it was clear there was little chance of her pulling through. The next day I went in again to say goodbye, holding her hand as she lay there, frail and almost immobile.

For Aaron, Jo and Rudi, the final parting was much harder, a gruelling day and night vigil would follow, in which Beryl's emaciated body refused to give up its final breath, improbably hanging on to life in a way that was deeply distressing for those who had to witness it. Finally, in the early hours of 2 July, Beryl stopped breathing and was at last at peace.

B ERYL HAD SPENT A long time thinking about her death and making preparations for it. She had written letters to be post-humously given to those close to her, tucking them away in the top drawer of the huge scroll-top writing desk[1] in the front room. In one of the larger drawers further down she kept a folder containing all her legal documents – deeds of the house, will, bank statements – ready to be passed over to her solicitor. She had also put aside a building society passbook, earmarked to cover the cost of her funeral. She had been topping it up with money over the years, though in fact it represented only a fraction of the price of a burial plot in her preferred resting place – Highgate Cemetery.

The day before the funeral, she was laid out in an open coffin in the front room of Albert Street, and her family and some of her close friends came to pay their last respects. In death she was as defiantly anti-conventional as she had been in life, and the viewing of her embalmed corpse was not to everyone's taste. Afterwards those who braved the ordeal sat on the front steps of the house, talking and drink-ing, as they had many times before, only for once Beryl remained inside.

The funeral was held at St Silas's in Kentish Town, after which she was interred in Highgate Cemetery. At the graveside, the band of mourners sang for the last time 'Did You Think I Would Leave You Dying (When There's Room On My Horse For Two)?', as they had at Beryl's parties in the past.

The news of Beryl's death provoked an outpouring of affectionate recollections, both from those who knew her well and those who had only met her once but who had never forgotten the experience. She was described in the press as 'much loved' – a term one couldn't imagine being applied to Iris Murdoch or Doris Lessing – and referred to as a 'national treasure'. In what seemed like an access of guilt, the Booker

Prize committee decided to award her a posthumous Booker, leaving it up to the public to decide which of the five previously shortlisted novels should win – the vote went to *Master Georgie*.

A decision had to be taken about the manuscript of *The Girl in the Polka Dot Dress*, so tantalizingly close to being completed. No one wanted to let all the work Beryl had done on the book, the time and energy she had spent on it over the last years of her life, count for nothing. As I had been editing the book since its conception, I prepared a final version from my working manuscript, incorporating the last pages she'd worked on and making some of the adjustments I'd talked about with her before she died. The sequence of events now ran from Rose's first meeting with Harold at the airport up to the moment prior to the shots being fired.

Had Beryl lived the ending would undoubtedly have been different. At one point she talked of Rose knocking Harold's gun just as he was about to shoot Dr Wheeler and that this would accidently kill Robert Kennedy. But I doubt the solution would have been quite so simple or so convenient if she'd got round to writing it. Would Rose's shot have anticipated those of Sirhan Sirhan, who was also in the room, armed and ready to kill, or simply added to them? We will never know. Beryl often said the end would be easy to do, but whenever she was blocked and I suggested she write it, she would always demur. I suspect she meant that while she didn't have the ending planned in detail, she trusted to the fact that it was almost always the easiest part to write, because by the time you get to the final page all the narrative problems have been solved and the logic of events takes over.

It is never ideal to publish an author's work in an unfinished state, but sometimes there is little choice. The best one can hope for is that the pleasure to be gained from the quality of the writing outweighs the disappointment of its lack of completeness. There was at least, as Ruth Scurr remarked in her review of the published novel, a certain appropriateness in its final state: 'It seems fitting that the novel which eluded Beryl Bainbridge for four decades should be published after her death as a testament to unresolvability, or the impossibility of ending.'[2]

Throughout her writing career Beryl encouraged the notion that her books were straightforwardly autobiographical. 'I can't write fiction,'[3] she would tell interviewers; 'my life's all in the novels.'[4] If this biography demonstrates one thing, it is that there is a more complicated relationship than has commonly been supposed between the facts of Beryl's life and the representations of it contained in her fiction. In truth this should come as no surprise. However closely a novel seems to be based on real-life source material, it is not a slice of authentic autobiography. To function as a novel it has to be shaped, it requires narrative structure, form, plot and character – and in this fictionalizing process the truth of an individual's experience is inevitably distorted, sometimes beyond recognition. The fact that Beryl worked in a wine-bottling firm does not make *The Bottle Factory Outing* a trustworthy guide to the emotional circumstances of her life at the time, any more than the fact that she was an actress at the Liverpool Playhouse makes *An Awfully Big Adventure* a reliable source of information about her adolescent experiences as a student there.

This is not to say that Beryl's fiction wasn't shaped by her experiences, but if parallels are to be drawn between the two, then at the very least they need be based on something more substantial than the anecdotes and stories she published in newspapers. Like many literary celebrities, Beryl was in a position where the things she said about herself and her motivations as a writer acquired a public prominence – and therefore a historical permanence – that was out of all proportion to the casual and often off-hand manner in which they were recounted.

In presenting Beryl's life honestly and openly for the first time, therefore, I hope this biography will help dispel the myths that surround her name and lead to a fresh evaluation of her, both as a woman and as a writer.[5] Only by understanding how the emotional traumas she lived through shaped her complex, contradictory personality can we begin to unravel the process by which she converted these experiences into the novels for which she will be remembered.

NOTES

ABBREVIATIONS

BL Beryl Bainbridge collection, British Library, London
JH Joseph Hansen papers, Huntington Library, San Marino, California

INTRODUCTION

1 Interview with George Yeatman for the Booker Prize in 1973.

2 Willa Petschek, 'Beryl Bainbridge's tenth novel', *The New York Times*, 1 March 1981.

3 *Forever England*, Duckworth, 1987, p. 66.

4 *Front Row: Evenings at the Theatre*, Continuum, 2005, pp. 2–3.

5 'The year I grew up', *Independent*, 11 July 1999.

6 See 'The non-fiction film in post-war Britain' by Leo Enticknap, PhD thesis, University of Exeter, 1999.

7 The only reference in her early writing to these events is in a fictionalized account of her relationship with a German prisoner of war, 'My Song is Done', written in 1949. Although it contains a grim description of a prisoner of war camp in America, concentration camps are only mentioned in passing, not described: 'Often [Loo] would ask him about Germany and the narzis and the concentration camps.' 'My Song is Done', BL MS 83743.

8 Diary entry for 17 February 1944. BL MS 83816.

9 'The year I grew up', *Independent*, 11 July 1999.

10 The closest Beryl gets to such a statement is in her 1949 diary, under the date 3 June, when she comes home to find her father hasn't washed or shaved since the previous day and she remarks: 'I loathe him at times.'

11 Diary entry for 23 January 1946. BL MS 83817.

12 'True colours', *Guardian*, 14 February 2004.

13 Beryl got the date and information about the numbers killed from her copy of the *Chronicle of the 20th Century*, Longman, 1988, p. 572. Also see note 15.

14 'The year I grew up', *Independent*, 11 July 1999.

15 See *Chronicle of the 20th Century*, Longman, 1988, p. 621. While the information she copied about Mussolini and his mistress being killed on 28 April is true, the *Chronicle* does not mention that it was actually the following day on which their bodies were taken to Milan and strung up, and not until the start of May that British newspapers printed the grisly photographs.

16 'Rubble, toil and troubles', *Evening Standard*, 21 April 1988.

17 Diary entry for 15 June 1953. BL MS 83819.

18 Compare the paragraph printed in 'Beryl Bainbridge says...', *The Times*, 3 September 1981, with that contained in the published edition on p. 54.

19 This and the subsequent quote: *Authors' Lives*, British Library sound recording (Track 2, December 2008). The passage has been edited to remove hesitations and repetitions.

20 'My week', *Observer*, 6 July 2008.

21 Mark Bostridge, *Lives for Sale: Biographers' Tales*, Continuum, 2004.

22 These annotations are often subject to the same carelessness with regard to fact as her published memoirs. This is especially true of those added in 2003–4 to the material bought by the British Library. She had been encouraged in this practice by Austin, who told her to write biographical information on the backs of her paintings as it would make them more valuable when she came to sell them. As Beryl did not bother to research or check the details beforehand, many of them are wildly inaccurate.

CHAPTER 1

1 Journal 1955–65. BL MS 83820.

2 William Foster, 'Childhood stories', *Scotsman*, 15 October 1977.

3 *Daily Mail*, 10 March 1992.

4 Martyn Harris, 'Biting hard on the bullet-hole', *Sunday Telegraph*, 24 March 1991.

5 Alan Franks, 'Act one, scene two', *The Times*, 7 April 1992.

6 Quoted in 'The sad, mad, funny world of Beryl Bainbridge', interview with Pat Garratt, *Woman's Journal*, 1979.

7 'My father, cabin boy', *Sunday Telegraph*, 5 December 1999.

8 William spent the last years of his life working as an 'ale store keeper' in Romilly Street. After his death his effects amounted to £154.

9 Although it should be noted that these genealogical databases are themselves minefields in which it is easy to come a cropper. The sheer repetition of names within a family and the small errors that creep into official records mean that everything has to be confirmed by secondary sources before it can be relied on.

10   The cause was given as kidney failure, though it is hard not to think that bearing thirteen children before the age of forty wasn't a contributory factor.

11   There was a seven-year gap between the birth of Marion (also known as Miriam) and that of Ellen's second daughter, Deborah, so it is likely that Marion was not William Bainbridge's child. In any event, Deborah, though born out of wedlock in 1875, was christened a Bainbridge, whereas Marion had been registered as a Kidd.

12   'Pinny for your thoughts', *Evening Standard*, 23 February 1990. Beryl also mentioned her father's singing of 'Lily of Laguna' in *A Weekend with Claud*, p. 57.

13   *A Weekend with Claud*, New Authors, 1967, p. 45.

14   'Learning to live with my mum and dad', *Observer*, 23 December 1984.

15   'Made in England', Arts Council, 2008.

16   See 'Facing backwards', *New Review*, October 1977; 'The year I grew up', *Independent*, 11 July 1999; 'How landscape influences an author's work', unpublished draft, c. 1986.

17   'Made in England', Arts Council, 2008.

18   Among the hundreds of other bankruptcies during this period was the creditor who pulled the plug on Bainbridge & Co., Thomas Gascoign. He was declared bankrupt on the same day as Richard. The slump affected every aspect of Richard's business life: Bickerton & Co., for whom he had acted as director, a position presumably gained through Margo's in-laws, was also wound up in February 1931.

19   Programme for *Little Women*, Salisbury Theatre, March 1953.

20   Information gathered from 'Ridge Hill Mine, near Chirbury: introduction & background' by Ivor Brown, in *Quarterly Journal of the Shropshire Caving & Mining Club*, Spring Issue, 2009.

21   *Liverpool Daily Post*, 13 June 1916.

22   Letter from Winnie Bainbridge, 10 March 1948.

23   Hilary Abbott, conversation with author, 13 May 2015.

24   Letter from Trevor Baines to author, 6 January 2014.

25   'Home is where the hearth is', *Evening Standard*, 17 March 1989.

26   See Winnie's letter to Beryl, c. 2 February 1948: 'I have been to Waterloo Hospital this morning to see a Dr. Plevin . . . He took a blood count & blood test and will communicate the result to Dr. Smythe tomorrow. I am feeling very much better but Dr. Smythe wants me to keep on with the injections, gradually lessening them to one a month.'

27   'Home is where the hearth is', *Evening Standard*, 17 March 1989.

28   *Liverpool Daily Post*, 11 September 1915.

29   Prospectus, Institut Notre-Dame aux Épines, 1920.

30   *Forever England*, Duckworth, 1987, pp. 13–14.

31   Beryl's recollection that Winnie was 'on the rebound from a cad called Walter who played tennis on the Isle of Wight' when she met Richard (see 'Women behaving badly', unidentified magazine, 1996), had at least some foundation. Photographs of Winnie on the Isle of Whithorn in July 1924 show her holding hands with a young man named Wallie. Given the similarity in the sound of the two place names, it seems probable that Beryl simply got them confused.

32   'Women behaving badly', unidentified magazine, 1996.

33   Significantly perhaps, given Beryl's later health problems, Ellen died from cardiac failure brought on by asthma and bronchitis.

34   Despite this, Beryl claimed that Winnie couldn't remember the names of her dead siblings.

35   Some of what Winnie felt during this early phase of her life with Richard is captured in a short story Beryl wrote in the mid-1960s, in which an older woman reflects on her past and recounts the moment she realized the future she'd dreamed of had been taken from her: 'I had a house, a whole house. I had a maid. In those days one could afford a maid you know. And I had a loving husband, and of course there was the baby . . . But one day when the baby was quite small, I woke up and I had the most curious feeling that I had lost something . . . or rather that something had been stolen from me. I played with the baby and I told the maid what we should have for dinner and I wound the clocks and dusted the ornaments, and I felt . . . cheated . . . it was all so boring, one man, one house, one child.' 'A walk in the park', BL MS 83793.

CHAPTER 2

1   'A treatise on justification', in 'Fragments 1951–53'. BL MS 83745.

2   'Sweet and sour idylls', *Daily Mail*, 13 November 1993.

3   Hilary Abbott, interview with author, 13 May 2015.

4   *Forever England*, Duckworth, 1987, p. 30.

5   Letter from Southport General Infirmary to Dr Kovachich, 4 March 1954.

6   'My Little Room', BL MS 83793.

7   *Forever England*, Duckworth, 1987, p. 41.

8   'Fragments 1951–53'. BL MS 83745.

9   Diary entries for 10 and 13 January 1949. BL MS 83818.

10   Diary entry for 4 March 1949. BL MS 83818.

11   Quoted in 'Yolanta May talks to Beryl Bainbridge', *New Review*, December 1976.

12   *The Times*, 7 April 1992. There are a number of inconsistencies in Beryl's account: first she says she was fourteen at the time, then that it happened

while she was at the Playhouse, when she would have been between the ages of seventeen and nineteen.

13 'Drape expectations', *Evening Standard*, 4 January 1991.

14 'A treatise on justification', in 'Fragments 1951–53'. BL MS 83745.

15 'Memories', in 'Fragments 1951–53'. BL MS 83745.

16 'More memories', in 'Fragments 1951–53'. BL MS 83745.

17 Diary entry for 31 January 1949. BL MS 83818.

18 *Liverpool Echo*, 20 December 1973.

19 'Fragments 1951–53'. BL MS 83745.

20 Diary entry for 2 March 1960. 1955–65 Journal. BL MS 83820.

21 Quoted in 'Yolanta May talks to Beryl Bainbridge', *New Review*, December 1976.

22 Quoted in 'Beryl Bainbridge: an ideal writer's childhood', interview with Craig Brown, *The Times*, November 1978.

23 Letter to Richard Bainbridge, c. 1948.

24 'Facing backwards', *New Review*, October 1977.

25 'I'm Not Criticising . . . I'm Remembering'. BL MS 83793.

26 'Another Friday', unpublished radio play. BL MS 83793.

27 Letter to Judith Shackleton, c. October 1963.

28 *Authors' Lives*, British Library sound recording (Track 2, December 2008).

29 Postcard to Winnie Bainbridge, c. 1944.

30 Birthday card to Winnie Bainbridge, c. 1948.

31 Letter to Winnie Bainbridge, January–February 1948.

32 A. N. Wilson, interview with author, 4 March 2015.

33 Letter to Judith Shackleton, c. 1 April 1965.

34 Beryl would frequently state that he was five or six years older than her, showing the extent to which, psychologically at least, she regarded him as being that much more mature than she was.

35 There was also no doubt an element of gender bias in this: Richard and Winnie simply expected more of Ian as a boy than of Beryl as a girl, or as Beryl put it: 'Boys were the ones that were supposed to achieve, then.' 'Mastering the art of the impossible', *Independent*, 24 August 1994.

36 Trevor Baines, interview with author, 6 January 2016.

37 Beryl's cousin Hilary spent a lot of time with Ian and his girlfriend, Janet, during this period and was sceptical about both claims.

38 'Beryl Bainbridge talks to Yolanta May', *New Review*, December 1976.

39 'Ghosts of Christmas past', undated article.

40 'A good death', BBC, March 2009.

41 This and subsequent quotes from 'Yolanta May talks to Beryl Bainbridge', *New Review*, December 1976.

42 *Forever England*, Duckworth, 1987, p. 42.

43 The song was made popular by the Three Flames, but there was also a slightly bawdier version by Walter Brown and the Tiny Grimes Sextet.

44 Although there are many photographs showing Richard at Chirbury looking relaxed and participating in the fun, Beryl implied that he often drove the family down and then left them there, taking advantage of the fact that the hotel faced directly onto the road: 'This was handy for my father, who on numerous occasions, spotting his detested father-in-law in the doorway, hand raised in welcome, would bring the car screeching to a halt within a yard of our destination . . . and when at last we were all out . . . he would fling himself back into the driving seat and reversing, roar off . . . like a man leaving a sinking ship.' *Forever England*, Duckworth, 1987, p. 140.

45 Hilary Abbott, interview with author, 13 May 2015.

46 Obituary of George Lyward, *The Times*, 28 June 1973.

47 Letter from Terry Alderman, 10 August 1946.

48 Letter from Terry Alderman, 9 August 1946.

49 According to Hilary Abbott her name was Helen Brown.

50 *Forever England*, Duckworth, 1987, p. 142.

51 Despite spending as much time in Chirbury as Beryl, Hilary Baines had no recollection of the ladder incident.

52 *Authors' Lives*, British Library sound recording (Track 2, December 2008).

53 Diary entry for 19 February 1946. BL MS 83817.

54 Hilary Abbott, interview with author, 13 May 2015.

55 Diary entry for 11 January 1949. BL MS 83818.

56 *Authors' Lives*, British Library sound recording (Track 2, December 2008).

57 'What I know about men', interview by Nicki Spritz, *Observer*, 15 January 2006.

58 Mary Kenny, *Catholic Herald*, 20 August 2004.

CHAPTER 3

1 'A treatise on justification', in 'Fragments 1951–53'. BL MS 83745.

2 Advertisement in Seed's Directory for Southport, 1924.

3 Advertisement in *Manchester Courier*, 6 July 1906. The exam boards included London Matriculation, Oxford Locals and Cambridge Higher. By the late 1930s the college was in decline, most of the original founders had already died, and the two remaining Misses Gill were both in their seventies. Alice Gill died in 1939, and the college closed down shortly after Beryl left in 1942.

4 Information from Formby Civic Society website.

5 'Basher's progress', interview in *Evening Standard*, 8 May 1967.

6 'I never thought I was worth anything as a writer', interview with Graham Turner, *Daily Telegraph*, 18 August 2001.

7 Diary entry for 10 March 1944. BL MS 83816.

8 Diary entry for 3 April 1944. BL MS 83816.

9 Recounted in an email to author by Anita Barry, 7 June 2013.

10 *Fifty Years 1900–1950: A History of S. Faith's Crosby*, compiled by G. W. Houldin, 1950.

11 Perhaps the teacher Beryl had most trouble with, and who represented the opposite of Miss Peck's more tolerant and encouraging approach, was Miss Williamson, the maths teacher. Beryl recalled being 'absolutely hopeless at maths' at school, and described 'Willie', as the pupils nicknamed her, as 'a horror, a real cross patch, always snappy and a fiend not just to me but to everybody'. This assessment is borne out by Beryl's fellow pupils – the most frequent epithet applied to Miss Williamson in their letters is 'bitch'. See 'My best teacher', interview with Pamela Coleman, *The Times Educational Supplement*, 29 January 1999.

12 Diary entries for 1944. BL MS 83816.

13 Diary entries for 1946. BL MS 83817.

14 Diary entry for 21 February 1944. BL MS 83816.

15 Beryl's later statement that she went to Mrs Ackerley twice a week for several years was a typical exaggeration.

16 Margaret Parsons, interview with author, 14 March 2014.

17 Diary entry for 19 June 1944. BL MS 83816.

18 In the introduction to a volume of her theatre criticism Beryl wrote: 'At the age of five I became a member of the Thelma Bickerstaff tap-dancing troupe', inventing a suitably comical and northern-sounding name, though in fact the principal of the Ainsdale School was Helen Jackson.

19 *Forever England*, Duckworth, 1987, p. 40.

20 Margaret Parsons, interview with author, 14 March 2014.

21 *Liverpool Echo*, 31 July 1945.

22 This and other early photographs show the extent to which Beryl's hair was permed, something carried out under the instigation of her mother and that she repeatedly claimed to detest, but which undoubtedly contributed to making her look much older than her years. 'From the age of six I always had a permanent wave,' she told one interviewer ('Spot the author', interview with Serena Allott, *Weekend Telegraph*, 11 April 1987); to another, she remarked that 'Perms in those days were fantastic.

You came out looking like a Zulu' ('Basher's progress', *Evening Standard*, 8 May 1967).

23 Letter from John James and Janet Baines, 1 August 1945.
24 Beryl's published account of her experiences working on *Children's Hour* are somewhat misleading. She didn't, as she claimed, travel 'during the war . . . to act on the wireless', nor did she spend 'the next two years . . . performing in various dramas'. See *Front Row: Evenings at the Theatre*, Bloomsbury Continuum, 2005, p. 2.
25 See diary entries for 15 and 25 August, and 2, 11 and 17 September 1944, for example. BL MS 83816.
26 'I Remember Peace Day', BL MS 83734.
27 A similar sense of embarrassment about her body, and a corresponding unease about the male gaze, features in a story she would write a few years later, in which the female narrator is handed a bouquet of flowers by a young man as a love token: 'I was very uncomfortable because even though it was extremely hot I was ashamed of my forming breasts and wore a thick cardigan to help disguise the fact that my summer frock was unwarrantably tight.' 'The Laird's Afternoon' in 'Fragments 1951–53'. BL MS 83745.
28 *The Magazine*, Merchant Taylors' School for Girls, 1944. Beryl would later say that the talk she remembered best was one about sewage, given by a man from the Water Board, but this is probably another piece of myth-making as she also mentions in the same article that Rex Harrison was among the school's guest speakers – he was not. See 'Waiting for stragglers', *The Listener*, 23 and 30 December 1982.
29 *Forever England*, Duckworth, 1987, p. 66.
30 Letter from Winnie Bainbridge, 29 February 1948.
31 Letter from Richard Malthouse, 24 October 1948.
32 Diary entry for 23 January 1949. BL MS 83818.
33 Diary entry for 8 April 1944. BL MS 83816.
34 'Ghosts of Christmas past', *Image*, December 1986.
35 Letter from Richard Bainbridge, 22 January 1948.
36 Diary entries for 1946. BL MS 83817.
37 Diary entry for 9 February 1946. BL MS 83817.
38 Diary entry for 24 February 1946. BL MS 83817.

CHAPTER 4

1 'Fragments 1951–53'. BL MS 83745.
2 *Formby Times*, 4 August 1945. Even this early newspaper report is erroneous in its dating of events. Beryl began at Mrs Ackerley's at the start

of 1944, when she was eleven, not ten, and she completed her gold medal in the space of a year, not two as stated. The *Liverpool Echo*, 31 July 1945, noted that Beryl's skill in composition was evidenced by 'a number of remarkably well-constructed and promising poems'.

3 'The Medvale Bombshell' is the earliest surviving example of Beryl's fiction, though one must assume there were earlier attempts that were subsequently lost or destroyed. The earliest reference to such work is in a section called 'More memories' in 'Fragments 1951–53': 'When I was nine or ten, perhaps younger I began to write a story in a red cash book. It was called "The Magic Carpet". I cannot remember much else about it.' In the introduction to *Filthy Lucre*, Beryl added that it was after seeing *The Thief of Bagdad* – which famously included scenes of a flying magic carpet – that she was inspired to write the story. The film was released late in 1940 and shown in the UK during 1941, when Beryl was between eight and nine. However, the other details about her early writings in the *Filthy Lucre* introduction seem more suspect, or at the very least erroneously dated.

4 The novel's hero lives in a house on Colgarth Road, which sounds very similar to Talgarth Road, where the LAMDA building was situated.

5 'The Medvale Bombshell'. BL MS 83738. All subsequent quotes are from the manuscript.

6 This is the title given in the manuscript, though at the top of the first chapter this has been overwritten at a later date with the title 'The Tragedy of Andrew Ledwhistle and Richard Soleways'.

7 'The Tragedy of Andrew Ledwhistle and Martin Andromiky'. BL MS 83740. When it was reproduced in *Filthy Lucre*, Beryl made a number of small and unnecessary changes to this paragraph, which reads better in the manuscript than in the published version. All subsequent quotes are from the ms version.

8 This and subsequent quotes relating to Christie/Lynda from 'My Song is Done'. BL MS 83743.

9 Letter from Lynda South, c. 20 March 1948.

10 Letter from Lynda South, c. late 1946.

11 Letter from Lynda South, c. 2 March 1952.

12 Poem dated Formby 1947. BL MS 83744.

13 Letter from Lynda South, c. February 1948.

14 Letter from Lynda South, c. 21 June 1952.

15 Extract of letter to Lynda South, c. 1952, in 'Fragments 1951–53'. BL MS 83745.

16 Note on Beryl's ammunition box.

17 This and subsequent quotations, 'Us Versus Them'. BL MS 83742.

CHAPTER 5

1   'Fragments 1951–53'. BL MS 83745.
2   Untitled poem dated 1947. BL MS 83744.
3   Draft version of 'The Summer of the Tsar'. BL MS 83761.
4   'The hermit is a learned man', *Formby Times*, 26 July 1947.
5   Little is known of Harry Franz, except that he lived near Kronach and worked for Siemens after the war, though the company no longer has any records relating to him. Beryl referred to him as Harry Arno Franz, though he himself always gave his name as Harry Franz.
6   Letter to Harry Franz, 21 August 1948.
7   Letter from Harry Franz, 25 November 1947.
8   The manuscript is dated 3 January 1949, but Beryl also puts her age as fifteen, which if correct means it must have been written between November 1947 and November 1948. The resulting novel was mixed at best, though it is difficult to judge it because it is impossible to know whether the unnumbered pages that form the current manuscript constitute all of those that were originally written, or indeed if they are in the right order. Nor is it clear whether all the pages belong to the same draft, or whether they represent alternative versions of the same story written at different periods. Beryl herself seems not to have been entirely satisfied with the result, and four years later in 1953 she recopied some or perhaps all of the pages, but the extent to which she may also have revised or rewritten them isn't clear.
9   Beryl had no photograph of Harry, but when the *Daily Telegraph* ran an article about her relationship with him in 2005, they incorrectly printed a photograph of another man she knew at the time called Harry Wesseling, even though his name is signed on the front. Beryl either didn't notice that this wasn't the 'real' Harry when she sent the photograph, or thought no one would know the difference.
10 'My Song is Done', 1949. BL MS 83743.
11 Ibid.
12 'Fragments 1951–53'. BL MS 83745.
13 'My Song is Done', 1949. BL MS 83743.
14 Letter from Alan Frost, c. March 1948.
15 *A Quiet Life*, Duckworth, 1976, p. 107.
16 Luke Salkeld, 'Love across enemy lines', *Daily Mail*, 16 August 2007.
17 'Fragments 1951–53'. BL MS 83745.
18 1947 Notebook.
19 Letter from Harry Franz, 28 July 1947.
20 The only Jimmy Clunie listed in birth records for Kinross was born in Cleish in 1915, which would make him thirty-two at the time.

21 'Fragments 1951–53'. BL MS 83745.
22 Ibid.
23 Letter from Harry Franz, 5 September 1947.
24 'Fragments 1951–53'. BL MS 83745.
25 Quoted in letter from Harry Franz, 11 September 1947.
26 Untitled poem dated Formby, 1947. BL MS 83744. The third and final stanza reads: 'For one day while walking/To meet you dear/Two loving figures went past/I heard you say, without a care/You are by far, more sweet than her/What a pity it had to end/What a pity it did'nt last.'
27 Letter from Harry Franz, 18 September 1947.
28 Quoted in letter from Harry Franz, 10 December 1947.
29 Quoted in letter from Harry Franz, 30 December 1947.
30 Quoted in letter from Harry Franz, 29 February 1948.
31 Quoted in letter from Harry Franz, 3 May 1948.
32 Quoted in letter from Harry Franz, 25 June 1948.
33 Letter from Bernard Blundell, c. 15 February 1948.
34 Letter from Jim Palmer, 17 January 1948.
35 Untitled poem, c. 1948. BL MS 83734.
36 Letter to Harry Franz, 21 August 1948.
37 Quoted in letter from Harry Franz, 15 May 1949.
38 Entry for 11 February 1949. 1949–53 Journal. BL MS 83818.
39 Entry for 20 February 1949. 1949–53 Journal. BL MS 83818.
40 'Fragments 1951–53'. BL MS 83745.

CHAPTER 6

1 'Fragments 1951–53'. BL MS 83745.
2 Ibid.
3 Beryl once let slip that the school authorities had told her parents it would be best for all concerned if she left, as there was no hope of her passing the school certificate. See *Terry Waite Takes a Different View*, Thames, 1986.
4 'It was a surprise for me to hear, that you next January go to London in the school.' Letter from Harry Franz, 6 August 1947.
5 Letter from Jacques Delebassée, 31 August 1947.
6 Beryl's assertion that the mansion was 'built by Charles II for Nell Gwynn' isn't true.
7 *Forever England*, Duckworth, 1987, pp. 112–13.
8 Julie Andrews, *Home: A Memoir of My Early Years*, Hachette, 2008.
9 Gillian Lynne, *A Dancer in Wartime*, Vintage, 2012, pp. 47–8.
10 Julie Andrews, *Home: A Memoir of My Early Years*, Hachette, 2008.

11 Letter from Ian Bainbridge, 18 January 1948 (misdated 1947). BL MS 83730A.

12 Letter from Ian Bainbridge, 25 January 1948 (misdated 1947). BL MS 83730A.

13 Letter from Rita Moody, 14 February 1948. BL MS 83730A.

14 Letter from Albert Riley, 16 January 1948.

15 Letter from Winnie Bainbridge, c. 29 January 1948. BL MS 83730A.

16 Letter from Richard Bainbridge, 19 January 1948.

17 Letter from Richard Bainbridge, 6 February 1949.

18 Letter from Richard Bainbridge, 15 February 1948. BL MS 83730A.

19 Letter from Winnie Bainbridge, c. 27 February 1948.

20 Or as her father put it: 'My own Darlin Berry, Now I sees by yer letter that yer fast settlin down, and mighty glad it is I find yer so.' Letter from Richard Bainbridge, 3 February 1948.

21 Letter from Winnie Bainbridge, 4 February 1948.

22 Julie Andrews, *Home: A Memoir of My Early Years*, Hachette, 2008.

23 Letter to Billy Cousins, 11 March 1948.

24 Letter from Ian Bainbridge, 15 February 1948. BL MS 83730A.

25 Letter from Ian Bainbridge, 18 January 1948 (misdated 1947). BL MS 83730A.

26 Eve Branson, *Mum's the Word: The High-Flying Adventures of Eve Branson*. AuthorHouse, 2013, p. 6.

27 Letter from Ian Bainbridge, 18 January 1948 (misdated 1947). BL MS 83730A.

28 Letter from Annette Moore, c. 24 January 1948.

29 Letter from Winnie Bainbridge, 15 February 1948.

30 Letter from Ian Bainbridge, 11 July 1948. BL MS 83730A.

31 Letter from Lynda South, c. 11 July 1948.

32 'Formby Forum', *Formby Times*, 5 March 1949.

33 'Formby Forum', *Formby Times*, 12 March 1949.

34 'Formby Forum', *Formby Times*, 19 March 1949.

35 See also diary entry for 24 January 1949. 1949–53 Journal. BL MS 83818.

36 Entry for 8 February 1949. 1949–53 Journal. BL MS 83818.

37 Entry for 1 March 1949. 1949–53 Journal. BL MS 83818.

38 Entry for 8 February 1949. 1949–53 Journal. BL MS 83818.

39 Entry for 26 January 1949. 1949–53 Journal. BL MS 83818.

40 Entry for 14 January 1949. 1949–53 Journal. BL MS 83818.

41 Entry for 22 February 1949. 1949–53 Journal. BL MS 83818.

42 Entry for 5 March 1949. 1949–53 Journal. BL MS 83818.

43 Entry for 9 March 1949. 1949–53 Journal. BL MS 83818.

44 Entry for 26 March 1949. 1949–53 Journal. BL MS 83818.

45 *Nottingham Evening Post*, 12 April 1949.

46 Letter from Winnie Bainbridge, 20 March 1949.

47 *Nottingham Evening Post*, 16 April 1949.

48 Letter from Richard Bainbridge, 13 March 1949.

49 Letter from Richard Bainbridge, 20 March 1949.

50 In *English Journey* Beryl claimed to have recited a monologue called 'The Bloke from Birkenhead', though there seems to be no poem or song with that title.

51 See letter from Jacques Delebassée, 1 May 1949: 'I should like to be in Bulwell during the week of Easter to see you on the theatre, and to dance with you.'

52 *English Journey*, Duckworth, 1984, p. 79.

53 In 2004 Beryl scribbled a hasty biographical note about Les Carr for the benefit of the British Library, who had just purchased some of her manuscripts: 'This was a man (23, 24) I met at the young Communist meetings in Formby. He was very Liverpudlian and I knew my parents would hate him. It was entirely platonic. I was 11.' Like many later comments about her early life this was factually misleading. Beryl was over sixteen when she met Les and there was a strong physical element to the relationship.

54 Letter from Les Carr, c. April 1949.

55 Les Carr exercise book, BL MS 83765.

56 Entry for May 1949. 1949–53 Journal. BL MS 83818.

57 Letter from Les Carr, c. 8 June 1949.

58 This and subsequent quote, entry for 7 June. 1949–53 Journal. BL MS 83818.

59 Letter from Harry Franz, 6 June 1949.

60 Entry dated 16 June 1949 but probably an error for 11 or 12 June. BL MS 83818.

61 Entry for 16 June 1949. 1949–53 Journal. BL MS 83818.

62 Entry for 20 June 1949. 1949–53 Journal. BL MS 83818.

63 Letter from Les Carr, c. 16 June 1949.

64 Entry for 7 June 1949. 1949–53 Journal. BL MS 83818.

CHAPTER 7

1 'Fragments 1951–53'. BL MS 83745.

2 Not 1895 as is often stated.

3 See *Liverpool Echo*, 19 November 1945. Beryl's assertion that Carpenter started as a barmaid at the theatre is purely fanciful.

4 Beryl herself often claimed to have started at the Playhouse at the age of fifteen, though this was not the case.

5 The only ASMs to be credited in the programmes during the period Beryl was at the Playhouse were Vivian Lloyd, who started just before her, and Monica Bell, who joined the company a year after.

6 Letter from Jacques Delebassée, 30 August 1949. 'Je crois que tu es contente de danser au "Playhouse"? . . . Je pense que vous devez être jolie avec votre costume bleu et rouge. Veux-tu m'envoyer une photographie ou tu es habillée avec les pantalons rouges et la blouse bleue.'

7 *English Journey*, Duckworth, 1984, p. 88. According to Hugh Paddick, who worked at the Playhouse in 1951, St John Barry used a hairbrush rather than a newspaper. Paddick found the incident amusing and whenever he passed his lodgings in Beryl's company would quip, 'Do pop up for a bit of the back of the hairbrush if you fancy a change.' Recounted by Nick Green, email to author, 7 March 2013.

8 Entry misdated '3 or 4 September'. In fact, the play opened on 6 September, but Beryl wrote up the diary a short time after the actual events, hence the error in dating. 1949–53 Journal. BL MS 83818.

9 Diary entry dated November 1949. 1949–53 Journal. BL MS 83818.

10 Entry for 16 June 1949. 1949–53 Journal. BL MS 83818.

11 *English Journey*, Duckworth, 1984, pp. 89–90.

12 Quoted in letter from Harry Franz, 16 August 1949. BL MS 83729.

13 Letter from Harry Franz, 16 August 1949. BL MS 83729.

14 Letter from Harry Franz, 6 October 1949.

15 Letter from Annette Moore, 19 October 1949.

16 *News Chronicle*, 28 November 1949.

17 *The Stage*, 1 December 1949.

18 *Liverpool Daily Post*, 1 December 1949.

19 *The Stage*, November 1949.

20 *Express*, 30 November 1949.

21 Entry for June 1950. 1949–53 Journal. BL MS 83818.

22 Review by HWR, *Liverpool Echo*, 29 March 1950.

23 Of the thirty-six productions that ran while Beryl was at the Playhouse, she appeared onstage in only half of them, the rest of the time being spent in understudying and other backstage duties.

24 Entry for June 1950. 1949–53 Journal. BL MS 83818.

25 Letter from Hugh Goldie, 7 June 1950.

26 Letter from Hugh Goldie, 25 September 1950.

27 Ibid.

28 Letter from Hugh Goldie, 18 January 1952.

29 Letter from Hugh Goldie, 25 September 1950.

30 This and subsequent quote, Ken Ratcliffe, interview with author, 26 October 2012.

31 Ken Ratcliffe, email to author, 9 December 2012.
32 Ken Ratcliffe, interview with author, 26 October 2012.
33 Ibid.
34 Review by SJ, *Liverpool Daily Post*, 25 October 1950.
35 Letter from Eric Colledge, 25 September 1952.
36 *Liverpool Echo*, 13 September 1950.
37 *Liverpool Daily Post*, 13 September 1950.

CHAPTER 8

1 'A treatise on justification', in 'Fragments 1951–53'. BL MS 83745.
2 Ibid.
3 *Liverpool Evening Express*, 23 April 1954.
4 Although Elizabeth, as a widow, was free to marry, Harold, being still legally married to Nora at the time of their affair, wasn't. To mitigate the appearance of living in sin Elizabeth changed her name officially to Hinchcliffe Davies in September 1939, making it seem as if she and Harold were already man and wife.
5 From information supplied by Belinda Davies, 2013.
6 Austin Davies, journal entry for 18 January 1952.
7 Ken Ratcliffe, interview with author, 26 October 2012.
8 'Fragments 1951–53'. BL MS 83745.
9 'Going spare in no man's land', *Evening Standard*, 5 November 1987.
10 Austin Davies, journal entry for 21 January 1952.
11 'Fragments 1951–53'. BL MS 83745.
12 Letter from Austin Davies, c. 23 August 1951.
13 Ibid.
14 Letter from Austin Davies, c. 27 August 1951.
15 Ibid.
16 Letter from Austin Davies, 10 September 1951.
17 This and subsequent quote, letter from Austin Davies, 3 September 1951.
18 Letter from Austin Davies, 18 September 1951.
19 Letter from Austin Davies, 27 September 1951.
20 Austin Davies, journal entry for 18 January 1952.
21 Letter from Austin Davies, 30 September 1951.
22 Letter from Austin Davies, 4–5 October 1951.
23 Austin Davies, journal entry for 21 January 1952.
24 Ken Ratcliffe, interview with author, 26 October 2012.
25 Austin Davies, journal entry for 21 January 1952.
26 Ibid.
27 *Beryl's Last Year*, directed by Charlie Russell, BBC, 2005.

28 Letter from Hugh Goldie, 7 June 1950.
29 *Liverpool Daily Post*, 10 October 1951.
30 Letter from Ken Ratcliffe, 15 January 1952.
31 Written on a programme belonging to Ken Ratcliffe, dated 20 January 1952.
32 Letter from Ken Ratcliffe, 31 January 1952.
33 Austin Davies, journal entry for 1 March 1952.
34 Letter from Ken Ratcliffe, 3 February 1952.
35 Ibid.
36 Letter from Ken Ratcliffe, 2 February 1952.

CHAPTER 9

1 'A treatise on justification', in 'Fragments 1951–53'. BL MS 83745.
2 Despite Beryl's repeated assertions in later life that she 'ran away to London' when she was sixteen (see *Forever England*, Duckworth, 1987, p. 11), this was not true. The facts of the issue have been made more confusing by journalists frequently mixing up Beryl's misleading account of leaving home for London when she was nineteen with a supposedly earlier attempt to run away from home to Liverpool. Although there are no references to this in her letters or diaries, and no direct evidence to support the story, Beryl claimed to have run away from home when she was fifteen, renting a room in Abercrombie Square until her father came a few days later and forcibly took her back (see 'Going spare in no man's land', *Evening Standard*, 5 November 1987). A piece in 'Fragments', entitled 'Falkner Square', refers to the narrator staying in a room there during the Festival of Britain in 1951, when Beryl was eighteen, and it is possible this is a reference to her first abortive attempt to leave home. There may also be a connection here to her anecdote about renting a room at the Aber House Hotel in Falkner Street when she thought her mother was going to leave her father: the similarities between Falkner Square and Falkner Street, and Aber House and Abercrombie, may signify an imperfect recollection of names or a mixing up of events in later memoirs.
3 'Fragments 1951–53'. BL MS 83745.
4 Ibid.
5 Although some pieces have been given titles and some bear dates of composition, most have been dated retrospectively and not entirely accurately.
6 Letter from Austin Davies, c. 26 March 1952.
7 Austin Davies, journal entry for 1 March 1952.
8 Letter from Austin Davies, 15 February 1952. BL MS 83730A.
9 Ibid.

10   Letter from Dorothy Green, 2 March 1952.

11   Letter from Lynda South, c. 29 February 1952.

12   Letter from Lynda South, c. 4 March 1952.

13   Austin Davies, journal entry for 1 March 1952.

14   Austin Davies, journal entry for 23 March 1952.

15   Letter from Austin Davies, 20 March 1952.

16   Letter from Austin Davies, 26 March 1952.

17   See obituary in the *Daily Telegraph*, 15 January 2003. In a newspaper article of 1974, Beryl later claimed she had been sacked by the manager after she refused to appear in a dirty film. In fact she left because she was offered an acting job. This is another example of Beryl's unthinking tendency to publish anything that came into her head. She was no doubt unaware that Rive was still alive in 1974 and that the things she made up for her articles and passed off as true were actually libellous.

18   'Fragments 1951–53'. BL MS 83745.

19   Letter from Lynda South, c. 8 March 1952. Written on a page torn out of an old diary dated 26 April 1950.

20   Letter from Lynda South, 4 April 1952. Written on a page torn out of an old diary dated 21 June 1950.

21   Letter from Lynda South, c. 2 April 1952. BL MS 83730A. Written on a page torn out of an old diary dated 15 June 1950.

22   In an article for the *Evening Standard*, Beryl once claimed that while she didn't approve of abortion she'd had a 'back-street' one 'in the days when to become pregnant before marriage was considered a mortal sin'. However, there is no external evidence to support this. See 'Picking up the pieces of life', *Evening Standard*, 28 April 1988.

23   Letter to Austin Davies, copied in journal entry for 30 March 1952.

24   Austin Davies, journal entry for 30 March 1952.

25   Letter from Austin Davies, c. 2 April 1952.

26   In an *Evening Standard* article published on 4 August 1988, Beryl made a very veiled allusion to the incident, but typically the version she gives here is deliberately misleading. The sexual assault is not mentioned at all, and she says that the man had slipped a 'Mickey Finn' into her coffee before knocking one of her teeth out. She also goes on to say that she reported the incident to the police, but that she gave them a false name and address as she was 'under age' at the time – though in reality she was nineteen. The fact that the 'fictionalized' account of the assault in *The Girl in the Polka Dot Dress* almost exactly matches the details given in her letter to Austin, which she had not seen since she wrote it fifty years before, shows she was aware that the account in the *Evening Standard* wasn't accurate.

27   *The Girl in the Polka Dot Dress*, Little, Brown, 2011, p. 14.

28 Diary entry, 27 May 1953. BL MS 83819.
29 Austin Davies, journal entry for 1 January 1953.
30 'Beryl's perils', interview with Lynn Barber, *Observer*, 19 August 2001.
31 'Beryl Bainbridge talks to Yolanta May', *New Review*, December 1976.
32 Letter from Lynda South, 1 April 1952. BL MS 83730A.
33 Austin Davies, journal entry for 18 January 1952.
34 Austin Davies, journal entry for 15 February 1952.
35 Austin Davies, journal entry for 1 March 1952.
36 The painting, completed in March, features in a list of works in his journal.
37 'Fragments 1951–53'. BL MS 83745.
38 Austin Davies, journal entry for 14 April 1952.
39 Letter from Dorothy Green, 21 May 1952.
40 'Fragments 1951–53'. BL MS 83745.
41 Letter from Lynda South, 16 May 1952.
42 Letter from Ken Ratcliffe, 18 May 1952.
43 Letter from Gareth Bogarde, 12 June 1952.
44 Letter from Dorothy Green, 11 June 1952.
45 Letter from Lynda South, 21 June 1952.
46 Frances Jordan, 'Studied atoms in sixth grade now ponders four scholarships', *Sunday Courier*, 10 June 1945.
47 Frohlich's intelligence was, if anything, even more abstruse than Fanchon's, and he became hugely influential in the developing fields of theoretical particle physics and quantum mechanics.
48 Austin Davies, journal entry for 14 April 1952.
49 Ibid.

CHAPTER 10

1 *Forever England*, Duckworth, 1987, p. 119.
2 *Dundee Courier*, 26 March 1946.
3 After giving up acting in the mid-1960s, Davis became a casting director. See obituary in the *Daily Telegraph*, 9 December 2002.
4 Paul Bailey, interview with author, 19 May 2015.
5 He later changed his name to Marc Bellomey.
6 Draft version of *A Weekend with Claud*. BL MS 83796.
7 Beryl would later use this scenario in *An Awfully Big Adventure*, where she makes her alter ego, Stella, fall in love with the director Meredith Potter, not realizing that he is gay. This is another example of the way Beryl would change and adapt her experiences and those of others for dramatic effect, and shows why it is unwise to assume a one-to-one relation between events in her novels and those of her life.

8 Maggie Dickie, interview with author, 9 October 2013.

9 Something that may have contributed to Beryl's feelings of 'guilt' and 'sin' was a recent incident concerning Lyn, whom she'd met in London prior to coming to Dundee. Shortly afterwards Lyn wrote to explain what had caused 'the awkwardness between us' at the time – her overpowering feeling of Beryl's beauty. She told her she had just wanted to sit and watch her, to study the things she loved about her – her mouth, her neckline, her hips, the clumsy-graceful gestures of her hands, the dimples in her cheeks. Lyn had drawn a portrait of Beryl in her art class, and her teacher was so struck by it he'd asked who it was. Lyn, nonplussed, went through possible answers in her mind – 'The most beautiful girl in the world? The girl I love? The heart of my heart?' – before replying, 'My friend' (letter from Lynda South, c. July 1952). It was probably in response to this effusive letter that Beryl cautioned Lyn 'it is not ever for us to lie together in such love' (extract from letter to Lynda South dated 1952 in 'Fragments 1951–53'. BL MS 83745).

10 Beryl would later joke that it was the 'hellfire and brimstone' (interview with Shusha Guppy, *Paris Review* no. 157, 2000) aspect of Catholicism that attracted her, and that she became disaffected with the Catholic Church after the liberalizing effects of Vatican II: 'No more Latin or sin or confession or penance. There's no longer any point to it' (interview with Laurie Taylor, *The New Humanist*, vol. 119, 2004). But this caricaturing of her motives is another way in which she sought to direct attention away from the real traumas that had affected her. Her sense of herself as sinful and impure was deeply felt, and at the time she looked to the Church for a cure. It was the failure of Catholicism to stop these feelings of self-disgust – not the liberalizing aspects of Vatican II – that led to her declining interest in and eventual abandonment of the tenets of Catholicism.

11 Beryl didn't tell her she had a problematic relationship with her parents. After she returned to Liverpool, Sister Mary Antony wrote to say she must be glad to have 'a little quiet time' to herself, enjoying 'the peace and comfort of "Home"'. Letter from Sister Mary Antony, 22 October 1952.

12 'Fragments 1951–53'. BL MS 83745.

13 Ibid.

14 *Dundee Courier*, 4 October 1952.

15 The tram system in Dundee was replaced by buses in 1956.

16 *Forever England*, Duckworth, 1987, p. 118.

17 Letter from Gerald Cross, c. 16 February 1953.

18 Extract from letter to Lynda South dated 1952 in 'Fragments 1951–53'. BL MS 83745.

19 Austin Davies, journal entry for 10 November 1952.

20 'Fragments 1951–53'. BL MS 83745.
21 Letter from Dorothy Green, 2 November 1952.
22 Austin Davies, journal entry for 10 November 1952.
23 Letter from Dorothy Green, 6 November 1952.
24 This and subsequent quote, Tom Davies, 'Alice in Wonderland: a writer's retreat', *The Times*, 18 August 1990.
25 Letter from Dorothy Green, mid-November 1952.
26 Austin Davies, journal entry for 19 November 1952.
27 Review in unidentified newspaper, October 1952.
28 Review in unidentified newspaper, November 1952.

CHAPTER 11

1 Diary entry, 10 January 1953. BL MS 83818.
2 This and subsequent quotations, Austin Davies, journal entry for 27 December 1952.
3 Austin Davies, journal entry for 1 January 1953.
4 Diary entry, 1 January 1953. BL MS 83819.
5 Austin Davies, journal entry for 1 January 1953.
6 These and subsequent quotes, letter from Austin Davies, 15 January 1953. BL MS 83730A.
7 Letter from Austin Davies, 19 January 1953.
8 Letter from Austin Davies, 22 January 1953.
9 Diary entry, 23 January 1953. BL MS 83818.
10 Letter from Austin Davies, 6 February 1953.
11 Letter from Austin Davies, c. 8 March 1953.
12 Diary entry, 14 February 1953, BL MS 83818.
13 Diary entry, 6 March 1953, BL MS 83818.
14 Diary entry, 27 May 1953, BL MS 83818.
15 Letter from Austin Davies, 11 February 1953.
16 Letter from Austin Davies, 14 February 1953.
17 Letter from Gerald Cross, c. 16 February 1953. Archive and BL MS 83730A.
18 This and subsequent quote: letter from Austin Davies, 18 February 1953.

CHAPTER 12

1 'A treatise on justification', in 'Fragments 1951–53'. BL MS 83745.
2 Review in unidentified newspaper, 17 March 1953.
3 Review in unidentified newspaper, c. 23 March 1953.
4 *Salisbury Times*, c. 23 March 1953.
5 Letter from Austin Davies, 20 March 1953.

6   Letter from Austin Davies, c. 13 March 1953.

7   Letter from Austin Davies, 20 March 1953.

8   Letter from Austin Davies, 26 March 1953.

9   Diary entries, 4, 5, 6, 7 April 1953. BL MS 83818.

10 Austin Davies, journal entry for 17 August 1953.

11 Letter from Hugh Goldie, 7 April 1953.

12 Diary entry, 22 April 1953. BL MS 83818.

13 Beryl spells the name erratically in the MS, at times 'Gospell', at times 'Gopsell', and once 'Gospel'. In her diary for 1953 she tends to spell the name correctly. I have standardized it to 'Gopsill' throughout.

14 'A treatise on justification', in 'Fragments 1951–53'. BL MS 83745.

15 This and subsequent quote, 'Salisbury March 1953' (but written 6 May 1953), in 'Fragments 1951–53'. BL MS 83745.

16 Diary entry, 26 April 1953. BL MS 83818.

17 Letter from Lynda South, c. April 1953.

18 Diary entry, 28 April 1953. BL MS 83818.

19 Diary entry, 29 April 1953. BL MS 83818.

20 Diary entry, 30 April 1953. BL MS 83818.

21 Diary entry, 1 May 1953. BL MS 83818. Anne Lindholm became a postulant at the Convent of Notre Dame, Ashdown Park, in October 1953. Three months later she spent some time in hospital suffering from a slipped disc, and a few months after that she was advised to wait a couple of years before resuming her postulancy. At the end of 1954 she started work at Leonard Cheshire's Mission for the Relief of Suffering in Ampthill, and six months later applied to enter the Carmelite convent at Presteigne, a small enclosed order set up only five years before and still undergoing construction work so that it could take on more postulants. After many months of discussion about her vocation, Anne was formally turned down at the start of 1956 as the building work at Carmel was taking longer than expected. However, by the time it was formally finished she was pregnant again, after having met Colin Haycraft a short while before. The two married in December 1956, and their first child was born seven months later.

22 Diary entry, 1 May 1953. BL MS 83818.

23 Ibid.

24 Diary entry, 5 May 1953. BL MS 83818.

25 Diary entry, 10 May 1953. BL MS 83818.

26 Diary entry, 11 May 1953. BL MS 83818.

27 Diary entry, 23 May 1953. BL MS 83818.

28 *Daily Sketch*, 24 May 1953.

29 Diary entry, 28 May 1953. BL MS 83818.

30 Diary entry, 4 June 1953. BL MS 83818.
31 Diary entry, 8 June 1953. BL MS 83818.
32 Diary entry, 16 June 1953. BL MS 83818.
33 Diary entry, 19 June 1953. BL MS 83818.
34 Diary entry, 22 June 1953. BL MS 83818.
35 Diary entry, 14 May 1953. BL MS 83818.
36 Diary entry, 19 May 1953. BL MS 83818.
37 Diary entry, 24 May 1953. BL MS 83818.
38 Diary entry, 23 May 1953. BL MS 83818.
39 Diary entry, 5 July 1953. BL MS 83818.
40 Diary entry, 7 July 1953. BL MS 83818.
41 Diary entry, 9 July 1953. BL MS 83818.
42 Diary entry, 11 July 1953. BL MS 83818.

CHAPTER 13

1 'Fragments 1951–53'. BL MS 83745. Beryl's inattention to factual detail is revealed here: while a thirty-inch waist might have been tubby for a twenty-year-old girl, it was positively slim for a sixty-year-old man.
2 Similar chance meetings between an older man and a younger girl recur in her later fiction.
3 Letter from Lynda South, c. March 1953.
4 Diary cntry, 25 July 1953. BL MS 83819.
5 Letter from Lynda South, c. 25 May 1952.
6 Letter from Lynda South, c. 3 March 1952.
7 Letter from Lynda South, 1 April 1952.
8 Letter from Lynda South, c. April 1953.
9 Letter from Lynda South, c. 3 March 1952.
10 Joseph Bartley Redman, who died on 25 February 1952 at the age of seventy-four.
11 Diary entry, 8 August 1953. BL MS 83819.
12 Diary entry, 11 August 1953. BL MS 83819.
13 Diary entry, 19 August 1953. BL MS 83819.
14 Diary entry, 21 August 1953. BL MS 83819.
15 Diary entry, 27 August 1953. BL MS 83819.
16 Diary entry, 27 August 1953. BL MS 83819.
17 Diary entry, 28 August 1953. BL MS 83819.
18 Diary entry, 29 August 1953. BL MS 83819.
19 Beryl would later claim that she was seventeen when she went to Paris with 'the Colonel', and had done so 'on a forged passport'. This was not true; the passport itself was legal, though it's possible Beryl forged her

parents' signature on the application form as she didn't want them to know she was going abroad.

20 Diary entry, 1 October 1953. BL MS 83819. In later accounts Beryl would say that the chambermaid said 'Courage mademoiselle', implying the hotel was used to unmarried couples coming for a 'dirty weekend' and the maid was trying to make her feel better about the ordeal to come. However, it is clear from the diary that the remark was directed at them both, and referred to the number of stairs to climb, not some kind of sexual innuendo.

21 Diary entry, 3 October 1953. BL MS 83819.

22 Diary entry, 4 October 1953. BL MS 83819.

23 Diary entry, 2 October 1953. BL MS 83819.

24 'Fragments 1951–53'. BL MS 83745.

25 Ibid.

26 Diary entry, 5 October 1953. BL MS 83819.

27 Diary entry, 8 October 1953. BL MS 83819.

28 Diary entry, 9 October 1953. BL MS 83819.

29 Diary entry, 13 October 1953. BL MS 83819.

30 Diary entry, 15 October 1953. BL MS 83819.

31 Diary entry, 17 October 1953. BL MS 83819.

32 Information from Stephen Peppiatt, email to author 23 March 2013.

33 Diary entry, 11 September 1953. BL MS 83818.

34 Diary entry, 13 September 1953. BL MS 83818.

35 Literally so in one instance. Ronnie's scheme to prevent his ex-wife getting access to his money, by opening an account with the Bank of Ireland under the fictitious name of Claude Bainbridge and using Beryl's address for correspondence purposes, didn't take into consideration how he could access the money, nor what would happen if he were to die. After his death, Beryl had been sent a new passbook for the account on its conversion to euros, and by 2010 it had some 7,000 euros in it. As it was of dubious legality, no one could get to the money or even make any legal claim on it. The existence of the account caused a certain amount of confusion during the probate of Beryl's estate after her death.

36 Diary entry, 10 October 1953. BL MS 83818.

37 Diary entry, 6 September 1953. BL MS 83818.

38 Letter from Lynda South, 13 October 1953.

39 Diary entry, 14 October 1953. BL MS 83818.

40 Diary entry, 28 November 1953. BL MS 83819.

41 Letter from Austin Davies, 3 December 1953.

42 Letter from Austin Davies, c. December 1953.

43 Letter from Austin Davies, 9 December 1953.

44 Austin Davies, journal entry for 15 January 1954.

45 Beryl managed to write one last entry in her diary before the illness overtook her: 'It is very late but I feel so ill. Suddenly I feel I have been ill for a long time and not known it. Yesterday the doctor came and said I was undernourished. I felt frightened suddenly sitting up in bed with him tapping my chest. When I looked down I looked so thin. I have lost weight, a stone, maybe more.' Diary entry, 17 January 1954. BL MS 83819.

46 Diary entry, 10 April 1955. BL MS 83820.

47 See letter from Sefton General Hospital to Cyril Taylor, 21 July 1954. To rule out the possibility of a tuberculous lesion Beryl was X-rayed again a few months later. She was subsequently given a bronchogram, but again the tests came back negative: 'There is no evidence of any tuberculosis infection.'

48 Austin Davies, journal entry for 15 January 1954.

CHAPTER 14

1 'The People in the Park', 'Fragments 1951–53'. BL MS 83745.

2 A sign of the growing emotional distance between them is reflected in the gift Lyn was given for being bridesmaid – a copy of *Under Milk Wood*. Beryl didn't write a message or even sign her name in the book, instead Austin wrote a slightly awkward dedication – 'For services rendered (i.e. bridesmaid)' – and signed it on Beryl's behalf. When Lyn married Rik in Greenwich six months later, neither Beryl nor Austin attended.

3 Austin wasn't the only one to find the choice of a Catholic church uncongenial: Uncle Len refused to attend the wedding on religious grounds.

4 'Drape expectations', *Evening Standard*, 4 January 1991.

5 Information from Robin Riley, interview with author, 15 March 2013.

6 Even at the height of her success it is doubtful whether Beryl could have afforded to buy the house she had once lived in as the wife of a university lecturer in art.

7 George Melly, *Revolt into Style*, Allen Lane/Penguin Press, 1970, p. 213.

8 *A Weekend with Claud*, New Authors, 1967, p. 51.

9 *Manchester Guardian*, 1 November 1954.

10 Diary entry, 10 April 1955. BL MS 83820.

11 Email from Belinda Davies to author, 26 January 2014.

12 Mayer-Marton was also a skilled mosaicist, and when Austin later moved down to London he used the techniques he had learned from him to produce a decorative mosaic commissioned by East Ham Technical College.

13 Peter Davies, *Liverpool Seen: Post-War Artists on Merseyside*, Redcliffe Press, 1992, p. 96.

14 J. F. Dewey, 'Robert Millner Shackleton. 1909–2001', *Biographical Memoirs of Fellows of the Royal Society*, 2004.

15 Interview with Brenda Haddon, 13 February 2013.

16 Interview with Chloë Buck, 13 April 2013.

17 Interview with Robin Riley, 13 December 2013.

18 By the time of his death in 2000, Taylor was recognized as a leading figure in the post-war movement for democratic health reform.

19 Gideon Ben-Tovim, 'Dr Cyril Taylor: a life of commitment', 21 December 2000.

20 Diary entry, 29 February 1960. BL MS 83820.

21 Diary entry, 10 April 1955. BL MS 83820.

22 This and subsequent quote, Austin Davies, journal entry for April 1955.

23 'Dockland ghosts', *Liverpool Daily Post*, 12 March 1955.

24 Austin Davies, journal entry for April 1955.

CHAPTER 15

1 Unfinished poem, 'Fragments 1951–53'. BL MS 83745.

2 Diary entry, 5 June 1953. BL MS 83818.

3 Letter to Judith Shackleton, c. September 1956.

4 Ibid.

5 Diary entry, 30 April 1953. BL MS 83818.

6 The tapes were sent back by the BBC and remained in Catharine Street after Austin and Beryl had left. Robin Riley found them when he moved in and took them to Huskisson Street, but what subsequently happened to them is unclear.

7 Letter from Denness Roylance, 14 August 1956. BL MS 83735. Also from information supplied by Nick Green and Robin Riley.

8 'Ceedy Man and the Bellringers'. BL MS 83793.

9 In all, Beryl wrote six Ceedy Man stories, though only four were broadcast. The last, 'Ceedy Man and the Music Festival', was recorded in London in November 1963.

10 It is for this reason that I have tried to avoid using Beryl's novels as a source of biographical information in this book, except in a few instances where it is supported by reliable documentary evidence.

11 Beryl's decision to make Harriet and the narrator fourteen and thirteen respectively was a way of disguising the book's origins. Given that her adventure with George occurred only six months before she married Austin, she might have felt it was too close for comfort to write about openly. Early draft versions shows that the decision to make the narrator thirteen was taken at a later date, and originally the girls were described

as being sixteen-year-olds – the same age as those in the New Zealand murder case. These references to age, along with others in which the narrator notes that it has been 'years and years' since she had last seen the Tsar, or that she was going to leave school and move to London, which wouldn't make sense if she was thirteen, were subsequently deleted from the final version.

12 Letter from Chapman & Hall, 18 December 1957. BL MS 83735.

13 Letter from Chapman & Hall, 1 January 1958.

14 Letter from Chatto & Windus, 7 May 1958. BL MS 83735.

15 She would continue to send the manuscript of 'The Summer of the Tsar' out over the next few years, to Weidenfeld & Nicolson in 1960, Anthony Blond in 1963, and Hutchinson in 1965.

16 'Another Friday'. BL MS 83793.

17 Letter to Judith Shackleton, c. 15 July 1957.

18 Letter to Judith Shackleton, c. September 1956.

19 Probably after the play *Léocadia* by Jean Anouilh, whose work Beryl had often used as audition pieces. She also used the name Leocardia for the station taxi in her children's story, 'Ceedy Man and Hopping Dog Day', which was written around the same period.

20 Letter to Judith Shackleton, c. 15 July 1957.

21 Interview with Brenda Haddon, 13 February 2013.

22 Interview with author, 13 February 2013.

23 'The Liverpool that I loved has gone for ever: Merseyside memories in the European Capital of Culture', *The Spectator*, 12 December 2007. In fact Eileen Wenton, née Hogan, was born in Liverpool, of Irish extraction, and though her husband's father was from Sierra Leone, her husband was also born in Liverpool. Nine children are recorded in the Birth Index, but their extended family may have given the impression it was much larger.

24 19 September 1959. 1955–65 Journal. BL MS 83820.

25 28 September 1959. 1955–65 Journal. BL MS 83820.

CHAPTER 16

1 Diary entry, 18 September 1959. BL MS 83820.

2 Interview with Brenda Haddon, 13 February 2013.

3 Maureen Cleave, 'Will the real Beryl Bainbridge sit down and write a novel?' *Over 21*, April 1979; Shusha Guppy, 'Beryl Bainbridge, the art of fiction', *The Paris Review*, no. 157, Winter 2000.

4 Sholto Byrnes, 'Beryl Bainbridge: echoes of a rackety life', *Independent*, 17 May 2004; and *Authors' Lives*, British Library sound recording (Track 6, March 2009). In a letter Beryl wrote to Austin on 13 January 2002,

she mentions that it was when she came back from giving birth to Aaron that she found two sets of breakfast plates and a note to a female student saying that Beryl would be coming back the following day.

5 Psiche Hughes, *Beryl Bainbridge: Writer, Artist, Friend,* Thames & Hudson, 2013, p. 32.

6 'Dame Beryl's gymslip secret', *Camden New Journal*, 7 February 2008.

7 Information based on account by Belinda Davies, email to author, 26 January 2014.

8 Letter from Austin Davies, c. 20 July 1959.

9 Letter from Austin Davies, 26 July 1959.

10 Letter from Austin Davies, c. 29 July 1959.

11 Draft of *A Weekend with Claud*. BL MS 83796.

12 21 September 1959. 1955–65 Journal. BL MS 83820.

13 Draft of *A Weekend with Claud*. BL MS 83796.

14 Interview with Ruth Green, 17 November 2014.

15 Letter to Mick Green, c. September 1962.

16 Letter to Judith Shackleton, c. 8 August 1959.

17 Ibid.

18 Diary entry, 17 September 1959. 1955–65 Journal. BL MS 83820.

19 This and subsequent four quotes, diary entry, 17 September 1959. 1955–65 Journal. BL MS 83820.

20 Diary entry, 18 September 1959. 1955–65 Journal. BL MS 83820.

21 Diary entry, 19 September 1959. 1955–65 Journal. BL MS 83820.

22 Diary entry, 22 September 1959. 1955–65 Journal. BL MS 83820.

23 Diary entry, 25 September 1959. 1955–65 Journal. BL MS 83820.

24 Ibid.

25 Diary entry, 29 September 1959. 1955–65 Journal. BL MS 83820.

26 Diary entry, 27 September 1959. 1955–65 Journal. BL MS 83820.

27 Diary entry, 28 September 1959. 1955–65 Journal. BL MS 83820.

28 The version of events Beryl gave in her *Evening Standard* article, 'The night I walked out on Lennon' (19 January 1990), is studded with errors. Beryl's date for the party, August 1957, was, like most of her dates, inaccurate.

29 Mark Lewison, *All These Years*, Little, Brown, 2013. Harrison's reference is to the British dance band leader Gerald ('Geraldo') Bright.

30 Not to be confused with Beryl's friend and Austin's student, Brenda Haddon, née Powell.

31 Diary entry, 19 September 1959. 1955–65 Journal. BL MS 83820.

32 Interview with Maggie Gilby, 5 November 2013.

33 Diary entry, 18 September 1959. 1955–65 Journal. BL MS 83820.

34 Letter from Austin Davies, c. January 1960.

35 Letter from Mick Green, 1 February 1960.

36 Diary entry, 29 February 1960. 1955–65 Journal. BL MS 83820.

37 Interview with Maggie Gilby, 5 November 2013.

38 Diary entry, 29 February 1960. 1955–65 Journal. BL MS 83820.

39 Information on antenatal record card, 1965.

40 Letter from Liverpool Stanley Hospital to Cyril Taylor, 2 February 1960.

41 Interview with Brenda Haddon, 13 February 2013.

42 Herbert J. Davis, the same firm her parents used.

43 Diary entry, 2 March 1960. 1955–65 Journal. BL MS 83820.

44 Diary entry, c. March 1960. 1955–65 Journal. BL MS 83820.

45 Diary entry, 2 March 1960. 1955–65 Journal. BL MS 83820.

46 *A Weekend with Claud*, New Authors, 1967, pp. 48–9.

47 Diary entry, c. Spring–Summer 1960. 1955–65 Journal. BL MS 83820.

CHAPTER 17

1 Draft of *A Weekend with Claud*. BL MS 83796.

2 Letter to Judith Shackleton, c. July 1961.

3 *A Weekend with Claud*, New Authors, 1967, pp. 77 and 39.

4 Born in Liverpool in 1894, Leah was the daughter of two Russian emigrés, Isaac Davis, who had a clock-repairing business, and his wife Nellie Cohen. She had not, as Beryl put it, been carried 'as a baby across the frozen steppes of Russia' by her mother.

5 'I'm Not Criticising . . . I'm Remembering'. BL MS 83793.

6 Letter from Leah Davis, 3 April 1965.

7 Draft of *A Weekend with Claud*. BL MS 83796. In the published version, the line becomes 'taken to extremes of eccentricity forty years along' (p. 123).

8 Letter to Judith Shackleton, c. 6 May 1963.

9 Letters to Judith Shackleton, 2 October 1962 and c. December 1962.

10 Letter to Judith Shackleton, c. June 1961.

11 Draft of *A Weekend with Claud*. BL MS 83796. A slightly different version appears in the published edition on p. 34.

12 Harry was also well liked by Aaron and Jo-Jo, whose mispronunciation of his name furnished him with the nickname by which he would be known in the house from then on: 'Harry the Lion'.

13 Information from interview with Rachel Mohin, 28 March 2014.

14 Draft of *A Weekend with Claud*. BL MS 83796.

15 *A Weekend with Claud*, New Authors, 1967, p. 124.

16 Ibid.

17 'I'm Not Criticising . . . I'm Remembering.' BL MS 83793.

18 Draft of *A Weekend with Claud*, deleted in the published edition. BL MS 83796.

19 Draft of *A Weekend with Claud*. BL MS 83796.

20 *A Weekend with Claud*, New Authors, 1967, p. 57.

21 Letter from Barley Allison, Weidenfeld & Nicolson, 29 June 1960. BL MS 83735.

22 It was run by an elderly lady in Lodge Lane called Miss Smith, known in the family as 'Miff Miff' after Jo-Jo's pronunciation of her name. According to Beryl, she died of a heart attack one day while playing the piano, with the children dancing around her.

23 Denis Forman, *Personal Granada*, André Deutsch, 1997, p. 126.

24 Letter to Judith Shackleton, c. September 1961.

25 Letter to Mick Green, c. August 1961.

26 Letter from Austin Davies, 23 August 1960. BL MS 83730A.

27 Brenda Haddon, interview with author, 13 February 2013.

28 Sally Vincent, 'Beryl Bainbridge: lady with the dangerous typewriter', *Cosmopolitan*, March 1979.

29 Letter from Derek Waring, c. 21 October 1960.

30 Voll would become a respected figure in his field when he returned to Germany a few years later.

31 Letter from Gerhard Voll, 30 November 1961.

32 *A Weekend with Claud*, New Authors, 1967, p. 166.

33 Letter to Judith Shackleton, c. August 1961.

34 Letter to Judith Shackleton, February 1974.

35 Name changed to protect family.

36 Letter to Judith Shackleton, c. August 1961.

37 *A Weekend with Claud*, New Authors, 1967, p. 167.

38 *A Weekend with Claud*, New Authors, 1967, p. 180.

39 Letter to Judith Shackleton, c. August 1961.

40 Quoted in letter from Edward L. Lohman, 20 September 1961.

41 Quoted in letter from Edward L. Lohman, 28 September 1961.

42 Letter from Edward L. Lohman, 20 September 1961.

43 Letter from Edward L. Lohman, 2 January 1962.

44 Letter to Mick Green, c. August 1962.

CHAPTER 18

1 Letter to Mick Green, c. September 1961.

2 Letter to Mick Green, c. August 1962.

3 This and subsequent two quotes, letter to Judith Shackleton, September 1962.

4   This and subsequent three quotes, letter to Mick Green, c. August 1962.

5   This and subsequent quote, letter to Judith Shackleton, September 1962.

6   This and subsequent quote, letter to Mick Green, c. August 1962.

7   Draft of *A Weekend with Claud*. BL MS 83796.

8   Draft of *A Weekend with Claud*. BL MS 83796. The same text appears in the published edition with minor changes on p. 43.

9   Letter to Mick Green, c. September 1961.

10   Letter from Edward L. Lohman, 20 September 1961.

11   This and subsequent quotes, letter to Mick Green, c. August 1962.

12   Letter to Mick Green, c. September 1962.

13   This and subsequent three quotes, letter to Mick Green, c. October 1962.

14   Letter to Judith Shackleton, mid-October 1962.

15   Letter from Austin Davies, c. September 1962.

16   Letter to Mick Green, c. September 1962.

17   Letter to Judith Shackleton, mid-December 1962.

18   Ibid.

19   Letter to Mick Green, c. November 1962.

20   Letter to Mick Green, undated, but probably 1962 given the reference to 'homecoming'.

21   Entry for 19 September 1959. 1955–65 Journal. BL MS 83820.

22   Draft of *A Weekend with Claud*. BL MS 83796. An expanded version of these paragraphs appears in the published version, pp. 63–5.

23   Ibid.

24   Brenda Haddon, interview with author, 6 December 2012.

25   Interview with Terry Waite, *Terry Waite Takes a Different View*, Thames, 1986.

26   Brenda Haddon, interview with author, 6 December 2012.

27   Interview with Terry Waite, *Terry Waite Takes a Different View*, Thames, 1986.

28   *Beryl's Last Year*, directed by Charlie Russell, BBC, 2005.

CHAPTER 19

1   Draft of unsent letter to Alan Sharp. BL MS 83730A.

2   Letter to Judith Shackleton, c. 6 May 1963.

3   Ibid.

4   Ibid.

5   Ken Doggett, interview with author, 24 June 2013.

6   Letter to Judith Shackleton, c. 6 May 1963.

7   Letter from Ken Doggett, 5 February 1964.

8   Ken Doggett, interview with author, 24 June 2013. These incidents would be used in *A Weekend with Claud*, where Ken was portrayed under the name of Edward.

9   Letter from Ken Doggett, 1 October 1963.

10 Letter to Judith Shackleton, c. September 1963.

11 Ibid.

12 Letter to Judith Shackleton, c. October 1963.

13 'William at the Harvest Festival', BL MS 83798.

14 Ibid.

15 Stephanie Nettell, 'We'll all go to Gedde when we go', *Books & Bookmen*, April 1965.

16 Haskel Frankel, 'Something to come home to', *Saturday Review*, 8 May 1965.

17 'William at the Harvest Festival', BL MS 83798.

18 This and subsequent quote, Alan Sharp letter to author, 13 February 2012.

19 Letter from Alan Sharp, c. October 1963.

20 Alan Sharp, letter to author, 13 February 2012.

21 Margaret Sharp, interview with author, 16 September 2014.

22 In later life, Beryl would state that she had met Alan's mother in Dundee in 1952, and that she was the wardrobe mistress there. In this she was mistaken. The wardrobe mistress was Dollie McKenzie and she was not Alan's mother.

23 Peter Craig Sr. featured in a string of newspaper reports for offences such as wife-beating, hen-stealing, drunkenness and burglary.

24 This and subsequent quote, Tom Shields, 'Chasing Hemingway on a galloping horse', *Herald*, 5 September 1992.

25 Later reprised as a television play in 1970 starring Ray Davies of the Kinks.

26 Haskel Frankel, 'Something to come home to', *Saturday Review*, 8 May 1965.

27 Letter from Ken Doggett, 24 October 1963.

28 Letter to Judith Shackleton, c. November 1963.

29 Letter from Ken Doggett, 14 November 1963.

30 Letter to Judith Shackleton, c. November 1963.

31 Ibid.

32 Ibid.

33 Ibid.

34 Letter from Ken Doggett, 17 November 1963.

35 Letter from Ken Doggett, 20 December 1963.

36 Letter from Alan Sharp, c. November 1963.

37 Letter to Judith Shackleton, c. January 1964.

38 Journal entry written c. May 1964.
39 Letter to Judith Shackleton, c. January 1964.
40 1964 Journal. BL MS 83821.
41 Letter from Alan Sharp to author, 13 February 2012.
42 Letter to Judith Shackleton, c. June 1964.
43 Letter to Judith Shackleton, c. November 1963.
44 Letter to Judith Shackleton, c. June 1964.
45 Letter to Judith Shackleton, c. March 1964. Beryl would reuse this incident in *Sweet William*, but in the novel her mother's disgust is over Ann's relationship with Gerald, rather than with William.
46 1964 Journal. BL MS 83821.
47 A few months later Beryl sent a copy of this, or one of her other radio plays, to Stephen Joseph at the Scarborough Theatre Trust. He wrote back declining the play on the ground that it wouldn't work in the theatre, but he encouraged her to continue, saying she had 'an extraordinary talent for writing'. Letter from Stephen Joseph, 30 October 1964. BL MS 83735.
48 Letter to Judith Shackleton, c. January 1964.
49 Letter to Judith Shackleton, c. June 1964.
50 Letter from Nina Froud, 29 April 1964.
51 Letter to Judith Shackleton, c. June 1964.
52 Letter to Judith Shackleton, c. 9 July 1964. Alan's excuse about Sal may have been another smokescreen. When Cecil and Lili Todes arrived at Arkwright Road to collect the keys, they noticed there was a woman with him. It was only when they finally met Beryl on her return months later that they realized she wasn't the woman they'd seen, and it dawned on them what Alan had been up to.
53 Letter from Ken Doggett, c. July 1964.
54 Letter to Judith Shackleton, c. mid-August 1964.
55 This and subsequent quotes, letter to Judith Shackleton, c. September 1964.
56 Letter to Judith Shackleton, c. October 1964.
57 Letter to Judith Shackleton, c. November 1964
58 This and subsequent quote, letter to Alan Sharp, c. November 1964. BL MS 83730A.
59 Untitled poem, c. 1964. BL MS 83793.

CHAPTER 20

1 Letter to Alan Sharp, c. mid-January 1965.
2 Letter from Alan Sharp, c. December 1964.
3 Letter to Alan Sharp, c. February 1965.

4   Letter to Alan Sharp, c. December 1964.

5   Ibid.

6   The mix-up was most probably due to Beryl's imprecision with dates. She also told her doctor she was born in 1934.

7   Letter to Judith Shackleton, c. 6 March 1965.

8   'Perils of Beryl', *The Sunday Times*, 5 January 1986.

9   Letter to Judith Shackleton, c. 1 April 1965.

10 Ibid.

11 Letter to Judith Shackleton, c. 24 April 1965.

12 Draft of *A Weekend with Claud*. BL MS 83796.

13 The *Guardian* even jokily compared Beryl to Nathalie Sarraute, an exponent of the *nouveau roman*, describing the book as 'an impressive first novel that made one think this was how Mme Sarraute might sound if she had the benefit of a Liverpool mind'. *Guardian*, 18 August 1967.

14 Letter from Graham Nicol, 4 August 1965. BL MS 83735. J. G. Farrell was one of the readers and later claimed to have 'discovered' Beryl. See Ralph Crane's 'A Man from Elsewhere: The Liminal Presence of Liverpool in the fiction of J. G. Farrell', in *Writing Liverpool*, Liverpool University Press, 2007.

15 Letter to Judith Shackleton, c. August 1965.

16 Letter to Judith Shackleton, c. 20 September 1965.

17 These and the negative comments that follow are excerpts from four reader's reports, compiled by Graham Nicol and sent to Beryl in 1965. BL MS 83735.

18 Letter to Judith Shackleton, c. 20 September 1965.

19 Details of the New Authors contract given by Alex Hamilton, *Writing Talk*, Matador, 2012, p. xiv.

20 Letter to Judith Shackleton, c. 20 September 1965.

21 Letter from Charles White, c. 1 July 1963.

22 Letter to Judith Shackleton, c. 20 October 1965.

23 Letter to Judith Shackleton, c. 20 September 1965.

24 Ibid.

25 *The Spectator*, 15 April 1965.

26 Letter from Alan Sharp, c. September 1965.

27 Nether her agent nor publisher mentioned Frankfurt at the time, and when in the 1990s Beryl did actually go to the Book Fair she made no mention of having attended before.

28 Letter to Judith Shackleton, c. 20 October 1965.

29 Ibid.

30 Letter to Judith Shackleton, c. 30 October 1965.

31 Ibid.

32 1964 Journal. BL MS 83821.

33 1964 Journal. BL MS 83821.

34 Letter to Judith Shackleton, c. February 1965.

35 Letter from Charles Rycroft to Dr Marcus, 11 November 1965.

36 Letter to Judith Shackleton, c. February 1966.

37 Letter from Alan Sharp, c. April 1966.

38 Letter from Alan Sharp, undated.

39 Letter to Judith Shackleton, c. August 1966. See also letter from Christy & Moore, 8 August 1966. This was probably a version of 'I'm Not Criticising . . . I'm Remembering'.

40 Letter to Judith Shackleton, c. September 1966.

41 Letter to Judith Shackleton, c. November 1966.

42 Letter from John Smith, Christy & Moore, c. April 1967. BL MS 83735.

43 Letter from John Smith, Christy & Moore, 5 January 1967. BL MS 83735.

44 Letter to Judith Shackleton, c. 5 April 1967.

45 Ibid.

CHAPTER 21

1 Letter to Harold Retler, October 1967.

2 Penny Jones, interview with author, 15 July 2013.

3 Letter to Judith Shackleton, c. June 1967.

4 Letter from John Smith, 2 June 1967.

5 Profile by Arthur Pottersman, *Sun*, 4 May 1967.

6 Quoted in letter from John Smith, 19 May 1967. BL MS 83735.

7 *Observer*, 18 June 1967.

8 *Sunday Telegraph*, 18 June 1967.

9 *Hampstead and Highgate Express*, 30 June 1967.

10 *Books & Bookmen*, July 1967.

11 Letter to Judith Shackleton, c. June 1967.

12 Letter from Leah Davis, 15 June 1967. BL MS 83730A.

13 Letter to Judith Shackleton, c. July 1967.

14 Letter to Judith Shackleton c. July 1967 and information from Harold Retler, May 2012.

15 Letter to Judith Shackleton, c. August 1967.

16 Letter to Harold Retler, c. August 1967.

17 Letter from Harold Retler, 19 August 1967.

18 Letter to Harold Retler, 1 September 1967.

19 Ibid.

20 Letter to Harold Retler, 26 September 1967.

21 Julian Symons, review of *A Weekend with Claud*, *The Sunday Times*, 9 July 1967.

22 Letter from Jilly Cooper, 10 July 1967. BL MS 83735.

23 Chloë Buck, email to author, 29 April 2013.

24 'You Could Talk to Someone,' *Intro*, September 1967. The version Beryl later published in *Mum & Mr Armitage*, 'Perhaps You Should Talk to Someone', is not the original unedited version, nor is it the version that appeared in *Intro*. Rather it is a version rewritten in 1984 especially for the collection. One of the most significant changes is in the passage quoted. The line about Moona's attempts to cover up her emotional fragility with laughter is cut altogether, and instead of Moona admitting she has fallen in love she says: 'I can't fathom him at all. First he says he loves me, then he says he doesn't', p. 65.

25 Letter to Harold Retler, c. September 1967.

26 This and subsequent references: 'A Walk in the Park'. BL MS 83793.

27 Letter to Harold Retler, 1 September 1967.

28 Letter from Jean Bowden, *Woman's Own*, 21 November 1967.

29 Letter from Camilla Shaw, *Woman*, 13 December 1967. Curiously, when Beryl came to publish a collection of her short stories she chose not to include 'A Walk in the Park'. The decision seems not to have been a literary one and was perhaps motivated by a feeling that it was too personal.

30 Letter to Judith Shackleton, c. October 1967.

31 Letter to Judith Shackleton, c. August 1967.

32 Letter to Harold Retler, 1 December 1967.

33 Letter from Harold Retler, 13 November 1967.

34 Letter to Harold Retler, 1 December 1967.

35 Letter to Harold Retler, 3 January 1968.

CHAPTER 22

1   Letter to Harold Retler, 3 January 1968.

2   Letter to Harold Retler, 25 January 1968.

3   Ibid.

4   Quoted in *Fiction and the Fiction Industry* by J. A. Sutherland, Bloomsbury Academic, 2013, p. 10.

5   Mick Farren, *Give the Anarchist a Cigarette*, Jonathan Cape, 2001, p. 352.

6   Letter from Michael Dempsey, 31 January 1968.

7   Letter to Judith Shackleton, c. February 1968.

8   Letter from John Smith, 27 March 1968. BL MS 83735.

9   Letter to Judith Shackleton, c. February 1968.

10 See letter from John Smith, 10 April 1968.

11 Letter from Maureen Woodhead, Anglia Television, 11 March 1968. BL MS 83735.

12 Letter to Harold Retler, 14 March 1968.

13 Ibid.

14 Letter to Harold Retler, 21 April 1968.

15 Letter to Harold Retler, 28 April 1968.

16 Telegram to Harold Retler, 17 May 1968.

17 Letter to Harold Retler, 24 May 1968.

18 Letter to Judith Shackleton, c. July 1967.

19 Eaves Farm Journal, 1969.

20 Email from Don McKinlay to author, 28 January 2013.

21 Letter from Harold Retler to author, 14 March 2015.

22 This and subsequent quotes taken from the American journal, May–June 1968, unless otherwise specified. Information provided by Larry Levine, letter to author 30 June 2014.

23 Letter from Psiche Hughes, 11 June 1968.

24 Letter from Don McKinlay, 5 June 1968.

25 Telegram from Don McKinlay, 5 June 1968.

26 Postcard to Brenda and Stanley Haddon, 7 June 1968.

27 Letter to Austin Davies and Winnie Bainbridge, c. 10 June 1968.

28 Ibid.

29 This and subsequent quote, letter from Don McKinlay, 18 June 1968.

30 Letter to Aaron, Jo and Rudi Davies, 8 June 1968.

CHAPTER 23

1 Eaves Farm journal, 1969.

2 Sheenagh McKinlay, email to author, 13 May 2013.

3 Letter to Judith Shackleton, c. July 1968.

4 This and subsequent quotes, Sheenagh McKinlay, email to author, 15 May 2013.

5 Draft letter to Alan Sharp, c. 1968. BL MS 83749.

6 Postcard from Harold Retler, 5 July 1968.

7 Letter to Harold Retler, 10 July 1968.

8 Letter to Judith Shackleton, c. July 1968.

9 Quoted in letter to Judith Shackleton, c. 1974.

10 Letter to Harold Retler, c. November 1968.

11 Letter to Harold Retler, 3 January 1968.

12 Letter to Harold Retler, c. November 1968.

13 *The Times Literary Supplement*, 14 November 1968.

14 Letter from John Smith, Christy & Moore, 29 October 1968. BL MS 83735.

15 Letter to Harold Retler, c. March 1969.

16 Postcard from Alison, 3 April 1969.

17 American Journal, 1968.

18 In the end the American journal wasn't included in the batch sold to the British Library as she was still using it to write her novel.

19 Alfred Green, 'Eyes left for Capt. Dalhousie', *Liverpool Echo*, 30 September 1972.

20 Draft of 'He's the Captain of the Team', c. 1969.

21 Ibid.

22 Quoted in Eaves Farm Journal, 1969.

23 Eaves Farm Journal, 1969.

24 Letter to Judith Shackleton, c. February 1974.

25 Letter to Harold Retler, 16 June 1969.

26 Eaves Farm Journal, 1969.

27 Ibid.

28 Ibid.

29 Ibid.

30 Jo Davies, diary entry, 26 August 1969.

31 Jo Davies, diary entry, 3 October 1969.

CHAPTER 24

1 'Christmas my delight', unpublished article, c. 1973. BL MS 83793.

2 Jo Davies, diary entry, c. September 1969.

3 Belinda Davies, email to author, 26 January 2014.

4 The other episodes in which Beryl featured were: 'The Devil's Sweets' (filmed 30–31 January 1970 and broadcast 23 March); 'Hear No Evil' (filmed 4 April 1970 and broadcast 4 May); 'Survival Code' (filmed 15 April 1970 and broadcast 11 May); 'No Room for Error' (filmed 15 September 1970 but not broadcast until 11 January 1971); and 'You Killed Toby Wren' (filmed 16 October 1970 and broadcast 14 December).

5 James Scott, email to author, 3 April 2011.

6 Letter from Don McKinlay, 7 February 1970.

7 According to the first draft of *The Bottle Factory Outing* (BL MS 83797), in the novel itself it is advertised in a newsagent.

8 Lili Todes, interview with author, 11 December 2012.

9 Willa Petschek, 'Beryl Bainbridge and her tenth novel', *The New York Times*, 1 March 1981.

10 'Pickled in a bottle factory – the very idea!', interview with Molly Parkin, *Evening Standard*, 16 November 1974.

11 Jan Dawson, *Sight and Sound*, Winter 1972.

12 That is the version she told me, at least, in 1987. James Scott doesn't recall her being uncomfortable during the shooting of the scene.

13 Clinical note dated 11 November 1969.

14 Letter from Don McKinlay, c. January 1970. Archive.

15 Letter from Don McKinlay, 17 March 1970. Archive.

16 Ibid.

17 Jo Davies, interview with author, 16 September 2013.

18 Letter to Don McKinlay, c. 1970–71.

19 'Mothers-in-law and firearms', draft version of the article that appeared in the *Daily Mail*.

20 'The day I was nearly shot dead by my mother-in-law', *Daily Mail*, 5 February 2009. When Beryl originally submitted the piece it was entitled 'Mothers-in-law and firearms'.

21 Martyn Harris, 'Biting hard on the bullet-hole', *Sunday Telegraph*, 24 March 1991; Nicholas Wroe, 'Filling the gaps', *Guardian*, 1 June 2002.

22 *Evening Standard*, 1 June 1995.

23 Air pistols of this sort were usually only capable of firing a single shot at a time, and would have had to be reloaded for a second shot.

24 Letter to Judith Shackleton, c. August 1967.

25 Letter to Harold Retler, 3 January 1968.

26 Shusha Guppy, 'The art of fiction: Beryl Bainbridge', *Paris Review*, no. 157, Winter 2000.

27 See *Authors' Lives*, British Library sound recording, 2009. This is an extended series of interviews with Sarah O'Reilly, conducted between December 2008 and July 2009. In them, Beryl talks at length, and in what appears to be specific detail, about many aspects of her life. However, the interviews are seriously marred by the fact that she gave them without recourse to any corroborative documentation. Not only are many of the dates of the anecdotes inaccurate, substantial errors of fact go unchallenged, making the whole sequence extremely unreliable as a guide to Beryl's life. The fact that the interviews have the imprimatur of the British Library, and will thus be taken by many to be authoritative, is a great pity. Although Beryl seemed to exhibit no signs of dementia in later life, at several points in the interview she struggles to remember the names of her novels: 'I did a book . . . oh dear . . . well, it was about the theatre . . . *A Pleasant Day* or something . . .' It is something of a shock to realize she means *An Awfully Big Adventure*. This memory lapse may have been the result of a stroke or her medication, but it may also be that she had taken too large a swig of whisky before going to the British Library, a tactic she often employed to get through interviews with people she didn't know, but one which wasn't conducive to accuracy.

28 Rudi Davies, interview with author, 6 August 2014.

29 This is the version Beryl told Colin, who recounted it in an article entitled 'Publishing Beryl Bainbridge', *Bookseller*, 5 September 1981.

CHAPTER 25

1   Colin Haycraft, 'Publishing Beryl Bainbridge', *Bookseller*, 5 September 1981.

2   Christopher Hurst, *The View from King Street: An Essay in Autobiography*, C. Hurst & Co. Publishers, 1997.

3   Colin Haycraft, 'How we met', *Independent on Sunday*, 21 October 1991.

4   The incident was reported in the newspapers at the time; see for example, *Aberdeen Journal*, 24 April 1929.

5   Michael Holroyd, interview with author, 25 June 2013.

6   Colin Haycraft, 'How we met', *Independent on Sunday*, 21 October 1991.

7   George Weidenfeld, 'At Weidenfeld & Nicolson', in *Colin Haycraft: Maverick Publisher*, ed. Stoddart Martin, Duckworth, 1995.

8   Alan Bennett was staying with Jonathan Miller when Colin and his family arrived in 22 Gloucester Crescent, but he moved in next door at number 23 – famously the setting for the events described in *The Lady in the Van* – in 1968.

9   Barry Baldwin, review of *Colin Haycraft: Maverick Publisher*, ed. Stoddart Martin, Duckworth, 1995, in *Bryn Mawr Classical Review*, 7.2, 1996, p. 131.

10 See, for example, Haycraft's comments in 'Publishing Beryl Bainbridge', *Bookseller*, 5 September 1981, and 'How we met', *Independent on Sunday*, 21 October 1991.

11 The late Oliver Sacks consistently testified to Colin Haycraft's gifts as an editor throughout his career, which was effectively launched by the success of *Awakenings* (Duckworth, 1973). Colin had encouraged Sacks to finish the book after Jonathan Miller had given him its first nine case histories in uncorrected typescript form. 'Colin did an amazing thing,' Sacks recalled, 'he gave me the nine case histories in proof, without consulting me or consulting anyone he'd gone straight from uncorrected manuscript into proof. It was proof for me that he really thought the book was good.' (See video interview on www.webofstories.com). After that, Sacks sent the remaining case histories as they were written down to Colin, and they would then go over them 'in minute detail'. See *On the Move*, Picador, 2015.

12 Zelide Cowan, interview with author, 10 September 2015.

13 Letter to Don McKinlay, c. 1971.

14 This wasn't so much of a concern for some Duckworth authors, as many were salaried academics who could afford to put up with small advances.

15 'Kindred spirits', *Guardian*, 19 March 2005.

16 The official title of the novel was *Harriet Said* . . . but I have deleted the ellipsis to avoid confusion over punctuation.

17 Letter to Judith Shackleton, c. November 1966.

18 This and subsequent two quotes, interview in *The Times*, 3 September 1981.

19 Letter from Colin Haycraft to the National Book League, 19 April 1972.

20 Duckworth press release, September 1972.

21 Karl Miller, 'A novelist worth knowing', *The New York Review of Books*, 16 May 1974.

22 Jo Davies, diary entry, May 1971.

23 'Pickled in a bottle factory: the very idea!', interview with Molly Parkin, *Evening Standard*, 16 November 1974.

24 'Beryl Bainbridge: lady with the dangerous typewriter', interview with Sally Vincent, *Cosmopolitan*, March 1979.

25 'Bitter sweet Beryl', *Liverpool Daily Post*, 19 October 1979.

26 'Pickled in a bottle factory: the very idea!', interview with Molly Parkin, *Evening Standard*, 16 November 1974.

27 'A visit with a friend – now a top British writer', interview with Judith Kirk (née Gleeson), *Focus*, 20 April 1979.

28 'Pickled in a bottle factory: the very idea!', interview with Molly Parkin, *Evening Standard*, 16 November 1974.

29 Interview with Terry Waite, *Terry Waite Takes a Different View*, Thames, 1986.

30 Letter to Anna Haycraft, c. April 1972.

31 Letter to Anna Haycraft, c. May 1972.

32 Letter from Colin Haycraft to Roger Hancock, 2 May 1972.

33 Letter to Anna Haycraft, c. June 1972.

34 Letter from Roger Hancock to Colin Haycraft, 19 January 1973.

35 Letter from Colin Haycraft to Roger Hancock, 23 January 1973.

36 'Exhibition of Contemporary Art', Camden Studios, 9–18 April 1968.

37 *Liverpool Echo*, 30 September 1972.

38 Quoted in Psiche Hughes, *Artist, Writer, Friend*, Thames & Hudson, 2013, p. 90.

39 Alfred Green, 'Eyes left for Capt. Dalhousie', *Liverpool Echo*, 30 September 1972.

40 Quoted in Psiche Hughes, *Artist, Writer, Friend*, Thames & Hudson, 2013, p. 90.

41 Letter from Nigel Mackenzie, c. October 1972.

42 See Psiche Hughes, *Artist, Writer, Friend*, Thames & Hudson, 2013, p. 104.

43 Alfred Green, 'Eyes left for Capt. Dalhousie', *Liverpool Echo*, 30 September 1972.

44 This and subsequent quote: draft of 'He's the Captain of the Team', BL MS 83793.

45 'Pickled in a bottle factory: the very idea!', interview with Molly Parkin, *Evening Standard*, 16 November 1974.

46 'Beryl Bainbridge: dressmaker novelist', interview with Gareth Marshallsea, *Books & Bookmen*, February 1974.

47 'Pickled in a bottle factory: the very idea!', interview with Molly Parkin, *Evening Standard*, 16 November 1974.

48 Karl Miller, 'A novelist worth knowing', *The New York Review of Books*, 16 May 1974.

49 'Bad old days', *The Times Literary Supplement*, 28 September 1973.

50 Anthony Clare, *In the Psychiatrist's Chair*, BBC Radio 4, 1999.

51 Interview with George Yeatman for the Booker Prize in 1973.

52 Letter to Judith Shackleton, c. February 1974.

CHAPTER 26

1 Letter to Judith Shackleton, c. February 1974.

2 Challenge Duplicate Notebook, 1974. BL MS 83795.

3 'Opponents in the generation game', *Guardian*, 5 April 1990.

4 Challenge Duplicate Notebook, 1974. BL MS 83795.

5 Letter to Judith Shackleton, c. March 1964.

6 'Opponents in the generation game', *Guardian*, 5 April 1990.

7 'Eric on the Agenda,' *Banana*s, no. 2, 1975.

8 Letter to Judith Shackleton, c. February 1974.

9 Ibid.

10 Draft letter to Alan Sharp, c. 1966. BL MS 83731A.

11 Megan Tresidder, 'The really awfully funny life of Beryl', *Guardian*, 8 April 1995.

12 *The Bottle Factory Outing*, Duckworth, 1974, p. 10.

13 Peter Straub, 'The novelists: five seekers of the dream', *Vogue*, August 1975.

14 Neil Lyndon, 'Beryl said . . .', *Radio Times*, 13 March 1976.

15 'Pickled in a bottle factory: the very idea!', interview with Molly Parkin, *Evening Standard*, 16 November 1974.

16 Interview with George Yeatman for the Booker Prize in 1973.

17 Letter to Edward Pearson, c. October 1974.

18 Two months later Greene selected *Bottle Factory* as one of his books of the year, describing it as 'an outrageously funny and horrifying story'. Graham Greene, *Observer*, 15 December 1974.

19 Ronald Blythe, *The Sunday Times*, October 1974.

20 Letter to Judith Shackleton, c. February 1974.

21 Letter to Belinda Davies, c. December 1974.

22 Letter from Austin Davies to Belinda Davies, c. December 1974.

23 Letter from Austin Davies to Belinda Davies, 3 January 1975.

24 Letter from Austin Davies to Jo Davies, 17 June 1975.

25 'Beryl's perils', interview with Lynn Barber, *Observer*, 19 August 2001. Beryl stated that the three most important men in her life – her father, her husband and her publisher – had all been bankrupts. In fact only her father was a bankrupt.

26 Letter to Belinda Davies, c. February 1975.

27 Postcard from Clive de Pass, 11 August 1973.

28 Letter from Clive de Pass, c. 1974.

29 Letter from Clive de Pass, c. 19 November 1974.

30 Letter to Anna Haycraft, c. September 1973.

31 Letter from Clive de Pass, c. November 1973.

32 Letter to Belinda Davies, c. December 1974.

33 Letter to Belinda Davies, c. February 1975.

34 *Sun*, 4 May 1967.

35 Peter Straub, 'The novelists: five seekers of the dream', *Vogue*, August 1975.

36 Letter to Edward Pearson, c. March 1974.

37 Quoted in 'It's been a long climb to the top', *Brandon Sun*, 15 May 1974.

38 'Beryl Bainbridge talks to Yolanta May', *New Review*, December 1976.

39 Alex Hamilton, 'Arts Guardian', *Guardian*, Friday 29 November 1974.

40 Susannah Clapp, 'Goings-on in North London', *The Times Literary Supplement*, 3 October 1975.

41 Peter Ackroyd, 'English tragedies', *The Spectator*, 10 October 1975.

42 Alan Sharp, letter to author, 13 February 2012.

43 Hansen would later dedicate his next Brandstetter novel, *The Man Everybody Was Afraid Of* (1978), to her.

44 Ronald Harwood, interview with author, 10 December 2013.

45 David Harsent, interview with author, 1 July 2013.

46 Ronald Harwood, interview with author, 10 December 2013.

47 Letter to Ronald Harwood, 14 March 1975. BL MS 88881/6/32.

48 This and subsequent quote, letter to Ronald Harwood, 28 March 1975. BL MS 88881/6/32.

49 Letter to Michael Holroyd, 11 April 1975.

50 Letter to Michael Holroyd, postmarked 11 April 1975. Such comments show how problematic it is to try to read Beryl's novels as autobiographical *romans à clef*.

51 In 1984 Colin sold the American rights to *Watson's Apology* to McGraw-Hill, being dissatisfied with George Braziller's offer. It was the first of Beryl's books not to be published by Braziller in the US. As a friend of Beryl's, George was understandably upset over the deal, which he blamed on Beryl's new agent, Andrew Hewson, even though he wasn't representing her at the time.

52 Telegram from George Braziller, 21 March 1975. Braziller offered her $1,000 expenses, but Beryl's irrepressible urge to exaggerate can be seen by the letter she wrote to Michael Holroyd two weeks later, in which she gives the figure as $2,000.

53 Letter from Michael Holroyd, 24 April 1975.
54 Letter from Michael Holroyd, 1 May 1975.
55 Postcard from Michael Holroyd, 24 May 1975.
56 Draft letter to Dennis Enright, c. June 1975. BL MS 83794.
57 Letter to Michael Holroyd, c. 23 June 1975.
58 Letter to Joseph Hansen, c. 30 June 1975. JH.
59 Letter to Joseph Hansen, c. 20 July 1975. JH.
60 Letter to Joseph Hansen, c. 5 September 1975. JH.
61 Letter to Michael Holroyd, c. September 1975.
62 Letter from Joseph Hansen, 15 September 1975.
63 Letter to Joseph Hansen, c. December 1975. JH.
64 Letter to Joseph Hansen, c. 4 March 1976. JH.
65 Letter to Colin Haycraft, c. 1976.
66 Nick Totton, *The Spectator*, 8 October 1976.
67 Letter to Joseph Hansen, c. 25 September 1975. JH.
68 Neil Lyndon, 'Beryl said . . .', *Radio Times*, 13 March 1976.
69 'Beryl Bainbridge talks to Yolanta May', *New Review*, December 1976.
70 Leslie Hanscom, 'A writer whose public consists of critics', *Newsday*, 14 March 1976.
71 Hugo Williams, *New Statesman*, 1 October 1976.
72 Francis Wyndham, 'Compression chamber', *The Times Literary Supplement*, 8 October 1976.

CHAPTER 27

1 Letter to Lili Todes, c. 12 January 1978.
2 Katharine Whitehorn, 'Novelist who can't write fiction', *The News*, 7 February 1978.

3 'It's my turn now . . . says writer Beryl Bainbridge', *Newsagent and Bookshop*, 18 September 1976.

4 'The peril of being Beryl', interview with Gerald Isaaman, *Camden New Journal*, 6 February 2003.

5 Letter to Penny Jones, c. 1977.

6 This and subsequent two quotes, letter from Clive de Pass, c. June 1976.

7 Draft letter to Clive de Pass, c. October 1976.

8 This and subsequent quote, letter from Clive de Pass, c. 24 August 1978.

9 Ibid.

10 Letter from Clive de Pass, 25 July 1978.

11 Unpublished extract from Dinah Swain's diary, 15 August 1978.

12 This and subsequent quotes to end of section, letter from Clive de Pass, c. 24 August 1978.

13 Letter to Judith Shackleton, c. September 1976.

14 A. N. Wilson, interview with author, 4 March 2015.

15 This and subsequent two quotes, letter to Joseph Hansen, c. 4 March 1976. JH.

16 Evelyn Straus, 'Panel of noted British literary figures talks with a Jerusalem audience', *Jerusalem Post*, 18 March 1977.

17 'How we met: Beryl Bainbridge and Bernice Rubens', interview with Caroline Boucher, *Independent*, 11 July 1993.

18 'A tale of two authors', interview with Dan Carrier, *Camden New Journal*, 4 November 2005.

19 This and subsequent quote: 'How we met: Beryl Bainbridge and Bernice Rubens', interview with Caroline Boucher, *Independent*, 11 July 1993.

20 'A tale of two authors', interview with Dan Carrier, *Camden New Journal*, 4 November 2005.

21 Mike Cullen, interview with Philip Saville and Beryl Bainbridge, 1981. In fact Payne devotes five pages to the incident, and some of the details it includes are used in *Young Adolf*.

22 *Reader's Almanac*, interview with Walter James Miller, WNYC, 30 June 1979.

23 During the writing of *Young Adolf*, Beryl made use of the only extracts of Bridget Hitler's diary then available, those published by Mike Unger in the *Liverpool Post* in 1973. Duckworth would publish Unger's edition of the diary under the titled *The Memoirs of Bridget Hitler* in 1979.

24 *Reader's Almanac*, interview with Walter James Miller, WNYC, 30 June 1979.

25 'Beryl Bainbridge writes portrait of young Hitler', interview with Carol Crotta, *Los Angeles Examiner*, 25 June 1979.

26 *Reader's Almanac*, interview with Walter James Miller, WNYC, 30 June 1979.

27 Letter to Colin Haycraft, 7 January 1978.

28 Written on the back of a first-day cover featuring breeds of horses, 6 July 1978.

29 Covering note to ms of *Young Adolf*, c. July 1978.

30 Philip Saville, interview with author, 28 February 2014.

31 *Small Talk*, with Edie Stevens, unidentified radio interview, 2001.

32 Television listing, *Observer*, 20 November 1977.

33 Richard Ingrams, 'Too gross', *The Spectator*, 24 December 1977.

34 Letter from Colin Haycraft to Simon King, 14 March 1979.

35 Letter to Michael Holroyd, c. 23 June 1975.

36 Nicholas Wroe, 'Filling in the gaps', *Guardian*, 1 June 2002.

37 Neil Lyndon, 'Beryl said . . .', *Radio Times*, 13 March 1976.

38 Maureen Cleave, 'Will the real Beryl Bainbridge sit down and write a novel?' *Over 21*, April 1979.

39 Letter to Colin and Anna Haycraft, c. March 1979.

40 Letter from Alan Sharp, 23 April 1979.

41 Letter to Don McKinlay, c. March 1979.

42 Harry Hoff, interview with author, 22 June 1989.

43 'Diary', *The Spectator*, 2 March 1985.

44 Harry Hoff, interview with author, 22 June 1989.

45 Entry in author's diary, 25 May 1989.

46 Letter to Psiche Hughes, 29 October 1984.

47 Ronald Hayman, 'A Russian experience', *Book Choice*, February 1981.

48 Entry in author's diary, 25 May 1989.

49 Ronald Hayman, 'A Russian experience', *Book Choice*, February 1981.

50 Frank Kermode, 'The Duckworth school of writers', *London Review of Books*, 20 November 1980.

51 Alice Thomas Ellis, 'I didn't miss Colin at all when he died', *The Times*, 27 October 2004.

52 Shirley Lowe, 'How we met: Colin Haycraft and Alice Thomas Ellis', *Independent*, 21 October 1991.

53 Alice Thomas Ellis, *A Welsh Childhood*, Michael Joseph, 1990, p. 164.

54 *The Clothes in the Wardrobe* (1987) contains what can be seen as a metaphorical allusion to the abortion incident: Margaret, nineteen (the same age as Anna was in 1952), has an affair with a young man she adores, who has murdered a gypsy girl. After Margaret helps him to dispose of the body, she is so stricken with feelings of guilt and shame that she wishes to atone for her actions by becoming a nun.

55 Information from Beryl's conversation with author on 6 October 1989.

56 Letter to Penny Jones, c. 1973. Beryl often signed notes to her friends 'Ethel', or more fully 'Ethel M. Dell', an ironic allusion to the popular Romantic novelist.

57 'A life in the day of novelist Beryl Bainbridge', interview with Victoria Jones, *The Sunday Times*, 17 August 1983.

58 Yolanta May, interview with author, 4 March 2015.

59 Michael Holroyd, interview with author, 18 September 2013.

60 Letter from Anna Haycraft, c. September 2001. BL MS 83731B. Significantly Beryl would annotate this letter and include it among the papers she sold to the British Library in 2004, so she clearly wanted the circumstances surrounding her falling out with Anna on public record.

61 To give just a few examples: in *The Birds of the Air*, Barbara's husband Sebastien is having an affair with a music teacher; in *Unexplained Laughter*, Lydia's lover, Finn, has gone off with another woman; in *Pillars of Gold*, Connie suspects her lover Memet of being unfaithful; and in *The Skeleton in the Cupboard*, Lili has an affair with Mrs Munro's husband Jack.

62 'A spoonful of matinee sugar', *Evening Standard*, c. 10 May 1991.

CHAPTER 28

1   Letter to Colin Haycraft, c. November 1984.

2   'Beryl in peril', *Evening Standard*, 15 September 1980.

3   Emma Fisher, review of *Another Part of the Wood*, *The Spectator*, 8 December 1979, p. 25.

4   Julian Symons, review of *Another Part of the Wood*, *The New York Review of Books*, 17 July 1980.

5   Gloria Valverde, *A Textual Study of Beryl Bainbridge's Another Part of the Wood and A Weekend with Claude*, PhD Thesis, University of Texas, 1985, p. 95.

6   *Birmingham Post*, November 1979.

7   'From Buffalo to Georgia by the Bainbridge route', interview with Matthew Lewin, *Ham & High*, 12 February 1982.

8   Ibid.

9   He wrote to John Pinsent at the Department of Greek, Liverpool University: 'Would you like a talk on the subject of wife-murder among classical scholars in 1871? So far I have only found one case.' Letter from Colin Haycraft to J. Pinsent, 13 November 1980. BL MS 83735.

10 'Mr Chips', in *Colin Haycraft: Maverick Publisher*, edited by Stoddart Martin, Duckworth, 1995, p. 52.

11 'Beryl in peril', *Evening Standard*, 15 September 1980.

12 'Pen friends', *Daily Express*, 17 November 1996.

13 *Motives*, interview with Anthony Clare, BBC, 22 August 1983.

14 Letter to Colin Haycraft, c. 10 April 1984.

15 From conversation with author, recorded in diary, 17 January 1989.

16 From conversation with author, recorded in diary, 3 February 1988.

17 Letter to Michael Holroyd, 30 June 1984.

18 Letter from Michael Holroyd, 3 August 2001.

19 Letter from Brian Masters, 16 October 1984. Masters first met Beryl in 1978 and would go on to become a close friend. His initial impressions of her are typical of many who encountered her during this period: 'She was a down-to-earth, sensible woman, prone to laughter and extravagance, smoking too much, drinking too much. There was nothing remotely over-whelming about her.' *Observer*, 29 October 2000.

20 Harriet Waugh, 'Love and rage', review of *Watson's Apology*, *The Spectator*, 3 November 1984.

21 Humphrey Carpenter, 'Kiss Me Hardy', review of *Watson's Apology*, *London Review of Books*, 15 November 1984.

22 Letter to Michael Holroyd, 24 October 1983.

23 Letter to Colin Haycraft, c. February 1984.

24 'Priestley: a message for all times', *The Times*, 17 August 1984.

25 Letters Page, *Radio Times*, 21 April 1984.

26 *Terry Waite Takes a Different View*, Thames, 1986.

27 Anatole Broyard, 'Books of the times', *The New York Times*, 6 September 1984.

28 Roger Mills, quoted in letter from Jimmy Dewar, 29 May 1984.

29 'Living with Ourselves', proposed outline for television series.

30 Letter to Psiche Hughes, c. September 1985.

31 This and subsequent quote, letter to Anna Haycraft, 3 September 1985.

32 Beatrix Campbell, 'South Yorkshire Republic', review of *Forever England*, *London Review of Books*, 4 June 1987.

33 Letter to Colin Haycraft, c. October 1984.

34 William Foster, 'Childhood stories', *The Scotsman*, 15 October 1977.

35 Letter to Colin Haycraft, 7 January 1978.

36 Letter from Jenne Casarotto to Colin Haycraft, 2 April 1979.

37 Letter from Jenne Casarotto to Colin Haycraft, 24 September 1979.

38 Beryl, as she always did in matters concerning money, took the loan seri-ously. It continued to play on her mind and she would later send them the manuscript of one of her novels as a thank-you gift.

39 Letter to Michael Holroyd, 5 December 1984.

40 Letter from Colin Haycraft, 11 December 1984.

41 Letter from Colin Haycraft to Jenne Casarotto, 11 December 1984.

42 See letter to Jenne Casarotto, c. 18 December 1984.

43 See letter to Colin Haycraft, c. January 1984.

44 Letter to Jenne Casarotto, c. 22 January 1985.

45 Letter from Colin Haycraft, 8 January 1985.

46 Letter to Andrew Hewson, c. 11 January 1985.

47 This and subsequent quote: letter to Colin Haycraft, c. 10 January 1985.

48 Letter to Andrew Hewson, 14 February 1985.

49 Letter to Jenne Casarotto, c. 22 February 1984.

50 Letter to Jenne Casarotto, 31 July 1985.

51 Letter to Andrew Hewson, c. 22 February 1985.

52 Letter from Colin Haycraft, 8 January 1985.

53 The most extreme form of this is in one of the last interviews she gave for the British Library in their *Authors' Lives* series: 'Colin would print no more than 3,000 books,' she told the interviewer. 'I never got any money when I was with Duckworth. All those years I'd done seventeen or eighteen books. I never got an advance, ever. I'd never earned more than about £4,000 a year.' See *Authors' Lives*, British Library sound recording (Track 10, May 2009).

54 See exchange of letters between Duckworth and BBC, covering the period 9 October–26 November 1986.

55 'Preface', *Filthy Lucre*, Duckworth, 1986, p. 8.

56 Letter from Andy McKillop, 5 June 1986.

57 Letter from Andrew Hewson, 10 June 1986.

58 Letter from Graham Greene, 4 May 1987.

CHAPTER 29

1 Letter to Judith Shackleton, c. March 1994.

2 See letter to Andy McKillop, c. October 1988. McKillop continued to hope Beryl would write something for him, and there was even a brief discussion about the possibility she might work with Billie Whitelaw on her autobiography. But this never got further than the discussion stage and like the history of Liverpool the idea was abandoned. See letter from Andy McKillop, 29 September 1988.

3 'Interview: Paul Taylor talks to Beryl Bainbridge', *Literary Review*, March 1986.

4 Details from author's diary, entries for 11, 17 and 23 March 1988. The book was later taken up by Melvyn Fairclough, whose *The Ripper and the Royals* was published by Duckworth in 1991.

5 'Banking on old remedies', *Evening Standard*, 21 January 1988. In this version Beryl tries to ring her bank, but in an interview in 1995 she says she tried to ring her mother. For a fuller discussion of the way Beryl massaged such stories to suit her needs, see Huw Marsh, 'Life's nasty

habit', in *Critical Engagements*, vol. 2. no. 1, UK Network for Modern Fiction Studies, 2008.

6   *Face to Face*, interview with Tony Wilson, Granada, 1989.

7   Beryl did in fact experiment for a while with the first-person narrator, but by the end of March, still dissatisfied with what she had written, she changed it all back as the tone wasn't right. Conversation with author, recorded in diary, 30 March 1988.

8   Peter Campbell, 'People who love people who love somebody else', *London Review of Books*, 25 January 1990.

9   Conversation with author, recorded in diary, 14 September 1989.

10 *Cumberland Evening Times*, 21 July 1971.

11 Colin Haycraft, account of Duckworth. BL MS 83736.

12 Conversation with author, recorded in diary, 26 October 1989.

13 Conversation with author, recorded in diary, 25 October 1988.

14 Conversation with author, recorded in diary, 26 September 1989.

15 Letter from Jonathan Reuvid to the editor of the *Evening Standard*, 12 September 1989. There is no record of Editione Duckworth Italiana ever publishing a book.

16 Ned Sherrin, 'Globe-warming for Wanamaker', 16 September 1989.

17 Beryl's account as recorded in author's diary, 26 September 1989.

18 Letter from Marie-Claude Shashoua to Colin Haycraft, 26 September 1989. BL MS 83736.

19 Letter from Jonathan Reuvid to Colin Haycraft, 30 September 1989. BL MS 83736.

20 Roger Shashoua, *Dancing with the Bear*, GMB Publishing, 2007, p. 9.

21 Beryl's account as recorded in author's diary, 26 September 1989.

22 Beryl's account as recorded in author's diary, 1 November 1989.

23 After Duckworth quit the building in 2000 it would become the site of Jay Jopling's uber-trendy White Cube gallery.

24 John Jolliffe, *Woolf at the Door*, Duckworth, 1998, p. 95.

25 Christopher Edwards, 'Minding his own business', *The Spectator*, 17 April 1992.

26 Letter to Andrew Hewson, 11 March 1992.

27 John Jolliffe, *Woolf at the Door*, Duckworth, 1998, pp. 95–6.

28 Latin exercise book, c. 1991–2,

29 Letter to Andrew Hewson, c. July 1992.

30 Letter from Malcolm Hill, c. February 2008.

31 Conversation between Beryl and author, recorded in diary, 20 April 1989. Colin eventually signed the form.

32 Latin exercise book, c. 1991–2,

33 Letter from Tony Ellis to Stephen Hill, 8 April 1992. BL MS 83736.

34 Letter from Tony Ellis to Jonathan Pearce, 30 October 1992. BL MS 83736.

35 Letter from Stephen Hill to Tony Ellis. 2 November 1992. BL MS 83736.

36 See letter from Stephen Hill to Beryl, 5 November 1992, in which he mentions the figure of £400,000, and letter from Bank of Ireland to Stephen Hill, 3 November 1992, which gives the amount of the loan as £600,000. BL MS 83736.

37 Letter from Tony Ellis to Stephen Hill, 6 November 1992. BL MS 83736.

38 Letter to Stephen Hill, 17 November 1992.

39 Letter to Stephen Hill, 19 November 1992.

40 *Authors' Lives*, British Library sound recording (Track 10, May 2009).

41 Letter to Andrew Hewson, c. May 1993.

42 Written on the bottom of a letter from Genevieve Cooper, 18 August 1992.

43 Beryl's income before tax for 1992 was a little over £89,400, of which just over £24,000 was from the *Evening Standard*.

44 Press release, c. 8 December 1992.

45 John Jolliffe, *Woolf at the Door*, Duckworth, 1998, p. 96.

46 Letter from Colin Haycraft to John Briggs, 26 May 1994.

47 Beryl's account as recorded in author's diary, 30 March 1988.

48 Ibid.

49 'Pen friends', *Daily Express*, 17 November 1996.

50 Information from Susan Hitch, interview with author, 20 March 2015.

51 This and subsequent quote: Peter Conradi, interview with author, 27 February 2015.

52 'Diary', *The Spectator*, 16 February 1985. Beryl's first reference to the book was in 1980, in *Winter Garden*, where she describes her alter ego Enid as having 'often read for pleasure Cherry-Gerrard's [*sic*] chilling account of the worst journey in the world' (p. 58).

53 Conversation with author, recorded in diary, 27 February and 24 April 1990.

54 Letter to Michelle Haycraft, c. 1990.

55 Letter to Mervyn Horder, c. 10 January 1991. That Beryl could claim her fictional representations of two such psychologically and temperamentally diverse figures as Adolf Hitler and Robert Scott were both based on her father shows that her statements can't be taken too literally.

56 Conversation with author, recorded in diary, 27 February 1990. During the 1970s Beryl had used the photograph of Queen Victoria and John Brown as a model for her experiments in engraving. The resulting pictures featured a naked woman on a horse in the same pose as the Queen, and

significantly, given Beryl's use of Napoleon as a symbol in her paintings, she is also wearing a Napoleonic hat.

57 'Act one, scene two', interview with Alan Franks, *The Times*, 7 April 1992.

58 Rowanne Pasco, 'Cold courage', *Tablet*, 1 February 1992.

59 Letter from Hugh Lloyd-Jones to Colin Haycraft, 16 June 1994.

60 Letter to Andrew and Margaret Hewson, c. July 1992.

61 Letters from Colin Haycraft, 20 June and 15 July 1994.

62 Letter from Colin Haycraft, 23 September 1994.

63 Unpublished draft of obituary, September 1994.

64 'Mr Chips', in *Colin Haycraft: Maverick Publisher*, edited by Stoddart Martin, Duckworth, 1995, pp. 53–5.

CHAPTER 30

1 Letter to Judith Shackleton, c. 1995.

2 Letter to Andrew Hewson, c. July 1993.

3 Letter from Robin Baird-Smith, 1 November 1994. BL MS 83736A.

4 Robin Baird-Smith, 'A not so quiet life', *Tablet*, 10 July 2010.

5 Letter from Andrew Hewson to Robin Baird-Smith, 25 February 1995.

6 Letter to Robin Baird-Smith, c. 25 February 1995.

7 Letter from Robin Baird-Smith to Andrew Hewson, 27 February 1995.

8 Letter from Robin Baird-Smith, 1 March 1995.

9 Robin Baird-Smith, 'A not so quiet life', *Tablet*, 10 July 2010.

10 Letter from Robin Baird-Smith, 4 January 1996.

11 Letter to Michael Holroyd, 29 June 2000.

12 Kate Kellaway, 'Beryl come on down', *Observer*, 25 October 1998.

13 Beryl wrote for *The Oldie* from its first appearance on 21 February 1992 until her death and rarely missed an issue.

14 Martin Wainwright, 'Scousers hit back at author's comments', *Guardian*, 4 March 1999.

15 A. N. Wilson, interview with author, 4 March 2015.

16 Nevertheless, Beryl's willingness to help others in their writing continued until the end of her life. During her final year, despite frequent bouts of illness, she spent time talking to the actor Sir Timothy Ackroyd, who had asked her for suggestions as to how to turn an undramatic murder trial monologue he'd written, entitled *It's a Dog's Life*, into something more conventionally dramatic. Despite a number of meetings, however, the project was begun too late and remained unfinished at her death, with only her suggested amendments to Act 1 having been incorporated. Ackroyd later finished the project himself, retitling it *The Fuse on the Hume Banger*.

17 Draft of 'Kiss Me Hardy', author's copy of working manuscript, c. 1988.

18 A few years later Beryl would reuse the title for an unrelated story about a man going on a cruise.

19 'I read and read and read and it all goes out of one ear', *Observer*, 5 April 1998.

20 *Springtime for Hitler*, *Mary Poppins* and *Bedknobs and Broomsticks* were other perennial favourites.

21 Script for 'The Last Battle', December 1990.

22 Kirk Freudenburg, *The Cambridge Companion to Roman Satire*, Cambridge University Press, 2005, p. 183.

23 Inevitably my working relationship with Beryl affected her previous reliance on Anna's editorial input. Beginning with *An Awfully Big Adventure* we spent many hours discussing the progress of her novels, from their initial conception to the final proofreading stage, a process that was formalized with *Every Man for Himself* when I took over the task of preparing Beryl's manuscripts. Describing our working relationship in an interview in 1999, Beryl said: 'Four or five years ago he started to help with my work, and nowadays we have long telephone conversations once I've written something. I give him pages to look at, and he'll say, "I'm not so sure about that word, Beryl. Did you mean to put that there?" He has fantastic input. He knows my work so well now; he knows the process and he knows what I'm trying to do.' ('Life support', *Observer*, 11 April 1999.)

24 Kent Carroll – who Beryl nicknamed 'Superman' – would publish Beryl's work in America until her death.

25 E. Jane Dickson, 'Hot on hellfire, strict on syntax', *Independent*, 19 February 1998.

26 Letter to Mary Thorne, c. 2004.

27 Derwent May, interview with author, 4 March 2015.

28 A. N. Wilson, interview with author, 4 March 2015.

29 Letter to Derwent and Yolanta May, 29 March 1993. In this letter Beryl gives the impression that Colin left her to walk home alone, but in a follow-up letter the next day she clarified that he had in fact offered to take her home but she'd refused because he was so tired.

30 Letter from Colin Haycraft, 2 April 1993.

31 A. N. Wilson, interview with author, 4 March 2015.

32 This and subsequent quote, letter to author, c. May 2004.

33 From conversation with author, recorded in diary, 8 June 1988.

34 'Relative values', *The Sunday Times*, 5 January 1986.

35 Message left on author's answer machine, c. October 2000.

36 'Crimea', *South Bank Show*, London Weekend Television, 1998.

37 'Welcome to the weird world of Beryl Bainbridge', interview with Judith Woods, *Scotsman*, 27 November 1997.

38 'Dead men live', *Sunday Express*, 13 December 1992. Barthorp also provided her with useful information on Crimean regiments and army surgeons.

39 Draft letter to Pamela Roberts, c. October 1996.

40 'The writing life interview', *Writer's Digest*, June 1999.

41 *South Bank Show: Crimea*, London Weekend Television, 1998.

42 Initially Robin was concerned that the book might be too short. Although at just over 47,000 words the novel is 10,000 words shorter than *Every Man for Himself*, it was still longer than both *The Dressmaker* and *Injury Time*.

43 Kate Kellaway, 'Beryl, come on down', *Observer*, 25 October 1998.

44 'Cold call: Beryl Bainbridge', interview with Jack O'Sullivan, *Independent*, 26 September 1998.

45 Julian Barnes betting slip, 27 October 1998. BL MS 83732A.

46 Valentine Cunningham, *The Times Literary Supplement*, 17 November 1978.

47 Quoted in Julian Barnes, 'How did she do it?', *Guardian*, 26 July 2008.

48 'Booker Prize: tears, tiffs and triumphs', *Guardian*, 8 September 2008.

49 *Independent*, 17 October 1998.

50 Letter from Robin Baird-Smith, c. 1998.

51 'Books: The loafer', *Guardian*, 10 July 1999.

52 See filings at Company Check website.

53 Letter from Stephen Hill to Andrew Hewson, 28 July 1999.

54 Letter from Stephen Hill to Margaret Hewson, 1 March 2000.

55 Fax to Margaret Hewson, 16 March 2001.

56 Unpublished blurb for *According to Queeney*, 16 March 2001.

57 'Beryl's perils', interview with Lynn Barber, *Observer*, 19 August 2001.

58 'I never thought I was worth anything as a writer', interview with Graham Turner, *Daily Telegraph*, 18 August 2001.

59 *Beryl's Last Year*, directed by Charlie Russell, BBC, 2005.

60 'I never thought I was worth anything as a writer', interview with Graham Turner, *Daily Telegraph*, 18 August 2001.

61 Letter from Anna Haycraft to *Daily Telegraph*, 27 August 2001. BL MS 83731B.

62 Letter from Anna Haycraft, September 2001. BL MS 83731B.

63 In an interview given the year before she died, Beryl said the only reason Anna had a house in Wales 'is because of the money that I've earnt'. (*Authors' Lives*, British Library sound recording, Track 8, April 2009.) This wasn't true, but it shows the extent to which the house in Trefechan

became a symbol in Beryl's mind of how she had been financially mistreated by Duckworth.

64　Draft letter to Anna Haycraft. September 2001. BL MS 83731B.

CHAPTER 31

1　Letter to Mary Thorne, c. 2004.

2　*South Bank Show: Crimea*, London Weekend Television, 1998.

3　The prize money of £40,000 was tax free, but one condition of the award was that recipients donate £10,000 to an organization of their choice to encourage writing and reading. The split prize meant that each writer received £20,000, out of which they each donated £5,000 to a good cause. Beryl chose the King's Lynn Literature Festival, which had its Arts Council grant cut a year or so previously.

4　Letter to Andrew Hewson, c. 14 April 2002.

5　Letter to Andrew Hewson, c. 16 August 2002. The performance was actually billed as *The Triumph and Tragedy of Dr Johnson*.

6　Susan Hill talks to Beryl Bainbridge, Hay-on-Wye Literary Festival, 9 June 2002.

7　'Knocked out into never-never land', *Sunday Telegraph*, 1 March 1992.

8　Letter to Margaret Hewson, 3 April 2002.

9　University College London (UCL) examination report, 15 March 2003.

10　Letter to Andrew Hewson, 13 March 2003.

11　Message on author's answer machine, 30 August 2003.

12　'Dear Brutus', author's copy of working manuscript.

13　'Echoes of a rackety life', interview with Sholto Byrnes, *Independent*, 17 May 2004.

14　'Coming to a bookshop near you', *Daily Telegraph*, 5 January 2004: 'That long-time Booker bridesmaid Beryl Bainbridge is throwing her hat in the ring again with *Dear Brutus* (September, Little, Brown).'

15　Letter to Andrew Hewson, c. July 2004.

16　Beryl was referred to a chest specialist at the Royal Free Hospital, who concluded that the hilar-node calcification on her X-rays was an indication of tuberculosis. As tests in 1954 had shown she didn't have TB as a child, this episode was determined to have happened subsequently. See letter from Dr Jeremy Brown to Dr Sackville-West, 3 July 2008.

17　Letter from Professor R. Pounder to Dr Steen, 3 January 1995.

18　Information contained in health records from the James Wigg Group Practice.

19　*Beryl's Last Year*, directed by Charlie Russell, BBC, 2005.

20　Letter from Peter Taylor, 6 January 2004.

21 Letter to Mary Thorne, c. 2004.

22 Information contained in health records from the James Wigg Group Practice.

23 'Nicotine teens and emphysemic adults', *Guardian*, 14 May 2007.

24 'Tragic Pauline was Beryl's inspiration', *Camden New Journal*, 30 October 2003.

25 Draft obituary for Margaret Hewson, c. 30 August 2002. In *According to Queeney*, Beryl named Mrs Thrale's servant Mags Hewson in her honour.

26 Lynn Barber, obituary of Margaret Hewson, *Guardian*, 3 September 2002.

27 Draft obituary for Margaret Hewson, c. 30 August 2002.

28 Alice Thomas Ellis, 'Diary', *The Spectator*, 24 April 2004.

29 Alice Thomas Ellis, 'I didn't miss Colin at all when he died', *The Times*, 27 October 2004.

30 'Kindred Spirits', *Guardian*, Saturday 19 March 2005.

31 In my own case, in a letter dated September 2004, it was regarding her work: 'Dearest Brendan, You have been my confidant all these years. Thank you so much. I'd like you to have a say in what happens to my novels . . . try to remember how we worked together. Every time you objected to something in my text, I argued and thought who the hell does he think he is. But every time you were right. Very much love, Beryl.'

32 Due to the huge amount of material and Beryl's erratic filing habits, a number of personal documents – such as drawings by her grandchildren – were included, while other papers that were more clearly literary in character – such as the American journal and pages of 'He's the Captain of the Team' she was using for *Polka Dot* – were excluded and remained scattered about in other filing cabinets and drawers until her death.

33 Letter from Joan Winterkorn, 18 January 2005.

34 Letter from Dr Karen Ling to Elizabeth Garrett Anderson Hospital, 18 November 2003.

35 James Wigg Practice records, entry for 16 August 1995.

36 James Wigg Practice records, entry for 11 August 2006.

37 Letter from J. R. Sainsbury to Juliet Glover, 24 August 2006.

38 Letter from J. R. Sainsbury to Dr Sackville-West, 29 August 2006.

39 'My heart attack worked wonders', *The Sunday Times*, 28 October 2008.

40 Letter from Dr J. Tobias to Dr Sackville-West, 7 February 2007.

41 A. N. Wilson, 'My week', *Observer*, 21 September 2008.

42 Letter from Richard Garlick to Dr Booth, 14 May 2008.

43 Letter from Jo Davies to Richard Garlick, 9 June 2008.

44 Letter from Dr K. Gowribalan to UCL neurology department, 8 January 2009.

45 *Authors' Lives*, British Library sound recording (Track 8, April 2009).

46 University College Hospital (UCH) discharge form, 29 March 2009.

47 *Authors' Lives*, British Library sound recording (Track 8, April 2009).

48 *Authors' Lives*, British Library sound recording (Track 12, July 2009).

49 *Beryl's Last Year*, directed by Charlie Russell, BBC, 2005.

50 Letter to Andrew Hewson, 28 September 2005.

51 Letter to Derwent and Yolanta May, 21 July 2009.

52 *Authors' Lives*, British Library sound recording (Track 10, May 2009).

53 Letter from Dr Richard Garlick to Dr Booth, 15 June 2008.

54 Letter to Derwent and Yolanta May, 21 July 2009.

55 Letter from Dr J. Tobias to Dr Sackville-West, 5 November 2009.

56 Letter to author, c. July 2009.

57 Letter to author, 24 September 2009.

58 Letter to Dr Sackville-West, c. January 2010.

59 Letter from Dr Sackville-West to Dr Ari Laurence, 14 January 2010.

60 Letter to Derwent and Yolanta May, February 2010.

61 Letter to author, 23 April 2010.

62 Mark Bostridge, unpublished diary entry for 17 April 2010.

63 Letter from James Crosbie to Dr Sackville-West, 10 May 2010.

64 Hospital diary, 2010. See also death certificate, dated 5 July 2010, where the cause of death is listed as (a) Bowel Obstruction (b) Metastatic Carcinoma.

AFTERWORD

1 The desk was rescued from the Duckworth offices when the firm moved out of the Old Piano Factory in 1990.

2 Ruth Scurr, 'Road trip', *Times Literary Supplement*, 27 May 2011.

3 Quoted in 'Novelist who can't write fiction', interview with Katharine Whitehorn, *The News*, 7 February 1978. Whitehorn went on to explain that 'presumably . . . she just lifts long strands of real life from the pot and cuts them off randomly'.

4 Mark Bostridge, 'Knowingly undersold', *New Statesman*, 30 May 2011.

5 Now that Beryl's personal papers in the British Library can be consulted, the published accounts of her home life and her family upbringing are beginning to face more serious critical scrutiny than in the past. This is evidenced by one of the best critical assessments of Beryl's work to date, Huw Marsh's *Beryl Bainbridge* (Northcote House, 2014), though it could be argued that Marsh still takes too many of Beryl's unsupported statements about her life at face value.

BIBLIOGRAPHY

NOVELS

A Weekend with Claud, New Authors, 1967.
Another Part of the Wood, Hutchinson, 1968.
Harriet Said . . ., Duckworth, 1972.
The Dressmaker, Duckworth, 1973 (US: *The Secret Glass*).
The Bottle Factory Outing, Duckworth, 1974.
Sweet William, Duckworth, 1975.
A Quiet Life, Duckworth, 1976.
Injury Time, Duckworth, 1977.
Young Adolf, Duckworth, 1978.
Another Part of the Wood, revised ed., Duckworth, 1979.
Winter Garden, Duckworth, 1980.
A Weekend with Claude, revised ed., Duckworth, 1981.
Watson's Apology, Duckworth, 1984.
Filthy Lucre, Duckworth, 1986.
An Awfully Big Adventure, Duckworth, 1989.
The Birthday Boys, Duckworth, 1991.
Every Man for Himself, Duckworth, 1996.
Master Georgie, Duckworth, 1998.
According to Queeney, Little, Brown, 2001.
The Girl in the Polka Dot Dress, Little, Brown, 2011.

NON-FICTION

English Journey, or The Road to Milton Keynes, Duckworth/BBC, 1984.
Forever England: North and South, Duckworth/BBC, 1987.
Something Happened Yesterday, Duckworth, 1993.
Front Row: Evenings at the Theatre, Continuum, 2005.

SHORT STORIES

Mum and Mr Armitage, Duckworth, 1985.

SELECTED JOURNALISM

'It's my turn now . . . says writer Beryl Bainbridge', *Newsagent and Bookshop*, 18 September 1976.

'Facing backwards', *New Review*, October 1977.

'Words fail me', *Radio Times*, 17 February 1979.

'The lullaby sound of houses falling down', *The Sunday Times*, 19 July 1981.

'Beryl Bainbridge says . . .', *The Times*, 3 September 1981.

'Priestley: a message for all times', *The Times*, 17 August 1984.

'Diary', *The Spectator*, 16 February 1985.

'Ghosts of Christmas past', *Image*, December 1986.

'Going spare in no man's land', *Evening Standard*, 5 November 1987.

'Banking on old remedies', *Evening Standard*, 21 January 1988.

'Rubble, toil and troubles', *Evening Standard*, 21 April 1988.

'Picking up the pieces of life', *Evening Standard*, 28 April 1988.

'Beryl Bainbridge and Alice Thomas Ellis chat', *Guardian*, 13 September 1988.

'Home is where the hearth is', *Evening Standard*, 17 March 1989.

'The night I walked out on Lennon', *Evening Standard*, 19 January 1990.

'Opponents in the generation game', *Guardian*, 5 April 1990.

'Drape expectations', *Evening Standard*, 4 January 1991.

'Knocked out into never-never land', *Sunday Telegraph*, 1 March 1992.

'Sweet and sour idylls', *Daily Mail*, 13 November 1993.

'Pen friends', *Daily Express*, 17 November 1996.

'The year I grew up', *Independent*, 11 July 1999.

'My father, cabin boy', *Sunday Telegraph*, 5 December 1999.

'Kindred spirits', *Guardian*, 19 March 2005.

'Bittersweet symphony', *Guardian*, 21 April 2007.

'The Liverpool that I loved has gone for ever: Merseyside memories in the European capital of culture', *The Spectator*, 12 December 2007.

'Made in England', Arts Council, 2008.

'My father would rant and rave for weeks – but he was still superior', *Daily Mail*, 9 February 2008.

'My heart attack worked wonders', *The Sunday Times*, 26 October 2008.

'The day I was nearly shot dead by my mother-in-law', *Daily Mail*, 5 February 2009.

SELECTED NEWSPAPER PROFILES AND INTERVIEWS

Anon. 'Bitter sweet Beryl,' *Liverpool Daily Post*, 19 October 1979.

Baker, John F. 'Beryl Bainbridge: total immersion in the past', *Publishers Weekly*, 9 November 1998.

Barber, Lynn. 'Beryl's Perils', *Observer*, 19 August 2001.

Boucher, Caroline. 'How we met: Beryl Bainbridge and Bernice Rubens', *Independent*, 11 July 1993.

Brooks, Richard. 'The Secret Lust of Bainbridge and Bonaparte', *The Sunday Times*, 23 January 2011.

Brown, Craig. 'Beryl Bainbridge, an ideal writer's childhood', *The Times*, 4 November 1978.

Byrnes, Sholto. 'Beryl Bainbridge: echoes of a rackety life', *Independent*, 17 May 2004.

Carrier, Dan. 'A tale of two authors', *Camden New Journal*, 4 November 2005.

Cleave, Maureen. 'Will the real Beryl Bainbridge sit down and write a novel?' *Over 21*, April 1979.

Cobb, Richard. 'Portrait of the dictator as a young artist', *New Society*, 16 November 1978.

Coleman, Pamela. 'My best teacher', *The Times Educational Supplement*, 29 January 1999.

Crotta, Carol. 'Beryl Bainbridge writes portrait of young Hitler', *Los Angeles Examiner*, 25 June 1979.

Crowley, Jeananne. 'In Priestley's footsteps', *Radio Times*, 24 March 1984.

Edwards, Christopher. 'Minding his own business', *The Spectator*, 17 April 1992.

Foster, William. 'Childhood stories', *Scotsman*, 15 October 1977.

Franks, Alan. 'Act one, scene two', *The Times*, 7 April 1992.

Garratt, Pat. 'The sad, mad, funny world of Beryl Bainbridge', *Woman's Journal*, 1979.

Green, Alfred. 'Eyes left for Capt. Dalhousie', *Liverpool Echo*, 30 September 1972.

Guppy, Shusha. 'Beryl Bainbridge: the art of fiction', *Paris Review*, no. 157, 2000.

Hamilton, Alex. 'Arts Guardian', *Guardian*, 29 November 1974.

Hanscom, Leslie. 'A writer whose public consists of critics', *Newsday*, 14 March 1976.

Harris, Martyn. 'Biting hard on the bullet-hole', *Sunday Telegraph*, 24 March 1991.

Haycraft, Colin, 'Publishing Beryl Bainbridge', *Bookseller*, no. 240, 5 September 1981.

Jones, Victoria. 'A life in the day of Beryl Bainbridge, novelist and playwright', *The Sunday Times Magazine*, 17 August 1983.

Kellaway, Kate. 'Beryl, come on down', *Observer*, 25 October 1998.

Lewin, Matthew. 'From Buffalo to Georgia by the Bainbridge route', *Ham & High*, 12 February 1982.

Lyndon, Neil. 'Beryl said . . .', *Radio Times*, 13 March 1976.

Marshallsea, Gareth. 'Beryl Bainbridge: dressmaker novelist', *Books & Bookmen*, February 1974.

May, Yolanta. 'Beryl Bainbridge talks to Yolanta May', *New Review*, December 1976.

Miller, Karl. 'A novelist worth knowing', *The New York Review of Books*, 16 May 1974.

Parkin, Molly. 'Pickled in a bottle factory: the very idea!', *Evening Standard*, 16 November 1974.

Petschek, Willa. 'Beryl Bainbridge and her tenth novel', *The New York Times*, 1 March 1981.

Price, Carol. 'The art of the novelist', *The Sunday Times Magazine*, 27 October 1985.

Salkeld, Luke. 'Love across enemy lines', *Daily Mail*, 16 August 2007.

Straub, Peter. 'The novelists: five seekers of the dream', *Vogue*, August 1975.

Taylor, Laurie. 'That's for the fellahs!', *New Humanist*, vol. 119, 2004.

Taylor, Paul. 'Interview: Beryl Bainbridge', *Literary Review*, March 1986.

Tresidder, Megan. 'The really awfully funny life of Beryl', *Guardian*, 8 April 1995.

Turner, Graham. 'I never thought I was worth anything as a writer', *Daily Telegraph*, 18 August 2001.

Vincent, Sally. 'Beryl Bainbridge: lady with the dangerous typewriter', *Cosmopolitan*, March 1979.

Whitehorn, Katharine. 'Novelist who can't write fiction', *News*, 7 February 1978.

Woodward, Richard B. 'Life's tragedy and farce', *Wall Street Journal*, 7 July 2010.

Wroe, Nicholas. 'Filling in the gaps', *Guardian*, 1 June 2002.

AUDIO-VISUAL SOURCES

Booker Prize interview with George Yeatman, 1973.

Omnibus: Words Fail Me, BBC2, 1979.

Reader's Almanac, interview with Walter James Miller, WNYC, 1979.

Motives, interview with Anthony Clare, BBC2, 1983.

Terry Waite Takes a Different View, interview with Terry Waite, BBC 2 North West, 1986.

In the Same Boat, interview with Kay Avila, Thames, May 1987.

Face to Face with Tony Wilson, Granada, 1989.

Book Talk, interview with Jill Kitson, ABC, 1996.

In the Psychiatrist's Chair, interview with Anthony Clare, BBC Radio 4, 1999.

Beryl's Last Year, documentary by Charlie Russell, BBC2, 2005.

SELECTED ACADEMIC CRITICISM

Anderson, Patricia. 'The novel as autobiography: the life and career of Beryl Bainbridge', *Quadrant*, vol. 53, no. 10, October 2009.

Carr, Helen. 'Beryl Bainbridge: unhomely moments', in *Writing Liverpool*, Liverpool University Press, 2007.

Grubisic, Brett Josef. *Understanding Beryl Bainbridge*. University of South Carolina Press, 2008.

Johnson, Diane. 'Young Adolf goes to Beryl Bainbridge's England', in *Terrorists and Novelists*, Knopf, 1982, pp. 97–104.

Lassner, Phyllis. 'Fiction as historical critique: the retrospective World War II novels of Maureen Duffy and Beryl Bainbridge', *Phoebe: A Feminist Journal of Interdisciplinary Studies*, 3 (Fall 1991), pp. 12–26.

Marsh, Huw. 'Life's nasty habit: time, death and intertextuality in Beryl Bainbridge's *An Awfully Big Adventure*', *Critical Engagements*, 2.1 (Spring/Summer 2008), pp. 85–110.

— 'From the "other side": mimicry and feminist rewriting in the novels of Beryl Bainbridge', in *Identity and Form in 20th and 21st Century Literature*, ed. Ana María Sánchez-Arce. Routledge, 2013.

— *Beryl Bainbridge: Writers and their Work*. Tavistock: Northcote House in association with the British Council, 2014.

Richter, Virginia. 'Grey Gothic: the novels of Beryl Bainbridge', *Anglistik und Englischunterricht*, 60 (1997), pp. 159–71.

Valverde, Gloria. A textual study of Beryl Bainbridge's 'Another Part of the Wood' and 'A Weekend with Claude', PhD Thesis, University of Texas, 1985.

Wennö, Elisabeth. *Ironic Formula in the Novels of Beryl Bainbridge*. Göteborg, 1993.

— 'Encased in ice: antarctic heroism in Beryl Bainbridge's *The Birthday Boys*', in *Cold Matters*, eds. Heidi Hansson and Cathrine Norberg. Northern Studies Monographs, 2009.

GENERAL REFERENCE

Andrews, Julie. *Home: A Memoir of My Early Years*. Hachette UK, 2008.

Blatchford, Robert. *Dismal England*. Walter Scott, 1899.

Bostridge, Mark. *Lives for Sale: Biographers' Tales*, Continuum, 2004.

Bowen, Phil. *A Gallery to Play To*. Liverpool University Press, 2008.

Branson, Eve. *Mum's the Word: The High-Flying Adventures of Eve Branson*. AuthorHouse, 2013.

Connolly, Cyril. *Enemies of Promise*. Routledge & Son, 1938.

Davies, Peter. *Arthur Ballard: Liverpool Artist and Teacher*. Old Bakehouse Publications, 1996.

— *Liverpool Seen: Post-War Artists on Merseyside*. Redcliffe Press, 1992.

Dewey, J. F. 'Robert Millner Shackleton. 1909–2001', *Biographical Memoirs of Fellows of the Royal Society*, 2004.

Ellis, Alice Thomas. *A Welsh Childhood*. Michael Joseph, 1990.

Fazan, Eleanor. *Fiz: And Some Theatre Giants*. Friesen Press, 2013.

Forman, Denis. *Persona Granada*. André Deutsch, 1997.

Furlong, June (with Jill Block). *June: A Life Study*. APML, 2000.

Haddon, Elizabeth. *Making Music in Britain*. Ashgate Publishing, 2006.

Hamilton, Alex. *Writing Talk: Conversations with Top Writers of the Last Fifty Years*. Matador, 2012.

Hirsch, Joshua. *Afterimage: Film, Trauma and the Holocaust*. Temple University Press, 2004.

Hughes, Psiche. *Beryl Bainbridge: Writer, Artist, Friend*. Thames & Hudson, 2012.

Hughes, Quentin. *Seaport: Architecture and Landscape in Liverpool*. Lund Humphries, 1964.

Hurst, Christopher. *The View from King Street: An Essay in Autobiography* C. Hurst & Co., 1997.

Jolliffe, John. *Woolf at the Door*. Duckworth, 1998.

Lee, Hermione. *Penelope Fitzgerald: A Life*. Chatto & Windus, 2013.

Lewison, Mark. *All These Years*. Little, Brown, 2013.

Loebl, Lili. *Don't Ask Me Where I Come From*. Book Guild, 2011.

Lynne, Gillian. *A Dancer in Wartime*. Vintage, 2012.

Martin, Stoddart (ed.). *Colin Haycraft: Maverick Publisher*. Duckworth, 1995.

Melly, George. *Revolt into Style*. Allen Lane, Penguin Press, 1970.

Morris, Mike and Tony Walley. *An Introduction to George Garrett*. Writing on the Wall, 2014.

Richmond, Peter. *Marketing Modernisms: The Architecture and Influence of Charles Reilly*. Liverpool University Press, 2001.

Roberts, John C. Q. *Speak Clearly into the Chandelier: Cultural Politics Between Britain and Russia 1973–2000*. Curzon Press, 2000.

Sacks, Oliver. *On the Move*. Picador, 2015.

Shashoua, Roger. *Dancing with the Bear*. GMB Publishing, 2007.

Sontag, Susan. *On Photography*. Penguin Books, 1977.

Taylor, A. J. P. *Essays in English History*. Pelican, 1976.

Wilkin, Fr Vincent. *The Image of God in Sex*. Sheed and Ward, 1955.

Willett, John. *Art in a City*. Methuen & Co., 1967.

Wyndham Goldie, Grace. *The Liverpool Repertory Theatre 1911–34*. University Press of Liverpool, 1935.

ACKNOWLEDGEMENTS

Special thanks to Beryl's children, Aaron, Jo and Rudi, for the support and encouragement they have given me throughout the writing process, as well as for allowing me to consult and quote from the papers in their possession. Many people were kind enough to let me copy documents they had relating to Beryl, but particular thanks go to Belinda Davies for access to Austin Davies's personal papers; Tom Haycraft for access to his archive of Duckworth material; Chloë Buck for her extensive collection of Beryl's letters to her mother, Judith Shackleton; Harold Retler for the letters Beryl wrote to him during the late 1960s; Andrew Hewson and Ed Wilson at Johnson & Alcock for access to the agency's files on Beryl dating back to the mid-1980s; and to Alan Sharp's Estate for permission to quote from his unpublished correspondence.

My thanks also go to all those who agreed to talk to me about their memories of Beryl or who helped to clarify information about her life and aspects of her work, including: Hilary Abbott, Helen Alexander, Paul Bailey, David Bainbridge, Trevor Baines, Robin Baird-Smith, Anita Barry, Nicole Bartos, Mark Bostridge, Melvyn Bragg, Alan Brookes, Chloë Buck, Janina Cebertowicz, Graham Clark, Margaret Clark, Charlotte Clement, David Coe, Peter Conradi, Rex Cowan, Zelide Cowan, Belinda Davies, Esme Davies, Florence Davies, John F. Dewey, Maggie Dickie, Ken Doggett, Maureen Duffy, Gwynne Dyer, August Ford, Inigo Ford, Luther Ford, Jason Fordham, Max Fordham, Lady Lucy French, Fanchon Frohlich, June Furlong, Maggie Gilby, Mark Gleeson, Chris Goldie, Nick Green, Ruth Green, Brenda Haddon, Sara Haddon, Alex Hamilton, David Harsent, Ronald Harwood, Arthur Haycraft, Richard Haycraft, William Haycraft, Sarah Haynes, Andrew Hewson, Susan Hitch, Sue Hodson, Harry Hoff, Michael Holroyd, Stephanie Howard, Philip Hughes, Psiche Hughes, Rebecca Hussey,

Margaret Jones, Penny Jones, Mike Laurence, Parvin Laurence, Larry Levine, Anna Lowther Harris, Stoddard Martin, Irene Matthews, Derwent May, Miranda May, Yolanta May, Viki McDonnell, Glenys McDougall, Roger McGough, Brian McGuinness, Luke McKernan, Don McKinlay, Sheenagh McKinlay, Helenka Medlik, Nicola Medlik, Bruce Moffat, Rachel Mohin, Rod Murray, Stephanie Nettell, Harvey Nicol, Sarah O'Reilley, Angela Ovenston, Margaret Parsons, Vicky de Pass, Stephen Peppiatt, Tristram Powell, Ken Ratcliffe, Harold Retler, Robin Riley, Bertie Russell, Charlie Russell, Natalie Russell, Nina Saville, Philip Saville, Prunella Scales, Alan Sharp, Margaret Sharp, Francesca Sheppard, Gail Stanhope, Ursula Starr, Dinah Swain, Mary Thorne, Lili Todes, Jeremy Trafford, Jack Treagus, Gertrud Watson, A. N. Wilson.

Research on this biography was greatly facilitated by a grant from the Authors' Foundation.

I would like to thank Robin Baird-Smith and Jamie Birkett at Bloomsbury Continuum for their editorial and technical assistance, Mark Bostridge for his editorial advice and input, and Richard Mason for his careful copy-editing of the final text.

INDEX

A NOTE ON THE TYPE

The text of this book is set in Adobe Caslon, named after the English punch-cutter and type-founder William Caslon I (1692–1766). Caslon's rather old-fashioned types were modelled on seventeenth-century Dutch designs, but found wide acceptance throughout the English-speaking world for much of the eighteenth century until replaced by newer types towards the end of the century. Used in 1776 to print the Declaration of Independence, they were revived in the nineteenth century and have been popular ever since, particularly amongst fine printers. There are several digital versions, of which Carol Twombly's Adobe Caslon is one.